Comic Art in Africa, Asia, Australia, and Latin America

Comic Art in Africa, Asia, Australia, and Latin America

A Comprehensive, International Bibliography

Compiled by **John A. Lent**

Forewords by
Effat Abdel Azim, Esmail, Abu Abraham, and
Ares (Aristides Esteban Hernández Guerrero)

Bibliographies and Indexes in Popular Culture, Number 7

Greenwood Press
Westport, Connecticut • London

Library of Congress Cataloging-in-Publication Data

Lent, John A.
   Comic art in Africa, Asia, Australia, and Latin America : a
comprehensive, international bibliography / compiled by John A. Lent
; forewords by Effat Abdel Azim, Esmail, Abu Abraham, and Ares
(Aristides Esteban Hernández Guerrero).
     p. cm.—(Bibliographies and indexes in popular culture,
ISSN 1066-0658 ; no. 7)
   Includes indexes.
   ISBN 0-313-29343-0 (alk. paper)
   1. Caricatures and cartoons—History—Bibliography. 2. Wit and
humor, Pictorial—Bibliography. I. Title. II. Series.
Z5956.C3L458 1996
[NC1325]
016.7415—dc20   95-31367

British Library Cataloguing in Publication Data is available.

Library of Congress Catalog Card Number: 95-31367
ISBN: 0-313-29343-0
ISSN: 1066-0658

First published in 1996

Greenwood Press, 88 Post Road West, Westport, CT 06881
An imprint of Greenwood Publishing Group, Inc.

Printed in the United States of America

The paper used in this book complies with the
Permanent Paper Standard issued by the National
Information Standards Organization (Z39.48–1984).

10 9 8 7 6 5 4 3 2

CONTENTS

LESS OUTSIDE INFLUENCE, FEWER COMMENTARY CARTOONS

Effat Abdel Azim, Esmail

Many would agree that basically, there exist two types of contemporary caricature. One might be called a "fixed line," meaning the cartoonist never reflects his/her mood toward anything. This is not even changed with the passage of time; it just is not preferable to have sensibility during the creative process. The second type of caricature is the opposite, where the artist is deeply interactive with the work.

Great cartoonists are usually freelancers. They are not engaged at a regular job so as to avoid being turned into a "registered" artist. The result is that such freelancers endure the frustration gap that exists between obtaining a means of sustenance and maintaining freedom of expression.

A genuine artist of cartoons must have a direct, cohesive connection of hand with mind. The mind crystallizes the cartoon drawing, after which it sends a message to the hand for implementation. The mind, in conceptualizing the cartoon, is affected by a number of factors, not least of which are the training modes and other artistic movements. In Africa and the Middle East, many cartoonists have been influenced by either a Western or Eastern school, depending on where they were sent to study. In many cases, such influences have made the artists' works less than totally comprehensible to local readers.

Moreover, one of the obvious drawbacks of the Western cartooning tradition is its noticeably wide divergence from that of Africa and the Middle East in the area of permissible topics. For example, there is an over sensitivity to tackling the subject of sex in African societies.

In both Africa and the Middle East, there is an absence of specialized academic study for the cartoonist, and of genuine talent, despite the afforded potentiality of the press.

A couple of remedies for the less than fully developed nature of African/Middle Eastern cartooning might be:

1. Encouragement of the use of more non-commentary cartoons, even though these are difficult to conceptualize and draw. The "oratorical" cartoon should be avoided because it causes, in some cases, distraction and distortion of the themes, and prevents the reader from the full enjoyment of the various aesthetical aspects of the work.

2. Emphasis must be placed on cartooning as an art, taking into consideration the famous words of Robert LaPalme, former director of the International Salon of Cartoons in Montreal—that each civilization is measured by the quality and quantity of its cartoon art.

That statement can be applied positively to the civilizations along the Nile; cartoon art in Egypt is very old, traceable to the Pharaonic period. Bess, the God of humor, is an actual allusion.

Since 1983, cartoonists in Egypt have been organized into an association established by pioneers such as Mohamed Abdel Moneim Rakha, Zohdey El-Adawy, and Ahmed Toghan. They had been preceded by a generation of cartoonists who had heavy Western influences, individuals such as Refki, Santos, Kairaz, and Saroukhan. Others counted among the pioneers are: Abdel-Samee, Salah El-Leithy, Salah Ghaheen, El-Labbad, Hegazi, Bahgat, George El-Bahgouri, Nagi, Hassan Hakim, Moustafa Hussein, Raouf Aiaad, Sherif Eleesh, Mohamed Hakim, Gomaa Farahat, and myself.

The Egyptian Association of Cartoonists has participated in the 1994 International Conference of Population and Development held in Cairo, sponsoring an appropriate exhibition, and the group has carried out other professional activities.

But, despite these activities, the Egyptian cartooning scene is plagued with difficulties, among them: an overabundance of commentary cartoons, a lack of international interaction (participation in international competitions and exhibitions), inadequate artistic background and an absence of cosmopolitanism among cartoonists, and a shortage of cartoon magazines. The latter is a severe problem as only one viable cartoon magazine is published in Egypt—in the entire Middle East for that matter.

It is not all bleak. One cannot ignore the increased activity and the positive movement towards achieving an optimum status for our cartoonists among the universe of artists.

Effat Abdel Azim, Esmail works as a freelance cartoonist in Cairo. He has carried out cartoon assignments for *Akhbaar El-Youm*, *Akher Saa Magazine*, *Literature News*, *Nesf El-Donia*, and *Hepdo*, among other publications. A member of both the British and Egyptian cartoonist clubs, the Egyptian Press Syndicate, and Plastic Arts Syndicate, Effat is the Egyptian editor for *WittyWorld International Cartoon Magazine*.

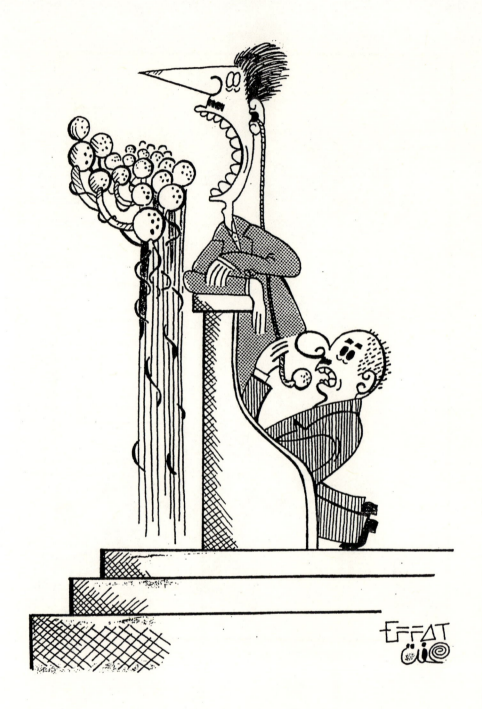

CARTOONING—ART OF THE UNDERDOG AND DISSENTER

Abu Abraham

Serious cartooning as distinct from the merely "comic" drawings, is the art of the underdog and the dissenter. It is their protest against oppression and discrimination. It is their way of cutting down to size those who are in power. It is the underdog's cry against his tormenters. It is a form of psychological warfare.

At the same time it has to be recognized that this form of dissent cannot thrive in a society where a tyranny (either of a government or of a social class or of the clergy) is so well organized that all dissent can be snuffed out. Cartoonists, thus, in certain countries, have had to suffer imprisonment. In one or two cases they have been physically eliminated by fundamentalist terrorism.

With all that, the art of the political cartoon has grown in strength and popularity throughout the world. The challenge to the cartoonists' freedom of expression has been greater when governments try to control the press, or actually stifle dissent. In many instances, cartoonists have found subtle ways of saying "objectionable" things without falling into the net of censorship.

Helen Vlachos, the Greek newspaper owner, who lived in exile during the rule of the colonels, once observed that cartoonists were able, even under dictatorship, to maintain some kind of opposition. The printed word was too precise, she said. In Greece the very ambiguity of the cartoons published gave them the subversive element so essential to the nature of this art. While the colonels were too dense to get the message, the readers worked it out with subtle skill.

Asia, Africa, South and Central America, and the Caribbean Islands, these constitute most of what has come to be known as the Third World. With a few notable

'What are you going to be when you grow up—illiterate, or unemployed?'

exceptions, the countries of these three continents have all suffered from foreign domination. In that sense, Australia and New Zealand could also be regarded as Third World countries, despite their very high standard of living.

There is, I think, a distinct acerbity in the work of the more celebrated cartoonists from the Third World, a certain radical feeling that can be traced to a history of colonial oppression.

If we include Australia also in the Third World, that is, in the sense that it was a British dominion, we have in David Low and Will Dyson examples of sharp political thinking. Low had Scottish and Irish ancestors; he was born in New Zealand and grew up in Australia before he left for England and started what is perhaps the most distinguished cartoon career of this century. His radical outlook must have come partly from his ancestry and partly from his Australian upbringing.

In India, cartooning as we know it today, began with the arrival of the printing press and the consolidation of British rule. When the art was taken up by Indian cartoonists, it became part of the nationalist struggle. In England, caricature and cartoons flourished as a means of tempering oligarchy. Indian cartoonists had the double role of tempering British oligarchy and, later on, the Indian version of it.

Indian cartoonists have been fortunate in that both the British rulers as well as Indian nationalist leaders had a sympathetic appreciation of caricatures and cartoons. While the viceroys were fond of collecting originals (especially those of Shankar who was the leading political cartoonist in pre-Independence days), Indian leaders, like Gandhi and Nehru and C. Rajagopalachari, the first governor-general of India, showed their profound sense of humor by publicly laughing with those who ridiculed them through cartoons. It was gentle fun, of course, in those days, but their encouragement helped the growth of cartooning. Today Indian cartoonists don't show any great restraint in their lampooning of contemporary politicians.

Because of the overwhelming influence of politics on newspapers and public life, Indian cartoonists have been mostly of the political variety. Therefore, cartoons satirizing social life, as in the *New Yorker*, or those that are pure fun, have remained somewhat under-developed though there are a few popular non-political comic magazines that are doing good business. Comic strips of the American kind are virtually absent. But the format is used to present folk and mythological stories and also the lives of heroes from Indian history. These are very popular among the young, but nowhere near as popular as "Dennis the Menace" or "Peanuts" or "Tarzan." I remember that my own two daughters, when young, couldn't quite figure out the sense of even the simplest of my cartoons, but they had no such problem in getting the point in Dennis, though the culture and way of life was really alien to them.

The American strip cartoon industry must surely be the biggest multinational corporation functioning in the modern world. How they have achieved this popularity and influence in all parts of the world is a subject worth serious investigation.

Humor, in my view, is really very national and regional. There is for instance, little connection between the Japanese and Indian sense of humor. But the American comics have, I suppose, a common humanity that has universal appeal.

The Pope and the Pill

Abu Abraham is considered one of the most prominent Indian cartoonists. For years, he was in England where he was staff cartoonist for the *Observer* and the *Guardian*. Upon his return to India, Abu drew for the *Indian Express* for 12 years. One of his features, "Salt and Pepper," is self-syndicated. Abu also served as a member of the Indian Parliament's Upper House (1972-1978).

LATIN AMERICAN CARTOONING: PROGRESS, PROSPECTS, AND PROBLEMS

Ares (Aristides Esteban Hernández Guerrero)

Christ is lowered from the cross and attended to by a group of intensive therapy specialists trying to save his life...."Even like this, you don't have any flavor!" a man tells his wife as he devours her at supper time....The wolf cries while in hiding because Little Red Riding Hood is being protected by bodyguards. This and much more happens in the cartoon world. Everything is possible there; the absurd lives a plentiful life; every frontier is broken, and the general and individual norms are violated. Everything succumbs or is reborn under the weight of a smile.

It's been more than a decade since I began cartooning, and along the way, I have discovered that humor is not only a medium to generate laughter, but also an attitude of life that takes for granted the use of the intellect and advances the understanding of human nature. With such characteristics, cartooning becomes great art. No one could say otherwise after seeing the works of Steinberg, Adolf Born, Ronald Searle, Moebius, Sempé, Folon, Zlatkovsky, and many others. To be sure, entering their world has not been easy, living in this continent, where we are isolated in great measure from cartoons done in other parts of the world, and even in countries of our own geographic area. As a rule, caricature and cartooning in the Third World remain isolated because there is little knowledge about them, even in the countries of origin where imported comics crush local artists.

Regardless of all the problems, our culture has had the good fortune of witnessing how cartooning in Latin America has reached a high level of accomplishment, with noticeable examples of works of excellent aesthetic quality. The styles and ways of making humor are different in each case, living together just as Lennon and Mozart live together in music. A list of a few names in this immense group of Latin American cartoonists might demonstrate the transcendental accomplishments of our creators: Quino,

Mordillo, Fontanarrosa, Ziraldo, Santiago, Helio Flores, Naranjo, Rius, Carlucho, Manuel, Ajubel, Roger, Tabaré, Palomo, or Zapata.

There are some elements that characterize the cartoon movement in Latin America. Particularly, we have observed an emphasis on the editorial cartoon with political content, but also misinformation, lack of publishing space and poor royalty payments to authors in this field. Another important factor in the evolution of cartooning in Latin America is, according to my knowledge, the lack of homogenous development. That is evident in the collective accomplishments of cartoonists in countries such as Argentina, Brazil, Cuba, and Mexico. Many talented cartoonists in the region are frequently forced to look to other frontiers for a place to grow, instead of remaining in their own lands. Lately, the cartooning that enjoys the best health is that of Mexico, since many new publications have emerged, affording space, new options, and new values. But Mexico is the exception and, as an exception, it only brings us back to the rule.

In Cuba's case, there is a long tradition in cartooning, going back to the small publications of a satirical nature during the beginning of the nineteenth century, and continuing with the creation of characters such as "Liborio" and "El Bobo," and caricaturists of great stature, such as Rafael Blanco, Conrado Massaguer, Eduardo Abela, and Juan David.

In order to talk about the actual state of Cuban cartooning, I consider it important to mention the innovative movement that emerged in the 1960s. The change occurred thanks to the cooperation of young caricature artists who were starting to work in a different social situation. In this way, two opposite sources—the conventional and the new ways of making humor—were created and are still going strong in Cuba. It was not until the decade of the 1970s that the boom of Cuban cartooning started. It initially resulted from the influence of United States comics and European cartoons, evidenced in works of Steinberg, Tiunin, Topor, etc. Cartooning was beginning to be seen as having aesthetic and conceptual aspirations that separated it from a minor plastic art.

The 1980s came and went, full of excellent cartoonists, some with previous experience, others with new criteria that shaped a more mature work. The humorous supplement, *Dedeté*, started in 1969, was in its greatest splendor, winning the award for world's best political satire publication in Forte Dei Marmi, Italy. The international humor salons offered Cubans the possibilities of making contact with the outside cartooning world and of showing their work. At the same time, Cuban cartooning has garnered, up to now, about 200 international awards and an accumulation of immeasurable influences.

Later, at the beginning of the 1990s, the fall of East Europe and the crudities of the American blockade injured the Cuban economy. The Cuban press reflected the seriousness of the situation as many newspapers and magazines folded or decreased the number of their issues. This notably affected Cuban cartooning since it took away many of the places where the artists were expressing themselves. This is still the situation in Cuba.

In other countries of Latin America, there are other reasons behind the problems faced by local cartooning. Regardless of other causes, many cartoonists have too few survival possibilities in a cultural colony where awareness starts and ends with what the United States does.

Maybe the problems of the Latin American and Third World cartoonists are minuscule when compared to problems faced by those starving, instead of smiling. In the midst of all those difficulties, cartoonists are convinced that life can be beautiful. They have forced us to look for a better world, knowing it is better to continue laughing and creating, hoping as the proverb says, that "when God closes a door, He opens a window."

On the other hand, if hunger kills so many people, misinformation and ignorance mutilate many of our talents. That is why I greet with a great sense of humor this new volume by my friend, John Lent, as a window where we can look out with new strength.

Translator: Dr. Maria C. Santana

Ares is both a psychiatrist and a cartoonist. His works, which feature fat people almost exclusively, have been compiled into two books, published frequently in Cuba and abroad, and awarded many prizes (more than 20 internationally). Ares is vice president of the Cuban Humorists Association.

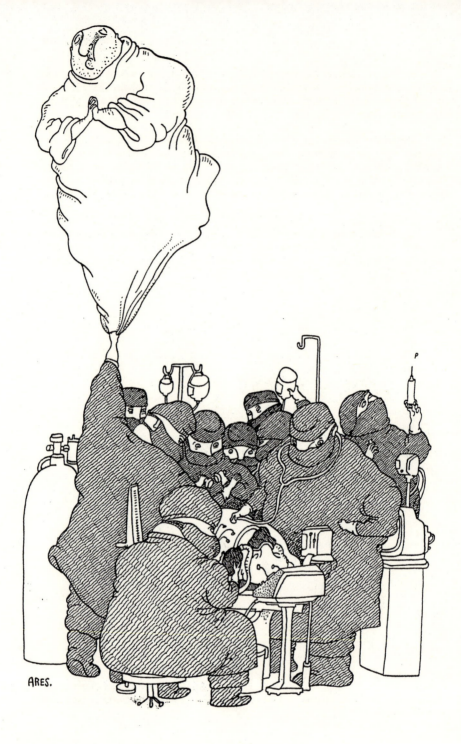

PREFACE

Journeying through the comic art worlds of Africa, Asia, Australia, and Latin America, one cannot help being deeply impressed with the longevity, magnitude, and versatility of their cartooning traditions.

A trip to a centuries-old Sri Lanka temple, with its sequentially-arranged panels—some with funny overtones—depicting Buddha's life, attests to the ancientness of comic art, as well as its possible Asian origins. A stop at a Japanese *manga* store confirms the huge business that comic books are, some selling millions of copies weekly, while a look at materials used to teach Islam in the Middle East or promote developmental goals in Asia and Africa, shows comics' varied use.

The "traveler" through these comic art realms will find a number of tourist attractions actually built around cartooning phenomena—a cartoon temple and a Disney theme park in Japan; a town called the "town of humor" in Cuba to honor its cartoon tradition, or a real-life dilapidated-looking pub built to the specifications of its comic strip model in Australia. He or she will read some of the world's oldest, continuously-drawn strips in Australia and the Philippines (the latter still drawn by its creator after six decades); comic books called *unka* (shit) that true to name feature defecation in Japan; volumes of "used" comic strip magazines, collected and bound together for sale at Arab bazaars; or an alternative newspaper, whose capital was donated by patrons of a series of cartoon exhibitions in Sri Lanka. If our "traveler" ventures to the movie house, he or she is most likely to enjoy Hollywood-credited animation that was drawn and totally produced in Asia, or feature films strictly based on comics (especially prevalent in the Philippines).

Despite the ubiquitous and often unique aspects of comic art in these regions, not much is known about African, Middle Eastern, Asian, Australian, and Latin American cartooning in the West. Worse yet, not much is known about what is happening within or between these regions. Trips throughout Asia and the Caribbean brought this home to me as cartoonists inquired about the nature of the profession in nearby countries. Some awareness has been generated through seminars and exchanges for cartoonists, funded by a Japanese foundation, the United States government, and other agencies, and through the research efforts of individual scholars and writers. Prominent among the latter are: Isao Shimizu and Frederik L. Schodt, Japan; Harold Hinds, Jr. and Charles Tatum, Mexico; Allen Douglas and Fedwa Malti-Douglas, the Arab world; Kosei Ono and John A. Lent, Asia; Germán Caceres, Argentina; Lim Cheong-San and Park Jae-Dong, Korea; John Ryan, Australia; Cynthia Roxas *et al.*, the Philippines; David W. Foster, Latin America, or Évora Tamayo, Lent, and Juan Blas, Cuba.

Other professional, academic, and fan-oriented activities have brought cartooning of these areas to a higher level and to the attention of the rest of the world. In at least Cuba and Japan, comic art collections have been established, while in India, Korea, Brazil, and Malaysia, colleges and universities have developed courses and programs in cartooning techniques and theory. Cartoonists' associations exist in many places, as do cartooning periodicals, including Iran's *Humour and Caricature* and *Kayhan Caricature*, Nigeria's *The Cartoonist*, Cuba's *Dedeté* and *Palante*, Argentina's *Trix*, Algeria's *Jornol do Man'kiko*, China's *World of Cartoons*, or Australia's *Inkspot*.

As comics and animation industries seek outside markets, Americans, Europeans, and the peoples of the continents featured in this book, are exposed to different stories, visual styles, and formats. Encouraging this interchange are many Japanese *anime* and *manga* fan clubs and fanzines that have sprouted up in the United States, England, and other parts of Europe.

Organization, Objectives, Emphases

This bibliography is the fourth of a series on comic art worldwide. The previous three volumes, all compiled by John A. Lent and published by Greenwood, appeared in 1994. They were: *Animation, Caricature, and Gag and Political Cartoons in the United States and Canada: An International Bibliography*; *Comic Books and Comic Strips in the United States: An International Bibliography*, and *Comic Art in Europe: An International, Comprehensive Bibliography*.

Comic art in this volume represents animation, caricature, comic books, comic strips, and gag, illustrative, magazine, and political cartoons. At times, it was difficult determining genre because of terminology used. The word "caricature" in some countries, especially those in Latin America, takes on more meanings than just exaggerated portraiture; in some cases, it refers to cartooning in general. In Korea and elsewhere, it can be a chore distinguishing between comic books, comic magazines, and comic strips.

This book is structured around the continents and regions of Africa, the Middle East, Asia, Australia and Oceania, Central and South America, and the Caribbean. The first chapter includes citations referring to comic art that crosses regional boundaries or that defies easy categorization or geographical placement.

Hard decisions had to be made concerning placement within some of the continental/regional chapters. Especially perplexing were sources on comics in the Islamic and/or Arab world. For convenience sake, they were put in the Middle East chapter, with full recognition that the Islamic/Arab world refers to a religion and national/ethnic groups that extend into North Africa, other parts of Asia, and elsewhere.

Sixty-seven countries have individual entries in the bibliography. Eighteen are in Asia, 16 in South and Central America, 15 in Africa, 8 in the Middle East, 6 in the Caribbean, and 4 in Australia/Oceania. Of course, the numbers of citations are very lopsided, ranging from hundreds on Argentina, Australia, Brazil, China, Japan, and Mexico, to one each on Liberia and Madagascar.

The disparity results because: 1. Some countries have longer and richer traditions of comic art from which literature can be generated; 2. Preservation and study of cartooning is more developed in some places, especially countries with stronger educational and cultural infrastructures, mass communication or art institutes, and comic art professional associations and activities; 3. The compiler has conducted first-hand research or has made professional contacts in certain countries, resulting in exposure to more sources from those places.

Common topics throughout the book include resources, general sources, historical aspects, cartooning and cartoons, cartoonists and their works, characters and titles, and the individual types of comic art—animation, comic books, comic strips, and political cartoons. Wherever they appear, sections on resources include any of the following: bibliographies, dictionaries, encyclopedias, catalogues, collections, libraries, checklists, guides, fanzines, and indices. Most continental/regional chapters contain a periodical directory, providing names, addresses, typical contents, and inaugural dates of comic art related journals, magazines, and fanzines. Ninety-two periodicals are featured, with 73 in Asia, 6 Central and South America, 5 Australia/Oceania, 4 the Middle East, 3 Africa, and 1 Caribbean.

Historical aspects include citations that by their approach or content denote history, as well as those sources that were published in the 1940s or before. Because the latter describe the cartooning scene in times that are now considered historical, they are included here. The category cartooning and cartoons takes in genres not provided separate headings, such as gag, illustrative, or magazine cartoons, as well as festivals, competitions, exhibitions, training, humor magazines, professionalism, business aspects, governmental and legal aspects, and multi-cartoonist anthologies.

Throughout this book, cartoonists and their works is a catch-all category, also including a few individuals who are not cartoonists but who are closely aligned to the profession. The criterion used in giving a cartoonist or cartooning-related individual a separate listing is that he or she was the subject of at least two citations. There were 242 cartoonists singled out, 138 hailing from Asia, 79 from Central and South America, 7 each from Africa and Australia/Oceania, 6 from the Caribbean, and 5 from the Middle

East. Some of the countries that had a large number of cartoonists individually listed were Japan, 49; Brazil, 48; China, 31; Argentina, 16; India, 12; the Philippines, 10, and Mexico, 9. The category "cartoonists and their works" consists of biographies, autobiographies, memoirs, profiles, interviews, sketchbooks, and obituaries.

Often, it was difficult to categorize cartoonists by genre and even by country. Japan's Tezuka is known for both his comic book and animation work and Mexico's Rius, his political cartoons and comic books. Other cartoonists are equally famous in more than one type of cartooning. Some cartoonists are split by countries—their places of origin and those where they make their living or gain their fame. Aubrey Collette was born and began his career in Sri Lanka, but was also identified with Singapore and Hong Kong, and very closely with Australia, where he spent a large part, including the later years, of his life. Miguel Covarrubias, born in Mexico, did much of his work in the United States. Alberto Breccia can be identified with either Uruguay or Argentina and Arturo del Castillo with Chile or Argentina. During recent economic downswings in their homeland, at least a half dozen Filipino cartoonists have moved to Singapore, just as a number of Chinese cartoonists migrated to Hong Kong, Taiwan, and elsewhere in 1949. Such multi-genre and multi-country cartoonists were usually placed where they were most prominent; admittedly, some placements were made rather arbitrarily.

One-hundred and seventy-three characters and titles of comic art are singled out with two or more citations. As would be expected, most, 129, are found in Japanese *manga* or *anime*. In some periodicals, cartoonist profiles are intermingled with accounts of their characters or the titled works for which they are known. Thus, the user of this bibliography will find in the sections on characters and titles much biographical information about the authors of those works, and conversely, much on characters and titles in cartoonists' profiles and interviews.

Placement of Japanese citations into animation or comic book categories presented problems because of frequent name changes of animation stories and comics titles (especially when they are exported) and because of the duplicitous nature of *anime* and *manga*. Many titles, of which "Doraemon" and "Akira" are just two well-known examples, have both *anime* and *manga* versions. The user of this bibliography is therefore encouraged to cross-reference the Japanese *anime* and *manga* characters and titles sections.

In the case of some countries, categories are expanded because of the nature of the development of cartooning and the relative number of citations. For example, China has "artistic aspects" and "woodcuts" categories to account for the close links between comic and more traditional art, especially highlighted by Feng Zikai, who merits a separate subcategory under "artistic aspects." India has a category on "development, education, and social consciousness" and Japan, one on "exports and imports." "Sports newspapers cartoons" merits a separate listing in Korea where they are considered a distinct genre. In both Korea and Thailand, where Japanese comics have been influential and oftentimes considered a threat to local comics and culture, a separate subcategory is provided. Under Brazil, culture and education, genres, and histórias are listed under comic books. Histórias is a rather vague category. Because the compiler had not seen many of those sources, he was not able to determine whether they were histories of comics or the genre of tales and legends. Histórias can refer to both.

With coverage of 67 countries, the citations are in a number of languages. In many cases, only the English translation of titles is given. When a translator was available, both the original and English titles were listed. Although an attempt was made to obtain the most accurate translations in all instances, there are shortcomings.

Most citations are full, but again, because of different ways of doing things (in this case, citing) in other cultures, sometimes page numbers and even specific dates are missing. Some periodicals, especially fanzines, are not dated and/or do not number pages. Others change series or alternate, without any seeming logic, between using dates and volume numbers or months and seasons of the year. Also, some citations were taken from clippings in obscure periodicals sent by cartoonists who had not fully documented them.

Nevertheless, a serious effort was put forth to compile a comprehensive and usable bibliography. No item was too small or insignificant to be listed; if it dealt with comic art, it could become a citation. The compiler works on the premise that both systematically-researched and ephemeral materials are useful during the course of developing a field of study.

Having said that, I must point out some limitations on comprehensiveness. Obviously, it is not possible to know of everything published in thousands of books and periodicals in all corners of the world. Even the so-called new information technology is incapable of knowing this. Oftentimes, the only way to obtain substantial information on a country's cartooning is to go there, an expensive and time-consuming process. Even then, librarians in some countries are not of much use in pointing out literature, partly because they have not concerned themselves with comic art, especially where it is considered a lowly popular culture form not worthy of study. So, much like an archeologist, the compiler of a bibliography of this scope and magnitude digs and scratches through all types of materials, looking for a "find."

The bibliography is representative in covering various publications, writing formats and styles, time periods, and languages. Most of the citations are current, although many date to the late nineteenth and early twentieth centuries.

Many problems surfaced in the course of doing this work. Some have already been discussed. One especially perplexing problem was the avoidance of duplication when dealing with such a voluminous amount of information presented (sometimes inaccurately) in different bibliographic styles. Although I have attempted to eliminate, or at least to minimize duplication, some is bound to exist.

The citations are arranged alphabetically by author, or by title of article when an author is not listed, and are numbered consecutively. Rather consistently, the first letters of all words, except short prepositions and conjunctions, are capitalized. Chinese and Korean proper names are cited without the comma.

Search Process

Besides using scores of libraries in the United States and beyond and the interlibrary loan services, the compiler employed other ways to track down sources on comic art of these regions.   Some key writers in the field were asked to submit bibliographies of their works; among those complying with this request were Isao Shimizu (Japan), Harold Hinds, Jr. (Mexico), Subhir Tailang (India), Darminto Sudarmo (Indonesia), Javad Alizadeh (Iran) with his periodical *Humour and Caricature*, and the editors of *Kayhan Caricature* (Iran).   Thirteen Chinese cartoonists responded to a letter request, sending lists of their comics-related books and articles which were translated by Dr. Hongying Liu-Lengyel.   They were Moy Low (Jiang Ke-An), Chen Shubin (Fang Tang), Su Guang, Wang Dazhuang, Lan Jian'an, Yong Fei, Cheng Huiling, Su Lang, Fang Cheng, Bi Keguan, Jiang Yousheng, Shen Tiancheng, and Zhou Fashu.   Numerous other cartoonists shared scrapbooks or clippings about their individual work; among these were Anant Pai, Suresh Sawant, and Vijay Seth (VINS), all of India; Larry Feign and Zunzi of Hong Kong; Johnny Lau and James Suresh of Singapore, and Johnny Hidayat of Indonesia.

Additional sources became available during my interviews with hundreds of cartoonists and comic art specialists around the world.   Since 1964, I have done research on Asian mass communication, living in the Philippines and Malaysia on two occasions for about three years and visiting for research purposes those and other countries on at least 16 occasions.   During the past decade, comic art has been the focus of this research; 205 interviews were conducted with cartoonists and comic art personnel in 15 Asian countries—in Taiwan and Malaysia in 1986; in the Philippines, 1988; in Korea, Taiwan, Hong Kong, the Philippines, Singapore, and Indonesia, 1992; in India, Sri Lanka, Bangladesh, Myanmar, Thailand, Malaysia, Vietnam, China, and Japan, 1993; and Korea, 1994.   Since 1968, I have been carrying out research on Caribbean mass communication, having made about 20 trips for the purpose of interviewing and collecting materials.   Trips to specifically interview cartoonists occurred in 1990 (Bahamas and Trinidad), 1991 (Cuba), and 1993 (Jamaica).

Also responsible for providing sources is a coterie of doctoral students working under my supervision in a loosely-structured group called Komiks and Manwha.   They have also searched libraries, conducted interviews, and otherwise gathered source materials on comic art in Japan (Rei Okamoto), China (Dr. Hongying Liu-Lengyel and Dr. Alfonz Lengyel), Taiwan (Dr. Hsiao Hsiang-Wen), India (Aruna Rao), and Korea (Yu Kie-Un).

Finally, the compiler sought sources by placing advertisements in *WittyWorld International Cartoon Magazine*, which he helped found and for which he has served as managing editor.   He also became familiar with much literature as he prepared his regular bibliographic column for *WittyWorld* from 1987 to the present.

The search of literature in libraries has been mostly manual, since that is the way the compiler works, and because much of the literature, being journalistic, anecdotal, or brief, is not in computerized databases.   However, for this particular volume, CD-ROM databases on business (January 1971-January 1994), education (January 1961-January

1994), psychology (January 1974-January 1994), and sociology (January 1974-January 1994), were accessed, but yielded very few sources. Many bibliographies, indices, and bibliographical periodicals, too numerous to list here, were used.

On a regular basis and rather systematically, the compiler has attempted to keep abreast of the literature on mass communication and popular culture for at least the past 30 years. For the most part, works on comic art are expected to be found in those fields, as well as in art. Hundreds of journal titles in these three fields, as well as geography-specific areas, published on all continents are scanned regularly by the compiler.

No effort will be made to list all of these periodicals, only those that would be expected to yield some articles. Among these, all numbers of the following were searched: *Animag, Animenonimous, Animerica, Anime UK, Apropos, Art? Alternatives, Canadian Cartoonist, The Cartoonist* (Nigeria), *Cartoonist PROfiles, Cine Cubano, Comic Art Studies, Comics Interview, Comics Journal, Comics Scene, Communication Abstracts, Communication Booknotes, Critical Studies in Mass Communication, European Journal of Communication, FECO News, Fushiga Kenkyu, Gauntlet, Gazette, Humor, Index on Censorship, Journal of Communication, Journal of Popular Culture, Journal of Popular Film, Journalism Quarterly, Kayhan Caricature, L'Ecran, Mangajin, Media Development, Media History Digest, Monthly Comic Magazine* (Hong Kong), *Nemo, Nordic Comics Revue, Protoculture Addicts, Public Culture, The Rose, Seriejournalen, Studies in Latin American Popular Culture, Target, To Za Now* (Taiwan), *Trix* (Argentina), *V-Max, Watcher,* and *WittyWorld.*

Additionally, the compiler looked at the following periodicals with varying degrees of exhaustiveness, depending upon availability and relevance: *AAEC Notebook, Animation, Animato, Ark/Arkensword, B and W, Bédésup, Bem, Big O, Boletim de HQ, Caricature* (Canada), *Caricature* (Egypt), *Caricature et Caricaturistes, Cartoon Quarterly, Comic Art, Comicguia, Comics, Comics Buyer's Guide, Comics Feature, Comics International, Comics Land, The Comics World, Comikaze, Comix, El Wendigo, Encyclopedia dei Fumetti, FA, Fumetti d'Italia, Funnyworld, Glimpse, Granma Weekly Review, Graphixus, Heavy Metal, Humour and Caricature, ICOM/Info, Il Fumetto, Inkspot, In Toon, IPI Report, Japanimation, The Jester, Jornol do Man'kiko, Karikatur, Keverinfo, La Borsa del Fumetto, Linus, Mangazine, Manwha Teo* (Korea), *Mecha Press, Mieux Vaut en Rire, National Cartoonists Society Newsletter, Newtype, Philippine Comics Review, Ran Tan Plan,* Seoul YWCA Comics Monitoring *Reports, Serieskaberen, Shpitz, Society of Strip Illustration Newsletter, Speakeasy, Story Board, Tratto, The World of Comic Art, Worldwide Classics Newsletter,* and *Yamete.*

"Fugitive" materials, such as dissertations not indexed through the University of Michigan system, theses, catalogues, conference papers, and pamphlets also make up part of the bibliography. For example, all 23 theses written on cartooning and comics at Mara Institute of Technology in Kuala Lumpur, Malaysia, the only two in the whole of Taiwan, the only three at Thailand's Thammasat, Chulalongkorn, and Chiang Mai universities, as well as most of those completed at the Institute of Mass Communication, University of the Philippines, and some at Korean universities are included.

ACKNOWLEDGMENTS

Bibliographic work, tedious and time-consuming (and even addictive) as it is, can have its moments of pleasure and fulfillment. In the course of finishing this bibliography, there were a number of such times—while scavenging through stacks of books and periodicals at comics festivals and stores, while finding a cache of fanzines or a list of references in library and commercial catalogues, or while interviewing cartoonists and comics authorities in all corners of the world.

The latter deserve my first words of gratitude. The hundreds of cartoonists I have interviewed in Asia, Canada, Caribbean, Europe, South America, and the United States are the most interesting, flexible, and generous professionals I have known. They have shared with me their experiences, cartoons, and scrapbooks and clippings, the latter especially useful for bibliographic purposes. They have showered me with hospitality, motored me around crowded cities, provided me translations, and, in some cases, given me the benefits of their own comic art research.

They should all be mentioned, but space does not permit. Especially helpful, and to whom I am very thankful, are: Norman Isaac, Tony Velasquez, Deng Coy Miel, and Nonoy Marcelo in the Philippines; Ramli Badrudin, Mahtum, Darminto M. Sudarmo, Gerardus Sudarta, and Johnny Hidayat in Indonesia; Suresh Sawant, Abu Abraham, Sudhir Tailang, Anant Pai, Pran, Ramesh Chande, Prakash Shetty, and Rajan Nair in India; K.M.K. Madagama, W.R. Wijesoma, S.C. Opatha, Winnie Hettigoda, and Camillus Perera in Sri Lanka; Harunoor Rasheed Harun, Nazrul Islam, Kazi Abul Kazem, Rafiqun Nabi, Knondokar Abu Sayeed and wife Gemy, Asiful Huda, the staffs of *Cartoon* and *Immad* magazines, particularly Ahsan Habib, in Bangladesh; the entire cartoonists club of Myanmar, and especially U Ngwe Kyi, Maung Maung Aung, Maung Maung and Shwe Min Thar; Chai Rachawat, Yootlachai Kaewdee, and Prayut

Ngaokrachang in Thailand; Lat and Zunar in Malaysia; Zhan Tong, Zhan Yong, Hong Jin Feng, and Zheng Xin Yao in China; Zunzi, Chan Ya, Larry Feign, Jimmy Pang, Paul Best, and David Ki in Hong Kong; Johnny Lau, James Suresh, and Heng Kim Song in Singapore; Yukio Sugiura, Sampei Sato, and Yoshiro Kato in Japan; Tom Hoong, Shan Li, Fang Wan-Nan, James Wang, Cheng Wen, and Lao Chung in Taiwan; Yoon Youngok, Kim Song Hwan, Ahn Hyun Dong, Park Soo-Dong, Park Jae-Dong, Chung Woon Kyung, and Lim Cheong San in Korea; Polito, Ares, Ajubel, Boligán, and Lillo in Cuba; Flavio Mario de Alcantava Calazans in Brazil, and DEW (D.E. Williams) in Trinidad.

Other individuals were also very kind during my travels and other quests for cartooning information: Rev. Samuel Meshack, Dr. Josephine Joseph, Dr. B.P. Sanjay in India; Lim Cheng Tju, Fong Pick-Huei, Vijay Menon, Vic Valbuena, Elsie Bong, and Elaine Song in Singapore; Sankaran Ramanathan and Mohd. Hamdan Adnan in Malaysia; Dr. Rho Byung Sung and Kie-ae Kim in Korea; Hane Latt, U Thiha (a) Thiha Saw, and Kyaw Lin in Myanmar; and Keiko Tonegawa, Yutaka Kaneko, Toshiko Nakano, Katsuhisa and Midori Ichitsuka, and Kosei Ono in Japan.

Former and current students, whose graduate work I proudly supervised during the past more than 20 years, lent much appreciated support, hosting me while in their countries, providing sources and valuable insights, recording and translating materials, and being the main scholarly stimulus in the academic factory where I work. Among them were: Professor Oranuj Lertchanyarak (and husband, Kanongdej), Thailand; Dr. Charles Elliott, Hong Kong; Dr. Hongying Liu-Lengyel (and husband, Dr. Alfonz Lengyel), and Dr. Fei Zhengxing, China; Dr. John V. Vilanilam and Aruna Rao, India; Dr. Myung Jun Kim, Dr. Hoon Soon Kim, Sang Kil Lee, and Yu Kie-Un, Korea; Dr. Hsiao Hsiang-Wen, Chyun-Fung Shi, Peng Hui Ching, and Chu-feng Tang, Taiwan; Rei Okamoto, Japan; Dr. Maria Santana, Puerto Rico; Kohava Simhi, Israel; Betsi Grabe, South Africa, and Dominique Monolesqu, Brazil.

Cartoonists and comic art specialists who kindly sent information, besides those already mentioned above, were: Muliyadi Mohamood on Malaysia; Isao Shimizu on Japan; Leif Packalen on Tanzania and other African countries; Harold Hinds, Jr., on Mexico; Moy Low, Chen Shubin, Lan Jian'an, Yong Fei, Wang Dazhuang, Su Guang, Cheng Huiling, Su Lang, Fang Cheng, Bi Keguan, Jiang Yousheng, Shen Tiancheng, and Zhou Fashu on China; Javad Alizadeh and M.H. Niroumand on Iran, and Vijay Seth (VINS) on India. Others who provided sources were Maurice Horn, Randall Scott, German Caceres, Robert Roberts, Joseph G. Szabo, Tim Ernst, and Dr. Chien-Chung Tsao.

Roseanne Lent typed the 1986 bibliography on comic art which I self published and Michael Taney prepared this one for publication. My daughter, Andrea Murta, and her husband, David, provided other services so that I could travel throughout Asia during the Summers of 1992 and 1993.

The reader of any scholarly work has a right to know who paid the research bill, for here lies the potential for influence peddling. As with my previous works, this bibliography was completed without grants and with very minimal (and that given begrudgingly) help from my workplace. Instead, it was financed from my personal income and from a loan that I good naturedly, but gratefully, call the Bovalino's Ristorante "Foundation," my brother Russ's restaurant in Westlake, Ohio.

To all the people mentioned above, and hundreds of others, I express my sincerest appreciation.

John A. Lent

Comic Art in Africa, Asia, Australia, and Latin America

1

MULTI-REGIONAL
PERSPECTIVES

GENERAL SOURCES

1. Castelli, Alfredo. "La Video-Invasione Riuscirà la TV a Sconfiggere Gli Eroi del Fumetto?" *If.* November 1982, pp. 51-52 (Hong Kong, Mexico, U.S.).

2. Hornung, Werner. "Comic-Strips. Eine Internationale Bibliographie." *NZ am Wochenende* (Munich). April 18, 1971.

3. "Humor in Art and Cartooning," pp. 243-249. In *Humor Scholarship: A Research Bibliography*. Westport, Connecticut: Greenwood Press, 1993.

4. Klaus Boldt, K. and Friedrich Schade. *Das Kann Doch Nicht die Erde Sein? Da Steht ja Noch ein Baum! Verschuldungskrise und Umweltzerstörung in Karikaturen und Zeichnungen aus der Dritten Welt.* Frankfurt: epd Entwicklungspolitik, 1990. 71 pp. (Third World).

5. Lan Jian'an. "Selection of the Famous Comic Strips in the World." *Culture and Entertainment Monthly* (Hangzhou). Vols 4, 7, 8, 10, 12, 1982; Vols 3, 7, 11, 1983; Vols 2, 6, 10, 1984; Vol. 3, 1987.

6. Lan Jian'an. *Selection of Comics from Foreign Countries*. Beijing: China Series Picture Books Publishing House, 1987.

7. Lan Jian'an. "Top Ten in the World Comic Strips." *Art of Picture-Story* (Beijing). 1 (1992).

8.   "Learning About the Environment: Magazines for Children." *Development Communication Report*. No. 76, 1992, pp. 12-13, 20. (Kenya, Zimbabwe, Zambia, Botswana, Nigeria, Bolivia, Argentina, Liberia, Ecuador).

9.   Lee Won-Bok. "Where Are Contemporary World Cartoons Going?" *Gha Nah Art* (Seoul). November-December 1990, pp. 35-37.

10.   Lent, John A. "The Historical and Global Dimensions of Comic Art." *Philippines Communication Journal*. March 1993, pp. 1-12.

11.   Lent, John A. "International Dimensions of Comic Art." Paper presented at Taipei cartoonists exhibition and seminar, Taipei, Taiwan, July 9, 1992.

12.   Lent, John A. "The World of Cartooning—Uses, Motivations, Problems, Achievements." Speech before "Cartooning and Cartoonists of World" seminar, Trivandrum, India, July 12, 1993.

13.   Medioni, Gilles. "Cartoons Abroad Are 'Stirring Things Up.'" *World Press Review*. October 1991, pp. 26-28.

14.   Moy Low. "The History of the World Periodical Cartoons." *International Communication Journal* (Beijing). December 1984, 3½ pp.; March 1985, 3 pp.; June 1985, 2 pp.; September 1985, 1 p.; March 1986, 4 pp.; June 1986, 6 pp.; September 1986, 5 pp.; March 1987, 7 pp.; June 1987, 9 pp.

15.   Regan, Colm, Scott Sinclair, and Martyn Turner. *Thin Black Lines: Political Cartoons and Development Education*. Birmingham, England: Development Education Centre, 1988.128 pp.

16.   "World Censorship Watch." *Comics Journal*. August 1993, p. 37. (South Asia, Middle East).

2

AFRICA

CONTINENTAL AND INTER-COUNTRY PERSPECTIVES

General Sources

17. "Africa." In *Cartoons: One Hundred Years of Cinema Animation*, by Giannalberto Bendazzi. Bloomington: Indiana University Press, 1994. (Egypt, pp. 391-392; Tunisia, p. 392; Algeria, pp. 392-393; Zambia p. 393; Liberia, p. 393; Mali, p. 393; Senegal, p. 393; Burkina Faso, p. 393; Ivory Coast, p. 394; Ghana, p. 394; Cameroon, p. 394; Zaire, pp. 394-395; Mauritius, p. 395; Mozambique, p. 395; Burundi, p. 395; The South African Republic, pp. 395-396).

18. Barber, Karin. "Popular Arts in Africa." *African Studies Review*. 30:3 (1987), pp. 1-78.

19. Hogarth, Paul. *People Like Us. Drawings of South Africa and Rhodesia*. London: Dennis Dobson, 1958. 47 pp.

20. McLellan, Iain. *Television for Development. The African Experience*. Ottawa: International Development Research Centre, 1986. 165 pp. (Animation in Africa).

21. *South-South North*. Exhibition. Swallows of Finland, Helsinki. Helsinki: Swallows of Finland and Finnida, 1994 [?]. (Katta Ka-Batembo, Tanzania; Frank Odoi, Ghana; Leif Packalén, Finland).

Beur Culture and Comics

22.   Boudjellal, Farid. *La Famille Slimani: Gags à l'Harissa*. Paris: Editions Humanos, 1989.

23.   Boudjellal, Farid. *La Gourbi: L'Oud II*. Paris: Futuropolis, 1985.

24.   Boudjellal, Farid. *Les Soirées d'Abdulah: Ratonnade*. Paris: Futuropolis, 1985.

25.   Boudjellal, Farid. *L'Oud*. Paris: Futuropolis, 1983.

26.   Boudjellal, Farid. *Ramadân: L'Oud III*. Paris: Futuropolis, 1988.

27.   Boudjellal, Farid and Larbi Mechkour. *Les Beurs*. Paris: L'Echo des Savanes/Albin Michel, 1985.

Comic Books

28.   [*Africaman*]. *WittyWorld*. Autumn/Winter 1994, p. 4.

29.   "Africana Comics at MSU." *Comic Art Collection*. May 2, 1988, pp. 3-5.

30.   African Images in Comics: file clippings and examples. Collected at Michigan State Universtiy in the Russel B. Nye Popular Culture Collection's Popular Culture Vertical File.

31.   Boyd, Robert. "Comics from the Old Country." *Comics Journal*. July 1993, pp. 27-29. (Nigerian Ossie Ogwo; Zimbabwian Boyd Maliki).

32.   Filippini, Henri. "BD pour l'Afrique." *Phénix* (Paris). No. 24, 1972.

33.   François, Edouard. "Raoul et Gaston, le Mythe Africain." *Phénix* (Paris). No. 13, 1970.

34.   Horn, Maurice. "L'Africa Nei Fuzetti: Il Continente Mitico." In *Striscie d'Africa*. Turin: Provincia Di Torino, 1985.

35.   "La Bande Dessinée, un Luxe pour l'Afrique." *Coccinelle*. June 1990, p. 8.

36.   Pierre, Michel. "Un Certain Rêve Africain." *Les Cahiers de la Bande Dessinée* (Grenoble). No. 56, 1984, pp. 83-86.

37.   "Voice of the Third World (Seraphina)." *Time*. November 4, 1966, pp. 79-80.

Political Cartoons

38.   Sahlström, Berit. "Political Posters in Ethiopia and Mocambique, Visual Imagery in a Revolutionary Context." Ph.D. dissertation, Uppsala (Sweden) University, 1990. (Acta Universitatis Upsaliensis, Nova Series 24. ISBN 91-554-2642-5).

39.   "Thus Spake the Cartoonists." *Index on Censorship*. November 1992, p. 38. (Gabon and Zaire).

40.   Watremez, Emmanuel. "The Satirical Press in Francophone Africa." *Index on Censorship*. November 1992, pp. 34-41. (West Africa).

Periodical Directory

41.   *Jornal do Man'Kiko*. Angolan periodical about comics. Includes articles, comics, news. Issue #5, May 1993. R.15, Bloco 51, 40° esq., B. Martires de Kifangondo, Luanda, Angola. Portuguese.

42.   *Caricature*. Published in Egypt by Arab Group for Publishing and Advertising. Thirty-five page weekly of short profiles of cartoonists, galleries of their work, and a sampling of caricature, gag, and strip cartoons. Started 1992.

43.   *The Cartoonist*. Published monthly from June 1992 by Link Studios Ltd., 19 Onayade St., Fadeyi, Lagos, Nigeria. Edited by Ebun Aleshinloye. Mainly Nigerian cartoons with some humorous prose.

ALGERIA

Comic Books

44.   Aïder, Mahfoud. *Histoires pour Rire*. Algiers: Entreprise Nationale du Livre, 1984.

45.   Bessaih, B., B. Bakhti, and B. Masmoudi. *L'Epoque du Cheikh Bouamama*. Algiers: Entreprise Nationale du Livre, 1986. 51 pp.

46.   Bil-Sâ'ih, Bû 'Allâm, Bin 'Umar Bakhîtî, and B. Masmûdî. *Malhamat al-Shaykh Bû 'Imâma*, part 1. Algiers: Entreprise Nationale du Livre, 1986.

47.   Brahim, Guerroui. *Les Enfants de la Liberte*. Algiers: Entreprise Nationale du Livre, ca. 1986. 31 pp.

48.   *Ca, C'Est du Sport!* Algiers: Entreprise du Livre, 1984. 50 pp.

49.   Hankour Mohamed. *Soloeïs: L'Ile du Grand Ordo*. Algiers: Entreprise Nationale du Livre, 1985.

50.   "La Scuola Algerina, a Cura di Mario Gomboli." *If*. November 1982, p. 34.

51.   Malek. *La Route du Sel*. Algiers: Entreprise Nationale du Livre, 1984.

52.   Masmûdi, B. and Ahmâd Bû Hilâl. *al-Amîr 'Abd al-Qâdir, part 1*. Algiers: Entreprise Nationale du Livre, 1985.

53.   Rafik, Ramzi. *SM15: Halte au "Plan" Terreur*. Algiers: Entreprise Nationale du Livre, 1983.

54.   Riyâd, 'Abd al-Halîm. *Mukhâtarât Muhtâl*. Algiers: al-Mu'assasa al-Wataniyya lil-Kitâb, 1986

55.   Tenani, Mustapha. *Le Fusil Chargé*. Algiers: Entreprise Nationale du Livre, 1986.

56.   Tenani, Mustapha. *Les Hommes du Djebel*. Algiers: Entreprise Nationale du Livre, 1985.

57.   Touat, D. and Ben-Abbas. *L'Orchestre aux Bananes*. Algiers: Entreprise Nationale du Livre, ca. 1984. 32 pp.

"Slim" (Menouar Merabtene)

58.   Slim. *L'Algérie de Slim*. Paris and St. Martin-D'Hères: Editions l'Harmattan and Revue "Grand Maghreb," 1983.

59.   Slim. *Réédition de Zid Ya Bouzid I & II!* Algiers: Entreprise Nationale du Livre, 1986.

60.   Slim. *Zid Ya Bouzid 3*. Algiers: Entreprise Nationale du Livre, 1986.

Comic Strips

61.   Achour, Kenza and Christiane Achour. "La B.D., l'Histoire, les Femmes: Formation par le Lecture." *Presence des Femmes*. 1987: 50-60.

62.   Amengual, Barthélemy. "Le Petit Monde de Pif le Chien." In *Travail et Culture d'Algérie*. Algiers: Argel, 1955.

63.   'Ammûrî, Mansûr and Ahmâd Bû Hilâl. *Al-Durûb al-Wa 'ra*. Algiers: al-Mu'assasa al-Wataniyya lil-Kitâb, 1984.

64. Garawî and 'Abbâs. *Abnâ' al-Hurriyya*. Algiers: al-Mu'assasa al-Wataniyya lil-Kitâb, 1986.

65. Kaci. *Bas les Voiles*. Paris: Les Editions Rochevignes, 1984.

Political Cartoons

66. Slyomovics, Susan. "Algeria Caricatures the Gulf War." *Public Culture*. Spring 1992, pp. 93-99.

ANGOLA

Comic Books

67. "Angola no Festival de Banda Desenhada da Amadora." *Jornal do Man'Kiko*. May 1993, p. 5.

68. Mantlo, Bill. "From Slavery to Freedom: A Comic Book from Angola." *Comics Journal*. March 1979, pp. 60-61.

69. "Regras Básicas para a Realização de Uma B.D." *Jornal do Man'Kiko*. May 1993, pp. 14-15.

CAMEROON

General Studies

70. Mbangwana, Paul. "Some Instances of Linguistic and Literary Resource in Certain Humorous Cameroonianisms." *Humor*. 6:2 (1993), pp. 195-222.

71. Watremez, Emmanuel. "Nyemb Populi: Candid Camera." *Index on Censorship*. November 1992, p. 37. (Political cartoons).

EGYPT

General Studies

72. Marsot, Affaf Lutifif Al-Sayyid. "The Cartoon in Egypt." *Comparative Studies in Society and History*. 13:1 (1971), pp. 2-15.

Historical Aspects

73.   Bauregard, Olivier. *La Caricature Egyptienne, Historique, Politique et Morale.* Paris: Thorin et Fils, 1894.

74.   Kees, Hermann. *Arte Egípcio.* Barcelona: Editorial Labor, 1932.

75.   Maspero, Gaston. *Egypte. Ars-Una. Species-Mille. Histoire Genérale de l'Art.* Paris: Hachette & Cie, 1912.

76.   Millet, Bertrand. "Egypte: Cent Ans de Bande Dessinée." In *Langues et Cultures Populaires dans l'Aire Arabo-Musulmane*, pp. 53-67. Paris: Association Française des Arabisants, 1988.

77.   Millet, Bertrand. *Samir, Mickey, Sinbad et les Autres: Histoire de la Presse Enfantine en Egypte.* Cairo: CEDEJ, 1987.

Cartoonists and Their Works

78.   Aladin Saad. *Flying Cartoons.* Cairo: 1993. 48 pp.

79.   al-Dhâkirî, Muhammad Nu'man *et al. Jamâl 'Abd al Nâsir.* Paris: Manshûrât al-Sihâfa al-Ifrîqiyya al-Mushtaraka, 1973.

80.   al-Labbâd, Muhyî al-Dîn. *Nazar.* Cairo: al-'Arabî lil Nashr wal-Tawzî', 1987.

81.   Bahjat ('Uthmân). *Al-Diktâtûriyya lil-Mubtadi'în*: Bahjâtûs, Ra'îs Bahjâtiyâ al-'Uzimâ. Cairo: Misriyya lil-Nashr wal-Tawzî', 1989.

82.   al-Bahjûrî, Jûrj. *Bahjar fî al-Mahjar.* London: Riad El-Rayyes, 1989.

83.   Mohamad Effat. *Effat. Humor Collection.1.* Cairo: 1993. 40 pp.

84.   Mohammed Effat Abdel Azim Esmail. "'I am Defending Myself Against the Idea of Committing Suicide by Satirizing It.'" *WittyWorld.* Winter/Spring 1989, pp. 36-37. (Hosam el-Sokkari).

85.   "Obituaries." *WittyWorld.* Autumn/Winter 1994, p. 7. (Zohdy).

Hijâzî, Ahmad

86.   Hijâzî, Ahmad. *Tambûl al-Awwal* (Tambûl the First). Beirut: Dâr al-Fatâ al Arabî, 1981.

87.   Hijâzî, Ahmad. *Tanâbilat al-Sibyân wa-Tanâbilat al-Khirfân* (The Lazy Boys and the Lazy Lambs). Cairo: Dâr al Hilâl, n.d.

88.   Hijâzî, Ahmad. *Yâ Halâwatak Ya Jamâlak.* Cairo: Dâr al-Hilâl, 1989.

Rakha (Mohamed Abdil Mooneim Rakha)

89.   Mohammed Effat Abd el-Azim Esmail. "Rakha, Egypt's Pioneer Critical Cartoonist, Dies at Age 79." *WittyWorld.* Summer/Autumn 1989, pp. 10-11.

90.   Said Aboul-Enein. *Rakha, the Cavalier of Caricature. Tears and Laughter of 60 Years in the Press.* Cairo: Akhbar el-Yom, 1990. 268 pp. Arabic.

Comic Books

91.   Aladin Saad. *Technical Relations Between Comics and Arts of Photography and Movies.* Cairo: Academy of Fine Arts, Graphics Section, Helwan University, 1993.

92.   Dimpre, Henry. "Les Héros Égyptiens S'Exprimaient Déjà dans les Ballons." *Pilote* (Paris). No. 283, 1967, p. 23.

93.   Douglas, Allen and Fedwa Malti-Douglas. *L'Idéologie par la Bande: Héros Politiques de France et d'Egypte au Miroir de la BD.* Cairo: CEDEJ, 1987.

94.   el Solami, Nabil. *Unter den Pyramiden.* Berlin: Eulenspiegel-Verlag, 1972.

95.   "It's a Bird! It's a Plane! It's Nabil Fawzil!" *Aramco World Magazine.* March-April 1970, pp 19-23.

Comic Strips

96.   Douglas, Allen and Fedwa Malti-Douglas. "Le Peuple d'Egypte et Son Chef: Tensions Iconographiques dans un Strip Nassérien." In *Images d'Egypte de la Fresque à la Bande Dessinée*, pp. 87-97. Cairo: CEDEJ, 1991.

97.   Ferro, Marc. *Comment on Raconte l'Histoire aux Enfants.* Paris: Payot, 1986, pp. 93-96.

98.   Gomaa, Farhat. *It's a Hot World. It's a Very Very Hot, Funny and Exciting World.* Introduction by Zohdy el-Adawy. Cairo: El-Aref Publishing House, 1990. 128 pp. Arabic.

Political Cartoons

99.   Boylan, Richard F. "Caricatures and Concerns: The Khwaga's View of Egypt Through Egyptian Cartoons." Paper presented at International Association for Mass Communication Research, Seoul, Korea, July 4, 1994.

100. Boylan, Richard F. "Political Press Cartoons During the Crisis." In *Media in the Midst of War*, edited by Ray E. Weisenborn, pp. 57-69. Cairo: The Adham Center for Television Journalism, 1992.

101. El-Tarabichi, Maha. "A Content Analysis of Cartoons in *Al-Ahram* Before and After Lifting of Press Censorship." Master's Thesis, American University in Cairo, 1975.

102. Gomaa, Farhat. *4 Governments and the Opposition*. Introduction by Adel Hammouda. Cairo: El-Aref Publishing House, 1990. 128 pp. Arabic.

103. Khalil, Nevine. "Cartoon Strips in the Egyptian Press During the Gulf Crisis." Unpublished research report, American University in Cairo, Department of Journalism and Mass Communication, 1991.

KENYA

General Sources

104. Gikonyo, Waithira. "Comics and Comic Strips in the Mass Media in Kenya." In *Comics and Visual Culture: Research Studies From Ten Countries*, edited by Alphons Silbermann and H.-D. Dyroff, pp. 185-195. Munich: K.G. Saur, 1986.

105. Shaw, Bernhard. *Visual Symbols Survey: Report on Recognition of Drawings in Kenya*. London: Center for Educational Development Overseas, 1969.

106. Tumusiime, James. *Bogi Benda*. Nairobi, Kenya: Stellascope, 198?

Joe

107. Frederiksen, Bodil Folke. "*Joe*, the Sweetest Reading in Africa: Documentation and Discussion of a Popular Magazine in Kenya." *African Languages and Culture*. 4:2(1991), pp. 135-155.

108. Frederiksen, Bodil Folke. "Living in the Neighbourhood of One's Dreams: The Role of Popular Writing in the Creation of the Ordinary." In *Culture in Africa: An Appeal for Pluralism*, edited by Raoul Granquist, pp. 96-106. Uppsala: Nordiska Afrikainstitutet, 1993.

109.   Lindfors, Bernth. "Interview with David Maillu.: *The African Book Publishing Record*. 5:2(1979), pp. 85-88.

LIBERIA

Political Cartoons

110.   Lent, John A. "Reading Between the Lines: Controversy Over Liberian Cartoonist's Plight." *WittyWorld*. Autumn 1987, pp. 8-9.

LIBYA

Caricature

111.   *Daffy Quddafi: Malice in Wonderland*. Staten Island, New York: Comics Unlimited, 1986.

112.   "Libyan Caricaturist Zovavi." *Kayhan Caricature*. February 1993.

MADAGASCAR

General Sources

113.   Saint-Michel, Serge. "Aventures dans L'Océan Indien...Ou L'Aventure de la B.D. Malgache?" *Le Nouveau Bédésup*. 34:12 (1985).

MOROCCO

General Sources

114.   Achache, Laurent and Anissa Abderrahim, *et al. Juba II: Roi des Maures*. Meknes: Enseignement Français au Maroc, Le Lycée Paul Valéry, 1991.

115.   Chahi, Zoubida. "La Production des Livres pour Enfants au Maroc (1947-1991)." Mémoire for Diplôme, Ecole des Sciences de l'Information, Morocco, 1992.

NIGERIA

General Sources

116.   Gboyega, "Dotun." *Kabiyesi: Selected Cartoons*. Ikeja, Nigeria: Concord Press, 1985. 80 pp.

117.   Ulansky, Gene. "It's Powerman: A Black 'Superman.'" *Cartoonews*. No. 9, 1975, 2 pp., not paginated. (Reprinted from *San Francisco Chronicle*).

Political Cartoons

118.   Akintunde, Olumuyiwa. "The Fun and Fury of Cartoons." *The Guardian* (Nigeria). August 7, 1988, pp. B-1, B-4, B-8.

119.   Aleshinloye, Ebun. "On the Education of Cartoonists." *The Guardian* (Nigeria). April 17, 1988, pp. 7.

120.   Jemie, Onwuchekwa. "On the Education of Cartoonists." *The Guardian* (Nigeria). March 27, 1988, p. 7.

121.   Lent, John A. "The Neglected Plight of Nigerian Cartoonists." *WittyWorld*. Summer/Autumn 1991, pp. 30-31.

122.   *National Concord, Sunday Concord: Selected Editorial Cartoons from Boye Gbenro's Portfolio: First Series, 1985*. Ikeja, Nigeria: Concord Press, 1985. 80 pp.

123.   "On the Road to Sedition." *The Guardian* (Nigeria). August 7, 1988, p.B-4.

SENEGAL

Comics Anthologies

124.   Fall, Samba. *Sangomar*. Senegal: Nouvelles Editions Africaines du Senegal, 1989. 77 pp.

125.   *Les Aventures de Leuk-Le-Lievre: d'Apres un Texte de L.S.Senghor et A. Sadji*. Dakar: Nouvelles Editions Africaines, 1975. 43 pp.

126.   *L'Ombre de Boy Melakh*. Senegal: Nouvelles Editions Africaines du Senegal, 1989. 80 pp.

SOUTH AFRICA

Comic Books

127. Africana. South African Comics: File of clippings and miscellany. Collected at Michigan State University in the Russel B. Nye Popular Culture Collection's Popular Culture Vertical File.

128. "Comics in South Africa." *Comics Journal*. May 1992, p. 15.

129. Corral, James. "The Blue Beetle." *Komix*. April 1963.

130. *Equiano: The Slave Who Fought To Be Free*. Illustrations by Rick Andrew; script by Joyce Ozynski and Harriet Perlman. Braamfontein, South Africa: Raven Press, 1988. 48 pp.

131. Everett, Bill. "Hydroman." *Komix* (Port Elizabeth). December 1963.

132. Gifford, Denis. "McClelland, Hugh (1912-)." In *Enciclopedia Mondiale del Fumetto*, edited by Maurice Horn and Luciano Secchi, p. 541. Milan: Editoriale Corno, 1978.

133. [*Madam and Eve*]. *WittyWorld*. Autumn/Winter 1994, p. 4.

134. Mantlo, Bill. "Alternating Currents: 'South African Comics.'" *Comics Journal*. December 1978, pp. 75-79.

135. Peirce, Bronwyn N. "Toward a Pedagogy of Possibility in the Teaching of English Internationally: People's English in South Africa." *TESOL Quarterly*. September 1989, pp. 401-420

136. Willenson, K., *et al.* "Caped Crusader; Mighty Man Comics Carrying Law and Order Message to South African Blacks." *Newsweek*. June 14, 1976, p. 48.

137. Wren, Celia M. "South Africa: Empowerment Through Comics." *Comics Journal*. October 1990, pp. 23-25.

Censorship

138. "Comics Ban Lifted in S. Africa." *Comics Journal*. August 1992, p. 10.

139. "Comics Banned in South Africa." *Comics Journal*. May 1992, pp. 13-15.

140. "South African Censorship Law." *Comics Journal*. May 1992, p. 14.

Political Cartoons

141. Abramson, Glenda. "Mightier Than The Sword: Jewish Cartoons and Cartoonists in South Africa." *Humor: International Journal of Humor Research*. 4:2 (1991), pp. 149-164.

142. *Drawing the Line: Cartoonists Against Apartheid: A Selection of Illustrations from 20 Years of Anti-Apartheid News*. London: Anti-Apartheid Movement, 1985. 38 pp.

143. *Fighting Apartheid: A Cartoon History*. London: International Defence and Aid Fund for Southern Africa and UNESCO, 1988. 76 pp.

144. Grogan, Tony. *Up the Creek*. Diep River: Chameleon Press, 1986. 80 pp.

145. Keillor, G. "Mission to Mandala." *New Yorker*. May 25, 1981, pp. 38-40.

146. Kundu, Mariam. "Media Output During the South African Elections." *Action*. October-November 1994, Special report, 4 pp.

147. Shain, Milton. "From Pariah to Parvenu: The Anti-Jewish Stereotype in South Africa, 1880-1910." *Jewish Journal of Sociology*. December 1984, pp. 111-127.

148. "Zapiro Exhibited at SVA." *Comics Journal*. April 1989, p. 23.

Anderson, Dave ("Andy")

149. Anderson, Dave. *Cartoons of Andy*. Johannesburg: The Penrose Press, 1989. 220 pp.

150. Anderson, Dave. "No Laughing Matter." *WittyWorld*. Summer 1987, p. 11.

Berry, Abe

151. Williams, Roger. "Berry Here To 'Goad, Amuse.'" *Cape Times*. May 30, 1987, p. 24.

152. Williams, Roger. "South Africa's Abe Berry on the Move at 77." *WittyWorld*. Winter/Spring 1989, pp. 70-71.

Jackson, J.H.

153. Jackson, J.H. *Through Jackson's Eyes*. Capetown and Pretoria: Citadel Press, 1961.

154. MacKenzie, Vic. "Africa's Cartoon Leader: Jackson of Cape Town." *Target*. Autumn 1983, pp. 18-20.

Leyden, Jock

155. Haas, Kathleen. "Leyden: An Artist of Unique Talent and Charisma." *Witty-World*. Summer 1987, pp. 8-10.

156. Leyden, Jock. *The Best of Leyden*. Durban: Durban Rotary Club in association with *Daily News*, 1988.

157. Leyden, Jock. "'It Happened to Me': An Affair of the Heart." *Personality*. December 3, 1993, pp. 76-77.

158. Leyden, Jock. "Unremitting Opposition." *Target*. Spring 1986, pp. 16-17.

159. Said, Benedict. "Jock Leyden." *Review* (Rhodes University). December 1993, pp. 42-45.

SWAZILAND

Cartoons

160. Epskamp, Kees. "Cross-Cultural Interpretations of Cartoons and Drawings." *Media Asia*. 11:4 (1989), pp. 208-214.

161. Epskamp, Kees. "Cross-Cultural Interpretations of Cartoons and Drawings." *Media Development*. 3/1984, pp. 38-42.

TANZANIA

Comics

162. Packalén, Leif. *Say It With Comics!* Morogoro: Tanzania Popular Media Association, 1994. 20 pp. (Also Kenya, Malawi, Senegal, Zimbabwe, Ivory Coast, Cameroon, Nigeria, Mozambique, Ghana).

163. "Witty Wire." *WittyWorld*. Autumn/Winter 1994, p. 4. (Cartoonists Association).

TUNISIA

Comic Books and Strips

164. al-Aqqâd, Abbâs Mahmûd. *Juhâ al-Dâhik al-Mudhik*. Cairo: Dâr al-Hilâl, n.d.

165.   al Shâdhilî, Bikhâmisa. *Jâbir wal-Samak al-'Ajîb*. Tunis: Manshûrât Tûnis Qartâj, n.d.

166.   Darwish, Adel. "The Strip Cartoon Koran." *Index on Censorship*. April 1990, pp. 24-25.

167.   "Koran Comic Causes Stir." *Comics Journal*. April 1990, pp. 23-24.

168.   "Voice of the Third World." *Time*. November 4, 1966, pp. 79-80.

3

MIDDLE EAST

REGIONAL AND INTER-COUNTRY PERSPECTIVES

General Sources

169. Helali, Abdelhamid. "La Littérature Enfantine Extra-Scolaire dans le Monde Arabe: Analyse Formelle et Thématique des Revues pour Enfants." Thèse d'Etat, Université de Paris V, 1986.

170. [Interview: Mohsen Nouri Najafi]. *Kayhan Caricature*. February 1993.

171. "Middle East." *WittyWorld*. Winter/Spring 1989, pp. 24-30.

172. "Popular Culture." Special issue. *Middle East Report*. No. 159, 1989.

173. Qutb, Sayyid. *Ma'rikatunâ ma'a...al-Yahûd*. Cairo: Dâr al Shurûq, 1988.

174. Stauth, Georg and Sami Zubaida, eds. *Mass Culture, Popular Culture, and Social Life in the Middle East*. Frankfurt and Boulder: Campus Verlag and Westview, 1987.

Islam and Comic Art

175. Abon, Ghoudda, Abdel Satar, and Clave Florencio. *L'Avènement de l'Islam*. Translated by Dalal Khoury. Paris: Robert Laffont/Al Marifa, 1985.

176.   Alkange, Jaafar, Gabriel Garcia, and Mohammed Baina. *L'Encyclopédie de l'Histoire Islamique en Bandes Dessinées*. Paris: Editions La BBD, 1990-.

177.   Aziza, Mohamed. *L'Image et l'Islam*. Paris: Albin Michel, 1978.

178.   Binmas'ûd, Muhammad and 'Abd al-'Azîz Ishbâbû. *Silsilat Ta'rîkt al-Islâm*. Mohamedia: Manshûrât Dâr al-Afâq al-Jadîda, 1988-.

179.   Hane, Djeynab. "A Travers l'Afrique: Non au Coran en Bandes Dessinées." *Jeune Afrique*. January 29, 1990, p. 31.

180.   "Islam's Satanic Comics." *Newsweek*. February 5, 1990, p. 36.

181.   Kada, Mohamed and H. ben Hafsi. *Histoire de l'Islam en Bandes Dessinées*. Paris: Magma-Média, 1989-.

182.   [On Islamic Animation.] *Kayhan Caricature*. February 1993.

183.   Péroncel-Hugoz, Jean-Pierre. "Le Coran en Bandes Dessinées." *Le Monde*. January 7-8, 1990.pp. 1, 9.

184.   Rosenthal, Franz. *Humor in Early Islam*. Leiden: E.J. Brill, 1956.

185.   Seddik, Youssef and Benoît de Pelloux. *Si le Coran M'État Conté: Abraham* (Arabic title: *Ibrâhîm*). Geneva and Tunis: Editions Alif, 1989.

186.   Seddik, Youssef and Gioux. *Si le Coran M'Était: Les Hommes de l'Eléphant* (Arabic title: *Ashâb al-Fîl*). Geneva and Tunis: Editions Alif, 1989.

187.   Seddik, Youssef, Philippe Teulat, and Philippe Jouan. *Si le Coran M'Était Conté: Peuples Maudits* (Arabic title: *Hûd, Sâlih, Yûnus*). Geneva and Tunis: Editions Alif, 1989.

188.   Tawfîq, 'Aliyya and Kamâl Darwîsh. *Hikâyât 'Arabiyya wa-Islâmiyya: Al-Qâdi al-'Adil wa-Hikâyât Ukhrâ*. Cairo: Matâbi'al-Ahrâm al-Tijâriyya, 1986.

189.   Tawfîq, 'Aliyya and Kamâl Darwîsh. *Hikâyât 'Arabiyya wa-Islâmiyya: Sâlim wal-Asîr wa-Hikâyât Ukhrâ*. Cairo: Matâbi' al-Ahrâm al-Tijâriyya, 1986.

Caricature

190.   Ahmad Ka'abi Falahieh. "Finding Ideas in Caricature." *Kayhan Caricature*. April 1993.

191.   *al-Intifâda bil-Kârîkâtîr*. Tunis: al-Ahâlî lil-Tibâ'a wal-Nashr wal-Tawzî.' 1988.

192. Hussein Niroumand. "Exaggeration in Caricature." *Kayhan Caricature*. April 1993.

Comic Books and Strips

193. Abdi, Nidam. "Du Sultan au Beur les Arabes Vus par le BD." *Libération*. Supplement Special Angoulême 1992, p.xiii.

194. Douglas, Allen and Fedwa Malti-Douglas. *Arab Comic Strips. Politics of an Emerging Mass Culture*. Bloomington: Indiana University Press, 1994. 263 pp.

195. Mu' Taz Sawwaf. "La B.D. Arabe." In *Histoire Mondiale de la Bande Dessinée*, edited by Pierre Horay, pp. 274-277. Paris: Pierre Horay Editeur, 1989. (Lebanon, Syria, Iraq, etc.).

196. "Palestine." *Big O Magazine* (Singapore). July 1994, pp. 44-45.

197. Shaheen, Jack G. "Jack Shaheen Versus the Comic Book Arab." *The Link*. November-December 1991, pp. 1-11.

198. Tiberi, J.P. "La BD Arabe." *Phénix* (Paris). No. 23, 1972.

Political Cartoons

199. Ghareeb, Edmund, ed. *Split Vision: Portrayal of Arabs in the American Media*. Washington, D.C.: American Arab Affairs Council, 1983. (Includes George H. Damon, Jr., "A Survey of Political Cartoons Dealing with the Middle East," and Neal G. Lendenmann, "Arab Stereotyping in Contemporary Arab Political Cartoons").

200. Olivieri, Angelo. *La Lampada di Saladino. La Satira Degli Arabi Sulla Guerra del Golfo*. Bari: Edizioni Dedalo, 1991. 213 pp.

Naji Salim al-Ali

201. Ahmad Kaabi Flahieh. "Naji Al Ali." *Kayhan Caricature*. September 1993.

202. Ali Taihami. "How a Satirist Saw the PLO." *Middle East*. October 1987, p. 16.

203. "Cartoonist Shot in London Street." *Index on Censorship*. September 1987, p. 5.

204. "Cartoonist Shot on London Street." *WittyWorld* Autumn 1987, p. 3.

205. "Hanzaleh." *Kayhan Caricature*. May 1992, pp. 41-42.

206. "Murdered Cartoonist Honoured." *IPI Report*. March 1988, p. 7.

207. Naji al-Ali. "Cartoons." *Index on Censorship*. December 1984, pp. 12-13.

208. "Palestinian Cartoonist Dies of Wounds." *CPJ Update*. September-October 1987, p. 5.

209. Szabo, Joseph George. "Naji Salim al-Ali and 'Hanzala.'" *WittyWorld*. Spring 1988, pp. 5-7.

Periodical Directory

210. *Humour and Caricature*. Published in Arabic as cartoon magazine. 36 pages, mainly of cartoons, but also columns and interviews. Six issues a year; No. 21 was August/September 1992. Javad Alizadeh, P.O. Box 16765-531, Tehran, Iran.

211. *Kayhan Caricature*. Published beginning March 1992, as monthly magazine for Iranian cartoonist community. 68 pages, only two of which are in English—table of contents and running article on history of Iranian caricature. Many articles and cartoons, a number of which have been "borrowed" from *WittyWorld* and other cartoon magazines. M.H. Niroumand, *Kayhan Caricature*, Martyr Shah Cheraghi St., Ferdowsi Ave., P.O. Box 11365/9631, Tehran, Iran.

212. *Mad*. "A magazine in our mother tongue [Hebrew]." Mainly works of Israeli cartoonists; meant for more popular appeal. Published by Modan. No. 1, June 1994.

213. *Shpitz* (Sharp Edge). Hebrew quarterly of the Israeli Cartoonist Section, P.O. Box 29211, Jerusalem 91291 Israel. Generally includes caricatures, comics, humorous and satirical articles. No. 4 in October 1993.

IRAN

General Sources

214. A'li, Abolfazl. *The Graphic Art of the Islamic Revolution*. Bethesda, Maryland: Iranbooks, 1985, 100 pp.

215. "4-Dimensional Humour." *Humour and Caricature*. November-December 1993, p. 32.

216. Iradj Hashemizadeh. *Cartoons from Persia*. Graz, Austria: Druk Phil, 1994.

217.   "Iran's News Agency Reports Rushdie Caricature Contest." *AAEC Notebook.* Spring 1993, p. 12.

218.   *Kayhan Caricature.* March 1993. Editorial, History of Caricature in Iran, Caricature for Children, The History of Caricature in the World, Interview with Foreign Caricaturists, Foreign and Domestic Reports, Animation.

219.   *Kayhan Caricature.* April 1992. "Caricature Teachings," "Bureaucracy," "Why We Laugh," "A Report on Belgium Exhibition," "Book Review: 'The Wounded Volume,'" by Mohsen Nouri Najafi, "Selected," "Cartooning," by John Adkins Richardson, "History of Caricature in the World," "Caricature in Iran 2."

220.   *Kayhan Caricature.* July 1992. "The Future Has Just Begun for Computer Comics"; collection of sports cartoons by French caricaturist Blachon; Ahmad Falahieh Kaabi, "Laughter in the Far East"; cartoons on Olympics; interview with Javad Alizadeh; conversation with Iranian cartoonists on Abrar international contest; Mohsen Ibrahim, "Gourmelin Makes Everybody Scared"; Hussein Niroumand on finding ideas in caricature; comics on stamps by Pierre Horn; Masoud Shojai Tabatabai, "Caricature in Iran 5."

221.   *Kayhan Caricature.* October 1992. "Caricature in Iran," caricature teaching, psychological basis of laughter in children, body design, news caricature, "From Imagination to Thinking" (Zagreb animation), caricature on communication.

222.   Mohsen Ibrahim. "Gourmelin Makes Everybody Scared." *Kayhan Caricature.* July 1992.

223.   "'Our Team, Their Team' Animation." *Kayhan Caricature.* June 1994.

224.   "TV." *Kayhan Caricature.* June 1994.

Tehran Cartoon Biennial

225.   "A Report on Prize Giving Ceremony of the 1st Tehran International Cartoon Biennial—1993." *FECO News.* No. 16, 1994, pp. 7-11.

226.   "Caricature Competition by Readers and Amateur Cartoonists." *Humour and Caricature.* November-December 1993, pp. 30-31.

227.   [Reports on First Tehran International Caricature Biennial, 1993]. *Kayhan Caricature.* October 1993.

228.   "Tehran Cartoon Biennial." *Comics Journal.* January 1994, p. 25.

229.   *Tehran Cartoon Biennial. The First International Exhibition.* Tehran: Visual Art Association with cooperation of Tehran Contemporary Art Museum, 1994. 150 pp.

Cartoonists

230. [Ali Farzat]. *Kayhan Caricature*. July 1993.

231. "Closeness of Caricature with Comics Cinema." *Kayhan Caricature*. January 1993.

232. "Exhibition of the Works of Massoud Shojai Tabatabai." *Kayhan Caricature*. June 1994, p. 3.

233. [Hussein Khosrowjerdi]. *Kayhan Caricature*. December 1992.

234. "Interview: Bahman Abdi." *Kayhan Caricature*. September 1992.

235. "Interview: Ms Parvin Kermani." *Kayhan Caricature*. November 1992.

236. "Javad Alizadeh: Interview." *Kayhan Caricature*. July 1992.

237. "Massoud Mehrabi, Tehran, Iran." *FECO News*. No. 6, 1988, p. 4.

238. Massoud Shojai. "The First Iranian Caricaturist." *Kayhan Caricature*. September 1992.

Pouyan, Javad

239. "Interview: Javad Pouyan." *Kayhan Caricature*. October 1992.

240. "Javad Pouyan Show." *Kayhan Caricature*. October 1944.

Caricature

241. Ahmad Kaabi Falahieh. "Frame Work in Caricature." *Kayhan Caricature*. May 1993.

242. Ali Reza Khamseh." Caricature and the Comedy Art." *Kayhan Caricature*. January 1993.

243. Hussein Niroumand. "Caricature Is Not Simple." *Kayhan Caricature*. June 1994.

244. Javad Pouyan. "About Caricature." *Kayhan Caricature*. November 1992.

245. "Understanding Caricature Contest." *Humour and Caricature*. November-December 1993, p. 8.

Historical Aspects

246. Hassan Beigi. "Caricature in Iran: Those Who Paved the Way." *Kayhan Caricature*. December 1992.

247. Massoud Shojai Tabatabai. "Caricature in Iran." *Kayhan Caricature*. March 1992, pp. 48-49.

248. Massoud Shojai Tabatabai. "Caricature in Iran 2." *Kayhan Caricature*. April 1992, p. 49.

249. Massoud Shojai Tabatabai. "Caricature in Iran 3." *Kayhan Caricature*. May 1992, pp. 49-50.

250. Massoud Shojai Tabatabai. "Caricature in Iran 5." *Kayhan Caricature*. July 1992, p. 65.

251. Massoud Shojai Tabatabai. "Caricature in Iran." *Kayhan Caricature*. August 1992.

252. Massoud Shojai Tabatabai. " Caricature in Iran." *Kayhan Caricature*. October 1992, p. 57.

253. Massoud Shojai Tabatabai. "Caricature in Iran." *Kayhan Caricature*. November 1992.

254. Massoud Shojai Tabatabai. "Caricature in Iran." *Kayhan Caricature*. January 1993.

255. Massoud Shojai Tabatabai. "Caricature in Iran." *Kayhan Caricature*. June 1993.

256. Massoud Shojai Tabatabai. "Caricature in Iran—Hasharat al Arz." *Kayhan Caricature*. April 1993.

257. Massoud Shojai Tabatabai. "Caricature in Iran: The Review of Kaskul Weekly." *Kayhan Caricature*. February 1993.

258. Massoud Shojai Tabatabai. "Tanbih: Caricature in Iran." *Kayhan Caricature*. July 1993.

Political Cartoons

259. "Drawn and Quartered." *Yellow Press*. June/July 1994, p. 6.

260. Gumucio, Juan Carlos. "Mr. Flowers Dares To Joke." *IPI Report*. May 1992, p. 23.

261. Sreberny-Mohammadi, Annabelle and Ali Mohammadi. "The Islamic Republic and the World: Images, Propaganda, Intentions, and Results." In *Post-Revolutionary Iran*, edited by Hooshang Amirahmadi and Manoucher Parvin, pp. 75-106. Boulder, Colorado: Westview Press, 1988.

IRAQ

General Sources

262. Makkî, Adîb. *Al-Ayyâm al-Tawîla*. Baghdad: Dâr Thaqâfat al-Atfâl, 1981.

ISRAEL

General Sources

263. "Cartoon Exhibition in Holon." *Shpitz* (Israel). No. 5, 1994, p. 66.

264. Jago, Mik. "News from Israel." *FECO News*. No. 16, 1994, p. 19.

265. "Kibbutz Cartoon Workshop Gains Popularity in Israel." *WittyWorld*. Winter/ Spring 1990, p. 14.

266. "MAD To Appear." *Shpitz* (Israel). No. 5, 1994, p. 67.

267. [Pencom]. *WittyWorld*. Autumn/ Winter 1994, p. 4.

268. "Portugal Also Discovers Israeli Comic Art." *Shpitz* (Israel). No. 5, 1994, p. 65.

Cartoonists

269. "Cartoonist from Ga'aton Kibbutz: Shmulik Katz." *Shpitz* (Israel). No. 5, 1994, p. 66.

270. "Censored: Moshik Lyn." *Shpitz* (Israel). No. 5, 1994, p. 67.

271. "Comic-Strip Artist Sues U.S. Publisher." *Shpitz*. No. 6, 1994. (Michael Netser).

272. "14 Israelis in Italian Cartoon Festival." *Shpitz*. No. 6, 1994.

273. Hofmekler, Ori. *Hofmekler's People*. New York: Holt, Rinehart and Winston, 1982. 128 pp.

274.   "Kichka in Singapore." *Shpitz*. No. 6, 1994.

275.   "Moldovenu Nicolae." *FECO News*. No. 8, 1989, p. 8.

276.   "Moshik Lyn, Public Envoy to Boston." *Shpitz*. No. 6, 1994.

277.   Perry, Smadar. "How Arabic Cartoonists [Media] Deal with Israeli Issues."
        Yediot Aharonot. October 22, 1993, pp. 48-49.

278.   "Ranan Lurie." *Cartoonist PROfiles*. No. 19, 1973, pp. 48-53.

279.   Saner-Lamken, Brian. "Israeli Cartoonists Hold Exhibition." *Comics Buyer's
        Guide*. November 12, 1993, p. 54.

280.   "30 Israeli Cartoonists Exhibited in Lisbon." *Shpitz* (Israel). No. 5, 1994, pp. 69-
        70. (Moshik Lyn, Shmulik Katz, Ze'ev, Michel Kichka).

Fink, Uri

281.   Fink, Uri. *Zbang!* Tel Aviv: Adar, 1989.

282.   "Uri Fink." *Shpitz* (Israel). No. 5, 1994, p. 65.

Gardosh, K. ("Dosh")

283.   Dosh (K. Gardosh). *220 Israel Cartoons by Dosh*. n.p.: Karni Publishers, Ltd.,
        1956. 130 pp.

284.   Honig, Sarah. "The Many Names of Dosh." *Jerusalem Post*. December 6, 1991.

Ze'ev (Ya'acov Farkas)

285.   Association of Israeli Cartoonists. *The Golden Book of Ze'ev*. Tel Aviv: Zmora
        Bitan, 1993. Hebrew.

286.   Benziman, Uzi. "Political Process in a Few Lines." In *Ze'ev: Eyewitness with a
        Smile*, pp. 24-28. London: National Museum of Cartoon Art, 1994.

287.   "Egy Keeskemétröl Induló Világhírü Karikaturistáról." *Kecskeméti Lapok*.
        September 6, 1991.

288.   Éva, Róna. "Zeév Sikeres Kiállitása." *Ahet Tukre*. October 24, 1991, p. 38.

289.   Maranz, Felice. "The Cutting Edge." *The Jerusalem Report*. November 21, 1991,
        p. 34. (Reprinted in *The Jester*. April 1992, p. 13).

290.   Naor, Daphna. "Ze'ev: Eyewitness with a Smile." In *Ze'ev: Eyewitness with a
        Smile*, pp. 11-19. London: National Museum of Cartoon Art, 1994.

291. Ronnen, Meir. "In Bed with the Pols." *Magazine*. November 15, 1991.

292. Silver, Eric. "Paprika Makes Cartoonists' Pens Flow with Spice." *The Jester*. March 1993. (Reprinted from *Jewish Chronicle*. February 5, 1993).

293. *Ze'ev: Eyewitness with a Smile*. London: National Museum of Cartoon Art, 1994. 56 pp.

294. Ze'ev. *From Bad to Worse*. Political Cartoons 1972-78. Tel Aviv: Zmora Bitan Modan, 1978. Hebrew.

295. Ze'ev. *Headlines*. Political Cartoons 1962-68. Tel Aviv: Levin Epstein, 1968. Hebrew.

296. Ze'ev. *Marriage Israeli Style. A Collection of Caricatures Between 1978-1991*. Introduction by Dan Patir. Tel Aviv: Zmora-Bitan, 1991.

297. Ze'ev. *Package Deal*. 170 Political Cartoons, 1967-72. Tel Aviv: Eked, 1972. Hebrew and English.

298. Ze'ev. *The Peace Process*. Tel Aviv: Eked, 1979. Hebrew.

299. Ze'ev. *Ze'ev Három Év*. Bnei Brak: Ahét Tükre, 1987. Hungarian.

300. "Zeev Draws the Israeli Political Scene." *In Jerusalem*. January 11, 1991.

301. "Ze'ev: Eyewitness with a Smile: Exhibition." *Shpitz*. No. 6, 1994.

302. "Ze'ev to London." *Shpitz*. No. 6, 1994.

Comic Books and Strips

303. Fogel, Sheva. "An Interview with Michael Netzer." *Comics Journal*. April 1991, pp. 35-36.

304. "Israeli Comic Art." *Yediot Aharonot*. March 19, 1993, pp. 32-34. Hebrew.

305. Kirschen, Ya'akov. *Dry Bones: Israel's Comic Strip*. Tel Aviv: Jerusalem Post and Cherryfield Associates, 1976.

Political Cartoons

306. Fogel, Sheva. "Drawing on Politics and Chutzpah." *Comics Journal*. April 1991, pp. 31-34.

307.   Gardosh (Dosh), K. "Political Caricature As a Reflection of Israel's Development." In *Jewish Humor*, edited by Avner Ziv, pp. 203-214. Tel Aviv: Papyrus, 1986.

308.   Kempe, Frederick. "Cartoonists in Israel, Cutting Very Deeply, Draw Begin's Blood." *Wall Street Journal*. November 30, 1982, pp. 1, 20.

LEBANON

General Sources

309.   Day, Richard C. and Maryam Ghandour. "The Effect of Television-Mediated Aggression and Real-Life Aggression on the Behavior of Lebanese Children." *Journal of Experimental Child Psychology*. August 1984, pp. 7-18.

310.   "Lebanese Cartoonist." *Group Media Journal*. 7:3/4 (1988), p. 25.

QATAR

General Sources

311.   "Cartoons and Comics on Qatar Football Tournament." *Humour and Caricature*. November-December 1993, pp. 18-19.

312.   [Salman Al Malek]. *Kayhan Caricature*. January 1993.

SAUDI ARABIA

General Sources

313.   Davis, Ed and Dick Massey. "Freelancing in the Middle East and Other Frightening Tales." *Cartoonist PROfiles*. March 1979, pp. 88-91.

314.   Greene, Jay. "Euro Disney's Prince Comes Through." *Variety*. June 6-12, 1994, p. 31.

315.   Neal, Jim. "Disney Characters To Travel to Saudi Arabia Under Pact." *Comics Buyer's Guide*. April 1, 1994, p. 54.

SYRIA

General Sources

316. Ba'labakkî, Fâtima, Nabîl Qaddûh, and Sarmad Junayd. *Rihlât Ibn Battûta.* 2 Vols. Beirut: Mu'assasat Bisât al-Rûh, n.d.

317. "Syrian Comic Art." *Yediot Aharonot.* March 5, 1993, pp. 12-13. Hebrew.

UNITED ARAB EMIRATES

Comic Books and Strips

318. al-Nuways, 'Abd Allâh. *Wasâ 'il al-I'lâm fî Dawlat al-Imârât al-'Arabiyya al-Muttahida.* Abu Dhabi: Shirkat Abû Zabî lil-Tibâ 'a wal Nashr, 1982 [?]. (Comics magazine, *Mâjid*).

319. Badr, Anwar and Muhammad Bayram. *al-Naqîb Khalfân wal-Musâ'id Fahmân wal-Khârijûn 'alâ al-Qânûn.* Abu Dhabi: Mu'assasat al-Ittihâd lil-Sihâfa wal-Nashr wal-Tawzî, n.d. (Crime comics).

320. Salîm, Jamâl and Hijâzî. *'Isâbat al-Khamsa wal-Maharâjâ.* Abu Dhabi: Matâbi' Mu'assasat al-Ittihâd lil-Sihâfa wal-Nashr, n.d. (Crime comics).

321. 'Umar, Ahmad and Hijâzî. *Dâ'irat Ma'ârif Zakiyya al-Dhakiyya.* Abu Dhabi: Maktabat Mâjid, n.d. (Strip, "Zakiyya al-Dhakiyya").

322. 'Umar, Ahmad and Mustafâ Rahma. *Kaslân Jiddan Hawl al-'Alam wa-Qisas Ukhrâ.* Abu Dhabi: Maktabat Mâjid, 1984. (Strip, "Kaslân Jiddan").

4

ASIA

CONTINENTAL AND INTER-COUNTRY PERSPECTIVES

General Sources

323. Ahmad Falahieh Kaabi. "Laughter in the Far East." *Kayhan Caricature*. July 1992.

324. Atsev, Kroum. "The Grotesque Realism of the East." *Apropos*. No. 1, 1983, pp. 140-143.

325. *Chôjū giga*. (Scrolls of Animal Caricatures). 2 Vols. Honolulu: East-West Center Press, 1969.

326. "Cute Little Round Profits." *Asiaweek*. October 12, 1990, pp. 72-73.

327. Feinberg, Leonard, ed. *Asian Laughter: An Anthology of Oriental Satire and Humor*. New York: Weatherhill, 1971, pp. 419-541.

328. Ono, Kōsei. *Ima Ajia Ga Omoshiroi: Manga, Eiga, Animēshon* [Now Asia Is Interesting: Comics, Films, and Animation]. Tokyo: Shōbunsha, 1983. 216 pp.

329. "Two More Bans." *Asiaweek*. January 18, 1980, p. 13.

330. "Violent Video Games Causing Concern in Asian States." *Asian Mass Communication Bulletin*. March-April 1994, p. 4.

331.   Yang Changjun, ed. *Cartoons and Jokes from Hong Kong and Taiwan*. Beijing: Huaji Publishing House, 1989.

Cartooning, Cartoons

332.   "Cartoonists Back to Work." *Asian Messenger*. Autumn 1979/Spring 1980, p. 8.

333.   "Cartoons Communicate." *Action*. July 1984. p. 8.

334.   "Cartoons Funny and Feisty." *Asiaweek*. January 30, 1981, pp. 10-11.

335.   "Cartoons with Health Messages." *ABU Newsletter*. September 1973, p. 25.

336.   Davies, Derek. "Traveller's Tales." *Far Eastern Economic Review*. January 7, 1988, p. 25. (China, Hong Kong cartoons).

337.   Lent, John A. *Asian Cartooning and Comics* (tentative title). Jackson, Mississippi: University Press of Mississippi, forthcoming.

338.   Lent, John A. "Aspects of Asian Cartooning." Talk before Myanmar Cartoonist Association, Yangon, Myanmar, July 30 1993.

339.   Lent, John A. "Cartooning in Asia." Paper presented at 11th Annual International Salon du Dessin de Presse et d'Humour, St. Just le Martel, France, October 4, 1992.

340.   Lent, John A. "Cartooning in Vietnam and Cambodia." *WittyWorld*. Forthcoming.

341.   Lent, John A. "Cartooning Malaysia and Singapore Style." Paper presented at Popular Culture Association, Chicago, Illinois, April 8, 1994.

342.   Lent, John A. "Cartoons and Comics in the Philippines, Singapore, and Indonesia." Paper presented at Popular Culture Association, New Orleans, Louisiana, April 10, 1993.

343.   Lent, John A. "Cartoons in Hong Kong and South Korea." *Asian Culture Quarterly*. Summer 1993, pp. 16-32.

344.   Lent, John A. "Comic Art and Film in Taiwan and the Philippines." Paper presented at Third International Conference, Asian Cinema Studies Society, New York, New York, June 12, 1992.

345.   Lent, John A. "Comic Art in Asia: History and Present Status." *Asian Thought & Society*. March-July 1983, pp. 94-111.

346.   Lent, John A. "Comic Art in Asian Mass Media." Public lecture, National Art Gallery, Kuala Lumpur, Malaysia, November 2, 1973.

347.   Lent, John A. "Comic Art in Hong Kong and South Korea." Paper presented at Mid-Atlantic Region, Association for Asian Studies, West Chester, Pennsylvania, November 1, 1992.

348.   Lent, John A. "Comic Art in Hong Kong, South Korea, and Taiwan." Paper presented at Popular Culture Association, Louisville, Kentucky, March 20, 1992.

349.   Lent, John A. "Comic Books, Funnies and Political Cartoons: The Asian Experience." *International Popular Culture*. 2:2 (1982), pp. 22-51.

350.   Lent, John A. "Confucius, Common Man, Kenkoy: The Fascinating World of Asian Cartooning." Paper presented at 2nd Annual Comic Arts Conference, San Diego, California, August 18, 1993.

351.   Lent, John A., ed. "Asian Cartooning." Special number. *Philippines Communication Journal*. March 1993. 80 pp. (Cambodia, India, Japan, Malaysia, Philippines, Taiwan).

352.   Park Byung-Ho. "Autopsy of Adult Cartoons in Korea and Japan." *Monthly Hot Wind* (Seoul). May 1993, pp. 19-23.

353.   "Serving Up the Cartoons." *Media for Asia's Communications Industry*. December 1979, p. 3.

354.   Shimizu, Isao. "Cultural Research on Southeast Asian Comics—Singapore, Brunei, and Indonesia." *Fūshiga Kenkyū*. No. 12, 1994, pp. 9-14.

Animation

355.   "Anima Vision." *ABU Newsletter*. January 1975, p. 27.

356.   "BVI Closes Subdistribution Deals in Four Areas." *Variety*. September 21, 1992, p. 62.

357.   "Cartoons with Health Messages." *ABU Newsletter*. September 1973, p. 25.

358.   "Children's Programmes." *Broadcaster*. March 1990, p. 18.

359.   "Children's Television Run by Children." *ABU Newsletter*. October/November 1970, p. 35.

360.   Crosby, Darin. "Drawing Up New Rules for Animation." *Asia Pacific Broadcasting*. May 1994, pp. 10, 12.

361.   Feazel, Mike, Mike Galbraith, Nick Demuth. "Asia Gains from Animation Boom." *Asia Pacific Broadcasting.* October 1991, pp. 12-13, 15-16.

362.   Goldrich, Robert. "Can American Animators Help Losing Work to the Far East." *TV World.* August 1982, p. 10. (Taiwan, Korea).

363.   Halligan, Fin. "Turner Takes Toons to Asian Viewers." *Variety.* October 10-16, 1994, p. 50.

364.   Johnstone, Bob. "Dream Machines." *Far Eastern Economic Review.* December 24-31, 1992, pp. 66-68.

365.   Karp, Jonathan. "Disney's World of Fantasy." *Far Eastern Economic Review.* December 30, 1993-January 6, 1994, p. 40.

366.   Lent, John A. *The Asian Film Industry.* London: Christopher Helm, 1990. 310 pp. (Burma, p. 221; Japan, p. 57; Korea, p. 132; Philippines, pp. 156, 182; Thailand, p. 220).

367.   Lent, John A. "Offshore Animation in Asia." Paper presented at 16th Annual Ohio University Film Conference, Athens, Ohio, November 4, 1994.

368.   "The Making of Turtle Power." *Asiaweek.* December 6, 1991, p. 67.

369.   "New Realities in Asia." In *Cartoons: One Hundred Years of Cinema Animation,* by Giannalberto Bendazzi. Bloomington: Indiana University Press, 1994. (Israel, pp. 397-398; Turkey, pp. 398-399; Iran, pp. 399-401; China, pp. 401-402; Vietnam, pp. 403-404; India, pp. 404-407; Sri Lanka, p. 407; Indonesia, p. 407; Thailand, pp. 407-408; Taiwan, p. 408; Mongolia, pp. 408-409; Singapore, p. 409; Malaysia, p. 409; The Philippines, pp. 409-410; Hong Kong, p. 410; North Korea, p. 410; South Korea, p. 411; Japan's Expansion, pp. 411-418).

370.   Palmer, Rhonda. "Asia Feeds the Cartoon World." *Variety.* May 27, 1991, pp. 41, 66.

371.   Poole, Bernard. "Cartoons Provide Light Relief for Film Men." *Media for Asia's Communications Industry.* March 8, 1982, pp. 6-7.

372.   "Television for Children." *ABU Newsletter.* September 1970, p. 51.

373.   *Television for Very Young Children and Their Parents. Reports and Papers of a Seminar (Kuala Lumpur, March 7-12, 1976).* [ERIC # ED 164 005]. (Bangladesh, Hong Kong, Indonesia, Korea, Japan, Malaysia, Pakistan, Singapore, Thailand).

374.   Williams, Michael. "Gallic Toonster To Ankle Asia." *Variety.* June 3, 1991, pp. 43, 76.

Comic Books

375. "Asian and Asian-American Portrayals in Comics." Clipping file, 194?-. 1 portfolio. Michigan State University, Russel B. Nye Popular Culture Collection's Popular Culture Vertical File.

376. "Asian Tales for Young Readers." *Asiaweek.* July 8, 1988, p. 30.

377. "Cartoons and Comics." *Asian Culture.* Special issue, January 1980.

378. "Comic Book Economics." *Asian Mass Communication Bulletin.* 17:5 (1987), p. 7.

379. "Comics: Asia's Factories of Fantasy." *Asiaweek.* December 4, 1981, pp. 51-52, 55.

380. Deverall, Richard L.-G. "American Comic Books In Asia." *America.* December 22, 1951, pp. 333-335; February 26, 1952, p. 494.

381. "Hooked on Comics." *Asiaweek.* May 6, 1988, pp. 42-44.

382. Lent, John A. "Asian Comics: As Different As Durian, Kaki, and Rambutan." *Jurnal Komunikasi* (Malaysia). Forthcoming.

383. Lent, John A. "Asian Comics: As Different As Durian, Kaki, and Rambutan." Lecture presented at Omiya cartoons exhibition opening, Omiya, Japan, November 4, 1993.

384. Lent, John A. "Asian Manga Industry." Paper presented at 1st AnimEast, New Brunswick, New Jersey, November 13, 1994.

385. Lent, John A. "Comic Books in Asia: The Findings from 200 Interviews." Paper presented at International Association for Mass Communication Research, Seoul, Korea, July 4, 1994.

386. Lent, John A. "Comic Books in Bangladesh, Myanmar, Sri Lanka, Thailand, and Vietnam." Paper presented at Mid-Atlantic Region, Association for Asian Studies, Ramapo, New Jersey, October 31, 1993.

387. Lent, John A. "Comics in Hong Kong, Korea, and Taiwan." *Journal of Popular Culture.* Forthcoming.

388. Lent, John A. "Comics Off the Beaten Path: Bangladesh, Burma, Vietnam." Paper presented at Popular Culture Association, Chicago, Illinois, April 9, 1994.

389. Lent, John A. "Southeast Asian Cartooning: Comics in Philippines, Singapore and Indonesia." *Asian Culture Quarterly.* Winter 1993, pp. 11-23.

390. Lent, John A. "Southeast Asian Cartooning: Comics in Philippines, Singapore, and Indonesia." *Humor*. Forthcoming.

391. Lent, John A. "Young Dinosaurs, *Oishimbo, Maus*: Comics for Literacy, Education, Consciousness Raising." Paper presented at World Association of Christian Communication, Manila, Philippines, October 1989.

392. Lim Cheng Tju. "Comic Book Confidential: Meet John Lent, Who's Giving Comics a Scholatic [sic] Slant." *Big O Magazine*. January 1993, pp. 64-65.

393. "Moving Pictures." *Asiaweek*. May 6, 1988, p. 43.

394. Neal, Jim. "Marvel Plans To Sell Comics in Japan, China." *Comics Buyer's Guide*. July 2, 1993, p. 22.

395. Ono, Kōsei. *Asia no Manga* (Comics in Asia). Tokyo: Taishūkan Shoten, 1993. Japanese.

396. "Popular Comics in Asia and the Pacific." *Asian Book Development Newsletter*. 19:2 (1988), pp. 3-6.

397. Vittachi, Nury. "That's Entertainment?" *Far Eastern Economic Review*. December 29, 1994 and January 5, 1995, pp. 74-75.

Political Cartoons

398. Ali, Saleha. "Corky's Caustic Cartoons." *Straits Times* (Singapore). September 27, 1989.

399. Allison, Tony, Angela Jeffs, Joyce Moy, Helen Ann Peters, and Henry Yap. "Figure It Out." *Asia Magazine*. January 7-9, 1994, pp. 8-13. (Profiles Lat, Chai Rachawat, Larry Feign, Jess Abrera, James Suresh, Johnny Lau, Yu Cheng, Hari Sunao).

400. "ASEAN Cartoonists Urge Regional Publication on Editorial Cartoons." *Asian Mass Communication Bulletin*. September/October 1989, pp. 8-9.

401. Borromeo, Tom. "Political Cartoonists." *Feedback*. Summer 1984, pp. 8-13.

402. Chua, Morgan. *Ying and Yang*. Hong Kong: Michael Stevenson Ltd., 1975. 124 pp.

403. "The Communicative Power of the Humble Political Cartoon." *Media Asia*. 13:4 (1986), pp. 195, 234.

404. "How Asia's Cartoonists Saw the Year." *Far Eastern Economic Review.* December 26, 1991- January 2, 1992, pp. 33-37.

405. "How Asia's Cartoonists Saw the Year." *Far Eastern Economic Review.* December 24-31, 1992, pp. 36-38.

406. Lent, John A. "Few Laughs Left for Asia's Cartoonists." *Leader.* 2:4 (1973), pp. 10-12.

407. Lent, John A. "Political Adversaries and Agents of Social Change: Editorial Cartoonists in Southeast Asia." *Asian Thought and Society.* May-August 1994, pp. 108-124.

408. Lent, John A. "Political Adversaries and Agents of Social Change: Editorial Cartoonists in Southeast Asia." Paper presented at Mid Atlantic Region, Association for Asian Studies, Pittsburgh, Pennsylvania, October 22, 1994.

409. "More Trouble for Cartoonists." *WittyWorld.* Autumn/Winter 1994, p. 5. (Cambodia, India).

410. Valbuena, Vic. *Editorial Cartooning: Workshop Report, Kuala Lumpur, Malaysia, 18-21 September 1989.* Singapore: Asian Mass Communication Research and Information Centre, 1989.

411. "A Wit That Travels Well." *Asiaweek.* February 9, 1990, p. 32. (ASEAN).

412. Zunzi. *Postliticians. 100 Caricatures of China, Taiwan and Hong Kong.* Hong Kong: Jimmy Pang C. Ming, 1993. 64 pp.

Periodical Directory

413. *Animag.* Published quarterly by Pacific Rim Publishing Company, 3833 Lakeshore Ave., Oakland, California. Devoted to Japanese animation.

414. *The AniManga Nuzu.* "An anime/manga newsletter" published by M.C. Ling. No.3, 1988.

415. *Anime-Club.* Hong Kong periodical devoted to Japanese animation.

416. *Anime Exchange.* A monthly fanzine of advertisements for anime trade, sales, clubs, etc., and reviews, reports, art. Chris Young, 826 Park Ave., Wilmette, Illinois 60091. 1987-.

417. *Anime Fandom Organization.* Monthly of 20 pages with synopses, episode guides, commentary, news on Japanese animation. James Staley, P.O. Box 268, Jones, Oklahoma 73049.

418. *Anime Illustrated.* Bi-monthly of synopses, fan fiction and manga, art on Japanese comics. James Lomax, 615 Las Lomas Rd., Duarte, California 91010.

419. *Animeland.* Quarterly French-language periodical devoted to Japanese animation. Animarte, 15 Rue de Phalsbourg, 75017 Paris, France.

420. *Animenominous!* Scheduled quarterly (but less frequent) magazine of Japanese animation. Reviews, news, editorials, mainly plot summaries. BDC Enterprises, PO Box 549, Indian Lake, New York 12842. Since Summer 1990.

421. *Animerica.* Published monthly by Viz Communications, P.O. Box 77010, San Francisco, California 94107. Designed to bring Japanese animation and manga information to Americans. First issue, November 1992.

422. *Anime UK Magazine.* Published by Helen McCarthy, 147 Francis Road, Leyton, London E10 6NT, England. Monthly of news, plot summaries, reviews, interviews, letters concerning Japanese animation.

423. *Anime Zasshi.* Fanzine of Japanese animation with synopses, song lyrics, news, episode guides. Steve Chaney, 7033 53rd Ave., Sacramento, California 95828.

424. *Anime-Zine.* Science fiction and fantasy animation quarterly of 42 pages, including letters, reviews, and news about Japanese animation. Minstrel Press Inc., P.O. Box 87, Rahway, New Jersey 07065-9998. First issue, 1986.

425. *A.T. Newsletter.* Published quarterly in 1986-87 with news of its sponsor, Yoyogi Institute of Animation, Tokyo.

426. *Big O* (Before I Get Old). Monthly published by Options Publications, P.O. Box 663, Robinson Road, Singapore. Country's only independent rock and roll magazine, the monthly carries articles, reviews, and interviews concerning comics. Since 1986.

427. *Cartoon Magazine.* Monthly Bangladeshi periodical devoted to all aspects of comic art in that country and others. Published since 1980 in Bengali, *Cartoon Magazine* was credited for providing a significant outlet for Bangladeshi cartoonists. Defunct as of late 1993. 33/1, Purana Paltan, Dhaka 1000, Bangladesh.

428. *The Cartoonist.* Irregularly published periodical of The Cartoonist Association of the Republic of China. News of association activities, information on the cartoon arts. Third issue published in 1990.

429. *Comic Box.* Monthly for comic, cartoon, and animation fans in Japan, Asia "and all over the world." Price lists, features, highlights of various titles. In Japanese. Vol. 95, August 1993.

430. *Daejoong Manwha* (Popular Cartoons) created in January 1990 by the Saeachim Publishing Company, Seoul, Korea.

431. *Dirty Pair Fanzine*. Episode guides, fan fiction, character guide on Japanese animation, "Dirty Pair." Richard Andreoli, 6369 Lake Alturas Ave., San Diego, California 92119.

432. *Duli Manhua* (Independent Cartoons). Published in Shanghai, September 1935 - February 1936.

433. *Fact Sheet Five*. Directory of fanzines and clubs. P.O. Box 170099, San Francisco, California 94117-0099.

434. *From Side to Side*. Monthly fanzine of episode guides and synopses of Japanese animation. Alec Orrock, 24950 Via Florecer #35, Mission Viejo, California 92692.

435. *Fūshiga Kenkyū* (The Study of Satiric Cartoons). Quarterly with many articles on Japanese comics and cartoons. In Japanese. Isao Shimizu, Akitsu 3-2-1-4, Narashino-shi, Chiba-ken, Japan.

436. *Ikkoku-kan Times*. Monthly fanzine geared towards Los Angeles anime fandom. News, directory, reviews. 1441 Armacost Ave., #1, Los Angeles, California 90025-2230. No. 3 in 1994.

437. *JAC Victoria Fangazine*. Bi-monthly fanzine of episode guides and news on Japanese comics. Ed Sum, 1807 Francisco Terrace, Victoria, B.C. V8N 4W2, Canada.

438. *JAM Japanese Animation Magazine*. Fanzine of reviews and articles on Japanese animation. JAM, 7017 Burnside Dr., San Jose, California 95120. Started in 1988.

439. *Japanese Animation Movement*. "The Animation News Magazine" first published in Summer 1992. Mainly reviews of anime. Quarterly of about 32 pages. Jam Publications, 32 Market Street, New York, New York 10002.

440. *Japanese Animation News and Review*. Newsletter of the club Hokubei Anime-kai. Japanese animation news, synopses, etc. P.O. Box 279, Botsford, Connecticut 06404.

441. *Japanimation*. Published quarterly by Eclectic Press (Detroit, Michigan) beginning in late 1980s. Interviews on Japanese animation and its U.S. invasion; polls, reviews, columns.

442. *Jiuwang Manhua* (National Salvation Cartoons). Published in Shanghai, September-November 1937.

443. *Kappa Magazine*. Italian-language monthly with color features and black and

white manga. Edizioni Star Comics, Viadi Vallingegno 2/a, Bosco, PG, Italy.

444. *Kiasu Magazine.* Quarterly made up of "Kiasu" comics, started in 1992, by Comix Factory Pte Ltd., 50A, Burnfoot Terrace, Singapore 1545.

445. *Let's Anime!* Reviews, interviews. David Merrill, P.O. Box 724182, Atlanta, Georgia 31139-1182. No. 5 in 1994.

446. *Mangajin.* Published ten times yearly to help teach Japanese language and culture through manga. Each issue includes comics in Japanese with detailed annotations on their linguistic and cultural qualities. 200 N. Cobb Parkway, Suite 421, Marietta, Georgia 30062. Begun in 1990.

447. *Manga Mania.* Monthly with strips and articles on Japanese comics. Park Horse International, 16-24 Underwood St., London N1 9EF, England.

448. *Manga Vizion.* Billed as "North America's First Monthly Manga Anthology." First issue in early 1995. 96 pages with three to four titles in each issue. Viz Comics, P.O. Box 77010, San Francisco, California 94107.

449. *Mangazine.* Monthly Italian-language periodical dealing with Japanese comics. Granata Press, Via Marconi No. 47, 40122 Bologna, Italy.

450. *Mangazine.* Anime and comics magazine published by Antarctic Press, P.O. Box 290221, San Antonio, Texas 78210-1621. Includes comics, articles, interviews, reviews. Since 1991.

451. *Manwha Gwangjang* (Cartoon Square). Monthly comic magazine which made its debut in Seoul, Korea, in December 1985.

452. *Manwha Shinmun.* Started in September 1986 as a cartoon newspaper by Minjok Misool Hyupuiwhoe (National Folk Art Association), Seoul.

453. *Manwha Sidae.* Weekly Korean cartoon magazine, started by Samji Moonwha Company, Seoul, Korea, in December 1988.

454. *Manwha Sosik* (Cartoon News). Newsletter of Cartoonist Association of Korea, started January 1976.

455. *Manwha Teo* (Cartoon Field). Quarterly of 62 pages published by The Korean Cartoonists Association. Articles, news, interviews about Korean cartooning. No. 8 in Winter 1994; started in late 1992 or early 1993. Korean.

456. *Mecha Press.* Started as bi-monthly mecha, gaming magazine with articles, reviews, editorials. Ianus Publications, 2360 de LaSalle Avenue, Studio 211, Montreal, Quebec, Canada H1V 2L1. Since 1991.

457. *Mongolcomics.* Started in 1993. Comic strips of Mongolia. Hiimori Publishing

House, P.O. Box 371, Ulanbatar 49, Mongolia.

458. *Monthly Comic Magazine*. Published by Jimmy Pang in Hong Kong. Six issues, usually of 80 pages or more, from 1990 through July 1991. Articles, critiques, new releases, reviews, interviews dealing with U.S., Hong Kong, China, Taiwan, and Japanese comics and animation. In Chinese language.

459. *Newtype*. Japanese movie and animation magazine in Japanese. No. 7 was July 1988.

460. *Oklahoma Megazone*. Monthly fanzine of anime reviews, articles, con reports, commentaries, manga and CD reviews. Burke Rukes, 2937 SW 26th, Oklahoma City, Oklahoma 73108.

461. *199X 1/2 Chicago Megazone*. Bi-monthly magazine of news, articles, interviews, translations, episode guides, commentary on Japanese comics. D.B. Killings, P.O. Box 59167, Chicago, Illinois 60659.

462. *The Philippine Comics Review*. At least one issue published (First Quarter 1979) by Ros H. Matienzo at temporary address in Manila, Philippines. Many articles on Philippine comics figures, historically and now, in the Philippines and abroad. Interviews, articles, illustrations.

463. *Protoculture Addicts*. Anime and manga bimonthly published by Ianus Publications Inc., 5000 Iberville Street, Studio 332, Montreal, Quebec, Canada H2H 2S6. Editorials, news, reviews, feature articles on Japanese comic art.

464. *The Rose*. Quarterly organ of Anime Hasshin (Animation Blast Off!), "independent organization servicing animation and manga fans worldwide." Subscription to *The Rose* constitutes membership. Art, articles, reviews, news, synopses, songs, commentaries, anime fanzines, interviews. Also provides 20 "synopsis packets" of articles, other materials. *The Rose* is 36-44 pages. No. 41, June 1994. Lorraine Savage, P.O. Box 391036, Cambridge, Massachusetts 02139-0011.

465. *Shanghai Manhua* (Shanghai Cartoons). Published in Shanghai, 1928-1930.

466. *Shidai Manhua* (Modern Cartoons). Published in Shanghai, January 1934 - June 1937.

467. *Sisa Manpyung* (Comic Criticism). Started in January 1990 by the Sisamanpyung Company, Seoul, Korea.

468. *Super Play*. Monthly magazine dedicated to Super Nintendo Entertainment System. News, columns on Japanese animation and comics. Future Publishing, Cary Court, Somerton, Somerset, England TA116TB.

469. *This Is Animation*. Published beginning in 1982, by Shōgakukan, 2-3-1,

Hitotsubashi, Chiyoda-ku, Tokyo, Japan. Includes profiles of animators, techniques, showcases. Japanese.

470. *To Za Now*. Published by To Za Now Comics Magazine Club of Taipei, this monthly was first issued August 1993. Chinese political cartoon magazine.

471. *Tsunami*. Monthly French-language periodical on Japanese comics. Durendal, 1 Rue Eugene Varlin, 93170 Bagnolet, France.

472. *Unmad* (Immad) *Magazine*. Satire magazine patterned after *Mad* of the United States. First published in 1978. Includes some articles about Bangladeshi cartooning. House #838, Road #19 (Old), Dhanmondi R/A, Dhaka, Bangladesh. In Bengali.

473. *Viz-In*. Published by Viz Comics, a San Francisco, California publisher which translates and publishes Japanese comics for an English-speaking audience.

474. *V-Max*. Anime with reviews, news on video, games, comics. No. 11 in September 1994. P.O. Box 3292, Santa Clara, California 95055.

475. *Woori Manwha*. Newsletter published by Association of Woori Manwha (Our Cartoons), promoting greater acceptance of Korean cartooning. Volume 3 in April 1994.

476. *The World of Cartoons*. Published twice monthly in Chinese, this 16-page magazine carries articles, profiles, columns, news, and cartoons of Chinese cartoonists. Some foreign artists are also included. Beginning Volume 10 in 1995. 839 Yan An Road (Middle), Shanghai, China.

477. *Yamete*. Annual supplement to *Yamato* devoted to Japanese eroticism, much of which emanates from comics. French language, first number, 1992. Illustrated. Articles. Yamato, Via Solferino 41, 20035 Lissone (Milano), Italy.

478. *Zasshi Anime*. Monthly fanzine with original artwork, manga strips, articles about new manga and anime, interviews, game and con news. 502 Harvest Hill, Lewisville, Texas 75017. Since 1994.

BANGLADESH

General Sources

479. Ahsan Habib. *Selected Cartoons of Ahsan Habib*. Dhaka: Jesim Ahmed, 1992. Bengali.

480. Lent, John A. "Cartooning in Bangladesh and Myanmar: Off the Beaten Path." *Comics Journal*. Forthcoming.

481. Mohammad Badrul Ameen Khan. *Pathikrit Chitrashilpi Kazi Abul Kasen* (Pioneer Artist Kazi Abul Kasem). Dhaka: Saleha Khatun Baishistya, 1988.

482. Qureshi, Mahmud Shah. "Cartoons: Mirror of Bangladesh Society." *Asian Culture*. January 1980, pp. 26-28.

483. *Who Is Not a Clown? Cartoon Magazine*. April 1991. Special Issue. Bengali.

BURMA (MYANMAR)

Historical Aspects

484. "He Hurts the One He Loves Most." *Thadin*. January 1971. Burmese.

485. Mayzar. [Cartoon History]. Rangoon: Sabe Baman, 1982. Burmese.

486. "Shwe Ta Lay Started Burmese Cartoons." *Thadin*. October 23, 1971. Burmese.

Cartoons

487. Mayzar. *Mayzar Cartoons*. Rangoon: Dawkhinhla, 1976. Burmese.

488. *Rangoon Si Pin Tha Yar Ya Committee*. Rangoon: Secretary for Captain Hlamyint, 1992. Burmese.

Animation

489. Sudan, I.M. "Origin and Growth of Cinema in Burma." *Cinema India-International*. January-March 1985, pp. 113-115. (Animation films on p. 114).

Political Cartoons

490. Lintner, Bertil. "Avoiding the Draft." *Far Eastern Economic Review*. September 12, 1991, pp. 32-33.

491. "A Most Censored Man: Burma: Cartoons." *Index on Censorship*. July/August 1994, p. 101.

492. Smith, Martin. "Confronting Fear with Laughter." *Index on Censorship*. January 1992, pp. 8-10.

CAMBODIA

Political Cartoons

493.   Chongkitthawon, Kawi. "Khmer Political Cartoonists as Social Critics." *The Nation* (Bangkok). January 2, 1990, p. 6.

494.   Chongkitthawon, Kawi. "Khmer Political Cartoonists as Social Critics." *Philippines Communication Journal*. March 1993, pp. 45-46.

495.   Dodd, Mark. "Cambodia Cartoonists Celebrate New-Found Freedom." Reuters Dispatch, July 19, 1993.

496.   Richardson, Michael. "Sann's Travelling Salesmen. Using Broadcasts and Caricatures, the Heng Samrin Government Fights a Propaganda Campaign Against the Anti-Communists." *Far Eastern Economic Review*. February 19, 1982, pp. 21-22.

CHINA

Resources

497.   Jiang Yihai, ed. *Manhua Zhishi Cidian* (Dictionary of Cartoon Knowledge). Nanjing: Nanjing University Press, 1989.

498.   Liu-Lengyel, Hongying. "An Overview of Chinese Cartooning — A Television Series." Paper presented at Popular Culture Association, Chicago, Illinois, April 9, 1994.

General Sources

499.   Adkins, Marian K. "Children's Drawing in the People's Republic of China." *Theory into Practice*. December 1978, pp. 401-409.

500.   "China Draws upon Humour." *Asiaweek*. October 30, 1987, p. 53.

501.   Ge Boxi. "Xiaohai Yuebao Kaozheng" (An Examination of Child's Monthly). *Xinwen Yanjiu Ziliao*. July 1985, pp. 168-175.

502.   Hung Mao. *Lectures of Comics Arts*. N.p.: Hsing-Yu Publishing Company, 1967. Chinese.

503.   Jiang Weitang. "Qimeng Huabao Wukao" (A Fifth Study of Primer Pictorial). *Xinwen Yanjiu Ziliao*. April 1985, pp. 191-203.

504.   Neils, Patricia. *China Images in the Life and Times of Henry Luce*. Savage, Maryland: Rowman and Littlefield, 1990. (China images in U.S. comics, pages 76-77).

Anthologies

505.   Association de Amities Franco-Chinoises, ed. *Images du Peuple Chinois*. Paris: AAFC and ARC, 1975.

506.   Cartoon Art Commission. *Selected Works of Chinese Cartoonists*. Chengdu: The Cartoon Art Commission of the National Chinese Artists Association and Fine Arts Publishing House of Sichuan, 1988. 198 pp.

507.   Daoyi District Cultural Federation. *Little Chili Peppers*. Guiyang: Guizhou Art Publishing House, 1981. Chinese.

508.   *Fuyu Manhua* (Fuyu Cartoons). Harbin: Liberation Army Arts and Culture Publishing House, 1991.

509.   Government Information Service, Taiwan. *Mai Xiang Weilai* (From the Past to the Future: Cartoon Collection). Taipei: 1989.

510.   Government Information Service, Taiwan. *Zhonghua Ernu de Nuhou* (Angry Roar of the Chinese: Cartoon Collection). Taipei: 1989.

511.   *The Historical Trial: Cartoon Collection of Criticism to "Gang of Four."* Shanghai: People's Art Publishing House, 1979.

512.   Hong Peiqi, ed. *Shenghuo, Aiqing, Yiumuo* (Life, Love and Humor). Nanjing: Yi Lin Publishing House, 1989.

513.   Huang Yongyu. *Liqiu Yansu Renzhen Sikao de Zhaji* (Collection That Tried To Have Serious Thinking). Beijing: Sanlian Bookstore, 1985.

514.   Lan Jian'an and Shi Jicai, comps. *Cartoons from Contemporary China*. Beijing: New World Press, 1989. 320 pp.

515.   Lengyel, Alfonz and Hongying Liu-Lengyel. "Looking at Columbus in the Cartoons of the Shanghai Artists." In *Ray Leight and the Shanghai Cartoonists' View of Columbus*, pp. 9-18. Ambler, Pennsylvania: Fudan Museum Foundation, 1992.

516.   Lewis, J. "China Through the Eyes of Chinese Cartoonists." In *Fulbright Hays Summer Seminars Abroad Program, 1985. Curriculum Projects*. New York: National Committee on United States-China Relations, 1985. 241 pp.

517. Li Mu and Yi Xie, eds. *Mei Ri Yi Xiao* (One Laugh a Day). Guangzhou: Guangzhou Traveling Publishing House, 1991.

518. Long Shengming and Liu Yongguo, eds. *Zhongguo Dangdai Youmo Huajia Zuopinxuan* (Selected Works of Contemporary Chinese Humorous Drawings). Nanning: Guangxi Arts Publishing House, 1991.

519. Satire and Humour Editorial, ed. *Fengci Yu Youmo* (Satire and Humour). Beijing: People's Arts Publishing House, 1989.

520. Wu Zuwang, ed. *Cartoons of Literature*. Beijing: Literature and Culture Publishing House, 1988. 99 pp.

521. Wu Zuwang and Yijie Zhang, eds. *World Children Topics Cartoons*. Beijing: Culture and Literature Publishing House, 1991. 164 pp.

522. Wu Zuwang and Yintang Miao, eds. *World Humorous Cartoon Selection*. Beijing: Chinese Folkloric Literature Publishing House, 1986. 92 pp.

523. Wu Zuwang, Yintang Miao, and Kexin Wen. *Encyclopedia of Humorous Cartoons*. Shijiazhuang: Hebei Children's Publishing House, 1990. 150 pp.

524. Wu Zuwang, Yintang Miao, and Kexin Wen, eds. *Selection of Foreign Humorous Cartoons*. Nanjing: Jiangsu Arts Publishing House, 1989. 332 pp.

525. Xu Jingxiang, comp. *200 Cartoons From China*. Beijing: China Today Press, 1990. 200 pp.

526. Xu Jingxiang, ed. *Zhongguo Youmohua Xuan* (Selection of Chinese Humorous Drawings). Shanghai: Fudan University Press, 1989.

527. Yang Changfei, ed. *Shijie Yinyue Youmo* (World Cartoons on Music). Beijing: Chinese Youth Publishing House, 1991.

528. Yin Zuo'an and Wang Wei, eds. *Guoji Huojiang Manhua Xuan* (Collection of the Awarded Cartoons in the World). Xuzhou: Jiangsu Arts Publishing House, 1991.

529. Yu Henxi and Xu Jin, eds. *Disanjie Gongren Ribao Manhua Dasai Zuopin Xuan* (Selected Works of the Third Worker's Daily Cartoon Competition). Beijing: Popular Science Publishing House, 1990.

530. Zhang Bin and Sun Maoju, eds. *Junxiao Manhua Xuan* (Selection of Cartoons from the Military School). Jiefangjun Arts Publishing House, 1992.

531. Zhang Guangyu. *Xiyou Manji* (Journey to the West). Beijing. Renmin Meishu Chubanshe, 1983.

532.   Zhu Genhua and Shen Tongcheng, eds. *Manhua Xuankan* (Selected Cartoons). Beijing: People's Arts Publishing House, 1982-87.

Artistic Aspects

533.   Chen Shubin. "The Cultivation of the Innovational Creativity in Children's Painting." *Art*. May 1991. p. 69.

534.   Chiang Yea-Ha. *Comics and Appreciation*. Chianghsu: Chianghsu People's Publishing Company, 1989. 137 pp. Chinese.

535.   Fong Sing. "Drawings from China." *New Republic*. June 28, 1948, pp. 16-17.

536.   Huang Mao (Huang Mengtian). *Du Hua Suibi* (Essays on Painting). Hong Kong: Renjian Shuwu, 1949.

537.   Huang Mao (Huang Mengtian). *Huajia Yu Hua* (Artists and Art). Hong Kong: Shanghai Shuju Youxian Gongsi, 1981.

538.   Huang Mao (Huang Mengtian). "Huihua Zhongguohua Tanxie" (Remarks on the Sinification of Art). *Jiuwang Ribao*. May 12, 1940.

539.   Huang Mao (Huang Mengtian). *Manhua Yishu Jianghua* (Lectures on Cartoon Art). Shanghai: Shangwu Yinshuguan, 1947. Original work published 1943.

540.   Jiang Yihai. *Manhua Yu Xinshang* (Cartoons and Appreciation). Nanjing: Jiangsu People's Publishing House, 1989.

541.   Jianxun. "Xin Meishu Yundong Zhankai Zhong — Wo De Jidian Yijian" (My Personal Views of the New Art Movement). *Huashang Bao*. August 6, 1941.

542.   Lengyel, Alfonz. "A Kinai Muveszet Mao Utan" (Chinese Art after Mao). In *Proceedings of XXIXth Congress of the Arpad Academy*, pp. 165-172. Cleveland, Ohio: 1985.

543.   Lengyel, Alfonz. "Kinai Tradicionalis Metodussal Keszult Ecset Es Tinta Kartonok" (Cartoons Made in Chinese Traditional Brush and Ink Method). *Proceedings of the XXXIIIth Congress of the Arpad Academy*. Cleveland, Ohio: November 1993.

544.   Liu-Lengyel, Hongying. "Cartoons of Chinese Tradition: Ink and Brush." Paper presented at Mid-Atlantic Region/Association for Asian Studies, Ramapo, New Jersey, October 30, 1993.

545.   Miu Yintang. *Manhua Yishu ABC* (The Art of Cartooning). Beijing: Chinese Series Pictures Publishing House, 1990.

546. Ning. "Xin Meishu Yundong" (New Art Movement). *Huashang Bao*. June 19, 1941.

547. Wang Qi. *Xin Meishu Lunji* (Collected Essays on New Art). Shanghai: Xin Wenyi Chubanshe, 1951.

548. Ye Qianyu. *Hua Yu Lun Hua* (On Paintings). Tianjin: Renmin Meishu Chubanshe, 1985.

549. Yong Fei. "Implied Beauty in Cartoons." In *On Chinese Cartoon Art*, edited by Hong, Shi, p. 229. Changchun: Changchun Publishing House, 1991.

550. Zhang Guangyu. "Guonei Meishujie De Qingzhuang" (The Current Art Scene in China). *Huashang Bao*. June 25, 1941.

Feng Zikai

551. Feng Zikai. *Gushi Xinhua* (Old Poems in New Paintings). Shanghai: Kaiming Shudian, 1945.

552. Feng Zikai. *Huihua Yu Wenxue* (Painting and Literature). Shanghai: Kaiming Shudian, 1934.

553. Feng Zikai. *Husheng Huaji* (Paintings on the Preservation of Life). 6 Vols. Reprint. Taipei: Chunwenxue Chubanshe.

554. Feng Zikai. *Manhua De Miaofa* (Cartooning Methods). Shanghai: Kaiming Shudian, 1948. Original edition, Guilin, 1943.

555. Feng Zikai. *Manwen Manhua* (Easy Writing and Easy Cartoons). Hankou: Dalu Shudian, 1938.

556. Feng Zikai. *Shaonian Meishugushi* (Art Stories for the Young). Shanghai: Kaiming Shudian, 1937.

557. Feng Zikai. *Xiyang Meishu Shi* (A History of Western Art). Shanghai: Kaiming Shudian, 1928.

558. Feng Zikai. "Yishu Bineng Jianguo" (Art Must Be Able To Build Up a Country). *Yuzhou Feng Yikan*. March 16, 1939, pp. 52-53.

559. Feng Zikai. *Yishu Conghua* (Miscellaneous Talks on Art). Shanghai: Liangyou Gongsi, 1935.

560. Feng Zikai. *Yishu Mantan* (Talks on Art). Shanghai: Renjian Shuwu, 1936.

561. Feng Zikai. *Yishu Quwei* (Taste for Art). Shanghai: Kaiming Shudian, 1934. Reprinted 1946 [?].

Historical Aspects

562.   A Ying. *Zhongguo Nianhua Fazhan Shilüe* (A Brief History of the Development of Chinese New Year Pictures). Beijing: Zhaohua Meishu Chubanshe, 1954.

563.   Bi Keguan. "Anti-Imperialist Cartoons of the Boxer Group." *Art History*. No. 4, 1984.

564.   Bi Keguan. "Cartoons in Newspapers and Periodicals in the Late Qing Dynasty and the Early Republic." *News Research*. March 1985.

565.   Bi Keguan. "Cartoons Yesterday and Today." *Culture and Recreation*. 12 articles, December 1978 to April 1979.

566.   Bi Keguan. *Zhong Guo Man Hua Shi Hua* (History of Chinese Cartoons). Jinan: Shangdong People's Art Publishing House, 1982, 1984.

567.   Bi Keguan and Huang Yuanlin. *Zhongguo Manhua Shi* (A History of Chinese Cartoons). Beijing: Wenhua Yishu Chubanshe, 1986.

568.   Cao Bohan. *Jietou Bibao* (Street Wall Newspapers). Shanghai: Shenghuo Shudian, 1937.

569.   "Cartoons and Woodcuts." Column in *Jiuwang Ribao* (National Salvation Daily). Began November 1, 1939.

570.   "Cartoons Come to Stay." *New China*. February 1931, p. 101.

571.   Chen Chin-yun. "Art Chronicle." *T'ien Hsia Monthly*. December-January 1940-1941, pp. 270-273.

572.   Chen Wangdao, ed. *Xiaopinwen He Manhua* (Personal Essays and Cartoons). Shanghai: Shenghuo Shudian, 1935.

573.   "Chinese Cartoons of the Day." *Asia*. August 1936, p. 507.

574.   *Chinese Comics History*. Beijing: 1986. Chinese.

575.   Croizier, Ralph. *Art and Revolution in Modern China: The Lingnan (Cantonese) School of Painting, 1906-1951*. Berkeley: University of California Press, 1988.

576.   Ding Cong. *Wit and Humour from Ancient China*. Beijing: New World Press, 1986. 220 pp. Bilingual Edition.

577.   Feng Yi. "Manhua Zhongguo Jin Bainian Xuelei Shi" (China's Struggle in the Past Hundred Years in Cartoons). *Zazhi*. January 20, 1940, pp. 36-40.

578.   Fu Chen and Wang Wang. *Xiao Shi Manhua* (Historical Laughing Stories and

Cartoons). Shanghai: Shanghai Ancient Books Publishing House, 1991.

579.   Grand-Carteret, John. *Chinois d'Europe et Chinois d'Asie.* Paris: Montgrédien & Cie Edts, n.d.

580.   Hong Kong Institute for Promotion of Chinese Culture, ed. *Chinese Satirical Drawings Since 1900.* Hong Kong: 1987.

581.   Hu Feng. "Luctan 'Xiaopinwen' Yu 'Manhua'" (On Personal Essays and Cartoons). In *Xiaopinwen He Manhua* (Personal Essays and Cartoons), edited by Chen Wangdao, pp. 173-176. Shanghai: Shenghuo Shudian, 1935.

582.   Hu Kao. "Xiwang Yu Manhuajie" (Hopes for the Cartoon Circle). *Qianqiu.* January 1, 1934, pp.7-8.

583.   Huang Mengtian. "Huiyi *Maoguo Chunqiu* Manhua Zhan" (Reminisces of *The Cat Kingdom* Cartoon Show). *Dadi* (The Earth). July 1981, pp. 60-64.

584.   Huang Shiyang. "Manhua Gailun" (An Introduction to Cartoons). In *Xiaopinwen He Manhua*, edited by Chen Wangdao. Shanghai: Shenghuo Shudian, 1935.

585.   Hung Chang-Tai. "The Fuming Image: Cartoons and Public Opinion in Late Republican China, 1945 to 1949." *Comparative Studies in Society and History.* January 1994, pp. 122-145.

586.   Ke Ling. "Zhoubao Cangsanglu" (The Vicissitudes in the History of the Weekly). In *Zhuzi Shengya*, by Ke Ling, pp. 76-117. Taiyuan: Shanxi Renmin Chubanshe, 1986.

587.   Lan Jian'an. "New Discovery of the Earliest Chinese Cartoon Strips." *Art of Picture Story* (Beijing). 2 (1993).

588.   Lent, John A. "Chinese Comic Art: Historical and Contemporary Perspectives." *Asian Culture Quarterly.* Winter 1992, pp. 27-46.

589.   Lent, John A. "Comic Art." In *Handbook of Chinese Popular Culture*, edited by Wu Dingbo and Patrick D. Murphy, pp. 279-305. Westport, Connecticut: Greenwood, 1994.

590.   Li Hua. [Report on cartoon exhibition, Nanning, Guangxi Province]. *Jiuwang Manhua.* January 12, 1938, p. 3.

591.   Li Qun. "Xuanchuanhua Zai Nongcun" (Propaganda Pictures in Villages). *Dikang Sanrikan.* October 13, 1937, p.8.

592.   Ling He. Preface to *Manhua He Shenghuo* (Cartoons and Life). January 1936, p. 3.

593. Liu Zhenqing. *Manhua Gailun* (An Introduction to Cartoons). Changsha: Shangwu Yinshuguan, 1939.

594. Liu-Lengyel, Hongying. "A Brief History of Chinese Manga from the Beginning of the First Half of the Twentieth Century." *Fūshiga Kenkyū*. No. 12, 1994, pp. 1-6.

595. Liu-Lengyel, Hongying. "Chinese Cartoons As Mass Communication: The History of Cartoon Development in China." Ph.D. dissertation, Temple University, 1993.

596. Liu-Lengyel, Hongying. "Chinese Cartoons Before 1949." *Comics Journal*. August 1994 (in press).

597. Lu Xun (Qiejie). "Manhua Er You Manhua" (Cartoons, Again Cartoons). In *Xiaopinwen He Manhua*, edited by Chen Wangdao, p. 156+. Shanghai: Shenghuo Shudian, 1935.

598. Lu Xun (Qiejie). "Mantan 'Manhua'" (On Cartoons). In *Xiaopinwen He Manhua*, edited by Chen Wangdao, p. 10+. Shanghai: Shenghuo Shudian, 1935.

599. Mu Hui. "Cartoons in Ming Dynasty." *Outlook Weekly*. 22 (1991), p. 36.

600. Qianyu [Ye Qianyu]. "Manhua de Minzu Xingshi" (The National Form of Cartoons). *Huashang Bao* (Hong Kong). October 1, 1941, p.3.

601. Shen Qiyu. "Zhongguo Manhuajia Cong Sulian Dailai De Liwu" (Gifts Brought Back from the Soviet Union by a Chinese Cartoonist). *GM*. October 10, 1936, pp. 570-572.

602. *Shidai Manhua* (Modern Cartoons). November 20, 1935, p.37.

603. "Tougao Guiyue." (Rules for Submission). *Taibai*. September 20, 1934.

604. Wang Dunqing. "Manhua de Xuanchuan Xing" (The Propaganda Nature of Cartoons). *Shidai Manhua*. May 20, 1935, n.p.

605. Wang Dunqing. "Seqing Manhua De Zanyang" (In Praise of Erotic Cartoons). *Shidai Manhua*. February 20, 1936, n.p.

606. Xiao Jianqing. *Manhua Shanghai* (Shanghai in Cartoons). Shanghai: Jingwei Shuju, n.d.

607. Xinbo. "Xiang Sulian Ji Shijie Jinbu De Huajia Xuexi" (Learn from Russian and Other Progressive Artists of the World). *Huashang Bao*. July 30, 1941.

608. Ye Qianyu. "Lüetan Zhongguo de Manhua Yishu" (A Brief Discussion of Chinese Cartoon Art). *Renwen Yikan*. December 12, 1948, p. 30.

609. Yong, Fei. "Two Caricature Portraits in Qing Dynasty." *China Cartoons*. 5 (1994), p. 28.

610. Yu Yueting. "Woguo Huabao De Shizu — Dianshizhai Huabao Chutan" (The Pioneer of Chinese Pictorials: A Preliminary Study of Dianshi Studio Pictorial). *Xinwen Yanjiu Ziliao* (Beijing). 10 (1981), pp. 149-181.

611. Zhang Wenyuan. "Zhongguo Manhua Yundong De Huigu Yu Qianzhan" (The Past and Future of the Chinese Cartoon Movement). *Wenchao Yuekan*. January 1, 1947, pp. 604-608.

612. Zheng Zhenduo. "Chatu Zhi Hua." *Xiaoshuo Yuebao*. January 10, 1927, pp. 1-20.

613. Zhu Xingyi. "Wo Suo Xiji Yu Manhuajie De" (My Hopes for Cartoon Circles). *Duli Manhua*. November 10, 1935, p.3.

"Cartoon Warfare"

614. Bader, A.L. "China's New Weapon, Caricature." *American Scholar*. April 1941, pp. 228-240.

615. Bi Keguan. "Cartoons in the Anti-Japanese War." *Beijing Evening*. August 24, 1985.

616. Chen, Jack. "China's Militant Cartoons." *Asia*. May 1938, pp. 308-312.

617. "China's Propaganda Cartoons." *China Weekly Review*. June 25, 1938.

618. Chu, B.F. "Chinese Cartoonists in War-Time." *Far Eastern Mirror*. April 21, 1938, pp. 72-73.

619. Fang Zhizhong. "Minzu Ziwei Yu Manhua" (National Defense and Cartoons). *Manhua He Shenghuo*. January 10, 1936, p. 11.

620. Hu Feng. *Jian, Wenyi, Renmin* (Sword, Art and Literature, and the People). Shanghai: Nitu She, 1950.

621. Hu Kao. "Baodao Hua" (Reportage Picture). *Huashang Bao*. December 3, 1941.

622. Hu Kao. "Jianli Kangzhan Manhua De Lilun" (Formulative Theories for the National Resistance Cartoon). *Zhandi*. April 5, 1938, pp. 34-35.

623. Hu Kao. "Zhanshi De Manhuajie" (Cartoonists During the War). In *Kangzhan Yu Yishu*. Chongqing: Duli Chubanshe, n.d.

624. Huang Mao (Huang Mengtian). "Manhua De Xuanchuan Fangshi" (Propaganda Methods in Cartoons). *Kangjian Tongsu Huakan*. July 1, 1942, pp. 16-20.

625. Huang Miaozi. "Kangzhan Yilai de Zhongguo Manhua" (Chinese Cartoons Since the Beginning of the War of Resistance). Preface to *Quanguo Manhua Zuojia Kangzhan Jiezuo Xuanji*, edited by Huang Miaozi. N.p.: Zhanwang Shuwu, 1938.

626. Huang Miaozi, ed. *Quanguo Manhua Zuojia Kangzhen Jiezuo Xuanji (QGXJ)* (Selected Works of Chinese Cartoonists on the War of Resistance). N.p.: Zhanwang Shuwu, 1938.

627. Huang Yuanlin. "Kangzhan Shiqi Jiefangqu De Manhua" (Cartoons in the Liberated Areas During the War of Resistance). *Kangzhan Wenyi Yanyiu*. May 15, 1984, pp. 65-69.

628. Hung Chang-Tai. *War and Popular Culture: Resistance in Modern China, 1937-1945*. Berkeley: University of California Press, 1994. 432 pp. (Cartoons, pp. 28-39, 93-150).

629. Jiang Feng. "Guanyu 'Fengci Huazhan'" (On the 'Satirical Cartoon Show'). *Jiefang Ribao*. February 15, 1942.

630. Lu Shaofei. "Kangzhan Yu Manhua" (The War of Resistance and Cartoons). *Dikang Sanrikan*. October 6, 1937, pp. 8-9.

631. Shen Zhenhuang. "Duiyu Manhua Xuanchuan Gongzuo De Yijian" (My Views About Cartoon Propaganda Work). In *Kangzhan De Jingyan Yu Jiaoxun*, edited by Qian Jiaju, Hu Yuzhi, and Zhang Tiesheng. N.p.: Shenghuo Shudian, 1939.

632. Tang Yifan. "Kangzhan Yu Huihua" (The War of Resistance and Painting). *Dongfang Zazhi*. May 16, 1940, pp. 26-28.

633. Te Wei. "Faxisi He Yishujia" (Fascism and Artists). *Huashang Bao*. July 16, 1941.

634. Wang Dunqing. "Manhua Zhan" (Cartoon Warfare). *Jiuwang Manhua*. September 20, 1937, p. 1.

635. "Woodcuts and Cartoons." *Xinhua Ribao* (New China Daily). August 21, 1943, p. 4.

636. Xuan Wenjie. "Kang-Ri Zhanzheng Shiqi De Manhua Xuanchuandui" (The Cartoon Propaganda Corps During the War of Resistance). *Meishu*. July 25, 1979, pp. 37-39.

637. Ye Qianyu. "Manhua De Minzu Xingshi" (The National Form of Cartoons). *Huashang Bao*. October 1, 1941.

638. Yu Feng. "Yong Yanshe Poxiang Faxisi" (Let's Wage an Art War Against Fascism). *Huashang Bao*. July 16, 1941.

639.   Zhang Ding. "Manhua Yu Zawen" (Cartoons and Miscellaneous Essays). *Jiefang Ribao* (Liberation Daily). May 25, 1942.

Lien Huan Hua

640.   Cheng Chi. "New Serial Pictures." *Chinese Literature*. No. 2, 1974, pp. 111-117.

641.   Chiang Wei-Pu. "Chinese Picture Story Books." *Chinese Literature*. March 1959, pp. 144-147.

642.   Hwang, John C. "Lien Huan Hua: Revolutionary Serial Pictures." In *Popular Media in China*, edited by Godwin Chu, pp. 51-72. Honolulu: East-West Center, 1978.

643.   Ma Ke. "Cheers to the New Achievements of the Serial Picture." *People's Daily*. December 29, 1963.

644.   Peng Sheng. "Picture Story Books of China." *Asian Culture*. January 1980, pp. 2-3.

645.   Roblot, Daniel and Jean-Michael Graulle. "Retour de Chine. Deux Français au Monde des 'Lianhuanhua.'" In *L'Année de la Bande Dessinée 85-86*, edited by Stan Barets and Thierry Groensteen, pp. 182-188. Grenoble: Eds. Jacques Glénat, 1985.

646.   Sung Yin. "A Talk on Moulding the Characters of Serial Pictures." *People's Daily*. July 6, 1974.

647.   Yin A. *China Serial Story History*. Beijing: People Art Publishing, 1980. 1st Ed., 1957. 25 pp.

Cartooning, Cartoons

648.   Bi Keguan. "About The Images in Cartoons." *Guangming Daily*. November 12, 1960.

649.   Bi Keguan. "About the Initiation and Popular Usage of the Term 'Cartoon.'" *Yang Liu*. No. 2, 1994.

650.   Bi Keguan. "Contemporary Press Cartoons." *News Research*. March 1985.

651.   Bi Keguan. "Humor and Laughter." *Guangming Daily*. January 10, 1993.

652.   Bi Keguan. "Interesting Points in Cartooning." Hong Kong *Wenhui Bao*. Series between January 1991 and July 1992.

653. Bi Keguan. "The New Stage of Cartoon Creation." *Art Magazine*. April 1985.

654. Bi Keguan. "On Cartoons (Series 1-6)." *Guangming Daily*. December 1978 to April 1979.

655. Bi Keguan. "Strengthen the Monitoring Power of the Press Cartoons." *Chongqing Evening*. July 10, 1988.

656. Bi Keguan. "Wish for a Richer Variety in the Styles and Characteristics of Cartooning." *Worker's Daily*. [?] 1979.

657. "Cartoons from China." *Asian Messenger*. Spring 1977, pp. 26-27.

658. "Cartoons with Message." *Asian Messenger*. Winter 1978/Spring 1979, p. 3.

659. Chen, L. "Stories Behind Some Cartoons." *Free China Weekly*. May 25, 1980, p. 3.

660. "China: World of Cartoons." *FECO News*. No. 5, 1987, p. 5.

661. Choi Suk-Tae. "The Flows and Types of Chinese Cartoons." *Gha Nah Art* (Seoul). November-December 1990, pp. 72-77.

662. "First Chinese Cartoon Exhibition in Europe." *FECO News*. No. 13, 1992, p. 14.

663. Hong Shi. *Inspiration for Cartooning*. Shuangyashan: Beijing Literature and Art Training School, 1993. 90 pp.

664. Hong Shi, ed. *Discussions on Cartoon Art*. Harbin: Heilongjiang Arts Publishing House, 1993. 335 pp.

665. Hong Shi, ed. *Manhua Jianlun* (On Cartoons). Harbin: North Publishing House, 1991.

666. Hong Shi, ed. *Zhongguo Manhua Yishu Lun* (On Chinese Cartoon Art). Changchun: Changchun Publishing House, 1991.

667. Lengyel, Alfonz. "China's Brief Cartooning Tradition." *WittyWorld*. Summer/Autumn 1989, pp. 16-19.

668. Li Jia. *Manhua Qutan* (On Cartoons). Heifei: Anhui Fine Arts Publishing House, 1986.

669. Li Su-Yuan. "The Colour Cartoon 'Monkey Makes Havoc in Heaven.'" *Chinese Literature*. No. 4, 1978, pp. 114-118.

670. Liu-Lengyel, Hongying. "Chinese Classical Literature and Folklore in Modern Chinese Caricatures." Paper presented at International Conference of the

American Association of Chinese Comparative Literature, Princeton, New Jersey, July 24, 1994.

671. Liu-Lengyel, Hongying. "Duhou Suigan" (Comments After Reading an Article on the Present Situation of Chinese Cartooning). *Manhua Xinxi* (Cartoon Information). March 1, 1994, p. 3.

672. Liu-Lengyel, Hongying. "Liu Hongying Boshi Tan Wuya" (Dr. Hongying Liu Speaks on "Crow"). *Wuya* (Crow). July 1993, p. 2.

673. Liu-Lengyel, Hongying. "Manhua Yao Zhagen Guyuan Yu Benguo Tude" (Chinese Cartoon Creation Should Be Resourced from Its Own Land). *Gongren Ribao* (Worker's Daily). September 2, 1992, p. 4.

674. Liu-Lengyel, Hongying. "Meiji Manhua Pinglunjia Liu Hongying Gei Yimei Manhua Zuozhe De Fuxin" (American-Chinese Cartoon Critic Hongying Liu's Letter to a Chinese Cartoonist). *Xiandai Gongren Bao* (Modern Worker's News). November 4, 1992, p. 2.

675. Liu-Lengyel, Hongying. "Wei Zhongguo Manhua Yaoqi Nahan" (Voicing for Chinese Cartooning). *Manhua Xinxi* (Cartoon Information). March 15, 1994, p. 1.

676. Moy Low. "Animal Images with Personifications." *The Economy Daily*. January 10, 1988, p. 4.

677. Moy Low. "Birthday Cards with Cartoons." *The Economy Daily*. December 7, 1991, p. 4.

678. Moy Low. "Cartoons and Advertisements." *The Economy Daily*. January 31, 1988, p. 4.

679. Moy Low. "Cartoons on the Candies' Papers." *The Economy Daily*. February 11, 1990, p. 4.

680. Moy Low. "Cartoons on T-Shirts." *The Economy Daily*. May 13, 1990, p. 3.

681. Moy Low. "Cartoons with the Subject Matter of 'Using Electricity.'" *The Economy Daily*. October 18, 1987, p. 4.

682. Moy Low. "Drawing Is Ended But Its Conception Is Endless." *The Economy Daily*. January 8, 1989, p. 4.

683. Moy Low. "Drawing Kangaroos by Cartooning Brushes." *The Economy Daily*. November 27, 1988, p. 4.

684. Moy Low. "Everyday Life and Humorous Interests." *The Economy Daily*. January 8, 1994, p. 4.

685. Moy Low. "Finding the New Subject Matter of Families." *The Economy Daily*. May 1, 1988, p. 4.

686. Moy Low. "Hospitals in the Eyes of Cartoonists." *The Economy Daily*. May 18, 1986, p. 3.

687. Moy Low. "Humor and Satire." *The Economy Daily*. March 5, 1989, p. 4.

688. Moy Low. "Large and Small, Moving and Still — Expressible Methods of Cartoons." *The Economy Daily*. August 9, 1987, p. 4.

689. Moy Low. "Peculiar Conception." *The Economy Daily*. December 28, 1986, p. 4.

690. Moy Low. "Peculiarity and Reverie." *The Economy Daily*. November 15, 1987, p. 4.

691. Moy Low. "'Raining' Under the Brushes of Cartoonists." *The Economy Daily*. July 19, 1987, p. 4.

692. Moy Low. "Scientific Subjects of Cartoons." *The Economy Daily*. July 5, 1987, p. 4.

693. Moy Low. "Seeing Humor within Seriousness." *The Beijing Daily*. June 4, 1986, p. 4.

694. Moy Low. "Thrilling Subject of Cartoons." *The Economy Daily*. June 22, 1986, p. 4.

695. Moy Low. "To Draw the Ancients in Cartoons." *The Economy Daily*. November 27, 1993, p. 4.

696. Moy Low. "Unexpected Brushes." *The Shanxi Daily*. June 28, 1994, p. 3.

697. Yong Fei. "A Beneficial Searching." *Chongqing Daily*. November 11, 1990, p. 4.

698. Yong Fei. "Bits of Chats on Cartooning." Column in *Zhejiang Worker's Daily*. Nine appeared in 1986 on page 4, titles and dates not provided; April 30, 1987, p. 4; August 20, 1987, p. 4; September 13, 1987, p. 4; 3 other columns in 1987, without dates specified; August 26, 1993, p. 4; January 15, 1994, p. 4; February 15, 1994, p. 4; March 15, 1994, p. 4; May 15, 1994, p. 4.

699. Yong Fei. "Cartooning's Developing Trends." In *On Chinese Cartoon Art*, edited by Hong Shi, p. 57. Changchun: Changchun Publishing House, 1991.

700. Yong Fei. "Choices of Schemes and Imaginations in Cartooning." *Cartoon Fudao Bao* (Shanxi). 6 (1986), p. 1.

701. Yong Fei. "Comments on the Cartoon Exhibition of Six-City and One-County." *Journal of the Masses' Art* (Hangzhou). 50 (n.d.), p. 7.

702. Yong Fei. "Creating New Styles of Cartoons." *Hangzhou Daily*. June 21, 1989, p. 4.

703. Yong Fei. "First Time Searching the Going-Away." *Hangzhou Daily*. November 17, 1987, p. 4.

704. Yong Fei. "From 'The Mouth Is Reaching the Sky and the Earth.'" *Shanxi Worker's Newspaper*. November 29, 1985, p. 4.

705. Yong Fei. "Gather-Together of Laughters." *Chongqing Evening*. November 5, 1987, p. 4.

706. Yong Fei. "The Humorous Cartoons That Are Daily Blossoming." *Hangzhou Daily*. April 11, 1990, p. 4.

707. Yong Fei. "Is Cartooning Opportunism?" *News Frontier* (Beijing). 1 (1991), p. 45.

708. Yong Fei. "Jumping Out from the Low Valley." *Yingkou Daily* (Liaoning). November 28, 1990, p. 3.

709. Yong Fei. "Let People Have More Fun." *Zhejiang Daily*. October 22, 1988, p.3.

710. Yong Fei. "Maintaining High Quality, New, and Skillful Styles in Numerous Cartoon Creations." *Taizhou Daily*. July 30, 1989, p. 3.

711. Yong Fei. "Mistaking Areas in Humorous Cartoons." *Zhejiang Daily*. August 19, 1990, p. 3.

712. Yong Fei. "News Cartoons Are of Various Styles." *World of Cartoons* (Shanghai). 8 (1989).

713. Yong Fei. "New Sparkles from the Old Scheme." *Zhejiang Daily*. October 8, 1988, p. 3.

714. Yong Fei. "On the Characteristics of Humor in Cartoons." *Arts* (Beijing). 4 (1986), p. 59.

715. Yong Fei. "Prospering Cartoon Creation." *Tazshou Daily*. September 22, 1990, p. 4.

716. Yong Fei. "Reading Cartoons and Talking about Cartoons." Column in *Cartoon Monthly* (Zhengzhou). 9 (1989), p. 18; 10 (1989), p. 14; 12 (1989), p. 12; 1 (1990), p. 19; 4 (1990), p. 7; 5 (1990), p. 19; 6 (1990), p. 19; 4 (1991), p. 24; 10 (1991), p. 22; 1 (1992), p. 10; 2 (1992), p. 20; 3 (1992), p. 24; 5 (1992), p.

10; 6 (1992), p. 9; 8 (1992), p. 10; 9 (1992), p. 23; 10 (1992), p. 21; 11 (1992), p. 10; 1 (1993), p. 20; 2 (1993), p. 9; 3 (1993), p. 2; 6 (1993), p. 13; 7 (1993), p. 29; 9 (1993), p. 2; 11 (1993), p. 23; 12 (1993), p. 32; 4 (1994), p. 10; 5 (1994), p. 28; 6 (1994), p. 18.

717.   Yong Fei. "Searching, Innovating, and Opening." *Chongqing Evening*. May 28, 1989, p. 3.

718.   Yong Fei. "There are Successors." *Taizhou Daily*. October 10, 1986, p. 4.

719.   Yong Fei. "Understanding, Consultation, and Goals." In *On Chinese Cartoon Art*, edited by Hong Shi, p. 575. Changchun: Changchun Publishing House, 1991.

720.   Yong Fei. "Zhuangxi in Cartoons." *Zhejiang Daily*. March 5, 1988, p. 3.

721.   *Xinwen Yanjiu Ziliao* (Research Materials on Journalism). December 1981, pp. 149-181.

722.   *Xinwen Yanjiu Ziliao* (Research Materials on Journalism). April 1985, pp. 191-203.

723.   *Xinwen Yanjiu Ziliao* (Research Materials on Journalism). July 1985, pp. 168-175.

724.   Zhou Fashu. "Analysis of the Selected Cartoons in the National Cartoons Exhibition." *Guizhou Daily*. September 17, 1993, p. 8.

725.   Zhou Fashu. "Learn from the Cartoonists In Sichuan and Yunnan Provinces." *Guizhou Daily*. February 13, 1988, p. 3.

726.   Zhou Fashu. "New Development in Cartoon Creations in Guizhou Province." *Guizhou Province*. November 11, 1990, p. 4.

727.   Zhou Fashu. "On the Cartoons Created by [People in] Eight Provinces." *Guizhou Daily*. November 8, 1986, p. 4.

Training

728.   *Duli Manhua*. November 10, 1935, p. 23; December 10, 1935, p. 40.

729.   *Liangyou*. July 1929, p. 38.

Woodcuts

730.   Ji Zhi. "Guanyu 'Muke Manhua'" (On Woodcut Cartoons). *Xinhua Ribao*. March 19, 1942.

731.   *Jin-Sui Jiefangqu Muke Xuan* (Selected Woodcuts from the Shanxi-Suiyuan

Liberated Region). Chengdu: Sichuan Renmin Chubanshe, 1982.

732. *Kangzhan Banian Muke Xuan* (Woodcuts of Wartime Japan). Edited by Zhonghua Quanguo Muke Xiehui (China Woodcut Association). Shanghai: Kaiming Shudian, 1946.

733. Lai Shaoqi. "Manhua Yu Muke" (Cartoons and Woodcuts). In *Kangzhan De Jingyan Yu Jiaoxun*, edited by Qian Jiaju, Hu Yuzhi, and Zhang Tiesheng. N.p.: Shenghuo Shudian, 1939.

734. Li Hua. "Kangzhan Qijian De Muke Yundong" (The Woodcut Movement During the War of Resistance). *Xin Zhonghua*. September 16, 1946, pp. 36-40.

735. Li Qun. "Xizhanchang Shang De Muke Yundong" (The Woodcut Movement on the Western Front). *Wenyi Zhendi*. January 1, 1940, pp. 1377-1378, 1383.

736. Liao Bingxiong. "Guanyu Manmu Hezuo" (On the Cooperation Between Cartoonists and Woodcut Artists). *Jiuwang Ribao*. February 22, 1940.

737. Lin Jianqi. "Zhongguo De Manhua Yu Muke." *Yue Bao*. February 15, 1937, pp. 452-453.

738. Lu Di. "Muke Zai Baozhi Shang De Zhendi" (The Woodcut Front in the Newspapers). *Xinwen Yanjiu Ziliao*. December 1981, pp. 182-191.

739. Lu Xun. "Tan Muke Yishu" (On Woodcuts). *Wenlian*. January 5, 1946, pp. 5-6.

740. Sun, Shirley Hsiao-Ling. "Lu Hsun and the Chinese Woodcut Movement, 1929-1936." Ph.D. dissertation, Stanford University, 1974.

741. Sun, Shirley Hsiao-Ling. *Modern Chinese Woodcuts*. San Francisco: Chinese Culture Foundation, 1979.

742. Wang Shucun. "Shanxi Wood Print New Year's Pictures." *People's Daily*. January 2, 1993, p. 8.

743. Xu Baishi. "Tan Muke" (On Woodcuts). *Shen Bao*. December 2, 1933.

Cartoonists: Profiles and Perspectives

744. Bi Keguan. "An Initial Research on Huang Wenhong." *Art History*. January 1982.

745. Bi Keguan. "Cartoonist Xiao Tongbai." *Satire and Humor*. March 20, 1988.

746. Bi Keguan. "Introductions of Chinese Cartoonists." Hong Kong *Wenhui Bao*.

Series for three years, from 1988.

747. Bi Keguan. "Lu Shaofei — a Hard Worker." *Satire and Humor*. No. 16, 1982.

748. Bi Keguan. "Zheng Zhenduo and Zikai Cartoons." *Book Forest*. No. 1, 1980.

749. Bi Keguan and Wang Dejuan. *Art Works of Bi Keguan and Wang Dejuan*. Singapore: Haozhen Art Gallery, 1990.

750. "Cartoonists Back to Work." *Asian Messenger*. Autumn 1979/Spring 1980, p. 8.

751. Chang Tiejun. *Chang Tiejun Manhua Xuan* (Selected Cartoons of Chang Tiejun). Beijing: Chinese Worker's Publishing House, 1989.

752. Chen Huiling. "Husband and Wife Cartoonists — Peasant Cartoonists Chen Bozi and Li Qing'ai." *Guangming Daily*. May 1, 1993, p. 5.

753. "The Chinese Cartoonist's Art." *Asiaweek*. November 16, 1979, pp. 62-64.

754. Croizier, Ralph. "Crimes of the Gang of Four: A Chinese Artist's Version." *Pacific Affairs*. Summer 1981, pp. 311-322.

755. Duan Jifu. *Lao Ma Zhengzhuan* (Series of Lao Ma). Tianjin: Yanhliuqing Pictorial House, 1990.

756. Hebei Qiuxian "Frog" Cartoonist Group. *Hebei Qiuxian Nongmin Manhua Xuan* (Selected Cartoons of the Peasants in Qiu County). Shijiazhuang: Hebei Arts Publishing House, 1989.

757. Horn, Maurice, ed. *The Encyclopedia of Comics*. New York: Chelsea House, 1976. (Pages 282, 575).

758. Huang Kuan-Lien. "The Unknown Comic Master Peng-Ti." *Monthly Comic Magazine* (Hong Kong). July 1991, pp. 18-19.

759. Ji Xiaopo. "A Story about Zhang Zhengyu." *Chongqing Evening*. January 5, 1992, p. 3.

760. Li Qing. *Li Qing Manhua* (Cartoons of Li Qing). Yiantai: Shandong Arts Publishing House, 1989.

761. Liu-Lengyel, Hongying. "Profile of Oldtime Chinese Cartoonists." Paper presented at Mid-Atlantic Region/Association for Asian Studies, West Chester, Pennsylvania, November 1, 1992.

762. Liu-Lengyel, Hongying. "The Peasant Cartoonist Group of Hebei Province, China." Paper presented at Popular Culture Association, New Orleans, Louisiana, April 3, 1993.

763.   "Look at This Very Interesting Three Generation Man." *Passages.* August 1993, pp. 84-91. (Huang Yongyu).

764.   Mao Chik, ed. *Cartoonists Talk About Comics.* Beijing: Technology of Art Publishing Company, 1989. Chinese.

765.   Miu Yintang. *Miu Yintang Manhua Xuan* (Selected Cartoons of Miu Yintang). Beijing: Knowledge Publishing House, 1990.

766.   Mo Ce, ed. *Manhuajia Tan Manhua* (Cartoonists on Cartoons). Beijing: Beijing Arts and Handicrafts Publishing House, 1989.

767.   Moy Low. "Building the Bridge Between the Sino-American Cartoonists." *International Communication Journal* (Beijing). March 20, 1994. 2 pp.

768.   People's Arts Publishing House, ed. *Chen Jinyan Meishu Zuopin Xuanji* (Selected Artistic Works of Chen Jinyan). Beijing: People's Arts Publishing House, 1981.

769.   Qian Wen. "The Old Man and Peace." *Wenhui Bao.* November 23, 1993. (Ji Xiaopo).

770.   Ren Zhou. "Cartoonists Miao Yintang and Wu Zuwang." *Hangzhou Daily.* November 9, 1988, p. 4.

771.   *The Series of Chinese Cartoons.* Shijiazhuang: Hebei Educational Publishing House, 1994. 18 Volumes. Chinese. (Among those included: Fang Cheng, Feng Zikai, Zhang Guangyu, Zhang Leping, Mi Gu, Ye Qianyu, Liao Bingxiong, Hua Junwu, Ding Cong, Zhang Ding, Han Yu, Miao Di, Jiang Yousheng, Zhan Tong, Yu Huali).

772.   Sun Yizeng. *Sun Yizeng Manhua Xuan* (Selected Sun Yizeng Cartoons). Beijing: Knowledge Publishing House, 1991.

773.   Wang Dazhuang. "About Mr. Dou Zonggan." *Chongqing Evening.* April 7, 1991, p. 3.

774.   Wang Dazhuang. "About Zhang Er." *Chongqing Evening.* January 21, 1990, p. 3.

775.   Wang Dazhuang. "A Conversation with Jiang Fan." *Chongqing Evening.* May 20, 1988, p. 3.

776.   Wang Dazhuang. "A Da, Who Died Too Young." *Chongqing Evening.* April 13, 1992, p. 3.

777.   Wang Dazhuang. "A Fighter in Cartoon Circles—Ying Tao." *Chongqing Evening.* April 17, 1988, p. 3.

778. Wang Dazhuang. "A Multi-Talented Person, Li Binsheng." *Chongqing Evening*. June 10, 1988, p. 3.

779. Wang Dazhuang. "An Old Man with Childish Characters—Mr. Che Fu." *Chongqing Evening*. December 23, 1990, p. 3.

780. Wang Dazhuang. "An Old, Still Running Horse—Shen Tongheng." *Chongqing Evening*. April 3, 1988, p. 3.

781. Wang Dazhuang. "A Pioneer Cartoonist Wang Dunquing." *Chongqing Evening*. January 22, 1989, p. 3.

782. Wang Dazhuang. "A Sketch of Hong Huang." *Chongqing Evening*. July 7, 1991, p. 3.

783. Wang Dazhuang. "A Visit to the Home of the Late Zhang Guangyu." *Chongqing Evening*. August 20, 1989, p. 3.

784. Wang Dazhuang. "Cartoonist Zhou Yuequan." *Chongqing Evening*. March 12, 1990, p. 3.

785. Wang Dazhuang. "'Father of Sanmao'—Zhang Leping." *Chongqing Evening*. February 3, 1989, p. 3.

786. Wang Dazhuang. "'Feetless General,' Yu Suoya." *Chongqing Evening*. March 31, 1989, p. 3.

787. Wang Dazhuang. "Gao Longsheng and His Cartoons Left Behind." *Chongqing Evening*. January 20, 1991, p. 3.

788. Wang Dazhuang. "Having a Cold Face But a Warm Heart—Wang Zimei." *Chongqing Evening*. November 25, 1990, p. 3.

789. Wang Dazhuang. "He Is a 'Gold Mine'—Mr. Ji Xiaobo." *Chongqing Evening*. October 14, 1990, p. 3.

790. Wang Dazhuang. "Ma De of Qingyu Lane." *Chongqing Evening*. November 27, 1988, p. 3.

791. Wang Dazhuang. "Meeting with Mr. Cai Ruohong." *Chongqing Evening*. October 20, 1989, p. 3.

792. Wang Dazhuang. "Mr. Hu Kao's Visit." *Chongqing Evening*. July 8, 1990, p. 3.

793. Wang Dazhuang. "Mr. Lu Zhixiang." *Chongqing Evening*. March 5, 1990, p. 3.

794. Wang Dazhuang. "Searching for Treasure in Mountain City—Xie Qusheng and His Cartoons." *Chongqing Evening*. January 6, 1991, p. 3.

795. Wang Dazhuang. "Talking with Mr. Zhang Wenyuan." *Chongqing Evening*. September 3, 1989, p. 3.

796. Wang Dazhuang. "The 'Bo Le' in Cartooning Field—Lu Shaofei." *Chongqing Evening*. June 3, 1988, p. 3.

797. Wang Dazhuang. "To Be a Guest in the Home of Miao Di." *Chongqing Evening*. April 24, 1988, p. 3.

798. Wang Dazhuang. "Visiting Mr. Jiang Mi." *Chongqing Evening*. February 3, 1991, p. 3.

799. Wang Dazhuang. "Visit of Tian Yuan at Night." *Chongqing Evening*. December 11, 1988, p. 3.

800. Wang Dazhuang. "Wang Letian." *Chongqing Evening*. July 8, 1988, p. 3.

801. Worker's Daily Agency, ed. *Dierjie Gongren Ribao Manhua Dasai Zuopin Xuan* (Selected Works of the Second Worker's Daily Cartoon Competition). Beijing: Worker's Daily Agency, 1987.

802. Xu Changming. *Xu Changming Manhua Xuan* (Selection of Xu Changming Cartoons). Shanghai: Translation Company, 1991.

803. Ye Chunyang. *Ye Chunyang Manhua Xuan* (Selected Cartoons of Ye Chunyang). Beijing: Chinese Worker's Publishing House, 1990.

804. Yong Fei. "The Amateur Humor of Cartoonists." *Zhejiang Daily*. November 4, 1987, p. 4.

805. Yong Fei. "Renewal of the Concepts in Cartoonists' Minds." *Chinese Arts* (Beijing). 38 (1988), p. 3.

806. Zhang E. "Wo Hua Manhua De Jingguo" (My Experience in Cartooning). In *Xiaopinwen He Manhua*, edited by Chen Wangdao. Shanghai: Shenghuo Shudian, 1935.

807. Zheng Xinyao. *Zheng Xinyao Manhua Xuan* (Selected Cartoons of Zheng Xinyao). Shanghai: Shanghai Cartoonist Studies, 1988.

Bi Keguan

808. Bi Keguan. *Bi Keguan Manhua Xuan* (Selected Cartoons of Bi Keguan). Chengdu: Sichuan Arts Publishing House, 1985.

809. Bi Keguan. "Jindai Baokan Manhua" (Cartoons in Modern Journalism). *Xinwen Yanjiu Ziliao* (Beijing). November 1981, pp. 68-87.

810. Bi Keguan. *Manhua Shitan* (Ten Discussions on Cartoons). Shanghai: People's Art Publishing House, 1981. Chinese.

811. Bi Keguan. *Selected Cartoons of Bi Keguan.* Tianjin: People's Art Publishing House, 1981.

812. Gao, Shuxun. "Art Historian and Cartoonist Bi Keguan." *China Culture News.* April 25, 1990.

813. Huang Mengtai. "The First Book on the History of Chinese Cartoons." Hong Kong *Dagong Bao.* March 31, 1983.

814. Huang Shulin. "Returning Humor Back to the Masses." *Union Morning News* (Singapore). October 13, 1987.

815. Huang Yuyun. "Cartoons, Uglification and Humor." *Union Morning News* (Singapore). July 19, 1988.

816. Lin Yushan. "The Interview of Bi Keguan." *The World of Cartoons.* No. 1, 1990.

817. Qing Lan. "Satire Is the Main Scheme in Chinese Cartoons." Hong Kong *Wenhui Bao.* October 11, 1987.

818. Qu Fengming. "He Never Gives Up." *Yantai Daily.* December 27, 1985.

819. Wang Dazhuang. "A Scholar in the Cartooning Circle." *Heilongjiang Daily.* November 18, 1986.

820. Xia Qingquan. "Self-Cultivation, Style and Others." *Satire and Humor.* No. 1, 1994.

821. Yong Fei. "Impression of Bi Keguan." *Zhejiang Daily.* September [?], p. 4.

822. Zhan Tong. "A Man Who Is Serious in Learning." *The World of Cartoons.* No. 7, 1990.

Chen Huiling

823. Bi Keguan. "A Strong, Older Man Chen Huiling." *Wenhui Bao* (Hong Kong). December 1988.

824. Chen Huiling. "Experience of Cartooning Based on Operas," "Movable Cartoons." In *On Chinese Cartoon Art*, edited by Hong Shi, pp. 156-158. Changchun: Changchun Publishing House, 1991.

825. Chen Huiling. "To Learn the Skills from a Good Butcher." Paper read at Cartooning Seminar of Sixth China National Art Exhibition, 1984.

826. Lu Jianhua. "Cartoonists: Father and His Sons." *Outlooks*. 11 (1985).

827. Lu Jianhua. "A Family of Cartoonists." *Throned Roses* (Hunan). 1982.

828. Ma Ding. "Digging the Well Every Day." *Sino-Foreign Exchange Pictorial* (Chongqing). 6 (1993), p. 32.

829. Miao Yintang. "Keeping Forever the Artistic Youth." *Satire and Humor*. December 1990.

830. Shang Gong. "Qian Xuesen's Comments on [Chen Huiling's] Cartoon." *China Cartoons*. 1 (1989), p. 10.

831. Wang Dazhuang. "An Old Cartoonist Chen Huiling." *Chongqing Evening*. November 13, 1988, p. 3.

832. Xu Zhihao. *Chronicle of 1911-1949 Chinese Art Publications*, p. 140. Shanghai: Calligraphy and Paintings Publishing House, 1992.

833. Zhan Tong. "Father and Sons Cartoonists." *Cartoon Monthly* (Henan). 1989.

Chen Shubin (Fang Tang)

834. "Chen Shubin and His Cartoons." In *Learn to Cartoon*, by Xu Pengfei, pp. 115-116. Changchun: Jilin University Press, 1992.

835. Fang Cheng. "Cartoonists' Knowledge." *Yangcheng Evening*. April 7, 1987, p. 2.

836. Liao Bingxiong. "A Good Head for Cartooning." *Beyond Eight Hours*. No. 1, 1987, pp. 30-31.

837. Shen Tongcheng. "Cheers for Press Cartoons." *News Frontier*. No. 1, 1985, pp. 26-27, 48.

838. Sun Yizeng. "Implication, Humor and Great Senses — On Chen Shubin's Cartoons." *Art*. No. 4, 1988, pp. 16-19.

Ding Cong

839. Bi Keguan. "Veteran Cartoonist Ding Cong." *Selected Cartoons*. April 1983.

840. Ding Cong. *Zuotian De Shiqing* (Yesterday's Events). Beijing: Sanlian Shudian, 1984.

841. Ding Cong, ed. *Wit and Humor from Ancient China: 100 Cartoons by Ding Cong*. Beijing: New World Press, 1986. 219 pp.

842.   Wang Dazhuang. "The Impression of Ding Cong." *Chongqing Evening*. December 18, 1988, p. 3.

843.   Wu Dunn, Sheryl. "Chinese Cartoonist Is the Master of the Fine Line." *New York Times*. December 31, 1990, p. 2.

Fang Cheng

844.   Ai Qing. "Wisdom, Cleverness, and Humor." (Beijing) *Reading Magazine*. 11 (1982).

845.   Fang Cheng. *Baokan Manhua* (Press Cartoons). Wuhan: Wuhan University Press, 1989.

846.   Fang Cheng. *Cartoon Collection of Fang Cheng*. Chengdu: Sichuan Art Publishing House, 1987. 102 pp. Chinese.

847.   Fang Cheng. *Cartoons of Fang Cheng*. Hong Kong: Hueng Kong Publishing Co., 1994. Chinese.

848.   Fang Cheng. *Fang Cheng Cartoon Selection*. Shijiazhuang: Hebei Publishing House, 1994.

849.   Fang Cheng. *Fang Cheng Lianhuan Manhua Yuanji* (Collection of Comic Strips of Fang Cheng). Changchun: Jilin Arts Publishing House, 1985.

850.   Fang Cheng. *Fang Cheng Manhua Xuan* (Selected Cartoons of Fang Cheng). Tianjin: Tianjin People's Arts Publishing House, 1981.

851.   Fang Cheng. *High Nutrition*. Shangsha: Hunan Publishing House, 1993.

852.   Fang Cheng. *Huaji yu Youmou* (Hilarity and Humor). Beijing: Overseas Chinese Publishing Co., 1989.

853.   Fang Cheng. *Humorous Cartoons*. Shanghai: New Art Publishing House, 1953.

854.   Fang Cheng. *Poems and Cartoons*. Beijing: Sino-Foreign Culture Publishing Co., 1990.

855.   Fang Cheng. *Political Cartoons of Fang Cheng and Zhong Ling*. Beijing: Zhao Hua Publishing House, 1954.

856.   Fang Cheng. *Selection of Essays*. Beijing: People's Daily Press, 1987.

857.   Fang Cheng. *Selection of Fang Cheng's Cartoons*. Shanghai: People's Art Publishing House, 1982.

858.   Fang Cheng. *Special Selected Cartoons of Fang Cheng*. Hong Kong: Nanyu Publishing House, 1991.

859.   Fang Cheng. *Squeezing Collection*. Beijing: People's Daily, 1987. Chinese.

860.   Fang Cheng. *Wang Xiaoqing*. Beijing: Workers Publishing House, 1951.

861.   Fang Cheng. *Xiao de Yishu* (The Art of Laughing). Shenyang: Chunfeng Cultural Publishing House, 1984.

862.   Fang Cheng. *Yiumuo, Fengci, Manhua* (Humor, Satire and Cartoons). Beijing: Life, Reader New Knowledge, San-Lian Bookstore, 1984.

863.   Fang Cheng, ed. *Dangdai Zhongguo Manhua Jing Xuan* (Contemporary Chinese Cartoons Selection). Hong Kong: Nan Yu Publishing House, 1991.

864.   Fang Cheng and Zhong Ling. *Fang Ling Cartoons Selection*. Beijing: Tian Xia Publishing House, 1952.

865.   He Wei and Jin Xu. "A Researcher of Cartoon Art." *Worker's Daily*. August 9, 1980.

866.   Huang Mengtian. "Fang Cheng, Kang Bo, and Cartoons." Hong Kong *Dagongbao*. October 2, 1980.

867.   I-Su. "Cheng Fang: The Man and His Paintings." *Monthly Comic Magazine* (Hong Kong). December 1990, pp. 4-6.

868.   Liao Bingxiong. "Fang Cheng — An Outstanding Cartoonist." Hong Kong *Wenhui Bao*. March 22, 1985.

869.   Liao Bingxiong. "The Endless Meaning in (Fang Cheng's) Cartoons." (Guangzhou) *Yangcheng Evening*. February 17, 1981.

870.   Lu Yaoshi. "Implication of Fang Cheng's Cartoon 'Wu Da Lang's Restaurant.'" *People's Daily*. August 21, 1980.

871.   Luo Mingyuan. "After Fang Cheng's Cartoon Exhibition." *Chengdu Daily*. December 18, 1980.

872.   Ma Ding. "Being Educated While Laughing." *Chongqing Daily*. January 11, 1981.

873.   Ma Ke. "Implying Satire into Humor." *Chinese Youth News*. August 4, 1980.

874.   Song Lin Zhong. "Cartoonist Fang Cheng's Successful Career." (Tianjin) *Outside of Eight Hours Magazine*. 6 (1982).

875. Tian Yuan. "The Art of Laughter." (Nanjing) *Xinhua Daily*. August 9, 1981.

876. Vink, Michele. "Cartoonist Draws a Political Line in People's Daily." Special to *Asian Wall Street Journal*. April 4, 1981.

877. Wang Dazhuang. "Interviewing Fang Cheng." *Chongqing Evening*. March 13, 1988, p. 3.

878. Xia Shuoqi. "The Fighting of Laughter." *Guangming Daily*. October 28, 1980.

879. Xu Zhankun. "The Big Fellow in Wu Da Lang's Small Restaurant." *People's Daily*. November 3, 1980.

880. Yang Weidong. "Do Not Learn from Wu Da Lang's Operation of His Restaurant." *People's Daily*. December 28, 1980.

881. Yu Suoya. "Implied and Vigorous Art in Satire." *Guangzhou Daily*. February 13, 1981.

882. Yu Wentao. "Cartoons Portray Chinese Humor." *China Daily*. July 9, 1981.

883. Zhong Ling. "The Person and the Cartoons of Fang Cheng." *Shenzhen Special Zone News*. March 22, 1985.

884. Zhong Ling. "The Sword Is Never Old." *Wenhui Magazine*. Supplement. 7 (1980).

885. Zuo Ting. "Fang Cheng — A Humorist and Caricaturist." *China Reconstructs*. 6 (1983).

Feng Zikai

886. Bi Keguan. "A Beautiful Story of the First Edition of *Zikai Cartoons.*" *People's Political Consultation News*. March 31, 1992.

887. Bi Keguan. "Feng Zikai Xiansheng De Liangzhang Zhenguide Fengmian Sheji" (Two Precious Cover Illustrations by Feng). *Meishuyuekan*. No. 2, 1980, pp. 13-14.

888. Bi Keguan. "Huai Zikai Laoshi" (Remembering My Teacher Feng Zikai). *Xinwenxueshiliao*. 5 (1981), pp. 91-95.

889. Bi Keguan. *My Teacher Feng Zikai*. Beijing: New Literature Historical Material, 1979.

890. Bi Keguan. "On Feng Zikai's Cartoons." *Chinese Literature*. No. 8, 1981, pp. 73-80.

891.   Bi Keguan. "On the Selection for the *Feng Zikai Cartoon Selection.*" *People's Daily.* May 6, 1983.

892.   Bi Keguan. "Remembering Artist Feng Zikai." *Culture and Recreation.* No. 2, 1980.

893.   Bi Keguan. *Selected Cartoons of Feng Zikai.* Chengdu: Sichuan People's Art Publishing House, 1983.

894.   Bi Keguan. "Tan Shuqing Manhua" (Talking About the Lyrical Cartoons). *Guangming Ribao.* February 11, 1979.

895.   Bi Keguan. "Ten-Year Anniversary of Feng Zikai's Death." *Southern Sea Business News.* September 14, 1985.

896.   Bi Keguan. "To Clearly Understand Mr. Feng's Cartoons." *Jiaxing Daily.* November 17, 1993.

897.   Bi Keguan. "Zhu Ziqing and Feng Zikai." *The World of Art.* No. 1, 1980.

898.   Chen Huijian. *Hong Yi Dashi Zhuan* (Biography of Li Shutong). Taipei: Sanmin Shuju, 1970.

899.   Fang Cheng. "Feng Zikai De 'Jiefang'" (Feng's Liberation). In *Xiandai Wentan Baixiang* (100 Phenomena from the Contemporary Cultural Scene), by Fang Cheng, pp. 61-65. Hong Kong: 1953.

900.   Feng Huazhan. "Feng Zikai Chuanlüe" (Biographic Note on Feng Zikai). *Jinyang Yuekan.* 4 (1982).

901.   Feng Huazhan. "Feng Zikai Jie Fangqianxi De Manhua" (Feng Zikai's Cartoons on the Eve of Liberation). *Yitan.* (Hefei). 2 (1982).

902.   Feng Huazhan. "Feng Zikai Yu Lu Xun" (Feng Zikai and Lu Xun). *Jiefang Ribao.* December 9, 1980.

903.   Feng Huazhan. "Huiyi Fuqin Feng Zikai Sai Changsha" (Remembering My Father Feng Zikai in Changsha). *Hunan Ribao.* April 28, 1982.

904.   Feng Huazhan. "Jinian Wode Fuqin Feng Zikai" (In Memory of My Father Feng Zikai). *Wenhui Bao.* April 4, 1979.

905.   Feng Huazhan. "Wo Fuqin Feng Zikai De Manhua" (The Cartoons of My Father Feng Zikai). *Wenhui Bao.* February 10, 1982.

906.   Feng Huazhan. "Wo Fuqin Feng Zikai De Wannian Shenghuo" (The Later Life of My Father Feng Zikai). *Suibi.* January 1982.

907. Feng Wanyin. "Feng Zikai He Ertong" (Feng Zikai and Children). *Wenhui Bao*. June 6, 1981.

908. Feng Yiyin. "Feng Zikai Xuehua De Gushi" (The Story of Feng's Learning To Paint). *Xiaopengyou*. No. 7, 1981.

909. Feng Yiyin. "Suiyue Bu Dai Ren" (Times Do Not Wait for People). *Guangming Ribao*. June 8, 1979.

910. Feng Yiyin, *et al*. *Feng Zikai Zhuan* (Biography of Feng Zikai). Hangzhou: Zhejiang Renmin Chubanshe, 1983.

911. Feng Yiyin, *et al*. "Feng Zikai Zhuan" (Biography of Feng Zikai). *Xin Wenxueshiliao*. Nos. 2, 3, 4, 1980, and No. 1, 1981.

912. Feng Zikai. *Bishun Xizitie* (Smooth Brush Calligraphy Exercise Book). Beijing: Baowentang Shudian, 1952.

913. Feng Zikai. *Boshi Jiangui* (Dr. X Sees Ghosts). Shanghai: Ertong Shuju, 1948.

914. Feng Zikai. *Chexiang Shehui* (Compartment Society). Shanghai: Liangyou Tushu Yinshua Gongsi, 1935.

915. Feng Zikai. *Dashu Huace* (The Big Tree Picture Book). Shanghai: Wenyixinchaoshe, 1942.

916. Feng Zikai. *Douhui Zhi Yin* (Voices from the City). Shanghai: Tianma Shudian, 1935.

917. Feng Zikai. *Ertong Shenghuo Manhua* (Cartoons on Children's Life). Shanghai: Ertong Shuju, 1932.

918. Feng Zikai. *Ertong Xiang* (Sketches of Children). Shanghai: Kaiming Shudian, 1945. Original edition, 1932.

919. Feng Zikai. *Feng Zikai Ertong Manhua* (Feng Zikai's Children's Cartoons). Beijing: Waiwen Chubanshe, 1956. English, Polish, German.

920. Feng Zikai. *Feng Zikai Huacun* (Repository of Cartoons by Feng Zikai). Tianjin: Minguo Ribao She, 1948. 2 vols.

921. Feng Zikai. *Feng Zikai Huaji* (Pictures by Feng Zikai). Shanghai: Renmin Meishu Chubanshe, 1963.

922. Feng Zikai. *Feng Zikai Jiezuoxuan* (Outstanding Works by Feng Zikai). Shanghai: Xinxiang Shudian, 1947.

923. Feng Zikai. *Feng Zikai Lian Huan Manhua Ji* (Linked Cartoons by Feng Zikai).

Hong Kong: Ming Chuang Chubanshe, 1979.

924. Feng Zikai. *Feng Zikai Manhua Xuan* (Selection of Cartoons by Feng Zikai). Beijing: Zhishi Chubanshe, 1982.

925. Feng Zikai. *Feng Zikai Manhua Xuanyi* (Interpretations of Selected Cartoons by Feng Zikai). Hong Kong: Chunyi Chubanshe, 1976.

926. Feng Zikai. *Feng Zikai Sanwen Xuanji* (Selected Essays of Feng Zikai). Shanghai: Shanghai Wenyi Chubanshe, 1981.

927. Feng Zikai. *Feng Zikai Shuhuaji* (Feng Zikai Calligraphy and Pictures). Singapore: Yufen Sezhibangongsi, 1976.

928. Feng Zikai. *Feng Zikai Shuhua Xuan* (Selections from Feng Zikai's Cartoons and Pictures). Hong Kong: Nantongtushugongsi, 1976.

929. Feng Zikai. *Feng Zikai Zhi Guang Qia Fashi Shuxinxuan* (Feng's Letters to the Monk Guang Qia). Singapore: Shiquangqia, 1977.

930. Feng Zikai. "Gao Yuanyuantang Zai Tian Zhi Ling" (Commemorating the Spirit of the Yuanyuan Studio). *Yuzhou Feng* (Shanghai). May 1, 1938, pp. 28-32.

931. Feng Zikai. *Guangming Huaji* (Pictures of Brightness). Shanghai: Guoguang Yin Shuju, 1931.

932. Feng Zikai. *Huazhong You Shi* (The Poetry of Painting). Chongqing: Wenguang Shudian, 1943.

933. Feng Zikai. *Huihua Lu Xun Xiaoshuo* (Illustrated Short Stories by Lu Xun). Shanghai: Wanye Shudian, 1950. 4 vols.

934. Feng Zikai. *Husheng Huaji* (Cartoons on the Preservation of Life). Shanghai: Kaiming Shudian, 1928.

935. Feng Zikai. *Husheng Hua Liuji*. Vol 6. Hong Kong: Shidaitushuyouxiangongsi, 1969.

936. Feng Zikai. *Husheng Hua Sanji*. Vol. 3. Shanghai: Dafa Lun Shuju, 1950.

937. Feng Zikai. *Husheng Hua Siji*. Vol. 4. Singapore: Zhanbuyuan, 1960.

938. Feng Zikai. *Husheng Hua Wuji*. Vol. 5. Singapore: Zhanbuyuan, 1965.

939. Feng Zikai. *Husheng Hua Xuji*. Vol. 2. Shanghai: Kaiming Shudian, 1940.

940. Feng Zikai. *Jiaoshi Riji* (A Teacher's Diary). Chongqing: Wanguang Shuju, 1944.

941. Feng Zikai. *Jieyu Manhua* (Cartoons After a Narrow Escape). Shanghai: Wanye Shudian, 1947.

942. Feng Zikai. *Kechuang Manhua* (Traveller's Cartoons). Guilin: Jinri Wenyishe, 1943. Original edition, 1942.

943. Feng Zikai. *Manhua A Q Zhengzhuan* (Cartoon Version of Lu Xun: The Story of Ah Q). Beijing: Kaiming Shudian, 1939.

944. Feng Zikai. *Maobi Huace* (The Brush Picture Book). Shanghai: Wanye Shudian, 1946. 4 vols.

945. Feng Zikai. *Renjianxiang* (Pictures of Human Life). Shanghai: Kaiming Shudian, 1935.

946. Feng Zikai. *Rensheng Manhua* (Cartoons on Human Life). Chongqing: Wanguang Shuju, 1944.

947. Feng Zikai. "Shengji" (The Instinct for Life). In *Yuanyuantang Zaibi* (Essays from the Yuanyuan Studio, Supplement). Shanghai: Kaiming Shudian, 1948.

948. Feng Zikai. *Shitai Huaji* (Cartoons on the Current Scene). Guilin: Wenguang Shudian, 1944.

949. Feng Zikai. *Shuaizhenji* (Honesty Collection). Shanghai: Wanye Shudian, 1946.

950. Feng Zikai. "Shushan Tongxun" (A Letter from Sichuan). *Wanxiang* (Shanghai). January 1, 1944, pp. 66-67.

951. Feng Zikai. *Ting Wo Changge Nanshang Nan* (Extremely Difficult To Hear Me Sing). Beijing: Zhongguo Shaonian Ertong Chubanshe, 1957.

952. Feng Zikai. *Tongnian Yu Guxiang* (Youth and Home). Shanghai: Wenhua Shenghuo Chubanshe, 1951.

953. Feng Zikai. *Wenmingguo* (The Enlightened State). Shanghai: Zuojiashuwu, 1944.

954. Feng Zikai. *Xiaochaopiao Lixianji* (The Dangerous Life of a Little Banknote). Shanghai: Wanye Shudian, 1947.

955. Feng Zikai. *Xuesheng Manhua* (Students' Cartoons). Shanghai: Kaiming Shudian, 1931.

956. Feng Zikai. "Yanhui Zhi Ku" (The Pain of Dinner Parties). *Lunyu* (Shanghai). July 1, 1947, pp. 621-622.

957. Feng Zikai. *Youer Keben* (A Reader for the Young). Shanghai: Dazhongguotu Shuju, 1950, 4 vols.

958.   Feng Zikai. *Yousheng Huaji* (Second Life Cartoons). Shanghai: Kaiming Shudian, 1947.

959.   Feng Zikai. *Youyou Huaji* (Cartoons for the Little Ones). Shanghai: Ertong Shuju, 1949. Original edition, 1947.

960.   Feng Zikai. *Yuanyuantang Jiwai Yiwen* (Supplement to *Essays from the Yuanyuan Studio*). Edited by Ming Chuan. Hong Kong: Wenxue Chubanshe, 1979.

961.   Feng Zikai. *Yuanyuantang Suibi* (Informal Essays from the Yuanyuan Studio). Shanghai: Kaiming Shudian, 1948. Original work, 1931.

962.   Feng Zikai. *Yuanyuantang Suibi* (Informal Essays from the Yuanyuantang Studio). N.p.: Renmin Wensue Chubanshe, 1957.

963.   Feng Zikai. *Yuanyuantang Zaibi* (Further Essays from the Yuanyuantang Studio). Kaiming Shudian, 1937.

964.   Feng Zikai. *Yunni* (Rainclouds). Shanghai: Tianma Shudian, 1935.

965.   Feng Zikai. *Zhandi Manhua* (Battleground Cartoons). Hong Kong: Yingshang Buliedian Tushu Gongsi, 1939.

966.   Feng Zikai. *Zhanshi Xiang* (Wartoon Cartoons). Shanghai: Kaiming Shudian, 1945.

967.   Feng Zikai. "Zhongguo Jiu Xiang Ke Dashu" (China Is Like a Big Tree). *Yuzhou Feng Yikan*. March 1, 1939, pp. 5-6.

968.   Feng Zikai. *Zikai Ertong Manhua* (Feng's Children's Cartoons). Tianjin: Tianjin Shaonian Ertong Meishu Chubanshe, 1959.

969.   Feng Zikai. *Zikai Huaji* (Pictures by Feng Zikai). Shanghai: Kaiming Shudian, 1927.

970.   Feng Zikai. *Zikai Jinzuo Manhuaji* (Recent Cartoons by Feng Zikai). Chengdu: Puyitu Shuguan, 1941.

971.   Feng Zikai. *Zikai Manhua* (Zikai's Cartoons). Shanghai: Kaiming Shudian, 1931. Original edition, Wenxue Zhou Baoshe, 1925.

972.   Feng Zikai. *Zikai Manhua Quanji* (Complete Collection of Feng Zikai's Cartoons). Shanghai: Kaiming Shudian, 1945. 6 vols.

973.   Feng Zikai. *Zikai Manhua Xuan* (Selection of Feng Zikai's Cartoons). Shanghai: Wanye Shudian, 1946.

974.   Feng Zikai. *Zikai Manhua Xuan* (Selection of Feng Zikai's Cartoons). Beijing:

Renmin Mei Shu Chubanshe, 1955.

975. [Feng Zikai letter]. *Wanxiang*. January 1, 1944, p. 67.

976. Harbsmeier, Christoph. *The Cartoonist Feng Zikai: Social Realism with a Buddhist Face*. Oslo: Universitetsforlaget, 1984. 215 pp.

977. Hua Ran. "Xinli Meiyou Yinmi De Jiaoluo" (No Secret Corners in His Heart). *Wenhui Bao* (Shanghai). December 29, 1981.

978. Hung Chang-Tai. "War and Peace in Feng Zikai's Wartime Cartoons." *Modern China*. January 1990, pp. 39-83.

979. Hung Shuen-Shuen. "Feng Tzu-K'ai: His Art and Thoughts." M.A. thesis, Michigan State University, 1986.

980. Ji Chengxing. "Feng Zikai Xiansheng" (Mr. Feng Zikai), *Xin Shidai*. January 1, 1937, pp. 75-76.

981. Ji Chengxing. "Zikai Xiansheng Gei Wo De Yinxiang" (My Impressions of Feng Zikai). *Yifeng*. February 1935.

982. Ke Ling. "Kangzhan Zhong De Feng Zikai Xiansheng" (Mr. Feng Zikai in the War). In *Biangu Ji*, edited by Wen Zaidao, *et al.*, pp. 354-362. Shanghai: Yingshang Wenhui Youxian Gongsi, 1938.

983. Li Huiying. "Feng Zikai Yu Feng Zikai De Manhua" (Feng Zikai and His Cartoons). *The Asia Weekly* (Hong Kong). April 2, 1972.

984. Li Shutong. *Qianchen Yingshi Ji*. Illustrated by Feng Zikai. Shanghai: Kangle Shudian, 1949.

985. Liu Xinhuang. *Hong Yi Fashi Xinzhuan* (New Biography of Li Shutong). Taipei: Renjian Shuwu, 1965.

986. Liu Yichang. "Ji Feng Zikai" (Remembering Feng Zikai). *Wenlin* (Hong Kong). January 5, 1973, pp. 2-3.

987. Ming Chuan. "Feng Zikai Xiansheng Er San Shi" (A Few Remarks on Mr. Feng Zikai). *Mingbao Yuekan*. March 1973, pp. 38-48.

988. Qi Zhirong. "Feng Zikai Manhua Xuan Wenshi" (The Publication of the Collection of Feng Zikai's Cartoons). *Xinmin Wanbao* (Shanghai). May 1982.

989. Qi Zhirong. "Feng Zikai Yu Tonghua" (Feng Zikai and Fables). *Wenxuebao*. December 10, 1981.

990. Tang Yun. "Yin Shui Si Yuan" (When Drinking Water Thinking of the Source).

Jiefang Ribao. May 26, 1981.

991. Tanizaki Jun'ichiro. "Du Yuanyuantang Suibi" (On Essays from the Yuanyuan Studio). In *Shuaizhen Ji* (Sincerity Collection), by Feng Zikai, pp. 6-10. Shanghai: Wanye Shudian, 1946.

992. Tao Ying. "Du Feng Zikai De Ertong Manhua" (Appreciating Feng's Children's Cartoons). *Wenhui Bao*. July 14, 1981.

993. Wang Zhaowen. *Wang Zhaowen Wenyi Lunji* (Collected Writings on Art). 3 vols. Shanghai: 1980.

994. Ye Shengtao. "Huainian Feng Zikai" (Remembering Feng Zikai). *Wenhui Bao* (Shanghai). April 11, 1979.

995. Ye Shengtao. "Zikai De Hua" (The Pictures of Feng Zikai). *Baikezhishi*. September 1981.

996. Yu Liu. "Zikai Yu Cikai" (Feng Zikai and Feng Zikai the Second). *Yuzhou Feng*. July 16, 1939, pp. 452-454.

997. Zhao Jingshen. "Feng Zikai He Tade Xiaopinwen" (Feng Zikai and His Personal Essays). *Renjian Shi*. June 20, 1935, pp. 14-16.

998. Zhen Ru. "Tan Feng Zikai" (Talking about Feng Zikai). *Refeng* (Hong Kong). January 6, 1955.

He Wei

999. He Wei: *Cartoons of He Wei*. Beijing: China Worker's Daily Publishing House, 1994.

1000. Li Rongsheng. "The Gardener of the Brush-and-Ink Humorous Cartoons." *Liaoning Economic Daily*. March 21, 1994, p. 4.

1001. Wang Dazhuang. "Mr. He Wei." *Chongqing Evening*. October 2, 1988, p. 3.

1002. Yu Fu. "The Expression of People's Humor by He Wei." In *World Cartoons Small Encyclopedia*. Taipei: n.p., n.d.

1003. Zhou Xigao. "He Wei—The Envoy of Laughter." *Beijing Daily*. July 15, 1994, p. 4.

Hua Junwu

1004. Hua Junwu. *Chinese Satire and Humour. Selected Cartoons of Hua Junwu (1955-1982*. Translated by W.J. Jenner. Beijing: New World Press, 1984, 1986, 1989. 328 pp.

1005. Hua Junwu. *Hua Junwu Manhua, 1983* (Cartoons of Hua Junwu, 1983). Chengdu: Sichuan Arts Publishing House, 1984.

1006. Hua Junwu. *Satire and Humour from a Chinese Cartoonist's Brush. Selected Cartoons of Hua Junwu ('83-'89)*. Beijing: China Today Press, 1991. 276 pp. Bilingual Edition.

1007. Hua Junwu. "Xiangcha Buduo" (Close Resemblance). *Jiefang Ribao*. August 2, 1943.

1008. Wang Dazhuang. "Visiting Hua Junwu." *Chongqing Evening*. March 6, 1988, p. 3.

1009. Yong Fei. "Hua's (Junwu) Style." *Labor Times* (Hangzhou). May 29, 1990, p. 4.

1010. Yong Fei. "Hua's Style with the Chinese Characteristics." *Zhejiang Daily*. November 17, 1990, p. 3.

Huang Miaozi

1011. Huang Miaozi. "Tan Manhua" (Speaking of Cartoons). *Manhuajie*. November 5, 1936, n.p.

1012. Huang Miaozi. "Wo De Manhua Lilun" (My Cartoon Theory). In *Xiaopinwen He Manhua*, edited by Chen Wangdao. Shanghai: Shenghuo Shudian, 1935.

1013. Wang Dazhuang. "Retired Cartoonists—Huang Miaozi and His Wife, Yu Feng." *Chongqing Evening*. October 29, 1989, p. 3.

Jiang Yousheng

1014. Jiang Yousheng. *Jiang Yousheng's Cartoons*. Shanghai: People's Art Publishing House, 1959. Chinese.

1015. Jiang Yousheng. *Selected Cartoons of Jiang Yousheng*. Tianjin: People's Art Publishing House, 1981. Chinese.

1016. Miao Yintang. "Cartoonist Jiang Yousheng." *China Cartoons*. 2, 1993, pp. 12-13.

1017. Wang Dazhuang. "The First Meeting with Jiang Yousheng." *Chongqing Evening*. June 17, 1988, p. 3.

Li Shutong

1018. Bi Keguan. "Li Shutong, Chen Shizeng and Feng Zikai." *Art History*. No. 3, 1983.

1019. Bi Keguan. "The Pioneers of the Contemporary Woodprints — Li Shutong and Feng Zikai." *Art History*. No. 4, 1993.

Liao Bingxiong

1020. Chen Shubin. "Reading [the Article by Zhu Jinlou] 'On Liao Bingxiong.'" *Guangzhou Art Studies*. No. 3, 1989, pp. 81-82.

1021. Huang Mao (Huang Mengtian). "Liao Bingxiong Jiushi" (Reminisces of Liao Bingxiong). *Dagong Bao* (Hong Kong). September 17, 1983.

1022. Lengyel, Alfonz. "Liao Bingxiong's 60 Years of Cartooning in China." Paper presented at Popular Culture Association, Chicago, Illinois, April 9, 1994.

1023. Liao Bingxiong. *Bingxiong Manhua* (Liao Bingxiong's Cartoons). Guangzhou: Lingnan Meishu Chubanshe, 1985. 121 pp.

1024. Liu-Lengyel, Hongying and Alfonz Lengyel. "Liao: 62 Years in the Forefront of Chinese Cartooning." *WittyWorld*. Autumn/Winter 1994, pp. 24-26.

1025. Wang Dazhuang. "Liao Bingxiong, a Man Made of Steel and Iron." *Chongqing Evening*. July 21, 1991, p. 3.

1026. Zhu Jinlou. "Lun Liao Bingxiong" (On Liao Bingxiong). *Xinan Ribao*. August 11, 1946, "New Art" column.

Lu Xun

1027. Chen Yanqiao. "Lu Xun Xiansheng Yu Banhua" (Mr. Lu Xun and Wood Carvings). *GM*. November 25, 1936, pp. 780-783.

1028. Li Hua. "Lu Xun Xiansheng Yu Muke" (Mr. Lu Xun and Woodcuts). *Minzhu Shijie*. November 1, 1946, p. 23.

Lui Liu

1029. Hunter, Joan. "Lui Liu." *Tops Magazine*. November 1993, pp. 8-9.

1030. *Lui Liu*. Introduction by Barry Callaghan. Exhibition catalogue. Toronto: Madison Gallery, 1994.

Ma Ding

1031. Xiao Ling. "Ma Ding and His Ciga." *Real Estates Market News*. March 23, 1994, p. 4.

1032. Yang Xiaoyi. "A Trouble Caused by a Cartoon of Ma Ding." *Economic Daily*. March 19, 1994, p. 4.

Mi Gu

1033. Bi Keguan. "Mi Gu's Theory of Cartooning — for Both Satire and Artistic Value." *Press Cartoon Communication*. September 27, 1991.

1034. Chen Huiling. "Salute to Big Brother Mi Gu Who Was Two Years Junior to Me." *China Cartoons*. 5 (1991).

1035. Mi Gu. *Mi Gu Manhua Xuan* (Selected Cartoons of Mi Gu). Chengdu: Sichuan People's Publishing House, 1982.

1036. Wang Dazhuang. "Memorial of the Brave Fighter, Mi Gu." *Chongqing Evening*. September 29, 1989, p. 3.

1037. Yong Fei. "A Great Master Cartoonist, Mi Gu." *Hangzhou Daily*. September [?], 1988, p. 3.

Pan Shunqi

1038. Pan Shunqi. *Pan Shunqi Youmo Hua* (Humorous Drawings of Pan Shunqi). Shanghai: People's Arts Publishing House, 1991.

1039. "The Selected Caricatures of Pan Shunqi, China." *FECO News*. No. 6, 1988, p. 3.

Shen Tiancheng

1040. Bao Siwen and Zijin Zhou. "The Interview of Shen Tiancheng." *Yiejin Bao*. October 8, 1988, p. 4. Chinese.

1041. Shen Tiancheng. *Life, Humor, and Cartoons*. Beijing: Knowledge Publishing House, 1992. Chinese.

1042. Shen Tiancheng. *Selected Cartoons of Tiancheng*. Chengdu: Sichuan Publishing House, 1992. Chinese.

Su Guang

1043. Su Guang. *Looking at the Water Fall* (Su Guang Cartoon Selection). Taiyuan: Shanxi People's Publishing House, 1961.

1044. Su Guang. *Su Guang Cartoon Selection*. Taiyuan: Beiyue Art Publishing House, 1992.

1045. Wang Dazhuang. "Su Guang." *Chongqing Evening*. September 1, 1991, p. 3.

Su Lang

1046. Cao Changguang. "The Impression from Su Lang's Cartoons." *China Cartoons*. 4 (1994), pp. 12-13.

1047. Fu Yuan. "Su Lang: With a Deep Affection Crossing the Ocean of Art." *Gansu Daily*. May 7, 1994, p.7.

1048. Guan Guo. "Cartoonist Su Lang." *Cartoon Monthly*. 9 (1993), p. 8.

1049. Guan Guo. "On Su Lang's Prize-Winning Cartoon at the 1993 Chinese National Cartoon Exhibition." *Guangming Daily*. December 5, 1993, p. 5.

1050. Su Lang. *Selected Cartoons of Su Lang*. Lanzhou: Gansu People's Art Publishing House, 1990.

1051. "Su Lang." *Guangming Daily*. March 20, 1994, p. 5.

Te Wei

1052. Wang Dazhuang. "An Old Gardener, Te Wei." *Chongqing Evening*. March 24, 1989, p. 3.

1053. Xinbo. "Wusheng De Zhadan" (Silent Bombs). *Huashang Bao*. May 7, 1941.

Wang Fuyang

1054. Wang Dazhuang. "A Working Model of Cartooning, Wang Fuyang." *Chongqing Evening*. September 8, 1988, p. 3.

1055. Wang Fuyang. *Wang Fuyang Manhua Xuan* (Cartoon Collection of Fuyang Wang). Chengdu: Sichuan Art Publishing House, 1990. 109 pp.

1056. Wang Fuyang, *et al.*, eds. *Shixiang Baitu* (Hundred Cartoons on Social Phenomena). Beijing: People's Daily Publishing House, 1991.

Wang Shuchen

1057. Wang Dazhuang. "Remember Mr. Wang Shuchen." *Chongqing Evening*. December 8, 1991, p. 3.

1058. Zhou Fashu. "Memory of Cartoonist Wang Shuchen." *Guiyang Evening*. January 18, 1992, p. 8.

Wu Zuwang

1059. Bi Keguan. "Wu Zuwang's Preference for Humorous Cartoons." *Hong Kong Wenhui Bao*. April 27, 1990, p. 24.

1060. Jiang Li. "Zuwang's Humor." *China Cultural News* (Beijing). February 22, 1987, p. 4.

1061. Li Boda. "Humorous Cartoonist Wu Zuwang: Increasing Smiles to People." *Hong Kong Ming Bao*. March 3, 1990, p. 19.

1062. Wang Letian. "Humorous Cartoons by Wu Zuwang and Zheng Xinyao." (no other information).

1063. Wu Zuwang. "Liberation of the Humorous Feeling." *Guiyang Evening*. July 25, 1986.

1064. Wu Zuwang. *Life, Humor and Cartoon: Cartoon Selections of Wu Zuwang*. Beijing: Knowledge Publishing House, 1992. 127 pp.

1065. Wu Zuwang. "My Opinions on Humorous Cartoon Creation." *Zhengzhou Evening*. June 28, 1986.

1066. Wu Zuwang. "Old Thoughts About Cartooning." *Satire and Humor*. No. 13 and No. 14, 1989.

1067. Xiao Yian. "A Person Who Is Making Humorous Cartoons." *Wenhui Bao*. April 11, 1987, p. 2.

1068. Yi Yang. "Wu Zuwang and His Humorous Cartoons." *Artists' Communication*. No. 6, 1987, p. 18.

Xiao Qian

1069. Bi Keguan. *Mr. Wang and Xiao Chen*. Beijing: People's Art Publishing House, 1986.

1070. Xiao Qian (Hsiao Ch'ien). *Wei Dai Ditu De Lüren — Xiao Qian Huiyilu* (Traveler Without a Map — The Memoirs of Xiao Qian). Hong Kong: Xiangjiang Chuban Gongsi, 1988.

Ye Qianyu

1071. Bi Keguan. *Selected Cartoons of Ye Qianyu*. Chengdu: Sichuan People's Art Publishing House, 1988.

1072. Bi Keguan. *Ye Qianyu's Cartoons*. Shanghai: People's Art Publishing House, 1981.

1073. Wang Dazhuang. "A Fairyman Ye Qianyu." *Chongqing Evening*. January 8, 1989, p. 3.

1074. Ye Qianyu. *Ye Qianyu Manhua Xuan, 1928-1959* (Selected Cartoons of Ye Qianyu, 1928-1959). Chengdu: Sichuan Arts Publishing House, 1986.

1075. Ye Qianyu. *Ye Qianyu Manhua Xuan — Sanshi Niandai Dao Sishi Niandai* (Selected Cartoons of Ye Qianyu from the 1930s to the 1940s). Shanghai: Renmin Meishu Chubanshe, 1985.

Yong Fei

1076. Ai Yi. "Cartoonist Yong Fei." *Hygiene News of the Special Zone* (Hainan Province). November 22, 1992, p. 4.

1077. Bi Keguan. "The Cartoonist Yong Fei at the West Lake." *Wenhui Bao* (Hong Kong). May 28, 1988, p. 16.

1078. Bo Xing. "Yong Fei's Cartoons." *The Communists.* 8 (1986).

1079. "Cartoonist Yong Fei's Perspectives on Consumption." *Economic Life.* March 5, 1991, p. 1.

1080. Fan Li. "Bits on the Well-Known Cartoonist Yong Fei." *Yuzhou Daily* (Zhejiang). January 19, 1993, p. 4.

1081. Gu Hanchang. "The Half-Bitter and Half-Happy Cartooning Career of Yong Fei." *Journal of the Masses' Art.* 31 (1987).

1082. Li Jia. "About the Veteran Cartoonist Yong Fei." *Cartoon Monthly.* 8 (1993), p. 13.

1083. Li Jia. "Worried About the Very Day." *Culture Weekly* (Hefei). July 5, 1987, p. 1.

1084. Nie Lili. "Yong Fei and Cartoons." *Taizhou Daily.* December 3, 1988, p. 3.

1085. Yang Fangfei. "About the Cartoonist Yong Fei Himself." *Economic Life* (Hangzhou). 1986, p. 4.

1086. Yang Fangfei. "Cartoonist Yong Fei." *Satire and Humor* (Beijing). 9 (1986), p. 3.

1087. Yao Zhenfa and Fang Cheng. "About Yong Fei." *Zhejiang Daily.* May 26, 1993, p. 8.

1088. Yao Zhenfa and Fang Cheng. "A Cartoonist in the Eye of Editors." *China Cartoons.* 9 (1993), p. 16.

1089. Yong Fei. "Cartoons and I." *World of Comedies* (Xian). 10 (1992), p. 62.

1090. Yong Fei. "My Opinion on Humorous Cartoons of Chinese Characteristics." In *On Chinese Cartoon Art*, edited by Hong Shi, p. 186. Changchun: Changchun Publishing House, 1991.

1091. Yong Fei. "My Opinions on Press Cartoons." In *Discussions on Cartoon Art*, edited by Hong Shi, p. 35. Harbin: Heilongjiang Arts Publishing House, 1993.

1092. Yong Fei. "On Humorous Cartoons." *Cartoon Arts* (Beijing). 48 (1988), p. 3.

1093. Yong Fei. "On the Topics of Cartooning." *Hangzhou Daily*. November 15, 1989, p. 4.

1094. Zhang Zhengming. "Life of Cartooning — Interview of Mr. Yong Fei." *Lianyi Bao*. December 4, 1992, p. 4.

1095. Zhang Zhengming and Mu Shui. "Yong Fei and His Cartoon Career." *Hangzhou Art and Culture News*. 10 (1992), p. 2.

1096. Zhu Jin and Tian Xing. "Interview with Cartoonist Yong Fei." *Nantong Daily*. June 5, 1988, p. 4.

Zhan Tong

1097. Wang Dazhuang. "Mr. Zhan Tong." *Chongqing Evening*. March 15, 1992, p. 3.

1098. Zhan Tong. *My Cartooning for Fifty Years*. Shanghai: Wen Hui Publishing House, 1994. 305 pp.

1099. Zhan Tong. *Zhan Tong Cartoon Selection*. Jinan: Shandong Art and Literature Publishing House, 1993. 61 pp.

1100. Zhan Tong. *Zhan Tong Ertong Manhua Xuan* (Selected Children's Cartoons of Zhan Tong). Chengdu: Sichuan Children Publishing House, 1985. 120 pp.

Zhang Ding

1101. Wang Dazhuang. "Visit of the Well-Known Cartoonist, Mr. Zhang Ding." *Chongqing Evening*. March 9, 1989, p. 3.

1102. Zhang Ding. "Sharen de Yanmu" (The Killing Smoke Screen). *Dongbei Manhua* (Northeast Cartoons). November 1, 1946.

1103. Zhang Ding. *Zhang Ding Manhua* (The Cartoons of Zhang Ding, 1936-1976). Shenyang: Liaoning Meishu Chubanshe, 1985.

Zhao Wangyun

1104. Cao Juren. "Ping Zhao Wangyun *Nongcun Xiesheng Ji Ji Qi Tishi*" (A Review of Zhao Wangyun's *Rural Sketches* and His Poetic Inscriptions). *Shen Bao*. January 30, 1934.

1105. Zhao Wangyun. *Zhao Wangyun Nongcun Xiesheng Ji* (Zhao Wangyun's Rural Sketches). Tianjin: Dagong Bao She, 1934.

1106. [Zhao Wangyun]. *Yuzhou Feng*. March 1, 1936, pp. 588-589.

Zhou Fashu

1107. Guizhou People's Publishing House and Guizhou Artist Association. *Guizhou Cartoon Selection*. Managing editors, Zhou Fashu and Fu Guorong. Guiyang: Guizhou People's Publishing House, 1958. Chinese.

1108. Ji Xinqiong. "Zhou Fashu and His Cartoons." *Guiyang Evening*. June 8, 1991, p. 8.

Characters and Titles

1109. Horn, Maurice. "Blue Sea and Red Heart." In *Enciclopedia Mondiale del Fumetto*, edited by Maurice Horn and Luciano Secchi, p. 195. Milan: Editoriale Corno, 1978.

1110. Horn, Maurice. "The Red Detachment of Women." In *Enciclopedia Mondiale del Fumetto*, edited by Maurice Horn and Luciano Secchi, pp. 648-649. Milan: Editoriale Corno, 1978.

1111. Li Su-yuan. "The Colour Cartoon 'Monkey Makes Havoc in Heaven.'" *Chinese Literature*. No. 4, 1978, pp. 114-118.

1112. "Niubizi." *Duli Manhua*. September 25, 1935, p. 29.

1113. "Tao Ger." *Liangyou*. March 31, 1929, p. 37.

"Girl from the People's Commune"

1114. "Girl from the People's Commune." In *A History of Komiks of The Philippines and Other Countries*, by Cynthia Roxas and Joaquin Arevalo, Jr., p. 243. Manila: Islas Filipinas Publishing, 1985.

1115. Horn, Maurice. "Girl from the People's Commune, The (Cina)." In *Enciclopedia Mondiale del Fumetto*, edited by Maurice Horn and Luciano Secchi, p. 426. Milan: Editoriale Corno, 1978.

"Hot on the Trail"

1116. Horn, Maurice. "Hot on the Trail (Cina)." In *Enciclopedia Mondiale del Fumetto*, edited by Maurice Horn and Luciano Secchi, p. 464. Milan: Editoriale Corno, 1978.

1117. "Hot on the Trail." In *A History of Komiks of the Philippines and Other Countries*, by Cynthia Roxas and Joaquin Arevalo, Jr., p. 243. Manila: Islas Filipinas Publishing, 1985.

"Sanmao"

1118. *Dazhong Dianying* (Popular Film). November 11, 1953, pp. 18-19.

1119. Farquhar, Mary Ann. "*Sanmao*: Classic Cartoons and Chinese Popular Culture." In *Asian Popular Culture*, edited by John A. Lent. Boulder, Colorado: Westview Press, forthcoming.

1120. "The Film *Orphan on the Streets* Abroad." *China Screen*. 1, 1982.

1121. Wen Chuan. "Talking About Zhang Leping's 'Three-Hair' Comics." *Monthly Comic Magazine* (Hong Kong). October 1990, pp. 33-36.

1122. Zhang Leping. *Adventures of Sanmao the Orphan*. Hong Kong: Joint Publishing Co., 1981. 154 pp.

1123. Zhang Leping. "Fujin-sixi Hua San Mao" (Recalling Sanmao). *Dazhong Dianying* (Popular Film). December 11, 1957, pp. 8-9.

1124. Zhang Leping. "San Mao." *Duli Manhua*. October 25, 1935, n.p.

1125. Zhang Leping. "San Mao." *Shidai Manhua*. February 20, 1936, n.p.

1126. Zhang Leping. *San-mao the Vagrant*. Beijing: People's Arts Publishing House, 1991. 214 pp. Chinese.

1127. Zhang Leping. *San Mao Liulang Ji* (Adventures of San Mao). Beijing: People's Arts Publishing House, 1991.

1128. Zhang Leping. *San Mao Liulangyi Quanji* (The Complete 'Wanderings of Sanmao'). Beijing: Renmin Meishu Chubanshe, 1984.

"Si Yeoo Ki"

1129. Horn, Maurice. "Si Yeoo Ki (Cina)." In *Enciclopedia Mondiale del Fumetto*, edited by Maurice Horn and Luciano Secchi, pp. 692-693. Milan: Editoriale Corno, 1978.

1130. "Si Yeoo Ki." In *A History of Komiks of the Philippines and Other Countries*, by Cynthia Roxas and Joaquin Arevalo, Jr., p. 244. Manila: Islas Filipinas Publishing, 1985.

Animation

1131. "Afanti International Animation Company." *China Screen*. 3/1991, p. 33.

1132. "Animation Studio Seeks American Partnership." *Variety*. May 4, 1988, p. 470.

1133. "BBC, China Agree on Cartoon Feature." *Variety*. November 12, 1980, pp. 1, 42.

1134. Biagini, Alessandra. "Lo Stile Nazionale nel Cinema d'Animazione Cinese: Proposta di Analisi Attraverso l'Esame di Danao Tiangong di Wan Laiming." MS thesis, Venezia, 1993. 131 pp.

1135. Cheng Jihua. *History of the Development of Chinese Cinema* (Zhongguo Dianying Fazhanshi). Beijing: China Film Press, 1963.

1136. Farquhar, Mary Ann. "Monk and Monkey: A Study of 'National Style' in Chinese Animation." Paper presented at Third International Asian Cinema Studies Conference, New York, New York, June 11, 1992.

1137. Geddes, Andrew. "Disney Will Return to China." *Advertising Age International*. April 27, 1992, p. I-12.

1138. Hutchinson, Harry. "Tooners Hanging on the Rim." *Variety*. June 20-26, 1994, p. 38.

1139. "The Ides of October." *Asiaweek*. September 25, 1992, p. 32.

1140. Jin Xi. "The Development of Chinese Animation Film." *Dianying Yishu* (Film Art). Nos. 4/5, 1959.

1141. Leigh, Will. "The Shanghai Animation Studio." *Animation*. Winter 1989, pp. 84-85.

1142. Li Jianguo. "Shanghai's Animated Film Studio." *China Reconstructs*. June 1989, pp. 67-68.

1143. "Mickey Mouse Back in China." *Far Eastern Economic Review*. November 4, 1993, p. 46.

1144. "Mickey Mouse Returns to China." *Comics Journal*. July 1993, p. 25.

1145. Palmer, Rhonda. "China's Jade in $5-Mil Co-Prod Pact." *Variety*. May 27, 1991, p. 44.

1146. "Pirates Kidnap Walt Disney." *Far Eastern Economic Review*. January 19, 1995, p. 7.

1147. "Puppet and Cartoon Film." *People's China.* May 1, 1956, p. 41.

1148. Quiquemelle, Marie-Claire. "The Wan Brothers and Sixty Years of Animated Film in China." In *Perspectives on Chinese Cinema*, edited by Chris Berry, pp. 175-186. London: British Film Institute, 1991.

1149. "Robt. Chua Awaits Canton Cartoonery for Chinese TV." *Variety*. October 15, 1980, p. 221.

1150. Scher, Mark J. "Film in China." *Film Comment*. Spring 1969, pp. 9-20.

1151. Segers, Frank and Laurence Michie. "Yank Coin To Finance China Animation Site." *Variety*. February 10, 1988, pp. 1, 133.

1152. *Shanghai Animation Film Studio 1957-1987*. Shanghai: Shanghai Animation Film Studio, 1987.

1153. *Shanghai International Animation Film Festival, 1992. 12. 5-12. 10.* Shanghai: Shanghai International Animation Film Festival Organizing Committee, 1992. 59 pp.

1154. Shi Cu. "About Cartoons" (Donghua Manhua). *Dazhong Dianying* (Popular Film). Nos. 5-6, 1962.

1155. Tanzer, Andrew. "China's Dolls." *Forbes*. December 21, 1992, pp. 250-252.

1156. Wan Laiming. "Fifty-Five Years of Activity in the Art of Animation" (Donghua Yishu Shengya Wushiwu Nian). *Yingju Meishu*. No. 1, 1981.

1157. Wan Laiming, Wan Guchan, and Wan Chaochen. "Talking About Cartoons." *Mingxing Huabao*. 1936.

1158. Yao Fangzao. "The Wan Brothers and *Uproar in Heaven*." *Yishu Shijie*. No. 1, 1979.

Comic Books

1159. *Bandes Dessinées Chinoises*. Paris: Centre Georges Pompidou, 1982.

1160. Bauer, Wolfgang, ed. *Chinesische Comics — Gespenster, Mörder, Klassenfeinde.*

Düsseldorf/Cologne: 1976.

1161. Berckman, Edward M. "Images of Women in the Comics — American and Chinese." Available through *Abstracts of Popular Culture*, Bowling Green State University, Bowling Green, Ohio.

1162. "The Big Bad Running Dog." *Asiaweek*. November 9, 1986, p. 15.

1163. Britton, Basil. "Chine." In *Histoire Mondiale de la Bande Dessinée*, edited by Pierre Horay, pp. 290-291. Paris: Pierre Horay Éditeur, 1989.

1164. Bromley, Dorothy D. "U.S. Tells Asia of China Reds in Comic Books." *New York Herald Tribune*. November 28, 1950.

1165. "Captain Capitalist." *Asiaweek*. March 3, 1993, p. 30.

1166. Chesneaux, Jean. "Die Chinesischen Comics als Gegenkultur." In *Das Mädchen aus der Volkskommune — Chinesische Comics*, pp. 306-317. Reinbek: Rowohlt, das neuebuch, 1972. Vol. 2.

1167. Chesneaux, Jean, comp. *The People's Comic Book; Red Women's Detachment, Hot on the Trail and Other Chinese Comics*. New York: Anchor Press, 1973. 252 pp.

1168. *Chūgoku No Gekiga: Renkanga* (Chinese Drama Comics: Renkanga). Tokyo: Tabata Shoten, 1974. 220 pp.

1169. *Das Mädchen aus der Volkskommune — Chinesische Comics*. Reinbek: Rowohlt, das neuebuch, 1972. Vol. 2.

1170. Destenay, Pierre. "Les Bandes Dessinées." *La Nouvelle Chine* (Paris). 4, 1971, pp. 38-43.

1171. "Disney Wins Suit." *Far Eastern Economic Review*. August 18, 1994, p. 55.

1172. Eco, Umberto. "Sur les Bandes Dessinées Chinoises: Contre-Information et Information Alternative." *Versus* (Milan). I, 1971, pp. 111-130.

1173. Eco, Umberto. "Vorsichtige Annäherung an Einen Anderen Code." In *Das Mädchen aus der Volkskommune — Chinesische Comics*, pp. 318-331. Reinbek: Rowohlt, das neuebuch, 1972. Vol. 2.

1174. "Egmont Starter Anders And Blad i Kina." *Seriejournalen*. Summer 1993, p. 19

1175. Eversberg, Gerd. "Chinesische Comics." *Science Fiction Times* (Bremerhaven). 14:4 (129), 1972, pp. 21-22.

1176. "Good Deed of Dai Bee-lun: A Comic Book Distributed to Children in

Communist China." *New York Times Magazine*. February 20, 1972, pp. 12-15.

1177.   Kaku, Michio. "Media: Racism in the Comics." *Bridge*. February 1974, pp. 23-24.

1178.   Kampl, Herbert. "Comics in China." *Comic Forum. Das Magazin für Comicliteratur* (Vienna). 8:32 (1986), pp. 13-17.

1179.   Nebiolo, Gino. "Einleitung." In *Das Mädchen aus der Volkskommune — Chinesische Comics*, pp. 7-15. Reinbek: Rowohlt, das neuebuch, 1972. Vol. 2.

1180.   Nebiolo, Gino. *The People's Comic Book*. Garden City: Doubleday, 1973.

1181.   "New Publications." *Heavy Metal*. June 1980, p. 89.

1182.   Szabo, Joseph George. "Chinese Comic Book Sparks Riots." *Inklings*. Summer 1994, p. 14.

Maoist

1183.   Bitsch, Hannelore. "Mao auf dem Comic-Trip." *Pardon* (Munich). No. 3, 1972, pp. 52-55.

1184.   Chesneaux, Jean, Umberto Eco, and Gino Nebiolo. *I Fumetti di Mao*. Rome: Editori Laterza, 1970 or 1971. 284 pp.

1185.   Kreinz, Glória. "Os Quadrinhos de Mao." *Boletim de HQ*. May-June 1992, p. 2.

1186.   "Mao — A Star in the Comics." *Asia Magazine*. September 26, 1971, pp. 10-11.

1187.   "Maos Comics." *Bulletin: Jugend + Literatur* (Hamburg). No. 6, 1972, Kritik 4, p. 43.

1188.   "Mao-Tse-Tung Comic-Geschichte." *Bunte Illustrierte* (Munich). No. 30, 1971, p. 74.

1189.   Moritz, Frederic. "Chinese Comics Teach Mao's Lessons." *Christian Science Monitor*. August 15, 1973.

1190.   Roux, Antoine. "Les Bandes Rouges du Président Mao." *Communication et Langages* (Paris). 12, 1971, pp. 101-117.

Comic Strips

1191.   "Comic Strips über Chinas Geschichte." *Der Spiegel* (Hamburg). No. 35, 1971, p. 16.

1192. Kramer, Barry. "A Newspaper Turns from Lies, Rudeness to 'Truth,' Funnies." *Wall Street Journal*. April 23, 1980, pp. 1+.

Political Cartoons

1193. Chen, L. "Cartoons Ain't Just for Fun." *Free China Weekly*. August 31, 1980, p. 3.

1194. Chen, L. "How Cartoons Have Been Used." *Free China Weekly*. May 18, 1980, p. 3.

1195. Chua, Morgan. *Tiananmen: A Cartoon Series*. Hong Kong: Chinatown Publications, 1989.

1196. Fang Cheng. "Cartoons in China." *WittyWorld*. Summer 1987, pp. 36-37.

1197. Findlay, Ian. "Drawing the Party Line: From Fallen Leaders to Consumerism." *Far Eastern Economic Review*. November 15, 1984, p. 108.

1198. Lengyel, Alfonz. "Kinai Karikaturistak, Mint a Politikai Es Tarsadalmi Elet Kritikusai" (Social and Political Satire in Chinese Cartoons). In *Proceedings of the Orientalistic Section of the Arpad Academy*, pp. 235-239. Cleveland, Ohio: November 1987.

1199. Lengyel, Alfonz. "Social Political Cartoons After Mao." Paper presented at Mid-Atlantic Region/Association for Asian Studies, Bethlehem, Pennsylvania, November 1, 1987.

1200. Lengyel, Alfonz. "Protest Art and Cartoons After Mao." Paper presented at Mid-Atlantic Region/Association for Asian Studies, Washington, D.C., October 27, 1985.

1201. Lengyel, Alfonz. "Protest Art and Socio-Political Cartoons After Mao." *Proceedings of Facing East/Facing West: North America and the Asia/Pacific Region in 1990*, pp. 387-394. Kalamazoo, Michigan, September 13-15, 1990.

1202. Liu-Lengyel, Hongying. "Effects of Post-Mao Policy on Chinese Cartoons." Paper presented at Mid-Atlantic Region/Association for Asian Studies, Lock Haven, Pennsylvania, November 21, 1991.

1203. "Look Who're Cartoon Characters." *Malaya*. August 19, 1986, p. 6.

1204. Min Zheng. "Irresistible Laughter: A Q-Methodological Study of Chinese Humour and Communication." Master's thesis, University of Windsor, Windsor, Canada, 1993. 169 pp.

1205. Schnell, Jim. "The Lack of Political Cartoons in the People's Republic of China." Paper presented at Speech Communication Association, Atlanta, Georgia, October 31-November 3, 1991. 13 pp.

1206. "Sketching China's Scoundrels." *Asiaweek*. September 2, 1983, pp. 52-53.

HONG KONG

General Sources

1207. Cheng Chia-chen. *Comics Art in Hong Kong*. Hong Kong: Joint Publishing (H.K.) Co., Ltd., 1992.

1208. Choi Po-King. "Popular Culture." In *The Other Hong Kong Report 1990*, edited by Richard Y.C. Wong and Joseph Y.S. Cheng, pp. 537-563. Hong Kong: Chinese University of Hong Kong, 1990. ("Comics," pp. 559-563).

1209. Wei-Chung. "The Change of the Age." *Monthly Comic Magazine*. October 1990, p. 15.

Cartooning, Cartoons

1210. Bowring, Philip. "Traveller's Tales." *Far Eastern Economic Review*. September 8, 1988, p. 47.

1211. "Cartoons Come into the Kitchen." *Media*. December 1979, p. 3.

1212. "Cartoons Funny and Feisty." *Asiaweek*. January 30, 1981, pp. 10-11.

1213. Chiu, Vivian. "Laughing at the World We Live In." *South China Morning Post*. September 14, 1991.

1214. *Contemporary Hong Kong Columnist Cartoon*. Hong Kong: Hong Kong Arts Centre, 1989.

1215. Ho Oi Wan. *How To Draw Cartoons*. Hong Kong: China Student Weekly Society, n.d. Chinese.

1216. "Hong Kong Style." *Esquire*. August 1973, pp. 78-79.

1217. Law, S.L. "China Accused of Bid To Thwart Magazine." *Hongkong Standard*. July 4, 1991.

1218. Mosher, Stacy. "Cocking Last Snooks." *Far Eastern Economic Review.* July 11, 1991, pp. 28-30.

Cartoonists

1219. Chou Po-Tang. "My Opinion of Chih-Ta Li." *Monthly Comic Magazine.* July 1991, pp. 42-43.

1220. Feign, Larry. "Hong Kong Cartoonists." *Cartoonist PROfiles.* June 1986, pp. 66-73.

1221. Mo. "An Interview with Hong Kong Cartoonist Ching-Chen Hsu." *Monthly Comic Magazine.* January 1991, pp. 19-22.

1222. Peng Chih-Ming, Yuan Chien-Tao. "Wan-Yu Chang Has Endless Will to Fight." *Monthly Comic Magazine.* December 1990, pp. 16-23.

1223. Yeh Fei. "An Interview with Cartoonist Siu-Man Kam." *Monthly Comic Magazine.* October 1990, pp. 19-22.

Feign, Larry

1224. Barrett, Hope. "Feign: Is He the Character He Creates?" *Hongkong Standard.* April 23, 1987, p. 3.

1225. Basler, Barbara. "Help! Wicked Satirist Is Loose, Colony Skewered." *New York Times.* January 12, 1990.

1226. Camens, Jane. "Drawing the Line." *Hongkong Standard/Extra.* October 28, 1987, p. 2.

1227. Chiu, Vivian. "Laughing at the World We Live In." *South China Morning Post.* September 14, 1991, p. 10.

1228. Feign, Larry. *How the Animals Do It.* Fort Lee, New Jersey: Barricade Books, 1992.

1229. Graham, Mark. "Feign Draws the Line at Hong Kong's Indifference." *South China Morning Post.* February 17, 1990.

1230. Sinclair, Alexis. "Into the World of Larry." *South China Morning Post.* November 12, 1988, p. 7.

1231. Sinclair, Kevin. "Smug, Self-Satisfied — and Happy." *Hongkong Standard.* November 8, 1986.

1232. Vanderkuyff, Rick. "He Draws on His Experiences in Hong Kong." *Los Angeles Times*. September 18, 1990.

Feng Chih-Ming

1233. Mao-Mao. "Talking About 'The Smile of Swords.'" *Monthly Comic Magazine*. January 1991, pp. 69-71.

1234. Ying-Ning. "An Interview with Cartoonist Chih-Ming Feng." *Monthly Comic Magazine*. No. 0, 1990, pp. 10-17.

Ho Chih-Wen

1235. Peng Chih-Ming. "An Interview with Chih-Wen Ho." *Monthly Comic Magazine*. December 1990, pp. 33-36.

1236. Tseng Ting-Chia. "The Records of Chih-Wen Ho's Words. *Monthly Comic Magazine*. December 1990, pp. 37-40.

Ke Wenyang

1237. Bi Keguan. "An Enjoyable Meeting with Ke Wenyang in Hong Kong." *The World of Cartoons*. December 1987.

1238. Bi Keguan. "The Exhibition of Hong Kong Cartoonist Ke Wenyang." *Beijing Evening*. March 26, 1988.

Ken Yuen Ka Po

1239. "Ken Yuen Ka Po." *Big O Magazine*. March 1994, p. 69.

1240. Lim, C.T. "The Deadly Duo." *Big O Magazine*. March 1994, pp. 68-69. (Wan Yat Leung and Ken Yuen Ka Po).

Ma Wing Shing

1241. "Tales by Ma." *Big O Magazine*. March 1991, p. 79.

1242. Yuan Chih-Pai. "Yuan Chih-Pai's Opinion of Paper Battles." *Monthly Comic Magazine*. December 1990, pp. 30-32. (Ma Wing-Shing and Ho Chih-Wen).

Wong, Tony

1243. Barnett, Will and Tina Wong. "Comics King Takes on the West." *Asian Advertising and Marketing*. July 1988, pp. 24-26, 29.

1244. Chan, Gary. "War Breaks Out in Land of the Comic King." *South China Morning Post*. July 25, 1993, p. 4.

1245. "Former Jademan Chief Faces New Charges." *Far Eastern Economic Review.* August 8, 1991, p. 65.

1246. "Hong Kong's Comic King." *Asiaweek.* May 6, 1988, p. 44.

1247. Keating, John. "Comics King Heads for New Conquests." *Asian Business.* October 1987, pp. 16-23.

1248. "Tony Wong." *Big O Magazine.* September 1993, p. 67.

1249. Wong, Kerry. "King of Comics Returns." *Sunday Morning Post.* July 18, 1993, Money, p. 6.

Zunzi

1250. Chang, Gypsy. "Lampooning 1997 with the Hong Kong Cartoonist Zunzi." *Sinorama.* August 1987, pp. 34-37.

1251. Ho Ling. "An Interview with Hong Kong Cartoonists Zunzi and Chan Ya." *Monthly Comic Magazine.* July 1991, pp. 11-14.

Characters and Titles

1252. Nung-Fu. "Characters in Comics." *Monthly Comic Magazine.* January 1991, pp. 66-68.

"The Gathering of Heroes"

1253. Nung-Fu. "Talking About "The Gathering of Heroes.'" *Monthly Comic Magazine.* October 1990, pp. 24-27.

1254. Pu Chin-Hung. "Talking About 'The Gathering of Heroes.'" *Monthly Comic Magazine.* July 1991, pp. 38-41.

1255. Sun Yu-Chiang. "A Rebuttal of 'Talking About the Gathering of Heroes.'" *Monthly Comic Magazine.* December 1990, p. 41.

"Lao-Fu-Tzu"

1256. Chai-Li. "'Lao-Fu-Tzu' Always Has a Childish Heart." *Monthly Comic Magazine.* July 1991, pp. 26-27.

1257. Liang Wang-Tsu. "A Retrospective of 'Lao-Fu-Tzu' and 'Lao-Pai-Shu.'" *Monthly Comic Magazine.* July 1991, pp. 20-22.

1258. Peng Chih-Ming. "The Acknowledgment of the Feature 'Lao-Fu-Tzu.'" *Monthly*

Comic Magazine. July 1991, pp. 16-17.

1259. Wang Ling-Wu. "Behind 'Lao-Fu-Tzu's' Joy." *Monthly Comic Magazine.* July 1991, pp. 23-25.

1260. Wang Tse. "'Lao-Fu-Tzu' and I." *Monthly Comic Magazine.* July 1991, pp. 30-32. (Originally in *Taiwan Huang-Kuan Comic Collection.* January 1980).

1261. Wu Hao. "'Lao-Fu-Tzu's' Violent World." *Monthly Comic Magazine.* July 1991, pp. 28-29.

"Teenage Mutant Ninja Turtles"

1262. Armstrong, Nigel. "'Turtles' Hurdles to a Hong Kong Chow-Down." *Variety.* April 4, 1990, pp. 1, 14.

1263. Gubernick, Lisa. "Turtle Power." *Forbes.* May 28, 1990, pp. 52-58.

1264. "The Ides of October." *Asiaweek.* September 25, 1992, p. 32.

1265. "Life After the Ninja Turtles." *Asiaweek.* November 6, 1992, p. 71.

1266. Ling Chung. "Not Ninja Turtles." *Monthly Comic Magazine.* No. 0, 1990, pp. 28-29.

1267. "Return of the Ninja Turtles." *Asiaweek.* April 19, 1991, p. 60.

1268. "The Turtles Take Hollywood." *Asiaweek.* May 18, 1990, p. 33.

"The World of Lily Wong"

1269. Browning, Michael. "The China Syndrome." *Miami Herald.* Sunday Magazine Supplement. May 3, 1992, pp. 21-22.

1270. Feign, Larry. *The Adventures of Superlily. A Cartoon Cavalcade Through Pre-1997 Hong Kong.* Hong Kong: Macmillan Publishers, 1989. 130 pp.

1271. Feign, Larry. *Quotations from Lily Wong: Cartoons from Pre-1997 Hong Kong.* Hong Kong: Macmillan, 1990. 146 pp.

1272. Feign, Larry and Nury Vittachi. *Execute Yourself Tonite! The 'Lilygate' Letters.* Hong Kong: Hambalan Press, 1993. 128 pp.

1273. Field, Catherine. "Lily Shows Three Fingers to the Establishment." *Sunday Observer.* October 3, 1993.

1274. "Lily Wong and Her Gweilo Say 'I Do' in Happy Ending." *South China Morning Post.* November 16, 1990, p. 4.

1275. Nelson, Dean. "Real-Life Irony Sharpens the Wit of Lily." *Sunday Morning Post* (Hong Kong). May 7, 1989.

Animation

1276. "Anime Hong Kong Style—in London." *Anime UK Magazine.* 3:5, p. 44.

1277. "Chinese Ghost Story To Haunt Theatres — Animatedly." *Animerica.* June 1993, p. 13.

1278. Groves, Don and Rhonda Palmer. "Hong Kong Firm Bids for Don Bluth Ent." *Variety.* November 9, 1992, p. 38.

1279. "H.K. Film's Cartoon 'Cute' Sweet at B.O., with More To Follow." *Variety.* October 14, 1990, p. 196.

1280. Neal, Jim. "Firms To Pay Damages to Disney." *Comics Buyer's Guide.* July 29, 1994, p. 58.

1281. Poole, Bernard. "Cartoons Provide Light Relief for Film Men." *Media for Asia's Communication Industry.* March 8, 1982, pp. 6-7.

Comic Books and Strips

1282. Chang Tan. "The Death of Hong Kong Comics, Part I." *Monthly Comic Magazine.* January 1991, pp. 30-31.

1283. Chang Tan. "The Death of Hong Kong Comics, Part II." *Monthly Comic Magazine.* July 1991, pp. 34-35.

1284. Chen Kuo-Hsien. "To Refrain from Going to Extremes." *Monthly Comic Magazine.* October 1990, pp. 28-29.

1285. Chien-Tao. "The Frolic Carefree Man." *Monthly Comic Magazine.* No. 0, 1990, pp. 24-27.

1286. Chiu, Vivian. "A Comic That Gets a Laugh Out of Hong Kong." *South China Morning Post* (Hong Kong). July 10, 1992.

1287. Chu Shao-Pin. "Who Won and Who Lost? A Glance at 1990's Hong Kong Comics." *Monthly Comic Magazine.* December 1990, pp. 26-29.

1288. Chung Jen-lin. "The Decline of the Publishing of Comic Strips in Hong Kong." *Publisher's Monthly.* April 1959, pp. 7-8.

1289. Courtney, Christine. "The Comic Side of Hong Kong." *Los Angeles Times*. January 28, 1992, p. H-3.

1290. Ho Chang-Shuo. "Where To Find Out-of-Print Comic Books." *Monthly Comic Magazine*. October 1990, pp. 74-75.

1291. "Hong Kong Comics Invade America." *Comics Journal*. March 1988, p. 6.

1292. "Hong Kong Invasion." *Retail Express*. January 8, 1988, p.1.

1293. Hsieh Pao-Yu. "The Publications of the Comrade Organizations in Hong Kong." *Monthly Comic Magazine*. October 1990, pp. 63-68.

1294. Kwang Nan-Lun. "Comics Are My Life." *Monthly Comic Magazine*. January 1991, p. 76.

1295. Lam, Jason. "The Comic Research Organization — The Pioneer of the Comrade Organizations." *Monthly Comic Magazine*. October 1990, pp. 59-62.

1296. Lent, John A. "The Brutal World of Hongkong Comics." *Big O Magazine*. May 1993, pp. 70-72.

1297. Lim, C.T. "Comics in Hongkong." *Big O Magazine*. October 1992, pp. 91-92.

1298. "Looking Forward to 91's Hong Kong Comics." *Monthly Comic Magazine*. January 1991, pp. 34-37.

1299. Lung Cheng-Feng. "My Sweetheart." *Monthly Comic Magazine*. No. 0, 1990, pp. 56-57.

1300. Marchand, Christopher. "Comic-Book Heroes." *Far Eastern Economic Review*. December 24, 1987, p. 85.

1301. "A Publishing Schedule of Main Comic Publications in Hong Kong." *Monthly Comic Magazine*. January 1991, pp. 32-33.

1302. "A Retrospective of 1990's Hong Kong Comics." *Monthly Comic Magazine*. January 1991, pp. 24-29.

1303. Wu Hao. "Hong Kong in Comics." *Monthly Comic Magazine*. No. 0, 1990, pp. 54-55.

1304. Wu Hao. "Satirizing Comics Should Catch Up with the News." *Monthly Comic Magazine*. January 1991, p. 78.

1305. Yuan Chih-Pai. "Nobody Has Ever Won When His Comic Topic Is Gambling." *Monthly Comic Magazine*. January 1991, pp. 64-65.

1306. Yuan Chih-Pai. "Talking About Producer System." *Monthly Comic Magazine.* July 1991, pp. 36-37.

Historical Aspects

1307. Bi Keguan. "The First Peek into the History of Cartooning in Hong Kong." *Hong Kong Wide-Angle Lense Magazine.* August 1985.

1308. Cheung Ka-Chun. "Brief History of Hong Kong Cartoon Development 1934-1980." In *Contemporary Hong Kong Columnist Cartoon*, p. 1. Hong Kong: Cartoonist Association, 1989. Chinese.

1309. Lim, C.T. "Looking Back: A History of Chinese Comics." *Big O Magazine.* March 1991, p. 80.

1310. Wen Chuan. "The First Comics I Read." *Monthly Comic Magazine.* No. 0, 1990, pp. 58-59.

1311. Wu Chia-Hsiung. "Chinese Current Event Comics in Early Days." *Monthly Comic Magazine.* July 1991, p. 46.

1312. Wu Hao. "Eight Families Sleeping in a Bed." *Monthly Comic Magazine.* October 1990, pp. 30-31.

Jademan

1313. Gomez, Rita. "Jademan Wins $52m Claim in Wong Case." *South China Morning Post.* June 18, 1992, Business, pp. 1-2.

1314. "Jade Dynasty." *Big O Magazine.* October 1993, pp. 66-67.

1315. *Jademan Comics.* File of clippings and advertising material. 1 portfolio. Michigan State University, Russel B. Nye Popular Culture Collection's Popular Culture Vertical File, East Lansing, Michigan.

1316. Jademan (Holdings) Limited. *Annual Report 1991-92.* Hong Kong: 1992. 64 pp.

1317. Rutledge, Charles. "What About Jademan?" *Comics Buyer's Guide.* March 3, 1989, p. 64.

Political Cartoons

1318. Barrett, Hope. *Crisis Chinatoon Tales.* Hong Kong: B Publications, 1989.

1319. Pomfret, John. "Cartoonists Help Colony Express Its Fears of 1997." *The Straits Times* (Singapore). February 6, 1990.

1320. "Tiananmen to Square Book." *Comics Journal*. April 1991, p. 24.

1321. Tyson, James L. "It's a Hard Place To Raise Hackles." *Christian Science Monitor*. August 11, 1989, p. 6.

INDIA

General Sources

1322. Atkinson, G.F. *"Curry and Rice" on Forty Plates, or the Ingredients of Social Life at "Our Station in India."* New Delhi: The Book International, 1982.

1323. Gupta, Ashish. "Taking the Mickey Out." *Sunday Indian Express Magazine*. September 21, 1993, p. 9.

1324. Khare, Adrian. "Hieroglyphic Humour!" *Blitz*. April 14, 1990, pp. 14-15.

1325. Krishnan, Jay R. "Is There Any Sense of Humor Among Indians?" *Express Magazine (Indian Express)*. September 15, 1985.

1326. Ramani, S. and V.S.R.D. Varma, eds. *Humour and Productivity*. 2 vols. Pune: Vijaya and Venkat Publishers, 1989. 438 and 381 pp.

1327. Sehgal, Rashme. "Satire in Art." *India Magazine of Her People and Culture*. February 1990, pp. 74-80.

1328. Siegel, L. *Laughing Matters: Comic Tradition in India*. Chicago, Illinois: University of Chicago Press, 1987, pp. 409-464.

1329. Tailang, Sudhir. "No Laughing Matter!!" *IJU Souvenir* (India). 1993. (Originally in *Gentleman's Magazine* (Bombay). December 1992).

1330. Triphathi, S. "Wagle Kiduniya." *India Today*. March 15, 1990, p. 157.

Cartooning

1331. *Communicator* (New Delhi). Special issue on cartooning, January-April 1986. ("Laxman on Cartoons," p. 10; Sudhir Dar, "Cartoonist Is a Social Critic," p. 13; "Cartoons: Abu's Viewpoint," p. 15; O.V. Vijayan, "National Lampoon," p. 19; Ranga, "Evolution of Cartooning," p. 22; Ravi Shankar, "Need for Social Cartoon," p. 24; John A. Lent, "Comic Art: An International Bibliography," p. 26).

1332. Gavankar, V.D. *Happy Moments with Cartoons*. Bombay: India Book House, 1986.

1333. Hateria, Nergish. "Cartooning Is a Grim Business." *Youth Times*. June 23-July 6, 1978, p. 12.

1334. Jain, Bina. "Role and Preference of Cartoons: A Survey." *Interface*. 4: 1 (1980), p. 9.

1335. Kamath, M.V. "Cartoon Capers." *Mid-Day*. February 17, 1993, p. 23.

1336. Lister, David. "Cartoon Cult Peddles Sex and Violence." *The Independent* (Bombay). October 18, 1993.

1337. Mehta, Anupa. "Changing Colours." *Sunday Mid-Day* (Bombay). August 9, 1992.

1338. Moorthy, Jar. "Humour in Indian Periodicals." *Indian Press*. November 1976, pp. 19-20.

1339. "Novel Idea." *The Times of India*. October 22, 1987.

1340. Samuel, Thomas. "Professional Cartooning or Sitting on the Volcano?" *Indian Press*. March 1977, pp. 49-50.

1341. Sathyanarayana, Y. "A United Nations of Humour." *Economic Times* (Bombay). March 3, 1985, p. 3.

1342. "The Story of the Cartoon in the Indian Press." *The Word*. December 1970, pp. 13-15.

1343. Vijayan, O.V. "National Lampoon." *Communicator*. January-April 1986, pp. 19-21.

Anthologies

1344. Abraham, Abu, ed. *The Penguin Book of Indian Cartoons*. New Delhi: Penguin, 1988.

1345. *Gandhi in Cartoons*. Ahmedabad: Navjivan Trust, 1970.

1346. Gopal, Ajit S. *As Indians Do*. New Delhi: Media Transasia Ltd., 1987. 102 pp.

1347. Ramamurthy, B.V. *Mr. Citizen*. Bangalore: Bangalore Printing and Publishing Co., 1975.

1348. Samuel, Thomas. *Babuji: 100 Selected Cartoons*. Delhi: Hind Pocket Books, 1971. 108 pp.

1349. Sarkar, Kamal. *Cartoons*. Calcutta: Niran Books, 1971.

Development, Education, and Social Consciousness

1350. Behl, Karuna and Hugh Gash. "Role-Taking Skills and Classification Abilities in Children in India." *Journal of Genetic Psychology*. June 1980, pp. 265-274.

1351. "Brushing Aside Communalism." *Times of India*. February 1, 1994.

1352. "Cartoonists 'Helped Fight' Communalism." *Hindustan Times*. January 31, 1994.

1353. "Cartoons Confront Women's Issues in Kerala." *Action*. November/December 1987, p. 3.

1354. Kumar, Keval Joe. "Media Education: An Indian Perspective." Paper presented at International Television Studies Conference, London, England, July 10-14, 1987. 28 pp.

1355. Menon, Sadanand. "Cartoonists Take on Communalists." *Economic Times* (Bombay). February 7, 1993.

1356. "Publishing a Comic Book with Health Messages in India." *Ideas and Action*. 167: 2 (1986), pp. 11-14.

1357. Rana, Indi. *Adaptation Kit for Stories of Adventure: Instructions for Adapting Story-Texts and Pictures*. New Delhi: World Health Organization, 1988. 90 pp.

1358. Rana, Indi. *Developing a Pictorial Language: An Experiment of Field Testing in Rural Orissa*. New Delhi: Danida Mission, 1990.

1359. Rana, Indi. "Comics — for Health." *Development Communication Report*. No. 4, 1987, pp. 1, 3.

1360. Rana, Indi. "Immunization in India: How Comic Books Can Teach Children What They Need To Know." *World Health Forum*. 7 (1986), pp. 279-280.

1361. Shankar, Ravi. "Need for Social Cartoon." *Communicator*. January-April 1986, pp. 24-25.

1362. Upadhyay, Madhuker, comp. *Punch Line: A Selection of Cartoons Against Communalism*. New Delhi: Sahmat, 1994.

Governmental and Legal Aspects

1363. "Cartoon Case Rocks Goa Press." *Times of India*. August 30, 1993.

1364. "Cartoonist Mishandled." *Indian Press*. February 1978, p. 33.

1365. "Cartoonists: 'Fired with the Spirit of Revolt.'" *Asiaweek*. August 31, 1984, p. 31.

1366. "Cartoons on the Media under Emergency." *Vidura*. October 1977, pp. 311-312.

1367. "Editor Jailed Over a Cartoon in India." *WittyWorld*. Autumn 1987, p. 9.

Historical Aspects

1368. Bhaskaran, Gautaman. "The World of Graphic Satire." *The Hindu*. August 4, 1991, p. 23.

1369. Chattopadhyay, Devasis. "Drawing on Humorous Lines." *The Statesman* (Delhi). June 20, 1992.

1370. Haridass, Srilatha. "Laughing Matters, No But Seriously!" *The Hindu* (Madras). April 17, 1993.

1371. Padmanabhan, R.A. "Earliest Cartoons in South India." *Vidura*. July-December 1991, p. 51.

1372. Ranga. "Evolution of Cartooning." *Communicator*. January-April 1986, pp. 22-23.

1373. Rao, Aruna. "Comic Art Traditions in India." Paper presented at Popular Culture Association, New Orleans, Louisiana, April 1993.

1374. Rao, Aruna. "Immortal Picture-Stories: Comic Art in Early Indian Art." In *Asian Popular Culture*, edited by John A. Lent. Boulder, Colorado: Westview Press, forthcoming.

1375. Rao, Aruna. "Tracing Comic Art Traditions to Pre-colonial Times." Paper presented at Mid-Atlantic Region/Association for Asian Studies, West Chester, Pennsylvania, October 1993.

1376. Rao, Aruna and Beth Heller. "Historic Images of Disability: Indian and European Comic Art Traditions." Paper presented at Association for Education in Journalism and Mass Communication, Kansas City, Missouri, August 1993.

1377. Sarkar, Kamal. "India's First Comic Journal." *Vidura*. July-October 1991, pp. 4-5.

1378. Sawant, Suresh. "Indian Cartooning: Then and Now." *WittyWorld*. Autumn 1987, p. 40.

1379. Srinivasan, Sumitra Kumar. "Ajanta Rediscovered Through the Magic Lens." *The Hindu*. July 27, 1993, p. XII.

Cartoonists

1380. Athale, Gouri Agtey. "Laughing All the Way." *Indian Express*. September 12, 1993. (Shivram D. Phadnis).

1381. "Cartoonists 'Prefer To Be Outsiders.'" *Economic Times* (New Delhi). February 1, 1994.

1382. Cherian, V.K. "A Cartoonist on Cartoons." *Vidura*. August 1981, pp. 258-259.

1383. "A Festival Offering of Cartoons." *Vidura*. July-October 1991. Special number featuring works of Gaganendra Nath Tagore, Shankar, Chandi Lahiri, Kamal Sarkar, Sudhir Dar, Abu, Ranga, Vijayan, Mickey Patel, Vishnu, Laxman, *et al.*

1384. "Indian Cartoonists Confer." *Vidura*. August 1973, pp. 267-268.

1385. Joseph, Jaiboy. "The Man with the Golden Pen." *Hindu Magazine*. March 27, 1994. (Srinivasa Vasu).

1386. Kutty, P.K.S. *Laugh with Kutty*. New Delhi: Ananda Publishers, 1982.

1387. Mahadevan, Uma. "Making Light of Dark Matters." *The Independent*. August 17, 1992. (Ponnappa).

1388. Mahesh. "Who Framed Ajit Ninan? *Sunday Mid-day*. August 26, 1990.

1389. Mehta, Anupa. "The Artist As Artisan." *The Independent* (Bombay). August 4, 1992, p. 12.

1390. Menon, Sadanand. "Cartoonist as a Conservative." *Economic Times* (Bombay). February 20, 1994, p. 11.

1391. Nangia, Vinita Dawra and Sheila Vesuna. "They Said It." *Times of India*. March 13, 1993.

1392. Prakash (Shetty). *Kittoo. Collection of Cartoon Strips by Prakash*. Mangalore: Prakash Shetty, 1988.

1393. Sami, A., ed. *Sami — The Pioneer Cartoonist of the Subcontinent*. Karachi: Sami Art Publications, n.d. (Cartoons from 1925-58).

1394. Shetty, Prakash. "Strip-Tease Artists: American Professor Goes Cartoonist-Chasing." *The Week*. August 1, 1993, p. 55.

1395. "Suresh Sawant." *Humour and Caricature*. April/May 1994, pp. 14-15.

1396. Tagore, Gogonendranath. *The Humorous Art of G.T.* Introduction by Prof. O.C. Gangoly. Calcutta: Birla Academy of Art and Culture, n.d.

1397. Unny. "The Aravindan I Knew." *Sunday Mail* (India). March 24, 1991.

Abu (Abu Abraham)

1398. Abraham, Abu. *Arrivals and Departures: Abu on Janata Rule*. Ghaziabad: Vikas Tarang Paperbacks, 1983.

1399. Abraham, Abu. "Cartoons: Abu's Viewpoint." *Communicator*. January-April 1986, pp. 15-18.

1400. Abraham, Abu. *The Games of Emergency*. New Delhi: Vikas Publishing House, Bell Books, 1977.

1401. Abu. *100 of the Best Private View*. New Delhi: Sterling Publishers, 1974.

1402. Abu, alias A.M. Abraham. "The Problems of a Cartoonist." *IPI Report*. August 1966, p. 7.

1403. Narayan, S. Venkat. "A Conversation with Abu Abraham." *Indian Press*. March 1974, pp. 25-30.

1404. Shoeb. "Abu on Abu." *Interface* (Hyderabad). 3: 2 (1979), pp. 55-56.

1405. Sivanand, Mohan. "The Private View of Abu Abraham." *Reader's Digest*. June 1993, pp. 47-49.

1406. Tailang, Sudhir. "The Best of Abu." *Illustrated Weekly of India*. July 1, 1984, p. 36.

1407. Warrier, Shobha. "In the Shade of the Swaying Palms." *The Independent*. December 11, 1992.

Chande, Ramesh

1408. Chande, Ramesh. *Mirror No. 1. 200 Cartoons*. Bombay: Janmabhoomi Group, 1968. Gujarati.

1409. Chande, Ramesh. *Mirror No. 2. 200 Cartoons*. Bombay: Janmabhoomi Group, 1979. Gujarati.

1410. Chande, Ramesh. *Variety of Satires. Part 1*. Bombay: Janmabhoomi Group, 1961. Gujarati.

1411. Chande, Ramesh. *Variety of Satires. Part 2*. Bombay: Janmabhoomi Group, 1961. Gujarati.

Dar, Sudhir

1412. Dar, Sudhir. *The Best of This Is It!* Calcutta: Rupa and Co., 1988.

1413. Dar, Sudhir. "Cartoonist Is a Social Critic — Sudhir Dar." *Communicator*. January-April 1986, pp. 13-14.

1414. Dar, Sudhir. *This Is It!* Delhi: Vikas Publishing House, 1976.

1415. Tailang, Sudhir. "The Best of Sudhir Dar." *Illustrated Weekly of India*. March 17, 1985, p. 30.

Gopalakrishnan, V.S.

1416. Gopalakrishnan, V.S. *Bureaucrat Goes Bananas*. Bombay: V.S. Gopalakrishnan, 1993. 96 pp.

1417. Gopalakrishnan, V.S. *Bureaucrat Goes Berserk, Cartoons*. Bombay: V.S. Gopalakrishnan, 1987.

1418. Gopalakrishnan, V.S. *Bureaucrat Goes Bonkers*. Bombay: V.S. Gopalakrishnan, 1990. 92 pp.

Laxman, L.K.

1419. "The Best of Laxman." *Sunday Midday*. February 3, 1991, p. 5.

1420. "Cartoon Is Not a Joke, But a Satire: Laxman." *The Hindu*. January 31, 1994, p. 15.

1421. De, Aditi. "He Said It." *Sunday Herald*. December 20, 1992, p. 8.

1422. Laxman, R.K. *The Best of Laxman*. New Delhi: Penguin Books, 1990. 224 pp.

1423. Laxman, R.K. *The Best of Laxman*. Vol. 2. New Delhi: Penguin, 1993. 250 pp.

1424. Laxman, R.K. *Doodles*. Bombay: India Book House, 1975.

1425. Laxman, R.K. *Eloquent Brush*. Bombay: Times of India, 1988. 303 pp.

1426. Laxman, R.K. "Freedom To Cartoon, Freedom To Speak." *Daedalus*. Fall 1989, pp. 69-91.

1427. Laxman, R.K. *Idle Hours*. Bombay: IBH, 1982. 167 pp. ("Bumping into David Low," pp. 143-146; "Distorted Mirror," pp. 164-167).

1428. Laxman, R.K. "Laxman on Cartoons." *Communicator*. January-April 1986, pp. 10-12.

1429. Laxman, R.K. *Science Smiles*. Bombay: India Book House, 1982.

1430. Laxman, R.K. *You Said It*. (4th Series). Bombay: India Book House Publishing Co., 1970. 108 pp. 7th series published in 1987.

1431. Laxman, R.K. *You Said It*. Vol. 1. Bombay: IBH, 1992. 106 pp. 1st Ed., 1961.

1432. Laxman, R.K. *You Said It*. Vol. 2. Bombay: IBH, 1992, 102 pp. 1st Ed., 1971.

1433. Laxman, R.K. *You Said It*. Vol. 3. Bombay: IBH, 1992. 106 pp. 1st Ed., 1968.

1434. Laxman, R.K. *You Said It*. Vol. 4. Bombay: IBH, 1992. 110 pp. 1st Ed., 1972.

1435. Laxman, R.K. *You Said It*. Vol. 5. Bombay: IBH, 1992. 102 pp. 1st Ed., 1974.

1436. Laxman, R.K. *You Said It*. Vol. 6. Bombay: IBH, 1992. 112 pp. 1st Ed., 1979.

1437. Laxman, R.K. *You Said It*. Vol. 7. Bombay: IBH, 1992. 114 pp. 1st Ed., 1984.

1438. Lent, John A. "R.K. Laxman." In *Cartoonometer: Taking the Pulse of the World's Cartoonists*, edited by Joe Szabo and John A. Lent, p. 50. North Wales, Pennsylvania: WittyWorld Books, 1994.

1439. Lent, John A. "R.K. Laxman and India's Common Man." *Philippines Communications Journal*. March 1993, pp. 63-70.

1440. Menon, Sobha. "I Am a Camera with In-Built Emotion: R.K. Laxman." *The Telegraph* (Calcutta). July 21, 1990.

1441. Moraes, Dom. "The Crow and the Little Man." *Sunday Midday*. October 14, 1990, p. 5.

1442. "R.K. Laxman." *Amusement Today and Tomorrow*. October/November 1990, pp. 22-23.

1443. "R.K. Laxman Serial Evokes Instant Empathy." *India Today*. March 15, 1990, p. 157.

1444. "View from the Bridge: His Contemporaries Assess Laxman and His Work." *Illustrated Weekly of India*. February 27, 1989.

Miranda, Mario

1445. Menezes, Ervell. "Around the World with Mario & Co." *Indian Express*. August 15, 1993.

1446. Miranda, M. *Are You Ready, Miss Fonseca?* Bombay: Jaico Publishing House, 1980.

1447. Nadkarni, Dev. "Well-Known Cartoonist Mario Miranda." *Amusement Today and Tomorrow*. October/November 1990, pp. 11-12.

1448. Pestonji, Meher. "Cartoonist in a Kibbutz." *Times of India*. May 8, 1994.

Pai, Anant

1449. Bhade, Abhijit. "Where Has Sad Sack Gone?" *The Island*. May 1993, pp. 38-39.

1450. Gangadhar, V. "Anant Pai and His *Amar Chitra Kathas*." *Reader's Digest* (India Edition). August 1988, pp. 137-141.

1451. "Man of the Month." *Eve's*. January 1993, p. 9.

1452. Narayan, Ambuja. "Disney of India." *Eve's*. January 1993, p. 8.

1453. Rao, Shobha. "Anant Pai." *Amusement Today and Tomorrow*. October/November 1990, pp. 18-19.

1454. R.G.K. "Uncle's Remedy for Self-Development." *Sunday Herald* (Bombay). March 7, 1993, p. 3.

Pran (Pran Kumar Sharma)

1455. "Adventures in India." *Inklings*. Summer 1994, p. 15.

1456. Buragohain, Jonali. "Man Behind 'Chacha Choudhary' [sic]" *Hindustan Times*. November 2, 1994, p. 7.

1457. Kumar, V.K. Santhosh. "Comic Genius: The King of Comics Is Sore at the English Press." *The Week*. June 27, 1993, p. 58.

1458. Nirula, Smita. "World of Comic Strips." *Hindustan Times*. May 23, 1992, p. 2.

1459. Sharma, Ashish. "Laughing Is Big Business." *Indian Express*. June 5, 1994, p. 5.

Shankar (K. Shankar Pillai)

1460. "Cartoon Journalism: Shankar." *Alpha*. August 1972, p. 17.

1461. "Cartoonist Shankar Is Dead." *The Independent* (Bombay). December 27, 1989, pp. 1, 4.

1462. Dewar, S. ed. *Shankar: His Cartoons and His Weekly*. New Delhi: Indraprastha Press, n.d.

1463. "Don't Spare Me Shankar." *Democratic Journalist*. November 1989, p. 7.

1464. Lal, Anupa. "The Pied Piper of Delhi." *Reader's Digest* (India). October 1987, pp. 83-85, 88-89, 91-92.

1465. Malhotra, Jyoti. "The Pioneer of Indian Cartooning." *The Independent* (Bombay). January 3, 1990.

1466. Narayan, S.V. "Doyen of Indian Cartoonists Is 69." *Illustrated Weekly of India*. August 1, 1971, pp. 40-41.

1467. Pillai, K. Shankar."Shankar Doffs His Dunce Cap." *Communicator*. October 1975, pp. 3-7.

1468. Pillai, K.S., ed. *Shankar's Weekly Souvenir*. New Delhi: Indraprastha Press (Children's Book Trust), 1975.

1469. Shankar, A. *Shankar*. New Delhi: Children's Book Trust of India, 1984.

1470. "Shankar—A Legend in His Lifetime." *Times of India*. December 27, 1989.

1471. Tailang, Sudhir. "The Best of Shankar." *Illustrated Weekly of India*. May 10, 1987, p. 44.

Tailang, Sudhir

1472. Browne, Sujata. "Drawing a Response." *Office Skills* (New Delhi). November 1986, p. 9.

1473. Karir, Gauvav. "Making Cartoons: A Way of Life." *The Pioneer*. November 14, 1994, p. 10.

1474. Nag, Madhumita. "Humour, Satirical Style." *Observer of Business and Politics*. November 17, 1992.

1475. Pourie, Jang. "Personality." *Sunday Mail*. August 5, 1990.

1476. Sharma, Lokesh. "Comic Retaliation." *Sunday Mail*. March 2-8, 1986.

1477. Subramaniam, Meenakshi. "HT's Fun Man." *Network*. March 1992, pp. 46-47.

1478. Tailang, Sudhir. *The World of Sudhir Tailang. A Collection of Cartoons*. Foreword by Abu Abraham. New Delhi: UBSPD, 1992.

VINS (Vijay N. Seth)

1479. Balachandran, Chhaya. "Saying It With Cartoons." *The Independent* (Bombay). April 3, 1991.

1480. "Cartoonists' Niche." *Indian Express*. July 27, 1987.

1481. Chatterji, Shoma A. "Exhibitors of a Lesser Gallery." *Financial Express* (Bombay). March 26, 1989, p. 4.

1482. "Humour at the Plaza." *Blitz*. November 4, 1989, p. 23.

1483. "Illustration: Vijay N. Seth." *Amusement Today and Tomorrow*. October/November 1990, p. 28.

1484. "Mit Andern Augen Gesehen." *Nebelpalzer*. No. 42, 1987, pp. 38-39.

1485. "Ripples in the Water." *P.S. The Indian Post*. March 19, 1989, p. 5.

1486. Thakore, Dilip. "Thakore's People." *Business World*. November 21-December 4, 1990, p. 109.

1487. "Vins." *Bombay*. August 22-September 6, 1982, p. 68.

1488. "[Vins]." *Bombay*. December 22, 1990-January 6, 1991, p. 55.

Vishnu

1489. Mala, Vaijayanthi. *Vishnu and His Cartoons*. Madras: Author, n.d.

1490. Vishnu. "The Cartoonist's Art: Its Social Relevance." *Alpha*. April 1973, pp. 22-23.

Animation

1491. Burra, Rani. "Animator—Conversation with Ram Mohan." *Vidura*. February 1977, p. 54.

1492. Groves, Don. "Dino Dub Rubs Coin In India, Pakistan." *Variety*. April 25 - May 1, 1994, pp. 27-28.

1493. Groves, Don and Uma da Cunha. "India's Dino-Size Legacy." *Variety*. August 15-21, 1994, pp. 41-42.

1494. Karp, Jonathan. "Bollywood Blues." *Far Eastern Economic Review*. December 22, 1994, pp. 50-51

1495. Khurana, Kireet. *World of Animation Cinema*. Bombay: Bombay International Film Festival, 1992.

1496. "Mickey Mouse Goes to India." *Asiaweek*. April 7, 1993, p. 55.

1497. Mishra, Vijay. "Decentering History: Some Versions of Bombay Cinema." *East-*

West Film Journal. January 1992, pp. 110-155.

1498. Sen, Jayanti. "Animation: The NID Style." *Cinema India-International.* 6:3/4 and 7:1 (1989-90), pp. 13-16.

1499. Swami, Ravi N. "Ramayana: The Legend of Prince Rama." *Anime UK Magazine.* 2:4, pp. 12-17.

Caricature

1500. *The Hindustan Times Book of Best Indian Caricatures.* Introduction by Abu Abraham. New Delhi: UBS Publishers' Distributors, 1992. 67 pp.

1501. Soni, I.M. "Caricatures and Cliches." *Vidura.* March - April 1987, pp. 25-28.

Comic Books

1502. Aggarwal, Anju D. "We Need More Children's Magazines." *Mid-Day.* February 20, 1984.

1503. Baria, Farah. "A Twist in the Tale." *Mid-Day.* February 19, 1992, pp. V, 5.

1504. Brandes, Ada. "Wave of Violence and Sadism Sweeps Comic-Book Market." *Communicator.* October 1977, pp. 44-45.

1505. Chand, Adelaide. "Comics." *Indian Journal of Communication Arts.* March-April 1979, pp. 13-16, 18.

1506. Chinai, Rupa. "Mizoram's Comic Cowboy." *Indian Express.* July 22, 1990.

1507. "The Comic Culture." *Business Standard.* November 29, 1984, p. 6.

1508. Cowell, E.B., ed. *The Jataka or Stories of the Buddha's Former Births.* Vol. 1. London: Luzac and Co., 1957.

1509. "India CI Research Breakthrough." *The Classics Collector.* February-March 1990, p. 9.

1510. Joshi, O.P. "Contents, Consumers and Creators of Comics in India." In *Comics and Visual Culture: Research Studies from Ten Countries,* edited by Alphons Silbermann and H. -D. Dyroff, pp. 213-224. Munich: K.G. Saur, 1986.

1511. Kothandaraman, Bala. "Colourful Years—And How! Indian Comics in English." In *Literature and Popular Culture,* edited by R.S. Sharma, K.N. Chandran, S.

Singh, and A. Uma. Hyderabad: Cauvery Publications, 1989.

1512. Kumar, Kamalini. "Confused Ideals in Fantasy Land." *The Telegraph*. May 8, 1983, p. 7.

1513. Lal, Lakshmi. "Classics and Comics." *Vidura*. August 1976, p. 169.

1514. Menon, Sadanand. "Clean Bowled for a Duck." *Economic Times* (Bombay). November 29, 1992, p. 11. (Disney Comics).

1515. Pal, Bulbul. "Angry Young Men and Weepy Women." *Express Magazine*. November 22, 1987.

1516. Pal, Bulbul. "Comic Interludes." *Express Magazine*. November 22, 1987.

1517. Punwani, Jyoti. "Comics Are Big Business." *Sunday Observer*. September 4, 1983.

1518. Rao, Aruna. "Constitution of Identity in Indian Comics." Paper presented at Mid-Atlantic Region, Association for Asian Studies, Pittsburgh, Pennsylvania, October 22, 1994.

1519. Rao, Aruna. "Immortal Picture Stories: Indian Comics Today." Paper presented at Mid-Atlantic Region/Association for Asian Studies, Mahwah, New Jersey, October 31, 1993.

1520. Rao, Aruna. "The Workings of the Comic Book Industry of India." Paper presented at Popular Culture Association, Chicago, Illinois, April 9, 1994.

1521. Sharma, Vashini. "Non-Verbal Communication in Comics (in Reference to Hindi-English)." *Psycho-Lingua*. January 1987, pp. 21-37.

1522. Singh, Chander Uday. "Comics: Fortune from Fantasy." *India Today*. September 30, 1982, pp. 146-147.

1523. Singh, Jacquelin. "Kids n' Komics." *Vidura*. August 1976, pp. 163-165.

1524. "Sudden Muanga." *Amusement Today and Tomorrow*. October/November 1990, p. 4.

1525. Suraiya, Bunny. "Comics Emerge from the Satchel As the Voice of India's Heritage." *Far Eastern Economic Review*. February 2, 1984, pp. 38-39.

1526. Uncle Omi. "The Great Epic." *Evening News*. April 3, 1985, p. 4.

1527. Varghese, A.V. "Funny Business in a Spin." *Deccan Herald*. May 31, 1992.

Amar Chitra Katha

1528. Bakshi, Rajni. "ACKS: Distorted History or Education?" *The Telegraph.* November 13, 1983, p. 8.

1529. Comic Books from India in English (microform): A Collection. *Series: Amar Chitra Katha/Gaurav Katha.* New York: New York Public Library, 1983.

1530. Hindi Comic Books (Microform): A Collection. *Series: Amar Chitra Katha/Gaurav Katha.* New York: New York Public Library, 1983.

1531. Kapada, Surekha. "The Story of Amar Chitra Katha." *Free Press Journal.* July 26, 1986, pp. 6-7.

1532. McCarthy, Brendan. "Amar Chitra! Zoom! Zoom! Zoom!" *Revolver* (United Kingdom). October 1990.

1533. Parekh, Mehool. "ACK: The Closing Chapters." *Business World.* November 20 - December 3, 1991, pp. 17-18.

1534. *Proceedings of the Seminar on the Role of Chitra Katha in School Education.* Bombay: India Book House Education Trust, 1978. 10 pp. (Includes: Anant Pai, "Chitra Katha in School Education," pp. 2-3; M.C. Joshi, "Chitra Katha Through The Ages," p. 4; V.P. Dwivedi, "The Role of Chitra Katha in Promoting Cultural Awareness," p. 5; Subba Rao, "The Chitra Katha in Teaching History," p. 6; K.R. Mitra, "Language Development Through the Ages," p. 7).

Comic Strips

1535. "Amitabh Supremo Bachchan: Superstar Turned Comic Strip." *India Magazine.* June 1984, pp. 50-53, 55, 57-59.

1536. Menon, Sadanand. "The Great 'Duck'tator Moves to India." *Economic Times* (Bombay). November 29, 1992, p. 11.

1537. Nadkarni, Dev. "The Art of the Cartoon Strip." *Amusement Today and Tomorrow.* October/November 1990, pp. 6-10.

1538. Nadkarni, Dev. "What's What in a Comic Strip." *Amusement Today and Tomorrow.* October/November 1990, p. 27.

"Chacha Chaudhary"

1539. "Chacha Chaudhary's Silver Jubilee." *Hindustan Times.* February 5, 1994, p. 20.

1540. Dhar, Aarti. "Chacha Chaudhury Is 25 Now." *The Hindu*. December 2, 1994, p. 18.

1541. "Indian Comic Strips for World Museum." *Times of India*. July 6, 1993, p. 11.

1542. "1994-Silver Jubilee Year of Chacha Chaudhary. Exhibition of Original Drawings of Comics by Pran." New Delhi: 1994. 4 pp.

Political Cartoons

1543. Abraham, Abu. "Mr. Punch in Old Age." *Vidura*. July-October 1991, pp. 17, 19.

1544. C.I.B. "Of Life and Limb." *Financial Express*. August 1986.

1545. "Creative, Contemporary Cartoons." *The Statesman* (New Delhi). August 10, 1986.

1546. Dar, Sudhir. "Cartoonists Must Be Critics, Not Cynics." *The Pioneer*. April 25, 1994.

1547. Hettigoda Gamage, Winnie. "Political Cartooning in India." Master's thesis, M.S. University of Baroda, 1991 (?). 106 pp.

1548. Kamdar, Neema. "Wood for Thought." *Midday*. March 6, 1994, pp. I, III.

1549. Mandoo, M.P. Saxena. *Cartoons for Peace*. Ahmedabad: Allied Publishers Pvt. Ltd., 1987. 108 pp.

1550. Menon, Sadanand. "The Politics of the Cartoon." *Economic Times* (Bombay). February 20, 1994, p. 11.

1551. Menon, Sadanand. "When You Put the Cart(oons) Before the Horse." *Economic Times* (Bombay). February 19, 1994, p. 11.

1552. Pereira, Myron J. "The Political Cartoon." *Group Media Journal*. 7: 3/4 (1988), pp. 13-15.

1553. Pereira, Rehina. "Funny Side Up!" *The Times of India*. August 15, 1990, p. 11.

1554. Ranga. "Cartooning in India." *Vidura*. July - October 1991, pp. 49-50.

1555. "Strokes That Make or Mar." *Times of India*. January 31, 1994, p. 9.

1556. "30 Questions." *Illustrated Weekly of India*. November 12, 1989, pp. 30-31.

1557. Unny. "Triangle of Half-Truths: (Love Triangle Between Gandhi, Congress and

Cartoonists Over Time)." *The Economic Times* (Bombay). October 2, 1994, pp. 11-12.

1558. *Vidura.* New Delhi. Various issues. (Includes Mohan Ram on Indian cartoons, August 1965, pp. 1-4; Abu on problems of a cartoonist, May 1966, pp. 8-9; Charles Gardosh on problems of a cartoonist, August 1966, p. 40; *Berliner Morgenpost* on problems of a cartoonist, August 1966, p. 41; Kamil Sarkar on cartooning in India, February 1966, p. 28).

INDONESIA

General Sources

1559. "Bali—Artist's Island." *Time.* November 22, 1937, pp. 25-26.

1560. "Dari Luar Negeri Banyak Yang Daftar." *Suara Merdeka.* November 28, 1987, p. 1.

1561. Handry, TM. "Dapat Sambutan di Norwegia." *Suara Merdeka.* September 20, 1987, p. 7.

1562. "HumOr Data dan Pembaca 1992." Jakarta: *HumOr,* 1992. 12 pp.

1563. "Humor Is Tawa Is Tangis." *Wawasan.* October 11, 1987, p. 1.

1564. Soedarmo, Darminto M. "Semarang dan Humor." *Wawasan.* August 30, 1987.

Cartooning, Cartoons

1565. Anderson, Benedict R. O'G. "Cartoons and Monuments: The Evolution of Political Communication under the New Order." In *Political Power and Communications in Indonesia,* edited by Karl D. Jackson and Lucian W. Pye, pp. 282-321. Berkeley: University of California Press, 1978.

1566. Handry, TM. "Jawab Kegelisahan Potensi Daerah." *Suara Merdeka.* March 29, 1987, p. 7.

1567. "Kehadiran Srimulat dan Gepeng Jangan Dijadikan Musuh." *Wawasan.* June 15, 1987, p. 3.

1568. "Menjual Senyum Lewat Kartun." *Kompas.* December 1, 1985.

1569. "Profesi Lucu, Makin Laku." *HumOr.* November 1990, pp. 65-66.

1570. Sjachran R. "Kumala, Kartun Pertama di Layar Putih." *Jawa Pos*. March 27, 1989, pp. 1, 16.

1571. Sjachran R. "Melongok Laboratorium PPFN." *Jawa Pos*. April 10, 1989, p. 9.

1572. Sudarmo, Darminto M. "Dominasi Humor dalam Film Indonesia Sebuah Mode Atau Fenomena Budaya." *Minggu Legi*. August 2, 1987, p. 5.

1573. Sudarmo, Darminto M. "Kartun Indonesia di Tengah Peta Kartun Dunia." *Wawasan*. October 27, 1987, p. 10.

1574. Sudarmo, Darminto M. "Merentang Sayap Pergaulan Budaya." *Jakarta*. January 26, 1989.

1575. Sudarmo, Darminto M. "Perlu Kerja Keras dalam Melaksanakan Diplomasi Kebudayaan." *Suara Merdeka*. February 25, 1988, p. 2.

Festivals

1576. "Banyak Peminat Festival Kartun dari Luar Negeri." *Kompas*. November 28, 1987, p. 1.

1577. "Borislav Stankovic (Yugoslavia) Raih Golden "Suara Merdeka' Award." *Suara Merdeka*. January 12, 1988, p. 1.

1578. *Canda Laga Mancanegara I*. International Cartoon Festival 1988, Semarang, Indonesia. Semarang: PT Masscom Graphy, 1988. 181 pp.

1579. "Festival Kartun Internasional di Semarang." *Kompas*. September 25, 1987, p. 1.

1580. "Festival Kartun Internasional di Semarang." *Suara Merdeka*. November 7, 1987.

1581. "Kartun Internasional Gaya Semarangan." *Tempo*. February 6, 1988, p. 94.

1582. "Para Kartunis Asing Dominasi 'Candalaga Mancanegara I.'" *Wawasan*. January 17, 1988, p. 10.

1583. "Pemenang Lomba Kartun Internasional." *Kompas*. January 17, 1988.

1584. Soebijoto, Hertanto S. "Festival Kartun Internasional di Semarang: Jaring Wisatawan Lewat Canda." *Wawasan*. December 20, 1987, p. 10.

1585. Soepriyanto G.S. "Semarang Yang 'Gelisah' Sampai Canda Laga Manca Negara I." *Suara Merdeka*. October 6, 1987.

1586. Sudarmo, Darminto M. "Menawarkan Sikap Optimis Melalui Candalaga Kartun." *Minggu Wage*. January 17, 1988.

1587. Sudarmo, Darminto M. "Yang Aneh—Unik di Balik Canda Laga Mancanegara I." *Minggu Ini*. January 1988, p. 8.

1588. Suprana, Jaya. "Hewan Apakah Candalaga Itu?" *Editor*. February 6, 1988, pp. 41-42.

1589. "Tercatat 125 Peserta Festival Kartun Internasional." *Wawasan*. November 27, 1987, p. 1.

Governmental and Legal Aspects

1590. "Indonesia: Criminal Charges for Political Caricatures." *Asia Watch*. May 13, 1991, pp. 1-5.

1591. "Jakarta Journalist Sacked Over Offensive Cartoon." *Asian Mass Communication Bulletin*. March-April 1993, p. 6.

Historical Aspects

1592. Ah Iseng Saja Kok. "Kartun-Kartun Kita. Yang Ha...Ha dan Yang Astaga." *Junior*. February 7, 1975, pp. 8-9, 64-65.

1593. Sudarta, G.M. *Indonesia 1967-1980*. Jakarta: Penerbit P.T. Gramedia, 1980. 380 pp. (Anthology with some cartoon history).

Cartoonists

1594. Odios. "Kartunis Yang Ngobral Karyanya." *Wawasan*. March 15, 1987, p. 4.

1595. "Pakyo: Terkatung-katung Setelah Main Secac." *HumOr*. November 1990, pp. 46-47. (Pakyo Cartoonist Association).

1596. Purnomo, Stephanie. "3 Kartunis Peraih Tingkat Penghargaan Internasional." *Minggu Ini*. Minggu III, January 1987, pp. 7-8.

1597. Sudarta, G. M. "Kepahitan Yang Humoristis." *Kompas*. December 21, 1985. (Sibarani).

Hidayat, Johnny

1598. "Johnny Hidayat." *Junior*. December 7, 1973, pp. 48-49; October-November 1972, p. 5.

1599. "Johnny Hidayat." *Metro*. October-November 1972, pp. 5-7.

1600. "Johnny Hidayat Ar. Disangka Tukang Kode Nomor." *PMM*. December 30, 1977, pp. 10-11.

1601. "Johnny Hidayat, Kartunis Laris." *Tempo*. January 31, 1976, pp. 24-26.

1602. "Johnny Hidayat-Sebulan Rp 200,000." *Romansa*. June 1975, pp. 12-13.

1603. "Johnny Hidayat Tinggalkan Masa Sendirinya." *Vista*. November 1978, p. 32.

1604. "Kalau Johnny Hidayat Bercinta." *Fortuna*. No. 38, pp. 4-7.

1605. "Kartoonis Johny Hidayat Man Nikau." *Ria Remaja*. June 1976, pp. 40-41.

1606. "Meski Sudah 22 Kali Bercinta Tak Pernah Sampai Kejenjang Perkawinan." *Flambojan*. 079, pp. 32, 38.

1607. "Meski Sudah 22 Kali Bercinta Tak Pernah Sampai Kejenjang Perkawinan." *Flambojan*. May 18, 1974, pp. 12-13.

1608. Nasco. "Johnny Hidayat. Pacar Sudah Ke 23, Belum Kawin Kawin Juga!" *Adam & Eva*. July 17, 1977, pp. 10-11, 38.

1609. Odios. "Johnny Hidayat: Kartunis Yang Gagal Berwiraswasta." *Wawasan*. March 8, 1987.

1610. "Potret Kartunis Yang Sukses." *Vista*. June 1977, pp. 14-15.

1611. "Siapa Sebenarnya Pelukis Kartoon Yang Bernama: Johny Hidayat." *Contessa*. No. 54, 1973, pp. 20-21.

1612. "Tampang 'James John' Johnny Hidayat. ar." *Metro*.

Koendoro, Dwi

1613. Darmawan, Ari. "Citra Audivistama: Kreativitas, Manajemen dan Bonafiditas." *Cakram*. June 1992, pp. 32-33.

1614. "Dunia Impian Dwi Koendoro." *Mode*. June 7, 1992, pp. 54-58.

1615. "Penyulam Kitik Dwi Koendoro." *Jakarta Jakarta*. February 8-14, 1992, pp. 28-39.

Lionar, Thomas A.

1616. Badrudin, Ramli. "Indonesia in a Golden Era of Cartooning." *WittyWorld*. Summer/Autumn 1991, pp. 84-86.

1617. Badrudin, Ramli. "Thomas A. Lionar." In *Cartoonometer: Taking the Pulse of the World's Cartoonists*, edited by Joe Szabo and John A. Lent, p. 106. North Wales, Pennsylvania: WittyWorld Books, 1994.

Pramono, S.H.

1618. Pramono. *Karikatur Karikatur 1970-1981*. Jakarta: Sinar Harapan, 1981. 122 pp.

1619. Pramono, S.H. "Wadah Kartunis Bukan Untuk Bikin Kartu Nama." *Sinar Harapan*. October 2, 1985, pp. V, VI.

1620. Sudarmo, Darminto M. "Kartunis Pramono Ya Kartunis Ya Jurnalis." *Kartika Minggu*. July 26, 1987.

1621. Sudarmo, Darminto M. "Pramono, Ya Kartunis, Ya Seniman." *Minggu Ini*. January 1987, p. 8.

1622. Sudarmo, Darminto M. "Pramono, Ya Kartunis, Ya Seniman." *Suara Merdeka*. n.d.

Sudarta, G.M.

1623. Badrudin, Ramli. "G.M. Sudarta." In *Cartoonometer: Taking the Pulse of the World's Cartoonists*, edited by Joe Szabo and John A. Lent, p. 82. North Wales, Pennsylvania: WittyWorld Books, 1994.

1624. Badrudin, Ramli. "Indonesian Cartoonists Cannot Have Authoritative Opinions." *WittyWorld*. Autumn 1988, pp. 34-36.

1625. "[G.M. Sudarta]." *Matra*. March 1989, pp. 14-23.

1626. Soedarmo, Darminto M. "Kartun Tenggang Rasa GM Sudarta." *Minggu Ini*. May 1987, p. 2, 7-8.

1627. Sudarta, G.M. "Karikatur: Mati Ketawa Cara Indonesia." *Prisma*. May 1987, pp. 49-53.

Animation

1628. Hertanto." Karyawan Boleh 'Berkemah di Kantor.'" *Tiara*. July 1992, pp. 82-83.

1629. "Si Unyil: A New Symbol for Indonesian Children." *Indonesia Magazine*. March-April 1982, p. 7.

1630. Soebijoto, Hertanto S. "Film Animasi Mancanegara Masih Mendominasi." *Suara Merdeka*. March 12, 1989, p. 7.

Caricature

1631. Agus. "Karikatur." *Hai*. June 16-22, 1987, pp. 28-29. (Arwah).

1632. Mas Agus. "Kartun, Karikatur, Gambar Ilustrasi." *Sisipan Majalah Gadis*. August 26, 1981, pp. 1-15.

Comic Books

1633. Atwowiloto, Arswendo. "Komik Kota Mereka." *Jakarta*. May 27-June 2, 1988, pp. 12-13.

1634. "Bisnis Komik di Indonesia (1)." *Jakarta*. May 27-June 2, 1988, pp. 4-5.

1635. "Bisnis Komik di Indonesia (2)." *Jakarta*. May 27-June 2, 1988, pp. 6-7.

1636. Bonneff, Marcel. "Deux Images pour un Reve, la Bande Dessinée et le Cinema Indonesiens." *Archipel* (Paris). 5 (1973), pp. 197-208.

1637. Bonneff, Marcel. *Les Bandes Dessinées Indonésiennes: Une Mythologie en Image*. Paris: Puyraimond, 1976.

1638. Hanna, Willard A. *Indonesian Komik*. Hanover, New Hampshire: American Universities Field Staff, No. 16, 1979.

1639. "In Indonesien Entdeck." *Comic!* September/October 1994, p. 5.

1640. "Komik [Gong!] Impor: Suka Tak Suka?" *Jakarta*. May 27-June 2, 1988, p. 1.

1641. "Komik Riwayatmu Dulu (1)." *Jakarta*. May 27-June 2, 1988, pp. 18-19.

1642. "Nyt Gnuff-album på Indonesisk." *Serieskaberen*. March 1990, pp. 6-7.

1643. "Perjalanan Komik Indonesia (1)." *Jakarta*. May 27-June 2, 1988, pp. 8-9.

1644. "Perjalanan Komik Indonesia (2)." *Jakarta*. May 27-June 2, 1988, pp. 10-11.

1645. Santana, Rudy. "Indonésie." In *Histoire Mondiale de la Bande Dessinée*, edited by Pierre Horay, pp. 288-289. Paris: Pierre Horay Éditeur, 1989.

Comic Strips

1646. "Tokah Khayal Paman Sam." *Jakarta*. May 27-June 2, 1988, pp. 16-17.

"Panji Koming"

1647. Koendoro, Dwi. *Panji Koming*. Jakarta: Gramedia, 1992. 195 pp.

1648. Priyanto, S. "Perlambang Koen Koming." *Tempo*. August 1, 1992, p. 108.

1649. Siregar, Arif B. "Panji Koming, Pailul, dan Walt Disney." *Matra*. October 1989, pp. 143-146.

JAPAN

Resources

1650. Durkin, Dan. "Magazine Review—*Anime* V." *The Rose*. September 1989, p. 7.

1651. Felton, Jay. "Magazine Review: Mangazine: The Official Manga Video Newsletter." *The Rose*. October 1993, p. 23.

1652. Hinata, Shigeo. "To Advance the Preservation and Study of Japanese Comics—On Visiting 'Library of Contemporary Comics.'" *Gengo Seikatsu*. 329 (1979), pp. 48-52.

1653. Ishikawa, Hiroyoshi, *et al.*, eds. *Taishū Bunka Jiten* (Encyclopedia of Popular Culture). Tokyo: Kōundō, 1991. 1,034 pp.

1654. *The Japanese Cartoonists Catalog*. Tokyo: The Japan Cartoonists Association, 1992. 260 pp.

1655. Keller, Chris. "What is V. Max?" *V. Max*. No. 1, pp. 2-3.

1656. Lent, John A. "Anime Periodicals." *Asian Cinema*. 6:1 (1995).

1657. Monkī, Panchi. *Komikku Nyūmon* (A Guide of Comics). Tokyo: Futabasha, 1968. 192 pp.

1658. "MSU Manga Collection Begins." *Comic Art Collection*. November 2, 1990, p. 1.

1659. Nihon Manga Gakuin and Tadao Kimura, eds. *Mangaka Meikan* (A Directory of Comic Artists). Tokyo: Kusanone Shuppankai, 1989. 192 pp.

1660. *Nihon Manga-ka Meikan 500, 1945-1992* (500 Japanese Cartoonists, 1945-1992). Tokyo: Acua Planning, 1992. 1,074 pp.

1661. Nihon Manga Kyōkai, ed. *Nihon Manga Nenkan '76* (The 1976 Annual of Japanese Comics). Tokyo: Gurafikkusha, 1976.

1662. Pearl, Steve. "Anime Shopper's Guide to New York City." *The Rose*. January 1992, pp. 24-25.

1663. Santoso, Widya. "Magazine Review: Animerica." *The Rose*. January 1993, p. 13.

1664. Santoso, Widya. "Magazine Review: Anime UK Magazine." *The Rose*. July 1992, p. 27.

1665. Santoso, Widya. "Magazine Review: Japanese Animation Movement." *The Rose*. April 1993, p. 15.

1666. Santoso, Widya. "Manga Manga Manga—A Celebration of Japanese Animation at the ICA Cinema." *The Rose*. July 1993, p. 26.

1667. Savage, Lorraine. "Anime Magazine Reviews." *The Rose*. July 1993, pp. 20-23.

1668. Savage, Lorraine. "Fanzine Reviews." *The Rose*. September 1990, pp. 18-19.

1669. Savage, Lorraine. "Magazine Review: Mangajin." *The Rose*. November 1990, p. 16.

1670. Schodt, Frederik L. "Magazines of Manga Criticism." *Mangajin*. No. 11, 1991, pp. 9, 61.

1671. Shimizu, Isao. *Chōshō Esekai Eno Tabi: Fūshi No Mangakan* (A Trip to the Ridiculous Picture World: A Museum of Caricature). Tokyo: Chūōkōronsha, 1982. 248 pp.

1672. Shimizu, Isao, ed. *Nihon Manga No Jiten* (The Dictionary of Japanese Comics). Tokyo: Sanseidō, 1985. 254 pp.

1673. Suyama, Keiichi. *Manga Hakubutsushi: Nipponhen* (An Almanac of Comics: Japan). Tokyo: Banchō Shoten, 1972.

1674. Town Mook. *Gekigaka/Mangaka Ōru Meikan* (Town Mook's Complete Encyclopedia of Comic Artists). Tokyo: Tokuma Shoten, 1979.

1675. Valente, Joyce. "A Bibliography of Articles Written in English on Japanese Animation." *Fanta's Zine*. May 1980-June 1981, pp. 53-61.

1676. Yanase, Takashi. *Manga Nyūmon: Anata No Tame No Yūmoa Seizōhō* (A Guide of Comics: A Recipe of Humor for You). Tokyo: Ashi Shobō, 1965. 214 pp.

1677. Yanase, Takashi and Danji Tachikawa. *Manga Gakkō* (The School of Comics). Tokyo: San'ichi Shobō, 1966. 216 pp.

General Sources

1678. "Anime and Manga News." *Mangazine*. February 1993, pp. 1-3.

1679. "Appetite for Literature." *Time*. August 1, 1983, pp. 85, 87.

1680. Fulford, Adam. "Shūkanshi: Purveyors of Sex, Gossip, Comics, Booms, Exposés, Scoops and Scandals." *Mangajin*. No. 32, 1993, pp. 14-18, 44.

1681. Hajek, Lubor. *Japanese Graphic Art*. Leicester: Galley Press, 1989. 38 pp.+. Earlier edition, Octopus Press, 1976.

1682. Hillier, Jack. *The Japanese Picture Book; A Selection from the Ravicz Collection*. New York: Abrams, 1991. 136 pp.

1683. Horn, Maurice, ed. *The World Encyclopedia of Comics*. New York: Chelsea House, 1976. (Pages 23, 72-73, 84-85, 88-89, 113, 122-123, 168-169, 191, 193, 230, 268, 270-271, 277, 285-286, 300, 304, 307, 318, 321, 327-328, 332, 347, 418, 420-421, 425-426, 430, 432-435, 442-443, 484, 499-500, 511, 520, 522-523, 525-527, 532, 586-588, 595-597, 599-600, 613-614, 628, 630, 640-641, 648-649, 652-654, 656-657, 665, 672-673, 679, 712-714.)

1684. Johnson, Chalmers. "A 'Modern Emakimono.'" *Mangajin*. March 1995, pp. 22, 33.

1685. Rheault, Sylvain. "To Bodly [sic] Go...to Tokyo." *Protoculture Addicts*. March-April 1993, pp. 28-29.

1686. Sanches, Mary. "Contemporary Japanese Youth: Mass Media Communication." *Youth and Society*. June 1977, pp. 389-416.

1687. Sato, Tomoko and Toshio Watanake, eds. *Japan and Britain: An Aesthetic Dialogue 1850-1930*. London: Lund Humphries, 1991. 175 pp.

1688. Shimizu, Isao. "Sōkan no Kotoba" (Words for the First Issue). *Fūshiga Kenkyū*. January 20, 1992, p. 1.

1689. Tagawa, Suihō. *Kokkei No Kōzō* (The Anatomy of Humor). Tokyo: Kōdansha, 1981. 285 pp.

1690. Teraoka, Masami. "Life As a Beach." *Shambhala Sun*. March 1995, pp. 26-31.

1691. "Tokyo Resents Vanity Fair Quip at Son of Rising Sun." *News Week*. August 10, 1935, p. 19.

1692. Watanabe, Kazan. *Isso Hyakutai* (A Hundred Figures in a Single Stroke). Japan: 1884, 42 pp.

1693. "What Makes Japan Laugh?" *Asiaweek*. July 10, 1981, p. 53.

Business Aspects

Anime (Animation)

1694. "A.D. Vision: A Brief History." *Protoculture Addicts*. March-April 1993, pp. 40-41.

1695. "AnimEigo." *Protoculture Addicts*. November-December 1992, p. 9.

1696. "Around the Dealers Room." *Anime UK Magazine*. 2:5, pp. 16-17.

1697. Carr, John T. "Happy Birthday Tatsunoko." *Anime UK Magazine*. 2:1, pp. 24-25.

1698. Cormier-Rodier, Béatrice and Béatrice Fleury-Vilatte. "The Cartoon Boom." *Unesco Courier*. October 1992, pp. 17-20.

1699. "French-Japanese Cartoon Co-production for $2.5-Mil." *Variety*. April 30, 1980, p. 153.

1700. "Japanese Company Joins Kurtz' Outfit on Animation Pic." *Variety*. May 4, 1984, p. 342.

1701. "Japan-France 'Toon.'" *Variety*. October 14, 1981, p. 196.

1702. Johnstone, Bob. "Here Come the Titans." *Far Eastern Economic Review*. December 24-31, 1992, pp. 70-72.

1703. Joseph, P.C. "Rendering Animation at U.S. Renditions." *Animag*. 2:3, pp. 24-25.

1704. "Making Anime Dreams Come True at Pioneer." *Animerica*. March 1994, p. 10.

1705. "Moebius, Kurosawa Team on 'The Airtight Garage.'" *Comics Buyer's Guide*. March 26, 1993, p. 6.

1706. Moscato, John and Martin Ouellette. "U.S. Renditions: Reviews." *Protoculture Addicts*. November-December 1992, pp. 28-29.

1707. "Movie Int'l Co's Cartoons." *Variety*. April 16, 1980, p. 140.

1708. Oscar, Michael. "A Retail Roundup." *Anime UK Magazine*. 3:2, p. 43.

1709. Oshiguchi, Takashi. "The Animation Industry's Response. *Animerica*. April 1994, p. 13.

1710. Oshiguchi, Takashi. "Japanese Video Sales and Rentals—Fickle or Failing?" *Animerica*. October 1994, p. 18.

1711. Ouellette, Martin. "U.S. Renditions Subs and Dubs." *Protoculture Addicts*. March-April 1993, pp. 34-35.

1712. Patten, Fred and Emru Townsend. "Streamline Pictures." *Protoculture Addicts*. July-August 1992, pp. 10-15.

1713. "Pioneer Launches at Last!" *Anime UK Magazine*. 3:5, pp. 18-19.

1714. "Pioneering the Anime Frontier." *Animerica*. December 1993, p. 14.

1715. "Retail Roundup." *Anime UK Magazine*. 3:3, p. 16.

1716. Robson, Autumn. "Retail Roundup." *Anime UK Magazine*. 3:4, p. 40.

1717. "Set Japanese, French, and U.S. Coproduction for Animated Skein." *Variety*. October 15, 1980, p. 221.

1718. "Shochiku Active in Animation Projects." *Variety*. May 12, 1982, p. 332.

1719. "Tatsunoko Stresses Co-Prods, Cartoons." *Variety*. April 18, 1979, p. 132.

1720. "Toei Co. Makes Hay with Merchandising Based on Its Animation Characters." *Variety*. April 22, 1981, p. 121.

1721. "Toei Co. Still Selling Animated Shows to TV Asahi Network." *Variety*. April 27, 1988, p. 252.

1722. "Toei To Roll Two Animated Features." *Variety*. October 15, 1980, p. 224.

1723. Werba, Hank. "Animation in Japan Nears $1-Bil Mark." *Variety*. June 4, 1980, pp. 5, 38.

Manga (Comic Books)

1724. "The Comics Explosion." *Publishers Weekly*. October 19, 1992, p. 40.

1725. Eiji, Otsuka. "Comic-Book Formula for Success." *Japan Quarterly*. July-September 1988, pp. 289+.

1726. "The Japan Pulp-Paper Company Report: Special Edition on Comics." *JP Ripôto: Tokushū-Manga*. No. 36, 1981.

1727. "Japan's New Magazine Boom." *Asiaweek*. April 18, 1980, p. 51.

1728. "Magazines." *Japan Marketing/Advertising*. 1985/1986, pp. 96-100.

1729. "Magazines." *Japan Marketing/Advertising*. 1987, pp. 126-130.

1730. "The Manga Market." *Mangajin*. April 1991, pp. 14-17.

1731. "The Manga Market." In *Mangajin's Basic Japanese Through Comics*, pp. 10-12. Atlanta, Georgia: Mangajin, 1993.

1732. Ojo Bolaji. "A Not-So-Funny Business." *Asia, Inc*. June 1994, pp. 36-39.

1733. Ono, Kōsei. "Japan's Remarkable Comic Book Culture." *Tokyo Business Today*. February 1989, pp. 32-35.

1734. Perton, Marc. "Middle-Aged Psychic Samurai Beancakes...How Japanese-Style Comics Are Taking Over the World." *Business Tokyo*. February 1991, pp. 32-36.

1735. "Promise You'll Be Lost in Love at Viz." *Animerica*. November 1993, p. 36.

1736. Solo, Sally. "Japanese Comics Are All Business." *Fortune*. October 9, 1989, pp. 143-149.

1737. Thorn, Matt. "Extreme Close-up." *Animerica*. November 1993, p. 37.

Cartooning, Cartoons

1738. *The Best Cartoons of Nippon '93*. Omiya: The Preparatory Committee for the Establishment of the Omiya City Humor Center, 1993. 120 pp.

1739. "The Best Cartoons of Nippon '93." *Humour and Caricature*. November-December 1993, p. 33.

1740. *The Best Cartoons of Nippon '94*. Omiya: The Preparatory Committee for the Establishment of the Omiya City Humor Center, 1994. 134 pp.

1741. Carlton, Ardith. "Manga and Anime: Japanese Comics and Animated Cartoons." *Comics Collector*. Summer 1984, pp. 67-73, 89-90.

1742. "Cartoons Dominate Nippon Publishing; Hence Pix an Echo." *Variety*. May 12, 1982, pp. 328, 346.

1743. Clancy, Patricia M. "Referential Strategies in the Narratives of Japanese Children." Paper presented at Boston University Conference on Language Development, Boston, Massachusetts, October 8-10, 1982. 14 pp.

1744. "Drawing Heroes." *Chinese Literature*. No. 12, 1970, pp. 105-109.

1745. Ejiri, Susumu. "Japanese Cartoons." *The East*. March-April 1969, pp. 23-25, 75.

1746. FECO Nippon. *Shibui Otoko-tachi '91* (Guys in Good Taste). Tokyo: Kagyusha, 1991. 126 pp.

1747. Gibson, Robert W. "Manga and Anime Update." *Comics Buyer's Guide*. April 22, 1988, p. 34.

1748. *Humor Photo Omiya '93. 1993 Omiya City Humor Photo Contest*. Omiya: The Preparatory Committee for the Establishment of the Omiya City Humor Center, 1993. 48 pp.

1749. *Illustration in Japan. Vol. 2*. Introduction by Mamoru Yonekura. Tokyo: Kodansha International Ltd., 1982. 261 pp.

1750. Imajo, Shuzo. "Effects of Psychological Reactance on Emotional Experience: Evaluations of a Cartoon." *Japanese Journal of Psychology*. December 1984, pp. 268-274.

1751. Imajo, Shuzo. "Effects of Reactance and Impression Management on Evaluation of a Cartoon." *Tohoku Psychologica. Folia*. 41:1-4, pp. 7-15.

1752. "Japan." *WittyWorld*. Winter/Spring 1990, pp. 16-19.

1753. Kim Seung-Hee. "Yesterday and Today of Japanese Cartoons." *Gha Nah Art* (Seoul). November-December 1990, pp. 79-83.

1754. "Nippon FECO." *FECO News*. No. 12, 1991, p. 17.

1755. Sadao, Yamane. "Cartoons and Comics in Japan: Putting Laughter in Everyday Life." *Asian Culture*. January 1980, pp. 6-12.

1756. Saitamaken-Ritsu Kindai Bijutsukan (The Museum of Modern Art, Saitama), ed. *Nippon No Fūshi* (Subtle Criticism: Caricature and Satire in Japan). Saitama: Saitamaken-Ritsu Kindai Bijutsukan, 1993.

1757. Sasaki, Nagao. "'Kodomo Asobi-e' to E-rōsoku" ("Pictures of Children's Play" and Picture Candles). *Fūshiga Kenkyū*. April 20, 1993, p. 5.

1758. Shimizu, Isao. *The Collected Essays of Japanese Modern Cartoons*. Tokyo: Sinsindo, 1984. 264 pp. Japanese.

1759. Shimizu, Isao. *Going for a Cartoon World Ramble*. Tokyo: Kyoikusha, 1989. 248 pp. Japanese.

1760. Shimizu, Isao. "Kindai Manga to Āru to Nūbō" (Modern Cartoons and Art Nouveau). *Fūshiga Kenkyū*. July 20, 1992, pp. 14-15.

1761. Shimizu, Isao. "'Kodomo Asobi-e' Kō" (A Study on "Pictures of Children's Play"). *Fūshiga Kenkyū*. July 20, 1992, pp. 1-3.

1762. Shimizu, Isao. *The Modern Japan Drawn by Cartoons*. Tokyo: Kyoikusha, 1988. 264 pp. Japanese.

1763. Shimizu, Isao. "Ōkushon no O-shirase" (Announcement of an Auction). *Fūshiga Kenkyū*. January 20, 1992, pp. 14-15.

1764. Shimizu, Isao. "Saikin no Manga Kanren-ten Zuroku Shiryō to Ronbun" (Recent Exhibition Catalogs and Essays in Them Concerning Cartoons). *Fūshiga Kenkyū*. July 20, 1993, pp. 11-13.

1765. Shimizu, Isao. *The Way of Conception in Cartoons*. Tokyo: Kodansha, 1985. 256 pp. Japanese.

1766. Troelstrup, Glenn C. "Japanese Cartoons." *Cartoonist PROfiles*. Summer 1969, pp. 73-80.

1767. Wetherall, William. "Bashers at Wits' End." *Far Eastern Economic Review*. August 2, 1990, pp. 25-26.

1768. *Witty Land. A Collection of Drawings by Graduates of Prof. Yoshitomi's Cartoon Seminar*. Kyoto: Kyoto Seika University, 1993. 61 pp.

1769. Yamane, Sadao. "Cartoons and Comics in Japan: Putting Laughter in Everyday Life." *Asian Culture*. January 1980, pp. 6-12.

Festivals and Competitions

1770. "Anime Con." *Animenominous!* Spring 1993, pp. 17-20.

1771. "Anime Expo '93." *Animerica*. September 1993, p. 15.

1772. "Anime Express—'94 Con Report." *Anime UK Magazine*. 3:4, pp. 14-15.

1773. "Anime Film Festival." *Anime UK Magazine*. October/November 1992, pp. 3-4.

1774. "Con Reports." *The Rose*. October 1994, pp. 26-27.

1775. Evans, Peter. "Hamacon." *Anime UK Magazine*. October/November 1992, pp. 31-33.

1776. "For Every Con, There Is a Season—Anime Conventions Bloom." *Animerica*. January 1994, p. 17. (In England).

1777. Kidde, Rune."Krigen og Tegneserierne." *Seriejournalen*. Winter 1993, p. 24. (Omiya Fest).

1778. Lapointe, Pierre. "AnimeCon '91." *Protoculture Addicts*. May-June 1992, p. 9.

1779. McCloy, Stephen and Lorraine Savage. "Convention Reports: Anime Fest, Arisia, AnimEast." *The Rose*. January 1995, p. 28.

1780. McLennan, Jim. "Anime Expo '92." *Anime UK Magazine*. October/November 1992, pp. 20-21.

1781. Matsuzaki, James. "AnimeCon '91." *V. Max*. No. 2, pp. 13, 31.

1782. Matsuzaki, James and Elizabeth Bales. "Con or Expo, What's in a Name?" *V. Max*. No. 5, pp. 24-26.

1783. Quintanar, Derek. "Anime Expo '92." *Animag*. 2:3, pp. 6-7.

1784. "Report on Omiya '93: Peace and Caricature Festival." *Humour and Caricature*. November-December 1993, pp. 12-13.

1785. San Diego Comic Convention. *Japanese Animation Guide 1992*. San Diego: San Diego Comic Convention, 1992. 48 pp.

1786. Santoso, Widya. "KABOOM: An Exhibition of American and Japanese Animation in Sydney, Australia." *The Rose*. January 1995, pp. 25, 30.

1787. "Shake, Rattle and Roll with Streamline's Festival of Animation." *Animerica*. March 1994, p. 15.

1788. Watson, Paul. "Anime America Report." *Anime UK Magazine*. 3:5, p. 27.

1789. Wepman, Dennis. "Cartoons and Bonsai in Omiya." *WittyWorld*. Winter/Spring 1994, pp. 16-17.

Cartoonists

1790. "Animal Scrolls by the Father of Japanese Caricature, Toba Sojo." *Asia*. June 1930, pp. 417-419.

1791. Bravard, Jonathan. "Ajin and His Paper-Sculptures." *WittyWorld*. Autumn 1987, pp. 41-43.

1792. Brown, Azby. "An Interview with Takeuchi Akira, Creator of *Garcia-kun*." *Mangajin*. September 1993, pp. 42-52.

1793. Buronson [Jō Fumimura]. "My Comic Road." *Shōnen Sunday Interview*. June 5, 1988.

1794. "Cartoonists Work Hard in Japan." *Editor and Publisher*. July 11, 1959.

1795. Chang, Yvonne. "Cartoonists' Mix of *Manga* and Art Reflects Pressing Environmental Issues." *Japan Times*. December 24, 1989, p. 10.

1796. Contreras, Cynthia. "War Memories and Rice Farmers: A Conversation with Masahiro Shinoda." *Asian Cinema*. 5:2 (1990), p. 6-8.

1797. Costa, Jordi. "Bola de Drac." Catalogue. 10è Saló Internacionl del Comic de Barcelona, 1992. Barcelona: 1992. 16 pp. (Akira Toriyama).

1798. "Creators of Animation: Akihiko Matsuda." *This Is Animation*. No. 3, 1982, pp. 56-57.

1799. "Creators of Animation: Hiroshi Sasagawa." *This Is Animation*. No. 3, 1982, pp. 50-53.

1800. "Creators of Animation: Masatoshi Tsurubuchi." *This Is Animation*. No. 3, 1982, pp. 54-55.

1801. "Creators of Animation: Masayuki Yamamoto." *This Is Animation*. No. 3, 1982, pp. 58-59.

1802. "Creators of Animation: Shichirō Kobayashi." *This Is Animation*. No. 2, 1982, pp. 58-60.

1803. "Creators of Animation: Yoshio Kuroda." *This Is Animation*. No. 2, 1982, pp. 50-53.

1804. "Creators of Animation: Yoshiyuki Tomino." *This Is Animation*. No. 2, 1982, pp. 54-57.

1805. Davies, Julie. "An Animator for All Seasons. We Need Tenchi! (Hiroki Hayashi Tells Us Why." *Animerica*. April 1994, pp. 4-9.

1806. Delorme, Ted. "The Manga of Hikaru Yuzuki." Privately printed. First appeared in *APAratus*.

1807. "An Eccentric Artist." *Apropos*. No. 3, 1986, pp. 119.

1808. Fujii, Yumiko. "A Comics Artist Pursues Happiness." *Awake*. February 22, 1988, pp. 23-27.

1809. "Gene Pelc." *Comics Interview*. May 1983, pp. 54-55.

1810. Horn, Maurice, ed. *Contemporary Graphic Artists*. Detroit, Michigan: Gale Research, 1986, 1987. (Vol I, 1986: Taku Furukawa, pp. 114-115; Osamu Tezuka, pp. 241-243; Vol. II, 1987: Keiji Nakazawa, pp. 173-175).

1811. Ichinoe, Masashi. *Mangaka No Seikatsu* (Lives of Comic Artists). Tokyo:

Hamano Shuppan, 1989. 227 pp.

1812. "Interview with John O'Donnell." *Protoculture Addicts*. May-June 1992, pp. 15-19.

1813. "Interview with Robert Woodhead." *Protoculture Addicts*. November-December 1992, pp. 10-11.

1814. "Interview with Tom Mason and Chris Ulm." *Protoculture Addicts*. December 1990, pp. 10-13.

1815. "Interviews: Johji Manabe, Haruhiko Mikimoto, Yoshiyuki Sadamoto." *Protoculture Addicts*. May-June 1992. pp. 10-12.

1816. Ishigami, Yoshitaka. "Toei Anime Collection Doodles of a Kitten—The World of Yasuji Mori." *Animerica*. January 1994, p. 58.

1817. Itō, Ippei. *Nihon No Mangaka* (The Cartoonists of Japan). Tokyo: Sangyō Keizai Shimbun, 1972.

1818. Ito, Junco. "Oh! My Goddess! It's Kosuke Fujishima." *Animerica*. February 1994, pp. 4-9.

1819. "Japanese Animated Pix Show Lotsa Talent but Lack Market." *Variety*. January 15, 1974, p. 273.

1820. Kanoh, Masahiro. "BD Japonaise. Au Commencement Était Tezuka." *Les Cahiers de la Bande Dessinée* (Grenoble). 72, 1986, pp. 39-41. (Hayao Miyazaki, Katsuhiro Otomo, Takao Saito, Yoshihiro Tatsumi, Osamu Tezuka).

1821. Karahashi, Takayuki. "Giant Robo: An Imagawa Runs Through It." *Animerica*. March 1994, pp. 4-9. (Yasuhiro Imagawa).

1822. Karahashi, Takayuki and Dana Fong. "Yuzo Takada's 3x3 Eyes." *Animag*. 2:1, pp. 18-19.

1823. Kato, Hisao. "Hirata, Hiroshi (1937-)." In *Enciclopedia Mondiale del Fumetto*, edited by Maurice Horn and Luciano Secchi, p. 461. Milan: Editoriale Corno, 1978.

1824. Kato, Hisao. "Kawanabe, Gyōsai (1831-1889)." In *Enciclopedia Mondiale del Fumetto*, edited by Maurice Horn and Luciano Secchi, p. 498. Milan: Editoriale Corno, 1978.

1825. Kato, Hisao. "Kojima, Koo (1928-)." In *Enciclopedia Mondiale del Fumetto*, edited by Maurice Horn and Luciano Secchi, p. 510. Milan: Editoriale Corno, 1978.

1826. Kato, Hisao. "Kuwata, Jirō (1935-)." In *Enciclopedia Mondiale del Fumetto*, edited by Maurice Horn and Luciano Secchi, p. 518. Milan: Editoriale Corno, 1978.

1827. Kato, Hisao. "Mizushima, Shinji (1939-)." In *Enciclopedia Mondiale del Fumetto*, edited by Maurice Horn and Luciano Secchi, p. 572. Milan: Editoriale Corno, 1978.

1828. Kato, Hisao. "Nagashima, Shinji (1937-)." In *Enciclopedia Mondiale del Fumetto*, edited by Maurice Horn and Luciano Secchi, p. 583. Milan: Editoriale Corno, 1978.

1829. Kato, Hisao. "Saitō, Takao (1936-)." In *Enciclopedia Mondiale del Fumetto*, edited by Maurice Horn and Luciano Secchi, p. 669. Milan: Editoriale Corno, 1978.

1830. Kato, Hisao. "Shimizu, Kon (1912-1974)." In *Enciclopedia Mondiale del Fumetto*, edited by Maurice Horn and Luciano Secchi, pp. 685-686. Milan: Editoriale Corno, 1978.

1831. Kato, Hisao. "Yokoyama, Taizō (1917-)." In *Enciclopedia Mondiale del Fumetto*, edited by Maurice Horn and Luciano Secchi, p. 778. Milan: Editoriale Corno, 1978.

1832. Koike, Kazuo. "My Comic Road." *Shōnen Sunday Interview*. May 4, 1988.

1833. Kruger, Dave. "'Gaijin' Cartoonist Lampoons Expat Life." *Japan Times*. October 22, 1992. (Tim Ernst).

1834. [Kuriyagawa Hakuson]. *Shidai Manhua*. October 20, 1934, n.p.

1835. Kuwata, Masakazu. *Japan Unbuttoned*. Cartoons by Masakazu Kuwata. Text and captions by Charles E. Tuttle. Tokyo: Charles E. Tuttle, n.d.

1836. Kyōdō Hōkoku-Jōhō Kyampusu V. *Teihen Emaki No Gakōtachi/Gekigaka* (Unsung Painters of Picture Scrolls: The Drama Comic Artists). Tokyo: Sangyō Hōkoku, 1972.

1837. Larson, Randall D. "Scoring Space Cruiser Yamato: A Profile of Hiroshi Miyagawa." *Animag*. No. 6, 1990, pp. 56-58.

1838. Laurent, Patrick. "Natacha et Yoko Tsuno Fêtent Leurs 20 Ans." *Coccinelle*. January-April 1990, p. 27.

1839. Ledoux, Trish. "Ryoichi 1/2." *Animerica*. September 1993, pp. 5-9. (Ryoichi Ikegami).

1840. Ledoux, Trish. "Take Ten at Anime Expo '93." *Animerica*. September 1993, pp.

16-17. (Keita Amemiya, Yasuhiro Imagawa, and Makoto Kobayashi).

1841. Ledoux, Trish. "Take Ten at Anime Expo, Part Two." *Animerica*. November 1993, pp. 16-17. (Takayuki Takeya, Masatoshi Tahara, Scott Frazier).

1842. Lin Chi-Tao. "The Originator of Alien." *Monthly Comic Magazine* (Hong Kong). No. 0, 1990, pp. 2-4.

1843. Lin Maiko. "Profile: Naoyuki Onda." *V. Max*. No. 1, p. 22.

1844. Lu Tzu-Ying. "First Animation: Illusory War." *Monthly Comic Magazine* (Hong Kong). October 1990, pp. 79-80.

1845. Lu Tzu-Ying. "In Memory of a Japanese Cartoonist." *Monthly Comic Magazine* (Hong Kong). January 1991, pp. 3-6.

1846. McCarthy, Helen. "Robert De Jesus." *Anime UK Magazine*. 2:6, p. 14.

1847. McCarthy, Helen. "Tim Eldred." *Anime UK Magazine*. 2:6, p. 15.

1848. McCarthy, Helen. "Yuuki Nobuteru: The Anime Expo Interview." *Anime UK Magazine*. 3:5, pp. 12-14.

1849. "Mad Ad." *Mangajin*. May 1992, pp. 8-9. (Mad Amano).

1850. Matsuyama, Fumio. *Gashu Matsuyama Fumio No Sekai* (The World of Fumio Matsuyama). Tokyo: Aishin Shuppan, 1980. 134 pp.

1851. Matsuzaki, James. "A Visit with Seiji Horibuchi of Viz Comics." *V. Max*. No. 4, pp. 5-8.

1852. Matsuzaki, James and Kensaku Nakata. "Hideaki Anno." *V. Max*. No. 3, p. 31.

1853. Mikimoto, Haruhiko. *Haruhiko Mikimoto Illustrations: Macross/Macross II/Orguss/Top O Nerae/Mobile Suit Gundam*. Tokyo: Yutaka Takahashi, 1992. 96 pp.

1854. Minejima, Masayuki. *Kondō Hidezō No Sekai* (The World of Hidezō Kondō). Tokyo: Seiabō, 1984. 380 pp.

1855. "Nakataro Takamizawa Dod, 90 År." *Seriejournalen*. September 1990, p. 20.

1856. "Nakazawa, Keiji." In *Contemporary Graphic Artists. Vol. II*, edited by Maurice Horn, pp. 173-175. Detroit, Michigan: Gale Research, 1987.

1857. "One Hundred Tales: The Seventh: Apparation of an Eel." *Mangajin*. November 1994, pp. 74-81. (Sugiura Hinaka).

1858. Ono, Kōsei. "Cartoon Capers of Momotaro and His Merry Men of War." *Far Eastern Economic Review*. August 16, 1984, pp. 46-47.

1859. Oshiguchi, Takashi. "Spotlight on Anime Music—Shiro Sasaki's Magic Carpet Ride." *Animerica*. August 1994, pp. 4-8.

1860. Oshiguchi, Takashi. "Totally Takaya." *Animerica*. January 1994, pp. 4-9. (Yoshiki Takaya).

1861. Ouellette, Martin. "Faces of Anime Expo." *Protoculture Addicts*. November-December 1992, pp. 10-11.

1862. Ouellette, Martin. "Nagano's Previous Works." *Mecha Press*. December 1992, pp. 22-23. (Mamoru Nagano).

1863. P.C. "The Rough Touch on My Mind from Mitsuru Adachi." *Monthly Comic Magazine*. December 1990, pp. 68-69.

1864. "Portrait of the Artist—Interview with Monkey Punch." *Anime UK Magazine*. 2:5, pp. 12-13.

1865. "Q and A: James D. Hudnall." *Japanimation*. No. 3, 1987, pp. 14-15.

1866. Quigley, Kevin. "Takashi Nemoto: The S. Clay Wilson of Japan." *Comics Journal*. November 1992, pp. 31-34.

1867. Rosenfeld, David M. "From 'Mangaholic' to Guru: The Rise of an American Journalist in Japan." *Mangajin*. May 1994, pp. 20-21, 44.

1868. Santoso, Widya. "A Chat at Anime Expo '93. Part 1: Helen McCarthy of Anime UK." *The Rose*. October 1993, pp. 16-17.

1869. Savage, Lorraine. "Interview: Robert Gibson, Writer of Eclipse's Captain Harlock Comic." *The Rose*. May 1990, pp. 4-5.

1870. Schodt, Frederik. "About the Author...." *Mangajin*. September 1994, p. 63. (Shungiku Uchida).

1871. Schodt, Frederik. "Mary Kennard: A New Breed of American." *Animerica*. September 1994, pp. 36-37.

1872. Shimizu, Isao. "Dentan Manga-ka 'Okayama Ippei' no Nazo" (The Mystery of a Cartoonist of Propaganda Leaflets, "Ippei Okayama"). *Fūshiga Kenkyū*. July 20, 1992, pp. 6-7.

1873. Shimizu, Isao. "Fūshiga-ka Shōkai (1): Shimokawa Hekoten" (Introduction of a Cartoonist, I: Hekoten Shimokawa). *Fūshiga Kenkyū*. January 20, 1992, pp. 6-7.

1874. Shimizu, Isao. "Fūshiga-ka Shōkai (3): Asō Yutaka" (Introduction of a Cartoonist, III: Yutaka Asō). *Fūshiga Kenkyū*. July 20, 1992, pp. 6-9.

1875. Shimizu, Isao. "Kindai Manga Kankei-sha no Ryakureki o Shiru Tame no Bunken" (The Literature That Includes a Brief History of People Concerned with Modern Cartoons). *Fūshiga Kenkyū*. January 20, 1993, p. 14.

1876. Shimizu, Isao. "Kindai Manga Kankei-sha Ryakureki (1)" (A Brief History of People Concerned with the Modern Cartoons, I). *Fūshiga Kenkyū*. January 20, 1993, pp. 12-13.

1877. Shimizu, Isao. "Niizeki Kennosuke no Dōga-teki Manga Sekai" (Kennosuke Niizeki's World of Children's Comics). *Fūshiga Kenkyū*. January 20, 1994, pp. 1-6.

1878. Shimizu, Isao. "Sen-nin no Manga-ka Jiten" (A Dictionary of One Thousand Cartoonists). *Fūshiga Kenkyū*. April 20, 1993, pp. 7, 9.

1879. Shimizu, Isao. "Shiryō, Nihon Manga-ka Renmei Kiyaku" (Policies of the Japanese Cartoonist League). *Fūshiga Kenkyū*. July 20, 1992, p. 12.

1880. Shimizu, Isao. *The Sketch Album of Japan by Charles Wirgman*. Tokyo: Iwanami Shoten, 1987. 224 pp. Japanese.

1881. Shintani, Kaoru. "My Comic Road." *Shōnen Sunday Comics*. June 1, 1988.

1882. Smith, Toren. "An Interview with Maria Kawamura: The Lady Behind the Voice." *Animag*. No. 7, 1989, pp. 27-29.

1883. Stefánsson, Halldór. "Foreign Myths and Sagas in Japan: The Academics and the Cartoonists." Unpublished paper.

1884. Swallow, Jim. "The Role Playing Connection: Anime UK Interviews Palladium Books' Kevin Siembieda." *Anime UK Magazine*. 2:5, pp. 36-37.

1885. Taylor, James S. "Explaining Minmay: The Allure of the Idol Singer." *Protoculture Addicts*. March-April 1994, pp. 26-30.

1886. Thorn, Matt. "Girls' Stuff." *Animerica*. December 1993, p. 39. (Yumiko Oshima, Taku Tsumugi, Ryoko Yamagishi, Akemi Matsunae).

1887. Thorn, Matt. "Girls' Stuff, Part Two." *Animerica*. January 1994, p. 41. (Keiko Takemiya, Riyoko Ikeda, Yasuko Aoike, Yukari Ichijo, Mariko Iwadate, Akimi Yoshida).

1888. Thorn, Matt. "'Mania-Muki' Mini Bios." *Animerica*. February 1994, p. 35. (Clamp, Minami Ozaki, Yun Koga, and Natsumi Itsuki).

1889. Thorn, Matt. "Moto Hagio, the Beethoven of Shojo Manga?" *Animerica*. July 1993, p. 38.

1890. Tom, Avery M. "Never Forget Your Protective Headgear!" *Animerica*. June 1994, p. 6. (Akemi Takada, Kazunori Ito, Mamoru Oshii, Yutaka Izubuchi).

1891. "Toshimichi Suzuki." *The Rose*. April 1993, p. 6.

1892. Tsao Sheng-Te. "Character Designers." *The Rose*. July 1992, p. 28.

1893. Uekusa, Jin'ichi. *Boku Ga Suki Na Gaikoku No Kawatta Mangakatachi* (Unique Foreign Comic Artists I Like). Tokyo: Seidosha, 1971. 224 pp.

1894. Velasquez, Phil. "Lea Hernandez." *The Rose*. July 1994, p. 26.

1895. Winchester, James R. "Works of Kentarō Yano." *The Rose*. September 1989, p. 10.

1896. Yang, Jeff. "Anime Q and A: Ken Iyadomi." *Animerica*. December 1993, p. 16.

1897. Yang, Jeff. "Anime: Q and A—Marvin Gleicher." *Animerica*. October 1994, p. 15.

1898. Yang, Jeff. "Anime Q and A: Naoju Nakamura." *Animerica*. March 1994, p. 16.

1899. Yang, Jeff. "Anime Q and A: Steve Wang." *Animerica*. January 1994, p. 18.

1900. Yoshida, Toshifumi. "Editing Legends with Shogakukan's Katsuya Shirai." *Animerica*. December 1993, pp. 8-9.

1901. Yoshida, Toshifumi. "Silent Möbius." *Animerica*. June 1993, pp. 4-10. (Kia Asamiya).

Akatsuka, Fujio

1902. Akatsuka, Fujio. *Warawazuni Ikirunante: Boku No Jijoden* (What If I Live Without Laughing: My Biography). Tokyo: Kairyūsha, 1978. 254 pp.

1903. Akatsuka, Fujio, *et al. Tokiwasō Monogatari* (Tokiwa Apartment Story). Tokyo: Suiyōsha, 1983. 166 pp.

1904. "Fujio Akatsuka." In *A History of the Komiks of the Philippines and Other Countries*, by Cynthia Roxas and Joaquin Arevalo, Jr., p. 264. Manila: Islas Filipinas Publishing, 1985.

1905. Kato, Hisao. "Akatsuka, Fujio." In *Enciclopedia Mondiale del Fumetto*, edited by Maurice Horn and Luciano Secchi, pp. 142-143. Milan: Editoriale Corno, 1978.

Amano, Yoshitaka

1906. *The Art of Yoshitaka Amano: Hiten.* Carson, California: Books Nippon, 1990 [?].

1907. Lippolis, Alessandro. "Yoshitaka Amano." *The Rose.* January 1995, p. 24.

Bigot, Georges

1908. "Bigot—A Letter Remembering Meeting Bigot's Wife." *Fūshiga Kenkyū.* No. 12, 1994, p. 7.

1909. Haga, Tōru, Isao Shimizu, Tadayasu Sakai, and Kōji Kawamoto, eds. *Bigot Sobyō Collection 1: Meiji No Fūzoku* (Collection of Bigot's Drawings 1: Customs in the Meiji Period). Tokyo: Iwanami Shoten, 1989. 164 pp. Japanese.

1910. Haga, Tōru, Isao Shimizu, Tadayasu Sakai, and Kōji Kawamoto, eds. *Bigot Sobyō Collection 2: Meiji No Sesō* (Collection of Bigot's Drawings 2: Social Conditions in the Meiji Period). Tokyo: Iwanami Shoten, 1989. 160 pp. Japanese.

1911. Haga, Tōru, Isao Shimizu, Tadayasu Sakai, and Kōji Kawamoto, eds. *Bigot Sobyō Collection 3: Meiji No Jiken* (Collection of Bigot's Drawings 3: Incidents in the Meiji Period). Tokyo: Iwanami Shoten, 1989. 156 pp. Japanese.

1912. Katayori, Mitsugu. "Bigot—The Power of Caricature That Exists in *Modern Japan.*" *Fūshiga Kenkyū.* No. 12, 1994, p. 8.

1913. Shimizu, Isao. "Bigō Dōbanga-shū 'Asa' no Nazo" (The Mystery of "Asa," Bigot's Copperplate Print Collection). *Fūshiga Kenkyū.* January 20, 1993, pp. 1-4.

1914. Shimizu, Isao. "Bigō no Nihon Shashin-kai Nyūkai" (Bigot Joins Japan Photography Association). *Fūshiga Kenkyū.* July 20, 1994, p. 16.

1915. Shimizu, Isao. "Dai 6-Satsu-Me no Bigō Dōbanga-shū" (The Sixth Copperplate Print Collection by Bigot). *Fūshiga Kenkyū.* January 20, 1993, p. 5.

1916. Shimizu, Isao. *The Essay Drawn by G. Bigot's Japanese Sketches.* Tokyo: Chuoukouronsha, 1981. 240 pp. Japanese.

1917. Shimizu, Isao. "F. Ganesuko to G. Bigō" (F. Ganesco and G. Bigot). *Fūshiga Kenkyū.* April 20, 1994, pp. 1-6.

1918. Shimizu, Isao. "Fūshiga no Meisaku (1): G. Bigō" (A Masterpiece of Caricature, I: G. Bigot). *Fūshiga Kenkyū.* January 20, 1992, p. 1.

1919. Shimizu, Isao. *Meiji No Fūshi Gaka: Bigō* (Georges Bigot, a Satiric Cartoonist in Meiji Era). Tokyo: Shinchōsha, 1971. 214 pp. Japanese.

1920. Shimizu, Isao. *The Sketch Album of Japan by Georges Bigot*. Tokyo: Iwanami Shoten, 1986. 228 pp. Japanese.

1921. Shimizu, Isao. *The Sketch Album of Japan by Georges Bigot, Continued*. Tokyo: Iwanami Shoten, 1992. 232 pp. Japanese.

1922. Shimizu, Isao. *The Work Album of Georges Bigot*. Tokyo: Bijutsudoujinsha, 1970. 120 pp. Japanese.

Chiba, Tetsuya

1923. Kato, Hisao. "Chiba, Tetsuya (1939-)." In *Enciclopedia Mondiale del Fumetto*, edited by Maurice Horn and Luciano Secchi, p. 248. Milan: Editoriale Corno, 1978.

1924. "Tetsuya Chiba." In *A History of the Komiks of the Philippines and Other Countries*, by Cynthia Roxas and Joaquin Arevalo, Jr., p. 262. Manila: Islas Filipinas Publishing, 1985.

Dunn, Ben

1925. Dubreuil, Alain. "Ben Dunn: Part 2." *Protoculture Addicts*. January-February 1992, pp. 14-16.

1926. Yang, Jeff. "Anime Q and A: Ben Dunn." *Animerica*. June 1994, p. 18.

Fujiko-Fujio

1927. "Creators of Animation: Fujiko-Fujio." *This Is Animation*. No. 3, 1982, pp. 46-49.

1928. Schodt, Frederik. "Frederik Schodt Interviews Fujiko Fujio (A), Creator of 'The Laughing Salesman.'" *Mangajin*. June 1994, pp. 28-30, 32, 78.

1929. Schodt, Frederik. "Frederik Schodt Interviews Fujiko Fujio (A), Creator of 'The Laughing Salesman.' (Part 2)." *Mangajin*. August 1994, pp. 28-30, 32, 56.

Go, Nagai

1930. Evans, Peter. "An Interview with Go Nagai." *Anime UK Magazine*. December 1992/January 1993, pp. 28-33.

1931. "Go Nagai: The Man Behind Mazinger Z." *Animag*. No. 8, p. 44.

1932. "Go Nagai's Cutey Honey." *Animenominous!* Summer 1991, pp. 5-11.

Hayashibara, Megumi

1933. Keller, Chris. "Profile: Megumi Hayashibara." *V. Max*. No. 8, pp. 8-9, 32.

1934. Okamoto, Jeff and Julie Davie. "The Nurse Who Would be Kitty: Megumi Hayashibara." *Animerica*. December 1993, pp. 4-

1935. "The Voice of Anime—Interview with Hayashibara Megumi." *Anime UK Magazine*. 2:5, pp. 8-9.

Hisaichi, Ishii

1936. "Selected Works of Ishii Hisaichi." *Mangajin*. September 1994, pp. 48-49.

1937. "Selected Works of Ishii Hisaichi." *Mangajin*. October 1994, pp. 56-58.

Hisaishi, Jo

1938. "My Neighbor Jo Hisaishi." *Animerica*. August 1994, p. 9.

1939. "A Selected Filmography of Jo Hisaishi." *Animerica*. August 1994, p. 10.

Hokusai, Katsushika

1940. Bowie, Theodore. *The Drawings of Hokusai*. Bloomington: Indiana University Press, 1964. 190 pp.

1941. Bowie, Theodore. "Hokusai and the Comic Tradition in Japanese Painting." *College Art Journal*. Spring 1960, pp. 210-224.

1942. de Goncourt, Edmond. *Hokusaï*. Paris: 1895.

1943. Dickens, F. W. *The Mangwa of Hokusai*. London, Transactions and Proceedings of the Japan Society, 1901-1904 and 1906.

1944. Focillon, Henri. *Hokousai*. Paris: 1914.

1945. Hillier, J.R. "Drawings by Hokusai's Followers: Taitō and Hokkei." *Connoisseur*. May-June 1957, pp. 157-161, 232-233.

1946. Hillier, J.R. "Hokusai Drawings in The Harari Collection." *Connoisseur*. June 1960, pp. 17-21.

1947. Hillier, J.R. *Hokusai; Paintings, Drawings and Woodcuts*. London: 1955.

1948. Hillier, J.R. "Hokusai; Some Drawings and Problems of Attribution." *Connoisseur*. May 1956, pp. 167-174.

1949. Hillier, J.R. *The Art of Hokusai in Book Illustration*. Berkeley, California: University of California Press; London: Sotheby Parke Bernet, 1980. 288 pp.

1950. *Hokusai Paintings and Drawings in the Freer Gallery of Art*. Washington, D.C.: Smithsonian Institution, 1960. 37 pp.

1951. Iijima, Hanjuro. *Katsushika Hokusai den*. Tokyo: 1893.

1952. Inouye, K. *The Fragments of the Study of Hokusai*. Tokyo: Ukiyoyeshi, 1929.

1953. Kato, Hisao. "Hokusai, Katsushika (1760-1849)." In *Enciclopedia Mondiale del Fumetto*, edited by Maurice Horn and Luciano Secchi, p. 463. Milan: Editoriale Corno, 1978.

1954. "Katsushika Hokusai." In *A History of the Komiks of the Philippines and Other Countries*, by Cynthia Roxas and Joaquin Arevalo, Jr., p. 263. Manila: Islas Filipinas Publishing, 1985.

1955. Kubota, Jean K. "The *Mangwa* Books of Hokusai." Master's thesis, State University of Iowa, 1954.

1956. Michener, James A., ed. *The Hokusai Sketchbooks: Selections from the Manga*. Tokyo: Charles E. Tuttle, 1958.

1957. Narazaki, M. and K. Yamaioto. *Hokusai*. Tokyo: 1958.

1958. Revon, Michel. *Stude sur Hoksaï*. Paris: 1896.

1959. Segi, Shin'ichi. *Hokusai Manga Saijiki* (Hokusai Cartoons Seasonal Diary). Tokyo: Bijutukōronsha, 1981. 210 pp.

1960. Shimizu, Isao. "Katsushika Hokusai, 'Sōma Kuge' no Shin'i" (The Real Intention of "Sōma Kuge" by Hokusai Katsushika). *Fūshiga Kenkyū*. April 20, 1992, p. 12.

Ishimori, Shōtarō

1961. Ishimori, Shōtarō. *Boku No Manga Zenbu* (All of My Comics). Tokyo: Kōsaido Shuppan, 1977. 191 pp.

1962. Kato, Hisao. "Ishimori Shōtarō (1938-)." In *Enciclopedia Mondiale del Fumetto*, edited by Maurice Horn and Luciano Secchi, pp. 473-477. Milan: Editoriale Corno, 1978.

Izubuchi, Yutaka

1963. Ledoux, Trish. "A Selected Filmography for Yutaka Izubuchi." *Animerica*. June 1984, p. 10.

1964. Oshiguchi, Takashi. "Yutaka Izubuchi, Toiler in the Vineyards of Anime." *Animerica*. June 1994, pp. 4-5, 7-9.

Kakinouchi, Narumi

1965. Leahy, Kevin. "The Beautiful Blood-Chilling World of Narumi Kakinouchi." *The Rose*. October 1993, pp. 8-10.

1966. Tsao Sheng-Te. "More on Narumi Kakinouchi." *The Rose*. January 1994, p. 11.

Katō, Yoshirō

1967. Kato, Hisao. "Kato, Yoshirou (1925-)." In *Enciclopedia Mondiale del Fumetto*, edited by Maurice Horn and Luciano Secchi, p. 497. Milan: Editoriale Corno, 1978.

1968. Katō, Yoshirō. *Gendai Manga 4, Katō Yoshirō Shū* (A Collection of Yoshirō Katō's Work: Modern Comics Vol. 4). Tokyo: Chikuma Shobō, 1969. 316 pp.

1969. Katō, Yoshirō. *Mappira-kun* (Mr. Mappira). Vol 10. Tokyo: Mainichi Shimbunsha, 1988. 134 pp.

1970. Katō, Yoshirō. *Senbiki No Ninja* (A Thousand Ninja). Tokyo: Farao Kikaku, 1990. 108 pp.

Kitazawa, Rakuten

1971. "Introducing Japan's Modern Cartoon Father." *Humour and Caricature*. November-December 1993, pp. 16-17.

1972. Kato, Hisao. "Kitazawa, Rakuten (1876-1955)." In *Enciclopedia Mondiale del Fumetto*, edited by Maurice Horn and Luciano Secchi, p. 506. Milan: Editoriale Corno, 1978.

1973. Kitazawa, Rakuten. *Yasashii e no Kakikata* (How To Draw Easily). Omiya: Kitazawa Rakuten Kenshōkai, 1981.

1974. *Kitazawa Rakuten, "Founder of the Modern Japanese Cartoon."* Omiya: International and Cultural Section Planning Department, City of Omiya, 1991. 60 pp.

Kitazume, Hiroyuki

1975. Ledoux, Trish. "A Selected Filmography for Hiroyuki Kitazume." *Animerica*. October 1994, p. 10.

1976. Oshiguchi, Takashi. "Make Mine Moldiver: Kitazume Can!" *Animerica*. October 1994, pp. 4-9.

Kobayashi, Kiyochika

1977. Kato, Hisao. "Kobayashi, Kiyochika (1847-1915)." In *Enciclopedia Mondiale del Fumetto*, edited by Maurice Horn and Luciano Secchi, p. 509. Milan: Editoriale Corno, 1978.

1978. Shimizu, Isao. *The Satiric Cartoons of Kiyochika Kobayashi*. Tokyo: Iwasakibijutsusha, 1982. 92 pp. Japanese.

Kojima, Goseki

1979. "Goseki Kojima." In *A History of the Komiks of the Philippines and Other Countries*, by Cynthia Roxas and Joaquin Arevalo, Jr., pp. 263-264. Manila: Islas Filipinas Publishing, 1985.

1980. Kato, Hisao. "Kojima, Goseki (1928-)." In *Enciclopedia Mondiale del Fumetto*, edited by Maurice Horn and Luciano Secchi, pp. 509-510. Milan: Editoriale Corno, 1978.

Kuri, Yoji

1981. Kuri, Yoji. "Only Festivals?" *Animation*. Nos. 2-3-4, 1972, pp. 28-31.

1982. Popova, Silvia. "Love and Humour—The World of Yoji Kuri." *Apropos*. No. 4, 1986, pp. 97-101.

1983. "Yoji Kuri." *Comics*. May 1973, pp. 28-29.

1984. Zanotto, Piero. "Yoji Kuri." *Comics*. May 1972, p. 50.

Macek, Carl

1985. Greenspan, Abra. "Interview (Carl Macek)." *Animag*. 2:1, pp. 21-23.

1986. "Interview with Carl Macek." *The Rose*. July 1988, pp. 8-9. Excerpted from Peter Payne's article, San Diego *C/FO Magazine*, April 1988.

1987. Savage, Lorraine. "Carl Macek at San Diego Comic Con." *The Rose*. November 1990, pp. 12-13.

1988. Velasquez, Phil. "Interview: Carl Macek." *The Rose*. April 1994, pp. 26-27.

1989. Yang, Jeff. "Anime Q and A: Carl Macek, Part One: The Tao of Dubbing." *Animerica*. September 1993, p. 18.

1990. Yang, Jeff. "Carl Macek, Part Two: Johnny Appleseed or Anime Antichrist." *Animerica*. October 1993, p. 18.

Matsumoto, Reiji

1991. Kato, Hisao. "Matsumoto, Reiji (1938-)." In *Enciclopedia Mondiale del Fumetto*, edited by Maurice Horn and Luciano Secchi, p. 557. Milan: Editoriale Corno, 1978.

1992. Ledoux, Trish. "Reiji Matsumoto." *Animag*. No. 6, 1988, pp. 16-22.

1993. "Leiji Matsumoto Returns to the Cockpit." *Animerica*. October 1993, p. 13.

1994. "Matsumoto Reiji No Sekai" (The World of Reiji Matsumoto). Supplement of *Shimpyō*, in a series on authors. Autumn 1979.

1995. Schodt, Frederik L. "The Manga of Matsumoto Reiji." *Mangajin*. December 1990, pp. 18-21, 29.

Miyazaki, Hayao

1996. Greenfield, Larry. "Greenfield's Guide to Miyazaki." *Animerica*. July 1993, p. 10.

1997. "Hayao and the Beast." *Animerica*. February 1994, pp. 10-11.

1998. "Hayao Miyazaki." *Animag*. No. 9, 1989, pp. 6-21.

1999. Miyazaki, Hayao. "'Why I Don't Make Slapstick...Now." *Comic Box*. October 1989.

2000. "Miyazaki and SF." *Comic Box*. November 1991.

2001. "Miyazaki Interview." Translated by Na Choon Piaw. *Anime-Club* (Hong Kong). June 10, 1987.

2002. "Money Can't Buy Creativity: Hayao Miyazaki." *Pacific Friend*. January 1991, pp. 7-8.

2003. Oshiguchi, Takashi. "The Whimsy and Wonder of Hayao Miyazaki." *Animerica*. July 1993, pp. 4-9.

2004. Ott, John. "Nausicaa's Creator, Hayao Miyazaki." *The Rose*. May 1990, pp. 10-11.

2005. Rheault, Sylvain. "Hayao Miyazaki." *Protoculture Addicts*. November-December 1992, p. 12.

2006. Schilling, Mark. "Animation for Grownups." *Japan Times*. August 7, 1991.

Mizuki, Shigeru

2007. Kato, Hisao. "Mizuki, Shigeru (1924-)." In *Enciclopedia Mondiale del Fumetto*, edited by Maurice Horn and Luciano Secchi, p. 572. Milan: Editoriale Corno, 1978.

2008. Schodt, Frederik L. "Mizuki Shigeru and the Spirit World." *Mangajin*. April 1993, pp. 24-26.

Moriyama, Yuji

2009. Ledoux, Trish. "A Selected Filmography for Yuji Moriyama." *Animerica*. September 1994, p. 11.

2010. Oshiguchi, Takashi. "Project A-Ko Is A-Okay! An (Unknown) Legend in His Own Time." *Animerica*. September 1994, pp. 6-10. (Yuji Moriyama).

Ohata, Koichi

2011. "Interview: Mr. Koichi Ohata." *Protoculture Addicts*. March-April 1994, pp. 19-20.

2012. Yang, Jeff. "Anime Q and A: Koichi Ohata." *Animerica*. April 1994, p. 16.

Okamoto, Ippei

2013. Kato, Hisao. "Okamoto, Ippei (1886-1948)." In *Enciclopedia Mondiale del Fumetto*, edited by Maurice Horn and Luciano Secchi, p. 598. Milan: Editoriale Corno, 1978.

2014. Okamoto, Ippei. *Ippei Zenshū* (The Collected Works of Ippei). Tokyo: Senshinsha, 1930.

2015. Shimizu, Isao. *The Biography of Ippei Okamoto—The Father of Modern Cartoons*. Tokyo: Bungei Shunjō, 1994. 304 pp. Japanese.

2016. Shimizu, Isao. *The Complete Works of Ippei Okamoto, An Enlarged Edition*. 20 Vols. Tokyo: Ozorasha, 1991. Average pp., 500. Japanese.

2017. Shimizu, Isao. "Okamoto Ippei no Shōkai Shita Miruto Gurosu" (Milt Gross Introduced by Ippei Okamoto). *Fūshiga Kenkyū*. July 20, 1994, p. 5.

2018. Yumoto, Gōichi. "Kenkyū: Ippei no Chichi, Okamoto Katei" (A Study: Katei Okamoto, the Father of Ippei). *Fūshiga Kenkyū*. January 20, 1992, p. 8.

2019. Yushima, Gōichi. "Okamoto Ippei Kankei-sha, Kikigaki" (Interviews with People Concerned with Ippei Okamoto). *Fūshiga Kenkyū*. July 20, 1993, p. 14.

Ono, Kōsei

2020. Lu Tzu-Ying. "Kōsei Ono: A Big Boy in Comic World." *Monthly Comic Magazine.* July 1991, pp. 63-65.

2021. Ono, Kōsei. *Battoman Ni Naritai: Ono Kōsei No Komikku Sekai* (I Want To Be the Batman: Ono Kōsei's World of Comics). Tokyo: Shōbunsha, 1974. 291 pp.

2022. Ono, Kōsei. *Chikyūgi Ni Notta Neko: Ono Kōsei No Komikku Wārudo* (The Cat on a Globe: Ono Kōsei's World of Comics). Tokyo: Tōjusha, 1982. 222 pp.

2023. Ono, Kōsei. *Manga Ga Baiburu* (Comics Is My Bible). Tokyo: Shinchōsha, 1984. 238 pp.

Ōtomo, Katsuhiro

2024. Boschi, Luca. "Referenze." *Comic Art.* June 1992, pp. 17, 21-40.

2025. Ōtomo, Katsuhiro. "My Manga Road." *Shōnen Sunday Interview.* September 7, 1988.

Sakamoto, Ryuichi

2026. Napton, Robert and David Riddick. "Sounds of the New Earth: The Music and Vision of Ryuichi Sakamoto." *Animag.* No. 12, pp. 25-26.

2027. Riddick, David Keith. "The Balance: A Look at Japan's Premier New Music Composer Ryuichi Sakamoto." *Anime-zine.* No. 3, p. 32.

Satō, Sanpei

2028. Kunihiro, Masao and Sanpei Satō. *Eigo Wa Kowaai?* (English Is Scary?). Tokyo: Pana Kyoiku Shisutemu, 1984.

2029. Lo, Jeannie. "Imagination, Courage and *Some* Money." *Look Japan.* August 1989, p. 41.

2030. Roseff, Lisa M. "Salaryman Comics: Fuji Santarō. Live and Laugh." *Look Japan.* August 1989, pp. 39-41.

2031. Satō, Sanpei. *Fuji Santarō* (500 Strips from April 1965 to June 1991). Tokyo: Asahi Shimbunsha, 1991.

2032. Yancey, Don. "Imagination and Creativity: Sato Sanpei." *Asahi Weekly.* August 24, 1975, p. 4.

Schodt, Fred

2033. Clements, Jonathan. "Virtual Japan: Fred Schodt." *Anime UK Magazine*. 3:4, pp. 26-29.

2034. "Interview: Fred Schodt." *Mangazine*. 2:15 (1992), pp. 36-38.

Shirato, Sanpei

2035. Kato, Hisao. "Shirato, Sanpei (1932-)." In *Enciclopedia Mondiale del Fumetto*, edited by Maurice Horn and Luciano Secchi, p. 686. Milan: Editoriale Corno, 1978.

2036. Kato, Hidetoshi. "Sampei Shirato's Marxist Funnies." *East-West Perspectives*. Fall 1980, pp. 26-31.

Shirow, Masamune

2037. Savage, Lynn. "Appleseed by Masamune Shirow." *The Rose*. January 1992, pp. 16-17.

2038. Smith, Toren. "Masamune Shirow: Interview with a Manga Artist." *Comics Buyer's Guide*. March 25, 1994, pp. 28, 30, 34.

Shoten, Nakamura

2039. Shimizu, Isao. "Nakamura Shoten Manga-bon Ichiran" (A List of Nakamura Shoten's Comic Books). *Fûshiga Kenkyû*. January 20, 1994, pp. 7-8.

2040. Yamashita, Takeshi. "Nakamura Manga to Shabana Bontarō no Shigoto" (Nakamura Shoten's Comics and the Works of Bontarō Shabana). *Fûshiga Kenkyû*. October 20, 1992, pp. 9-10.

Smith, Toren

2041. Savage, Lorraine. "Interview with Toren Smith. Part 2." *The Rose*. September 1990, p. 4.

2042. Savage, Lorraine. "Toren Smith." *The Rose*. July 1990, p. 7.

2043. Swallow, Jim. "Toren Smith: The Interview." *Anime UK Magazine*. 3:3, pp. 26-30.

2044. Velasquez, Phil. "Interview: Toren Smith." *The Rose*. January 1995, pp. 20-21, 31.

2045. Yang, Jeff. "Anime Q and A: Toren Smith." *Animerica*. February 1994, p. 16.

Sugiura, Shigeru

2046. Kato, Hisao. "Sugiura, Shigeru (1908-)." In *Enciclopedia Mondiale del Fumetto*, edited by Maurice Horn and Luciano Secchi, p. 711. Milan: Editoriale Corno, 1978.

2047. "Shigeru Sugiura." In *A History of the Komiks of the Philippines and Other Countries*, by Cynthia Roxas and Joaquin Arevalo, Jr., p. 264. Manila: Islas Filipinas Publishing, 1985.

Sugiura, Yukio

2048. Sugiura, Yukio. *Sugiura Yukio No Manga Kōyūroku* (Sugiura Yukio's Friendship Through Comics). Tokyo: Ie No Hikari Kyōkai, 1978. 328 pp.

2049. Sugiura, Yukio. *Sugiura Yukio Shū* (The Work of Yukio Sugiura). Tokyo: Chikuma Shobō, 1971. 314 pp.

2050. Sugiura, Yukio and Fuyuhiko Okabe. *Zukai Shukujo no Mihon* (Illustrated Models of the Lady). Tokyo: Jitsugyō no Nihonsha, 1961. 156 pp.

2051. Sugiura, Yukio and Isao Shimizu. *Shōwa Manga Fūzokushi: Sugiura Yukio Manga de Tadoru 50-Nen* (The Social History of the Shōwa Period Through Comics: The 50 Years in the Cartoons by Yukio Sugiura). Tokyo: Bungei Shunjūsha, 1984. 240 + iv pp.

Taguchi, Beisaku

2052. Shimizu, Isao. "Taguchi Beisaku Shiryō Kara Mita Kobayashi Kiyochika" (Kiyochika Kobayashi's Influence in the Works of Beisaku Taguchi). *Fūshiga Kenkyū*. October 20, 1992, p. 16.

2053. Yushima, Gōichi. "Taguchi Beisaku Nenpu, Beisaku Manga Shiryō" (Chronology of Beisaku Taguchi, and the Materials of Beisaku's Cartoons). *Fūshiga Kenkyū*. October 20, 1992, pp. 6-8.

Takachiho, Haruka

2054. "Haruka Takachiho." Transcribed by Lorraine Savage. *The Rose*. October 1992, pp. 6-7.

2055. Karahashi, Takayuki. "Haruka Takachiho's Dirty Stormy Destiny." *Animerica*. April 1994, pp. 4-9.

2056. "The Writer's Craft—Interview with Takachiho Haruka." *Anime UK Magazine*. 2:5, pp. 10-11.

Takahashi, Rumiko

2057. Hernandez, Lea. "Rumiko Takahashi: An Appreciation." *Comics Buyer's Guide.* July 8, 1994, p. 46.

2058. Horibuchi, Seiji. "Rumiko Takahashi: The Manga Wunderkind." *Animerica.* April 1993, pp. 4-10.

2059. Jones, Gerard. "Gerard Jones, Rewriter to the Stars!" *Animerica.* April 1993, p. 9.

2060. Ledoux, Trish. "My Dinner with Rumiko." *Animerica.* September 1994, p. 2.

2061. "My Comic Road: An Interview with Rumiko Takahashi." Translated by James R. Winchester. *Shōnen Sunday Comics.* January 9-15, 1988.

2062. Oshiguchi, Takashi. "Rumiko Takahashi." *Animerica.* November 1993, p. 13.

2063. "The Other Takahashi: Rumic World." *Animenominous!* Summer 1991, pp. 29-32.

2064. "Rumiko Takahashi at San Diego Comic Con." *The Rose.* October 1994, pp. 18-19.

2065. "Rumiko Takahashi Will Attend." *Comics Buyer's Guide.* July 8, 1994, p. 46.

2066. Santoso, Widya. "Rumiko Takahashi's Dustspot." *The Rose.* March 1991, p. 11.

2067. Smith, Toren. "Princess of the Manga, Rumiko Takahashi—Japan's Best-Loved Cartoonist." *Amazing Heroes.* May 15, 1989, pp. 20-27.

2068. "Takahashi, Takezaki Lead Spring Line-Up from Viz." *Animerica.* April 1993, p. 37.

2069. "Wrap Up Rumiko for the Holidays." *Animerica.* December 1993, p. 38.

Tanaka, Yoshiki

2070. Flórez, Florentino. "King—Gon." *El Wendigo.* No. 63, 1994, pp. 14-15.

2071. "Yoshiki Tanaka Interview." Translated by Masashi Suzuki. *The Rose.* April 1992, pp. 6-7. Reprinted from *B-Club 66.* May 1991, pp. 6-8.

Terasawa, Buichi

2072. McLennan, Jim. "Buichi Terasawa." *Anime UK Magazine.* October/November 1992, p. 22.

2073. Matsuzaki, James and Elizabeth Bales. "Buichi Terasawa." *V. Max.* No. 6, pp. 11-12, 29.

Tezuka, Osamu

2074. *The Animation Filmography of Osamu Tezuka.* Shinjuku-ku: Tezuka Productions, 1991. 96 pp.

2075. *The Art of Osamu Tezuka.* Shinjuku-ku: Tezuka Productions, 1994. 12 pp.

2076. Ashby, Janet. "Time Out Japanese: Tezuka Osamu." *Japan Times.* August 17, 1990.

2077. Ashby, Janet. "Time Out Japanese: Tezuka Osamu." *Japan Times.* August 24, 1990.

2078. Covert, Brian. "The Tezuka Controversy." *Mangajin.* June 1992, pp. 8-11.

2079. "Creators of Animation: Osamu Tezuka." *This Is Animation.* No. 2, 1982, pp. 45-49.

2080. De Stains, Ian. "Osamu Tezuka, a Veteran Animator of Distinction." *TV World.* March 1984, pp. 27-28.

2081. Dlin, Doug, trans. "Osamu Tezuka: Japanese Animation/Manga Founding Father." *Mangazine.* 2:15 (1992), pp. 27-35.

2082. "Exhibit Lauds Godfather of Comic Books." *Mainichi Daily News.* September 26, 1990.

2083. Fujiko, Fujio. "Tezuka Osamu Wa Uchūjin Da (Osamu Tezuka Is an Alien). *Bungei Shunjū.* 67:5 (1989), pp. 208-214.

2084. Goba, Mike. "Osamu Tezuka Speaks at Hartford." *The Rose.* November 1987, p. 5.

2085. Ishigami, Mitsutoshi. *Tezuka Osamu No Kimyō Na Sekai* (The Strange World of Osamu Tezuka). Tokyo: Kisōtengaisha, 1977.

2086. Ishiko, Jun. "Tezuka Osamu No Shigoto: Inochi No Daijisa o Utaitsuzuketa Manga Shijin (The Work of Osamu Tezuka: A Poet of Comics Who Kept Appealing the Value of Life). *Bunka Hyōron.* 338 (1989), pp. 209-216.

2087. Iwaya, Kokushi, Isao Shimizu, Ippei Itō, Mitsutoshi Ishigami, Michio Tanaka, and Yasuo Yoshitomi. *Gendai Manga Shiatā 1: Tezuka Osamu* (The Comic Theater 1: Osamu Tezuka). Tokyo: Seizansha, 1979.

2088. Kato, Hisao. "Tezuka, Osamu (1926-)." In *Enciclopedia Mondiale del Fumetto,* edited by Maurice Horn and Luciano Secchi, p. 724. Milan: Editoriale Corno, 1978.

2089. Kure, Tomofusa. "Tezuka Osamu No Imi: Aru Sengo Sēshin No Igyō (The Meaning of Osamu Tezuka: A Great Work of a Post-War Spirit). *Bungakukai.* 43:4 (1989), pp. 234-240.

2090. McCarthy, Helen. "Tezuka Osamu—A Tribute." *Anime UK Magazine.* 3:1, pp. 28-29.

2091. *Osamu Tezuka.* Tokyo: The National Museum of Modern Art in collaboration with Tezuka Production Co., Ltd., 1990. 348 pp.

2092. "Osamu Tezuka." *Banc-Titre.* October 1984, pp. 26-30.

2093. "Osamu Tezuka." *Speakeasy.* April 1989, p. 25.

2094. [Osamu Tezuka]. *WittyWorld.* Autumn/Winter 1994, p. 4.

2095. "Osamu Tezuka Dead at 62." *Comics Journal.* March 1989, p. 22.

2096. "Osamu Tezuka Dies, Created 'Astro Boy.'" *The Rose.* March 1989, p. 3.

2097. "Osamu Tezuka: 40 Years of Comics." *Animenominous!* Summer 1990, pp. 14-17.

2098. *The Osamu Tezuka Manga Museum.* Shinjuku-ku: Tezuka Productions, 1994. 50 pp.

2099. Saito, Jiro. *What Osamu Tezuka Wished For.* Tokyo: Iwanami Shoten, 1989.

2100. Sato, Sadao. "King of the Toons." *Look Japan.* July 1989, pp. 4-7.

2101. Schodt, Frederik L. "Osamu Tezuka—In Memorium." In *San Diego Comic Convention 1989, Program,* p. 89. San Diego, California: Comic-Con Committee, 1989.

2102. Schodt, Frederik L. "Osamu Tezuka: The Storyteller, the Artist, and the Man." *Animag.* No. 7, 1989, pp. 19-20.

2103. Schodt, Frederik L. "Tezuka Osamu—Japan's 'God of Manga.'" *Mangajin.* May 1992, pp. 22-43.

2104. Shimizu, Isao. *The Fascinating World of Osamu Tezuka Works.* Tokyo: Seizansha, 1979. 188 pp. Japanese.

2105. Shimizu, Isao. "Shin-hakken! Tezuka Manga 'Kasei Tanken-tai" (A Newly Discovered Tezuka Comics, "An Exploration Party to the Mars"). *Fūshiga*

Kenkyū. July 20, 1992, p. 7.

2106. Skidmore, Martin. "Obituary: Osamu Tezuka." *FA.* March 1989, pp. 28-29.

2107. Tezuka, Osamu. *Boku Wa Mangaka: Tezuka Osamu Jiden 1* (I Am a Cartoonist: Volume 1 of Osamu Tezuka's Autobiography). Tokyo: Yamato Shobō, 1979.

2108. Tezuka, Osamu. *Little Known Episodes About Osamu Tezuka.* Tokyo: Shin-Nihonshuppansha, 1990.

2109. Tezuka, Osamu. *Tezuka Osamu No Subete* (Everything about Osamu Tezuka). Tokyo: Daitosha, 1981. With English notes.

2110. Tezuka, Osamu. *Tezuka Osamu Rando* (Osamu Tezuka-Land). Tokyo: Yamato Shobō, 1977.

2111. Tezuka, Osamu. *Tezuka Osamu Rando 2* (Osamu Tezuka-Land Volume 2). Tokyo: Yamato Shobō, 1978.

2112. "Tezuka Filmography." *Anime UK Magazine.* 3:1, p. 30.

2113. Wheelock, Janet. "The King of Japanese Comics, Part One." *Comics Scene.* No. 3, 1982, pp. 49-51.

2114. Wheelock, Jim. "Osamu Tezuka's World." *Comics Scene.* July 1982, pp. 24-28.

2115. "Where'd Ya Get Those Peepers?" *Wild Cartoon Kingdom.* 7:13 (1993), p. 51.

2116. "The World of Osamu Tezuka." *Asahi Journal.* Extra number, 1989.

Tsuge, Yoshiharu

2117. Kato, Hisao. "Tsuge, Yoshiharu (1937-)." In *Enciclopedia Mondiale del Fumetto*, edited by Maurice Horn and Luciano Secchi, p. 738. Milan: Editoriale Corno, 1978.

2118. Tsuge, Yoshiharu. *Tsuge Yoshiharu To Boku* (Tsuge Yoshiharu and I). Tokyo: Shōbunsha, 1977. 230 pp.

Tsukioka, Yoshitoshi

2119. Kato, Hisao. "Tsukioka, Yoshitoshi (1839-1892)." In *Enciclopedia Mondiale del Fumetto*, edited by Maurice Horn and Luciano Secchi, pp. 738-739. Milan: Editoriale Corno, 1978.

2120. "Yoshitoshi Tsukioka." In *A History of the Komiks of the Philippines and Other Countries*, by Cynthia Roxas and Joaquin Arevalo, Jr., p. 265. Manila: Islas Filipinas Publishing, 1985.

Utagawa, Kuniyoshi

2121. Iizawa, Takumi. "Utagawa Kuniyoshi, 'Kitsune no Yomeiri-zu' no Nazo" (The Mystery of Kuniyoshi Utagawa's "A Picture of a Fox's Wedding"). *Fūshiga Kenkyū*. January 20, 1992, pp. 9-10.

2122. Kato, Hisao. "Utagawa, Kuniyoshi (1797-1861)." In *Enciclopedia Mondiale del Fumetto*, edited by Maurice Horn and Luciano Secchi, p. 744. Milan: Editoriale Corno, 1978.

Yanase, Masamu

2123. Katayori, Mitsugu. "Yanase Masamu no Hansen Manga ni Tsuite" (About Masamu Yanase's Anti-War Cartoons). *Fūshiga Kenkyū*. July 20, 1992, pp. 8-9.

2124. Shimizu, Isao. "Fūshiga-ka Shōkai (2): Yanase Masamu" (Introduction of a Cartoonist, II: Masamu Yanase). *Fūshiga Kenkyū*. April 20, 1992, pp. 6-9.

2125. Shimizu, Isao. "Yanase Masamu no Shoki Fūshiga Sakuhin" (Masamu Yanase's Early Works of Caricature). *Fūshiga Kenkyū*. July 20, 1994, pp. 14-15.

Yasuhiko, Yoshikazu

2126. Matsuzaki, James. "Yasuhiko Yoshikazu." *V. Max*. No. 4, pp. 23-24.

2127. Ott, John. "Yoshikazu Yasuhiko's Star of the Kurds." *The Rose*. September 1990, p. 13.

2128. Swint, Lester. "Venus Wars." *The Rose*. January 1992, p. 21.

Yokoyama, Ryūichi

2129. Kato, Hisao. "Yokoyama, Ryūichi (1909-)." In *Enciclopedia Mondiale del Fumetto*, edited by Maurice Horn and Luciano Secchi, p. 778. Milan: Editoriale Corno, 1978.

2130. "Ryuychi Yokoyama." In *A History of the Komiks of the Philippines and Other Countries*, by Cynthia Roxas and Joaquin Arevalo, Jr., p. 263. Manila: Islas Filipinas Publishing, 1985.

2131. Yokoyama, Ryūichi. *Ryūichi Kona (Ryūichi Corner)*. Tokyo: Rokkō Shuppan, 1982. 270 pp.

2132. Yokoyama, Ryūichi. *Waga Yūgiteki Jinsei* (My Playful Life). Tokyo: Nihon Keizai Shimbunsha, 1972.

Characters and Titles

Anime (Animation)

2133. "A.D. Vision Burns Up the Screen." *Animerica*. December 1993, p. 15.

2134. "A.D. Vision's End of Summer." *Animerica*. June 1994, p. 17.

2135. Adolf, Julie, et al. "CD Reviews." *The Rose*. January 1995, p. 26. ("Gatchaman," "Gundam," "Captain Harlock," World of Leiji Matsumoto).

2136. "Animation Update." *Animag*. No. 8, pp. 3-5.

2137. "Anime News." *Mangazine*. November 1994, pp. 3-9.

2138. "AnimEigo." *Mangazine*. November 1994, p. 5.

2139. "AnimEigo's Happy New Year—With Lum." *Animerica*. February 1994, p. 15.

2140. "Area 88—The Story Thus Far." *Animerica*. October 1983, pp. 20-38.

2141. "Armageddon Now!" *Animerica*. June 1994, p. 16.

2142. Ashmore, Darren. "The Secret of Blue Water." *Anime UK Magazine*. December 1992/January 1993, pp. 20-25.

2143. Ashmore, Darren and Yuko Abe. "Video Reviews." *Anime UK Magazine*. 3:1, pp. 31-33.

2144. "Aura Battler Dunbine." *Animag*. 1:2 (1987), pp. 11-30.

2145. Baskin, Marg. "Dragonar." *Anime-Zine*. No. 3, pp. 33-38.

2146. Beauchamp, Marc and Hiroko Kataya. "Mickey Mouse, Meet Hello Kitty." *Forbes*. May 18, 1987, pp. 68, 70.

2147. "Best of the West." *Animerica*. April 1993, p. 60.

2148. "Beta's Counter Attack." *Newtype*. July 1988, pp. 42-47.

2149. "Big Wars Rages Across Japan This Summer." *Animerica*. April 1993, p. 13. ("Big Wars").

2150. "The Biography of Guscoe Budori." *Animerica*. December 1993, pp. 10-11.

2151. "Blue Seed." *Mangazine*. November 1994, p. 10.

2152. Carlson, Bruce. "Ask IQ 9." *The Rose*. January 1995, p. 5.

2153. "CD Reviews." *Animenominous!* Summer 1991, pp. 22-25.

2154. "CD Reviews." *The Rose.* October 1994, p. 31.

2155. Clarke, Jeremy. "The Sensualist." *Anime UK Magazine.* October/November 1992, pp. 16-17.

2156. Clements, Jonathan. "Alien Nations." *Anime UK Magazine.* 3:3, pp. 34-36.

2157. Clements, Jonathan. "Building Bridges, Building Walls." *Anime UK Magazine.* 2:5, p. 31. ("Monkey Brain Sushi").

2158. Clements, Jonathan. "KO Century Beast Warriors." *Anime UK Magazine.* 3:3, pp. 20-21, 23-25.

2159. Clements, Jonathan. "Tetsuo—The Iron Man by Shinya Tsukamoto." *Anime UK Magazine.* 2:4, p. 20.

2160. "Compact Disc Review." *Animenominous!* Autumn 1990, pp. 24-25.

2161. "Compiler." *Anime UK Magazine.* 3:5, p. 25.

2162. Connell, Ed. "Touch 2." *Out of Chaos.* No. 10.

2163. "Coo from a Faraway Sea." *Animerica.* January 1994, p. 13.

2164. "Cyborg of the People, Cashan." *Animerica.* June 1993, pp. 12-13.

2165. "Dark Angel." *Newtype.* July 1988, pp. 49-63.

2166. Davis, Julie. "Mermaid's Scar." *Animerica.* November 1993, pp. 4-8.

2167. "Demon Century Water Margin." *Animerica.* November 1993, p. 11.

2168. "Demon City Shinjuku, U-Jin Brand Lead February Releases from U.S.M.C." *Animerica.* January 1994, pp. 16-17.

2169. "Don't Make Me Smack You, Sinchan." *Inklings.* Summer 1994, p. 4.

2170. "DNA^2." *Mangazine.* November 1994, p. 12.

2171. Durkin, Dan. "Baoh." *The Rose.* July 1990, p. 4.

2172. Durkin, Dan. "Twinkle^2 Idol Stars." *The Rose.* September 1991, p. 5.

2173. Eldred, Tim. "Cybersuit Arkadyne: An Introduction." *Protoculture Addicts.* January-February 1992, pp. 12-13.

2174. Endresak, Dave. "Magic Knight RayEarth." *The Rose*. January 1995, p. 6.

2175. Evans, Meg. "Prince Planet." *The Rose*. January 1990, pp. 12-13.

2176. Evans, Peter. "Live from Hell City." *Anime UK Magazine*. August/September 1992, pp. 12-13.

2177. "Even Bigger Wars—The Dark Blue Fleet." *Animerica*. September 1993, pp. 10-11.

2178. "Even More Desperate Love." *Animerica*. September 1994, p. 12.

2179. "Fabulous Fighting Females of the U.S.M.C.—Iczer 3 and Project A-Ko." *Animerica*. May 1994, p. 16.

2180. Feldman, Steven. "Robot Carnival." *The Rose*. September 1991, pp. 8-9.

2181. Fong, Dana. "Gall Force." *Animag*. No. 6, 1990, pp. 20-28.

2182. Freiberg, Freda. "Tales of Kageyama." *East-West Film Journal*. January 1992, pp. 94-110.

2183. "Galactic Pirates." *Anime UK Magazine*. 3:2, p. 20.

2184. Gavigan, Ryan. "The Humanoid." *The Rose*. April 1992, p. 18.

2185. "Get Ready for Gigantor!" *Animerica*. February 1994, p. 14.

2186. "The Girl from Phantasia." *Animerica*. January 1994, p. 16.

2187. Grey, Simon. "Galaxy Express 999." *Animenominous!* Spring 1991, pp. 22-25.

2188. Grimes, Ethel M. "Toward the Terra." *The Rose*. May 1989, p. 4.

2189. "Guyver, Orguss Lead the Pack in LAH/USR's New Releases." *Animerica*. February 1994, p. 15.

2190. "The Hakkenden—Tale of the Eight Dogs." *Animerica*. November 1993, pp. 10-11.

2191. "Have Scalpel, Will Travel." *Animerica*. September 1993, p. 11. ("Blackjack").

2192. "Heroic Legends and Legendary Heroics—U.S.M.C.'s Heroic Legend of Arislan and RG Veda." *Animerica*. December 1993, pp. 14-15.

2193. "Hey Hey! It's Rei Rei." *Animerica*. March 1994, p. 14.

2194. Hoffman, Curtis. "Gunsmith Cats." *V. Max*. No. 8, pp. 10-14.

2195. Ishigami, Yoshitaka. "Best of the East." *Animerica*. April 1993, pp. 58-59.

2196. Ishigami, Yoshitaka. "Best of the East." *Animerica*. May 1993, pp. 58-59. ("Ellcia," "Oz," "Green Legend Ran").

2197. Ishigami, Yoshitaka. "Best of the East." *Animerica*. June 1993, pp. 58-59. ("Lovely Soldier Sailor Moon," "All-Purpose Cultural Cat Girl," "This Is Greenwood").

2198. Ishigami, Yoshitaka. "Best of the East." *Animerica*. July 1993, pp. 52-53. ("Armored Dragon Legend Villgust," "Takamaru," "Download").

2199. Ishigami, Yoshitaka. "Casshan, 'The Return from Legend.'" *Animerica*. February 1994, p. 60.

2200. Ishigami, Yoshitaka. "Natsuki Crisis." *Animerica*. May 1994, p. 56.

2201. Jang, Galen and Kensaku Nakata. "Cyber City Oedo 808." *V. Max*. No. 3, pp. 24-26.

2202. Jerng, Henry. "Time Strangers." *C/FO San Antonio Newsletter*. March 1987.

2203. "Jo Jo's Bizarre Adventure." *Animerica*. June 1994, p. 64.

2204. "Kekkō Kamen." *Mangazine*. November 1994, p. 4.

2205. Keller, Chris. "Star of the Kurds." *V. Max*. No. 6, pp. 5, 7-9.

2206. Kodaira, Sachiko Imaizumi and Takashiro Akiyama. *"With Mother" and Its Viewers: Behavior Monitoring of 2- and 3-Year-Olds*. Tokyo: Japan Broadcasting Corporation, 1988. 48 pp.

2207. Kurtin, Dana. "Basic Saga Salamander." *Animag*. No. 11, p. 15.

2208. Kurtin, Dana. "High Speed Jecy." *Animag*. No. 11, pp. 26-27.

2209. La Rue, John, Jr. "The Jungle Book: Anime in the Bargin [sic] Bin." *The Rose*. May 1991, pp. 15-16.

2210. Leahy, Kevin. "Makaitoshi Hunter." *The Rose*. October 1992, p. 5.

2211. Leahy, Kevin. "Ragnarok Guy." *The Rose*. September 1991, p. 14.

2212. Leahy, Kevin. "Things That Go 'Ge Ge Ge' in the Night." *The Rose*. October 1992, pp. 14-15. ("Ge Ge Ge No Kitaro").

2213. "Leave It to Scrappers!" *Animerica*. May 1994, p. 12.

2214. "Legend of Syrius, from Japan Fantasy Film Journal." *The Rose*. September 1990, p. 11.

2215. "Love City." *Anime UK Magazine*. 3:2, p. 21.

2216. Lufkin, Kamara and Kay Lillibridge. "Dragon Century, Part 1, 1990." *Protoculture Addicts*. May-June 1992, pp. 22-24.

2217. McCarthy, Helen. "Eternal Anime." *Anime UK Magazine*. June/July 1992, p. 30.

2218. McCarthy, Helen. "Manga Video Preview: Doomed Megalopolis and Crying Freeman." *Anime UK Magazine*. 2:4, p. 35.

2219. McCarthy, Helen. "New Releases." *Anime UK Magazine*. October/November 1992, p. 24.

2220. McCarthy, Helen and Wil Overton. "Masumune Shirow's Orion." *Anime UK Magazine*. August/September 1992, pp. 20-21.

2221. McLennan, Jim. "Kabuto." *Anime UK Magazine*. October/November 1992, p. 23.

2222. "'Mai' Unveiled as a Movie Musical." *Comics Buyer's Guide*. July 19, 1991, p. 20.

2223. "Manga Video's Most Recent Tapes Reviewed." *Anime UK Magazine*. 2:5, p. 29.

2224. Martin, Richard. "Locke the Superpower." *Protoculture Addicts*. January-February 1993, pp. 27-30.

2225. "Metamorphose Moldiver." *Animerica*. September 1994, p. 16.

2226. Moisan, David. "Kiki's Delivery Service Guidebook." *The Rose*. November 1990, p. 15.

2227. Moisan, David. "Labyrinth Tales (Manic-Manic)." *The Rose*. March 1991, p. 6. ("Labyrinth-Labyritos").

2228. "More Anime To Watch." *Protoculture Addicts*. January-February 1994, pp. 36-37.

2229. "Mr. Anime's Wild Ride Through Willow Town." *Animerica*. October 1993, p. 12.

2230. Munson-Siter, Patricia A. "The 8th Man." *Protoculture Addicts*. July-August 1993, pp. 32-34.

2231. Munson-Siter, Pat. "RG Veda." *Anime UK Magazine*. 2:4, pp. 21-26.

2232. Munson-Siter, Pat. "Tekkaman Blade/'D-Boy.'" *Anime UK Magazine*. 2:3, pp. 6-19.

2233. "Now That the Boys of Summer Are Gone...Look Out for the Girls of U.S.M.C.'s 'Destruction'!" *Animerica*. October 1993, p. 17.

2234. "The October CD Revue!" *Anime UK Magazine*. 2:6, p. 28.

2235. "Oruorane the Cat Player." *Animag*. 2:3, p. 4.

2236. Ouellette, Martin. "Fatal Fury 2." *Protoculture Addicts*. March-April 1994, p. 39.

2237. Ouellette, Martin. "I Can Hear the Sea." *Protoculture Addicts*. July-August 1994, p. 44.

2238. Ouellette, Martin and C.J. Pelletier. "The Weathering Continent." *Protoculture Addicts*. January-February 1994, p. 38.

2239. "Passport for the Ultra Zone, Part 3." *Starlog*. May 1979, pp. 46-49.

2240. Payne, Harry. "Manga Video 92: A Year in the Life." *Anime UK Magazine*. 2:1, pp. 28-29.

2241. Peacock, Dirk. "OAV Review: Dragon Knight." *The Rose*. January 1995, pp. 21, 29.

2242. Pelletier, Claude J. "Aladdin from the East to the West; Japanese's Aladdin Version." *Protoculture Addicts*. March-April 1993, pp. 30-32.

2243. Pelletier, Claude J. "Introducing The Gates of Pandragon." *Protoculture Addicts*. February 1991, p. 22.

2244. "Pin-Up in Feature." *Anime UK Magazine*. 2:6, pp. 20-21. ("Cat's Eye").

2245. Primer, Ken. "Cypher." *The Rose*. September 1991, p. 19.

2246. Primer, Ken. "Moeru! Oniisan." *The Rose*. May 1991, p. 7.

2247. "Reviews." *Protoculture Addicts*. November-December 1992, pp. 26-28.

2248. Ross, Dave. "CD Reviews." *Anime UK Magazine*. 3:3, p. 18. ("Ah My Goddess," "The Gunbuster 'Dramadisk'").

2249. Santoso, Widya. "Riding Bean (English Dub)." *The Rose*. October 1994, p. 7.

2250. Savage, Lorraine. "Battle for Moon Station Dallos." *The Rose*. November 1991, pp. 16-17.

2251. Schilling, Mark. "Movie Depicts Greek Myth." *Japan Times*. August 11, 1992, p. 16.

2252. Schilling, Mark. "Red Pig Rushes to the Rescue." *Japan Times*. July 28, 1992, p. 18.

2253. "School Should Always Be Fun! Comet Machine Gakusaver." *Animerica*. September 1993, p. 10.

2254. Sertori, Julia. "Reviews: Angry Young Men." *Anime UK Magazine*. 3:5, pp. 34-38.

2255. Simmons, Mark. "Heavy Metal L-Gaim." *Animag*. No. 12, pp. 36-39.

2256. Simmons, Mark. "Walker Machine Xabungle." *Animag*. 2:2, pp. 50-56.

2257. "The SM Girls of Saber Marionettes." *Animerica*. September 1994, p. 13.

2258. Smith, Toren. "U-jin Brand." *Animerica*. May 1994, p. 59.

2259. Smith, Toren. "Wings of Oneamis." *Anime-Zine*. 2, 1987, pp. 22-29. ("Oneamis No Tsubasa").

2260. "SPT Layzner." *Animag*. 2:2, pp. 6-15.

2261. Staley, James. "The Cockpit." *The Rose*. January 1995, pp. 8-10.

2262. Staley, James. "Kitsune Kun. The Bad Anime Dub." *Protoculture Addicts*. September-October 1994, pp. 28-29.

2263. Staley, James. "Rumic World, Volume 1." *The Rose*. January 1993, p. 24.

2264. Steele, Richard. "Genesis Surviver Gaiarth." *Anime UK Magazine*. 2:4, pp. 6-9.

2265. Sternbach, Rick. "Neo-Tokyo." *Animerica*. March 1994, p. 55.

2266. "The Story of Arion." *Animag*. 1:2, 1987, pp. 3-8.

2267. Swallow, Jim. "Dynamo Joe." *Anime UK Magazine*. 2:1, pp. 30-31.

2268. Swett, Chris. "Demon Warrior Luna Varga." *V. Max*. No. 5, pp. 9-11, 13.

2269. Swint, Lester. "Little Norse Prince." *The Rose*. November 1990, pp. 6-7.

2270. Swint, Lester. "Promise." *The Rose*. July 1994, pp. 6-7.

2271. Swint, Lester. "The Six God Union Godmars Television Series and the Godmars OAV." *The Rose*. July 1992, p. 16.

2272. Swint, Lester. "2001 Nights." *The Rose*. March 1991, p. 7.

2273. Swint, Lester. "Yoma. Part 1: The Great Warlord." *The Rose*. January 1992, p. 11.

2274. "A Tale of Seven Cities." *Animerica*. July 1993, p. 12.

2275. Teal, James and Takayuki Karahashi. "Legend of Heavenly Sphere Shurato." *Animag*. 2:2, pp. 57-65.

2276. "They Ride Again! Wild Seven Returns." *Animerica*. November 1993, p. 11.

2277. "Tico of the Seven Seas Sets Sail." *Animerica*. March 1994, p. 10.

2278. "Two Dubbed Guys and a Hard Day's Dragon Knight from A.D. Vision." *Animerica*. April 1994, p. 15.

2279. "Vampire Hunter D." *Animenominous!* Autumn 1990, pp. 26-27.

2280. Van Melkebeke, Emanuel and Steven Smet. "Mysterious Cities of Gold." *Anime UK Magazine*. 2:6, pp. 6-11.

2281. "Video Fest Streamline Reviews." *Protoculture Addicts*. July-August 1992, pp. 22-26.

2282. "Video Recommendations for the Absolute Beginner." *Animenominous!* Spring 1993, pp. 7-15.

2283. "Video Reviews." *Anime UK Magazine*. 2:6, p. 33.

2284. "Video Reviews." *Anime UK Magazine*. 3:3, pp. 31-33.

2285. "Video Reviews: Kamasutra, Laughing Target, Gigolo, Little Angel Alita, Guyver Part 1, Cat Girl: Nuku-Nuku." *Anime UK Magazine*. 3:2, pp. 28-31.

2286. Winchester, James R. "Tensai Bakabon." *The Rose*. July 1991, p. 16.

2287. "Yokoyama Rides to War with Mars." *Animerica*. March 1994, p. 11.

2288. Yoon, John. "Shonan Bakusozoku 1." *The Rose*. July 1994, pp. 8-9.

2289. Yoon, John. "Tsuyoshi Shikkari Shinasai." *The Rose*. July 1993, pp. 16-17.

2290. "'You're Terminated Otaku': Rhea Gall Force." *Animerica*. October 1994, p. 14.

2291. "Yuugen Kaisha." *Anime UK Magazine*. 3:4, pp. 20-21, 23-24.

"Ah My Goddess"

2292. "Ah My Goddess." *The Rose*. April 1994, pp. 8-9. Reprinted from *New Type*. June 1993.

2293. "Animation Update: Ah! My Goddess Taiho Shichauzo (I'll Arrest You)." *Animag*. 2:2, pp. 3-5.

2294. Ashmore, Darren, *et al*. "Reviews: Anime. Oh My Goddess! Manga Video." *Anime UK Magazine*. 3:4, pp. 30-35.

2295. Evans, Peter. "Ah My Goddess. Vol. 1. Moonlight and Cherry Blossoms." *Anime UK Magazine*. 2:3, pp. 30-31.

2296. "Oh! My AnimEigo." *Animerica*. June 1994, pp. 16-17.

2297. Swint, Lester. "OAV Review: Oh My Goddess!" *The Rose*. October 1994, pp. 8-9.

2298. Swint, Lester. "Oh My Goddess!" *The Rose*. October 1994, pp. 9-10.

"Akira"

2299. "Akira: Epic Comics Enters Japanese Manga Field with Color Series About Post-Holocaust Mutants." *Comics Buyer's Guide*. January 1, 1988, pp. 1, 3.

2300. "Akira's Neo-Tokyo Beat." *Protoculture Addicts*. March-April 1993, p. 14.

2301. Akurt, Dan and Toshifumi Yoshida. "Akira." *Animag*. No. 7, 1989, pp. 30-35.

2302. Baltake, Joe. "'Akira' Looks Beautiful, Feels Terrifying." *Sacramento Bee*. June 7, 1990.

2303. Bernardi, Luigi. "Corri, Kaneda, Corri!" *Comic Art*. July 1990, p. 49.

2304. Blodrowski, Steve. "Japanese Animation: Wonders Overcoming Western Prejudice." *Cine Fantastique*. March 1990, p. 47.

2305. Drennen, Eileen M. "Despite Muddled Plot, 'Akira' Packs Big Punch with Dazzling Animation." *Atlanta Constitution*. May 11, 1990.

2306. Harrington, Richard. "Not Just Kids' Stuff." Cleveland, Ohio *Plain Dealer*. April 27, 1990, pp. 8, 15.

2307. Kehr, David. "Japanese Cartoon 'Akira' Isn't One for the Kids." *Chicago Tribune*. March 30, 1990, p. D-7.

2308. Komai, Chris. "'Akira' Breaks Barriers of Animated Films." *Los Angeles*

Japanese Daily News. March 28, 1990, pp. 1, 3.

2309. Miller, Bob. "'Akira' Production Report." *Comics Buyer's Guide.* October 19, 1990, p. 67.

2310. Rayns, Tony. "Akira." *Monthly Film Bulletin.* March 1991, pp. 61+.

2311. Solomon, Charles. "'Akira': High Tech Hokum from Japan." *Los Angeles Times.* March 14, 1990.

2312. Sternbach, Rick. "A Strange and Violent Future: Akira." *Animerica.* September 1994, pp. 61-62.

2313. Webber, Brad W. "'Akira' Draws on Top 'Japanimation.'" *Chicago Sun-Times.* March 25, 1990, p. E.

"Arislan"

2314. "Arislan Battle Story III and IV." *The Rose.* July 1994, p. 11.

2315. "Heroic Record of Arislan." *The Rose.* April 1992, p. 21.

2316. McCarthy, Helen. "Heroic Legend of Arislan." *Anime UK Magazine.* 2:4, pp. 32-33.

2317. Savage, Lorraine. "Heroic Legend of Arislan. Part I." *The Rose.* July 1994, p. 10.

2318. Savage, Lorraine. "Heroic Legend of Arislan. Part II." *The Rose.* July 1994, pp. 10-11.

"Armored Trooper"

2319. Eldred, Tim. "Armored Trooper Votoms." *Animag.* No. 11, pp. 42-44.

2320. Ishigami, Yoshitaka. "Armored Trooper Votoms, 'The Glorious Defiance.'" *Animerica.* August 1994, p. 59.

2321. Kelly, Victoria. "Armored Samurai Troopers African Travelogue." *The Rose.* November 1990, pp. 4-5.

"Astro Boy"

2322. *Astroboy Episode Guide: The Official Astroboy Reference Manual Containing Synopses of All 104 Original Episodes.* Des Moines, Iowa: Right Stuff, 1992. 55 pp.

2323. "Astro Boy Returns for Now." *Four Color Magazine.* May 1987, p. 24.

2324. Swint, Lester. "Astro Boy: The Official Reference Manual." *The Rose*. October 1992, pp. 18-19.

2325. "The Words by the Author on 'Astro Boy.'" In *Golden Comics: Collected Works of Osamu Tezuka—Astro Boy 20*. Tokyo: Shogakukan, 1970.

"Bastard"

2326. "Bastard." *Animag*. 2:3, p. 5.

2327. Evans, Peter. "Bastard!!" *Anime UK Magazine*. December 1992/January 1993, pp. 36-37.

"The Beastketeers"

2328. "The Beastketeeers." *Animag*. 2:3, p. 4.

2329. Ishigami, Yoshitaka. "KO Century Three Beastketeers II." *Animerica*. September 1993, p. 54.

"Black Magic M-66"

2330. Connell, Ed. "Black Magic M-66." *Out of Chaos*. No. 13.

2331. Steele, Richard. "Black Magic M-66." *The Rose*. April 1994, p. 7.

2332. Swallow, Jim. "Black Magic—Manga into Anime." *Anime UK Magazine*. August/September 1992, pp. 32-34.

"Blue Sonnet"

2333. "Blue Sonnet." *Animenominous!* Autumn 1990, pp. 16-20.

2334. "Sing a Sonnet of Sixpence." *Animerica*. September 1994, p. 15.

"Borgman"

2335. "Hey Hey, It's the Borgman!" *Animerica*. July 1993, p. 12.

2336. "I'm the Borgman." *Newtype*. July 1988, pp. 16-19.

"Bubblegum Crisis"

2337. "And Then, Riding a Dark Horse, Came Manga...! *Animerica*. February 1994, p. 34.

2338. Baker, Ed. "Bubble Gum Crash 2." *The Rose*. November 1991, p. 7.

2339. "Bubblegum Crisis." *Anime UK Magazine*. June/July 1992, pp. 24-29.

2340. "Bubblegum Crisis." *The Rose*. July 1991, p. 3.

2341. "Bubblegum Crisis in Color from Dark Horse." *Animerica*. May 1993, p. 36.

2342. Chow, Kong. "Bubblegum Crash I: Illegal Army." *Japanese Animation Movement*. Summer 1992, pp. 13-14.

2343. Chow, Kong. "Bubblegum Crash III: Meltdown." *Japanese Animation Movement*. Summer 1992, pp. 17-18.

2344. "Cyberpunk Classic Finds Its Voice." *Animerica*. October 1994, p. 13.

2345. Duarte, Roger. "Bubblegum Crash!" *Anime UK Magazine*. October/November 1992, pp. 26-29.

2346. Duarte, Roger. "Bubblegum Crisis." *Anime UK Magazine*. August/September 1992, pp. 14-17.

2347. Edwards, Jacob. "Bubblegum Crash II: Geo Climbers." *Japanese Animation Movement*. Summer 1992, pp. 15-16.

2348. Horibuchi, Seiji. "Bubble, Bubble, Genom Means Trouble." *Animerica*. May 1993, pp. 4-9.

2349. Karahashi, Takayuki. "Voices of the Bubblegum Pop." *Animerica*. May 1993, p. 11.

2350. "Merchandise Madness at AnimEigo." *Animerica*. March 1994, p. 15.

2351. Ouellette, Martin. "Bubblegum Crisis Characters." *Mecha Press*. August-September 1992, pp. 22-23.

2352. Ouellette, Martin. "Why 'Bubblegum Crisis.'" *Mecha Press*. August-September 1992, pp. 16-17, 21.

2353. Savage, Lorraine. "OAV Review: Bubblegum Crisis." *The Rose*. October 1994, p. 12.

2354. Savage, Lynn. "Subtitled Bubblegum Crisis I." *The Rose*. September 1991, p. 15.

2355. Spray, Carmen. "Bubblegum Crash." *The Rose*. November 1991, p. 6.

2356. Sternbach, Rick. "Best of the West: Bubblegum Crisis." *Animerica*. July 1993, p. 55.

2357. Swint, Lester. "Bubblegum Crisis: Grand Mal." *The Rose*. January 1995, pp. 11, 29.

2358. "Takezaki's AD Police on the Mean Streets of Bubblegum Crisis." *Animerica*. May 1994, p. 36.

   "Catgirl: Nuku-Nuku"

2359. Carrières, Jean. "Super Cat Girl Nukunuku." *Protoculture Addicts*. March-April 1993, p. 38.

2360. Cowie, Geoff. "Manga in Focus." *Anime UK Magazine*. 3:2, p. 32.

2361. Swallow, James. "Catgirl: Nuku Nuku." *Mangazine*. November 1994, p. 11.

2362. Weber, Christof. "Cat Girl Nuku Nuku." *The Rose*. July 1994, p. 13.

   "Cat's Eye"

2363. Bierbaum, Tom and Mary. "The Cats [sic] Pajamas." *The Rose*. January 1987, pp. 5-6.

2364. Savage, Lorraine. "Cat's Eye Live Action." *The Rose*. September 1988, p. 9.

   "Chibi Maruko Chan"

2365. Ashby, Janet. "Time Out Japanese: 'Chibi Maruko-Chan.'" *Japan Times*. October 12, 1990 [?].

2366. "'Chibimaruko-chan'—Cartoon of a Different Era." *Mainichi Daily News*. July 23, 1990.

2367. "Chibi Maruko-Chan." *Nihongo Journal*. November 1990.

2368. Kageyama, Yuri. "Oriental Female Bart Simpson Is the Latest Rage in Japan." *Muncie* (Indiana) *Evening Press*. November 12, 1990, p. 14.

2369. Leahy, Kevin. "Bride of Bart: Chibi Maruko-Chan." *The Rose*. November 1990, p. 7.

   "City Hunter"

2370. "City Hunter." *Animag*. No. 11, p. 4.

2371. Kuo Chih-Ping. "City Hunter the Movie." *The Rose*. July 1991, pp. 12-14.

2372. Kuo Chih-Ping. "City Hunter the Movie: Part 2." *The Rose*. September 1991, pp. 6-7.

2373. Staley, James. "City Hunter 3." *The Rose*. July 1991, p. 19.

2374. "XYZ City Hunter." *Animenominous!* Summer 1991, pp. 33-38.

"Crayon Shin-Chan"

2375. "Crayon Shin-Chan." *Mangajin*. December 1994, pp. 53-59.

2376. "Crayon Shin-Chan." *Mangajin*. March 1995, pp. 52-59.

2377. "Crayon Shin-Chan Says 'Aloha.'" *Animerica*. February 1994, p. 14.

2378. "Theatrical Release, Musical Planned for Crayon, Sailor Moon." *Animerica*. July 1993, p. 13.

2379. Yoon, John. "General Guide for Crayon Shin-Chan." *The Rose*. January 1994, pp. 6-7.

"Crusher Joe"

2380. Kurtin, Dana. "Crusher Joe." *Animag*. 2:2, pp. 16-23.

2381. McCarthy, Helen. "Crusher Joe." *Anime UK Magazine*. 2:6, pp. 22-25.

"Cutey Honey"

2382. "Android Undercover Angel Cutey Honey." *Animerica*. January 1994, pp. 12-13.

2383. Newton, Cynthia J. "Much Better Developed: Cutey Honey." *Animerica*. October 1994, pp. 57-58."

"Cyborg 009"

2384. "Cyborg 009." In *A History of the Komiks of the Philippines and Other Countries*, by Cynthia Roxas and Joaquin Arevalo, Jr., p. 244. Manila: Islas Filipinas Publishing, 1985.

2385. Grimes, Ethel M. "Cyborg 009: Review and Character Outline." *The Rose*. January 1988, pp. 5-7.

2386. Grimes, Ethel M. "Defenders of the Vortex." *The Rose*. March 1989, pp. 4-5.

2387. Kato, Hisao. "Cyborg 009 (Giappone)." In *Enciclopedia Mondiale del Fumetto*, edited by Maurice Horn and Luciano Secchi, p. 270. Milan: Editoriale Corno, 1978.

"The Dagger of Kamui"

2388. Ashmore, Darren. "The Dagger of Kamui." *Anime UK Magazine*. 3:2, pp. 6-9.

2389. Horn, Carl G. "The Dagger of Kamui." *Animerica*. December 1993, p. 60.

2390. Savage, Lorraine. "Video Review: Dagger of Kamui (Subbed)." *The Rose*. January 1995, p. 22.

"Dangaio"

2391. "Dangaio." *Animag*. No. 6, 1988, pp. 26-29.

2392. Savage, Lynn. "Dangaio." *The Rose*. November 1991, pp. 12-13.

"Devil Hunter Yohko"

2393. Doi, Hitoshi and Peter Evans. "Mamono Hunter Yohko 5." *Anime UK Magazine*. 3:5, pp. 4-5.

2394. Leahy, Kevin. "'Fantastic Adventure of Yohko: Leda' Is Returning." *The Rose*. March 1988, p. 6.

2395. "Move Over, Buffy: Devil Hunter Yohko." *Animerica*. October 1994, p. 13.

2396. Steele, Richard. "Devil Hunter Yohko." *Anime UK Magazine*. 2:5, pp. 29-31.

"Dirty Pair"

2397. Andreu, Carlos. "Dirty Pair English Novel." *The Rose*. September 1988, p. 7.

2398. Collett, Tony. "Dirty Pair: Flight 005 Conspiracy." *The Rose*. October 1994, p. 24.

2399. Cunningham, Jonathan. "Dirty Pair." *Anime-Zine*. No. 3, pp. 8-16.

2400. "Dirty Pair." *Animag*. No. 8, pp. 6-16.

2401. "Dirty Pair Raises Virtual Hell in New Series." *Animerica*. May 1993, p. 36.

2402. Durkin, Dan. "Dirty Pair." *The Rose*. September 1989, p. 4.

2403. Durkin, Dan. "The Dirty Pair Do It Again!" *The Rose*. November 1989, p. 5.

2404. Dyar, Dafydd N. "A Decade of the Dirty Pair." *Anime UK Magazine*. June/July 1992, pp. 4-14.

2405. "Everything Old Is New Again—New Lil' Pair Adventures Come Bustin' Out of the Old Tradition." *Animerica*. December 1993, p. 10.

2406. Ishigami, Yoshitaka. "Dirty Pair Flash." *Animerica*. April 1994, p. 60.

2407. Lyon, Matt. "Mini Review: Dirty Pair: The Anime Comic." *The Rose*. January 1995, p. 22.

2408. Morse, Roger. "TV Series Review: Dirty Pair Flash #1-6." *The Rose*. January 1995, p. 24.

2409. Ouellette, Martin. "Dirty Pair Flash." *Protoculture Addicts*. September-October 1994, p. 45.

2410. Sternbach, Rick. "A Pair That's One-of-a-Kind." *Animerica*. August 1994, pp. 61-62.

2411. "Streamline's New Conspiracy." *Animerica*. September 1994, p. 15.

2412. Swallow, Jim. "Girls with Guns." *Anime UK Magazine*. 2:3, pp. 34-35.

2413. Swint, Lester. "The Great Adventures of the Dirty Pair." *The Rose*. April 1992, pp. 22-23.

2414. Yang, Jeff. "Anime Q and A." *Animerica*. September 1994, p. 18.

"Dominator"

2415. "Get a Grip, Dominator." *Animerica*. November 1993, p. 36.

2416. "Straight from the Subsonic Realm of Hell—Kodansha's Dominator." *Animerica*. October 1993, p. 39.

"Dominion"

2417. Christiansen, James and Grant Kono. "Dominion." *Animag*. No. 9, 1989, pp. 24-26.

2418. "Crusher Police Dominion." *Anime UK Magazine*. 3:1, pp. 10-11.

2419. Gagnon, Etienne. "Dominion." *Mecha Press*. August-September 1992, pp. 28-30.

2420. Kim, Andy, James E. Christiansen, and Grant Kono. "Dominion." *Animag*. No. 7, 1989, pp. 21-26.

2421. McCarthy, Helen. "Dominion." *Anime UK Magazine*. August/September 1992, pp. 28-31.

2422. "Special Tank Division Dominion, 'Tank Police...Go!'" *Animerica*. February 1994, p. 61.

2423. "Tank-up Time! Dominion." *Animerica*. November 1993, p. 10.

"Doraemon"

2424. Minami, Horoshi, ed. *Doraemon Kenkyu: Kodomo Ni Totte Manga Towa Nanika* (A Study of Doraemon: What Is the Comics for Children). Tokyo: Burēn Shuppan, 1986. 240 pp.

2425. Walker, Brad. "Fantastics [in an] Animation Festival." *Comics Feature*. No. 23/24, 1983, pp. 124-132.

"Dragon Ball"

2426. Alegado, Eric. "Dragonball: (Hoi Poi?) Do Don Pa? Kamehameha?" *Animenominous!* Summer 1991, pp. 12-18.

2427. Saeki, Daichi. "Dragon Ball Characters." *Protoculture Addicts*. May-June 1993, pp. 22-24.

2428. Saeki, Daichi. "Dragon Ball Overview." *Protoculture Addicts*. May-June 1993, pp. 16-20.

"Dragon Half"

2429. Chan, Ronald. "Dragon Half." *The Rose*. October 1992, pp. 20-21.

2430. O'Connell, Kevin. "Dragon Half." *The Rose*. May 1990, p. 15.

"Fist of the North Star"

2431. Arago, Michael. [Fist of the North Star]. *SF* (San Francisco) *Weekly*. October 23, 1991, p. 24.

2432. Armstrong, David. "A 'Splattertoon.'" *SF* (San Francisco) *Weekly*. October 23, 1991, p. 24.

2433. Bardy, John. "Fist of the North Star." *The Rose*. January 1992, p. 21.

2434. Dlin, Doug. "Fist of the North Star." *Mangazine*. 2:15 (1992), pp. 44-45.

2435. "Fist of the North Star." *Anime UK Magazine*. June/July 1992, p. 15.

2436. Harrington, Richard. "Cartoon Carnage!" *Washington Post*. October 25, 1991.

"Five Star Stories"

2437. Christiansen, James. "The Five Star Stories." *Animag.* No. 8, pp. 17-23, 38.

2438. Christiansen, James. "Five Star Stories. Book Two." *Animag.* No. 12, pp. 18-23.

2439. "The Five Star Stories." *Animag.* No. 7, 1989, pp. 6-18.

2440. "Mecha Synopsis: Five Star Stories." *Mecha Press.* December 1992, pp. 17-20.

2441. "The Official Art of The Five Star Stories." *Newtype.* July 1988, pp. 123-129.

2442. Ouellette, Martin. "Five Star Stories Characters." *Mecha Press.* December 1992, pp. 10-11.

2443. Ouellette, Martin. "Five Star Stories Overview." *Mecha Press.* December 1992, pp. 8-9.

2444. Ouellette, Martin. "What's Five Star Stories." *Mecha Press.* December 1992, p. 5.

"Fushigi No Umi No Nadia"

2445. O'Connell, Kevin, *et al.* "Nadia of the Sea of Mystery." *The Rose.* September 1990, pp. 8-10.

2446. Payne, Peter. "Fushigi No Umi No Nadia." *The Rose.* April 1992, p. 25.

2447. Santoso, Widya. "Nadia—Streamline's Episode One." *The Rose.* July 1992, p. 11.

"Future Boy Conan"

2448. Dunn, Ben. "The World of Future Boy, Conan." *Mangazine.* February 1993, pp. 4-8.

2449. "Future Boy Conan Episode Guide." *Mangazine.* February 1993, pp. 13-18.

2450. "Who's Who in Future Boy Conan." *Mangazine.* February 1993, pp. 9-12.

"Gatchaman"

2451. "Gatchaman Flies Again." *Mangazine.* November 1994, p. 13.

2452. Long, James and Dana Kurtin. "Science Ninja Team Gatchaman. The Show That Defined the Anime Team." *Animag.* 2:1, pp. 32-38.

2453. Munson-Siter, Pat. "Gatchaman and Gatchaman II Background." *C/FO San*

Antonio Newsletter. September 1986.

2454. Rogers, Alara. "Gatchaman." *Animenominous!* Spring 1993, pp. 32-48.

2455. Triger, Susan. "Battle of the Planets: *Episode Guide.*" *The Rose.* November 1991, p. 15.

2456. Triger, Susan. "Culture Shock." *The Rose.* November 1991, p.14.

2457. "Who Was That Masked Gatchaman?" *Animerica.* September 1994, p. 12.

"Ghost Sweeper Mikami"

2458. Chan, Ronald. "GS Mikami: Gokuraku Daisakusen!" *The Rose.* July 1993, pp. 5-6.

2459. Leahy, Kevin. "Ghost Sweeper Mikami." *The Rose.* July 1993, pp. 5, 7.

2460. Steele, Richard. "Ghost Sweeper Mikami." *Protoculture Addicts.* September-October 1994, pp. 22-25.

2461. Sukimoto, Nobuyuki. "Anime America/Anime Expo." *V. Max.* No. 8, pp. 5-7.

"Giant Robo"

2462. "Giant Robo I and II. The Music." *Protoculture Addicts.* March-April 1993, p. 15.

2463. Lapointe, Patrick. "Giant Robo Character Guide." *Protoculture Addicts.* March-April 1993, pp. 9-11.

2464. Lapointe, Patrick. "Giant Robo Synopsis." *Protoculture Addicts.* March-April 1993, pp. 12-13.

2465. Leahy, Kevin. "Getter Robo Go." *The Rose.* April 1992, p. 19.

2466. Ouellette, Martin. "Giant Robo Overview." *Protoculture Addicts.* March-April 1993, p. 8.

"Ginrei"

2467. Ouellette, Martin. "Ginrei Anime Story." *Protoculture Addicts.* September-October 1994, pp. 17-18.

2468. Ouellette, Martin. "Ginrei Characters." *Protoculture Addicts.* September-October 1994, pp. 14-16.

2469. Staley, James. "Barefoot Ginrei." *The Rose.* July 1994, p. 29.

"Godzilla"

2470. Dubois, André. "Godzilla vs. Ghidra." *Protoculture Addicts*. November-December 1992, pp. 18-21.

2471. Gomez, Jeffrey. "Godzilla Approaches." *Gateways*. August 1987, p. 34.

2472. Napier, Susan J. "Panic Sites: The Japanese Imagination of Disaster from *Godzilla* to *Akira*." *Journal of Japanese Studies*. Summer 1993, pp. 327-352.

"Grave of the Fireflies"

2473. Feldman, Steven. "Grave of the Fireflies." *The Rose*. April 1992, pp. 10-11.

2474. "Subtitled Grave of the Fireflies from CPM." *Animerica*. June 1993, p. 16.

"Gunbuster"

2475. Alldridge, Richard and Chris Tilley. "Gunbuster: Aim for the Top." *Anime UK Magazine*. 3:3, pp. 6-10.

2476. Durkin, Dan. "Gunbuster: Aim for the Top! Volume 3." *The Rose*. March 1990, p. 9.

2477. Fong, Dana. "Aim for the Top! Gunbuster." *Animag*. No. 11, pp. 19-24.

2478. "Gunbuster—Ships & Mecha." *Protoculture Addicts*. June-July 1991, pp. 13-14.

2479. "Gunbuster—Uh?!" *Protoculture Addicts*. June-July 1991, p. 11.

2480. Riddick, David and Robert Napton. "Gunbuster—Mini Interview." *Protoculture Addicts*. June-July 1991, p. 12.

2481. Sternbach, Rick. "Best of the West: Aim for the Top! Gunbuster." *Animerica*. May 1993, p. 61.

"Hades Project Zeorymer"

2482. "Clash of the Titans! USMC's Genocyber and Hades Project Zeorymer." *Animerica*. March 1994, p. 14.

2483. Diaz, Richard. "Hades Project Zeorymer." *The Rose*. July 1994, p. 7.

2484. "Hades Project Zeorymer." *Animag*. No. 8, pp. 30-32.

"Iczer"

2485. Feldman, Steven, "Horror in Japanese Animation—Iczer One." *The Rose*. November 1991, pp. 4-5.

2486. "Fight! Iczer-One and Antarctic Press." *Animerica*. March 1994, p. 34.

2487. "Iczer 1." *Animag*. 1:3 (1987), pp. 8-11.

2488. Leahy, Kevin. "Iczer 1—Golden Warrior." *The Rose*. September 1988, p. 11.

2489. Leahy, Kevin. "Iczer 1—Golden Warrior Chapter 3." *The Rose*. November 1988, p. 9.

2490. Leahy, Kevin. "Iczer 1—Golden Warrior Chapter 4." *The Rose*. January 1989, p. 13.

2491. Leahy, Kevin. "Iczer Update." *The Rose*. July 1988, pp. 5-6.

2492. Martin, Rick. "Iczer-3, Acts 1 and 2." *The Rose*. January 1991, p. 5.

2493. Rogers, Alara. "Adventure Iczer-3." *Animenominous!* Spring 1991, pp. 2-9.

2494. Staley, James. "Iczer Three." *The Rose*. October 1994, p. 25.

"Jungle Emperor"

2495. "Japan's Kimba vs. Disney's Simba." *The Rose*. October 1994, p. 18.

2496. Ledoux, Trish. "Whose Lion Is It Anyway?" *Animerica*. August 1994, p. 38.

2497. Tomiyasu, Stephanie and Frederik Schodt. "Kimba vs. Simba." *Mangajin*. February 1995, pp. 4, 34.

"Kimagure Orange Road"

2498. Dubreuil, Alain. "Whimsical Episode Guide." *Protoculture Addicts*. March-April 1993, pp. 21-24.

2499. Dubreuil, Alain. "Whimsical Episode Guide." *Protoculture Addicts*. May-June 1993, pp. 9-13.

2500. Dubreuil, Alain. "Whimsical Episode Guide." *Protoculture Addicts*. July-August 1993, pp. 25-29.

2501. Dubreuil, Alain and Patrick Lapointe. "Kor Alive! OVAS." *Protoculture Addicts*. July-August 1993, pp. 30-31.

2502. Dubreuil, Alain and Patrick Lapointe. "Lights, Camera, Settings!" *Protoculture Addicts*. March-April 1993, pp. 25-26.

2503. Dubreuil, Alain and Patrick Lapointe. "Orange Road Characters." *Protoculture Addicts*. March-April 1993, pp. 18-19.

2504. Dubreuil, Alain and Patrick Lapointe. "Whimsical Secret Dossiers." *Protoculture Addicts*. May-June 1993, p. 8.

2505. Durkin, Dan. "Kimagure Orange Road." *The Rose*. January 1990, p. 4.

2506. Higgins, Walter. "Take Me to Summer Side: Kimagure Orange Road." *Animenominous!* Summer 1990, pp. 20-22.

2507. Lapointe, Patrick. "Kimagure Orange Road." *Protoculture Addicts*. March-April 1993, pp. 16-17.

2508. Tsao Sheng-Te. "Orange Road Movie." *The Rose*. July 1990, p. 11.

"Kurenai No Buta"

2509. Ott, John. "Kurenai No Buta." *The Rose*. July 1992, pp. 18-19.

2510. Ott, John. "A New Film by Hayao Miyazaki: Kurenai No Buta." *The Rose*. January 1992, pp. 12-13.

"Laputa"

2511. "American Premiere—Laputa: The Castle in the Sky." *The Rose*. November 1987, p. 8. Reprinted from *Animation Magazine*. No. 1.

2512. Connell, Ed. "Laputa—Castle in the Sky." *Out of Chaos*. No. 3.

2513. Feldman, Stephen. "Fantastic Voyage: The Art of Anime." *The Newspaper* (Providence, Rhode Island). July 20, 1989, pp. 4, 12.

2514. Garrett, Robert. "Adventures on the Far Side of Clouds." *Boston Globe*. June 16, 1989.

2515. Janusonis, Michael. "The Characters Are Cartoons, Too." *Providence* (Rhode Island) *Journal*. July 22, 1989.

2516. "Laputa: Jonathan Swift Inspires Japanese Filmmaker." *Comics Buyer's Guide*. n.d. 1989.

2517. Lawson, Terry. "Remarkable Animation Takes Us to 'Castle in the Sky.'" *Dayton Daily News*. September 2, 1989.

2518. Miller, Bob. "The Lure of 'Laputa.'" *Comics Scene*. No. 7, p. 69.

2519. Patten, Fred. "Laputa and Twilight of the Cockroaches." *Animation Magazine*. Spring 1989, pp. 21, 59.

2520. Phillips, Thomas E. "Laputa: Castle in the Sky (English)." *The Rose*. May 1989, p. 5.

2521. Segaloff, Nat. "Confusion Sinks Animated 'Laputa.'" *Boston Herald*. June 16, 1989, p. S-4.

2522. Tucker, Ernest. "'Laputa' Sets New Standards for Animation from Orient." *Chicago Sun-Times*. April 21, 1989, p. 35.

"Legend of the Galactic Heroes"

2523. Jang, Galen, Andy Kim, and James Matsuzaki. "Legends of the Galactic Heroes." *V. Max*. No. 2, pp. 15-24.

2524. Karahashi, Takayuki. "Legend of the Galactic Heroes." *Animag*. 2:3, pp. 36-44.

2525. "Legend of the Galactic Heroes." *Animerica*. June 1994, pp. 12-13.

"Lensman"

2526. Feldman, Steven. "Lensman." *The Rose*. July 1991, p. 11.

2527. Janusonis, Michael. "The Force Is Not with 'Lensman.'" *Providence Journal*. May 17, 1991.

2528. Orrock, Alec. "Lensman." *The Rose*. November 1990, p. 13.

2529. Payne, Harry. "Quagdop the Mercotan Lives! Lensman Reviewed." *Anime UK Magazine*. 2:4, p. 34.

2530. Solomon, Charles. "'Lensman' Animated Clone of 'Star Wars.'" Cleveland, Ohio *Plain Dealer*. April 19, 1991, p. 8.

2531. Sternbach, Rick. "Best of the West." *Animerica*. June 1993, p. 61.

"Lone Wolf and Cub"

2532. Beatty, Terry. "Lone Wolf and Child: An Outsider's View." *Comics Buyer's Guide*. June 29, 1984, pp. 66, 68.

2533. Feldman, Steven. "Lone Wolf and Cub." *The Rose*. May 1991, pp. 8-9.

"Lupin"

2534. House, Michael and Carl G. Horn. "Lupin III 'The Fabulous Gold of Babylon.'" *Stray Particles* (Denver Anime International). November 1989.

2535. Janusonis, Michael. "Cartoon Cuts to the Chase." *Providence* (Rhode Island) *Journal-Bulletin.* February 7, 1992, p. D-7. ("Castle of Cagliostro").

2536. Leahy, Kevin. "Lupin III—Then and Now." *The Rose.* January 1992, pp. 18-19.

2537. "Lupin III." *Anime UK Magazine.* 2:4, pp. 21.

2538. Patten, Frederik. "Lupin III—The Castle of Cagliostro." *Animation.* Winter 1989, p. 72.

2539. Payne, Harry. "Lupin III: The Castle of Cagliostro." *Anime UK Magazine.* 2:2, p. 29.

"Majo No Takyubin"

2540. Leahy, Kevin. "Majo No Takyubin—Witch's Delivery Service." *The Rose.* November 1989, p. 4.

2541. Schilling, Mark. "'Majo' Delivers Innovative World of Animation." *Japan Times.* August 29, 1989.

"Megazone 23"

2542. Kennard, Mary, Jean Dewey, and Vince Richards. "Megazone 23." *Anime-Zine.* No. 1, 1986, pp. 2-10.

2543. King, Martin. "A Review of Megazone 23." *Anime-Zine.* 2, 1987, pp. 38-40.

2544. Leahy, Kevin. "Megazone 23 Part III." *The Rose.* March 1990, p. 8.

2545. Okamoto, Jeff. "Megazone 23, Part One." *Animag.* No. 11, pp. 28-31.

"Mekton"

2546. Pelletier, Claude J. "Put Some Magic in It: A Mekton Magical System." *Protoculture Addicts.* January-February 1992, pp. 17-18.

2547. Vézina, Marc-Alex. "Mecha Designs Adaptation for Mekton." *Mecha Press.* August-September 1992, pp. 10-11.

2548. Vézina, Marc-Alex. "Mecha Designs Adaptation for Mekton." *Mecha Press.* November 1992, p. 26.

2549. Vézina, Marc-Alex. "Mekton: Closer to Japanimation." *Mecha Press*. November 1992, pp. 24-25.

2550. Vézina, Marc-Alex. "Mekton 30." *Mecha Press*. August-September 1992, pp. 8-9.

"Mermaid's Forest"

2551. Chan, Ronald. "Mermaid's Forest." *The Rose*. October 1993, pp. 6-7.

2552. "Mermaid's Forest (Ningyo No Mori)." *The Rose*. January 1991, p. 9.

"Minky Momo""

2553. Endresak, Dave. "Minky Momo (Magical Girls and Shinin' Dreams)." *The Rose*. October 1994, pp. 20-21.

2554. "Minky Momo: 'The Station of Embarcation.'" *Animerica*. September 1994, pp. 59-60.

2555. "Minky Momo's Magical Mystery Tour." *Animerica*. December 1993, p. 11.

2556. "New Minky Momo." *Mangazine*. July 1992, 3 pp.

2557. Troutman, James. "A Gathering of Angels." *The Rose*. July 1992, p. 17.

2558. Troutman, James. "Around the Minky Momo's Dreams." *The Rose*. May 1990, p. 12.

"Mobile Suit Gundam"

2559. Carlson, Bruce. "G Gundam." *The Rose*. July 1994, p. 21.

2560. Davies, Julie and Toshifumi Yoshida. "Mobile Suit Gundam 0083: Stardust Memory." *Animag*. 2:3, pp. 46-54.

2561. Del Grosso, Tony. "The Mad Modeler." *V. Max*. No. 8, pp. 30-31.

2562. Dyar, Dafydd N. "Mobile Suit Gundam. Century." *Anime UK Magazine*. December 1992/January 1993, pp. 6-17.

2563. Dyar, Dafydd N. "Mobile Suit Gundam. Century: Part 2." *Anime UK Magazine*. 2:1, pp. 12-23.

2564. Dyar, Dafydd N. "Mobile Suit Gundam. Century: Part 3." *Anime UK Magazine*. 2:2, pp. 6-18.

2565. "Gundam." *Protoculture Addicts*. April-May 1991, pp. 26-27.

2566. Howell, Mike. "MS Senki and MS Era: Mobile Suit Gundam 0001-0080." *The Rose*. January 1991, p. 16.

2567. "It's Victory for Gundam Fans." *Animerica*. April 1993, p. 12.

2568. "I Wanna Have a Pure Time...Everyone's an LD Mind." *Animerica*. January 1994, p. 12.

2569. Lapointe, Patrick. "Gundam 0083 0080." *Protoculture Addicts*. May-June 1993, pp. 14-15.

2570. Leahy, Kevin. "Standing Up to the Victory: Victory Gundam." *The Rose*. January 1994, pp. 8-10.

2571. MacDonald, Mike and Matthew Anacieto. "History of the Mobile Suit." *Animag*. 1:1 (1987), pp. 27-29.

2572. "Mobile Suit Gundam." *Animag*. 1:1 (1987), pp. 14-18.

2573. "Mobile Suit Gundam." *Animag*. No. 8, pp. 33-37.

2574. "Mobile Suit Gundam F 91." *V. Max*. No. 3, pp. 14-16, 18-22.

2575. "Mobile Suit Zgundam." *Animag*. No. 9, 1989, pp. 27-31.

2576. Ouellette, Martin. "Gundam F91 Characters." *Mecha Press*. November 1992, pp. 10-15.

2577. Ouellette, Martin. "Gundam Formula 91 Overview." *Mecha Press*. November 1992, pp. 8-9.

2578. Ouellette, Martin. "Gundam Formula 91: Technology in UC 0123." *Mecha Press*. November 1992, p. 9.

2579. Ouellette, Martin. "Gundam 0080: War in the Pocket." *Mecha Press*. August-September 1992, pp. 17-20.

2580. Ouellette, Martin. "Gundam 0080: War in the Pocket." *Mecha Press*. November 1992, pp. 17-20.

2581. Ouellette, Martin. "Mobile Suit V Gundam TV Series." *Protoculture Addicts*. July-August 1993, pp. 38-39.

2582. Ouellette, Martin. "V-Gundam Continued." *Protoculture Addicts*. January-February 1994, p. 39.

2583. Ouellette, Martin. "V-Gundam Continued." *Protoculture Addicts*. July-August 1994, p. 38.

2584. Ouellette, Martin. "V-Gundam: The Final Episodes." *Protoculture Addicts*. March-April 1994, p. 46.

2585. Savage, Lynn. "Mobile Suit Gundam I: The Awakening." *The Rose*. September 1990, p. 19.

2586. Schumann, Mark. "A Chronicle of the Future: Yoshiyuki Tomino's Gundam Universe." *V. Max*. No. 6, pp. 14-18.

2587. "Street Fighting Gundam-Style (Or, You Call That Gundam!?)." *Animerica*. April 1994, p. 10.

2588. Swint, Lester. "Gundam Mobile Suit Volume I: Awakening." *The Rose*. January 1991, pp. 14-15.

2589. Swint, Lester. "Gundam Mobile Suit Volume II: Escalation." *The Rose*. May 1991, pp. 12-14.

2590. Swint, Lester. "Mobile Suit Gundam 0083." *The Rose*. July 1994, pp. 20-21.

2591. Teal, James. "Mobile Suit Zeta Gundam." *Animag*. No. 6, 1990, pp. 30-35.

2592. Teal, James. "Mobile Suit Zeta Gundam: Episodes 31-36." *Animag*. No. 7, 1989, pp. 36-41.

2593. "Tominoism Is the Enjoyment of Gundam." *The Rose*. January 1992, pp. 8-10.

"Mongo's Manga"

2594. House, Michael. "Mongo's Manga: Gokuu Midnight Eye." *Animag*. No. 12, pp. 14-15.

2595. "Mongo's Manga." *Animag*. No. 6, 1988, pp. 36-38.

2596. Okamoto, Jeff. "Mongo's Manga: Maison Ikkoku." *Animag*. 2:2, pp. 24-26.

"My Youth in Arcadia"

2597. "My Youth in AnimEigo." *Animerica*. November 1993, p. 15.

2598. "My Youth in Arcadia." *Animag*. No. 6, pp. 6-15.

"Omoide Poroporo"

2599. Kettering, Chat and Kevin Leahy. "Omoide Poro Poro." *The Rose*. October 1994, p. 28.

2600. Leahy, Kevin. "Omoide Poroporo." *The Rose*. January 1991, p. 8. From *Animage*. January 1991.

2601. Moisan, David. "Thoughts on Omoide Poroporo." *The Rose*. March 1991, p. 13.

2602. Payne, Peter. "Omoide Poro Poro." *The Rose*. April 1992, p. 24.

"Orguss II"

2603. Ouellette, Martin. "Orguss 2: Volume 1." *Protoculture Addicts*. July-August 1994, p. 45.

2604. Spencer, John. "Orguss: Super Dimension Century." *Anime UK Magazine*. 2:3, pp. 22-25.

2605. Wade, Calvin. "Superdimensional Century Orguss." *Animag*. No. 11, pp. 16-18.

2606. "Where Are You Going, When Are You Coming Home? Orguss II." *Animerica*. October 1993, p. 12.

"Patlabor"

2607. "Calling All Mobile Police Units! Civil Unrest Expected This Summer." *Animerica*. June 1993, p. 12.

2608. Ishigami, Yoshitaka. "Mobile Police Patlabor 2." *Animerica*. November 1993, p. 60.

2609. Kim, Andy. "Mobile Police Patlabor." *V. Max*. No. 1, pp. 18-19.

2610. "Mobile Police Patlabor Storylines." *Anime UK Magazine*. June/July 1992, pp. 21-23.

2611. "Patlabor the Movie." *Anime UK Magazine*. 2:5, pp. 20-21.

2612. Rittler, Steve. "Police Presence Patlabor: Mobile Police Force." *Animenominous!* Summer 1990, pp. 10-13.

2613. Simmons, Mark. "Mobile Police Patlabor." *Animag*. No. 6, 1990, pp. 46-53.

2614. Williams, John and Kensaku Nakata. "Mobile Police Patlabor." *V. Max*. No. 3, pp. 5-9.

"Phoenix"

2615. Patten, Fred. "The Film Boom." *Noumenon*. April 1978, pp. 15-16.

2616. Patten, Fred. "Fred's Film Notes." *Noumenon*. July 1979, pp. 10-11.

2617. Tezuka, Osamu. "The Phoenix." *Mangajin*. June 1992, pp. 45-61.

"Plastic Little"

2618. "Plastic Little." *Anime UK Magazine*. 3:2, pp. 22-24, 27.

2619. "The Secret of Cloud Water." *Animerica*. April 1993, pp. 12-13.

"Porco Rosso"

2620. McCarthy, Helen. "Porco Rosso." *Anime UK Magazine*. 3:1, pp. 22-23.

2621. McCarthy, Helen. "Porco Rosso." *Anime UK Magazine*. October/November 1992, p. 30.

2622. Matsuzaki, James. "The Crimson Pig." *V Max*. No. 8, p. 16-22.

2623. Ouellette, Martin. "Porco Rosso Characters." *Protoculture Addicts*. January-February 1994, pp. 10-11.

2624. Ouellette, Martin. "Porco Rosso Synopsis." *Protoculture Addicts*. January-February 1994, pp. 12-17.

2625. Ouellette, Martin. "Porco Rosso Technology." *Protoculture Addicts*. January-February 1994, p. 18.

2626. "Porco Rosso." *Protoculture Addicts*. November-December 1992, p. 13.

"Project A-Ko"

2627. "Introducing Project A-KO RPG." *Protoculture Addicts*. July-August 1994, pp. 12-13.

2628. "Let's Sing Along with Project A-Ko." *Animerica*. April 1994, pp. 14-15.

2629. McCarthy, Helen. "Project A-Ko." *Anime UK Magazine*. August/September 1992, pp. 5-10.

2630. McLennan, Jim. "Project A-Ko." *The Rose*. October 1992, pp. 16-17.

2631. Ouellette, Martin. "Project A-Ko." *Protoculture Addicts*. May-June 1992, p. 21.

2632. "Project A-Ko." *Animenominous!* Spring 1991, pp. 12-15.

2633. "Project A-Ko Is A-OK As Brand-New Malibu Manga." *Animerica*. October 1993, p. 39.

2634. Rispoli, Joseph. "Project A-K4: Final." *The Rose*. January 1991, pp. 6-7.

"Ranma"

2635. Koos, Michael. "Ranma 1/2 Not Just Another Martial Arts Story." *Japanese Animation Movement*. Summer 1992, pp. 5-10.

2636. Ledoux, Trish. "Voicing Miss Ranma." *Animerica*. December 1993, p. 7.

2637. "Ranma 1/2." *Animenominous!* Autumn 1990, pp. 7-12.

2638. "Ranma 1/2, The Movie." *Animerica*. April 1994, p. 14.

2639. Savage, Lynn. "Ranma 1/2." *The Rose*. July 1992, pp. 22-23.

2640. Swett, Chris. "'Ranma in America' Goes to Japan." *Animerica*. April 1993, p. 10.

2641. Sorfleet, Winston. "Ranma Nibunnonichi: Synopsis and Design." *Protoculture Addicts*. April-May 1991, pp. 15-25.

2642. Sternbach, Rick and Roberta Nakamura. "Ranma 1/2: TV Vol. 1." *Animerica*. April 1994, p. 57.

2643. Szeto, Vincent. "Ranma 1/2 Desperately Seeking Shampoo." *The Rose*. July 1994, p. 25.

2644. Warren, Wayne. "OAV Review: Ranma 1/2: Big Trouble in Nekkonron China." *The Rose*. October 1994, p. 21.

2645. Watson, Paul. "Ranma 1/2: Game Review." *Anime UK Magazine*. 3:1, pp. 20-21.

"Raven Tengu Kabuto"

2646. "Raven Tengu Kabuto." *Animag*. 2:3, p. 3.

2647. Samuels, Mitch. "A New Kind of Hero: Raven Tengu Kabuto." *Animerica*. August 1994, pp. 62-63.

"Record of Lodoss War"

2648. Jang, Galen. "Lodoss Wars: The Conclusion." *V. Max*. No. 6, pp. 30-35.

2649. Jang, Galen, Andy Kim, and James Matsuzaki. "Record of Lodoss Wars." *V. Max*. No. 4, pp. 15-21.

2650. Karahashi, Yoshiyuki and Albert Wang. "Record of Lodoss War." *Animag*. 2:2, pp. 38-45.

2651. Karahashi, Yoshiyuki and Albert Wang. "Record of Lodoss War." *Animag.* 2:3, pp. 28-33.

2652. McCarthy, Helen. "Record of Lodoss War." *Anime UK Magazine.* 2:1, pp. 4-9.

2653. McCarthy, Helen. "Stories of Record of Lodoss War." *Anime UK Magazine.* 2:2, pp. 26-27.

2654. Ouellette, Martin. "Record of Lodoss War Characters." *Protoculture Addicts.* July-August 1994, pp. 14-15.

2655. Pelletier, Claude J. "Record of Lodoss War Episodes 3 to 13." *Protoculture Addicts.* July-August 1994, pp. 16-26.

2656. "Record of Lodoss War: Synopsis and Design." *Protoculture Addicts.* January-February 1992, pp. 20-27.

"Roujin Z"

2657. Carr, John T., III. "Roujin Z." *Anime UK Magazine.* August/September 1992, pp. 18-19.

2658. Carr, John T., III. "Roujin-Z: Anime Towards the 21st Century." *Japanese Animation Movement.* Summer 1992, pp. 19-21.

2659. Keller, Chris. "Roujin Z." *V. Max.* No. 4, pp. 10-13.

"Saint Seiya"

2660. Chang, Jennie. "Boys Be-Saint Seiya." *The Rose.* July 1991, p. 19.

2661. Chiu Feng-Nien. "An Introduction of 'Saint Seiya.'" *Monthly Comic Magazine* (Hong Kong). July 1991, pp. 44-45.

2662. Leahy, Kevin. "More Manga—Saint Seiya Style." *The Rose.* July 1988, p. 7.

2663. Leahy, Kevin. "Saint Seiya: Warriors of the Final Crusade." *The Rose.* March 1989, p. 10.

2664. Merrill, David. "New Saint Seiya Rules Forever." *The Rose.* January 1989, p. 6.

2665. Simmons, Janet. "Saint Seiya." *The Rose.* March 1988, pp. 4-5.

2666. Switzer, Madeline. "St. Seiya." *Anime-Zine.* 2, 1987, pp. 4-10.

2667. Thomas, Matt. "The Battle for Athena." *The Rose.* July 1989, p. 6.

"Silent Möbius"

2668. Carr, John T., III, and Helen McCarthy. "Silent Möbius." *Anime UK Magazine.* October/November 1992, pp. 6-13.

2669. Evans, Peter and Wil Overton. "Silent Möbius 2." *Anime UK Magazine.* 2:2, pp. 19-21.

2670. Jang, Galen. "Silent Möbius." *V. Max.* No. 6, pp. 19-24.

2671. Saeki, Daichi. "Silent Möbius: The Manga." *Protoculture Addicts.* May-June 1993, pp. 28-30.

2672. "Silent Möbius: The Motion Picture." *Protoculture Addicts.* July-August 1992, pp. 16-19.

"Sol Bianca"

2673. "Avast There, Anime Fans! Sol Bianca Sighted in Local Waters." *Animerica.* April 1993, p. 16.

2674. Baker, Ed. "Sol Bianca II." *The Rose.* April 1992, p. 20.

2675. Matsuzaki, James. "Fashionable and Deadly Sol Bianca." *V. Max.* No. 5, pp. 15-21.

2676. "Sol Bianca." *Anime UK Magazine.* 2:5, 1994, pp. 22-25.

"Space Cruiser Yamato"

2677. Amos, Walter. "Yamato, the Star Blazers You Didn't See." *Mangazine.* November 1994, pp. 16-19.

2678. Burns, James H. "Make Way for Star Blazers." *Starlog.* June 1980, pp. 51-53.

2679. Carlton, Ardith. "Space Cruiser Yamato." *Comics Collector.* Spring 1984, pp. 62-63, 91.

2680. Crawley, Tony. "Space Cruiser." *Starburst.* March 1978, pp. 24-26.

2681. Dlin, Douglas. "Farewell to Space Battleship Yamato: A Review." *Mangazine.* November 1994, p. 230.

2682. Fenelon, Rob. "So Which Is Which?" *Mangazine.* November 1994, p. 20.

2683. Fenelon, Rob. "Tales from the Inside." *Mangazine.* November 1994, p. 21.

2684. Fenelon, Rob. "Yamato Filmography." *Mangazine.* November 1994, p. 19.

2685. Fenelon, Rob and Martin King. "Yamato Academy." *Mangazine*. November 1994, p. 24.

2686. Kimura, Kuni. "Did You Know...?" *Mangazine*. November 1994, p. 25.

2687. King, Martin. "Yamato III: T-Minus 52 and Counting." *Mangazine*. November 1994, pp. 26-27.

2688. King, Martin and Robert Fenelon. "After the Comet Empire: Yamato 3." *Anime-Zine*. 2, 1987, pp. 11-19.

2689. Leahy, Kevin. "Crisis on Infinite Cruisers: The Yamato Comic Adaptations." *The Rose*. July 1992, pp. 12-13.

2690. Lee, Eugene. "Video Games and Other Amusements: Space Cruiser Yamato." *Animerica*. June 1993, p. 57.

2691. Napton, Robert. "Space Cruiser Yamato." *Animag*. No. 6, 1990, pp. 6-14, 16-19.

2692. Pym, John. "Uchusenkan Yamato." *Monthly Film Bulletin*. April 1979, pp. 31-32.

2693. Staley, James. "Dub Review: Farewell to Space Battleship Yamato." *The Rose*. January 1995, p. 23.

2694. "The Yamato Experience." *Animenominous!* Autumn 1990, pp. 21-23.

"Space Fortress Macross"

2695. Kawamori, Shoji and Haruhiko Mikimoto. "Superdimensional Fortress Macross." *Animag*. No. 11, pp. 10-14.

2696. "Lovers Again...at Last!" *Animerica*. November 1993, p. 14.

2697. "Macross." *Animerica*. November 1992, pp. 12-13.

2698. "Macross Plus." *Animerica*. May 1994, p. 12.

2699. "Macross Plus." *Animerica*. October 1994, p. 68.

2700. "Macross 7." *Mangazine*. November 1994, pp. 14-15.

2701. "Macross II CD Soundtrack from U.S. Renditions." *Animerica*. October 1993, p. 17.

2702. "Macross II Graphic Novel, Illustration Book Available at Last." *Animerica*. March 1994, p. 34.

2703. "Macross II Movie Update." *Animerica*. April 1993, pp. 16-17.

2704. Ouellette, Martin. "Episodes I and II: Macross II." *Protoculture Addicts*. November-December 1992, pp. 14-17.

2705. Patten, Fred. "Reviews: Space Fortress Macross: Volume One, Booby Trap." *Get Animated!* February 1985, p. 8.

2706. "Relive the Magic of Macross Once More." *Animerica*. October 1994, p. 40.

2707. Swint, Lester. "Super Dimensional Fortress Macross II." *The Rose*. April 1994, pp. 22-23.

"Speed Racer"

2708. Palmaira, Michael. "Speed Racer." *The Rose*. October 1993, p. 24.

2709. Savage, Lorraine. "TV Review: New Speed Racer." *The Rose*. October 1993, p. 25.

2710. Schubert, Ann. "Speed Racer." *Animag*. No. 11, pp. 34-37.

2711. Swint, Lester. "Speed Racer: Manga, Anime and Comics (Part 1)." *The Rose*. October 1992, pp. 12-13, 15.

2712. Swint, Lester. "Speed Racer: Manga, Anime and Comics (Part 2)." *The Rose*. January 1993, pp. 14-15.

"Star Blazers"

2713. Friedman, Arnold J. "Star Blazers: A Conflict of Culture." *Animag*. No. 6, 1990, pp. 54-55.

2714. Nishizaki, Yoshinobu. *Star Blazers*. W.C.C. Animation Comics, Vols. 1-5. Tokyo, Japan: West Cape, 1983.

2715. Rowe, Allen. "Star Blazers Episode Guide." *Japanimation*. No. 3, 1987, pp. 22-27.

2716. "Star Blazers Character Guide." *Japanimation*. No. 3, 1987, pp. 20-21.

"Street Fighter"

2717. "Fight! Animated Street Fighter II." *Animerica*. August 1994, p. 12.

2718. "In THIS Corner...! Tokuma's Street Fighter II." *Animerica*. February 1994, p. 34.

2719. Luse, Jonathan. "Street Fighter II." *The Rose*. January 1995, pp. 7, 30.

2720. "Street Fighter II Leaps to the Screen." *Animerica*. July 1993, p. 37.

"Tenchi Muyo!"

2721. McCarthy, Helen. "Tenchimuyo Ryo Oh Ki." *Anime UK Magazine*. 2:6, pp. 30-31.

2722. "No Need for Tenchi!" *Animerica*. February 1994, pp. 60-61.

2723. "Pioneer's Special Need." *Animerica*. May 1994, p. 17.

2724. Steele, Richard. "Tenchi Muyo!" *Protoculture Addicts*. July-August 1994, pp. 22-23.

2725. Steele, Richard. "Tenchi Muyo! Characters." *Protoculture Addicts*. July-August 1994, pp. 24-25.

2726. "Tenchimuyo Ryo Oh Ki." *Anime UK Magazine*. 3:1, pp. 8-9.

"3 x 3 Eyes"

2727. Fredericks, Deborah. "3x3 Eyes." *The Rose*. September 1991, pp. 16-17.

2728. Kim, Andy and Galen Jang. "3x3 Eyes." *V. Max*. No. 2, p. 25.

"Tonari No Totoro"

2729. Brockman, Terra. "My Neighbor Totoro: An Enchanting Japanese *Anime* Is Dubbed into English—With Mixed Results." *Mangajin*. October 1994, pp. 30-31.

2730. Nakamura, Roberta. "A Magical Adventure for You: My Neighbor Totoro." *Animerica*. September 1994, pp. 62-63.

2731. O'Connell, Kevin. "Tonari No Totoro (My Neighbor Totoro)." *The Rose*. November 1989, p. 12.

2732. Rittler, Steve and Camille Cauti. "What's That Big Fuzzy Thing Anyway?" *Animenominous!* Spring 1991, pp. 16-21.

2733. "The Theatrical Release of My Neighbor Totoro by Troma, Inc." *The Rose*. July 1993, pp. 18-19.

2734. "Totoro's Big Screen Debut (in English!)." *Animerica*. April 1993, p. 16.

"Urotsuki Doji"

2735. "Double Your Dreams, Double Your Fun—Urotsuki Doji II." *Animerica*. October 1993, p. 16.

2736. McCarthy, Helen. "Urotsukidoji—The Legend of the Overfiend." *Anime UK Magazine*. December 1992/January 1993, p. 35.

2737. "Urotsuki Doji Penetrates Video Stores, Theaters Nationwide." *Animerica*. April 1993, p. 17.

"Urusei Yatsura"

2738. Alegado, Eric. "'It Isn't Urusei Yatsura.'" *Animenominous!* Spring 1991, pp. 26-29.

2739. "Area 88, Urusei Yatsura To Return." *Animerica*. July 1993, p. 37.

2740. Ashmore, Darren. "Urusei Yatsura." *Anime UK Magazine*. 3:3, pp. 12-15.

2741. Ashmore, Darren. "Urusei Yatsura Revisited." *Anime UK Magazine*. 3:4, pp. 16-17.

2742. Holleran, Jeff. "Viz's Urusei Yatsura Translation. Part Two." *The Rose*. March 1989, p. 7.

2743. Holleran, Jeff. "Viz's Urusei Yatsura Translation. Part 3." *The Rose*. May 1989, p. 13.

2744. Holleran, Jeff. "Viz's Urusei Yatsura Translation—What You May or May Not See." *The Rose*. January 1989, p. 9.

2745. "There's More to This Show Than Just Tiger Stripes." *Animenominous!* Summer 1990, pp. 23-30.

2746. "'Urusei Yatsura' by Takahashi Rumiko." *Mangajin*. March 1991, pp. 43-57.

2747. "'Urusei Yatsura' by Takahashi Rumiko." *Mangajin*. April 1991, pp. 49-65.

2748. "Urusei Yatsura Episode Guide Part 3 (Episodes 104-117)." *Mangazine*. February 1993, pp. 19-20.

"U.S. Manga Corps"

2749. Ouellette, Martin. "U.S. Manga Corps." *Protoculture Addicts*. July-August 1993, pp. 36-37.

2750. Pelletier, Claude J. "Spotlight: U.S. Manga Corps." *Protoculture Addicts*. May-June 1992, p. 14.

"Venus Wars"

2751. Kurtin, Dana and Toshifumi Yoshida. "Venus Wars." *Animag*. No. 9, 1989, pp. 40-44.

2752. Sternbach, Rick. "Venus Wars." *Animerica*. November 1993, p. 59.

2753. Swint, Lester. "Venus Wars." *The Rose*. March 1990, p. 5

2754. "Venus Wars Rage at Dark Horse Comics." *Animerica*. November 1993, p. 36.

"Video Girl Ai"

2755. Leahy, Kevin. "Video Girl Ai." *The Rose*. November 1991, p. 11.

2756. Vézina, François. "Video Girl Ai: BGM 1&2." *Protoculture Addicts*. January-February 1994, p. 34.

2757. Vézina, François. "Video Girl Ai Characters." *Protoculture Addicts*. January-February 1994, pp. 26-27.

2758. Vézina, François. "Video Girl Ai: The Movie." *Protoculture Addicts*. January-February 1994, p. 33.

2759. Vézina, François. "Video Girl Ai: The OVA's." *Protoculture Addicts*. January-February 1994, pp. 28-32.

2760. Wilkinson, Bryan. "Video Girl Ai." *V. Max*. No. 1, pp. 16-17.

"Voltes V"

2761. Dupea, Bobby. "SF In the East." *Starburst*. January 1980 [?], pp. 52-55.

2762. Gonzalez, E.T. and E.M. "Japan's Voltes V vs. America's Superman." *Diliman Review*. January-March 1979, outside front cover +.

"Wicked City"

2763. Marlo, Kim E. "OAV Review: Wicked City." *The Rose*. October 1994, p. 13.

2764. Taylor, James S. "Wicked City Toronto." *Protoculture Addicts*. July-August 1994, p. 34.

2765. "When Desire Turns Deadly, There's No Place To Hide in Streamline's Wicked City." *Animerica*. September 1993, p. 14.

"The Wings of Honneamise"

2766. Horn, Carl G. "The Wings of Honneamise." *Anime UK Magazine*. 3:5, pp. 8-11.

2767. Horn, Carl G. "Wings of Honneamise." *Protoculture Addicts*. November-December 1992, pp. 18-26.

"Yotoden"

2768. Hedman, Eric. "Yotoden, Strange Tale from a War Torn Land." *Animag*. No. 8, pp. 24-29.

2769. Kurtin, Dana. "Yotoden. Part Three: Chapter of Blazing Flames." *Animag*. No. 12, pp. 8-13.

"You're Under Arrest"

2770. "No Rest for the Wicked When You're Under Arrest." *Animerica*. June 1994, p. 12.

2771. "You're Under Arrest." *Animerica*. October 1994, pp. 68-69.

"Zillion"

2772. Staley, James. "Zillion." *The Rose*. March 1991, p. 5.

2773. "Zillion." *Animag*. No. 6, 1988, pp. 30-35.

Manga (Comic Books)

(This section includes characters in and titles of *manga* and newspaper strips.)

2774. Adams, Kenneth A. and Lester Hill, Jr. "Graveyard of the Gods." *Journal of Psychohistory*. Fall 1989, pp. 103-153.

2775. Andreoli, Richard. "From Side to S.I.D.E." *The Rose*. March 1991, p. 15.

2776. "Arerugen." *Mangajin*. May 1994, pp. 67-83.

2777. Baker, Ed. "Comic Gaia #1." *The Rose*. May 1991, p. 5.

2778. "'Bakuhatsu Senzen' (On the Verge of Explosion) by Tanioka Yasuji." *Mangajin*. April 1991, pp. 21-37.

2779. Barber, Lee. "The Ghost in the Shell." *The Rose*. July 1992, p. 7.

2780. "Beranmei Tōchan." *Mangajin*. March 1995, pp. 50-51.

2781. Bernardo, Carmen. "Pixy Junket." *The Rose*. October 1993, p. 22.

2782. Bilodeau, Normand and Patrick Lapointe. "Manga Reviews." *Protoculture Addicts*. May-June 1993, pp. 36-37.

2783. "Bio-Booster Armor Guyver Metamorphs to Manga!" *Animerica*. October 1993, pp. 39-40.

2784. Buruma, Ian. "Kakusan, the Heroic Villain Who Betrayed His Roots." *Far Eastern Economic Review*. November 3, 1983, pp. 58-60.

2785. Chan, Ronald. "Olfina." *The Rose*. January 1995, pp. 18-19.

2786. Chan, Ronald. "Otōsan To Isshyo." *The Rose*. July 1994, p. 19.

2787. Chan, Ronald. "Peach Colored Sabbath." *The Rose*. October 1994, pp. 22-23.

2788. Christiansen, James and Kensaku Nakata. "Beast War Madara." *V. Max*. No. 2, pp. 6-8, 10.

2789. "Coming Soon to a Comic Store Near You...A Plague of Angels." *Animerica*. June 1994, pp. 40-41.

2790. Craig, Andrew. "Return." *The Rose*. October 1994, p. 19.

2791. "Cry Havoc, and Let Slip the Dogs of War—Dark Horse's Hellbounds." *Animerica*. May 1994, p. 36.

2792. Deluxe Company. "Zusetsu Gendai Yōgo. A Visual Glossary of Modern Terms." *Mangajin*. December 1994, pp. 46-51.

2793. "Director Hira Namijirō, by Nitta Tatsuo." *Mangajin*. March 1995, pp. 70-92.

2794. Durand, Sylvain and Jean Carrières. "Manga Reviews." *Protoculture Addicts*. July-August 1994, pp. 36-37.

2795. "Everything Old Is New Again: Tetsujin 28 FX." *Mangazine*. July 1992, 3 pp.

2796. "Fancy Dance by Okano Reiko." *Mangajin*. December 1994, pp. 68-91.

2797. Fermín Pérez, Ramón. "La Amenaza Amarilla." El *Wendigo*. No. 59, 1993, pp. 6-7.

2798. Gagnon, Etienne, Sylvain Durand, and Jean Carrières. "Manga Reviews." *Protoculture Addicts*. September-October 1994, pp. 30-32. ("Horobi," "Dominion Book 1," "The Rebel Sword").

2799. "Garcia-kun by Takeuchi Akira." *Mangajin*. November 1994, pp. 56-59.

2800. Gyū Jirō. "Eigyō Tenteko Nisshi." *Mangajin*. June 1992, pp. 29-43.

2801. "Hiragana, Katakana and Manga." *Mangajin*. September 1990, pp. 8-14.

2802. Horn, Maurice. "Tanku Tankurō (Giappone)." In *Enciclopedia Mondiale del Fumetto*, edited by Maurice Horn and Luciano Secchi, p. 717. Milan: Editoriale Corno, 1978.

2803. "Imadoki No Kodomo (Kids These Days) by Kubō Kiriko." *Mangajin*. February 1995, pp. 55-65.

2804. "It's Mighty Morphin' Time! Power Comic." *Animerica*. June 1994, p. 40.

2805. Jang, Galen and Kensaku Nakata. "Dark Angel." *V. Max*. No. 5, pp. 4-7.

2806. Karahashi, Yoshiyuki. "Chinmoku No Kantai, The Silent Service." *Animag*. 2:3, pp. 20-22.

2807. Kato, Hisao. "Akadō Suzunosuke." In *Enciclopedia Mondiale del Fumetto*, edited by Maurice Horn and Luciano Secchi, p. 142. Milan: Editoriale Corno, 1978.

2808. Kato, Hisao. "Ashita No Joe." In *Enciclopedia Mondiale del Fumetto*, edited by Maurice Horn and Luciano Secchi, p. 160. Milan: Editoriale Corno, 1978.

2809. Kato, Hisao. "Billy Pack (Giappone)." In *Enciclopedia Mondiale del Fumetto*, edited by Maurice Horn and Luciano Secchi, p. 188. Milan: Editoriale Corno, 1978.

2810. Kato, Hisao. "Bōken Dankichi (Giappone)." In *Enciclopedia Mondiale del Fumetto*, edited by Maurice Horn and Luciano Secchi, p. 197. Milan: Editoriale Corno, 1978.

2811. Kato, Hisao. "Chikaino Makyū (Giappone)." In *Enciclopedia Mondiale del Fumetto*, edited by Maurice Horn and Luciano Secchi, p. 249. Milan: Editoriale Corno, 1978.

2812. Kato, Hisao. "Daiheigenji (Giappone)." In *Enciclopedia Mondiale del Fumetto*, edited by Maurice Horn and Luciano Secchi, p. 271. Milan: Editoriale Corno, 1978.

2813. Kato, Hisao. "8 Man (Giappone)." In *Enciclopedia Mondiale del Fumetto*, edited by Maurice Horn and Luciano Secchi, p. 605. Milan: Editoriale Corno, 1978.

2814. Kato, Hisao. "Fushigina Kuni No Putcha." In *Enciclopedia Mondiale del Fumetto*, edited by Maurice Horn and Luciano Secchi, pp. 349-350. Milan: Editoriale Corno, 1978.

2815. Kato, Hisao. "Futen (Giappone)." In *Enciclopedia Mondiale del Fumetto*, edited by Maurice Horn and Luciano Secchi, p. 350. Milan: Editoriale Corno, 1978.

2816. Kato, Hisao. "Gaki Deka (Giappone)." In *Enciclopedia Mondiale del Fumetto*, edited by Maurice Horn and Luciano Secchi, p. 418. Milan: Editoriale Corno, 1978.

2817. Kato, Hisao. "Gekkō Kamen." In *Enciclopedia Mondiale del Fumetto*, edited by Maurice Horn and Luciano Secchi, p. 422. Milan: Editoriale Corno, 1978.

2818. Kato, Hisao. "Golgo 13 (Giappone)." In *Enciclopedia Mondiale del Fumetto*, edited by Maurice Horn and Luciano Secchi, p. 429. Milan: Editoriale Corno, 1978.

2819. Kato, Hisao. "Hakaba No Kitaro (Giappone)." In *Enciclopedia Mondiale del Fumetto*, edited by Maurice Horn and Luciano Secchi, p. 445. Milan: Editoriale Corno, 1978.

2820. Kato, Hisao. "Harisu No Kaze (Giappone)." In *Enciclopedia Mondiale del Fumetto*, edited by Maurice Horn and Luciano Secchi, p. 448. Milan: Editoriale Corno, 1978.

2821. Kato, Hisao. "Hatanosuke Hinomaru (Giappone)." In *Enciclopedia Mondiale del Fumetto*, edited by Maurice Horn and Luciano Secchi, p. 451. Milan: Editoriale Corno, 1978.

2822. Kato, Hisao. "Hi No Tori (Giappone)." In *Enciclopedia Mondiale del Fumetto*, edited by Maurice Horn and Luciano Secchi, pp. 460-461. Milan: Editoriale Corno, 1978.

2823. Kato, Hisao. "Jungle Tatei (Giappone)." In *Enciclopedia Mondiale del Fumetto*, edited by Maurice Horn and Luciano Secchi, p. 489. Milan: Editoriale Corno, 1978.

2824. Kato, Hisao. "Kibaō (Giappone)." In *Enciclopedia Mondiale del Fumetto*, edited by Maurice Horn and Luciano Secchi, p. 502. Milan: Editoriale Corno, 1978.

2825. Kato, Hisao. "Kozure Okami (Giappone)." In *Enciclopedia Mondiale del Fumetto*, edited by Maurice Horn and Luciano Secchi, p. 511. Milan: Editoriale Corno, 1978.

2826. Kato, Hisao. "Kyojin No Hoshi (Giappone)." In *Enciclopedia Mondiale del Fumetto*, edited by Maurice Horn and Luciano Secchi, p. 518. Milan: Editoriale Corno, 1978.

2827. Kato, Hisao. "Nagagutsu No Sanjūshi (Giappone)." In *Enciclopedia Mondiale del Fumetto*, edited by Maurice Horn and Luciano Secchi, p. 583. Milan: Editoriale Corno, 1978.

2828. Kato, Hisao. "Ninja Bugeichō (Giappone)." In *Enciclopedia Mondiale del Fumetto*, edited by Maurice Horn and Luciano Secchi, p. 591. Milan: Editoriale Corno, 1978.

2829. Kato, Hisao. "Nonkina Tousan (Giappone)." In *Enciclopedia Mondiale del Fumetto*, edited by Maurice Horn and Luciano Secchi, p. 594. Milan: Editoriale Corno, 1978.

2830. Kato, Hisao. "Norakuro (Giappone)." In *Enciclopedia Mondiale del Fumetto*, edited by Maurice Horn and Luciano Secchi, p. 594. Milan: Editoriale Corno, 1978.

2831. Kato, Hisao. "Ogon Bat (Giappone)." In *Enciclopedia Mondiale del Fumetto*, edited by Maurice Horn and Luciano Secchi, pp. 597-598. Milan: Editoriale Corno, 1978.

2832. Kato, Hisao. "O-Man (Giappone)." In *Enciclopedia Mondiale del Fumetto*, edited by Maurice Horn and Luciano Secchi, pp. 599-600. Milan: Editoriale Corno, 1978.

2833. Kato, Hisao. "Osomatsu-Kun (Giappone)." In *Enciclopedia Mondiale del Fumetto*, edited by Maurice Horn and Luciano Secchi, p. 605. Milan: Editoriale Corno, 1978.

2834. Kato, Hisao. "Robot Santōhei (Giappone)." In *Enciclopedia Mondiale del Fumetto*, edited by Maurice Horn and Luciano Secchi, pp. 658-659. Milan: Editoriale Corno, 1978.

2835. Kato, Hisao. "Sabaku No Maō (Giappone)." In *Enciclopedia Mondiale del Fumetto*, edited by Maurice Horn and Luciano Secchi, p. 667. Milan: Editoriale Corno, 1978.

2836. Kato, Hisao. "Sasuke (Giappone)." In *Enciclopedia Mondiale del Fumetto*, edited by Maurice Horn and Luciano Secchi, pp. 671-672. Milan: Editoriale Corno, 1978.

2837. Kato, Hisao. "Shochan No Bōken (Giappone)." In *Enciclopedia Mondiale del Fumetto*, edited by Maurice Horn and Luciano Secchi, p. 686. Milan: Editoriale Corno, 1978.

2838. Kato, Hisao. "Shōnen Oja (Giappone)." In *Enciclopedia Mondiale del Fumetto*, edited by Maurice Horn and Luciano Secchi, p. 686. Milan: Editoriale Corno, 1978.

2839. Kato, Hisao. "Tenpei Tenma (Giappone)." In *Enciclopedia Mondiale del Fumetto*, edited by Maurice Horn and Luciano Secchi, p. 721. Milan: Editoriale Corno, 1978.

2840. Kato, Hisao. "Tetsujin 28 Gō (Giappone)." In *Enciclopedia Mondiale del Fumetto*, edited by Maurice Horn and Luciano Secchi, pp. 723-724. Milan: Editoriale Corno, 1978.

2841. Kato, Hisao. "Tetsuwan-Atom (Giappone)." In *Enciclopedia Mondiale del Fumetto*, edited by Maurice Horn and Luciano Secchi, p. 723. Milan: Editoriale Corno, 1978.

2842. Kato, Hisao. "Todano Bonji (Giappone)." In *Enciclopedia Mondiale del Fumetto*, edited by Maurice Horn and Luciano Secchi, p. 732. Milan: Editoriale Corno, 1978.

2843. Klei, Volker. "Tanaka: Gon 1." *Comic!* September/October 1994, pp. 50-51.

2844. Leahy, Kevin. "Fuma No Kojiro." *The Rose*. October 1993, p. 19.

2845. Leahy, Kevin. "Magical Taruruto-Kun." *The Rose*. May 1991, pp. 6-7.

2846. Leahy, Kevin. "Thirsty for More D? The Vampire Hunter D Novels." *The Rose*. January 1995, pp. 16-17, 31.

2847. Leahy, Kevin. "What Are You Babbling About? Babel 2-Sei." *The Rose*. April 1994, pp. 24-25.

2848. "Lycanthrope Leo and Alita Graphic Novel—A Match Made in...Heaven!?" *Animerica*. January 1994, p. 40.

2849. Maekawa Tsukasa. "Sanshirō's Love." *Mangajin*. September 1993, pp. 52-61.

2850. Mergenthaler, Andreas. "Crying Freeman." *Comic!* September/October 1994, p. 50.

2851. Nemoto, Susumu. *Kuri-Chan* (Little Kuri). Tokyo: Self-published, 1965. Japanese.

2852. "New Ultraman Live-Action TV Series." *Animerica*. December 1993, p. 38.

2853. Nishimura, Sō. "Assari-kun." *Mangajin*. 1:1 (1990), pp. 32-33.

2854. "Obatarian by Hotta Katsuhiko." *Mangajin*. November 1994, pp. 44-48.

2855. "Osaru No Monkichi, Monkichi the Monkey." *Mangajin*. February 1995, p. 8.

2856. Ott, John. "Gun Frontier and V2 Panzer." *The Rose*. January 1990, p. 5.

2857. Ott, John. "Maps and Legend of Myu." *The Rose*. September 1989, p. 5.

2858. Ott, John. "Mugen-Shinshi." *The Rose*. March 1990, p. 10.

2859. Ott, John. "Shuho Itahashi's Alien Crash and Lucky Route Runaway." *The Rose*. July 1990, p. 9.

2860. Palmaira, Michael A. "Intron Depot." *The Rose*. January 1993, p. 5.

2861. Saito, T. *Into the Wolves' Lair*. Golgo 13 Graphic Novel Series, No. 1. Tokyo: Lead Publishing, 1986. 167 pp.

2862. Santoso, Widya. "A Winter's Tale." *The Rose*. May 1990, p. 13. ("Winter Story").

2863. Savage, Lorraine. "Shion: Blade of the Minstrel." *The Rose*. March 1991, p. 10.

2864. Savage, Lorraine. "Shuna's Journey." *The Rose*. September 1990, p. 3.

2865. "Shōjo Manga." Special edition of *Eureka: Shi To Hihyō*. July 1981.

2866. "Shoot! by Ōshima Tsukasa." *Mangajin*. October 1994, pp. 61-79.

2867. Staley, James. "Jamka's Big Adventure." *The Rose*. July 1994, p. 24.

2868. Swallow, Jim. "Air Force: Manga in Focus." *Anime UK Magazine.* 3:1, pp. 26-27.

2869. Swallow, Jim. "The Hunt for Red Nippon." *Anime UK Magazine*. December 1992/January 1993, pp. 18-19. ("The Silent Service").

2870. "Takahashi's Uniquely Macabre 'Mermaid Saga' To Continue with Mermaid's Promise." *Animerica*. August 1994, pp. 36-37.

2871. Tomisawa Chinatsu. "Katsushika Q." *Mangajin*. August 1993, pp. 49-63.

2872. Weiland-Pollerberg, Florian. "Das Selbstmordparadies." *Comic!* September/October 1994, p. 50.

2873. Winchester, James R. "Laughing Salesman." *The Rose*. May 1990, p. 15.

2874. Yamafuji Shōji's Black Angel." *Mangajin*. March 1993, p. 11.

2875. Ying-Chi. "Stay Crazy—Ran Xerox." *Monthly Comic Magazine* (Hong Kong). October 1990, pp. 5-8.

"After Zero"

2876. "After Zero by Okazaki Jirō." *Mangajin*. December 1994, pp. 60-67.

2877. "After Zero by Okazaki Jirō. 'Memories of the Future,' Part II." *Mangajin*. February 1995, pp. 67-75.

2878. "After Zero by Okazaki Jirō. 'Memories of the Future,' Part III." *Mangajin*. March 1995, pp. 60-68.

2879. "After Zero, Okazaki Jirō." *Mangajin*. October 1993, pp. 42-29.

2880. "After Zero, Okazaki Jirō. Part III." *Mangajin*. No. 32, 1993, pp. 55-63.

"Anmitsu Hime"

2881. "Anmitsu Hime." In *A History of the Komiks of the Philippines and Other Countries*, by Cynthia Roxas and Joaquin Arevalo, Jr., pp. 244-245. Manila: Islas Filipinas Publishing, 1985.

2882. Kato, Hisao. "Anmitsu Hime." In *Enciclopedia Mondiale del Fumetto*, edited by Maurice Horn and Luciano Secchi, pp. 156-157. Milan: Editoriale Corno, 1978.

"Barefoot Gen"

2883. "Barefoot Gen—Life After the Bomb." *Publishers Weekly*. March 18, 1988.

2884. Gleason, Alan. "Again Gen." *Comics Journal*. October 1982, pp. 40-41.

2885. LaFleur, W. "Barefoot Gen." *Los Angeles Times Book Review*. March 8, 1987, pp. 1, 6.

2886. Lent, John A. "A Different Japanese Comic Strip." *Media History Digest*. Fall 1985, p. 51.

2887. Luciano, Dale. "Gen of Hiroshima: Two-Fisted Pacifism." *Comics Journal*. December 1981, pp. 40-41.

2888. MacRae, Cathi. "Young Adult Perplex." *Wilson Library Bulletin*. October 1989, pp. 108-109.

2889. Nakazawa, Keiji. *Barefoot Gen: The Day After. A Cartoon Story of Hiroshima*. Philadelphia, Pennsylvania: New Society Publishers, 1988. 177 pp.

2890. Scholz, Carter. "Sgt. Rock Told Backward." *Comics Journal*. December 1981, p. 43.

2891. Walker, Brad. "Nuclear Family." *Comics Feature*. September-October 1981, pp. 70-75.

2892. Yronwode, Cat. "Gen of Hiroshima." *Comics Feature*. May 1980, pp. 30-31, 60.

"Battle Angel Alita"

2893. Horibuchi, Seiji. "Battle Angel Alita: The Thoroughly Postmodern Manga of

Yukito Kashiro." *Animerica*. October 1993, pp. 4-10.

2894. Steele, Richard. "Battle Angel Alita." *Anime UK Magazine*. 3:1, pp. 6-7.

"Bravo Theater"

2895. "'Bravo Theater': Political Cartoon by Gōda Yoshiie." *Mangajin*. September 1990, pp. 48-51.

2896. "Shiatā Appare 'Bravo Theater': Political Manga by Yoshiie Gōda." *Mangajin*. 1:1 (1990), pp. 34-35.

"Captain Harlock"

2897. "Captain Harlock Sets Sail Once More from Malibu Comics." *Animerica*. May 1993, p. 36.

2898. Dubois, André. "Captain Harlock." *Protoculture Addicts*. June-July 1991, pp. 15-18.

2899. Dubois, André. "Harlock." *Protoculture Addicts*. February 1991, pp. 26-29.

2900. Grey, Simon. "Captain Harlock: Looking for a Place To Die." *Animenominous!* Summer 1990, pp. 7-9.

2901. Johnson, Lynn. "Taking a Look at Captain Harlock." *The Rose*. March 1988, pp. 8-9.

2902. Leahy, Kevin. "Captain Harlock and Queen Emeraldus." *The Rose*. July 1992, pp. 14-15.

2903. Ott, John. "Captain Harlock." *The Rose*. November 1989, p. 7.

"Caravan Kid"

2904. Swint, Lester. "Caravan Kid." *The Rose*. October 1993, p. 11.

2905. Winchester, James. "Caravan Kidd." *The Rose*. January 1989, p. 8.

"Dai-Tōkyō Binbō Seikatsu Manyuaru"

2906. "Dai-Tōkyō Binbō Seikatsu Manyuaru (Manual for Cheap Living in Greater Tokyo) by Maekawa Tsukasa." *Mangajin*. September 1990, pp. 52-61; March 1991, pp. 35-41.

2907. "Dai-Tōkyō Binbō Seikatsu Manyuaru (Manual for Cheap Living in Greater Tokyo) by Maekawa Tsukasa." *Mangajin*. February 1995, pp. 84-91.

"Dr. Slump"

2908. "Toriyama Akira's Dr. Slump." *Mangajin*. No. 32, 1993, pp. 64-83.

2909. "Toriyama Akira's Dr. Slump. Part II." *Mangajin*. March 1994, pp. 73-83.

"Fuku-Chan"

2910. "Fuku-Chan." In *A History of the Komiks of the Philippines and Other Countries*, by Cynthia Roxas and Joaquin Arevalo, Jr., p. 244. Manila: Islas Filipinas Publishing, 1985.

2911. Kato, Hisao. "Fuku-Chan (Giappone)." In *Enciclopedia Mondiale del Fumetto*, edited by Maurice Horn and Luciano Secchi, p. 348. Milan: Editoriale Corno, 1978.

2912. Okamoto, Rei. "The Japanese Comic Strip 'Fuku-chan' (Little Fuku), 1936-1944." *Philippines Communication Journal*. March 1993, pp. 71-79.

"Furiten-kun"

2913. "Ueda Masashi's Furiten-kun." *Mangajin*. May 1994, pp. 42-44.

2914. "Ueda Masashi's 'Furiten-kun.'" *Mangajin*. September 1994, pp. 50-52.

2915. "Ueda Masashi's Furiten-kun." *Mangajin*. November 1994, pp. 49-51.

"Ginga Tetsudō 999"

2916. "Ginga Tetsudō 999." *Mangajin*. April 1991, pp. 66-75.

2917. "Ginga Tetsudō 999 (Galaxy Express 999)." *Mangajin*. March 1991, pp. 59-75.

2918. Matsumoto, Reiji. "Ginga Tetsudō 999, Galaxy Express 999." *Mangajin*. No. 10, 1991, pp. 61-73.

"Gunhed"

2919. "Gunhed." *Anime UK Magazine*. 3:3, p. 36.

2920. Swint, Lester. "Gunhed." *The Rose*. January 1991, p. 12.

"Guyver"

2921. Leahy, Kevin. "The Guyver." *The Rose*. January 1993, pp. 8-9.

2922. Peacock, Dirk. "Video Review: Guyver 4 (English Dub)." *The Rose*. January 1995, pp. 17, 31.

2923. "Sequel to Live-Action Guyver Announced." *Animerica*. June 1993, p. 16.

"Hotel"

2924. "'Hotel' by Shōtarō Ishinomori." *Mangajin*. 1:1 (1990), pp. 48-69.

2925. "'Hotel' by Ishinomori Shōtarō." *Mangajin*. 1:2 (1990), pp. 46-71.

2926. "Hotel by Ishinomori Shōtarō." *Mangajin*. October 1993, pp. 51-79.

"Jimi-Hen"

2927. "Jimi-Hen by Nakazaki Tatsuya." *Mangajin*. August 1990, pp. 36-39.

2928. "'Jimi-Hen' by Nakazaki Tatsuya." *Mangajin*. September 1990, pp. 44-47.

"Kachō Shima Kōsaku"

2929. "Kachō Shima Kōsaku (Part II)." *Mangajin*. September 1993, pp. 63-87.

2930. Reid, T.R. "Kachō Shima Kōsaku: Japan's Most Famous Salaryman." *Mangajin*. August 1993, pp. 65-87.

"Kamui-Den"

2931. Kato, Hidetoshi. "Comics, Rebellion, and Ecology." In *Essays in Comparative Popular Culture: Coffee, Comics, and Communication*, edited by Hidetoshi Kato, pp. 9-27. Honolulu, Hawaii: East-West Center, 1975.

2932. Kato, Hisao. "Kamui-Den (Giappone)." In *Enciclopedia Mondiale del Fumetto*, edited by Maurice Horn and Luciano Secchi, pp. 493-494. Milan: Editoriale Corno, 1978.

2933. Mergenthaler, Andreas. "The Legend of Kamui." *Comic!* September/October 1994, p. 51.

2934. Swint, Lester. "Dagger of Kamui." *The Rose*. April 1992, pp. 16-17.

"Maboroshi No Futsū Shōjo"

2935. "Maboroshi No Futsū Shōjo, by Uchida Shungiku." *Mangajin*. August 1994, pp. 57-73.

2936. "'Maboroshi No Futsū Shōjo' by Uchida Shungiku." *Mangajin*. September 1994, pp. 62-81.

"Maison Ikkoku"

2937. Houston, Susan. "Maison Ikkoku." *The Rose*. November 1988, p. 8.

2938. "Manga Series *Maison Ikkoku* Translated." *Comics Journal*. April 1993, p. 35.

2939. Pelletier, Claude J. "Maison Ikkoku." *Protoculture Addicts*. November-December 1992, pp. 24-25.

2940. Staley, James. "Maison Ikkoku." *The Rose*. April 1993, p. 7.

2941. Thorn, Matt. "And Now for Something Completely Different...Maison Ikkoku from Rumiko Takahashi." *Animerica*. June 1993, p. 37.

"Nadia"

2942. Dunn, Ben. "Nadia." *Mangazine*. 2:15 (1992), pp. 45-46.

2943. Jang, Galen. "Story." *V. Max*. No. 1, pp. 11-14.

2944. Johnson, Jenny and Mike Pondsmith. "Nadia, The Secret of Blue Water." *Animag*. 2:3, pp. 12-19.

2945. Kim, Andy. "Nadia of the Mysterious Seas." *V. Max*. No 1, pp. 8-11.

2946. McCarthy, Helen. "Nadia Phone Home: The Wonderful World of the Anime Phone Card." *Anime UK Magazine*. 2:1, pp. 10-11.

2947. Matsuzaki, James. "Liner Notes." *V. Max*. No. 1, p. 14.

2948. "Nadia's Theme." *Animenominous!* Spring 1993, pp. 22-30.

2949. P-Chan. "Nadia of the Mysterious Sea: Synopsis and Design." *Protoculture Addicts*. February 1991, pp. 18-21.

"Naniwa Kin'yūdō"

2950. "Naniwa Kin'yūdō by Aoki Yūji." *Mangajin*. April 1994, pp. 64-83.

2951. "Naniwa Kin'yūdō by Aoki Yūji." *Mangajin*. May 1994, pp. 45-66.

2952. "'Naniwa Kin'yūdō' by Aoki Yūji, Part 3." *Mangajin*. June 1994, pp. 79-91.

2953. "Naniwa Kin'yūdō, by Aoki Yūji, Part 4." *Mangajin*. August 1994, pp. 83-91.

2954. "'Naniwa Kin'yūdō' by Aoki Yūji, Part 5." *Mangajin*. September 1994, pp. 83-91.

2955.   "Naniwa Kin'yūdō by Aoki Yūji. Part 6." *Mangajin*. October 1994, pp. 89-97.

2956.   "Naniwa Kin'yūdō by Aoki Yūji. Part 7." *Mangajin*. November 1994, pp. 83-92.

"Nausicaä in the Valley of the Mind"

2957.   Dreiss, Jerry. "Nausicaä: Seven Times of Fire." *The Rose*. July 1991, p. 7.

2958.   Feldman, Steven. "Nausicaä." *The Rose*. May 1989, p. 9.

2959.   James, Walt. "Warriors of the Wind." *Animation News*. January/February 1987.

2960.   "Nausicaä of the Valley of Wind." *Protoculture Addicts*. January-February 1993, pp. 22-25.

2961.   "Nausicaä's Back." *Animerica*. June 1994, pp. 40-41.

2962.   "Nausicaä's 'Magical Adventure' from Tokuma." *Animerica*. June 1993, p. 36.

2963.   Nei Mo Han. "Nausicaä's World." *Anime-Zine*. No. 1, 1986, pp. 11-17.

2964.   Ott, John. "The Return of Nausicaä." *The Rose*. May 1990, pp. 8-9.

2965.   Suzuki, Masashi. "Manga—Nausicaä in The Valley of the Mind." *Animage Magazine*. April 14, 1990.

2966.   Thorn, Matt. "Translating Nausicaä." *Animerica*. July 1993, p. 10.

2967.   Wolfe, Ken. "Warriors of the Wind." *The Rose*. September 1988, pp. 4-5.

"Ningen Kōsaten"

2968.   Henderson, Ed. "Ningen Kōsaten." *Mangajin*. No. 11, 1991, p. 50.

2969.   Yajima, Masao. "Ningen Kōsaten." *Mangajin*. October 1992, pp. 51-81.

"Ninja High School"

2970.   Durkin, Dan. "Ninja High School." *The Rose*. May 1989, p. 7.

2971.   "Ninja High School Goes Multi-media." *Animerica*. December 1993, pp. 38-39.

2972.   "Ninja High School Returns to Its Roots." *Animerica*. April 1994, p. 34.

"Oishinbō"

2973.   Kariya, Tetsu. "'Oishinbō' 300 Man Bu No Himitsu" (The Secret of "Oishinbo," a 300 Million Seller). *Bungei Shunjū*. 64:4 (1986), pp. 340-344.

2974. Tetsu, Kariya. "Oishinbō: Japan's Ultimate Food Manga." *Mangajin*. April 1992, pp. 51-52, 57.

"OL Shinkaron"

2975. "OL Shinkaron." *Mangajin*. March 1995, pp. 46-49.

2976. "OL Shinkaron by Akizuki Risu." *Mangajin*. November 1994, pp. 60-61.

"Robotech"

2977. Duarte, Roger and Jim Swallow. "The Robotech Generation." *Anime UK Magazine*. 2:2, pp. 32-35.

2978. McKinney, Jack. "Robotech: Zentraedi Rebellion." *Protoculture Addicts*. March-April 1994, pp. 12-17.

2979. "New Life for Robotech." *Animerica*. September 1994, p. 36.

2980. Orrock, Alec. "Robotech #18 *The End of the Circle* by Jack McKinney." *The Rose*. January 1990, p. 10.

"Sailor Moon"

2981. Doi, Hitoshi. "Sailor Moon Synopsis." *Protoculture Addicts*. July-August 1993, pp. 14-17.

2982. Endresak, Dave. "Monsters and Girls and Sailor Suits, Oh My! (Sailor Moon)." *The Rose*. July 1994, pp. 22-23.

2983. Gelman, Morrie. "1. Sailor Moon." *Animation*. February 1995, p. 42.

2984. Oshiguchi, Takashi. "The Sailor Moon Boom." *Animerica*. June 1994, p. 15.

2985. "Over the Manga Moon." *Asiaweek*. July 20, 1994, p. 32.

2986. Pelletier, Claude J. "Sailor Moon Goods." *Protoculture Addicts*. July-August 1993, p. 18.

2987. "Sailor Moon: A Quick Review." *Protoculture Addicts*. July-August 1993, p. 19.

2988. Shimkevich, Sergei. "Lovely Soldier Sailor Moon." *Animerica*. December 1993, p. 59.

2989. Takahashi, Alan. "Sailor Moon Characters." *Protoculture Addicts*. July-August 1993, pp. 12-13.

2990. Takahashi, Alan. "Sailor Moon Overview." *Protoculture Addicts.* July-August 1993, pp. 10-11.

"Sanctuary"

2991. Pierson-Smith, Stephen M. "Sanctuary." *The Rose.* January 1993, pp. 6-7.

2992. "Sanctuary." *Big O Magazine.* May 1994, pp. 50-53.

2993. "Sanctuary, Part Two Resumes This May." *Animerica.* May 1993, pp. 36-37.

"Sazae-San"

2994. Hasegawa, Machiko. *Sazae-san Uchiakebanashi* (A Confession of Sazae-san). Tokyo: Shimaisha, 1979. 128 pp.

2995. Imamura, Taihei. "Comparative Study of Comics: American and Japanese—Sazae-san and Blondie." In *Japanese Popular Culture*, edited by Hidetoshi Kato, pp. 87-102. Cambridge, Massachusetts: MIT Press, 1959.

2996. Kato, Hisao. "Sazae-San (Giappone)." In *Enciclopedia Mondiale del Fumetto*, edited by Maurice Horn and Luciano Secchi, p. 673. Milan: Editoriale Corno, 1978.

2997. "Sazae-san, Animated Heroine of the Not-So-Typical Family Next Door." *Variety.* October 17, 1989, pp. 152-154.

Shonen Jump

2998. Ashby, Janet. "Jump *Manga* Provides Escape Fare for All Ages." *Japan Times.* January 3, 1992, p. 10.

2999. Lazarus, David. "*Jump* Rules Comics Kingdom." *Asian Advertising and Marketing.* June 1992, pp. 18-20, 22.

3000. "L'Impériale Ascension de la BD." *Libération* (Paris). April 12, 1982.

3001. "Shonen Jump Special." *Out of Chaos.* No. 18.

"Take'emon-ke No Hitobito"

3002. "Take'emon-ke No Hitobito by Satō Take'emon." *Mangajin.* November 1994, pp. 52-55.

3003. "Take'emon-ke No Hitobito, The Take'emon Clan, by Satō Take'emon." *Mangajin.* March 1994, pp. 36-37.

"Tanaka-kun"

3004. Tanaka, Hiroshi. "Naku Na! Don't Cry! Tanaka-kun." *Mangajin*. 1:1 (1990), pp. 26-31.

3005. "Tanaka-kun." *Mangajin*. March 1991, pp. 22-24.

3006. "Tanaka-kun by Tanaka Hiroshi." *Mangajin*. 1:2 (1990), pp. 40-44.

"Taro-san"

3007. Booth, Alan. "The Birth of Taro San." *Winds*. 1984, pp. 16-23.

3008. Funabashi, Yoichi. "Taro-san, Seen as Symbol of Japan's Economic Might." *Asahi Shimbun*. October 5, 1983.

3009. "Ranan R. Lurie Presents Taro-san, Japan's New National Cartoon Symbol!" *Cartoonist PROfiles*. December 1983, pp. 8-11.

"Warau Sērusuman"

3010. "Warau Sērusuman by Fujiko Fujio (A)." *Mangajin*. March 1994, pp. 65-72.

3011. "Warau Sērusuman, by Fujiko Fujio (A)." *Mangajin*. April 1994, pp. 56-63.

3012. "'Warau Sērusuman' by Fujiko Fujio (A)." *Mangajin*. June 1994, pp. 70-77.

3013. "Warau Sērusuman (Part 2), by Fujiko Fujio (A)." *Mangajin*. August 1994, pp. 74-82.

"What's Michael?"

3014. "Michael Goes to a Cat-baret." *Mangajin*. 1:2 (1990) , pp. 21-35.

3015. Savage, Lorraine. "Review: 'What's Michael?'" *The Rose*. November 1987, p. 9.

3016. "'What's Michael?'" *Mangajin*. April 1991, pp. 38-47.

3017. "What's Michael?" *Mangajin*. November 1994, pp. 62-69.

3018. "'What's Michael' by Kobayashi Makoto: O-miai." *Mangajin*. September 1990, pp. 22-35.

3019. "'What's Michael?' by Makoto Kobayashi." *Mangajin*. 1:1 (1990), pp. 36-47.

3020. "What's Michael? Japan's 'Garfield' Comes to the U.S." *Comics Buyer's Guide*. October 13, 1989, p. 9.

3021. "'What's Michael?' Maikeru Tōjō." *Mangajin*. March 1991, pp. 25-32.

"Yawara"

3022. Durkin, Dan. "Yawara." *The Rose*. September 1990, p. 5.

3023. "Yawara!" *Mangajin*. May 1993, pp. 69-87.

3024. "Yawara!" *Mangajin*. June 1993, pp. 59-79.

"Yūyake No Uta"

3025. Saigan Ryōhei. "Yūyake No Uta." *Mangajin*. September 1994, pp. 52-61.

3026. "Yūyake No Uta by Saigan Ryōhei." *Mangajin*. October 1994, pp. 80-88.

Exports and Imports

Anime (Animation)

3027. Alexander, Garth. "Cartoons Dominate Japan's Film Exports." *Variety*. May 27, 1991, p. 44.

3028. Alexander, Garth. "Disney Hopes Mickey Can Mind the Store." *Variety*. August 19, 1991, pp. 29, 32.

3029. "Anime and Manga in Germany." *The Rose*. July 1994, pp. 15-16.

3030. "Anime Cons in Britain." *The Rose*. July 1994, p. 30.

3031. "Anime News from Britain." *The Rose*. July 1994, p. 16.

3032. "The Battle Begins with A.D. Vision This Summer." *Animerica*. July 1993, pp. 16-17.

3033. Bessman, Jim. "Central Park Adds 'Japanimation' Vids." *Billboard*. July 27, 1991, pp. 47, 54.

3034. "Caution! High-Speed Ninjas Ahead." *Animerica*. June 1993, p. 36.

3035. "Cheech and Chong Go Japanese?" *Animation*. December 1987, p. 7.

3036. Clements, Jonathan. "Fairy Tales and Foreign Sales." *Anime UK Magazine*. 3:2, pp. 33.

3037. Clements, Jonathan. "Manga and Anime à la U.K." *Animerica*. April 1994, p. 34.

3038. "CPM Adapts Anime to New Comics Line." *Comics Buyer's Guide*. February 10, 1995, p. 76.

3039. "East Meets West in Cartoon Venture." *Business Week*. May 11, 1963, p. 105.

3040. Grossman, Scott. "Renting Japanese Animation Videos in America." *The Rose*. July 1988, p. 4.

3041. Hudnall, James D. "Influences from Abroad." *Animerica*. November 1992, p. 7.

3042. "Japanese Courtship of the Disney Audience." *Business Week*. May 22, 1978, p. 34.

3043. "Japanese Producer Animates Wolfman/Colan Dracula Series." *Comics Journal*. September 1981, p. 20.

3044. Korkis, Jim. "The New Japanese Invasion." *Comics Journal*. November 1979, pp. 78-79.

3045. "Learning about Americans from 'Mickey Mouse.'" *East-West Center Magazine*. Summer-Fall 1977, pp. 8-9.

3046. Lhoste, Philippe. "Animé? Oui Oui Oui! Anime in France." *Protoculture Addicts*. November-December 1992, pp. 22-23.

3047. Lippolis, Alessandro. "Anime on TV in Italy." *The Rose*. October 1994, p. 32.

3048. McCarthy, Helen. "European Anime." *Anime UK Magazine*. 2:3, pp. 20-22. (France, Italy).

3049. McCarthy, Helen. "It's a Stick-Up." *Anime UK Magazine*. 2:5, p. 33. (Italian publisher of anime).

3050. "Made in Japan Disney Cartoons." *Mainichi Daily News*. February 20, 1990, p. 6-B.

3051. Matsuzaki, James. "Across an Ocean." *V. Max*. No. 4, p. 2.

3052. "Mickey Mounts Major Move on Video Market." *Variety*. September 16, 1991, p. 52.

3053. Miller, Bob. "Streamline Pictures: Bringing Japanimation Stateside." *Animato*. No. 18, 1989, p. 6.

3054. Moline, Alfons. "Anime Olé!" *Anime UK Magazine*. 3:4, pp. 10-11.

3055. "More Japanimation on the Way." *Cartoon Heroes*. Spring 1987, p. 10.

3056. Nakagawa, Sakuichi, *et al.* "'Popeye'—A Case Study." *CBC Report*. January 1964, pp. 42-45.

3057. "Northern California 'Anime Week' Update." *Animerica*. May 1993, p. 16.

3058. Oldham, Alan D. and Lester Swint. "Manga American Style." *Japanimation*. No. 3, 1987, pp. 12-13.

3059. "Orion, Polygram Bring Anime to Mainstream—Budge Titles May End Japanese Genre's Cult Status." *Billboard*. December 24, 1994.

3060. Oshiguchi, Takashi. "Animation and Foreign Markets." *Animerica*. September 1994, p. 14.

3061. "Outlandish New Video from D.I.E." *Animerica*. May 1993, p. 17.

3062. Painter, Jamie. "Japanimania." *Wild Cartoon Kingdom*. 7:13 (1993), pp. 46-51.

3063. Patten, Fred. "Japan's 'Star Quest' Premieres in U.S." *Animation News*. March/April 1987.

3064. Patten, Fred. "Offshore Animation." *Get Animated*. April 1985, p. 13.

3065. Patten, Fred. "Offshore Animation." *Get Animated*. September 1985.

3066. Patten, Fred. "Offshore Animation." *Get Animated*. January 1986, p. 12.

3067. Perissinotto, Diego and Danila and Michele Salgarello. "Anime in Italy." *Anime UK Magazine*. 2:5, pp. 34-35.

3068. "Post-Apocalyptic Tale Genesis Survivor Gaiarth from AnimEigo." *Animerica*. June 1993, p. 17.

3069. Rubies, Jose. "A Sad Sight: Manga and Anime in Spain." *Protoculture Addicts*. July-August 1992, pp. 20-21.

3070. Sternbach, Rick. "Best of the West." *Animerica*. November 1992, pp. 35-37.

3071. "Streamline Does Distribution Deal with Orion." *Mangazine*. November 1994, p. 3.

3072. "Streamline Hits Cable Market on Network One." *Mangazine*. November 1994, p. 3.

3073. "Streamline Pictures Offers Japanese Animation." *Comics Buyer's Guide*. June 2, 1989, p. 20.

3074. Susman, Gary. "Tokyorama." *Boston Phoenix*. July 10, 1992.

3075. Swallow, Jim. "Canadian Club." *Anime UK Magazine*. 2:4, pp. 18-19.

3076. Swint, Lester. "The Japanese Invasion." *Japanimation*. No. 3, 1987, pp. 6-11.

3077. "Toei's Cartoon Sales Aim at Europe, Asia." *Variety*. April 16, 1980, p. 142.

3078. "Turner Sees Lotsa Loot in Japan-Made Cartoons." *Variety*. October 31, 1984, p. 61.

3079. "Two Features Ready from Toei Animation, Eight More To Come." *Variety*. April 16, 1980, p. 140.

3080. Wang, Albert Sze-Wei. "Subtitling American-Style." *Animag*. 2:1, p. 24, 29.

3081. Willis, Donald C. "The Fantastic Asian Video Invasion: Hopping Vampires, Annoying Aliens, and Atomic Cats." *Midnight Marquee*. 1990 [?], pp. 4-11.

Manga (Comic Books)

3082. "Adam Warren: Drawing Manga for Americans." *Comics Buyer's Guide*. March 25, 1994, pp. 27-28.

3083. "Back to Viz-ness with New Video Line." *Animerica*. July 1993, p. 16.

3084. Canby, Vincent. "One U.S. Export That's Thriving in Japan." *New York Times*. November 17, 1988, p. C-25.

3085. Cyphers, Luke. "Japanese Comics Are Poised To Grab More U.S. Turf Ruled by Superheroes." *Wall Street Journal*. October 25, 1991, p. B9C.

3086. "Dark Horse Rides to War This Summer with Venus Trade Paperback." *Animerica*. July 1993, p. 37.

3087. Dennett, John, *et al.* "Dark Horse Comics." *Protoculture Addicts*. May-June 1993, p. 32.

3088. "The Devil You Say! Subtitled Devilman from L.A. Hero/D.I.E." *Animerica*. May 1993, pp. 16-17.

3089. Duke, Pat. "From the Glacier." *Protoculture Addicts*. May-June 1993, p. 35.

3090. "Epic Adds Japanese Book." *Retail Express*. January 2, 1988, p. 4.

3091. "First To Publish *Manga* Here." *Retail Express*. January 22, 1988, p. 4.

3092. Fu Bo-Nin. "Let Japanese 'Iron Soldiers' Change Their Faces: Taiwan and South

Korean Publishers Do Not Allow Japanese Comic Books To Leave." *United Daily News* (USA edition). October 5, 1993, p. 16.

3093. Gomez, Jeffrey. "An Eclipse Over the Orient: Three More Manga Epics Arrive!" *Gateways*. August 1987, pp. 13-15.

3094. Gomez, Jeffrey. "Samurai Rising: Lone Wolf and Cub Arrive in America." *Gateways*. August 1987, pp. 7-9, 11.

3095. "Japanese Cartoons Flood Korea." *Newsreview*. April 20, 1991, p. 28.

3096. "Japanese Cartoons in Korea." *Asian Media Alert*. Winter 1992, pp. 8-9.

3097. "Japanese Comics Blasting Through American Market." *Indianapolis Star*. May 5, 1988.

3098. "Join the Corps and Escape the Heat-Harmagedon and Odin from U.S.M.C." *Animerica*. July 1993, p. 17.

3099. Jundis, Orvy. "Japanese and American Comics Reflecting Influences." *WittyWorld*. Summer 1987, pp. 20-21.

3100. Ledoux, Trish. "Vizions of America." *Protoculture Addicts*. May-June 1993, p. 34.

3101. McCarthy, Helen. "American Manga: Penquins Manqué—The Genesis and Growth of Antarctic Press." *Anime UK Magazine*. 2:6, pp. 12-13.

3102. Manache-Hirochi. *Skokuminti Nipon*. (American Influence in Japan). Tokyo: n.p., n.d. Japanese.

3103. "Manga Comes to America." *Comics Buyer's Guide*. March 27, 1987, pp. 1, 3.

3104. "Manga Mania at Malibu." *Animerica*. April 1993, pp. 37-38.

3105. "Marvel Cuts Merchandising Deal with Japanese Publishing Giant." *Comics Journal*. April 1993, p. 35.

3106. O'Brien, Geoffrey. "Zukaaa! Dokitsu! Kiiiii!" *Village Voice Literary Supplement*. December 1987, pp. 31-33.

3107. Oshiguchi, Takashi. "Japanese Manga and Anime in Asia." *Animerica*. December 1993, p. 13.

3108. Schodt, Frederik L. "Thoughts on Manga in America. *Animerica*. September 1993, p. 35.

3109. "Spider-Man Webs His Way to Japan To Launch Marvel Alliance with Sho Pro."

Comics Buyer's Guide. March 12, 1993, p. 6.

3110. "Ultra-Exciting News from Harvey Comics." *Animerica*. June 1993, p. 36.

3111. "U.S. Manga Corps To Release Subtitled Odin, Explorer Woman Ray." *Animerica*. May 1993, p. 17.

3112. "Viz Plans Color Media Tie-ins." *Comics Career Newsletter*. October 1990, p. 7.

3113. Wargelin, Paul. "Netrobber: Japanese *Manga* Come to American Shores." *Comic Culture*. March 1994, p. 5.

3114. "We Want Your Artists...but Not Your Bootlegs." *Comics Journal*. February 1991, p. 19.

3115. "Wolfman, Wein To Adapt Manga for Viz." *Comics Buyer's Guide*. September 29, 1989, p. 20.

3116. "Ye Gods! It's a Crop o' Celestials From Dark Horse Comics." *Animerica*. August 1994, p. 36.

Historical Aspects

3117. Akita, Takahiro. "Manga Ga Gensaku No Nihon Eiga Risuto, 1925-1993" (A List of Japanese Films Based on the Comic Art, 1925-1993). *Fūshiga Kenkyū*. April 20, 1994, pp. 11-14.

3118. Feng Zikai. "Tan Riben de Manhua" (On Japanese Cartoons). *Yuzhou Feng* (Shanghai). October 1, 1936, pp. 120-127.

3119. "GI Adventures in Japan; Cartoons by Claude." *New York Times Magazine*. January 26, 1947, pp. 20-21.

3120. "'The Japan Punch.'" *Oriental Affairs*. May 1939, pp. 259-270.

3121. Kajii, Jun. *Sengo No Kashibon Bunka* (Postwar Booklender Culture). Tokyo: Tokōsha, 1979.

3122. Katayori, Mitsugu. "'Pekin Yumemakura' to 'Jikyoku-zu'" ("Peking Dreams" and "A Picture of the Situation"). *Fūshiga Kenkyū*. April 20, 1993, pp. 8-9.

3123. Lent, John A. "Japanese Comics." In *Handbook of Japanese Popular Culture*, edited by Richard Gid Powers and Hidetoshi Kato, pp. 221-242. Westport, Connecticut: Greenwood Press, 1989.

3124. Miyao, Shigeo. *Nihon No Giga: Rekishi To Fūzoku* (Japanese Cartoons: Their History and Place in Popular Culture). Tokyo: Dai-ichi Hōki, 1967.

3125. Murase, Miyeko. *Emaki: Narrative Scrolls from Japan*. New York: Asia Society, 1983.

3126. Nagasse, T. *La Figure Humaine dans les Estampes Japonaises*. Paris: 1934.

3127. Netto, C. and G. Wagener. *Japanischer Humor*. Leipzig: F.A. Brockhaus, 1901. 284 pp.

3128. "Nihon No Warai: Manga Sennenshi" (The Humor of Japan: 1,000 Years of Comic Art). Special edition of *Bungei Shunjū Derakkusu*. September 1975.

3129. Okada, Osamoo. "Footprints of the Japanese Post-War Cartoons." *Gha Nah Art* (Seoul). November-December 1970, pp. 84-87.

3130. Okudairo, Hideo. *Emaki: Japanese Picture Scrolls*. Rutland, Vermont: Charles E. Tuttle, 1962.

3131. Okudairo, Hideo. *Narrative Picture Scrolls*. New York: Weatherhill, 1973.

3132. Reyes, Roger. *The Male Journey in Japanese Prints*. Berkeley: University of California Press, 1989. 189 pp.

3133. "Sashi-e/Manga Ni Miru Shōwa No Gojūnen: Kabashima Katsuichi Kara *Dame Oyaji* Made" (Fifty Years of the Shōwa Period, As Seen Through Illustrations and Comic Art: From Katsuichi Kabashima to *Dame Oyaji*). Special edition of *Asahi Graph*. October 30, 1974.

3134. Shimizu, Isao. *The Biography of the Peoples Drawn by Satiric Cartoons*. Tokyo: Maruzen, 1991. 214 pp. Japanese.

3135. Shimizu, Isao. *The Cartoon and Newspaper — Asahi Weekly Encyclopedia — History of Japan No. 101*. Tokyo: Asahi Shimbunsha, 1988. 32 pp. Japanese.

3136. Shimizu, Isao. *The History of the Japanese Cartoon*. Tokyo: Iwanami Shoten, 1991. 256 pp. Japanese.

3137. Shimizu, Isao. "'Ippyō Manga-shū Shohen,' Meiji 28-Nen" ("Ippyō Cartoon Collection, the First Edition," 1895). *Fūshiga Kenkyū*. July 20, 1993, pp. 1-4.

3138. Shimizu, Isao. *The Japan Images Drawn by Foreign Cartoonists*. Tokyo: Maruzen, 1994. Japanese.

3139. Shimizu, Isao. "Shiryō Shōkai (1): 'Hi-bijutsu Gahō'" (Introduction of a Material, I: "Non-art Graphic"). *Fūshiga Kenkyū*. January 20, 1992, p. 11.

3140. Shimizu, Isao. *The World of Satiric Cartoons*. Tokyo: Chuoukoronsha, 1982. 250 pp. Japanese.

3141. Yumoto, Gōichi. "'Panchi'-shi ni Egakareta Nihon" (Japan Portrayed in the "Punch"). *Fūshiga Kenkyū*. April 20, 1992, p. 11.

Anime (Animation)

3142. Anderson, J.L. "Spoken Silents in Japanese Cinema; or, Talking to Pictures: Essaying the *Katsuben*, Contextualizing the Texts." In *Reframing Japanese Cinema*, edited by Arthur Nolletti, Jr. and David Desser, pp. 259-311. Bloomington: Indiana University Press, 1992.

3143. "Anime Time Machine 1963-1982." *This Is Animation*. No. 2, 1982, pp. 13-28.

3144. Carter, Lloyd. "In the Beginning." *The Rose*. July 1992, p. 35.

3145. "History of Japanese Animation (Parts I and 2)." In *The Tenth Hong Kong International Film Festival*, pp. 86-87. Hong Kong: Urban Council, 1986.

3146. Mori, Takuya. "Short History of Japanese Animation." *Hiroshima Festival, Daily Bulletin*. No. 6, 1987.

3147. Namiku, Takashi, ed. "History of Japanese Animated Films." *Film 1/24*. Special Issue, June 10, 1977, pp. 1-27.

3148. Patten, Fred. "Fifteen Years of U.S. Anime Fandom. Part II: 1985-1992." *Anime UK Magazine*. 3:2, pp. 34-39.

3149. Patten, Fred. "1977-1992: Fifteen Years of North American Fandom." *Anime UK Magazine*. 3:1, pp. 12-17.

3150. Patten, Frederick. "Full Circle: Japanese Animation from Early Home Studios to Personal Workshops for Home Video." *WittyWorld*. Summer 1987, pp. 31-33.

3151. Slay, Richard. "Anime B.Y. (Before Yamato)." *The Rose*. April 1992, pp. 26-27.

Caricature

3152. Ishiko, Jun. *Shōwa No Sensō Karikathua* (War Caricature in the Shōwa Era). Tokyo: Horupu Shuppan, 1985. 317 pp.

3153. Matsuyama, Fumio. *Aka Shiro Kuro: Fūshiga Shijuyonen* (Red, White, Black: Caricature 40 Some Years). Tokyo: Zōkeisha, 1969. 115 pp.

3154. Noguchi, Y. "Japanese Humour and Caricature." *Bookman*. July 1904, pp. 473-475.

3155. Shimizu, Isao. "Bakumatsu Fūshiga No Seiritsu to Hatten Katei" (The Process of the Foundation and Development of Caricature in the Late Edo Period). *Fūshiga Kenkyū*. October 20, 1993, pp. 1-7.

3156. Shimizu, Isao. "Bakumatsu Fūshiga Shiryō (1): 'Kinsei Nishiki-e Sesō-shi,' Dai-1-2-kan" (The Materials on Caricatures in the Late Tokugawa Period, I: "Modern Social History by *Nishiki-e*," vols. 1-2). *Fūshiga Kenkyū*. April 20, 1992, pp. 14-15.

3157. Shimizu, Isao. "Bakumatsu Fūshiga Shiryō (2): 'Otona' Asobi-e" (The Materials on Caricatures in the late Tokugawa Period, II: "Adult's" Pictures of Play). *Fūshiga Kenkyū*. October 20, 1992, pp. 10-11.

3158. Shimizu, Isao. "Bakumatsu Fūshiga Shiryō (3): 'Dōraku-ji Ahodara Kyō'" (The Materials on Caricatures in the late Tokugawa Period, III: "Dōraku Temple Silly Sutras"). *Fūshiga Kenkyū*. January 20, 1993, p. 10.

3159. Shimizu, Isao. "Bakumatsu Fūshiga Shiryō (4): 'Aomono Sakana Gunzei Ōkassen No Zu'" (The Materials on Caricatures in the late Tokugawa Period, IV: "A Picture of the Great Battle of the Vegetables and the Fish"). *Fūshiga Kenkyū*. April 20, 1993, pp. 8-9.

3160. Shimizu, Isao. "Bakumatsu Fūshiga Shiryō (5): 'Kodomo Asobi Takara No Atarimono'" (The Materials on Caricatures in the late Tokugawa Period, V: "Children's Play, Treasure Game"). *Fūshiga Kenkyū*. July 20, 1993, p. 15.

3161. Shimizu, Isao. "Fūshiga No Meisaku: Ieyasu No Kaita Giga Manga" (A Peculiar Work of Caricature: *Giga* Cartoon Drawn by Ieyasu). *Fūshiga Kenkyū*. October 20, 1993, p. 7.

3162. Shimizu, Isao. "Fūshiga-shi Nenpyō (1): Meiji 10-Nen (1877)" (A Chronology of the History of Caricature, I: The Year of Meiji 10 [1877]). *Fūshiga Kenkyū*. January 20, 1992, p. 13.

3163. Shimizu, Isao. "Fūshiga-shi Nenpyō (2): Taishō 5-Nen (1916)" (A Chronology of the History of Caricature, II: The Year of Taishō 5 [1916]). *Fūshiga Kenkyū*. April 20, 1992, p. 13.

3164. Shimizu, Isao. "Fūshiga-shi Nenpyō (3): Taishō 12-Nen (1923)" (A Chronology of the History of Caricature, III: The Year of Taishō 12 [1923]). *Fūshiga Kenkyū*. July 20, 1992, p. 13.

3165. Shimizu, Isao. "Fūshiga-shi Nenpyō (4): Meiji 15-Nen (1882)" (A Chronology of the History of Caricature, IV: The Year of Meiji 15 [1882]). *Fūshiga Kenkyū*. October 20, 1992, p. 13.

3166. Shimizu, Isao. "Fūshiga-shi Nenpyō (5): 1868-Nen" (A Chronology of the History of Caricature, V: The Year of 1868). *Fūshiga Kenkyū*. Janaury 20, 1993, p. 15.

3167. Shimizu, Isao. "Fūshiga-shi Nenpyō (6): Meiji 35-Nen (1902)" (A Chronology of the History of Caricature, VI: The Year of Meiji 35 [1902]). *Fūshiga Kenkyū*. April 20, 1993, p. 11.

3168. Shimizu, Isao. "Meiji Giga Nishiki-e Kenkyū (1): Shōsai Ikkei" (A Study of *Giga Nishiki-e* in the Meiji Period, I: Ikkei Shōsai). *Fūshiga Kenkyū*. January 20, 1992, pp. 2-3.

3169. Shimizu, Isao. "Meiji Giga Nishiki-e Kenkyū (2): Tsukioka Yoshitoshi, 'Kigen Kurabe'" (A Study of *Giga Nishiki-e* in the Meiji Period, II: Yoshitoshi Tsukioka, "Contest of the Temper"). *Fūshiga Kenkyū*. April 20, 1992, pp. 4-5.

3170. Shimizu, Isao. "Taishō Demokurashī to Fūshiga: Kōen Yōyaku" (Taishō Democracy and Caricature: A Summary of a Lecture). *Fūshiga Kenkyū*. January 20, 1992, pp. 4-5.

3171. Shimizu, Isao. *The World of Portrait Cartoons*. Tokyo: Chikuma Shobō, 1984. 148 pp. Japanese.

Cartoon and Humor Magazines

3172. Okamoto, Rei. "*Manga*: Japanese Wartime Cartoon Magazine." Paper presented at Popular Culture Association, Chicago, Illinois, April 9, 1994. 16 pp.

3173. Okamoto, Rei. "World War II Manga Magazines." Paper presented at Mid-Atlantic Region, Association for Asian Studies, Pittsburgh, Pennsylvania, October 22, 1994.

3174. Shimizu, Isao. *"Mangashonen" and the Comic Books in the Early Period After the War*. Tokyo: ZΩION sha, 1989. 262 pp. Japanese.

3175. Shimizu, Isao. "Manga Zasshi wa Shiryō No Hōko" (Cartoon Magazines Contain Valuable Data). *Fūshiga Kenkyū*. January 20, 1993, p. 5.

3176. Shimizu, Isao. *The Museum of Japanese Modern Cartoon Magazines. Vol. 1 — Marumaruchinbun. Part 1*. Tokyo: Kokushokankoukai, 1986. 220 pp. Japanese.

3177. Shimizu, Isao. *The Museum of Japanese Modern Cartoon Magazines. Vol. 2 — Marumaruchinbun. Part 2*. Tokyo: Kokushokankoukai, 1986. 220 pp. Japanese.

3178. Shimizu, Isao. *The Museum of Japanese Modern Cartoon Magazines. Vol. 3 — Joutoupunch*. Tokyo: Kokushokankoukai, 1986. 140 pp. Japanese.

3179. Shimizu, Isao. *The Museum of Japanese Modern Cartoon Magazines. Vol. 4 —*

Kokkeikai. Tokyo: Kokushokankoukai, 1986. 224 pp. Japanese.

3180. Shimizu, Isao. *The Museum of Japanese Modern Cartoon Magazines. Vol. 5 — Tokyo Puck. Part 1.* Tokyo: Kokushokankoukai, 1986. 164 pp. Japanese.

3181. Shimizu, Isao. *The Museum of Japanese Modern Cartoon Magazines. Vol. 6 — Jijimanga. Part 1.* Tokyo: Kokushokankoukai, 1986. 164 pp. Japanese.

3182. Shimizu, Isao. *The Museum of Japanese Modern Cartoon Magazines. Vol. 7 — Tokyo Puck. Part 2.* Tokyo: Kokushokankoukai, 1986. 172 pp. Japanese.

3183. Shimizu, Isao. *The Museum of Japanese Modern Cartoon Magazines. Vol. 8 — Osaka Puck.* Tokyo: Kokushokankoukai, 1986. 176 pp. Japanese.

3184. Shimizu, Isao. *The Museum of Japanese Modern Cartoon Magazines. Vol. 9 — Tokyo Puck. Part 3.* Tokyo: Kokushokankoukai, 1987. 220 pp. Japanese.

3185. Shimizu, Isao. *The Museum of Japanese Modern Cartoon Magazines. Vol. 10 — Mangaman.* Tokyo: Kokushokankoukai, 1987. 224 pp. Japanese.

3186. Shimizu, Isao. *The Museum of Japanese Modern Cartoon Magazines. Vol. 11 — Jijimanga. Part 2.* Tokyo: Kokushokankoukai, 1987. 172 pp. Japanese.

3187. Shimizu, Isao. *The Museum of Japanese Modern Cartoon Magazines. Vol. 12 — Yomiuri Sunday Manga.* Tokyo: Kokushokankoukai, 1987. 154 pp. Japanese.

3188. Shimizu, Isao. "Nihon Manga Shiryō-kan Shozō Shiryō (1): 'Ōsaka Pakku'" (A Collection of Nihon Manga Shiryō-kan, I: "Ōsaka Punch"). *Fūshiga Kenkyū.* October 20, 1992, pp. 14-15.

3189. Shimizu, Isao. "Nihon Manga Shiryō-kan Shozō Shiryō (2): 'Tōkyō Ponchi'" (A Collection of Nihon Manga Shiryō-kan, II: "Tōkyō Ponchi"). *Fūshiga Kenkyū.* January 20, 1993, pp. 8-9.

3190. Shimizu, Isao. "Nihon Manga Shiryō-kan Shozō, Shōwa Sengo-ki No Manga Zasshi, Shōwa 20-Nen — Shōwa 37-Nen" (Cartoon Magazines During the Postwar Shōwa Period, 1945-62, Housed in the Nihon Manga Shiryō-kan). *Fūshiga Kenkyū.* April 20, 1994, pp. 7-10.

3191. Shimizu, Isao. "Nihon Manga Shiryō-kan Shozō, Taishō, Shōwa Senzen-ki No Manga Zasshi" (Cartoon Magazines during the Taishō and the Prewar Shōwa Period, Housed in the Nihon Manga Shiryō-kan). *Fūshiga Kenkyū.* July 20, 1993, pp. 7-10.

3192. Shimizu, Isao. "Shiryō Shōkai (2): 'Yūmoa'" (Introduction of a Material, II: "Humor"). *Fūshiga Kenkyū.* January 20, 1992, p. 12.

3193. Shimizu, Isao. "Tobai Kō" (A Study of *Tobae*). *Fūshiga Kenkyū*. July 20, 1994, pp. 1-5.

3194. Yumoto, Gōichi. "Meiji Ponchi-bon No Sekai (1)" (The World of Ponchi Books in the Meiji Period, I). *Fūshiga Kenkyū*. January 20, 1993, p. 11.

Manga (Comic Books)

3195. *Asahi Shimbun*, ed. *Shōwa No Manga Ten* (Catalog for Exhibition of Comics in Shōwa). Tokyo: Asahi Shimbun, 1989. Japanese.

3196. Bungei Shunjū, ed. *Maboroshi No Kashihon Manga Daizenshū* (Anthology of the Illusive Rental Comic Books). *Bunshun Bunko* (Bunshun Books) V110-4. Tokyo: Bungei Shunjūsha, 1987.

3197. Chang, Yvonne. "Japans Tagneseriehistorie." *Seriejournalen*. September 1990, pp. 28-29.

3198. Clements, Jonathan. "Trade Surplus: Japan and Post-War Sci-Fi." *Anime UK Magazine*. 2:2, pp. 22-23.

3199. Hasebe, Toshio, ed. *Shomin Manga No Gojūnen* (Fifty Years of the People's Comics). Tokyo: Nippon Jōhō Sentā, 1976.

3200. Ishiko, Jun. *Manga Meisakukan: Sengo Manga No Shujinkōtachi* (A Museum of Comic Classics: Heroes of Postwar Comics). Tokyo: Tokuma Shoten, 1977.

3201. Ishiko, Jun. *Nihon Mangashi* (A History of Japanese Comics). Vols. 1 and 2. Tokyo: Otsuki Shoten, 1979.

3202. Ishiko, Jun. *Nihon Mangashi* (A History of Japanese Comics). Tokyo: Shakaishisōsha, 1988. 460 pp.

3203. Ishiko, Jun. *Shim Mangagaku* (A New Comicology). Tokyo: Mainichi Shimbunsha, 1978.

3204. Ishiko, Junzō. *Shengo Mangashi Nōto* (Notes on the Postwar History of Comics). Tokyo: Kinokuniya Shoten, 1975.

3205. Itō, Ippei. *Nihon Shimbun Mangashi* (A History of Japanese Newspaper Comics). Tokyo: Zōkeisha, 1980. 165 pp.

3206. Kanamori, Takeo. *Manga Shōwashi* (A History of Shōwa Era Through Comics). Tokyo: Shakai Shisōsha, 1983. 299 pp.

3207. Katayori, Mitsugu. *Sengo Manga Shisōshi* (A History of the Postwar Thoughts of Comics). Tokyo: Miraisha, 1985. 196 pp.

3208. Katayori, Mitsugu. "Shimbun Mangashi 1: Shōwa Senzen, Senchūki" (A History of Newspaper Comic Strips 1: Showa Prewar and Wartime). In *Shōwa Shimbun Mangashi*. Special Issue of *Ichioku-nin No Shōwa-shi*, pp. 46-50. Tokyo: Mainichi Shimbunsha, 1981.

3209. *Kodomo No Shōwa-shi, Shōwa Gan-nen — 20-Nen: Meisaku Comic Shū* (A History of Children's Showa Period, 1926-1945: A Collection of Famous Comics). Special edition of *Taiyō*. Tokyo: Heibonsha, 1989. Japanese.

3210. *Kodomo No Shōwa-shi, Shōwa 35-Nen — 48-Nen* (A History of Children's Showa Period, 1960-1973). Special edition of *Taiyō*. Tokyo: Heibonsha, 1990. Japanese.

3211. Matsumoto, Reiji and Satoshi Hidaka, eds. *Manga Rekishi Dai Hakubutsukan* (A Giant Museum of Comic History). Tokyo: Buronzusha, 1980.

3212. Minejima, Masayuki. *Gendai Manga No Gojunen: Mangaka Puraibashi* (Fifty Years of Modern Comics: A Private History of Comic Artists). Tokyo: Aoya Shoten, 1975.

3213. Murakami, Tomohiko, Ei Takatori, and Yoshihiro Yonezawa. *Mangaden: "Kyojin No Hoshi" Kara "Oishinbō" Made* (A Legend of Comics: From "Kyojin No Hoshi" to "Oishinbō"). Tokyo: Heibonsha, 1987. 340 pp.

3214. Ono, Kōsei and Osamu Tezuka. "Japon." In *Histoire Mondiale de la Bande Dessinée*, edited by Pierre Horay, pp. 278-285. Paris: Pierre Horay Éditeur, 1989.

3215. Parrott, L. "Laughs from Tokyo; Japanese Comics Reappear." *New York Times Magazine*. May 12, 1946, p. 28.

3216. Saikibara, Seiki. *Nihon Mangashi* (A History of Japanese Comics). Tokyo: Yūzankaku, 1924. 235 pp.

3217. Sakuta, Keiichi, Michitarō Tada, and Toshihiro Tsuganesawa. *Manga No Shujinkō: Shōwaki Nihonjin No Ningengakuteki Kōsatsu* (Comic Heroes: A Humanistic Study of the Japanese in Showa Era). Tokyo: Shiseidō, 1965. 222 pp.

3218. Schodt, Frederik L. "Sugiura Hinako and the Roots of Japanese Comics." *Mangajin*. September 1992, pp. 8-9.

3219. Shimizu, Isao. *Edo No Manga* (The Cartoons of Edo Era). Tokyo: Bungei Shunjū, 1981. 224 pp. Japanese.

3220. Shimizu, Isao. *The History of Showa Seen by Cartoons and Illustrations*. Vol. 7. Tokyo: Kodansha, 1985. 172 pp. Japanese.

3221. Shimizu, Isao. *The Japanese Cartoon History Viewed from the Cartoon Books. Part 1*. Tokyo: Nihon Koshotsu Shinsha, 1987. 92 pp. Japanese.

3222. Shimizu, Isao. *The Japanese Cartoon History Viewed from the Cartoon Books. Part 2.* Tokyo: Kotsu Mamehon No. 76, Nihon Koshotsu Shinsha, 1987. 92 pp. Japanese.

3223. Shimizu, Isao. *The Japanese Modern Cartoons. Vol. 1 — The End of the Edo Era and the Meiji Restoration.* Tokyo: Chikuma Shobō, 1986. 112 pp. Japanese.

3224. Shimizu, Isao. *The Japanese Modern Cartoons. Vol. 2 — The Age of Democratic Rights Movement.* Tokyo: Chikuma Shobō, 1985. 112 pp. Japanese.

3225. Shimizu, Isao. *The Japanese Modern Cartoons. Vol. 3 — The Age of the Sino-Japanese War.* Tokyo: Chikuma Shobō, 1985. 112 pp. Japanese.

3226. Shimizu, Isao. *The Japanese Modern Cartoons. Vol. 4 — The Age of Russo-Japanese War.* Tokyo: Chikuma Shobō, 1985. 112 pp. Japanese.

3227. Shimizu, Isao. *The Japanese Modern Cartoons. Vol. 5 — The First Half of Taisho Era.* Tokyo: Chikuma Shobō, 1985. 112 pp. Japanese.

3228. Shimizu, Isao. *The Japanese Modern Cartoons. Vol. 6 — The Latter Period of Taisho Era.* Tokyo: Chikuma Shobō, 1986. 112 pp. Japanese.

3229. Shimizu, Isao. "Japan's Rich Tradition of Cartoons and Comics." *Echoes of Peace.* January 1993, pp. 13-15.

3230. Shimizu, Isao. *Manga No Rekishi* (A History of Comics). Tokyo: Iwanami Shoten, 1991. 240 pp.

3231. Shimizu, Isao. *"Manga Shōnen" To Akabon Manga: Sengo Manga No Tanjō* ("Manga Shonen" and Akabon Manga: Birth of Postwar Comics). Tokyo: Tōsui Shobo, 250 p. 198 pp.

3232. Shimizu, Isao. *Meiji Manga Yūransen* (An Excursion Into Meiji Comic Art). Tokyo: Bungei Shunjū, 1980. 232 pp. Japanese.

3233. Shimizu, Isao. *Meiji Mangakan* (The Cartoon Museum of Meiji Era). Tokyo: Kodansha, 1979. 224 pp.

3234. Shimizu, Isao. *Meiji Manyoushu.* Tokyo: Bungei Shunjō, 1989. 264 pp. Japanese.

3235. Shimizu, Isao. *Nihon Manga No Jiten* (The Encyclopedia of Japanese Cartoon History). Tokyo: Sanseido, 1985. 256 pp. Japanese.

3236. Shimizu, Isao. "Nihon Manga Shiryō-kan Shozō Shiryō (3): 'Shōnen Pakku'" (A Collection of Nihon Manga Shiryō-kan, III: "Boys' Puck"). *Fūshiga Kenkyū.* April 20, 1993, pp. 1-4.

3237. Shimizu, Isao. "Nihon Manga Shiryō-kan Shozō Shiryō (4): 'Nihon Manga-kai Dai-4-kai Ten Shuppin Sakuhin'" (A Collection of Nihon Manga Shiryō-kan, IV: Works Submitted at the Fourth Nihon Manga-kai Exhibition). *Fūshiga Kenkyū*. April 20, 1993, p. 10.

3238. Shimizu, Isao. "Nihon Manga Shiryō-kan Shozō Shiryō (5): 'Kōraku,' Taishō 10-Nen" (A Collection of Nihon Manga Shiryō-kan, V: "Kōraku," 1922). *Fūshiga Kenkyū*. October 20, 1993, p. 14.

3239. Shimizu, Isao. "Nihon Manga Shiryō-kan Shozō Shiryō (6): 'Harō Manga,' 5-Gō (A Collection of Nihon Manga Shiryō-kan, VI: "Hello Manga," the Fifth Issue). *Fūshiga Kenkyū*. October 20, 1993, p. 15.

3240. Shimizu, Isao. "Nihon Manga Shiryō-kan Shozō Shiryō (7): 'Manga No Kuni,' Shōwa 10—15-Nen" (A Collection of Nihon Manga Shiryō-kan, VII: "The Kingdom of Comics," 1935-40). *Fūshiga Kenkyū*. January 20, 1994, pp. 13-15.

3241. Shimizu, Isao. "Nihon Manga Shiryō-kan Shozō Shiryō (8): 'Jidō Manga,' Sōkangō" (A Collection of Nihon Manga Shiryō-kan, VIII: "Children's Comics," the First Issue). *Fūshiga Kenkyū*. April 20, 1994, p. 15.

3242. Shimizu, Isao. "Nihon Manga Shiryō-kan Shozō, Taishō, Shōwa Senzen-ki No Manga-bon, Shōwa 7-Nen — Shōwa 18-Nen" (Comic Books During the Taishō and the Prewar Shōwa Period, 1932-43, Housed in the Nihon Manga Shiryō-kan). *Fūshiga Kenkyū*. January 20, 1994, pp. 9-12.

3243. Shimizu, Isao. "Nihon Manga Shiryō-kan Shozō, Taishō, Shōwa Senzen-ki No Manga-bon, Taishō 1-Nen — Shōwa 7-Nen" (Comic Books During the Taishō and the Prewar Shōwa Period, 1912-32, Housed in the Nihon Manga Shiryō-kan). *Fūshiga Kenkyū*. October 20, 1993, pp. 8-11.

3244. Shimizu, Isao. *The Satiric Cartoons and the Chronological Table of Social Manners in Meiji Taisho Era.* Tokyo: Jiyoukokuminsha, 1982. 132 pp. Japanese.

3245. Shimizu, Isao. *The Satiric Cartoons and the Chronological Table of Social Manners in Showa Era.* Tokyo: Jiyoukokuminsha, 1984. 128 pp. Japanese.

3246. Shimizu, Isao. "Senryōka Kankō Manga-bon No Taikan" (An Overview of Comic Books Published During the Occupation). *Fūshiga Kenkyū*. July 20, 1994, pp. 6-12.

3247. Shimizu, Isao. *The Social Manners History Seen by Manga in Showa Era.* Tokyo: Bungei Shunjū, 1984. 248 pp. Japanese.

3248. Shimizu, Isao. *Taiheiyō Sensōki No Manga* (Cartoons During the Pacific War). Tokyo: Bijutsu Dōjinsha, 1971. 84 pp.

3249. Shimizu, Isao, ed. *Manga, Manga, Manga-ten: Nihon Manga No 300-Nen*

(Comics Exhibition: 300 Years of Japanese Comics). Tokyo: Yomiuri Shimbunsha, 1993. 64 pp.

3250. Shiokawa, Kanako. "'The Reads' and 'Yellow Covers': Pre-Modern Predecessors of Comic Books in Japan." Special issue of *Journal of Asian Pacific Communication*, edited by John A. Lent. Forthcoming.

3251. "Shōwa Shimbun Mangashi" (A History of Newspaper Comics in the Shōwa Period). Supplement in *Ichiokunin No Shōwashi*. Tokyo: Mainichi Shimbunsha, 1977, 1981.

3252. Suyama, Keiichi. *Manga Hyakunen* (A Hundred Years of Comics). Tokyo: Masu Shobō, 1956. 231 pp.

3253. Suyama, Keiichi. *Nihon Manga Hyakunen* (One Hundred Years of Japanese Comic Art). Tokyo: Haga Shoten, 1968. 269 pp.

3254. Takida, Yū. *Shōwa Yumezōshi* (Shōwa Dream Scroll). Tokyo: Shinchōsha, 1980. 207 pp.

3255. Terada, Hirō. *Manga Shōnen-shi* (A History of *Manga Shōnen*). Tokyo: Shōnan Shuppan, 1981.

3256. Teramitsu, Tadao. *Shōden Shōwa Manga: Nansensu No Keifu* (Showa Comics: Genealogy of Nonsensical Comics). Tokyo: Mainichi Shimbunsha, 1990. 270 pp.

3257. "Tokio Kid." *Time*. June 15, 1942, p. 36.

3258. Tsurumi, Shunsuke. *Manga No Sengo Shisō* (The Postwar Thoughts of Comics). Tokyo: Bungei Shunjū, 1973. 269 pp.

3259. Yashima, Taro. *The New Sun*. New York: Henry Holt, 1943.

3260. Yonezawa, Yoshihiro. *Sengo Gyaggu Mangashi* (A Postwar History of Gag Comics). Tokyo: Shimpyōsha, 1981.

3261. Yonezawa, Yoshihiro. *Sengo SF Mangashi* (A Postwar History of Science Fiction Comics). Tokyo: Shimpyōsha, 1980.

3262. Yonezawa, Yoshihiro. *Sengo Shōjo Mangashi* (A Postwar History of Girls' Comics). Tokyo: Shimpyōsha, 1980.

3263. Yoshihiro, Kōsuke. *Manga No Gendaishi* (Contemporary History of Comic Books). Maruzen Library 83. Tokyo: Maruzen, 1993.

Political and Propaganda Cartoons

3264. Heiwa Hakubutsukan o Tsukuru Kai (Japan Peace Museum). *Kami No Sensō, Dentan: Bōryaku Senden Bira Wa Kō Kataru* (The War of the Paper, Propaganda Leaflets: Propaganda Leaflets Thus Speak). Tokyo: Emīrusha, 1990. Japanese.

3265. Ishiko, Jun. "Oppajmattazo!: Gaikoku Manga Ga Egaku Sonohi To Sonogo" (Starting Something: The Day and the Day After Portrayed in Foreign Cartoons). In *Document, Shinjuwan No Hi* (The Document of the Day of Pearl Harbor), edited by Ryūchi Sasaki, Yōichi Kibata, Nobuyoshi Takashima, Yasuhiro Fukazawa, Gen Yamazaki, and Akira Yamada. Tokyo: Ōtsuki Shoten, 1991. Japanese.

3266. Iwashita, Tetsunori. "Political Information and Satirical Prints: The Popular Image of Political Authorities in Utagawa Kuniyoshi's 'Kitaina Meii Nanbyo Ryoji." Paper presented at Association for Asian Studies, Washington, D.C., April 9, 1995.

3267. Shimizu, Isao. "Nihon Manga Ni Egakareta the Day After" (The Day After Portrayed in Japanese Cartoons). In *Document, Shinjuwan No Hi* (The Document of the Day of Pearl Harbor), edited by Ryūchi Sasaki, Yōichi Kibata, Nobuyoshi Takashima, Yasuhiro Fukazawa, Gen Yamazaki, and Akira Yamada. Tokyo: Ōtsuki Shoten, 1991. Japanese.

3268. Shimizu, Isao. "Shinryaku o Hihan Kōgeki Shita Nihon-jin no Manga" (Cartoons by the Japanese Who Criticized and Attacked the Invasion). *Fūshiga Kenkyū*. April 20, 1992, pp. 1-3.

3269. Sodei, Rinjiro. "Satire Under the Occupation: The Case of Political Cartoons." Discussion by John W. Dower. In *The Occupation of Japan: Arts and Culture: The Proceedings of the Sixth Symposium.* Sponsored by the MacArthur Memorial, edited by Thomas W. Burkman, pp. 93-123. Norfolk, Virginia: General Douglas MacArthur Foundation, 1988.

3270. Suzuki, Akira and Akira Yamamoto. *Hiroku, Bōryaku Senden Bira: Taiheiyō Sensō No "Kami No Bakudan"* (The Secret Record of Propaganda Leaflets: "The Paper Bomb" in the Pacific War). Tokyo: Kōdansha, 1977. Japanese.

3271. Zarrow, Peter. "The Gentle Art of Fengci: Irony, Sarcasm and Savage Ridicule in the Early Twentieth Century." Paper presented at Association for Asian Studies, Washington, D.C., April 8, 1995.

Anime (Animation)

3272. Alexander, Garth. "If Pigs Had Wings...." *Variety.* August 10, 1992, p. 33.

3273. "Anicomic Set To Market Animated Programs, Comics." *Variety*. October 15, 1980, p. 223.

3274. "Animated Pix Still Dominate Tokyo." *Variety*. April 20, 1983, p. 29.

3275. "Animation Sensation." *Japan Pictorial* (North American Editon). 5:2 (1982), pp. 1-9.

3276. "Animation Update." *Animag*. 2:1, pp. 5-7.

3277. "Animation Update." *Animag*. No. 12, pp. 5-7.

3278. "AnimeCon." *Animag*. 2:1, pp. 8-16.

3279. "Anime Directory of United States." *Anime UK Magazine*. 2:5, pp. 14-15.

3280. "Animeland." *Newtype*. July 1988, pp. 64-73.

3281. "Anime News: Dateline Japan." *Animerica*. November 1992, pp. 3-7.

3282. "Anime Soapbox." *Anime UK Magazine*. 3:4, p. 25.

3283. "Anime Success." *Big O Magazine*. December 1993, p. 60.

3284. Arriola, George A. "Anime Update." *Toon Magazine*. Fall 1993, pp. 78-79.

3285. "Art." *Newtype*. July 1988, pp. 130-133.

3286. Bailey, James. "At the Movies." *Wilson Quarterly*. Summer 1985, pp. 46-79.

3287. Bailey, James. "Godzilla vs Doraemon: The Japanese Movie Industry in Transition." *Mangajin*. September 1994, pp. 14-19, 44, 50.

3288. Baricord, de Giovanni, Pietroni, Rossi, and Tunesi. *Cartoonia Anime, Guida al Cinema di Animazione Giappoese*. Bologna: Granata Press, 1991.

3289. Bernardo, Carmen. "Traces of Japanese Literature in Anime and Manga." *The Rose*. January 1993, p. 20.

3290. Bernhardi, Jill. "Anime Kyo UK — Britain's Only National Anime Fan Club." *The Rose*. January 1994, p. 27.

3291. Byrne, Chuck. "Animekomikkusu: Japanese Animation Comics." *Print*. November-December 1988, pp. 158-163.

3292. Carter, Lloyd. "Anime Shoppers' Guide to Atlanta." *The Rose*. April 1992, p. 34.

3293. "Catch Up! Kadokawa Anime." *Newtype*. July 1988, pp. 4-15.

3294. Chaney, Steve. "Animeigo; Licensed, Subtitled, Quality Japanese Animation." *The Rose*. September 1990, pp. 14-15.

3295. Clements, Jonathan. "The Nobility of Failure: Animated Classics of Japanese Literature." *Anime UK Magazine*. 3:4, pp. 8-9.

3296. "Combating Third World Illiteracy with Anime." *Animerica*. April 1993, p. 12.

3297. Cormier-Rodier, Béatrice and Béatrice Fleury-Vilatte. *Unesco Courier*. October 1992, pp. 17-20.

3298. Cotterill, David. "The Anime Network." *Anime UK Magazine*. 2:2, pp. 30-31.

3299. "Creation." *This Is Animation*. No. 3, 1982, pp. 61-71.

3300. Dunn, Bob and Joe Doughrity. "Readers' Poll." *Japanimation*. No. 3, 1987, pp. 16-17.

3301. "Early Summer Anime Headline." *Newtype*. July 1988, pp. 76-85.

3302. "Fanscene Roundup." *Anime UK Magazine*. 2:1, p. 34. (UK, Europe, USA).

3303. "Fanscene Roundup." *Anime UK Magazine*. 2:2, p. 37. (Canada, Belgium).

3304. "Fanscene Roundup." *Anime UK Magazine*. 2:3, p. 37; 2:4, p. 37; 2:6, p. 39; 3:1, p. 39; 3:2, p. 42; 3:3, p. 42.

3305. Felton, Jay. "Anime Fandom in Britain." *The Rose*. March 1991, p. 14.

3306. "Femme-Led Cartoons with Classical Music from Orient Films." *Variety*. April 16, 1980, p. 140.

3307. "From Red Rasher to Raccoon Dog...Studio Ghibli's Animal House." *Animerica*. April 1994, p. 11.

3308. Gibson, Robert W. "Hokuto No Ken." *Animag*. 1:3 (1987), pp. 14-20.

3309. "Girls with Guns." *Animenominous*! Summer 1990, pp. 2-6.

3310. Guevara, Adam. "San Francisco Guide to Anime Shopping." *The Rose*. October 1994, pp. 30-31.

3311. Imamura, Taihei. "Japanese Art and the Animated Cartoon." *The Quarterly of Film, Radio and Television*. Spring 1953, pp. 217-222.

3312. *Japanese Animation Film Festival*. Program. Sydney: Japan Foundation, 1990. 12 pp.

3313. Keenan, Woodie. "You Gotta Fight the Powers That Program." Brown Universtiy *Independent*. February 27, 1992, p. 17.

3314. Keller, Chris. "Why We Do What We Do." *V. Max*. No. 2, p. 2.

3315. Kenny, Glenn. "Manga Mania — A Beginner's Guide to Japanese Animation." *Pulse*! August 1992, pp. 77-78.

3316. Kister, D.M. "Japanimation." *Heavy Metal*. March 1984, p. 7.

3317. Kondo Masaki. "The Impersonalization of the Self in an Image Society." *Iris*. Spring 1993, pp. 37-48.

3318. Kurcfeld, Michael. "Animation: What's Next?" *Animag*. 2:1, pp. 43-45.

3319. Kyte, Steve. "A to Z of Anime." *Anime UK Magazine*. December 1991 and ongoing.

3320. Kyte, Steve. "Anime A to Z: A." *Anime UK Magazine*. June/July 1992, pp. 16-17.

3321. Kyte, Steve. "Anime A-Z: Part Two—'B.'" *Anime UK Magazine*. August/September 1992, p. 10.

3322. Kyte, Steve. "Anime A-Z: 'C.'" *Anime UK Magazine*. October/November 1992, p. 25.

3323. Kyte, Steve. "Anime A-Z: 'D.'" *Anime UK Magazine*. December 1992/January 1993, p. 34.

3324. Kyte, Steve. "A to Z of Anime: G." *Anime UK Magazine*. 2:1, p. 27.

3325. Kyte, Steve. "A to Z of Anime: I, J." *Anime UK Magazine*. 2:2, p. 24.

3326. Kyte, Steve. "A to Z of Anime: K, L." *Anime UK Magazine*. 2:3, p. 32.

3327. Kyte, Steve. "A to Z of Anime: M." *Anime UK Magazine*. 2:4, pp. 10-11.

3328. Kyte, Steve. "A to Z of Anime." *Anime UK Magazine*. 2:5, p. 18.

3329. Kyte, Steve. "A to Z of Anime: O." *Anime UK Magazine*. 2:6, p. 18.

3330. Kyte, Steve. "A to Z of Anime: P." *Anime UK Magazine*. 3:1, p. 25.

3331. Kyte, Steve. "A to Z of Anime: R." *Anime UK Magazine*. 3:2, p. 10.

3332. Kyte, Steve. "A to Z of Anime: R, S." *Anime UK Magazine*. 3:4, p. 18.

3333. Kyte, Steve. "A to Z of Anime: S." *Anime UK Magazine*. 3:5, p. 6.

3334. Ledoux, Trish. "The Animerica Ultimate Anime Guide." *Animerica*. June 1994, pp. 60-62.

3335. McCarthy, Helen. *Anime! A Beginner's Guide to Japanese Animation*. London: Titan Books, 1993. 64 pp.

3336. McCarthy, Helen. *Manga, Manga, Manga: A Celebration of Japanese Animation at the ICA Cinema*. London: Island World Communications, 1992.

3337. Malone, Patricia. "'But They Don't Look Japanese.'" *Anime-Zine*. No. 3, p. 5.

3338. "Marionette Generation." *Newtype*. July 1988, pp. 109-116.

3339. Martin, Kathy. "Manga Done Right." *Animag*. 1:3 (1987), pp. 12-13, 48.

3340. Matsuzaki, James. "Mikimoto Mania." *Animerica*. November 1992, pp. 9-11.

3341. "'Metamorphoses.'" *Funnyworld*. Fall 1978, pp. 48-50.

3342. Miller, August. "Language of Animation." *Los Angeles Japanese News*. February 4, 1991, pp. 1, 3.

3343. Nash, Scott. "Adventures in Japan: How To Find Anime in Japan." *The Rose*. January 1991, pp. 19-20.

3344. "Newtype Express." *Newtype*. July 1988, pp. 27-35.

3345. "Newtype Forum." *Newtype*. July 1988, pp. 98-105.

3346. "Newtype Press." *Newtype*. July 1988, pp. 36-47.

3347. Oshiguchi, Takashi. "Animation Events in Japan." *Animerica*. May 1994, p. 15.

3348. Oshiguchi, Takashi. "Animation Magazines." *Animerica*. February 1994, p. 13.

3349. Oshiguchi, Takashi. "Animation Schools." *Animerica*. March 1994, p. 13.

3350. Oshiguchi, Takashi. "From Manga to Anime." *Animerica*. April 1993, p. 15.

3351. Oshiguchi, Takashi. "The Portrayal of Sex in Japanese Animation." *Animerica*. August 1994, p. 15.

3352. "Paper Theater." *V. Max*. No. 6, p. 40.

3353. Patten, Fred. "Japan + Animation = Japanimation!" *Starlog*. April 1986, pp. 36-40.

3354. Patten, Fred. "Japan + Animation = Japanimation!" Part II. *Starlog*. May 1986, pp. 65-68.

3355. Patten, Fred. "Japanese Animation: The Cult Grows Up." *Animation Magazine*. Summer 1990, pp. 28-30.

3356. "Roman Album: No, They're Not Records." *Animenominous*! Autumn 1990, pp. 2-5.

3357. Santiago, Merlene. "Films Show Richness of Japanese Animation." Cleveland, Ohio *Plain Dealer*. April 19, 1991, p. 8.

3358. Savage, Lorraine. "Japanese vs English Translation." *The Rose*. May 1989, p. 8.

3359. "The Shaping of Protoculture." *Protoculture Addicts*. December 1990, p. 7; February 1991, pp. 8-10; April-May 1991, p. 7; June-July 1991, pp. 8-9.

3360. Shur, Mike. "Confessions of an Anime Junkie." Brown University *Independent*. February 27, 1992, p. 16.

3361. Simmons, Mark. "Anime Ja Nai." *Animag*. No. 12, pp. 34-35.

3362. Simmons, Mark and Julie Davis. "Anime Ja Nai: A Continuing Series on the World Behind the Screen." *Animag*. 2:2, pp. 66-68.

3363. Smith, Edward. "Japanese Animated Film: A Study of Narrative Intellectual Montage and Metamorphosis Structures for Semiotic Unit Sequencing." Ph.D. dissertation, University of Iowa, 1972.

3364. Smith, Toren. "News from Japan." *Anime-Zine*. 2, 1987, pp. 35-37.

3365. Smith, Toren and Graham Miyako. *A Viewer's Guide to Japanese Animation*, edited by Steven R. Johnson. 2nd Ed. Los Angeles: Books Nippon, 1987. 48 pp.

3366. Sternbach, Rick. "The Year in Anime, 1994." *Animerica*. January 1994, pp. 10-11.

3367. Strom, Frank E. "On the Trail of the Elusive Japanese Monster." *Anime-Zine*. No. 1, 1986, pp. 19-25.

3368. Taffler, Danny. "How To Fool an Anime Fan!" *Anime UK Magazine*. 2:3, pp. 28-29.

3369. Takahashi, Noboru. "Developmental Changes of Interests to Animated Stories in Toddlers Measured by Eye Movement While Watching Them." *Psychologia: An*

International Journal of Psychology in the Orient. March 1991, pp. 63-68.

3370. Takahashi, Noboru and Tsukiko Sugioka. "The Developmental Study of Children's Understanding of Animated Cartoon." *Japanese Journal of Educational Psychology.* June 1988, pp. 135-143.

3371. Teng Man-Chiu. "The Third International Animation Festival — Hiroshima '90." *Monthly Comic Magazine* (Hong Kong). December 1990, pp. 82-83.

3372. *This Is Animation 2: Fantasy, Meruhen Shōjo Anime* (Fantasy, Fables, Girls' Animation). Tokyo: Shōgakukan, 1982. 132 pp. Japanese.

3373. *This Is Animation 3: Sports, Gag, Life Anime.* Tokyo: Shōgakukan, 1982. 132 pp. Japanese.

3374. "Trends in Japanese Animation." *The Rose.* January 1993, pp. 18-19.

3375. "What Makes the Japanese Laugh?" *Apropos.* No. 4, 1986, pp. 90-96.

3376. Williams, John. "Profile." *V. Max.* No. 2, pp. 11-12.

3377. Wolfe, Ken. "Japan: Shop 'Til You Drop." *The Rose.* January 1991, p. 20.

3378. Yang, Jeff. "Anime Rising." *Village Voice.* November 1992.

3379. Yelverton, Brian. "Mondo Anime." *The Rose.* March 1991, p. 12.

Anthologies

3380. "Ah! New OAV Series from AnimEigo." *Animerica.* October 1993, p. 16.

3381. "Creation." *This Is Animation.* No. 2, 1982, pp. 61-85.

3382. "Dramatic Scenes." *This Is Animation.* No. 2, 1982, pp. 29-44.

3383. Grossman, Scott. "Synopses." *The Rose.* March 1989, p. 14; September 1989, pp. 14-15; January 1990, p. 18.

3384. Jones, Roy, *et al.* "CD Reviews." *The Rose.* July 1994, p. 27.

3385. Karahashi, Takayuki, Trish Ledoux, and Toshifumi Yoshida. "Animation Update." *Animag.* No. 6, 1990, p. 3.

3386. Keller, Chris. "Choice Cuts: Compact Discs." *V. Max.* No. 8, pp. 24-27.

3387. "Mini Synopses." *The Rose.* November 1990, p. 17; March 1991, p. 18; May 1991, p. 19; January 1992, p. 27; April 1992, p. 25; January 1993, p. 21; April 1993, p. 21; January 1994, p. 28.

3388. "Original Illustrations." *This Is Animation*. No. 3, 1982, pp. 77-92.

3389. Oshiguchi, Takashi. "TV Animation and OAVs." *Animerica*. September 1993, p. 13.

3390. *A Viewer's Guide to Japanese Animation*. Translated by Toren Smith and Miyako Graham; edited by Steven R. Johnson. 2nd Ed. Los Angeles, California: Books Nippon, 1987. 48 pp.

3391. Wiles, Wade and Bruce Carlson. "Mini Anime Reviews." *The Rose*. July 1994, p. 31 ("Plastic Little," "Barefoot Ginrei," Emblem of Gude," "Touch").

Games and Toys

3392. "Anime Game On!" *Anime UK Magazine*. June/July 1992, pp. 18-20.

3393. Batio, Christopher. "Japanese Phone Cards Are As Hot As the Sun." *Phone Card Collector*. November 18, 1994, pp. 26-27.

3394. Evans, Peter J. "It's Alive!" *Anime UK Magazine*. August/September 1992, pp. 24-27.

3395. "Fantasy South." *Anime UK Magazine*. 2:6, p. 32. (Model Club).

3396. "Fraser Gray's Modellers World." *Anime UK Magazine*. 2:3, pp. 26-27.

3397. Friedland, Jonathan. "Kid Stuff." *Far Eastern Economic Review*. June 9, 1994, pp. 61-62.

3398. Friedland, Jonathan. "Playing Games." *Far Eastern Economic Review*. January 20, 1994, pp. 42-44.

3399. Hudnall, James D. "The Games People Play." *Animerica*. April 1993, p. 18.

3400. "Japanese Win WWII in Video Games, Comics." *Korea Times Guide to English Study*. July 8, 1994, p. 1.

3401. Keller, Chris. "Confessions of a Game Show Host." *Animag*. 2:3, p. 8.

3402. Koh, Wayne. "Robotech." *Gateways*. September 1986, pp. 6-7, 26.

3403. McCarthy, Helen. "Model Club Special." *Anime UK Magazine*. December 1992/January 1993, pp. 26-27.

3404. "Mecha File." *Mecha Press*. December 1992, pp. 12-15.

3405. Oshiguchi, Takashi. "The RPG Connection." *Animerica*. July 1993, p. 15.

3406. Ouellette, Martin. "Model Reviews." *Protoculture Addicts*. July-August 1993, pp. 22-23.

3407. Overton, Wil. "Games Pocket." *Anime UK Magazine*. 2:3, p. 33.

3408. Pearl, Steve. "Game Review: Duo Anime—Urusei Yatsura CD-ROM Game." *The Rose*. January 1995, p .27.

3409. Perrin, Steve. "Games: DC, Japan and PSIS." *Comics Feature*. July 1986, pp. 42-45.

3410. Riddick, David and James Teal. "Animag Games Column." *Animag*. 2:1, pp. 46-47.

3411. Swallow, Jim. "The Roleplaying Connection." *Anime UK Magazine*. August/September 1992, pp. 22-23.

3412. Teal, James. "Video Games and Other Amusements: Dragon Ball Z, 'Super Legendary Battle.'" *Animerica*. July 1993, p. 56.

3413. Vézina, Marc-Alex. "Gencon 92." *Mecha Press*. August-September 1992, pp. 6-7.

3414. Vézina, Marc-Alex. "Palladium Games' Macross II." *Protoculture Addicts*. January-February 1994, p. 19.

3415. Ward, Brian. "Hokuto No Ken 6: For the Super Famicom." *The Rose*. July 1993, p. 15.

3416. Wark, McKenzie. "The Video Game As an Emergent Media Form." *Media Information Australia*. February 1994, pp. 21-30.

3417. Watson, Paul. "Game Zone." *Anime UK Magazine*. 3:4, pp. 12-13.

3418. Watson, Paul. "Game Zone: Dragon Ball Z 2." *Anime UK Magazine*. 3:2, pp. 12-13.

3419. Watson, Paul. "Game Zone: Latest Imports." *Anime UK Magazine*. 3:1, p. 18.

3420. Watson, Paul. "Model Club." *Anime UK Magazine*. 2:2, p. 25.

3421. Watson, Paul. "Model Club." *Anime UK Magazine*. October/November 1992, pp. 18-19.

3422. Wolfe, Gary. "The Force of Mekton." *Gateways*. September 1986, pp. 8-9.

Genres

3423. Crawley, Tony. "SF in the East." *Starburst*. January 1980[?], pp. 52-55. ("Future Robot Dartanias").

3424. Kyte, Steve. "Heavy Metal Heaven — A History of the Robot in Anime." Privately printed for distribution at 1990 National Science Fiction Convention. Reprinted in *Anime Kyo News*. 1992.

3425. Patten, Fred. "Dawn of the Warrior Robots." *Fangoria*. February 1980, pp. 30-35.

3426. Patten, Fred. "Force Five: Previewing an Ambitious New Animated Science Fiction Series!" *Fangoria*. October 1980, pp. 52-56.

3427. Schodt, Frederik. "Invasion of the Robots." *PHP Intersect*. December 1985, pp. 30-35.

3428. Sciacca, Tom. "Shogun: Battle of the Afternoon Warriors." *Mediascene*. January-February 1979, pp. 25-27.

3429. "Sci-Fi Cartoon Still Leads Tokyo B.O." *Variety*. September 3, 1980, pp. 32, 36.

3430. Siegel, Mark. "Foreigner As Alien in Japanese Science Fantasy." *Science Fiction Studies*. 12 (1985), pp. 252-263.

3431. Strom, Frank E. "On the Trail of the Elusive Japanese Monster." Anime-Zine. No. 2, 1987, pp. 30-34.

Music

3432. Altstaetter, Karl. "Robotech: The Music of an Era." *Protoculture Addicts*. January-February 1993, p. 13.

3433. Keller, Chris. "Consonance and Discord." *V. Max*. No. 3, pp. 10-12.

3434. Keller, Chris. "Shinjuku Loft." *V. Max*. No. 6, pp. 26-28.

3435. Keller, Chris. "The Music and the Madness." *V. Max*. No. 1, pp. 4-6.

3436. "Lyrics." *Protoculture Addicts*. February 1991, p. 13.

3437. Marin, Jean-Philippe. "Background Music Anime Style." *Protoculture Addicts*. January-February 1993, pp. 14-20.

3438. Overton, Wil. "A Beginner's Guide to Anime Music." *Anime UK Magazine*. 2:6, pp. 26-27.

3439. "Shinjuku Loft." *V. Max.* No. 5, pp. 22-23.

3440. Taylor, James S. "How To Access New Sources of Anime and Music." *Protoculture Addicts.* January-February 1994, pp. 20-24.

3441. Taylor, James S. "Japan Rocks." *Protoculture Addicts.* January-February 1993, pp. 9-12.

3442. Williams, John. "Ryūdō Gumi." *V. Max.* No. 4, pp. 25-27.

Technical Aspects

3443. "Animation Practical Guide." *This Is Animation.* No. 2, 1982, pp. 86-92.

3444. "Animation Practical Guide." *This Is Animation.* No. 3, 1982, pp. 72-76.

3445. "Another World of Animation: Commercial Animation, Model Animation." *This Is Animation.* No. 2, 1982, pp. 93-108.

3446. "Electronic Comics." *Asian Mass Communication Bulletin.* September 1980, p. 16.

3447. "The Great Debate, Subbing or Dubbing." *Anime UK Magazine.* 2:6, pp. 35-37.

3448. Kenji, Kira and Kazuo Fukui. "Input Techniques for 3D Animation." *NHK Laboratories Note.* June 1984, pp. 1-14.

3449. Kurtin, Dana. "Animated Plastic." *Animag.* 2:3, pp. 55-56.

3450. Ledoux, Trish. "Animated Plastic." *Animag.* No. 11, pp. 49-50.

3451. McCarthy, Helen. "How Anime Is Made." *Anime UK Magazine.* 3:2, pp. 16-18.

3452. Machida, Masahiko. "Recent Trends in the Application of Computer Graphics and Animation Technology in Television Broadcasting." *Studies of Broadcasting.* March 1984, pp. 5-16.

3453. Mayo, Bill. "Modeling." *The Rose.* March 1991, p. 16.

3454. Mayo, Bill. "Modeling: Those Eyes!" *The Rose.* May 1991, p. 23.

3455. Oshiguchi, Takashi. "Mecha Design." *Animerica.* June 1993, p. 15.

3456. Oshiguchi, Takashi. "Voice Actors." *Animerica.* May 1993, p. 15.

3457. Patten, Frederick. "All Those Japanese Animation Soundtracks." *Cinema Score.* Winter 1986 - Summer 1987, pp. 135-139.

3458. Simmons, Mark. "Mecha File." *Animag*. No. 12, pp. 42-47.

3459. Takahashi, J.K. "The Making of Ronin: A Stick Puppet Animation Adventure." *Super-Eight Filmmaker*. September-October 1975, pp. 14-17.

3460. Teal, James. "Mecha File: A Continuing Series on the Mechanics and Robots of Japanese Animation." *Animag*. No. 6, 1988, p. 40; No. 7, 1989, p. 42; No. 9, 1989. pp. 38-39; No. 11, 1989, pp. 38-40; No. 6, 1990, pp. 39-44; 2:2, pp. 46-49.

3461. Wickstrom, Andy. "Latest from Japan: Animated Adventures with Pop-Rock Sound." *Philadelphia Inquirer*. October 24, 1991, p. 10-D.

Television

3462. Akiyama, Takashiro and Sachiko Imaizumi Kodaira. *Children and Television: A Study of New TV Programs for Children Based on the Pilot of an Animated Production*. Tokyo: NHK (Japan Broadcasting Corporation), 1987. 31 pp.

3463. Burton, Jack. "Japanese TV Mixes Variety, Drama and Voyeurism." *Advertising Age*. March 12, 1984, pp. M-10-M-11, M-20.

3464. Henderson, Chris. "Fresh Japanese Films for Cable-TV." *Comics Scene*. March 1983, p. 14.

3465. Iwao, Sumiko, Ithiel de Sola Pool, and Shigeru Hagiwara. "Japanese and U.S. Media: Some Cross-Cultural Insights into TV Violence." *Journal of Communication*. Spring 1981, pp. 28-36.

3466. Katori, Atsuko. "A Content Analysis of Japanese T.V. Animation Films." *Soshioroji*. September 1983, pp. 39-57.

3467. "Kidvid Cartoons in Japan Stress Cuteness, Not Gore." *Variety*. November 3, 1982, pp. 49, 63.

3468. Kodaira, Sachiko Imaizumi. *Television for Children in Japan: Trends and Studies*. Tokyo: Japan Broadcasting Corporation, 1986. 57 pp.

3469. Leahy, Kevin. "Zutto Anime Ga Suki Datta." *The Rose*. April 1993, p. 19.

3470. Lin, Carolyn A. "Cultural Differences in Message Strategies: A Comparison between American and Japanese TV Commercials." *Journal of Advertising Research*. July/August 1993, pp. 40-48.

3471. Lu Tzu-Ying. "The Midsummer Night Beyond Time and Space." *Monthly Comic Magazine* (Hong Kong). No. 0, 1990, pp. 74-77.

3472. Media Factory, Inc. *Zutto Anime Ga Suki Datta*. N.p.: Media Factory, Inc., 1993. 196 pp.

3473. Miller, Bob. "Video Comics." *Comics Scene*. August 1991, pp. 38-39.

3474. Nakamura, Shoichi, *et al*. "Cartoon Programs on TV." *TV Programming* (YTV, Osaka). 1972, pp. 150-162.

3475. Patten, Fred. "TV Animation in Japan." *Fanfare*. Spring 1980, pp. 9-19.

3476. Patten, Frederick. "2½ Carrots Tall: TV's First Animated Cartoon Star." *Comics Scene*. November 1982; January 1983.

3477. Rowe, Allen. "Space Cobra." *Japanimation*. No. 3, 1987, pp. 18-19.

3478. "The Tokyo Television Report." *Animerica*. October 1994, pp. 16-17.

3479. "Unrivalled for Eager Viewing." *TV World*. August 1982, pp. 24-25.

Theme Parks

3480. do Rosario, Louise. "Woes in Wonderland." *Far Eastern Economic Review*. April 9, 1992, p. 54.

3481. "Of Mice and Yen." *Sojourn*. No. 33, 1994, pp. 4-9.

3482. "Under Disney's Magic Spell." *Asiaweek*. July 6, 1994, p. 40.

Comic Strips

3483. Allen, Caron. *Glimpses of Japan Through Comics*. Urbana, Illinois: University of Illinois, Center for Asian Studies, 1985. 80 pp.

3484. Bumiller, Elisabeth. "Cartoonist Highlights World of the 'OL.'" *Japan Times*. August 29, 1991.

3485. Grant, Vern. "Samurai Superstrips." *Comics Journal*. October 1984, pp. 91-94.

3486. Hisae, Shirai. "Reading 4-Frame Comic Strips." *Nihongo Journal*. July 1994, pp. 17-21.

3487. Horvat, Andrew. "By the Book or the Comic." *Far Eastern Economic Review*. June 20, 1991, pp. 69-70.

3488. Shimizu, Isao. "92-Nen No Shimbun Manga" (Newspaper Cartoons in 1992). *Fūshiga Kenkyū*. July 20, 1993, pp. 5-6.

3489. Yoyozuya, Ryuichi. "Evaluation of Oral Fluency in English As a Foreign Language." Master's thesis, Hiroshima University, 1982. 121 pp.

Manga (Comic Books)

3490. Balfour, Brad. "Japanese Comics." *Spin.* August 1988, p. 48.

3491. Barson, Michael S. "Mangal Horde." *Heavy Metal.* March 1984, p. 6.

3492. Beatty, Terry. "Book Guide." *Comics Buyer's Guide.* September 30, 1983, pp. 42, 44, 46.

3493. Buckley, Sandra. "Le Son de la Violence: Court-Circuiter la Voix dans la Bande Dessinée Japonaise." *Iris.* Spring 1993, pp. 49-56.

3494. Buckley, Sandra. "'Penguin in Bondage': A Graphic Tale of Japanese Comic Books." In *Technoculture*, edited by Constance Penley and Andrew Ross, pp. 163-195. Minneapolis: University of Minnesota Press, 1991.

3495. "Capitalist Comics." *East-West Perspectives.* Fall 1980, p. 31.

3496. Chang, Yvonne. "Tegneserie-Museer i Japan." *Seriejournalen.* September 1990, pp. 29-30.

3497. Clements, Jonathan. "Back to the Edge of the World." *Anime UK Magazine.* 2:3, p. 36.

3498. "College Students Like Comics." *NSK News Bulletin.* May 31, 1979, p. 8.

3499. *Comic Box.* August 1993. Issue devoted to "Summary of Comics in 1992." Japanese.

3500. "Cool Comics." *Animenominous*! Autumn 1990, pp. 13-15.

3501. Corcoran, E. "Laughing Matters." *Scientific American.* July 1988, p. 114.

3502. Cowie, Geoff. "Modern Japanese Graphic Art: The Best of Manga." *Anime UK Magazine.* 3:5, pp. 15-17.

3503. Darlin, Damon. "Grown Men in Japan Still Read Comics and Have Fantasies." *Wall Street Journal.* July 21, 1987, pp. 1, 13.

3504. Davies, Derek. "Traveller's Tales." *Far Eastern Economic Review.* March 1, 1990, p. 26.

3505. Desmond, Edward W. "They're Infectious! A Bout of Manga Mania." *Time*. November 1, 1993, pp. 46-47.

3506. Fallows, James. "The Japanese Are Different from You and Me." *Atlantic Monthly*. September 1986, pp. 35-41.

3507. Faur, Jean-Claude. "Japanese Comics." *Bédésup*. 3-4 Trimestre 1988, pp. 24-28.

3508. Ferrigno, Robert. "Made in Japan: These Cartoons Are Not Just for Kids." *Orange County* (CA.) *Register*. September 21, 1987, pp. E-1, E-8.

3509. Ford, Glyn and Nakajima Keiko. "Manga Mania in Japan." *New Statesman*. October 7, 1983, pp. 22-23.

3510. "Forlag Tilbagekalder 5 Mio. Seriehefter." *Seriejournalen*. March 1991, p. 11.

3511. Fujishima, Usaku. *Manga Bōkoku* (Degenerate Comics). Tokyo: Mainichi Shimbunsha, 1970. 254 pp.

3512. "Gendai Manga No Techō" (A Handbook of Modern Comics). Special edition of *Kokubungaku: Kaishaku to Kyozai No Kenkyū* (Japanese Literature: Study of Criticism and Teaching Materials). April 1981.

3513. Gomez, Jeffrey. "Manga! Manga! The Universe of Japanese Comics." *Gateways*. August 1987, p. 10.

3514. Groensteen, Thierry. *Il Mondo dei Manga*. Bologna: Granata, 1991.

3515. Groensteen, Thierry. *L'Universe des Mangas. Une Introduction à la Bande Dessinée Japonaise*. Brussels: Casterman, 1991. 136 pp.

3516. Haga, Tōru, Ai Maeda, Tadayasu Sakai, and Isao Shimizu. *Kindai Manga* (Modern Comics). 6 Vols. Tokyo: Chikuma Shobō, 1985.

3517. Halloran, Fumiko Mori. "Best Sellers." *Wilson Quarterly*. Summer 1985, pp. 46-79.

3518. Hirayama, Noriko. "Mystery of Kanashibari: Issues of the Sleep Paralysis Phenomenom in Japan." Unpublished manuscript, University of Pennsylvania, 1994. (In John A. Lent's collection).

3519. Hiroyuki, Nanba. "Yoshimoto Banana: 'Manga Sedai' No Jun-Bungaku." In *Josei Sakka No Shinryū*, special volume of *Kokubungaku: Kaishaku to Kanshō*, edited by Hasegawa Izumi. Tokyo: Shibundō, 1991.

3520. Horn, Maurice. "Comix International." *Heavy Metal*. November 1980, p. 7.

3521. Hososuga, Atsushi. "Gendai Komikku No Shinchoku Jōkyō" (The Progress of

Contemporary Comics). *Fūshiga Kenkyū*. January 20, 1992, pp. 10, 16.

3522. Ichikawa, Hirokazu. "Comics Aren't Just for Kids Anymore." *ST*. February 28, 1992, p. 6.

3523. "In Japan, a Rush for Comics." *Asiaweek*. March 21, 1980, pp. 44, 47.

3524. Ishiko, Junzō. *Gendai Manga No Shisō* (Intellectual Currents in Modern Comics). Tokyo: Taihei Shuppan, 1970.

3525. Ishiko, Junzō. *Manga Geijutsuron* (An Essay on the Art of Comics). Tokyo: Fuji Shoin, 1967. 271 pp.

3526. Ishiko, Junzō, Jun Kajii, Asajirō Kikuchi and Shin Gondō. *Gendai Manga Ronshū* (Essays on Modern Comics). Tokyo: Seirindo, 1969. 284 pp.

3527. "Japanese Comics." *Bédésup*. 3rd-4th Trimester 1989, pp. 24-28.

3528. "Japanese Comics." Clipping file. 1 portfolio. Russel B. Nye Popular Culture Collection's Popular Culture Vertical File, Michigan State University, East Lansing, Michigan.

3529. Kanoh, Masahiro. "Le Japon, Ce Continent Inconnu." *Les Cahiers de la Bande Dessinée*. (Grenoble). 71, 1986, pp. 86-88.

3530. Katagiri, Hiroe. "High School Students' Views on Comics: Results of a Questionnaire." *Dokusho Kagaku*. 22 (1979), pp. 39-50.

3531. Kato, Hisao. "A View of the Con from Across the Pacific." In *San Diego Comic Convention 1989*, pp. 78-79. San Diego: San Diego Comic-Con Committee, 1989.

3532. Kobayashi, Katsuyo. *Misesu Manga Gakkō e Iku* (A Married Woman Goes to a School of Comics). Tokyo: Kōdansha, 1970. 306 pp.

3533. Kosuke, Yoshihiro. *Manga-No Gendaishi*. Tokyo: Maruzen Library, 1993.

3534. Kusamori, Shin'ichi. *Mangakō* (A Study on Comics). Tokyo: Kodama Puresu, 1967. 267 pp.

3535. Leahy, Kevin. "News from the *Daily Yomiuri*." *The Rose*. July 1994, p. 18.

3536. Lin Chih-Tao. "Japanese Peculiar Comics." *Monthly Comic Magazine* (Hong Kong). December 1990, pp. 84-86.

3537. "A Love Affair with Comics." *Asian Mass Communication Bulletin*. November-December 1992, p. 7.

3538. Loveday, Leo and Satomi Chiba. "Aspects of the Development Toward a Visual Culture in Respect of Comics: Japan." In *Comics and Visual Culture: Research Studies from Ten Countries*, edited by Alphons Silbermann and H.-D. Dyroff, pp. 158-184. Munich: K.G. Saur, 1986.

3539. Loveday, Leo and Satomi Chiba. "At the Crossroads: The Folk Ideology of Femininity in the Japanese Comic." *Communications*. 7:2/3 (1981), pp. 135-150.

3540. Loveday, Leo and Satomi Chiba. "At the Crossroads: The Folk Ideology of Femininity in the Japanese Comic." *Fabula: Zeitschrift für Erzahlforschung*. 24:3/4 (1983), pp. 246-263.

3541. Lowenthal, Kevin. "Just Dancin' Through." *Comics Journal*. April 1989, pp. 51-54.

3542. MacLeod, John. "Speaking of Which." *The Comicist*. August 1990, p. 4.

3543. Maderdonner, Megumi and Eva Bachmayer. *Aspekte Japanischer Comics*. Vienna: Institut für Japanologie, Universität Wien, 1986.

3544. *Manga*. Catalogue for exhibition "Manga, Comic Strip Books from Japan," at Pomeroy Purdey Gallery, London, England, October-November 1991. London: Lowe Culture, 1991.

3545. "Manga." *Inklings*. March 1994, p. 13.

3546. "Manga Close Up." *Animerica*. November 1992, p. 14.

3547. "Manga Dai Zukan" (A Giant Pictorial of Comics). Supplement of series *Ichiokunin No Shōwashi*. Tokyo: Mainichi Shimbunsha, 1982.

3548. *Manga Sedai: Seinen Shinri 19* (Comics Generation: Adolescent Psychology 19). Tokyo: Kaneko Shobō, 1980. 168 pp.

3549. Martínez Peñaranda, Enrique. "La Mujer de Nieve (Legende Japonesa). Una Bellisima Historieta Japonesa." *Comicguia*. No. 21, 1991, pp. 23-26.

3550. Matsuzawa, Mitsuo. *Nihonjin No Atama o Dame Ni Shita Manga-Gekiga* (The Comics That Have Ruined Japanese Minds). Tokyo: Yamate Shobō, 1979.

3551. "Miles of Manga: Japan's Dream Mechanism." *Comics Journal*. October 1984, pp. 68-69.

3552. Mizuno, Ryutaro. *Mangabunkano Uchimaku* (Inside Comic Culture). Tokyo: Kawade Shobō, 1991.

3553. Moliterni, Claude. "La BD Japonaise." *Phénix* (Paris). No. 21, 1971.

3554. Nakajima, Azusa. "Dreams of Hermaphroditos." *Kiso Tengai*. December 1978.

3555. Nishimura, Shigeo. "The Japanese Manga." Foreign Press Center, Japan, 1994.

3556. Nitschke, Günter. "The Manga City." In *The Electric Geisha: Exploring Japan's Popular Culture*, edited by Atsushi Ueda, translated by Miriam Eguchi, pp. 231-242. Tokyo and New York: Kodansha, 1994.

3557. Ono, Kōsei. "Comics of Japan." *Cartoonist PROfiles*. No. 9, 1971, pp. 16-23.

3558. Orrock, Alec and Dan Durkin. "Convention Report: Project A-Kon '90." *The Rose*. September 1990, pp. 16-17.

3559. Oshiguchi, Takashi. "Dojinshi." *Animerica*. October 1993, p. 15.

3560. Oshiguchi, Takashi. "Translating Manga to Movies and Television." *Animerica*. January 1994, p. 15.

3561. Ōshiro, Noboru, Osamu Tezuka, and Reiji Matsumoto. *OH! Manga* (Oh! Comics). Tokyo: Shōbunsha, 1982. 210 pp.

3562. Otsuka, Eiji. "Comic-Book Formula for Success." *Japan Quarterly*. July-September 1988, pp. 287-291.

3563. Otsuka, Eiji. *The Structure of Manga*. Tokyo: Yudachisha, 1988.

3564. Ozaki, Hotsuki. *Gendai Manga No Genten: Warai Kotoba e No Atakku* (The Origin of the Modern Comic: An Attack on Laughter). Tokyo: Kōdansha, 1972.

3565. Ozaki, Hotsuki. *Manga No Aru Heya: Gendai Manga e No Shikaku* (A Room with Comics: A Perspective on Modern Comics). Tokyo: Jiji Tsūshinsha, 1978.

3566. Patten, Fred. "Mangamania!" *The Comics Journal*. October 1984, pp. 44-55.

3567. Pellegrini, Denise. "TV, Comic Books Provide Fodder For Nippon Cinema." *Variety*. September 16, 1991, p. 52.

3568. Philips, Adam. "Exotic Comics in a Faraway Land." *Comics Journal*. June 1984, pp. 59-60.

3569. "Popular Comics." *Asian Messenger*. Autumn 1979/Spring 1980, p. 21.

3570. Richie, Donald. *A Lateral View: Essays on Contemporary Japan*. Tokyo: Japan Times, 1987. 208 pp.

3571. Samuelson, R.J. "What Makes Japan Tick." *Newsweek*. July 25, 1988, p. 55.

3572. Santoso, Widya. "Manga: Comic Strip Books from Japan. Program Book from the UK Exhibition." *The Rose*. January 1992, p. 22.

3573. Satō, Tadao. *Nihon No Manga* (Japanese Comics). Tokyo: Hyōronsha, 1973.

3574. Schodt, Frederik L. *Inside the Robot Kingdom: Japan, Mechatronics, and the Coming Robotopia*. New York: Kodansha, 1988. 256 pp.

3575. Schodt, Frederik L. "Manga Communication." *Animerica*. May 1994, p. 37.

3576. Schodt, Frederik L. *Manga! Manga! The World of Japanese Comics*. Tokyo: Kodansha, 1983.

3577. Schodt, Frederik L. "Reading the Comics." *Wilson Quarterly*. Summer 1985, pp. 57-66.

3578. Shapiro, Margaret. "Comic Books: All the Rage in Highly Literate Japan." *Washington Post*. March 24, 1990, p. A-24.

3579. Shimizu, Isao. *Manga Kūkan Sansaku* (Wander into the Comics Space). Tokyo: Kyōikusha, 1989. 247 pp.

3580. Shirato, Sanpei. *Sasuke*. Tokyo: Shogakukan, 1978.

3581. "The Silent Service." *Seriejournalen*. March 1991, p. 11.

3582. Smet, Mårdøn. "De Drog Vest På." *Seriejournalen*. December 1990, pp. 31-33.

3583. Smith, Toren. "Manga in Japan." *Protoculture Addicts*. May-June 1993, pp. 25-27.

3584. Smith, Toren. "Manga in Japan — Comics' Popularity Is Unmatched." *Comics Buyer's Guide*. March 25, 1994, p. 26.

3585. Sneider, Daniel. "In Japan, Comics Aren't Just for Laughs." *Christian Science Monitor*. September 2, 1988, p. 1.

3586. Soeda, Yoshiya. *Gendai Mangaron* (A Theory of Modern Comics). Tokyo: Nihon Keizai Shimbunsha, 1975.

3587. Swallow, Jim. "Manga in Focus." *Anime UK Magazine*. October/November 1992, pp. 14-15.

3588. Swallow, Jim. "Manga in Focus: Mangamerican." *Anime UK Magazine*. 2:6, pp. 16-17.

3589. *Taiwaroku, Gendai Manga Aika* (Interview: An Elegy of Modern Comics). Tokyo: Seirindō, 1970. 280 pp.

3590. Takeuchi, Osamu, ed. *Manga Hihyō Taikei* (The Collection of Comics Critiques). Vol. 1. Tokyo: Heibonsha, 1987. 287 pp.

3591. Takeuchi, Osamu and Tomohiko Murakami, eds. *Manga Hihyō Taikei* (The Collection of Comics Critiques). Vols. 2-4. Tokyo: Heibonsha, 1987.

3592. Taylor, James S. "A Reflection of Japanese Culture." *Protoculture Addicts*. July-August 1994, p. 32.

3593. *Visions of the Floating World. The Cartoon Art of Japan*. Catalogue. Exhibition, Cartoon Art Museum, San Francisco, May 27-September 5, 1992. San Francisco: 1992, 32 pp.

3594. Yang, Jeff. "Pulp Culture." *Magazine Temptations '91*. 1991, pp. 18, 58.

3595. Yomota, Inuhiko. *Collected Manga Criticism*. Vol. 1. Tokyo: Heibonsha, 1989.

3596. Yoshida, Reiji. "Manga Mad." *Japan Times Weekly International Edition*. September 13-19, 1993, p. 17.

3597. Yoshida, Reiji. "'Manga' Magazines Zoom to New Heights." *Japan Times*. August 28, 1993, p. 3.

3598. *Zasshi No Mokuroku*. Tokyo: Shuppan Hambai Kabukigaisha, 1982.

Education

3599. Browne, Ray B. and Arthur G. Neal. "The Many Tongues of Literacy." *Journal of Popular Culture*. Summer 1991, pp. 157-186.

3600. "Cartoons? Strip Joints? Economics 101 Was Never Like This." *Newsweek*. July 27, 1987, p. 44.

3601. "Comics in Japan Are Not Just for Laughs." *Straits Times*. November 22, 1986, p. 2.

3602. Evans, Peter. "Educational Manga." *Mangajin*. February 1993, pp. 10-13.

3603. "'Gomics' Question Consumerism." *Asian Mass Communication Bulletin*. March-April 1992, p. 6.

3604. Ishimori, Shotaro. *Japan Inc.: Introduction to Japanese Economics*. Berkeley: University of California Press, 1988. ("Introduction" by Peter Duus).

3605. Johnson, Chalmers. "Comics-Sense of Economics." *Far Eastern Economic Review*. February 5, 1987, pp. 44-45.

3606. "Mangajin in the Classroom." *Mangajin*. October 1993, p. 20.

3607. "Medical Comics Catching On." *Japan Times*. August 2, 1990.

3608. Miyamoto, Tomohiro. "Manga Dokkai Ni Okeru 'Kaki Moji' No Kouka" (The Effect of Handwriting To Read Comics). *Dokusho Kagaku*. 34:2 (1990), pp. 68-75.

3609. Mizuno, Hirosuke. "On the Need for Stimulation As a Motivating Factor of Mass Media Exposure." *Japanese Journal of Experimental Social Psychology*. February 1978, pp. 77-87.

3610. Nesbitt, Scott. "No! Can It Be True? *Mangajin*: Learning Through Comics." *Comics Journal*. May 1993, pp. 100-101.

3611. Simmons, Vaughan P. "Translating Japanese *Manga* into English." In *Mangajin's Basic Japanese Through Comics*, pp. 8-9. Atlanta, Georgia: Mangajin, 1993.

3612. Takashima, Hideyuki. "Acculturation and Second Language Learning: Use of Comics To Measure the Degree of Acculturation." *IRAL*. February 1987, pp. 25-40.

3613. Waters, Ginny Skord. "Japan in Your Pocket!" *Mangajin*. August 1993, p. 18.

3614. Yoshida, Akira. "Manga To Daigaku Toshokan" (Comics and University Libraries). *Toshokan Zasshi*. 84:9 (1990), pp. 632-635.

Genres: General

3615. "Execs Snap Up Comic Book on Dealing with Gangsters." *Japan Times*. December 11, 1993.

3616. Kamata, Tōji. "Okaruto Manga Ryūsei No Shinsō" (The Depth of Prosperity of Horror Comics). *Chishiki*. 85 (1989), pp. 261-268.

3617. Umezu, Kazuo. *Jūyon-sai* (14 Years Old). Vol. 11. Tokyo: Shōgakukan, 1993. 210 pp.

3618. Yoshitomi, Yasuo. *Manga Manga No Miryoku* (The Charm of Funny Comics). Tokyo: Seizansha, 1978. 190 pp.

Genre: Boys'

3619. Fukuda, Yoshiya. *Miwaku No Shōnen Manga* (Fascinating Boys' Comics). Tokyo: Kawashima Shoten, 1968. 222 pp.

3620. Fujio-Fujiko. *Futari de Shōnen Manga Bakari Kaite Kita* (All We've Ever Done Is Draw Boys' Comics). Tokyo: Mainichi Shimbunsha, 1977.

Genre: Children's

3621. Fujikawa, Chisui. *Kodomo Mangaron* (An Essay on Children's Comics). Tokyo: Sanichi Shobō, 1967. 260 pp.

3622. Hatano, Kanji. "Children's Comics in Japan." In *Japanese Popular Culture*, edited by Hidetoshi Kato, pp. 103-108. Rutland, Vermont: Charles Tuttle, 1959.

3623. Manba, Haruo. "Kodomo To Manga: 'Hotto Rōdo' To 'Hana No Asukagumi!' o Tōshite" (Children and Comics: Through "Hotto Rōdo" and "Hana No Asukagumi!"). *Kyōiku.* 38:6 (1988), pp. 6-18.

3624. Nakahara, Mie. "Manga Bunka To Kodomo No Kakawari" (The Relationship Between Comics Culture and Children). *Sěshōnen Mondai.* 35:5 (1988), pp. 12-18.

3625. Saitō, Jirō. *Kodomo Manga No Sekai* (The World of Children's Comics). Tokyo: Gendai Shokan, 1979. 285 pp.

3626. Takehisa Yumeji. *Kodomo No Sekai* (The Children's World). Tokyo: Ryuseikaku, 1970.

Genre: Drama

3627. Ishiko, Junzō, Senjuro Kikuchi, and Shin Gondō. *Gekiga No Shisō* (The Thoughts of Drama Comics). Tokyo: Taihei Shuppansha, 1973. 277 pp.

3628. Kajiwara, Ikki. *Gekiga Ichidai* (One Generation of Drama Comics). Tokyo: Mainichi Shimbunsha, 1979. 224 pp.

Genre: Erotic and Adult

3629. Andrei, Silvio. "Intimo Desiderio: Fantasie in Mutandine e Reggiseno." *Yamete.* No. 2, 1993, pp. 22-40.

3630. Andrei, Silvio. "Mille Coperture: La Censura in Giappone: Un Gioco Senza Regole." *Yamete.* No. 2, 1992, pp. 14-18.

3631. Andrei, Silvio. "Video Girl Ai." *Yamete.* No. 2, 1993, pp. 46-49.

3632. Andrei, Silvio and Hiroko Saejima. "Lolita Complex: Un Complesso Solo Giapponese?" *Yamete.* No. 2, 1993, pp. 11-21.

3633. Ashby, Janet. "*Manga* Rebels or Kiddie Porn Pushers." *Japan Times.* November 5, 1993, p. 21.

3634. Bornoff, Nicholas. *Pink Samurai: Love, Marriage and Sex in Contemporary Japan.* New York: Simon and Schuster, 1991. 479 pp.

3635. Costa, Maurizio. "Segni Maliziosi: I Suoni dell' Eros." *Yamete*. No. 1, 1992, pp. 35-42.

3636. Costa, Maurizio, Francesco Prandoni, and Saburo. "La Porta del Corpo." *Yamete*. No. 2, 1993, pp. 58-64.

3637. "Ero Gekiga No Sekai" (The World of Erotic Comics). Supplement of *Shimpyō*. Series on authors. Spring 1979.

3638. Ito, Kinko. "Images of Women in Weekly Male Comic Magazines in Japan." *Journal of Popular Culture*. Spring 1994, pp. 81-95.

3639. Ito, Kinko. "Sexism in Japanese Weekly Comic Magazines for Men." In *Asian Popular Culture*, edited by John A. Lent. Boulder, Colorado: Westview Press, forthcoming.

3640. "Japanese Murders Influenced by Manga?" *Comics Journal*. February 1990, p. 12.

3641. Kusamori, Shin'ichi. *Manga-Erochishizumukō* (Comics and Thoughts on Eroticism). Tokyo: Burēn Bukkusu, 1971.

3642. Matsubara, Lily. "Comics for Adults." *Far Eastern Economic Review*. June 23, 1994, p. 70.

3643. Ono, Kōsei. "Female Genitalia with Chrolophyl [sic] ." *Collected Manga Criticism*. Vol. 1. Tokyo: Heibonsha, 1989.

3644. Prandoni, Francesco. "Solo un Bacio, L'Erotismo nei Manga dal Dopguerra a Oggi." *Yamete*. No. 1, 1992, pp. 3-13.

3645. Prandoni, Francesco. "Tokyo Decadence." *Yamete*. No. 1, 1992, pp. 57-64.

3646. Prandoni, Francesco. "U-Jin: Angeli e Liceali." *Yamete*. No. 1, 1992, pp. 19-34.

3647. Schodt, Frederik. "Sex and Violence in Manga." *Mangajin*. No. 10, 1991, pp. 9, 30.

3648. Seward, Jack. *Seward's Follies*. Houston, Texas and Tokyo: Yugen Press, 1994. 140 pp. ("Erotic Comics," pp. 113-116).

3649. Seward, Jack, ed. *Japanese Eroticism: A Language Guide to Current Comics*. Houston, Texas and Tokyo: Yugen Press, 1993. 168 pp.

3650. *Shigaisen*. Tokyo: Tsukuru Shuppan, 1993.

3651. Smith, Toren. "Miso Horny: Sex in Japanese Comics." *Comics Journal*. July 1991, pp. 111-115.

3652. *Yugai Comics Mondai-o Kangaeru*. Tokyo: Tsukuru Shuppan, 1991.

Genre: Fantasy

3653. Adams, Kenneth A. and Lester Hill, Jr. "Protest Anality in Japanese Group-Fantasies." *Journal of Psychohistory*. Fall 1987, pp. 113-145.

3654. Adams, Kenneth A. and Lester Hill, Jr. "Protest and Rebellion: Fantasy Themes in Japanese Comics." *Journal of Popular Culture*. Summer 1991, pp. 99-127.

3655. "Comic Book Types, TV Push Yields Japan's Sci-Fi Cat Hit." *Variety*. May 12, 1982, p. 328.

Genre: Girls'

3656. Hide, Takatori. "Shojo Manga Ni Okeru Ai To Sei" (Love and Sex in Comics-for-Girls). *Dacapo*. 164 (1988), pp. 6-11.

3657. "Move Over, Shonen! New OAVs Aimed at the Shojo Generation Debut from Shueisha." *Animerica*. May 1993, pp. 12-13.

3658. Schodt, Frederik L. "A Tale of Two Translations." *Mangajin*. October 1991, pp. 9, 51.

3659. *Shōjo Manga No Sekai I, Shōwa 20-37* (The World of Girls' Comics I, 1945-1962). "Kodomo No Shōwa-shi" (Children's History of Shōwa Period) series of *Bessatsu Taiyō*. Tokyo: Heibonsha, 1991. 144 pp.

3660. *Shōjo Manga No Sekai II, Shōwa 38-64* (The World of Girls' Comics II, 1963-1989). "Kodomo No Shōwa-shi" (Children's History of Shōwa Period) series of *Bessatsu Taiyō*. Tokyo: Heibonsha, 1991. 164 pp.

3661. Takeda, Michi. "Shōjo Manga No Kigō Naiyō" (The Symbol of Girls' Comics). *Kasēgaku Kenkyū*. 32:2 (1986), pp. 281-286.

3662. Takemiya, Keiko and Hagio Moto. *Shōjo Mangaka Ni Nareru Hon* (How To Become a Girls' Comic Artist). Tokyo: Futami Shobō, 1980.

3663. Thorn, Matt. "'Gay' Shojo and North American Fandom." *Animerica*. April 1994, p. 35.

3664. Thorn, Matt. "Girls' Stuff: Matt's Travel Diary." *Animerica*. October 1994, p. 41.

3665. Thorn, Matt. "Girls' Stuff: The Genius of Boku-Tama." *Animerica*. June 1994, p. 41.

3666. Thorn, Matt. "Shojo Manga — A Manual for Living." *Animerica*. October 1993, p. 40.

3667. Thorn, Matt. "Shojo Manga — Of, By, and For Women." *Animerica*. April 1993, p. 38.

3668. Thorn, Matt. "Those Eyes." *Animerica*. May 1993, p. 37.

3669. Thorn, Matt. "What is Shojo? What is Shonen? All About Genres." *Animerica*. August 1994, p. 37.

3670. Treat, John W. "Yoshimoto Banana Writes Home: *Shōjo* Culture and the Nostalgic Subject." *Journal of Japanese Studies*. Summer 1993, pp. 353-388.

Genre: Heroes and Superheroes

3671. Bertieri, Claudio. "Superman d' Oriente." *Comic Art*. April 1988, p. 78.

3672. Buruma, Ian. "The Flawed Myth of a Folk Hero Who Was Not Quite Japanese." *Far Eastern Economic Review*. October 6, 1983, pp. 79-80.

3673. Buruma, Ian. *A Japanese Mirror, Heroes and Villains of Japanese Culture*. London: Jonathan Cape, 1984.

3674. "Cartoon Heroes Captivate Japanese Young People." *Japan Quarterly*. April-June 1982, pp. 165-168.

3675. Evans, Peter J. "The Beautiful and the Terrible." *Anime UK Magazine*. 2:4, pp. 27-30.

3676. Fujiwara, Usaku. *Atomu Ga Ite Doraemon Ga Ite: Manga No Aidorutachi* (There Is Atomu, and There Is Doraemon: Heroes in Comics). Tokyo: Shimizu Shoin, 1985. 253 pp.

Genre: Salaryman

3677. Hay, Cameron. "Day-Laborer 'Manga' a Laugh at Society." *Japan Times*. November 11, 1993.

3678. Pepper, Anne G. "White Collar Comics." *Business Japan*. October 1987, p. 15.

3679. Skinner, Kenneth A. "Salaryman Comics in Japan: Images of Self-Perception." *Journal of Popular Culture*. Summer 1979, pp. 141-151.

Genre: Samurai

3680. Dohr, Chris. "Der Samuraikult in Comics." *Watcher of the Unknown*. April 1988, pp. 40-46.

3681. Grant, Vern. "Samurai Superstrips." *Comics Journal*. October 1984, pp. 91-94.

3682. Munson-Siter, Patricia A. "Mystic Warriors." *Anime UK Magazine*. 3:5, pp. 28-30.

Governance

3683. "Crackdown in Japan?" *Comics Journal*. July 1991, p. 15.

3684. "Japanese Kids To Be Protected from Porno Comics." *Asian Mass Communication Bulletin*. July-August 1991, p. 5.

3685. "Japanese Kids To Be Protected from Porn Comics." *Asian Media Alert*. Winter 1992, p. 9.

3686. "Official Control, Publishers' Restraint on Comics' Sexual Expressions." *NSK News Bulletin*. March 1991, pp. 4-5.

Portrayals

3687. Briscoe, David. "Family of Activists Accuses Cartoonist of Racism." *Japan Times*. August 27, 1991.

3688. Buckley, Sandra. *Phallic Fantasies: Sexuality and Violence in Japanese Comic Books*. Forthcoming.

3689. "Comic Book Looks at Job-Changing." *Japan Times*. December 24, 1990.

3690. Ledden, Sean and Fred Fejes. "Female Gender Role Patterns in Japanese Comic Magazines." *Journal of Popular Culture*. Summer 1987, pp. 155-176.

3691. Schodt, Frederik L. "Black and White Issues (II)." *Mangajin*. April 1992, pp. 9, 72. (Racism).

3692. Schodt, Frederik. "Gaijin in Manga." *Mangajin*. March 1995, pp. 14-19, 66.

3693. Schodt, Frederik L. "Race and Manga." *Animerica*. March 1994, p. 35.

Technical Aspects

3694. Kure, Tomofusa. *Mangaka Ni Naruniwa* (How To Become a Comic Artist). New Edition. Tokyo: Perikansha, 1983. 188 pp.

3695. Tezuka, Osamu. *Manga No Kakikata: Nigao Kara Chōhen Made* (How To Draw Comics: From Portraits to Story-Comics). Tokyo: Kōbunsha, 1977.

Political Cartoons

3696. Jeffs, Angela. "Political Cartoonist Having a Ball with 'Hawk Eyes' Hosokawa."
Japan Times. September 12, 1993.

3697. Ono, Kōsei, ed. *Komikku Nichi-Bei Masatsu: Waratte Bakari Wa Iraremasen*
(Comic Japan-US Friction: Not Just a Laughing Matter). Tokyo: Kodansha, 1992.
247 pp. Japanese.

3698. "A Political Cartoon." *Mangajin*. April 1993, p. 7.

3699. "A Political Cartoon." *Mangajin*. May 1993, p. 7.

3700. "Political Cartoon from the *Asahi Shimbun*." *Mangajin*. June 1993, p. 6.

3701. "Political Cartoon from the *Asahi Shimbun*." *Mangajin*. September 1993, p. 9.

3702. "Political Cartoon from the *Asahi Shimbun*." *Mangajin*. October 1993, p. 7.

3703. "Political Cartoon from the *Asahi Shimbun*." *Mangajin*. No. 32, 1993, p. 7.

3704. "Political Cartoon from the *Asahi Shimbun*." *Mangajin*. April 1994, p.7.

3705. "Political Cartoon from the *Asahi Shimbun*." *Mangajin*. May 1994, p. 7.

3706. "Political Cartoon from the *Asahi Shimbun*." *Mangajin*. June 1994, p. 11.

3707. "Political Cartoon from the *Asahi Shimbun*." *Mangajin*. August 1994, p. 11.

3708. "Political Cartoon from the *Asahi Shimbun*." *Mangajin*. September 1994, p. 11.

3709. "Political Cartoon from the *Asahi Shimbun*." *Mangajin*. October 1994, p. 11.

3710. "Political Cartoon from the *Asahi Shimbun*." *Mangajin*. November 1994, p. 11.

3711. "Political Cartoon from the *Asahi Shinbun*." *Mangajin*. December 1994, p. 9.

3712. "Political Cartoon from the *Asahi Shimbun*." *Mangajin*. February 1995, p. 9.

3713. "Political Cartoon from the *Asahi Shinbun*." *Mangajin*. March 1995, p. 7.

3714. "Political Cartoons." *Mangajin*. April 1993, p. 4.

3715. Saitamāken Kindai Bijutsukan (Museum of Modern Art, Saitama), ed. *Nippon No
Fūshi* (Satire of Japan). Saitama: Saitamaken Kindai Bijutsukan, 1993. 154 pp.

3716. Shimizu, Isao. "Fūshi Bijutsu Shōron" (A Short Discussion on the Satirical Art).
Fūshiga Kenkyū. January 20, 1993, pp. 6-7.

KOREA

General Sources

3717. Ahn Choon-Gun. *Theories of Magazine Publishing*. Seoul: Bumwoosa, 1988.

3718. Chun Young-Pyo. *Publication Theories*. Seoul: Dae Gwang Publishing Co., 1987.

3719. Han Tae-Yul. *Theories of Newspaper Study*. Seoul: Park Young-Sa, 1987.

3720. Kang Sang-Ho and Lee Won-Pak. *Current Capitalism and Mass Media*. Seoul: MiRaeSa, 1986.

3721. Kim Ji-Woon, ed. *Mass Media Political Economics*. Seoul: Nanam, 1990.

3722. Kim Jong Dae. *Theory of Korean Drawings*. Seoul: Iljisa, 1989.

3723. Kum Chang-Yun. "Study on Sensationalism of Korean Popular Magazines." Master's thesis, Yonsei University, Department of Administration, 1992.

3724. Lee Doo-Young. "Directions of Information Computerization for Publishing." *Chool Panyun-gu* (Publications Study). 1993.

3725. Lee Kang-Soo. *Mass Media Industry and the Audience Movement*. Seoul: Korean Press Institute, 1991.

3726. Lee Sang-Chul. *History of Communication Development*. Seoul: Iljisa, 1982.

3727. Park Hyung-Bok. "Study on the Characteristics of the Korean Publishing Industry." Master's thesis, Hanyang University, Department of Mass Communication, 1990.

3728. Roh Byung-Sung. "1980's Korean Book Industry: An Industrial Organization Analysis." Ph.D. dissertation, Sogang University, 1992. 282 pp. Korean.

3729. Sung Dong-Gyu. *Study on Structural Characteristics of Korean Publishing Industry*. Seoul: Choongang University, 1989.

3730. "USA Protesterer Mod Koreansk Serie." *Seriejournalen*. March 1991, p. 11.

3731. Woorimadang, ed. *Theories of Visual Media*. Seoul: Woorimadang, 1987.

Mass Culture

3732. Choi Min-Wha. "Key for the Truthful Mass Culture." *Newspaper of Hanyang University*. March 14, 1985.

3733. Choi Min-Wha. "The Role of Cartoons in Terms of Cultural Movement." *Uidae*

Hakbo ((Medical School newspaper). March 3, 1986.

3734. Cultural Development Institute, Korean Culture and Arts Department. *Study on Mass Culture Industry and Policies for It*. Seoul: 1989.

3735. Hong Ji-Ong. "Daejoong Yesooloceoui Manwha" (Cartoon as Popular Culture). *Godae Moonwha*. February 1982.

3736. Joo Dong-Whang. "Need for Policy for Cultural Preservation." *Sinmun Gwa Bangsong*. (Newspaper and Broadcasting). February 1994.

3737. Kang Hyun-Doo, ed. *Mass Culture of Korea*. Seoul: Nanam, 1987.

3738. Kang Hyun-Doo, ed. *Theories of Mass Culture*. Seoul: MinEumSa, 1984.

3739. Kim Jong-Hyup. "Postmodern Adventure." In *How To Study Culture*. Seoul: Hyunsuk Moon Jae-YunGooSa. (Institute for Contemporary Problems), 1994.

3740. Kum Chang-Yeon. "Hankook Adong Manwhaui Baldal." In *Hankookui Daejoong Moonwhna* (Korean Popular Culture), edited by Kang Hyun-Dew. Seoul: Nanam, 1986.

3741. Lim Choon-Hee. "New Leaps for Popular Culture." *Newspaper of Sangmyung University*. August 26, 1986.

Historical Aspects

3742. Choi Yeol. "The History of Korean Cartoons and Their Popularization Movement." *Yonsei*. 24, 1986.

3743. Choi Yeol. "Tradition and Modes of National Arts: 1900-1960." In *Arts Movements 1*, edited by The Institute of Visual Media. Seoul: 1988.

3744. Choi Yeol, *et al. Manwhawa Sidae* (Cartoons and the Times). Seoul: Gongdongchae, 1987.

3745. Kim Sung-Hwan. "Brief History of Korean Newspaper Cartoons." *Journalism*. Summer 1973.

3746. Kim Ui-Whan. *Manwha Hankooksa* (Cartoon Korean History). Seoul: Gumsung Publishing Co., 1980.

3747. Lee Hae-Chang. *Hankook Sisa Manwhasa* (History of Korean Political Cartoon). Seoul: Iljisa, 1982. 269 pp. Korean.

3748. Lent, John A. "Korean Cartooning: Historical and Contemporary Perspectives." *Korean Culture*. Forthcoming.

3749. Lent, John A. "Korean Cartoons: Historical and Contemporary Perspectives." *Sinmun Gwa Bangsong* (Newspaper and Broadcasting). 1/1994, pp. 94-103. Korean.

3750. Park Hung-Gyu. *Hankookui Yeoksa 1* (Korean History 1): *Gabose Gabose*. Seoul: Hyungsungsa, 1989.

3751. Whang Sun Kil. *Animation Movie History*. Seoul: Bak Soo Sa, 1990.

3752. Yoon Youngok. *The History of Korean Newspaper Cartoons*. Seoul: Youlwhadang, 1986. 345 pp. Korean.

Cartooning, Cartoons

3753. Ahn Dol. *Hyunjang Haksup Manwha: Gulo Kijoonbup* (Field Study Cartoons: Labor Basic Law). Seoul: Chungsa, 1986.

3754. Bang Hak-Ki. *Sesangmansa Arisamsam* (Everything in the World in Confusion). Seoul: Whamoongak, 1988.

3755. Barun Manwha Yeongoowhoe (Research Association for the Right Cartoons). *Manwha Changjak 1* (Cartoon Creation 1). Seoul: Taeam Publishing Company, 1990.

3756. Cartoon Section, Association of University Newspaper Reporters in Seoul Area. *It Takes Five Minutes To Be Exploded, Six Minutes To Hold On—The History of the 1980s from the Reporter's Perspective*. Seoul: Mirae Moon Haksa, 1990.

3757. Choi In Hyun. "Study of Functions and Values of Inserted Cartoons As an Educational Medium." Master's thesis, Gemyung University-Taegu, 1982.

3758. Choi Ji-Choong. *Manwha Jangja*. Seoul: Woori Publishing Company, 1987.

3759. Choi Min-Wha. "Boolbup Cheryuja" (Illegal Sojourner). *Moonhakui Jayuwa Silchunul Wihayeo 1* (For the Freedom and Practice of Literature 1). February 1985.

3760. Choi Min-Wha. "Cartoons As a Weapon of Life." *Hyunsil Gwa Balun* (Reality and Suggestion). 1984.

3761. Choi Min-Wha. "Nodungui Saebyuk: Sonmoodum" (Dawn of Labor: Tomb of Hands). *Moonhakui Jayuwa Sil-Chunul Wihayeo 3: Nodongui Moonhak, Moonhak Saebyuk*. Seoul: Leesak, 1985.

3762. Choi Min-Wha. "Salmui Moogorosoui Manwha" (Cartoons as Weapon of Life). *Moonhakui Jayuwa Silchunul Wihayeo2: Jayui Moonhak Silchunui Moonhak*. Seoul: Leesak, March 1985. Reprinted in *Hyunsil Gwa Balun*. Seoul: Yeolwhadang.

3763. Choi Myung Rak. "The Way Our Cartoons Should Take—In Light of Publishers." Paper presented to First Korean Cartoon Culture Development Seminar, Seoul, Korea, November 20, 1992.

3764. Choi Yeol. "The Blade of the Sword of Cartoons Is Still Not Sharp Enough." *Hyundae Gongron* (Contemporary Public Opinion). March 1988.

3765. Choi Yeol. "The Footprints of Contemporary Korean Cartoon." *Gha Nah Art*. November/December 1990, pp. 58-71.

3766. Choi Yeol. "How To Handle the Tasks of Cartoon Publishing." *Kookmin Dae Hakbo*. June 15, 1987.

3767. Choi Yeol. "New Winds Blown in the Golden Times of Cartoons." *Woori Sidae*. June 1987.

3768. Choi Yeol. "The Results of Cartoon Movements in the 1980s." *Uidae Hakbo* (Medical School Newspaper). March 18, 1986.

3769. Choi Yeol, *et al.*, eds. *Cartoons and Times 1*. Seoul: Gong Dong Chae, n.d.

3770. "The Current Problems of Cartoons." Conference sponsored by Sadariwhoe (Ladder Group), Seoul, Korea, October 1987. (Papers included "The Development of Korean Cartoons: What Are the Problems?" by Kim Dong-Wha, and "Censorship: Yesterday and Today," by Jang Tae-Sang).

3771. Do Jung-Il. *Cartoons and Psychology of Modern People: International Cartoons*. Seoul: Sedae, 1974.

3772. Gang Chul-Joo. "Kachee [Cartoon Character] Is Strong." *Ma Dang*. June 1986.

3773. Gang Chul-Joo. *Balriui Chooeok*. Seoul: Hanam Publishing Company, 1989. 6 Vols.

3774. Go Woo-Young. *Boribat Saitgil* (Sidewalks in Barley Field). Seoul: Dangsan Publishing Company, 1990.

3775. Go Woo-Young. *Samgookji (Three Countries)*. Seoul: Woosuk Samminsa, 1979.

3776. Go Woo-Young. *Soohoji*. Seoul: Woosuk, 1974.

3777. Go Woo-Young. *Yimgeokjung*. Seoul: Woosuk, 1979.

3778. Go Woo-Young. *Yim Kuk Jung*. Seoul: Woosuk, 1973.

3779. Go Woo-Young, *et al. Hold! President Rho Described by the Cartoonists*. Seoul: Hosan Moon Whasa, 1990.

3780. *Gongdan Maeari* (Echoes from the Factory). Inchon and Buchon: City Workers' Association, 1988.

3781. *Gwahak Haksup Manwha* (Science Study Cartoon). Seoul: Kumsung Publishing Co., 1981.

3782. Gwak Dae-Won. "Manwha Woondongron: Saraitnun Manwharul Wihayeo" (Essay on the Cartoon Movement: For the Living Cartoon). *Midaehakbo* (Seoul National University Art College newspaper). October 1988.

3783. Gwak Dae-Won. "Peculiarity and Generality of Cartoons As Media." *Woedae Hakbo* (Hankook University of Foreign Studies). March 11, 1986.

3784. Ha Jong-Won. "Possibilities and Directions of Cartoons As Mass Media." *Gha Nah Art*. November/December 1990, pp. 48-57.

3785. *Haksup Manwha Saegaesa*. Seoul: Gemongsa, 1988. 20 Vols.

3786. Han Seung Chul. "Cartoon Age Riding on Commercialism." *Sul Mut*. July 1989, pp. 53-59.

3787. Hasimoto, Masaroo. *Manwha Chaplain: Woosumsokui Kal* (Cartoon Chaplain: Knife in Laughing). Seoul: Ohwol, 1990.

3788. The Institute for Good Cartoons. *Cartoon Creation 1*. Seoul: Tae Am, 1990.

3789. Jakwhagongbang. *Heil, Rhotler*. Seoul: Manwha Journals, 1989.

3790. *Jakwhagongbang* (I Bury You in the Bosoms of the 10 Millions of Workers). Seoul: Dolbaegae, 1988.

3791. Jin Hyung-Jun. "Manwhawoondongui Bansung" (Reflection of the Cartoon Movement). *Saemi Gipun Mool* (Deep Spring Water). June 1988.

3792. Joo Duk-Yong. *Choomchoonun Gasibus* (Dancing Gasibusi). Seoul: Dangrae Publishing Company, 1990. 2 Vols.

3793. Joo Wan-Soo. *Botong Gorilla* (Ordinary Gorilla). Seoul: Saegae, 1988.

3794. Joo Wan-Soo. "Butege" (Dear Friend). In *Misool Woondong 1* (Art Movement 1). Seoul: Gondongche, 1988.

3795. Jung Jun-Young. "Cartoons." In *Understanding and Practices of Mass Media,* edited by Kang Sang-Hyun and Chae Baek. Seoul: Han Na Rae Publishing, Series of Mass Media 2, 1993.

3796. Keel Chang-Duk. *Soonakjil Yeosa* (Completely Vicious Lady). Seoul: Baekjae, 1979.

3797. Kim Chang-Nam. "A General Look at Cartoons." In *Manwha Wa Sidae*. Seoul: Gong Dong Chae, 1987.

3798. Kim Hyun. "Cartoons Are Art, Too?" *Manwha Jungshin* (Spirit of Cartoons). December 1986.

3799. Kim Hyun. "Cartoons As Literature." *Puri Gi Pun Na Moo* (Deep Rooted Tree). January 1977.

3800. Kim Hyun. "On Cartoon Semiotics." *Yesool Gwa Bipyung* (Arts and Criticism). Winter 1984.

3801. Kim Jae-Eun. "How To Appreciate Cartoon Culture." Paper presented at '90 Cartoon Development Symposium, Korean Publications Ethics Committee, Seoul, Korea, May 28, 1990.

3802. Kim Jang-Wook. "No More in This Way for the Cartoon Culture." Paper presented at First Korean Cartoon Culture Development Seminar, Seoul, Korea, November 20, 1992.

3803. Kim Joon-Ho. "Current Situation of Korean Cartoons and New Strategies To Be Considered." *Yonsei Choon Choo* (Journal of Yonsei University). February 27, 1984.

3804. Kim Joong-Bae. "Images of Critical Citizens." *Shimmun Yungoo* (Newspaper Studies). Spring 1977.

3805. Kim Kwang-Sung. *Weedaehan Sungboo* (The Great Competition). Seoul: Parangsae Publishing Company, 1988. 3 Vols. (Economic cartoons supported by National Businessmen's Alliance).

3806. Kim Tae-Sung. "Where Did Money and Jung Bae Go? Special Report, Manwha or Manga?" *Jibang Sidae*. August 1990, pp. 26-49.

3807. Korean Books, Magazines, and Weekly Newspapers Ethics Committee. *88 Cartoon Seminar—'The Problems of Cartoons and the Proposals.'* Seoul: October 11, 1988.

3808. Korean Publications Ethics Committee. *Analysis of the Deflation of the Cartoon Market*. Seoul: KPEC, April 1993.

3809. Korean Publications Ethics Committee. *The 90's Cartoons Development*

Symposium—What Are the Problems of Cartoons Culture. Seoul: KPEC, May 28, 1990.

3810. Lee Choon-Ok. "The Golden Age of Cartooning Is Coming." *Economist*. April 20, 1987.

3811. Lee Hee-Jae, Lim Cheong-San, and Park Jae-Dong. "Diagnosis of Today's Cartoon." *Gha Nah Art*. November/December 1990, pp. 38-47.

3812. Lee Jae-Wha. *Cartoon Encyclopedia*. Seoul: Seo Rim Munwha-sa, 1991.

3813. Lee Jong-Hyun. *Actual Materials for Cartooning*. Seoul: Sam Misa, 1983.

3814. Lee Jung-Moon. *Simsool Gajok* (Troublesome Family). Seoul: Baekjae, 1979.

3815. Lee Sang-Ho. *Galbici* (Mr. Rib). Seoul: Samjoongdang, 1979.

3816. Lee Won-Bok. "Cartoons As Education Media Standing in the Open Field." *Wolgan Echeonnyun* (Monthly 2000 Years). January 1988.

3817. Lee Won-Bok. "Cartoons As Mass Media." *Newspaper of Shungshin Women's University*. April 28, 1987.

3818. Lee Won-Bok. "Diagnosing the Current Situation of Korean Cartoons." Paper presented at '90 Cartoon Development Symposium, Korean Publications Ethics Committee, Seoul, Korea, May 28, 1990.

3819. Lee Won-Bok. *Meon Nara, Ewoot Nara* (Distant Country and Near Country). Seoul: Goryoga, 1987. 6 Vols.

3820. Lee Won-Bok. "Newly Emerging Mass Culture, Cartoons.' *Korean*. June 1986.

3821. Lee Won-Bok. "The Problems of Cartoons and Proposals." Paper presented at '88 Cartoon Seminar, Korean Book Publishing and Weekly Newspapers Ethics Committee, Seoul, Korea, October 11, 1988.

3822. Lee Won-Bok. *The World of Cartoons: Cartoons of the World*. Seoul: Meejinsa, 1991. 247 pp. Korean.

3823. Lee Young-Joo and Lee Hang-Bok. "Discussion of Our Cartoons." *Sogang*. Vol. 12, 1982.

3824. Lim Cheong-San. "Cartoon Aesthetics As Applied Arts." *Kongju Junior College Thesis Collection*. 16 (1989).

3825. Lim Cheong-San. "Directions for Development of Cartoon Culture." Paper presented at '90 Cartoon Development Symposium, Korean Publications Ethics Committee, Seoul, Korea, May 28, 1990.

3826. Lim Cheong-San. "The Foundation of Cartoon Art and Its Development." *The Journal of Kongju National Junior College*. 16 (1989), pp. 1-30.

3827. Lim Cheong-San. "Study on the Visual Image of Cartoon Characters." Master's thesis, Choongnam University (Taejun), Department of Arts, 1991.

3828. Manwha Sarang (Cartoon Loving). "Positioning of the Cartoon Movement." In *Moonhak Yesool Woondong* (Art and Literature Movement). Seoul: Pulbit, 1989.

3829. Manwha Sarang (Cartoon Loving). "Toojaengyi Saranguro Mannanun Saesang" (The World Where Fighting Becomes Love). *Yonsei* (Yonsei University newspaper). 28, November 1988.

3830. *Mook Sisamanwha* (Magazine Book of Contemporary Cartoons). Issue 1. Seoul: Yesoolgwan Publishing Company, 1988.

3831. Oh Kyu-Won. *Reality of Korean Cartoon*. Seoul: Yeolwhadang, 1981. 86 pp. Korean.

3832. Park Hung-Yong. *Bammada Woochako* (What Shall I Do Every Night?). Seoul: Gwangeowa Miraesa, 1988. 4 Vols.

3833. Park Mun-Yun. "How To Deal with Ill Fed Cartoons—Special Report. Manwha or Manga?" *Jibang Sidae*. August 1990, pp. 22-25.

3834. "Popular/National Styles of Cartoons Are Possible?" *Uidae Hakbo*. 4:2 (1986).

3835. "The Real Study of Cartoons in a Cartoon-Like World." *Wolgan Dokseo* (Monthly Reading). Special number. March 1979. "Adong Manwharon" (Study of Children's Cartoon), by Kang Chul-Soo; "Sungin Manwharon" (Study of Adult Cartoons), by Go Woo-Young; "Shinmun Manwharon" (Study of Newspaper Cartoons), by Oh Ryong; "Dokjakui Manwharon" (Study of Cartoon Readers), by Lee Sang-Woo.

3836. Roe Jae-Ryung. "Korean Art at Home and Abroad: Staging a Culture." *Art and Asia Pacific*. 1:4 (1994), pp. 48-55. (Kim Bong-Jun).

3837. *Sasangmanwharo Anun Hankook* (Korea Known Through Cartoons). Seoul: Wawoo Publishing Company, 1988.

3838. Seoul YWCA Children Department. *Collection of Cartoons Study Materials 2: Cartoons, Fun, the Eternal Handcuff*. Seoul: YWCA, 1990.

3839. Seoul YWCA Children Department. *Collections of Cartoon Study Materials 1*. Seoul: YWCA, 1989.

3840. Son Sang-Ik. *The Cartoon World Is Coming*. Seoul: Hankook Moonwhasa, 1992.

3841. Son Sang-Ik. "A Proposal for the Development of Korean Cartoon Industry." Paper presented at First Korean Cartoon Culture Development Seminar, Research Institute for Cartoon Culture, Korean Cartoonists Association, Seoul, Korea, November 20, 1992.

3842. Song Book-Ik. "Visual Media—Reinforcement of Cartoon Professionalism." *E Dae Hakbo* (Newspaper of Ewha Women's University). March 30, 1987.

3843. Sung Wan-Kyung. "Poongjawhaui Jungshingwa Gu Byunchunsa" (Satiric Spirit and Its History). *Gaegan Misool* (Quarterly Arts). September 1984.

3844. Um Gwan-Yong. "Cartoon Tycoons in the Cartoon Golden Times." *Ga-Jung Chosun* (Family Chosun). June 1987.

3845. University Newspaper Reporters Alliance's Cartoon Section. *Teojinun De 5boon, Butinun De 6boon* (5 Minutes To Be Exploded and 6 Minutes To Hold): *Daehak Manwha Gijaduri Bon 80nyundaesa* (The History of the 1980s Reflected by University Cartoon Reporters). Seoul: Mirae Moonhaksa, 1990.

3846. Wee Ki-Chul. "Cartoon As the People's Mode of Expression." In *Manwhawa Sidae*. Seoul: Gong Dong Chae, 1987.

3847. Whang Soo-Bang. "Cartoon Publishing in Light of Content Reviewing." Paper presented at '88 Cartoon Seminar, Korean Book Publishing and Weekly Newspapers Ethics Committee, Seoul, Korea, October 11, 1988.

3848. *Wooridulmanui Yiyagi.* (Story of Our Own). Seoul: Daewoong Publishing Company, 1989. (Sex education comic book).

3849. Yoon Joong-Ho. "Unleashed Cartoons in the Cartoon-Like World." *Woori Sidae.* April 1987.

Adult Cartoons

3850. Go Woo-Young. "Essay on Adult Cartoons." *Wolgan Dokseo.* (Monthly Reading). March 1979.

3851. Lee Tae-Ho. "Deleterious Cartoons Which Gnaw at People's Spirits." In *Actual Field of 70s.* Seoul: Hanma Dang Publishing, 1982.

3852. Lee Won-Bok. "Prerequisite for Adult Cartoons." *Ahjoo University Newspaper.* March 17, 1986.

3853. Suh Young-Suk. "Sae Sungin Kukjang Manwhasidae (New Adult Theater Cartoon Age.)" *Wolgan Kyunghyang.* March 1987.

Children's Cartoons

3854. Baek Eun-Hyun. "A Study of the Impacts of Cartoons Upon Children's Attitudes." Master's thesis, Ewha Women's University, 1973.

3855. Gang Chul-Soo. "Essay on Children's Cartoons." *Wolgan Dokseo* (Monthly Reading). March 1979.

3856. Jung Soon-Ja. "A Study of the Children's Cartoon." Master's thesis, Sogang University, 1979.

3857. Kim Ji-Young. "Killing and Destruction in Children's Cartoons, Is There Any Solution? Animated Movies, Now Let's Make Our Own with Our Hands." *Video Plaza*. August 1990.

3858. Korean Cartoonists Association for Children's Cartoons. *Collections of Korean Cartoons*. Seoul: Korean Cartoonists Association, 1975.

3859. Kum Chang-Yeon. "A Study on the Functional Characteristics of Korean Children's Cartoons." Master's thesis, Choongang University, 1986.

3860. Lee Hae-Chang and Yu-Jae Song. "An Analysis of Children's Magazines (Comic Magazines Included) and Suggestions. Part I—In Terms of Purpose, Readers, Publicity." *Shinmoongwa Bangsong*. June 1980.

3861. Lee Jong-Hyun. *Theories of Children's Cartoons*. Seoul: Woojoo Munwhasa, 1971.

3862. Lee Won-Bok. "Are Children's Cartoons OK in This Way?" Seoul: YWCA, April 28, 1987. Pamphlet.

3863. Lim Chang. "Dirty Business of Children's Cartoons." *Poorikipuen Namoo*. August 1976.

3864. Oh So-Baek. "The Children's Cartoon Arena in Dusty Wind." *Saedae*. November 1976.

Exhibitions

3865. "Cartoon Cultural Awards." *Monthly Publications Ethics Bulletin*. December 1993, p. 22. Korean.

3866. "Exposition of International Comic Books." *Monthly Publications Ethics Bulletin*. November 1993, p. 19. Korean. (Taejon Expo '93 International Cartoon Contest).

3867. *Taejon Expo '93 Int'l Cartoon Contest*. Taejon: Daehoon Books, 1993. 102 pp. Korean.

3868. *The Third Cartoon Art Exhibition. Cartoon, Caricature, Animation, Illustration, Fancy, Etc.* Kongju: Kongju Junior College, 1993. Korean. (Cartooning school graduates' work).

Realism and Cartoons

3869. Choi Yeol. "Realism in Cartoons." *Handae Shinmun*. December 4, 1986.

3870. Choi Yeol. *The Reality and Tasks of Korean Cartoons*. In *Manwha Wa Sidae*. Seoul: Gong Dong Chae, 1987.

3871. Gwak Dae-Won. "Cartoon Movement Clings to Reality." *Sogang Hakbo*. February 14, 1986.

3872. Gwak Dae-Won. "Reality of Newspaper Cartoons: Newspaper Cartoons Must Be Changed." *Ghanah Art*. No. 6, March 1989.

3873. "Logic and Reality of Newspaper Cartoons." *Shinmun Yeongoo* (Newspaper Studies). Special number. Spring 1977.

3874. Oh Gyu-Won. *Hankook Manwhaui Hyunsil* (Reality of Korean Cartoons). Seoul: Yeolwhadang, 1981.

3875. Shin Jae-Wook. "Cartoon Movements and Comic Realism." *EDae Hakbo* (Newspaper of Ewha Women's University). January 1986.

Training and Techniques

3876. Chun Sang-Gyun, ed. *Manwha Technic*. Seoul: Shindo Publishing, 1985.

3877. "If You Want To Be a Cartoonist." *Manwha Gwangjang* (Cartoon Square). February 1987. 3 Series.

3878. "Instructions for the Future Cartoonist: Cartoon Course." *Manwha Gwangjang* (Cartoon Square). January 1987.

3879. Jakwha Gongbang. *The Actual Field of Cartoon School*. Seoul: Yi Woot Publishing Co., 1989.

3880. Lee Jong-Hyun. *Materials For Cartoon Practice*. Seoul: Sang Misa, 1983.

3881. Lee Won-Bok and Lim Cheong-San. *Cartoon Technique*. Seoul: Dasut Sooyae, 1991.

3882. Lent, John A. "Cartoon Schools Around the World: Kongju National Junior College, Seoul." *WittyWorld*. Autumn/Winter 1994, p. 22.

3883. Lim Cheong-San. "Cartoonist Education and Training." Paper presented at

International Association for Mass Communication Research, Seoul, Korea, July 5, 1994.

3884. Lim Cheong-San. "Tasks of the Cartoon Department and the Future of the Comic Arts." *Junmun Dae Hakgyoyuk*. 5 (1991).

3885. *Manwha Gurigi* (Cartoon Drawing). Seoul: Jigyungsa Minjok Misool Hyupuiwhoe, 1988.

3886. Park Ki-Jun. *Manwha Jakbup* (Cartoon Drawing Skills). Seoul: Chungjagak, 1975.

3887. Park Ki-Jun. *Manwhakipup Kangjoa* (Cartoon Skills Lectures). Seoul: Wooram Moonwhasa, 1987.

3888. Park Ki-Jun. *Manwhayaga Doeryomyun* (If You Want To Be a Cartoonist). Seoul: Taegwang Munwhasa, April 1987.

3889. Seoul YWCA Children's Department. *Collection of Cartoon Study Materials 3: Cartoons—Very Difficult Work To Do*. Seoul: YWCA, 1991.

Cartoonists and Their Works

3890. Cho Yong-Man. "Woongcho, Kim Kyu-Taek, the First Commentary Cartoonist." *Gaegan Misool*. March 1985.

3891. Choi Yeol. "The National Cartoon Movement in the 1920s: Focusing on Kim Dong-Sung and Ahn Suk-Joo." *Yeoksa Bipyung* (History Criticism). March 1988.

3892. Chung Woon-Kyung. *Walsun the Housemaid*. Seoul: *Joong-Ang Ilbo*, 1991. 125 pp.

3893. Jang Mi-Jung. "The Great Drawing Battles Between Lim Kuk-Jung and Jang Gil-San." *Woori Sidae*. July 1987.

3894. Jung Jun-Young. "Cartoonists' Profiles." Paper presented at International Association for Mass Communication Research, Seoul, Korea, July 5, 1994.

3895. Jung Jun-Young. "The Comic Words of Cartoonist Park Bong-Sung." *Moonhak Gwa Sahoe* (Literature and Society). 1993.

3896. Jung Jun-Young. *Ilki Manwha Bogiwa Manwha* (Looking at Cartoons and Reading Cartoons). Seoul: Hannarae, 1994. 243 pp. Korean. (Lee Hyun-Se, Park Pongseung, Huh Youngman, Koh Haengseuk).

3897. Jung Jun-Young. "Kang Chul-Soo Vs. Lee Hyun-Se." *Sasang Moon Yewoon*

Dong (Thoughts and Literature Movements). 1993.

3898. Kim Soo-Jung. *Kim Soo-Jung Manwha Junjip* (Kim Soo-Jung Cartoon Collections). Seoul: Seoul Moonwhasa, 1990. 20 Vols.

3899. Korean Cartoonists Association. *The Records of 24th Annual General Meeting.* Seoul: KCA, 1990.

3900. Lee Hang-Won, *et al. Cartoon Collection of Eight Cartoonists for the Poor Students.* Seoul: Yoyo Comics Molder, 1988.

3901. Lee Jae-Hyun. "Memories of 'Balbari.'" *Mal.* June 1990.

3902. Lim Cheong-San. "The Problems of Korean Cartoons and Answers to the Problems in Light of Cartoonists." Paper presented at First Korean Cartoon Culture Development Seminar, Research Institute for Cartoon Culture, Korean Cartoonists Association, Seoul, Korea, November 20, 1992.

3903. Yoon Pil. *Jolboorosoyida* (I Am an Upstart). Seoul: Manwha Journal Company, 1990.

3904. Yoon Youngok. *Putting My Life into a Four-Cut Panel.* Seoul: Jinsol, 1991. 258 pp. Korean.

Kim Song-Hwan

3905. *Asahi Shimbun.* February 16, 1991. Article on Kim Song-Hwan.

3906. *The Exhibition of Political Cartoons "Kobau" In Commemoration of the 10,000th Issue. Kim Song-Hwan.* Seoul: 1987. Korean.

3907. Kim Song-Hwan. *The Half of Life with Kobau.* Seoul: Yeol Wha Dang, 1978.

3908. Kim Song-Hwan. *Kim Song-Hwan Manwhajip Kongsangwon* (Kim Song-Hwan's Cartoon Collection Kongsangwon). Seoul: Samjoongdang, 1979.

3909. Kim Song-Hwan. *Kobau.* Seoul: Samjoongdang, 1979. 10 vols.

3910. Kim Song-Hwan. *Kobau Contemporaries: 40 Years Since Independence from Japan and Commentary Cartoons.* Seoul: Koryoga, 1987.

3911. Kim Song-Hwan. *Modern History of Kobau: Between 1951-1961.* Seoul: Koryoga, 1987. 316 pp. Korean.

3912. Koh Sun-Ah. "Kim Song-Hwan Spokesman for the People, Cartoonist of Old Kobau." *Korea Today.* No. 4, 1988, pp. 28-32.

3913. Oh Kwang-Soo. *Kobau Kim Song Hwan: Daejoong Young-Woongron* (Essay on

Popular Hero). Seoul: Saedae, 1970.

Kim Sung-In

3914. Kim Sung-In. *Cartoon Exhibition*. Seoul: Gurim Madang Min, 1988.

3915. Kim Sung-In. *Jungchimanpyungjip: Essaramul Midujooseyo* (Political Cartoon Collections: Trust Me). Seoul: Georum, 1988.

Kim Yong-Whan

3916. Kim Yong-Whan. *Kojubu Pyoranggi*. Seoul: Yungsung, 1983.

3917. Kim Yong-Whan. *Kojubu Sisamanwhajip* (Kojubu Journalistic Cartoons). Seoul: Yungsung, 1983.

Lee Doo-Ho

3918. Lee Doo-Ho. *Puri* (Roots). Seoul: Hakwon Choolpansa, 1979.

3919. Lee Doo-Ho. *Tanggeomi* (Sunset Shadow). Seoul: Whamoongak, 1988.

Lee Hee-Jae

3920. Lee Hee-Jae. *Ganpan Star* (The Most Famous Star). Seoul: Ye-Um Publishing Company, 1987.

3921. Lee Hee-Jae. *Sungjil Soonan, Jebijun* (Sufferings of Sungjil, Swallow Story). Seoul: Goguryo Sung, 1988.

Lee Hyun-Se

3922. Lee Hyun-Se. *Cheolbooji Kachi 1* (Native Kachi 1). Seoul: Wonjung Publishing Company, 1988.

3923. Lee Hyun-Se. *Myunuri Bapulkote Daehan Bogoseo* (*Report on the Flower of Myunuri Bapul*). Seoul: Hosan Moonwhasa, 1988. 2 Vols.

Park Jae-Dong

3924. Park Jae-Dong. *Aiya Woori Siktaken Unzangpane*. (Children, There Is a Silver Plate on Our Table). Seoul: Theory and Practice Publishing, 1994. 328 pp. Korean.

3925. Park Jae-Dong. *Cartoons! My Love: Park Jae-Dong's Cartoon Essay*. Seoul: Jiin Publishing Co., 1994. 263 pp. Korean. (Japan, Korea, U.S.).

3926. Park Jae-Dong. *Hapdang Blues*. Seoul: Yiron Kwa Shilchoung, 1992. 346 pp.

3927. Park Jae-Dong. "Pictures Drawn in the Sky." In *Towards People's Arts*, Hyun Silgwa Bal Un. Seoul: Gwa Hak Gwa Sa Sang, 1990.

3928. Park Jae-Dong. *Whan Sang Yi Combi*. (Fantastic Combination). Seoul: Chingu, 1989. 228 pp.

3929. Whang Ji-Woo. "Laughs at Power—Iconic Analysis of Park Jae-Dong's Cartoons." In *Towards People's Arts*, Hyun Silgwa Bal Un 2. Seoul: Gwa Hak Gwa Sa Sang, 1990.

Park Soo-Dong

3930. Park Soo-Dong. *Goindol*. Seoul: Kachi, 1973.

3931. Park Soo-Dong. *Goindol Wangguk* (Goindol's Kingdom). Seoul: Moon Hang Sa, 1992. 229 pp.

3932. Park Soo-Dong. *Honggil Dong Kwa Heading Park*. Seoul Moon Hang Sa, 1992. 223 pp.

3933. Park Soo-Dong. *Wife Haengjin Kok* (Wife March). Seoul: Moon Hang Sa, 1992. 265 pp.

Animation

3934. "Korea Picks Cartoon Net." *Variety*. November 14-20, 1994, p. 37.

3935. Lee Sook-Yi, *et al*. "Special Edition: Study of Television Animated Movies." *Bangsong 90* (Broadcasting 90). July 1990.

3936. Lee Won-Bok. "Korean Comic Animation Industry." Paper presented at the Foreign Comic Movies and Videos Seminar, YWCA, Seoul, 1992.

3937. Lim Cheong-San. "The Principle and Practice of Animation As Total Arts." *Journal of the Kongju National Junior College*. 17 (1990), pp. 1-27.

3938. Park Ki-Joon. *The Skills of Cartoon Movies II*. Seoul: Woo Ram, 1988.

3939. Shin Gyu-Ho. "Animated Movies: Do We Still Need Other Countries' Cartoons?" *Sami Gipun Mool*. April 1985.

3940. Shin Jin-Sik. *Computer Animation*. Seoul: Hangook Moonyun, 1989.

3941. "South Korean Censors, Low Blows." *The Economist*. April 16, 1994, p.94.

3942. "Television: Sombre Comics," *Asiaweek*. December 23, 1977, p.39.

3943. Whan Sun-Gil. *Animation Movie History*. Seoul: Baeksoosa, 1990.

3944. Whan Sun-Gil. "The Present Situation and the Possibility of Animation." *Gha Nah Art*. November/December 1990, pp. 100-102.

3945. Whan Sun-Gil. "Understanding Animation." *Bang Song Sidae* (Broadcasting Age). Fall/Winter 1993.

Comic Books

3946. "Korean Comic Slams U.S. Policy." *Comics Journal*. February 1991, p.22.

3947. "Korean Comics Collection Stimulates New Level of Subject Access." *Comic Art Collection*. December 2, 1991, p.3.

3948. Lim Dong-Ahn. *Introduction to Animation*. Seoul: Myung Ji Publishing Co., 1990.

3949. Roh Byung-Sung. "The Comic Book Industry." Paper presented at International Association for Mass Communication Research, Seoul, Korea, July 5, 1994.

Circulation and Readership

3950. Choi Yeol. "Production and Circulation of Korean Cartoons." In *Hankookui Daejoong Moonwhna* (Korean Popular Culture), edited by Kang Hyun-Dew. Seoul: Nanam, 1987.

3951. Han Dae-Hee. "The Ways of Production and Distribution of Deleterious Cartoons." *Madang*. May 1985.

3952. Im Bum. "Because the Circulation Structure Changes, Korean Cartoons Are on the Edge." *Hankyoreh Shinmun*. October 29, 1994, p.8.

3953. Korean Gallup. *A Survey Research on Cartoon Rental Shops—Their Current Situation*. Seoul: Korean Gallup, 1990.

3954. Korean Publications Ethics Committee. *The Actual Situation of Cartoons Circulation and Better Strategies*. Seoul: KPEC, March 5, 1990.

3955. Korean Publications Ethics Committee. *Report of the Opinion Survey: The Cartoon Rental Shop Businessmen's Opinion on the Regulation of Monitoring Cartoon Publications*. Seoul: KPEC, December 1993.

3956. Korean Publications Ethics Committee. *Report on Circulation of Deleterious Publications and Content Analysis*. Seoul: KPEC, 1989.

3957. Korean Publications Ethics Committee. *A Survey on the Cartoon Rental Shops.* Seoul: KPEC, 1990.

3958. Korean Publications Ethics Committee. *A Survey Report on the Management of Cartoon Rental Shops.* Seoul: KPEC, 1989.

3959. Lee Won-Bok. *A Study of Reformation of Circulation Structure of Korean Cartoons.* Seoul: Korean Publications Ethics Committee, 1991.

3960. Lee Sang-Woo. "Cartoon Theories by Audience." *Wolgan Dokseo.* March 1979.

3961. Lim Cheong-San. *A Survey of Circulation Situation of Japanese Cartoon and Reading Patterns in Korea.* Seoul: Korea Publications Ethics Committee, 1993. 163 pp. Korean.

3962. "News about Exemplary Comic Rental Shop." *Monthly Publications Ethics Bulletin.* December 1993, p.21. Korean.

3963. Seoul YWCA. *The Second Survey Report on the Use of Cartoon Rental Shops in Seoul—Focusing on the Shops Near Railroad Stations.* Seoul: YWCA, 1989.

3964. Seoul YWCA. *A Survey Report on Reading Patterns of Comic Magazines During Youth Week.* Seoul: YWCA, 1992. Korean.

3965. Seoul YWCA. *A Survey Report on the Use of Cartoon Rental Shops Around Middle and High Schools in Seoul.* Seoul: YWCA, 1988.

3966. Seoul YWCA Cartoon Monitor Meeting. *Survey Report on the Youth's Readership of Weekly Cartoon Magazines.* Seoul: YWCA, 1992.

3967. "A Survey of Comic Circulation Through Comic Rental Shops." *Monthly Publications Ethics Bulletin.* May 1994, pp. 15-17. Korean.

Governance

3968. "Advisory Committee of Cartoon Reviewing." *Monthly Publications Ethics Bulletin.* October 1993, p. 24. Korean.

3969. Culture Ministry. *Publication Policy Reference Book.* Seoul: 1991.

3970. "Gonghae Manwha." (Cartoon Pollution). *Chosun Ilbo.* May 1990. Editorial.

3971. Kim Hyun-Bae. "Creation of Cartoons Suffering from the Double Value Structure." Paper presented at meeting, "Today and Tomorrow of Korean Newspaper Cartoons," Research Institute for Cartoon Culture, Korean Cartoonists Association, November 20, 1992.

3972. *Kim Satgat, the Walking Dictionary of Copyright*. Seoul: Committee of Copyright Monitoring and Adjustment, 1993.

3973. Korean Publications Ethics Committee. *The Annual Review Report in 1990*. Seoul: KPEC, 1990.

3974. Korean Publications Ethics Committee. *The Annual Review Report in 1992*. Seoul: KPEC, 1990.

3975. Korean Publications Ethics Committee. *The Annual Review Report in 1993*. Seoul: KPEC, 1993.

3976. Korean Publications Ethics Committee. *The Ethics Code and Practice Guidelines of Book Publishing*. Seoul: KPEC, October 1989.

3977. Korean Publications Ethics Committee. *The Publications Ethics, January 1993-April 1994*. Seoul: KPEC, 1994.

3978. Korean Publications Ethics Committee. *A Report for Deep Considerations on the Circulation of Deleterious Publications and the Readers*. Seoul: KPEC, 1990.

3979. Korean Publications Ethics Committee. *Report on the Deleterious Publications and Proposals for Their Annihilation*. Seoul: KPEC, December 1989.

3980. Korean Publications Ethics Committee. *A Study on the Publication Ethics*. Seoul: KPEC, 1990.

3981. Lee Hee-Jae. "Barun Manwha Yeongoowhoe (Research Association for the Right Cartoons). Which Gets Rid of Violent and Deleterious Cartoons." *Hankookin*. September 1990.

3982. "1993 Annual Reviewing Report." Seoul: Korean Publications Ethics Committee, 1994. Korean. (Comics, pp. 101-178, 207-230).

3983. "The People's Duty To Watch Journalism." *Sisa Journal*. January 10, 1992.

3984. Seoul YWCA Children's Department. *Article Collection of the Conference for "Sound Cartoon Culture Formation Campaign—Do We Need To Make a Law To Prevent Illegally Circulated Cartoons?"* Seoul: YWCA, May 3, 1993.

3985. Seoul YWCA Children's Department. *Collection of Cartoon Study Materials 4: Instructions of Cartoon Monitoring*. Seoul: YWCA, 1992 (?).

3986. Seoul YWCA Children's Department. *Report of Seoul YWCA Cartoon Monitoring Meeting*. Seoul: YWCA, 1991.

3987. Seoul YWCA Children's Department. *Report of the Children Cartoon Monitor Meetings (May 1988-April 1989)*. Seoul: YWCA Children's Department, 1989.

3988. Seoul YWCA Children's Department. *Report of Seoul YWCA Children Cartoon Monitor Meeting*. Seoul: YWCA, 1993.

Japanese Comics

3989. "Emergence of Pessimistic Opinions About Japanese Cartoons." *Monthly Publications Ethics Bulletin*. October 1993, p. 23. Korean.

3990. "How We Deal with Japanese Cartoons." *Monthly Publications Ethics Bulletin*. October 1993, pp. 8-15. Korean. (Panel discussion report).

3991. "Japanese Cartoons in Korea." *Asian Mass Communication Bulletin*. July-August 1991, p. 5.

3992. "Japanese Comics Craze Hits Korea." *Asian Mass Communication Bulletin*. January-February 1993, p. 8.

3993. "Korean Cartoonists Fight To Regain Their Market." *Asian Mass Communication Bulletin*. November-December 1993, p. 7.

3994. "Korean Cartoonists Fight To Regain Their Own Turf." *Korea Newsreview*. July 1993, pp. 31-32.

3995. Korean Publications Ethics Committee. *Research on the Copied Version of Japanese Cartoons*. Seoul: KPEC, December 1993.

3996. Korean Publications Ethics Committee. *A Review Report on the Adult Cartoons Which Were Not Reviewed by the Committee and Copied from the Japanese Cartoons*. Seoul: KPEC, May 1988.

3997. Korean Publications Ethics Committee. *Survey Report on the Copied or Plagiarized Cartoons from the Japanese and Comparative Analysis of Korean-Japanese Boys and Girls Comic Magazines*. Seoul: KPEC, 1990.

3998. Leahy, Kevin. "Anime and Manga in Korea." *The Rose*. July 1994, pp. 28-29.

3999. Lee Soon-Duk. "Japanese Publication Culture Opening the Age of New Media Publication." *Chool Pan Munwha* (Publication Culture). July 1991.

4000. Lee Sang Soo. "Youth Readership Survey of Translated Japanese Cartoons and Content Analysis." Paper presented at Campaign Meeting for Sound Cartoon Culture, YWCA, Seoul, Korea, May 30, 1993.

4001. Lim Cheong-San. *A Comparative Study on Activities of Cartoon Arts Between Korea and Japan*. Kongju: L.C.S. International Cartoon Institute, 1992. 34 pp. Korean.

4002. "Pirated Japanese Comics Floods [sic] Korea." *Comics Journal*. July 1993, p. 24.

4003. Seoul YWCA Cartoon Monitor Meeting. *Survey Report on Children's Recognition of Korean Translated Japanese Cartoons*. Seoul: YWCA, 1991.

4004. Seoul YWCA Children's Department. "Survey Report on the Students' Readership and Recognition of Translated Japanese Cartoons." Paper presented at Campaign Meeting for Sound Cartoon Culture, "Illegally Circulated Cartoons, Do We Need a Law?" YWCA Children's Department, Seoul, Korea, May 30, 1993.

4005. Sohn Tae-Soo. "Mixed Reaction Over Import of Japanese Culture." *Korea Newsreview*. March 1994, p. 28.

4006. "The True Aspect of Japanese Cultural Invasion of Korea, Part 1." *Monthly Publications Ethics Bulletin*. January-February 1994, pp. 2-11. Korean.

4007. "The True Aspect of Japanese Cultural Invasion of Korea, Part 2." *Monthly Publications Ethics Bulletin*. March 1994, pp. 2-17. Korean.

4008. "The True Aspect of Japanese Cultural Invasion of Korea, Part 3." *Monthly Publications Ethics Bulletin*. April 1994, pp. 2-20. Korean.

Comic Strips

4009. Chang Sang-Ok. "The Role of Enlightenment of Modern Korean Newspaper Cartoons." Master's thesis, Yonsei University, Department of Administration, 1991.

4010. "Comic Pollution." *Asian Messenger*. Winter 1978/Spring 1979, p. 14.

4011. "Dirty Strips." *Asian Mass Communication Bulletin*. December 1980, p. 17.

4012. Dredge, C. Paul. "Social Rules of Speech of a Comic Strip Character." *Korea Journal*. January 1976, pp. 4-14.

4013. Gwak Dae-Won. "The Reality of Korean Newspaper Cartoons: The Cartoons Need To Change." *Gha Nah Art*. March 1989.

4014. Oh Ryong. "Essay on Newspaper Cartoons." *Wolgan Dokseo* (Monthly Reading). March 1979.

4015. Park Ki-Joon, "Caricature and Comic Strips: Essential to Korean Journalism." *Asian Culture*. January 1980, pp. 4-5.

Political Cartoons

4016. Bantzogi. *Bantzogi's Sisa Manpyung 1: Minjoojoouirul Wihae Pogihaseyo* (Bantzogi's Commentary Cartoons 1: Just Give Up for Democracy). Seoul: Hangilsa, 1989.

4017. "Cartoon Aimed at Chun Is Banned in Seoul." *Far Eastern Economic Review.* February 13, 1986, p. 8.

4018. Choi Yeol. "The Current Situation of Korean Political Cartoons." *Suwon University Newspaper.* March 16 through April 13, 1988.

4019. Clifford, Mark. "A Funny Thing Happened on the Way to Democracy." *Far Eastern Economic Review.* May 26, 1988, pp. 52-53.

4020. Lee Hae-Chang. "Gundae Hankook Sisa Manwhaui Baljachi (Footprints of Korean Modern Commentary Cartoons). *Gaegan Misool* (Quarterly Arts). March 1984.

4021. Lee Hae-Chang. *Ideas of Korean Satirical Cartoons.* Seoul: SaeGul-sa, 1976.

4022. Lee Won-Bok. "The Social Impact of Newspaper Cartoons." Paper presented at First Journalism Conference, Korean Press Center, Seoul, December 8, 1990.

4023. Lee Woo-Jung. *Manwha Kim Young-Sam* (President Kim Young-Sam in Cartoons). Seoul: Dongwang Publishing Company, 1987.

4024. Lee Yeon-Tak. "Study of Korean Satirical Literature. Seoul: Ewoo Publishing Co., 1979.

4025. *Manwha Changjak.* Seoul: Barun Manwha Yunguhoe, 1980. 230 pp. Korean.

4026. Oh Gyu-Won. "Woorinara Sisa Manwharon" (Essays on Our Country's Commentary Cartoons). *Yichunnyun* (2000 years). December 1984. Reprinted in Kang Hyun-Dew, ed. *Hankookui Daejoongmoonwha* (Korean Popular Culture). Seoul: Nanam, 1984.

4027. Park Jae-Dong. "Political Cartoons." Paper presented at International Association for Mass Communication Research, Seoul, Korea, July 5, 1994.

4028. Shim Jae-Hoon. "A Hard Act To Follow." *Far Eastern Economic Review.* June 13, 1991, pp. 54-55.

Sports Newspapers Cartoons

4029. "Cartoons in Sports Newspapers Are Facing Critical Judgment." *Dong-A Ilbo*. June 19, 1992.

4030. Cha Ae-Ok. "Study of the Impacts of Newspaper Cartoons on Cartoon Culture—With Respect to Sports Newspaper Cartoons." Master's thesis, Sogang University, Graduate School of Public Policy, 1992.

4031. Choi Suk-Tae. "Current Situations of Newspaper Cartoons and Proposals for Betterment—in Terms of Daily Sports Newspapers." Paper presented at meeting, "Today and Tomorrow of Korean Newspaper Cartoons," Research Institute for Cartoon Culture, Korean Cartoonists Association, Seoul, Korea, September 25, 1992.

4032. Lee Sang-Soo. "A Proposal for the Sports Newspaper Cartoons With Reference to Impact on the Youth." Paper presented at meeting, "Today and Tomorrow of Korean Newspaper Cartoons," Research Institute for Cartoon Culture, Korean Cartoonists Association, Seoul, Korea, September 25, 1992.

4033. Park Joo-Pil. "The Pornography of Sports Newspapers." *Mal*. August 1990.

4034. Seoul YWCA. *Report of Readership Survey of Sports Newspapers and Analysis Results*. Seoul: YWCA, 1991.

4035. Seoul YMCA. *A Survey Report on the Youth's Readership of Sports Newspapers*. Seoul: YMCA, November 1990.

4036. Seoul YWCA Cartoon Monitor Meeting. *Report on Youth Readership Survey of Sports Newspapers*. Seoul: YWCA, 1991.

4037. "Serialized Cartoons in Sports Newspapers—There Is No Will To Correct." *Dong-A Ilbo*. January 30, 1992.

4038. "The Sports Newspapers Enter into Dirty Competition." *Un Lon Nobo*. June 7, 1992.

4039. "Sports Seoul Stops Its Extra Copies of Adult Cartoons." *Un Lon Nobo*. July 5, 1992.

MALAYSIA

General Sources

4040. Aznam, Suhaini. "Quipping Away at Racism." *Far Eastern Economic Review*. December 14, 1989, pp. 42, 46.

4041. Gallop, Annabel. "Koleksi Melayu di British Library, London." *Sari*. 6 (1988), pp. 75-86.

4042. "Moving Pictures." *Asiaweek*. May 6, 1988, p. 43.

4043. "Sketching Life's Colours." *Straits Times*. July 26, 1989.

4044. Wan Abdul Kadir Wan Yusoff. *Budaya Popular dalam Masyarakat Melayu Bandaran* (Popular Culture in Urban Malay Society). Kuala Lumpur: Dewan Bahasa dan Pustaka, 1988.

Cartooning, Cartoons

4045. Abdul Rahman Sallehhuddin. "Satu Kajian Mengenai Bahasa Tampak dalam Seni Lukis Kartun." Kursus Seni Reka Grafik, Thesis, Institut Teknologi MARA, Shah Alam, 1984.

4046. Ahmad Radzi Mohd Bedu. "Ilustrasi Kartun dalam Kad Ucapan Yang Mengutarakan Imej Malaysia." Kursus Seni Reka Grafik, Thesis, Institut Teknologi MARA, Shah Alam, 1981.

4047. A. Samad Ismail. "Kartunis Cabaran dan Masa Sepan." *Sasaran*. December 1992, pp. 118-122.

4048. "Dari Sinar Harapan, Orang-orang Jepun Tak Suka Kartun Berbau Kritik, Mingguan Malaysia." *Mingguan Malaysia*. January 16, 1983.

4049. Ismail Zain. *Seni dan Imajan*. Kuala Lumpur: Balai Senilukis Negara, 1980.

4050. Jamaliah Mahmud. "Seni Lukis Kartun Sebagai Media Sindiran." Kursus Seni Reka Grafik, Thesis, Institut Teknologi MARA, Shah, Alam, 1986.

4051. Muliyadi Mahamood. "Kartunis Perlu Wujudkan Persatuan Untuk Jaga Kepentingan Mereka." *Utusan Malaysia*. December 28, 1984.

4052. Muliyadi Mahamood. "Mengenal Senilukis Kartun Melayu Malaysia: Humor—Sindiran Ada di Dalamnya." *Harian Nasional* (Kuala Lumpur). April 5, 1984.

4053. Muliyadi Mahamood. "Picasso Sebegai Kartunis." *Dewan Budaya*. May 1989.

4054. Muliyadi Mahamood. "Sikap dan Sifat Masyarakat Melayu dari Kacamata Kartunis Melayi Malaysia Masakini." (Attitudes and Characteristics of Malay Society As Seen Through the Lenses of Malay Cartoonists of Malaysia at the Present Time). Thesis, Institut Teknologi MARA, Shah Alam, 1984. 111 pp.

4055. Sabri Said. "Kartun. Media Untuk Membentuk Masyarakat Cemerlang 2020."
       Sasaran. December 1992, pp. 126-128.

4056. Zambri. "Kartun dan Media." Kursus Seni Reka Grafik, Thesis, Institut
       Teknologi MARA, Shah Alam, 1981.

4057. Zulkifli Hamzah. "Peranan Seni Lukis Kartun." Kursus Seni Halus, Thesis,
       Institut Teknologi MARA, Shah Alam, 1981.

Anthologies

4058. Aza. *Fiesta*. Kuala Lumpur: Creative Enterprise Sdn. Bhd., 1993. 120 pp.

4059. Nan. *Koleksi Din Teksi*. Kuala Lumpur: Utusan Publications and Distributors
       Sdn. Bhd., 1992. 158 pp.

4060. *Pameran. Karikatur. Kartun & Komik*. Balai Seni Lukis Negara. 16 Jun-9 Julau
       1989. Kuala Lumpur: Balai Senilukis Negara, 1989.

4061. *Perjumpaan Kartunis Antarabangsa. Malaysia 1990. International Cartoonists
       Gathering. Sept. 27-Oct. 3, 1990*. Kuala Lumpur: 1990. 30 pp.

4062. *Selamatkanlah Malaysia*. Kuala Lumpur: n.p., 1990. 48 pp.

4063. "Selections of Works by Cartoonists [and] Illustrators, Creative Enterprise Sdn.
       Bhd." Kuala Lumpur: Creative Enterprise Sdn. Bhd., n.d. 8 pp.

Historical Aspects

4064. "The Malayan Punch." *British Malaya*. September 1927, p. 131.

4065. Redza. "Enlightening Cartoon Shows." *Sunday Times* (Malaysia). October 28,
       1973.

4066. Zailah Ishmail. "Turning to Our Own Legends To Delight the Children." *Straits
       Times*. October 21, 1973.

4067. Zainab Awang Ngah. "Malay Comic Books Published in the 1950's." *Kekal
       Abadi* (Berita Perpustakaan Universiti Malaya). 3:3 (1984), pp. 4-11.

4068. Zakiah Hanum. *Senda Sindir Sengat* (Karikatur Melayu Silam). Petaling Jaya:
       Penerbitan Lajmeidakh Sdn. Bhd., 1989. 122 pp.

Humor Magazines

4069. Provencher, Ronald. "Covering Malay Humor Magazines: Satire and Parody of
       Malaysian Political Dilemmas." *Crossroads*. 5:2 (1990), pp. 1-25.

4070. Provencher, Ronald. "Modern Malay Folklore: The Humor Magazines." In *Asian Popular Culture*, edited by John A. Lent. Boulder, Colorado: Westview, forthcoming

4071. Provencher, Ronald and Jaafar Omar. "Malay Humor Magazines As a Resource for the Study of Modern Malay Culture." *Sari*. 6 (1988), pp. 87-99.

4072. Sukardi Abdul Ghani. "Istimewanya Majalah Gila-Gila." *Mastika* (Kuala Lumpur). March 1980.

PEKARTUN

4073. *Mesyuarat Agung. Persatuan Kartunis Selangor dan Wilayah Persekutuan. 10 April 1993*. Kuala Lumpur: PEKARTUN, 1993. 12 pp.

4074. Muliyadi Mahamood. "Menyatukan. Pekartun Kartunis." *Peka*. 1, 1993, pp. 3-4.

4075. "Pekartun Jadi Tamu Kerajaan Negeri Sarawak." *Peka*. 1, 1993, p. 13.

Cartoonists

4076. *1st. Malaysian Apazine: A Collective Showcase of Original Comics Art*. Kuala Lumpur: Amateur Press Association of Malaysia and Berita Publishing Sdn. Bhd., 1985. 98 pp.

4077. Kerengge. *Siri Gila-Gila Produksi Dengan Kerengge*. Kuala Lumpur: Creative Enterprise Sdn. Bhd., 1986. 120 pp.

4078. Lee, Reggie. *Made in Malaysia*. Kuala Lumpur: Berita Publishing, 1984. 84 pp.

4079. Lim Cheng Tju. "Comicscene Forever!" *Big O Magazine*. February 1994, pp. 58-59. (Daniel Chan).

4080. Lim Kok Wing. *Guli Guli*. Petaling Jaya: Eastern Universities Press Sdn. Bhd., 1983.

4081. Nik Naizi Husin and M. Hafez M. Soom. "Cabai. Kartunis Wanita Yang Gigih." *Sasaran*. July 1993, pp. 110-112. (Woman cartoonist, Cabai).

4082. Provencher, Ron. "Malay Cartoonists and Humor Writers." *Philippines Communication Journal*. March 1993, pp. 15-43.

4083. "When Cartoonists Get Together." *The New Paper*. October 2, 1990.

4084. "Yankee Leong. An Obituary to Malaysia's Foremost Prewar Artist and Cartoonist." *Jurnal Kewartawanan Malaysia*. April-May-June 1986, pp. 45-46.

Jaafar Taib

4085. Jaafar Taib. *Gila-Gila Jungle Jokes*. Kuala Lumpur: Creative Enterprise Sdn. Bhd., 1991. 66 pp.

4086. Jaafar Taib. *Kalau. Jilid 2*. Kuala Lumpur: Creative Enterprise Sdn. Bhd., 1993. 121 pp.

Lat (Mohd. Nor Khalid)

4087. Abishegam, Joanna. "Lat's Kampung Legacy." *Sunday Style* (Kuala Lumpur). February 14, 1993, pp. 12-13.

4088. Chandy, Gloria. "Lat—The Malaysian Folk Hero." *The New Straits Times Annual 1980*. Kuala Lumpur: Berita Publishing, 1980, pp. 38-42.

4089. Dunfee, E.J. "The Joker's Wild." *Asia Magazine*. March 19, 1989, pp. 8-14.

4090. Hantover, Jeffrey. "Lat's Last Laugh." *Far Eastern Economic Review*. February 23, 1995, pp. 46-47.

4091. Lat. *Buku Conteng Lat*. Kuala Lumpur: Berita Publishing Sdn. Bhd., 1983.

4092. Lat. *Buku Mewarna Lat 4* (Lat's Colouring Book 4). Kuala Lumpur: Berita Publishing Sdn. Bhd., 1983.

4093. Lat. *Entah Lah Mak...!* Kuala Lumpur: Berita Publishing, n.d. 86 pp.

4094. Lat. *It's a Lat Lat Lat Lat World*. Kuala Lumpur: Berita Publishing, 1985. 146 pp.

4095. Lat. *The Kampung Boy*. Kuala Lumpur: Berita Publishing Sdn. Bhd., 1978.

4096. Lat. *Kampung Boy Yesterday and Today*. Kuala Lumpur: Berita Publishing, 1993.

4097. Lat. *Keluarga Si Mamat*. Kuala Lumpur: Berita Publishing Sdn. Bhd., 1994. 112 pp.

4098. Lat. *Lat and Gang*. Kuala Lumpur: Berita Publishing Sdn. Bhd., 1987. 107 pp.

4099. Lat. *Lat and His Lot Again!* Kuala Lumpur: Berita Publishing, 1983.

4100. Lat. *Lat 30 Years Later*. Petaling Jaya: Kampung Boy, 1994.

4101. Lat. *Lat with a Punch*. Kuala Lumpur: Berita Publishing, 1988. 157 pp.

4102. Lat. *Lots of Lat*. Kuala Lumpur: Berita Publishing, 1977. 140 pp.

4103. Lat. *Mat Som*. Petaling Jaya: Kampung Boy Sdn. Bhd., 1989. 187 pp.

4104. Lat. *Town Boy*. Kuala Lumpur: Berita Publishing Sdn. Bhd., 1981.

4105. "Lat a Favourite in Singapore." *New Straits Times*. January 1, 1991.

4106. "Lat's Lot." *Big O Magazine*. August 1991, p. 26.

4107. Lent, John A. "A Lot About Lat: An Exclusive Interview." *Berita*. Winter 1987, pp. 28-34.

4108. Lent, John A. "A Lot of Lat." *WittyWorld*. Summer 1987, pp. 28-30.

4109. Lent, John A. "What's Lat Got To Do With Us?" *Sasaran*. No. 8, 1987, pp. 12-15.

4110. Lim Cheng Tju. "Just a Simple Man. The Lat Interview." *Big O Magazine*. January 1994, pp. 59-60.

4111. McKinley, Robert. "Lat's Cartoons and the Ancient Tradition of Betel Chewing." Paper presented at Malaysia/Singapore/Brunei Studies Group, Ann Arbor, Michigan, August 2-4, 1984.

4112. "Malaysian Cartoonist Lat Makes Japanese Debut." *Asian Mass Communication Bulletin*. 15:1 (1985), p. 15.

4113. *New Straits Times*. April 20, 1986, April 17, 1988, and August 29, 1989. (On Lat).

4114. Yronwode, Cat. "Fit To Print." *Comics Buyer's Guide*. June 29, 1984, pp. 68, 70.

Rejab Had

4115. Provencher, Ronald. "Travels with the Headman: Rehab Had, Cartoonist and Teacher." Special edition of *Journal of Asian Pacific Communications*, edited by John A. Lent, forthcoming.

4116. Rejab Had. *Bengkel Kartun Rejabhad* (Rejabhad's Cartoon Workshop). Petaling Jaya: Rejab Had, 1990.

4117. Rejab Had. *Gila-Gila Tan Tin Tun*. Kuala Lumpur: Creative Enterprise Sdn. Bhd., 1992. 169 pp.

4118. Rejab Had. *Perwira Mat Gila* (A Grandly Humorous Legend). Kuala Lumpur: Creative Enterprise, 1988.

4119. Rejab Had. *Siri Gila-Gila Produksi Dengan Rejab Had*. Kuala Lumpur: Creative Enterprise Sdn. Bhd., 1983. 146 pp.

Animation

4120. Azitah Azmi. "Penyampaian Mesej Melalui Filem Animasi dan Keberkesanannya." Kursus Seni Reka Grafik, Thesis, Institut Teknologi MARA, Shah Alam, 1989.

4121. "A Bumpy Carpet Ride." *Asiaweek*. July 14, 1993, p. 28.

4122. "Film Ban Call." *Far Eastern Economic Review*. June 10, 1993, p. 14.

4123. Mohd Fauzi Hj. Hamzah. "Unsur-unsur Pendidikan Moral dalam Filem Animasi Kartun." Kursus Seni Reka Grafik, Thesis, Institut Teknologi MARA, Shah Alam, 1992.

4124. Muhd Marzuki Ibrahim. "Animasi di Malaysia; Sejauhmanakah Perkembangannaya." Kursus Seni Reka Grafik, Thesis, Institut Teknologi MARA, Shah Alam, 1988.

4125. Muliyadi Mahamood. "Sikap dan Sifat Masyarakat Melayu dari Kacamata Kartunis Melayu Malaysia Masa Kini." Kursus Seni Halus, Thesis, Institut Teknologi MARA, Shah Alam, 1984.

4126. Mustaffa Ahmad Hidzir. "Animasi dalam Seni Iklan Televisyen." Kursus Seni Reka Grafik, Thesis, Institut Teknologi MARA, Shah Alam, 1978.

4127. Roshadah Othman. "Kesedaran Yang Mempengaruhi Penggunaan Animasi dalam Pengiklanan di Malaysia." Kursus Seni Reka Grafik, Thesis, Institut Teknologi MARA, Shah Alam, 1992.

4128. Rozairi Omar. "Karikatur; Pendekatan dalam Menyampaikan Mesej di Malaysia Masa Kini." Kursus Seni Reka Grafik, Thesis, Institut Teknologi MARA, 1992.

4129. Zaili Sulan. "Animasi Moden, Nafas Baru Kepada Pengiklanan Kreatif." Kursus Seni Reka Grafik, Thesis, Institut Teknologi MARA, Shah Alam, 1983.

4130. Zamri Pahrul. "Pengaruh Kartun TV Terhadap Kanak-Kanak." Kursus Seni Reka Grafik, Thesis, Institut Teknologi MARA, Shah Alam, 1989.

Comic Books

4131. Abdul Malik Jamal. "Komik Melayu Sezaman." Kursus Seni Reka Grafik, Thesis, Institut Teknologi MARA, Shah Alam, 1979.

4132. Anuar Dan. "Garisan Terhadap Ilustrasi Komik, Kartun dan Cerita Bergambar untuk Kanak-kanak di Malaysia." Kursus Seni Reka Grafik, Thesis, Institut Teknologi MARA, Shah Alam, 1983.

4133. "EduComics' Rifas Visits Malaysia." *Comics Buyer's Guide*. December 23, 1983, p. 3.

4134. Halim Hj. Hassan. "Seni Lukis Komik dan Kartun Tempatan; Satu Tinjauan ke Atas Kemajuannya Dulu dan Sekarang." Kursus Seni Reka Grafik, Thesis, Institut Teknologi MARA, Shah Alam, 1985.

4135. "KL To Act Against Subversive Comic Publishers." *CAJ Quarterly Newsletter*. September 1985, p. 8.

4136. Lim, C.T. "The Comics Scene in KL." *Big O Magazine*. February 1994, p. 59.

4137. Mohd Rofi Yaakub. "Komik Sebagai Medan Ilmu." Kursus Seni Reka Grafik, Thesis, Institut Teknologi MARA, Shah Alam, 1990.

4138. Mohd Sah Mohd Deli. "Ilustrasi dalam Komik di Malaysia." Kursus Seni Reka Grafik, Thesis, Institut Teknologi MARA, Shah Alam, 1981.

4139. Nor Eliza Md. Nasir. "Ilustrasi Majalah, Komik dan Buku Kanak-kanak Tempatan: Satu Tinjauan Terhadap Teknik, Ilustrasi dan Penyerapan Unsur-unsur Islam." Kursus Seni Reka Grafik, Thesis, Institut Teknologi MARA, Shah Alam, 1984.

4140. Rifas, Leonard. "Comics in Malaysia." *Comics Journal*. October 1984, pp. 96-101.

4141. Salleh Hamzah. "Pelukis Komik Paling Gigih." *Berita Harian*. October 17, 1981.

4142. Suhaili Abd. Minal. "Pengaruh dan Unsur-unsur Pendidikan dalam Kartun dan Komik Tempatan Terhadap Kanak-kanak." Kursus Seni Reka Grafik, Thesis, Institut Teknologi MARA, 1984.

4143. Tajuddin Mohd. Yassin. "Komik dan Kartun Melayu." Kursus Seni Reka Grafik, Thesis, Institut Teknologi MARA, Shah Alam, 1979.

Comic Strips

4144. "Jurnalisme Kartun." In *Jurnalisme Akhbar*, edited by Mustaffa Suhaimi, pp. 108-120. Kuala Lumpur: Progressive Products, 1986.

4145. Lockard, Craig A. "Reflections of Change: Sociopolitical Commentary and Criticism in Malaysian Popular Music Since 1950." *Crossroads*. 6:1 (1991), pp. 1-106. (Lat, pp. 59-60; Kit Leee [M. Eeel], pp. 84-89).

Political Cartoons

4146. Maslina Yusuff. "Isu Sosial dan Politik Melalui Penyampaian Kartun." Kursus Seni Reka Grafik, Thesis, Institut Teknologi MARA, Shah Alam, 1984.

4147. Muliyadi Mahamood. "Kartunis Dianggap Binatang Politik Yang Melihat Dengan Mata Burung." *Utusan Malaysia*. November 19, 1984.

4148. Muliyadi Mahamood. "Mengenal Senilukis Kartun Melayu Malaysia: Sejak Lahir Jadi Senjata Politik—Kritik." *Harian Nasional*. April 6, 1984.

NEPAL

Cartoons and Development

4149. Comings, John. "Testing Literacy Materials—It's Worth It." *Development Communication Report*. 1, 1990, pp. 2-3.

4150. Walker, David A. "Pictures Open Unexpected Horizons in Nepal." *Development Communication Report*. Autumn 1986, p. 5.

PAKISTAN

General Sources

4151. Enayetullah, Anwar. "Many Young Cartoonists Appearing: Pakistan." *Asian Culture*. January 1980, pp. 24-25.

4152. "'Fired with the Spirit of Revolt.'" *Asiaweek*. August 31, 1984, p. 31.

4153. "Nigar Nazar." In *A History of Komiks of the Philippines and Other Countries*, by Cynthia Roxas and Joaquin Arevalo, Jr., p. 265. Manila: Islas Filipinas Publishing, 1985.

PHILIPPINES

General Sources

4154. Africa, Susana W. "Philippine Comics and Cartoons...." *Diliman Review*. July-August 1981, pp. 25-34.

4155. Alvina, Ma. Cristina B. "A Survey on Exposure to Newspaper Cartoon Strip/Comic Books and Attitude Toward Specific Types of Jokes and Joke Preferences." AB Thesis, University of Philippines, 1979. 93 pp.

4156. Balein, Jose. "Inkwell Heroes." *Sunday Times Magazine* (Manila). June 25, 1950, pp. 18-19.

4157. Cruz, E. Aquilar. "Filipino Humor." *Philippine Quarterly*. June 1952, pp. 8-12.

4158. Horn, Maurice, ed. *The World Encyclopedia of Comics*. New York: Chelsea House, 1976. (Pages 30, 74-75, 140-141, 210, 286, 328, 440-441, 474-475, 541, 577-578, 598, 621, 647, 687-688).

4159. Molina, Karolyn. "Filipino Humor: For All Seasons and Reasons." *Life Today*. March 1986, pp. 24-25.

Historical Aspects

Cartoons

4160. Esteban, Cirilo. "They Managed To Laugh." *Deadline*. September 1953, pp. 7-8.

4161. Matawaran, Ely. "Cartoons Through the Years." *Life Today*. March 1986, pp. 21-23.

4162. "Philippine Comics and Cartoons—How It All Began." *Diliman Review*. July/August 1981, pp. 25-34.

Comic Books (Komiks)

4163. Balein, Jose. "Philippine Comics." *Sunday Times Magazine* (Manila). June 25, 1950. p. 20.

4164. Buluran, Eduardo K. "A Historical Analysis of Super Hero Stories in Filipino Komiks." BA Thesis, University of the Philippines, 1986. 60 pp.

4165. Georges, Albert. "Philippines." In *Histoire Mondiale de la Bande Dessinée*, edited by Pierre Horay, pp. 286-287. Paris: Pierre Horay Éditeur, 1989.

4166. Roxas, Cynthia and Joaquin Arevalo, Jr. *A History of Komiks of the Philippines and Other Countries*. Quezon City: Islas Filipinas Publishing Co. Inc., 1984. 305 pp.

Comic Strips

4167. Mathay, Gabriel A.P. "A Case Study: The History and Development of the Filipino Newspaper Comic Strip." AB Thesis, University of the Philippines, 1976. 25 pp.

4168. Mayuga, Sylvia L. "From Kenkoy to Tisoy: Komiks and the Filipino Consciousness." *Sunburst*. April 1976, pp. 14-20.

Cartooning, Cartoons

4169. Santiago, Roni. "Cartooning in the Philippines." *PPI Press Forum*. 5:1 (1990), pp. 3-4.

4170. Santiago, Roni. "Cartooning in the Philippines." *PPI Press Forum*. 5:2 (1992), p. 5.

4171. Tsai, H.C. *Humor and Caricatures*. Manila: Regal, 1981. 75 pp.

Cartoonists and Their Works

4172. "Cartoonists Are Born, Not Made." *Life Today*. March 1986, pp. 21-25.

4173. "Cartoonists Get Together." *PPI Press Forum*. 5:1 (1990), pp. 2, 5.

4174. Delotavo, Antipas. "Through the Cartoonist's Eye." *Group Media Journal*. 7:3/4 (1988), pp. 11-12.

4175. Jundis, Orvy. "Aguila, Dani." In *Enciclopedia Mondiale del Fumetto*, edited by Maurice Horn and Luciano Secchi, p. 139. Milan: Editorial Corno, 1978.

4176. Jundis, Orvy. "Bulanadi, Danny (1946-)." In *Enciclopedia Mondiale del Fumetto*, edited by Maurice Horn and Luciano Secchi, p. 216. Milan: Editoriale Corno, 1978.

4177. Jundis, Orvy. "Gomez, Pablo S. (1931-)." In *Encliclopedia Mondiale del Fumetto*, edited by Maurice Horn and Luciano Secchi, pp. 429-430. Milan: Editoriale Corno, 1978.

4178. Jundis, Orvy. "Jodloman, Jesus M. (1925-)." In *Enciclopedia Mondiale del*

Fumetto, edited by Maurice Horn and Luciano Secchi, pp. 484-485. Milan: Editoriale Corno, 1978.

4179. Jundis, Orvy. "Martin, Menny Eusobio (1930-)." In *Enciclopedia Mondiale del Fumetto*, edited by Maurice Horn and Luciano Secchi, p. 554. Milan: Editoriale Corno, 1978.

4180. Jundis, Orvy. "Rodriguez, Emilio D. (1937-)." In *Enciclopedia Mondiale del Fumetto*, edited by Maurice Horn and Luciano Secchi, p. 660. Milan: Editoriale Corno, 1978.

4181. Jundis, Orvy. "Santos, Jesse F. (1928-)." In *Enciclopedia Mondiale del Fumetto*, edited by Maurice Horn and Luciano Secchi, pp. 670-671. Milan: Editoriale Corno, 1978.

4182. Jundis, Orvy. "Torres, Elpidio (1925-1973)." In *Enciclopedia Mondiale del Fumetto,* edited by Maurice Horn and Luciano Secchi, p. 736. Milan: Editoriale Corno, 1978.

4183. Matawaran, Ely. "Larry Alcala: Foremost Filipino Cartoonist." *WittyWorld.* Autumn 1987, pp. 30-31.

4184. Matienzo, Ros H. "J. Zabala Santos: Pioneer Cartoonist." *Philippine Comics Review.* First Quarter 1979, pp. 30-35.

4185. Matienzo, Ros H. "Vince Fago at the Plaza." *Philippine Comics Review.* First Quarter 1979, pp. 48-49.

4186. Miel, Deng Coy. *Cartoons of Deng Coy Miel.* Manila: Philippines Today, 1988. 94 pp.

4187. "Norman Isaac." *Humour and Caricature.* June/July 1994, pp. 14-15.

4188. Redondo, Sisenando P. "The First Philippine Comicbook Editor: Isaac Tolentino." *Philippine Comics Review.* First Quarter 1979, pp. 24-29.

4189. "Rights of Artists." *Philippine Comics Review.* First Quarter 1979, pp. 36-37.

Alcala, Alfredo P.

4190. Auad, Manuel. "Alfredo P. Alcala—Famed Comic Book Artist." *Cartoonist PROfiles.* No. 22, 1974, pp. 18-23.

4191. MacDonald, Heidi and Phillip D. Yeh. *Secret Teachings of a Comic Book Master: The Art of Alfredo Alcala.* Lompoc, California: International Humor Advisory Council, 1994. 72 pp.

Badajos, Ed

4192. "Ed Badajos: A Retrospective." *San Francisco*: Kearny Street Workshop Press, 1984.

4193. Jundis, Orvy. "In Memory of Ed Badajos." *East Wind*. Fall/Winter 1983, pp. 62-63.

Caparas, Carlos J.

4194. Matienzo, Ros. "'Do You Know How I Try, How I Agonize, I Suffer?'" *Philippine Comics Review*. First Quarter 1979, pp. 54-56.

4195. Vitug, Maritess. "Carlos Caparas: Komiks Is His Medium." *Celebrity*. April 15, 1980, pp. 48-52.

Coching, Francisco V.

4196. "A Capsule Biography of Francisco V. Coching." *Philippine Comics Review*. First Quarter 1979, pp. 12-13.

4197. Jundis, Orvy. "The Francisco V. Coching Art Exhibit." *WittyWorld*. Autumn 1987, p. 23.

4198. Matienzo, Ros H. "Is Coching Still Relevant?" *Philippine Comics Review*. First Quarter 1979, pp. 5-11.

Marcelo, Nonoy

4199. Borja, Maria Carmen. "A Study on The Readership and Impact of Nonoy Marcelo's 'Ikabod Bubwit.'" BA thesis, University of the Philippines, Institute of Mass Communication, 1985. 55 pp.

4200. Marcelo, Nonoy. *Ikabod. Dagang Sosyal*. Manila: Atis Palimbagan, 1981.

4201. Mendoza, Ivy Lisa. "A Comparative Analysis of Two Cartoon Strips, Ikabod and Kusyo at Buyok." BA thesis, University of the Philippines, 1986. 72 pp.

Niño, Alex

4202. Amigo, Celestino. "The Thoughts of Alex Niño." *Philippine Comics Review*. First Quarter 1979, pp. 44-47.

4203. Jundis, Orvy. "Niño, Alex (1940-)." In *Enciclopedia Mondiale del Fumetto*, edited by Maurice Horn and Luciano Secchi, pp. 591-592. Milan: Editoriale Corno, 1978.

4204. "A Lust for Experiment...Niño's Art." *Philippine Comics Review*. First Quarter 1979, pp. 38-43.

4205. Zavisa, Christopher. *Satan's Tears: The Art of Alex Niño*. Detroit, Michigan: The Land of Enchantment, 1977. 301 pp.

Ravelo, Mars

4206. "Rapping with Ravelo." *Philippine Comics Review*. First Quarter 1979, pp. 22-23.

4207. Matienzo, Ros H. "Ravelo, Iconoclast." *Philippine Comics Review*. First Quarter 1979, pp. 16-21.

Redondo, Nestor

4208. Jundis, Orvy. "Redondo, Nestor (1928-)." In *Enciclopedia Mondiale del Fumetto*, edited by Maurice Horn and Luciano Secchi, pp. 649-650. Milan: Editoriale Corno, 1978.

4209. "Nestor Redondo: Collector's Album." *Philippine Comics Review*. First Quarter 1979, pp. 57-62.

Rizal, José

4210. Redondo, Dando. "Rizal, Inventor of the Comics." *Philippine Comics Review*. First Quarter 1979, pp. 50-53.

4211. Villarroel, Fidel. "Jose Rizal: First Filipino Cartoonist." *Life Today*. March 1986, pp. 16-17.

Velasquez, Antonio

4212. Lent, John A. "Antonio Velasquez, Father of Philippine Komiks." *Philippines Communication Journal*. March 1993, pp. 47-50.

4213. Tejero, Constantino C. "Reintroducing Mister Francisco Harabas, a.k.a. Kenkoy." *Sunday Inquirer Magazine* (Manila). March 11, 1990, pp. 21+.

Characters and Titles

4214. Jundis, Orvy. "DI-13 (Filippine)" In *Enciclopedia Mondiale del Fumetto*, edited by Maurice Horn and Luciano Secchi, pp. 290-291. Milan: Editoriale Corno, 1978.

4215. Jundis, Orvy. "Indio, El (Filippine)." In *Enciclopedia Mondiale del Fumetto*, edited by Maurice Horn and Luciano Secchi, p. 470. Milan: Editoriale Corno, 1978.

4216. Jundis, Orvy. "Kenkoy (Filippine)." In *Enciclopedia Mondiale del Fumetto*, edited by Maurice Horn and Luciano Secchi, pp. 499-500. Milan: Editoriale Corno, 1978.

4217. Jundis, Orvy. "Kulafu (Filippine)." In *Enciclopedia Mondiale del Fumetto*, edited by Maurice Horn and Luciano Secchi, p. 517. Milan: Editoriale Corno, 1978.

4218. Jundis, Orvy. "Malaya (Filippine)." In *Enciclopedia Mondiale del Fumetto*, edited by Maurice Horn and Luciano Secchi, p. 547. Milan: Editoriale Corno, 1978.

4219. Jundis, Orvy. "Payaso (Filippine)." In *Enciclopedia Mondiale del Fumetto*, edited by Maurice Horn and Luciano Secchi, pp. 613-614. Milan: Editoriale Corno, 1978.

4220. Jundis, Orvy. "Reggie (Filippine)." In *Enciclopedia Mondiale del Fumetto*, edited by Maurice Horn and Luciano Secchi, pp. 650-651. Milan: Editoriale Corno, 1978.

4221. Jundis, Orvy. "Siopawman (Filippine)." In *Enciclopedia Mondiale del Fumetto*, edited by Maurice Horn and Luciano Secchi, p. 692. Milan: Editoriale Corno, 1978.

4222. Jundis, Orvy. "Tagisan ng mga Agimat (Filippine)." In *Enciclopedia Mondiale del Fumetto*, edited by Maurice Horn and Luciano Secchi, p. 715. Milan: Editoriale Corno, 1978.

4223. Jundis, Orvy. "Voltar (Filippine)." In *Enciclopedia Mondiale del Fumetto*, edited by Maurice Horn and Luciano Secchi, p. 752. Milan: Editoriale Corno, 1978.

4224. Nofuente, V. "Nangitlog ng Pantasya si Phantomanok." *Diliman Review*. October-December 1978, pp. 62-63.

Animation

4225. "Animator in Philippines Enters Offshore Lists with a Taiwan Coprod." *Variety*. May 1, 1985, p. 409.

4226. "Cartoons a Promising Filipino Export." *Asian Mass Communication Bulletin*. July-August 1993, p. 16.

4227. "Cartoons Banned in TV and Theatres of the Philippines." *Variety*. September 12, 1979, p. 53.

4228. Cheng, Deking L. "Exposure to Television Cartoons and Identification Behavior of School Children Toward Cartoon Characters." AB Thesis, University of the Philippines, 1974. 63 pp.

4229. Deocampo, Nick. *Short Film: Emergence of a New Philippine Cinema.* Manila: Communication Foundation for Asia, 1985, pp. 88-90; 118-121.

4230. Dioko, Lisa Mona N. "A Content Analysis of Filipino Values in Selected Cartoon Shows." BA thesis, University of the Philippines, Institute of Mass Communication, 1986. 66 pp.

4231. Durango-dela Rosa, Josefina B. "A Content Analysis of Not for Adult Only Movies: A Television Cartoon." BA thesis, University of the Philippines, 1974.

4232. Fernandez, Rudy A. "TV Can Play an Important Role in Children's Lives." *Philippine Star.* July 19, 1993, p. 35.

4233. Rivero, Isagani. "Anime in the Philippines." *The Rose.* July 1994, p. 28.

4234. Tamondong, Bleseda Irene. "Exposure to Tagalog Cartoon Programs and the Level of Identification of Elementary Students Towards the Cartoon Characters." BA thesis, University of the Philippines, 1988. 51 pp.

Comic Books (Komiks)

4235. Angeles, Enrique E. "A Subjective, Thematic Analysis of Pilipino Komiks." AB thesis, University of the Philippines, 1969. 55 pp.

4236. Anguluan, Milagros A. "Ang Kapisanan ng mga Publisista at Patnugot ng mga Komiks Magasin sa Pilipino." BA thesis, University of the Philippines, 1974. 16 pp.

4237. Bejo, Noel B. "'Komiks' in the Philippines: A Medium That Seeks Recognition." *Communicatio Socialis Yearbook.* 1986, pp. 155-170.

4238. Cabling, Mario S. *May Sining, Tagumpay at Salapi sa Pagsulat ng Komiks.* Manila: National Book Store, 1972.

4239. "Comics: Opiate of the Masses?" *Asiaweek.* November 23, 1984, pp. 57-58.

4240. "Comics Sale Soars." *Asian Mass Communication Bulletin.* December 1978, pp. 12-13.

4241. del Mundo, Clodualdo, Jr. "Komiks: an Industry, a Potent Medium, Our National 'Book,' and Pablum of Art Appreciation." *Sunday Malaya.* April 21, 1985, pp. 3-5.

4242. Enika and Eringa. "Nuts and Bolts." *Philippine Comics Review*. First Quarter. 1979, pp. 36-37.

4243. Jatulan, M.C. "U.S. Comics Made in the Philippines." *Examiner*. September 1977, pp. 23-25.

4244. Jundis, Orvy. "Panorama dell'Editoria a Fumetti nelle Filippine." In *Enciclopedia Mondiale del Fumetto*, edited by Maurice Horn and Luciano Secchi, p. 33. Milan: Editoriale Corno, 1978.

4245. "Komiks Bridging 7,000 Islands." *Illustrated Press*. November 1977.

4246. "*Komiks*: Most Widely Read." *Philippine News*. September 9, 1981, p.6.

4247. Lent, John A. "Komiks. National Book of the Philippines." *Comics Journal*. May 1989, pp. 79-84.

4248. Lent, John A. "Philippine *Komiks*: The National Book." Paper presented at International Association for Mass Communication Research, Bled, Yugoslavia, August 26-31, 1990.

4249. Lent, John A. "Risky Business." *Big O Magazine*. June 1993, pp. 67-68.

4250. Marcelo, Nonoy. "Komiks: The Filipino National Literature?" *Asian Culture*. January 1980, pp. 18-20.

4251. *May Sining, Tagumpay, at Salapi sa Pagsusulat ng Komiks*. Manila: Liwayway Publishing Inc., 1972.

4252. Perez, Ligaya D. "The Comics: A Potent Tool in Mass Media." *JESCOMEA Newsletter*. February 29, 1972, pp. 12-14.

4253. "A Philippine Komiks Collection." *Comic Art Collection*. November 2, 1990, p. 2.

4254. "Popular Komiks." *Asian Messenger*. Winter 1978/Spring 1979, p. 19.

4255. Reyes, Soledad S. "The Philippine Komiks." *International Popular Culture*. No. 1, 1980, pp. 14-23.

4256. Rodriguez, Chula M. "High-Tech Story Weavers." *Manila Chronicle*. September 25, 1988, pp. 19, 22.

4257. Sacerdoti, Guy. "Comics in a Campaign." *Far Eastern Economic Review*. January 9, 1986, p. 31.

4258. "Seminar Participants To Produce 'Komiks-Magasin.'" *Contact*. November-December 1978, p. 4.

4259. "Superaide Comic Book Launched." *Daily Express* (Manila). September 2, 1977, p. 28.

4260. Topacio, Marivel R. "Content Analysis of Pilipino Comic Books Before and After the Declaration of Martial Law." AB thesis, University of the Philippines, 1974. 22 pp.

4261. "2 M Comic Magazine Readers." *Philippine Today.* January 7, 1978, p. 48.

4262. Yalung, Susan G. "Komiks Exposure and Attitude Toward Early Marriage." AB thesis, University of the Philippines, 1974. 38 pp.

Development, Education, and Social Consciousness

4263. Adams, Patricia. "Jesus Christ: A 'Comic' Book." *Communicatio Socialis Year Book.* 1981-82, pp. 260-262.

4264. Amansec, Wihelmina. "Comics: A Potential Diversion in the Classroom." *Life Today.* March 1986, pp. 18-20.

4265. Bundoc-Ocampo, Nene J. "Komiks-Magasin: The PNA's Link to the Common Tao." In Asean Editors Conference, First, Manila, 18-22 January 1983, pp. 1-4. Manila: Philippine News Agency, 1983.

4266. Cantor, Filma B. "Relative Effectiveness of Two Comic Strip Formats in Disseminating Developmental Information to Rural Audience." Bachelor of Science thesis, University of the Philippines at Los Baños, 1983. 98 pp.

4267. Chen, Elena. "A Pilot Study on the Use of Comics for Evangelism Among Female Factory Workers." In *Case Studies in Christian Communication in an Asian Context*, edited by Ross W. James, pp. 137-159. Manila: OMF, 1989.

4268. "Comics-Magazine Promotes Technology." *Contact.* May-June 1978, p. 4.

4269. Cruz, Agustina Ortega C. "Interest-Stimulating Qualities of Comic Strip and Comics Magazines to Grade Six Children in Certain Elementary Schools in Manila." Master's thesis, Philippine Women's University, 1957.

4270. Florendo, A.C. "The Comic Strips As Social Commentary." *Mirror* (Manila). December 5, 1970, p. 6.

4271. Grieser, Mona. "Learning About Environment: Magazines for Children." *Development Communication Report.* No. 76, 1992, pp. 12-13, 20.

4272. Hembrador, Ma Theresa V. "Exposure to Comics-Magazines and Knowledge/Attitude Toward Family Planning of Rural Residents." AB thesis, University of the Philippines, 1975. 60 pp.

4273. Maglalang, Demetrio M. "Agricultural Approach to Family Planning." Manila: Communication Foundation for Asia, 1976. (Use of comic books to promote family planning in four Cavite villages).

4274. Maglalang, Demetrio M., editor. *From the Village to the Medium: An Experience in Development Communication*. Manila: Communication Foundation for Asia, 1976.

4275. Mag-uyon, Madeline G. "Comics Readership and Performance in Classes of Elementary and High School Students in Manila." AB thesis, University of the Philippines, 1972. 41 pp.

4276. Movido, Monica S. "The Attitude of Comics Magazines Readers on Family Planning." AB thesis, University of the Philippines, 1970. 92 pp.

4277. Movido, Monica S. "Comics—Magazine Exposure and Family Planning Knowledge, Attitudes, and Practices Among Murphy Libis Housewives." *Philippine Journal of Communication Studies*. September 1971, pp. 44-59.

4278. "The New Comic Books: Zap! Pow! and Social Significance." *Mirror* (Manila). March 6, 1971, p. 7.

4279. Ong, Genaro V., Jr. "Comics and Komiks." *Devcom*. March 1976, pp 8-9.

4280. Pajel, Efigenia A. "The Effects of Illustrated Classics on the Attitude of Children in Literature." BA thesis, University of the Philippines, 1985. 68 pp.

4281. Pontenila, Roberto J. "From Kenkoy to Zuma: A Look at Filipino Values in Komiks." In *Communication, Values and Society*, edited by Crispin C. Maslog, pp. 267-280. Los Baños: Philippine Association of Communication Educators, 1992.

4282. Quintos, Cresenciano. "The Potential Reach, Effectiveness and Acceptability of...One-Sheet Komiks in Delivering Health and Development Messages." BA thesis, University of the Philippines, 1985. 89 pp.

Images and Portrayals

4283. Berceño, Marila A. "The Filipina As Projected by the Local Komiks." BA thesis, University of the Philippines, 1985. 85 pp.

4284. Constantino-David, Karina. "The Changing Images of Heroes in Local Comic Books." *Philippine Journal of Communication Studies*. September 1974, pp. 1-22.

4285. Felipe, Virgilio Suerte. "Life Seen Through Filipino Komiks." *Life Today*. December 1984, pp. 10-11.

4286. Guevarra, Maribel S. "A Comparative Content Analysis of Filipino Komiks

Magazines (1972-1977) in the Portrayal of the New Society." AB thesis, University of the Philippines, 1978. 115 pp.

Komiks and Movies

4287. Lent, John A. *The Asian Film Industry*. London: Christopher Helm, 1990. 310 pp. (*Komiks*, pp. 155, 168, 173).

4288. Reyes, Emmanuel A. *Notes on Philippine Cinema*. Manila: De La Salle University Press, 1989. ("Black and White in Color: The Lure of *Komiks* Movies," pp. 71-78).

4289. Vinzons, Charity P. "Pilipino Komiks Exposure to Project 4 Residents and Their Attitude Toward Pilipino Movies." AB thesis, University of the Philippines, 1977. 48 pp.

Sex, Violence Controversy

4290. Abletez, Jose. "Comics, a Force for Good or Evil." *Philippines Free Press*. August 19, 1961, pp. 22-24.

4291. Carreon, B.A. "Komiks Even Mothers Enjoy." *Woman's Home Companion*. April 25, 1974, pp. 26-27.

4292. Diaz, Henrietta. "Comics Are Okay." *Weekly Women's*. March 9, 1956, p. 34.

4293. Espino, F.L. "Sidewalk Sex." *Mirror*. February 13, 1971, p. 10.

4294. Estepa, Pio. "The Myth of Love According to the Filipino Komiks." *DIWA 3*. October 1978, pp. 86-96.

4295. Florendo, A.C. "I Lost It in the Komiks." *Homelife*. April 1972, pp. 2-23.

4296. Guerrero, Amadis Ma. "Smut or Schmaltz." *Weekly Graphic*. October 8, 1969, pp. 26, 42-43.

4297. Hechanova, Conchita Melchor. "Our Comics Are No Laughing Matter." *Sunday Times Magazine*. April 24, 1966, pp. 28-30.

4298. Malay, Armando. "The Menace of the Comics." *Weekly Women's*. September 21, 1951, p. 10.

4299. "Pilipino 'Komiks': Sex and Deviation." *Philippine Press Forum*. June 1969, pp. 5, 12.

Technical Aspects

4300. Marcelino, Ramon R. *Komiks Magasin: Script Writing*. Manila: Communication

Foundation for Asia, 1980. 67 pp.

4301. Marcelino, Ramon R. *Teach Yourself Book. Komiks Magasin.* Manila: Communication Foundation for Asia, 1980. 67 pp.

Comic Strips

4302. Mercado, Lourdes K. "Local Comic Strips As Mirror of the Filipino Characters." BA thesis, University of the Philippines, 1972. 91 pp.

4303. Orap, Ana Maria. "A Content and Comparative Analysis of Three Newspapers' Local Comic Strips August 1985-August 1986." BA thesis, University of the Philippines, 1987. 80 pp.

4304. Villar, Rafael A.S. "Filipino-Authored Comic Strips in Newspapers and Readers' Perception of Their Factual and Synthetic Contents." MA thesis, University of the Philippines, 1987. 130 pp.

Political Cartoons

4305. Arcedera, Reynaldo S., Jr. "A Study on the Effectivity of the Editorial Cartoons of Bulletin Today." BA thesis, University of the Philippines, 1980. 81 pp.

4306. *The Book of Philippine Newspaper Cartoons.* Manila: Samahang Kartunista ng Pilipinas and Philippine Press Institute, with assistance from UNESCO, 1990. 75 pp.

4307. Isaac, Norman. "A Pessimistic View on the Prospects of New Features." *Witty-World.* Autumn/Winter 1994, p. 2.

4308. Ladrido, Rosa C.R.H. "The Newspaper As an Institution and the Editorial Cartoons in Two Manila Daily Newspapers." AB thesis, University of the Philippines, 1973. 187 pp.

American Era

4309. McCoy, Alfred and Alfredo Roces. *Philippine Cartoons: Political Caricature of the American Era 1900-1941.* Manila: Vera-Reyes, 1985. 370 pp.

4310. "A Portfolio of Political Cartoons (1900-1946)." In *General History of the Philippines. Part V. Vol. 1. The American Half-Century (1898-1946),* edited by Lewis E. Gleeck, Jr., pp. A-P. Quezon City: R.P. Garcia Publishing, 1984.

Marcos Era

4311. Campos, Jose Carlos G. "A Comparative Analysis of the Editorial Cartoons of the Bulletin Today 1970-1984." BA thesis, University of the Philippines, Institute of Mass Communication, 1986. 71 pp.

4312. Casimiro, Ma. Consuelo M. "The Editorial Cartoon As History: A Comparative Analysis (1966-1987)." BA thesis, University of the Philippines, 1988. 105 pp.

4313. Cruz, Andres Cristobal. *Editorial Cartoons '69: Selections from the Manila Press.* Manila: The National Library, 1969. 150 pp.

4314. Estepa, Pio C. "Humour Power: The Political Cartoon vs. Marcos." *Media Development.* 4, 1986, pp. 30-34.

4315. Knipp, Steven. "Marcos Blots." *Far Eastern Economic Review.* June 10, 1993, p. 37.

4316. Roces, Alfredo and Irene Roces. *Medals and Shoes: Political Cartoons of the Times of Ferdinand and Imelda Marcos, 1965-1992.* Manila: Anvil Publishing Co., 1992. 168 pp.

4317. Trinidad, Corky. *Marcos: The Rise and Fall of the Regime: A Cartoon History.* Honolulu: Arthouse Books, 1986.

SINGAPORE

Cartooning, Cartoons

4318. Anuar Othman. "Cartoons Present More Than Just Laughter." *Straits Times* (Singapore). September 11, 1986.

4319. Cheong, Teresa. "From Book to Stage to Cartoon." *Straits Times.* July 30, 1987, p. 23.

4320. "Details Make the Difference." *Straits Times.* July 28, 1991.

4321. Lee, Michelle. "Master Strokes." *Straits Times.* June 28, 1991.

4322. ["Think Green, Go Green"]. *WittyWorld.* Autumn/Winter 1994, p. 5.

4323. "Welcome to Rojak School." *The New Paper.* October 10, 1991.

Anthologies

4324. Kitchi Boy. *Oh No, It's the Kitchi Boy Gang!* Illustrations by K. Subra.

Singapore: Times Books International, 1986. 174 pp.

4325. Kitchi Boy (Siva Choy). *I'm Sorry, It's Kitchi Boy Again.* Singapore: Times Books International, 1986 [?]. 132 pp.

4326. Toh Paik Choo. *Lagi Goondu.* Singapore: Times Books International, 1986 [?]. 122 pp.

Censorship

4327. "Banned in Singapore." *Big O Magazine.* September 1993, p. 66.

4328. Mathews, Kevin M. "Censorship in Singapore." *Comics Journal.* July 1991, pp. 37-38.

Cartoonists

4329. "Egg Roll." *Big O Magazine.* August 1993, pp. 70-73. (Lee Lai Lai).

4330. Heng Kim Song. *A Selection of Editorial Cartoons by Heng Kim Song.* Singapore: 1993. 16 pp.

4331. Lee Hup. "Cartoonists Cut Out the Laughs." *The New Paper* (Singapore). September 28, 1989.

4332. "Provocative Artist in TNP." *The New Paper.* November 7, 1991.

4333. Vijaya, R. "This Cartoonist Doodles To Beat Boredom." *Straits Times.* January 18, 1992.

4334. "Zen Drives TNP's New Cartoonist." *The New Paper.* December 24, 1991.

Cheah Sin Ann

4335. "It's Cheah." *Straits Times.* March 6, 1990.

4336. Cheah Sin Ann. *The House of Lim: The Year of the Horse Collection.* Singapore: Imperial Publishing House, 1991. 220 pp.

4337. Yuen, Stefanie. "House of Cheah." *Straits Times.* June 15, 1991.

Khoo, Eric

4338. Lim Cheng Tju. "Dude in Toyland." *Big O Magazine.* March 1991, pp. 26-31.

4339. Lim Cheng Tju. "My Life As a Dog (Eric Khoo)." *Big O Magazine*. September 1989, pp. 18-19, 23.

Lau, Johnny

4340. Lau, Johnny. "Rusty Thunder." *Big O Magazine*. January 1991, pp. 82-87.

4341. Lim Cheng Tju. "How Kiasu Can Johnny Get?" *Big O Magazine*. August 1991, pp. 98-99.

4342. "New Guys in Toon Town." *Sunday Times*. December 29, 1991.

Comic Books

4343. "Chinese Comics Rage." *Big O Magazine*. March 1991, p. 79.

4344. "Dreams Are Made of These." *Big O Magazine*. March 1991, p. 79.

4345. *The Edge of the Fringe*. Singapore Festival of the Arts 1988. Singapore, 1988. 56 pp.

4346. Heng, K.C. and S. Arulanandam. "In Singapore: Superman Fights Nick O'Teen." *Development Communication Report*. No. 71, 4/1990, p. 10.

4347. Lent, John A. "The View from the Outside...A Critical Eye at the Singapore Comics Scene." *Big O Magazine*. July 1993, pp. 63-65.

4348. Lim Cheng Tju. "A Comics Killing." *Big O Magazine*. July 1993, p. 12.

4349. Lim Cheng Tju. "The Great Singapore Comics Jam." *Big O Magazine*. November 1993, p. 67.

4350. Lim Cheng Tju. "A Killing in the Afternoon." *Big O Magazine*. November 1992, pp. 91-92.

4351. Lim Cheng Tju. "Means of Escape." *Big O Magazine*. November 1991, p. 77.

4352. Lim Cheng Tju. "The *Song* Remains the Same." *Big O Magazine*. August 1992, p. 68.

4353. Lim Cheng Tju. "Thought Balloon." *Big O Magazine*. August 1992, p. 68.

4354. Lim Cheng Tju. "Thought Balloon." *Big O Magazine*. November 1992, pp. 91-92.

4355. "On a Roll." *Big O Magazine*. July 1991, p. 18.

4356. Quek, Angela. "Superman and Other Superheroes: Comic Books As a Form of Popular Culture in Singapore." BA paper, National University of Singapore, 1987. 58 pp. Available in NUS Library.

4357. "Rabbits with a Kick." *Asiaweek*. February 8, 1991, p. 68.

4358. "Singapore: Finding the Funny Bone." *Asiaweek*. September 1, 1993, p. 27.

4359. Tan, Stephen. "Laying It on the Line." *Big O Magazine*. December 1986, p.37.

4360. Tan, Stephen. "Open Season." *Big O Magazine*. September 1986, pp. 48-49.

Business Aspects

4361. Bertieri, Claudio. "Economia a Fumetti." *Comic Art*. July 1986, p. 75.

4362. Chuang Peck Ming. "A Comic Tragedy." *Singapore Business*. January 1989, pp. 28-30.

4363. Lim Cheng Tju. "Shopping Around." *Big O Magazine*. April 1993, p. 75.

4364. Lim Cheng Tju. "Shops." *Big O Magazine*. May 1993, p. 72.

4365. "SNP Sets Up Comic Book Business with HK Firm." *Straits Times*. July 19, 1991.

4366. Tan Cephah. "Price War Forces 6 Comics Shops To Call It Quits." *Straits Times*. July 2, 1991.

"Mr. Kiasu"

4367. Abdullah, Yohanna. "Funny Books Take the Cake at the Fair." *Straits Times*. September 3, 1991, p. 1.

4368. Ang, David. "Kick for Kiasuism." *New Paper*. June 2, 1993, p. 31.

4369. Choong Kit Son. "McDonald's New *'Kiasu'* Ads Leave Bad Taste in the Mouth." *Straits Times*. June 2, 1993.

4370. Chuang Peck Ming. "Kiasu." *Business Times*. August 25, 1990, p. 1.

4371. "Everything Also They Draw." *The Sunday Times*. July 28, 1991.

4372. "Kiasu Burgers Cross Million Mark in Sales." *Straits Times*. July 24, 1993.

4373. "Kiasuism: Biting Off More Than You Can Chew?" *Straits Times*. May 27, 1993. Advertisement.

4374. "Kuppies and Cartoonists." *World Executive's Digest*. November 1990, p. 70.

4375. Lim Cheng Tju. "The Trouble With Mr. Kiasu." *Big O Magazine*. October 1993, pp. 67-68.

4376. "Mr. Kiasu To Go Regional." *In Sync with the Arts*. September 2, 1994. (*Straits Times*. September 1, 1994).

4377. "'Mr. Kiasu' Woos Singapore Advertisers." *Asian Advertising and Marketing*. December 1990, p. 4.

4378. Ng, Lois. "Creators To Expand Comix Factory." *New Paper*. January 2, 1992.

4379. Ng, Lois. "Everything Also I Want." *The New Paper*. August 20, 1990.

4380. Ng, Lois. "Kiasu Ladio." *The New Paper*. February 21, 1991.

4381. Ng, Lois. "Mr. Kiasu Goes Abroad." *The New Paper*. January 2, 1992, p. 1.

4382. "Nuggets [Mr. Kiasu]." *Big O Magazine*. June 1993, pp. 12-13.

4383. Tripathi, Salil. "Capitalizing on Kiasu." *Asia, Inc.* September 1993, pp. 16-18.

4384. Woon Wui Jin. "'If the Simpsons Can, So Can the Kiasu Gang.'" *Sunday Times* (Singapore). June 4, 1993.

Readership

4385. "Big O Comics Poll." *Big O Magazine*. February 1987, pp. 21-23.

4386. Quek, Angela. "Who Reads Comics?" *Big O Magazine*. April 1987, pp. 25-26.

4387. Tan, Stephen. "Can We Count on You, Comics Fans?" *Big O Magazine*. January 1987, pp. 24-25.

Technical Aspects

4388. "Electric Dreams: First Full-Fledged Local Computer Comic Soon." *Big O Magazine*. January 1993, p. 62.

4389. Lim, C.T. "Shopping Around — Createch." *Big O Magazine*. November 1992, p. 92.

4390. Lim, C.T. "The Story of IT." *Big O Magazine*. February 1993, pp. 4-6, 8.

Comic Strips

4391. Dorai, Francis. "This Lot Will Draw Your Comic Strips." *Straits Times*. July 29, 1991.

4392. "Drawing Power." *Straits Times*. August 30, 1989.

4393. Koh, Nancy. "Sympathy for the Little Man." *Straits Times*. August 30, 1989.

4394. Lim Cheng Tju. "Cut and Dry (Humour)." *Big O Magazine*. August 1991, p. 99.

4395. Mariadass, Tony. "Kampung View of Progress." *The New Paper*. December 1991.

4396. Shukor, Abdul. "Paper Lions To Egg on Real Lions." *The Jester*. August 1992, p. 17.

Political Cartoons

4397. "Cartoonist Dishes Out Home-Grown Humor." *Business Times*. August 14, 1991.

4398. Nonis, George. *Hello Chok Tong, Goodbye Kuan Yew*. Singapore: Flame of the Forest, Angsana Books, 1991. 199 pp.

4399. "So, Have Political Cartoons Arrived." *Business Times*. September 14, 1991.

4400. Teo, Anna. "Are We Ready To Laugh at Ourselves?" *Business Times*. September 14, 1991.

4401. Wang Fuquan. "Drawing the Fine Line on Singapore." *South China Morning Post*. December 22, 1991.

SRI LANKA

General Sources

4402. Amunugama, Sarath. "Andare: Sinhala Folk Tale As Animated Film." *Cinema Asia/Cinema Africa*. No. 2, 1977, pp. 10-11.

4403. Hettiaratchi, D.E. *Sinhalese Encyclopaedia*. Vol. 6. Colombo: Department of Cultural Affairs, 1978. ("Cartoons").

4404. Rhodes, Lorna Amarasingham. "Laughter and Suffering: Sinhalese Interpretations of the Use of Ritual Humor." *Social Science and Medicine.* 17:4 (1983), pp. 979-984.

Cartoonists

4405. Hettigoda, Winnie. *Sketch of Reality. A Collection of Cartoons by Winnie Hettigoda.* Dehiwala: Sridevi Printers Pvt. Ltd., 1990.

4406. "Looking Good." *Asiaweek.* June 19, 1992, pp. 6-7.

4407. *20 Years. Yoonoos.* Colombo: Aththa, 1992.

4408. Weerarathna, Susil. "Most Prophetic and Versatile Cartoonist of Sri Lanka." *The Island.* Not dated.

Collette, Aubrey

4409. Chia, Corinne, K.K. Seet and Pat M. Wong. Cartoons by Collette. *Made in Singapore.* Singapore: Times Books International, 1986[?]. 128 pp.

4410. Collette. *Ceylon Since Soulbury Part I. A History in Cartoons by Collette.* Foreword by Frank Moraes. Colombo: Times of Ceylon, 1948.

4411. Collette, Aubrey. "Aubrey Collette: Cartoonist from 'Down Under.'" *Cartoonews.* June 1975, pp. 25-27.

4412. Collette, Aubrey. *The World of Sun Tan.* Hong Kong: Asia Magazine, 1970. 60 pp.

Opatha, S.C.

4413. "Opatha Among the World's Best." *Times of Ceylon.* June 20, 1977.

4414. "S.C. Opatha." *Worldpaper.* February 1984, p. 8.

Wijesoma, W.R.

4415. Dorakumbure, W.B. "Exhibition of Cartoons by Wijesoma." *The Island.* August 21, 1990, pp. 6-7.

4416. Pieris, Harold. "Humour Without Malice." *Dialogue* (Dhaka). April 22, 1992.

4417. Weerarathna, Susil. "An Exhibition of Cartoons by Wijesoma." *The Island.* November 2, 1985.

4418. Wijesoma, W.R. *A Collection of Cartoons by Wijesoma*. Colombo: Lake House, 1985. 182 pp.

Comics

4419. "Axa Stirs a Storm." *Asiaweek*. October 19, 1980, p. 84.

4420. "Comic War Looms in Sri Lanka." *Media*. March 1981, p. 11.

4421. Rifas, Leonard. "Cartooning in Sri Lanka: A Precarious Tight Rope Act." In *Asian Popular Culture*, edited by John A. Lent. Boulder, Colorado: Westview Press, forthcoming.

TAIWAN

General Sources

4422. Chang Shih-Min. "Hsu Shui-te Loves To Read Cartoons." *Central Daily News*. July 6, 1994, p. 3.

4423. Chang Yinchao. *Lectures on the Arts of Sketch Cartoon and Caricature*. Taipei: Taiwan Hsing-Sheng Pao Publishing Company, 1956. 160 pp. Chinese.

4424. Chi Szu-Ping. "Not a Silent Role." *Central Times*. November 18, 1979, p. 8.

4425. Hsiao Hsiang-Wen. "Popular Culture in Taiwan: The Change of Comic Art After 1988." Paper presented at Mid-Atlantic Region, Association for Asian Studies, Pittsburgh, Pennsylvania, October 22, 1994.

4426. Hsiao Min-Hui. "Don't Match a Boy to a Girl." *United Daily News*. July 25, 1991.

4427. Hsiao Min-Hui. "Getting Tired of Japanese Cartoons? Try the French Style." *United Daily News*. April 6, 1991, p. 27.

4428. Liang Hsuan. "Roaming in the Cartoon Area." *United Daily News*. April 21, 1984.

4429. *1991 Taiwan Creative Graphic Arts. Creative Illustration*. Taipei: Su-Chao Wang, 1991. 282 pp.

4430. *Toward Cleanliness, Calmness and Tranquility Tomorrow*. Taipei: Department of Information, Government of Republic of China, 1989.

Cartoonists

4431. Cartoonist Association of Republic of China. *ROC Cartoonist Register*. Taipei: Chun Liu, 1988.

4432. Chen Ying-Hua. "Studies on Cartoonists' Characteristics." Master's thesis, National Chengchi University, 1991.

4433. Dong Yu-Ching. "New Breed of Cartoonists for a Modern Chinese Life." *Philippines Communication Journal*. March 1993, pp. 51-52.

4434. Dong Yu-Ching. "New Breed of Cartoonists Mirror the Modern Way of Chinese Life, Trends and Politics." *Free China Journal*. July 28, 1985, p. 3.

4435. "Friends Express Sorrow for Passing of Liang Chung-Ming." *Min Sheng Pao*. July 21, 1994, p. 14.

4436. Hsai Chuan-Shu. "The Cool and Refreshing Water When You're Thirsty — What the World Cartoonists Offer Us." *China Times*. December 24, 1979.

4437. Hsiao Min-Hui. "Cartoon Comrades Started Underground Work." *United Daily News*. July 2, 1991, p. 20.

4438. Hu Chueh-Lung ("Kid Jerry"). *The Kid Jerry Show*. Taipei: Black and White Club, 1988. 126 pp.

4439. Hung Te-Lin. "1990 — Turn in Grade Reports, Taiwanese Cartoonists." *China Times*. June 16, 1991.

4440. Kuo Chun-Liang. "He Creates the Superdog, Pea Pea." *Min Sheng Pao*. December 31, 1981.

4441. Li Yu. "Please Give Cartoonists Justice." *Taipei Weekly*. January 5, 1980.

4442. Lim, C.T. "Ronald Chu: Labours of Love." *Big O Magazine*. May 1994, p. 22.

4443. Lin Wen-Yi. "Who Delivers Chinese Cartoons to the Next Generation? Introducing 11 Hard-working and Outstanding Chinese Cartoonists." *Review and Bibliography*. July 1, 1979, pp. 2-43.

4444. Liu Mei-Min. "Chi Lung-Sheng Draws Life 60 Years." *United Evening Post*. April 9, 1993, p. 19.

4445. "Mainland Chinese Illustrations Land in Taiwan Giving Children More Choices; Local Artists Feel Threatened with More Pressure." *United Daily News*. July 22, 1991, p. 15.

4446. Niu Ko. "My Comic Drawing Career — Drawing for Forty Years." *China Times*. December 18, 1979.

4447. "People." *Asiaweek*. December 20, 1991, pp. 48-49. (Yu Su-Lan of Taiwan).

4448. Phillips, Brian D. "Ta Yu K'an T'ou: Chinese Sexual Culture and the Cartoons of T'ung Chin-Mao." Paper presented at Popular Culture Association, Chicago, Illinois, April 7, 1994.

4449. "Satirizing the Excesses of Materialism." *Free China Review*. March 1993, pp. 18-19. (Huang Chin-Ho).

4450. "Taiwan's Cartoonists Intend to Issue Chronicle of Cartoonists." *World Daily News*. May 29, 1993, p. A-13.

4451. Yeh Fan. "Why Publishers Do Not Want To Print Our Cartoonists' Work." *United Daily News*. May 22, 1980, p. 9.

Animators

4452. Huang Pei-Lang. "Yu-Li Teng Indulges the Cartoons; His Sample Film Completed in Half Year; Confident of Exportation of Cartoon Films." *United Daily News*. December 30, 1975.

4453. Shao, Maria. "Meet James Wang, Asia's Walt Disney." *Business Week*. June 15, 198[?], p. 29.

Chao Ning

4454. Chin Heng-Wei and Ma Yi-Kung. "Poetaster Cartoonist Chao Ning — A Communication Doctor Who Loves Drawing." *China Times*. November 22, 1979.

4455. Lent, John A. "A Cartoonist's Perspective on Cartooning in Taiwan." *Philippines Communication Journal*. March 1993, pp. 13-14.

Dulu

4456. "Chat with Cartoonist Dulu." *Dragon Youth*. No. 5, 1994, p. 48.

4457. "Dulu's File Man's Talk." *Dragon Youth*. No. 5, 1994, pp. 49-50.

Tsai Chih-Chung

4458. Chang Meng-Jui. "Chih-Chung Tsai's Comics Are Entering the United States Market." *World Journal*. August 1, 1993, p. A-13.

4459. Huang Mei-Hui. "Chih-Chung Tsai's Comics Passed the Academic Challenge — Princeton University Publication Decided To Publish 'Chuang-Tzu Speaks' and

'Lao-Tzu Speaks.'" *World Journal*. June 14, 1992, p. 11.

4460. Tsai Chih-Chung. *Zhuangzi Speaks The Music of Nature*. Princeton: Princeton University Press, 1992.

Wen Cheng

4461. Hsieh Shu-Fen. "Cheng Wen — A Man Who Understands What Animates the Japanese." *Sinorama*. April 1992, pp. 94-95.

4462. Li Tsui-Ying. "Wen Cheng's Comic Book Beat Out Japanese Competitors." *China Times*. May 30, 1991.

4463. Liu Wei-Ming and Peng Chih-Ming. "Talking with Wen Cheng." *Monthly Comic Magazine* (Hong Kong). January 1991, pp. 13-17.

4464. Nung-Fu. "Ideology." *Monthly Comic Magazine* (Hong Kong). No. 0, 1990, p. 60.

Yeh Hung-Chia

4465. Chiu, Jennifer. "Yeh Hung-Chia: Hero Maker of Another Era." *Philippines Communication Journal*. March 1993, pp. 53-54.

4466. Chiu, Jennifer. "Yeh's Cartoons Lived in Every Child's Dreams." *Free China Review*. June 7, 1990, p. 6.

4467. Hsu Hai-Ling. "First Political Cartoonist Hung-Chia Yeh Dead." *Tzu-Li Early Newspaper*. April 25, 1990.

4468. Lin Tsung-Chi. "Goodbye, Szulang Chukeng!" *The Journalist*. April 30-May 6, 1990.

Yu Fu

4469. Yu Fu. *Cartoon Liberation*. Taipei, 1988. Second edition, 1989. 127 pp.

4470. Yu Fu. *Taiwan Without Martial Law 1988 Illustrated: A Collection of Yu Fu's Editorial Cartoons*. Taipei: Independence Evening Post, 1989. 144 pp.

Characters and Titles

Animation

4471. Chiao Hsiung-Ping. "Watching Cartoons Through 'Old Pedant.'" *United Daily News*. September 23, 1981.

4472. Chin Jen-Kuang. "'Old Pedant' Boxoffice Succeeded in Hong Kong; Taiwanese Cartoon Businessmen Then Shoot Cartoon Films in Same Fashion." *Min Sheng Pao*. August 3, 1981.

4473. "Chinese Cartoon Corp. Announce Shooting of 'Hung Yeh' (Red Leaf Little Baseball) Cartoon Film." *Min Sheng Pao*. March 16, 1979.

4474. "Color Cartoon 'Lao-Fu Tzu' Triumphed in Hong Kong; Morning and Midnight Shows Broke Box Office Records." *Min Sheng Pao*. July 25, 1981.

4475. Hsu Jui-Hsi. "Who Produced Ninja Turtles?" *United Evening News*. July 10, 1990.

4476. Kuo Ta-Ching. "Cartoon Film 'The Story of Three Countries': More Than 100 Technicians Worked for a Year and Drew 150,000 Pictures." *Taiwan Hsin-sheng Pao*. 1979.

4477. "'Lao-Fu Tzu' Coming to the Wide Screen, Famous Cartoon Will Be Shot As Animated Film." *Min Sheng Pao*. July 23, 1980.

4478. "'San Kuo Yen Yi' — Rumor of Hiring Japanese Director." *United Daily News*. February 15, 1979.

4479. "'The Story of Three Kingdoms' Difficult To Release, Imperfection in Production, Publishers Lost Confidence." *Min Sheng Pao*. July 19, 1979.

"Cousin Lee"

4480. "Cousin Lee To Debut in Film, Comic Books." *Free China Journal*. December 23, 1985, p. 1.

4481. "Cousin Lee: A Welcome Abstraction." *Free China Journal*. December 23, 1985, p. 2.

4482. Ge Sz-ming. "All About Cousin Lee, and How He Grew, What He Represents." *Free China Journal*. December 8-14, 1985, p. 1.

4483. Ge Sz-ming. "Cartoonist Ranan R. Lurie Searches for 'Chinese Symbol.'" *Free China Journal*. July 28, 1985, p. 1.

4484. Huang, Hamilton. "European Cartoonists Draw Most Inspiration from ROC's Symbol." *Free China Journal*. February 16, 1987, p. 1.

4485. Jeng, Arthur. Translated by Perer Eberly. "The International Cousin Lee Cartoon Contest." *Sinorama*. April 1987, pp. 94-97.

4486. "Lurie's Cousin Lee Offers New Image of the Modern Chinese." *Free China Journal*. December 8-14, 1985, p. 1.

Animation

4487. "Cartoon Businessmen Have Much Trouble. Two Companies — Shang-Shang and Hsing Hui — Were Forced To Stop Business." *Min Sheng Pao*. May 9, 1979.

4488. "Cartoon Contest Judged and Announced Yesterday; Exhibition Will Begin May 1." *Min Sheng Pao*. April [?] 1983.

4489. "Cartoon Films Sino-ized; Chinese and Foreign Experts Make Suggestions." *China Times*. November 1, 1979.

4490. Chen Kuo-Chen. "Developing the Domestic Cartoon Films in Taiwan; Sufficient in Personnel and Money But Lack of Market." *Min Sheng Pao*. August 2, 1978.

4491. Chen Kuo-Chen. "European and American Cartoon Films Decreased Gradually; Japanese Cartoon Films Tend to Evil Way; TV Cartoon Films Are in Shortage." *Min Sheng Pao*. July 5, 1981.

4492. Cheng Kuei Ping. "Our TV Cartoons Are Full of Foreign Tastes." *China Times*. March [?] 1979.

4493. Chien Wan. "Animated Cartoons and Comics — History, Typology and Present Situation." *Review and Bibliography*. August 1, 1979.

4494. "China TV Company Will Release 'I Love Cartoon' TV Program." *Min Sheng Pao*. July 29, 1981.

4495. "Chinese TV Service Wants To Produce Cartoon Series; Domestic Cartoon Businessmen Differ in Opinion." *China Times*. August 19, 1981.

4496. "Congressman Wen-Yi Chao Suggests Government Assist in Producing Children Cartoon Films." *United Daily News*. October 17, 1979.

4497. "Heads of Cartoon Corporations Appeal to Government To Supply, Fund and Unite Excellent Personnel To Produce Cartoons in the International Market." *United Daily News*. August 19, 1981.

4498. Lewis, Mark. "Taiwan Buyers Seek Toons n' Tough Guys." *Variety*. April 5, 1993, p. M-91.

4499. Liu Hsiao-Mei. "Cartoon Films Function Tremendously Well; Exportation Also Potential." *United Daily News*. June 8, 1979.

4500. Thurston, David. "The Art of Animation." *Asia Magazine*. July 13, 1986, pp. 24-26.

Cuckoo's Nest

4501. Chi Nai-Ho. "The Walt Disney of Taiwan. Taiwanese Cartoons Exported Overseas." *China Times*. June 1, 1982.

4502. Lee, Rachel F.F. "Cartoon Company Among World's Largest." *Free China Journal*. June 8, 1993, p. 5.

4503. Melliza, Cindy. "Donald Conceived in Hollywood but Born in ROC Cuckoos Nest." *Free China Journal*. February 9, 1987, p. 4.

Comic Books

4504. "Campaign Poster Copy Comics." *China Times*. December 8, 1980, p. 6.

4505. Chang, Winnie. "From Knights Errant to Errant Couples." *Free China Review*. January 1992, pp. 4-17.

4506. Chang Yu-Wei. *Comics Art*. Taipei: Chuan Ming Publishing Co., 1954. 88 pp. Chinese.

4507. Chen Ching-Ho. *Introduction to Comics Art*. Taipei: Li Ming Publishing Co. Ltd., 1982.

4508. Cheng Yu-Hang. "World Comics Exhibit." *China Times*. December 31, 1979.

4509. Chien Shu-Yuan. "When Children Read Comic Books, What Should Parents Do?" *Taipei Weekly*. May 3, 1980.

4510. Clements, Jonathan. "Comics in Taiwan." *Anime UK Magazine*. October/November 1992, p. 34.

4511. "Comic Books." *Asian Messenger*. Winter 1980/Spring 1981, p. 6.

4512. "Comics Are Pirated As Campaign Tool." *United Daily News*. December 8, 1980.

4513. "Easy Reading Comic Books Are Gaining in Popularity." *Free China Journal*. April 7, 1985, p. 3.

4514. Hanafi, Laurence. "Bulles de Taiwan." *Les Cahiers de la Bande Dessinée*. (Grenoble). 69, 1986, pp. 55-57.

4515. Hsu Cheng Chin. "Enthusiastic Comic Fans Get Big Chance." *United Daily News*. January 19, 1991. pp. 2, 7.

4516. Hu Chih-Yin. "Re-profiling Taiwan's Comics Industry." *Macroview*. April 15, 1994, pp. 29-31.

4517. Huang Pao-Ping. "Adult Cartoons Invade Children's Reading; Japan's Violence and Sex Cartoons Overflow Our Rental Bookstores." *Min Sheng Pao*. April 23, 1986.

4518. Hung Tei-Lin. "The Re-establishment of Comics Value." *Liberal Times*. June 23, 1994, p. 29.

4519. Lee Ching Hung. "Contribution Principals." *Popular Custom Graphic Monthly*. 1, 1953, p. 20.

4520. Lent, John A. "Millionaires, Pirates and Risk Takers." *Big O Magazine*. April 1993, pp. 74-75.

4521. Lent, John A. "The Renaissance of Taiwan's Cartoon Arts." *Asian Culture Quarterly*. Spring 1993, pp. 1-17.

4522. Lent, John A. "Taiwanese Cartooning: From Bust to Boom." *Comics Journal*. January 1994, pp. 27-30.

4523. Lent, John A. "Taiwan's Emerging Cartoon Arts: Interviews and Analyses." Paper presented at Mid-Atlantic Region, Association for Asian Studies, Lock Haven, Pennsylvania, November 2, 1991.

4524. Leu Chien-Ai. "Sardonically Yours." *Free China Review*. January 1992, pp. 24-29.

4525. Li Jo-Nan. *Ting-tang Mao te Meng* (The Dream of a Cartoon Cat). Taipei: Linking Publishing Co., 1990.

4526. Lin, Diana. "Today, Comic Books Are For Everyone." *Free China Journal*. October 14, 1994, p. 5.

4527. Ma Hsing-Yeh. "Comics." *Central Daily News*. November 17, 1974, p. 10.

4528. "Skill Show." *Dragon Youth*. No. 11, 1993, pp. 1-4.

4529. "Students Like Comics." *Asian Messenger*. Winter 1981, p. 13.

4530. Sun Yueh-Ping. "If the Textbook Is the Same As the Comic Book." *Independent Evening News*. June 30, 1980.

4531. Tsao Yun-Yi. "The Guarantee of the Creation of Comic Books." *United Daily News*. March 8, 1991, p. 29.

Business Aspects

4532. "Cartoon Businessmen Have Much Trouble." *Min Sheng Pao*. May 9, 1979.

4533. Chang Meng-Jui. "An American Who Has Enthusiasm in the Products of Chinese Culture — Brian Bruya Wants to Introduce to the U.S. the Comics Based on Chinese Classics." *World Journal*. August 1, 1993, p. A-13.

4534. Chen Fang-Jung. "How Much Do You Know About Publishing Comics?" *Publishing Monthly*. 51 (1976), pp. 93-99.

4535. Mai Chun-Yin and Chai Chun-Yin. "Japan Cartoon Runs Rampant; Translating To Get Profit Will Damage Our Descendants." *United Daily News*. September 2, 1982.

4536. *World Journal*. August 1, 1993, p. A-13. (Export of Taiwan cartoons).

Governance

4537. Chi En-Ping. "Compilation Committee Makes Mistakes Again." *Taipei Weekly*. January 12, 1980.

4538. "Different Standard of Censoring; Domestic Cartoonists Struggle for Their Right." *Min Sheng Pao*. September 27, 1982.

4539. "'Following Wind' Sweeps One Hundred Thousand Illegal Graphics and Books; Strip Drawing and Pornographic Are Very Very Abundant." *Min Sheng Pao*. July 25, 1983.

4540. Ho Shou. "Is the Institute of Compilation and Translation National or Private?" *Tsung Heng Monthly*. 5:4 (1983), p. 70.

4541. Hsiao Min-Hui. "The Examination Is Coming Back; Some Cartoonist Pioneers Begin Opening Outside Territory." *United Daily News*. August 17, 1991, p. 29.

4542. "Japan's Pirated Strip Overflow; Control Yuan Investigates Compilation Committee." *Min Sheng Pao*. December 14, 1982.

4543. Lin Ying-Chi. "Prohibit Japanese Comics; Encourage Domestic Cartoonists' Works; Compilation Committee and Cartoonists Should Examine Their Efforts for Readers' Benefit; They Should Improve Technique." *Min Sheng Pao*. October 6, 1982.

4544. Lin Ying-Chi. "Publishers' Pirating; Compilation Committee's Blind Cartoon Censorship Showing up Shortcomings." *Min Sheng Pao*. September 30, 1982.

4545. Lin Ying-Chi. "Why Doesn't Compilation Committee Set up a Procedure Schedule?" *Min Sheng Pao*. August 13, 1983.

4546. Lu Li-Chen. "Japanese Influence Harmful to Taiwan Comics." *Philippines Communication Journal*. March 1993, pp. 55-57.

4547. Niu Ching-Fu. "Japanese Violent and Pornographic Comic Books Flood Market; Parents Frightened." *United Daily News*. July 22, 1991, p. 15.

4548. "Pirated Strip Overflow; Compilation Committee Denies Losing Principle." *Min Sheng Pao*. September 26, 1982.

4549. "Restarting Examination? Opposition from the Cartoon Field; GIO Cleared Out." *Min Sheng Pao*. July 23, 1991.

4550. "There Is a Double Standard on Censorship; Publishers Don't Know What To Follow." *Min Sheng Pao*. September 27, 1982.

4551. Tsao Yun-Yi. "Examination of Comics (Cartoons) Hot Topic; Where Is the Focus?" *United Daily News*. August 3, 1991, p. 29.

4552. Wu Chia-Ling. "Restarting Prior Examination System? The Cartoon Field Reacts Severely." *China Times*. July 19, 1991, p. 20.

Historical Aspects

4553. Chen Yueh-Yun. "Thirty Years of Cartoons' Vicissitude." *Commercial Times* (Taipei). September 9, 10, 1981.

4554. Hu Ying-Ping. "Recall Comics Age." *Central Daily News*. March 15/16, 1994, p. 7.

4555. Hung Tei-Lin. *A Brief Review of Taiwanese Comics, 1949-1993*. Foreword by John A. Lent. Taipei: China Times, 1994. 199+ pp. Chinese.

4556. Ta Feng. "From the Rise of Comics to Cartoonists' Cultivation." *Popular Custom Graphic Monthly*. 5 (1954), p. 20.

Comic Strips

4557. Ching Jih. *Theatre*. Taipei: Courser Publishing, 1988. 109 pp.

4558. Fan Yen. "Expect a Harvest of Humor Cartoons." *Min Sheng Pao*. December 6, 1980.

4559. "Half White." "No Friend for Cartoons?" *Taipei Weekly*. January 19 and 26, 1980.

4560. Hatherly, Gerald. "Creative Cartooning in the Republic of China." *Sinorama*. April 1986, pp. 108-112.

4561. Hsu, Lina. "Taiwan Cartoons Technically, Culturally Unique." *Free China Journal*. November 22, 1990, p. 6.

4562. Lee Chan. "Wan Hsiang Comic Season." *United Daily News*. December 3, 1979.

4563. Lin Ching-Hsuan. "Beautiful Dream World — Unforgettable Comic Images." *China Times*. January 18, 1979.

4564. Lu Li-Chen. "When Chu-ko Szu-lang Meets City Hunter." *Sinorama*. August 1990, pp. 33-41.

4565. Peng Ching-Yang. "Our Own Cartoon — Y Y Is Coming." *United Daily News*. October 22, 1979.

4566. Tang Chu-Fen. "Taiwan Millionaire Cartoonists Find Success with Marital Spats, Sayings of Sages." *WittyWorld*. Winter 1993, pp. 12-13.

Political Cartoons

4567. "Aesthetic Dagger in Taiwan." *Independent Evening News*. January 5, 1991.

4568. Beeson, Diana. "Freedom of Expression and Editorial Cartoons: Political Change in Taiwan, 1972-1992." Paper presented at Association for Education in Journalism and Mass Communication, Atlanta, Georgia, August 10-13, 1994.

4569. Hsiao Hsiang-Wen. "Political Cartoons in Taiwan: Historical Profile and Content Analysis." Ph.D. Dissertation, Temple University, 1995. 242 pp.

4570. "In Defense of Cartoons." *Free China Review*. January 1992, pp. 18-23.

4571. Lin Ching-Wen. "Editorial Cartoonists Enjoy Newfound Freedoms." *Free China Journal*. July 9, 1990, p. 6.

4572. Lin Ching-Wen. "Freer Climate for Editorial Cartoonists." *Philippines Communication Journal*. March 1993, pp. 58-62.

4573. Lin, C.W. "Bringing Life to a Taboo: Editorial Cartoonists Enjoy Newfound Freedoms." In *Art and Culture*, pp. 53-57. Taipei: Chiu-yu Printing Co. Ltd., 1990.

4574. Lin Hung. "Political Cartoons Are the Index of Democracy." *Liberal Times Weekly*. 15 (1985), pp. 62-64.

4575. O Yang Yu. "Content Analysis of Political Cartoons in Daily Newspapers from July 1986 to June 1989." Master's thesis, Fu Jen University, Taipei, 1991.

4576. Peng Ching-Yang. *Caricature of Famous People*. Taipei: Independent Evening Post, 1993.

4577. "Satire Comes of Age." *Free China Review*. January 1992, p. 1.

4578. Weng Wen-Ching. "It's Easy To Caricature the President." *The Journalist Weekly*. January 15, 1990, pp. 77-80.

THAILAND

Cartooning, Cartoons

4579. "Cartoons — Virus That the Dictators Hated." *Lankeao* (Bangkok). March 10-16, 1985, pp. 48-51. Thai.

4580. Gesmankit, Pairote and Kullasap. "Cartoon Techniques Widely Applied in Thailand." *Asian Culture*. January 1980, pp. 21-23.

4581. *Lankbang* (Get Rid Of). Compilation of Cartoons. Bangkok: n.p., 1992. Thai.

4582. Michaelson, Helen. "Under Threat from the West? Thai Art and Culture." *Media Information Australia*. August 1993, pp. 59-61.

4583. "Thai Cartoons with Humor." *Feature Magazine* (Bangkok). August 1990, pp. 79-90. Thai.

4584. "A Witty World, As Seen Through a Cartoonist's Eye." *Bangkok Post*. September 16, 1992, p. 26.

4585. *Yim Yimm: Kartun yod Sanuk*. No. 4. Bangkok: Chun Ha San, 198? 96 pp. Thai. (Scatological cartoons).

Cartoonists

4586. "Cartoonists — People Who Work Behind the Scenes." *Feature Magazine* (Bangkok). August 1990, pp. 69-78. Thai.

4587. Chanyawong, Sudrak. "The Strategic Communication of Cartoon 'Kabuan Kan Kac Jon.'" Master's thesis, Chulalongkorn University, 1989. Thai.

4588. "Thai Cartoonist Gains Recognition Abroad." *Bangkok Post*. June 7, 1991, p. 32.

4589. Vatikiotis, Michael. "Wallop Manyun, Thailand: The Long Way Home." *Far Eastern Economic Review*. February 16, 1995, p. 62.

Chai Rachawat

4590. Chai Rachawat. *Compilation of Humor of Chai Rachawat*. 7 Vols. Bangkok: Green Thumb Artists, 1988. Thai.

4591. "Chai Rachawat Is Most Popular Cartoonist in Thailand." *Kukang*. May 17, 1993. Thai.

4592. Panacharoensawad, Chatree. "Analysis of Chai Rachawat's Satirical Comics Pooyai Ma and Tung Ma Mern BE 2521-2523." Srinakarunviroj University, 1986. Thai.

Animation

4593. Blaufarb, Ross. "Mickey Mouse Fit To Be Thaied." *Variety*. January 13, 1992, p. 84.

4594. Florance, Adam. "Thais Break Two-Decade Toon Drought." *Variety*. June 20-26, 1994, p. 36.

4595. Heng, Somporn. "Imagination in Motion." *The Nation* (Bangkok). September 20, 1992, p. B-4.

4596. Ngaokrachang, Payut. *Sud Sakorn*. Bangkok: Kuru Sapa, May 1986.

4597. "Target: Three Animation Films." *Cepta Circuit*. September 1978, pp. 9-10.

4598. "Thai Film Biz into Cartoon Field." *Variety*. August 2, 1978, p. 32.

4599. "Thailand vs. *Electric Man*." *Asiaweek*. July 24, 1981, p. 16.

Comic Books

4600. Chalanuchpong, Sirimas. "Thailand's Comic Relief." *The Nation* (Bangkok). October 24, 1993, p. B-1.

4601. Napattalung, Surangrat. "Comparison of Achievement in Health Education of Prathom Suksa Seven Students Through Learning with Comic Book and Conventional Method." Master's thesis, Chulalongkorn University, Bangkok, 1977. 138 pp. Thai.

4602. "Thai Publishers See Big Future in Comics." *Asian Mass Communication Bulletin*. September-October 1993, p. 6.

Japanese Comics

4603. *Doremon*. New Ed. Bangkok: Sam Dao, 198? 128 pp.

4604. *Doremon*. No. 20. Bangkok: Wibunkij, 1987. 181 pp.

4605. Srisantisuk, Oratai. "Japanese Comics and Thai Children." *Tawan Magazine*. May-July 1984, pp. 15-25. Thai.

4606. Sunkatiprapa, Suwanna. "Reading Behavior and Selection of Japanese Comic Books of Thai Students in Bangkok Metropolis." Master's thesis, Thammasat University, 1989. Thai.

Political Cartoons

4607. Chanjaroen, Chanyaporn. "Cartoons Pack Potent Message." *The Nation* (Bangkok). May 27, 1992, p. C-1.

4608. Kawwathanasakula, Jiamsakdi. "Political Cartoons During the Dictatorship Government. The Study of Political Cartoons from February 23, 1991 to December 9, 1991." Master's thesis, Chiang Mai University, 1992. 86 pp. Thai.

4609. Tansubhapol, Kulcharee. "Drawing on the Mind's Eye." *Bangkok Post*. February 1, 1994, p. 3-1.

VIETNAM

General Sources

4610. Florance, Adam. "Quality Gets New Focus in Vietnam." *Variety*. June 20-26, 1994, p. 36.

4611. Huxley, David. "'The Real Thing': New Images of Vietnam in American Comic Books." In *Vietnam Images: War and Representation*, edited by Jeffrey Walsh and James Aulich, pp. 160-170. New York; St. Martins, 1989.

4612. Seaford, Bruce. "Cartoon Capers." *Far Eastern Economic Review*. January 24, 1985, p. 3.

4613. Thuc-sinh. "Choe — Detained Cartoonist." *Index on Censorship*. December 1984, pp. 8-9.

4614. Trãn Van Can, Hũu Ngoc, and Vũ Huyên. *Vietnamese Contemporary Painters.* Hanoi: Red River, 1987. 162 pp.

4615. "Vietnam in Tinta China." *Primera Plana* (Buenos Aires). No. 199, 1966, p. 46.

5

AUSTRALIA AND OCEANIA

AUSTRALIA

Resources

4616. Dickinson, Pauline. *Index to the Comics in the Science Fiction and Fantasy Collection, University of Sydney Library*. Sydney, Australia: University of Sydney Library, 1984. 54 pp.

4617. National Library of Australia. "The John Ryan Comic Collection." Canberra, Australia: 1984. 81 pp.

4618. Swain, David. "Museum." *Inkspot*. March 1986, p. 9.

4619. Swain, David. "Museum." *Inkspot*. June 1986, p. 8.

Periodical Directory

4620. *The Australia Comic Collector*. Published 1977-1983 by Alumina Forests Publications, Subiaco, Western Australia. Articles, reviews, news of Australian comics; some by U.S. and British. Also called TACC.

4621. *Comic Hotline*. Monthly of 24 pages acts as tribute to Australian comics industry. Profiles, interviews, articles. St. James, Sydney, Australia.

4622. *Inkspot.* Quarterly of Australian Black and White Artists Club, Wayne Baldwin, P.O. Box 318, Strawberry Hills, NSW 2012, Australia. No. 6 in September 1987. Columns, news, interviews, and profiles of Australian comic artists.

4623. *John Dixon's Air Hawk.* First appeared Winter 1988, featuring episodes of John Dixon's aviation adventure and articles on the artist and other items of interest. Nat Karmichael, P.O. Box 549, Redcliffe 4020, Queensland, Australia.

4624. *Toon Art Times.* Published by The Cartoon Gallery, Shop 38, Level 2, Queen Victoria Building, Sydney, Australia 2000. Basically four page shopper with news of U.S. animation. Cartoon Gallery started in 1991.

Business and Legal Aspects

4625. Groves, Don. "Gaffney Intl. Finds Licensing Characters in Oz Marvelous." *Variety.* September 17, 1986, p. 82.

4626. Seeger, Colin. "Licensing and Merchandising." *Inkspot.* Autumn 1993, pp. 30-31.

4627. Seeger, Colin. "Moral Rights." *Inkspot.* Spring/Summer 1992, p. 35.

4628. Simpson, Shane. *The Visual Artist and the Law.* 2nd Ed. North Ryde, Australia: Law Book Company, 1992. 306 pp.

Historical Aspects

4629. Brannigan, Augustine. "Crimes from Comics: Social and Political Determinants of Victoria Law Reform 1938-1954." *Australian and New Zealand Journal of Criminology.* March 1986, pp. 23-42.

4630. Coleman, Peter and Les Tanner. *Cartoons of Australian History.* Melbourne: Thomas Nelson, 1973. 195 pp.

4631. Couperie, Pierre. "Australie." In *Histoire Mondiale de la Bande Dessinée*, edited by Pierre Horay, pp. 292-295. Paris: Pierre Horay Éditeur, 1989.

4632. *50 Years of the Newspaper Cartoon in Australia 1923-1973.* Adelaide: The News, 1973. 97 pp.

4633. "Fifty Years of the Potts." *Daily Telegraph.* October 31, 1970.

4634. Gordon, Ian. "Stop Laughing, This Is Serious: The Comic Art Form and Australian Identity 1880-1960." B.A. honors thesis, University of Sydney, 1986. 184 pp.

4635. King, T. "Social and Historical Aspects of the Australian Comic Strip." B.A. honors thesis, 1973. 25 pp.

4636. Lindesay, Vane. "Gurney: 1902-1955, Inklore." *Inkspot*. Spring/Summer 1992, pp. 26-28.

4637. Lindesay, Vane. *The Inked-in Image — A Survey of Australian Comic Art*. Melbourne: William Heinemann, 1970.

4638. Lindesay, Vane. *The Inked-in Image*. 2d. ed. Melbourne, Australia: Hutchinson, 1979. 336 pp.

4639. Openshaw, Robert. "'Worthless and Indecent Literature': Comics and Moral Panic in Early Post-War Australia." *History of Education Review*. 1986, pp. 1-12.

4640. Ryan, John. *Panel by Panel*. Stanmore, New South Wales, Australia: Cassell Australia, 1979. 223 pp.

4641. Ryan, John and Howard Siebel. "The Comic Book History of Australia. 1975 Edition. Typical Material from the Forties." *RBCC*. No. 119, 1975, pp. 36-37.

4642. Swain, David, ed. *200 in the Shade: An Historical Selection of Cartoons about Aborigines*. Sydney: Collins Australia, 1988. 193 pp.

Cartooning, Cartoons

4643. Adamson, Rob. "Why the Fishing's Good up in Arnhem Land." *Inkspot*. September 1988, p. 14.

4644. "Australasia." In *Cartoons: One Hundred Years of Cinema Animation*, by Giannalberto Bendazzi. Bloomington: Indiana University Press, 1994. (Australia, pp. 419-426; New Zealand, pp. 426-428).

4645. Buchanan, Cole. "AGM: Another Fine Mess." *Inkspot*. Spring/Summer 1992, p. 11.

4646. Buchanan, Cole. "Inc-ing in the Image." *Inkspot*. Winter 1992, p. 5.

4647. Budden, Earl. "Step by Step: Realism Matters." *Inkspot*. Spring/Summer 1992, pp. 36-39.

4648. "Cartooning and Education." *Inkspot*. Autumn 1993, p. 13.

4649. David, Mark. *Cartooning for Kids*. Sydney: A and R, 1992.

4650. [Fun Focus Syndicate]. *WittyWorld*. Autumn/Winter 1994, p. 4.

4651. Heimann, Rolf. "The Face of Australia." *WittyWorld*. Autumn 1987, pp. 32-33.

4652. Heimann, Rolf. "Respectable Graffiti." *WittyWorld*. Summer 1987, pp. 34-35.

4653. "A Letter from Jeff." *Inkspot*. Autumn 1990, pp. 32-33.

4654. "'Living Together': A Cartoon View of Australia." *Inkspot*. March 1988, p. 8.

4655. Lofo (Rolf Heimann). "Australian Cartooning Above and Below the Salt." *Access Magazine*. Autumn 1985, pp. 24-27.

4656. Russell, Jim. "Uncle Dick Meets Uncle Sam." *Inkspot*. September 1988, pp. 7-8.

4657. Shakespeare, John. "Ink with the Comic Touch." *Inkspot*. Winter 1992, pp. 16-19.

4658. "The Wrath of Nile." *Comic Hotline*. 1:1, 1986, p. 10.

Anthologies

4659. Bridges, Jim and Rolf Heimann, comps. *Australia — the Cartoon*. Carlton, Australia: McCullough Publication Inc., 1988. 96 pp.

4660. Heimann, Rolf. *No Emus for Antarctica!* Albert Park, Victoria: R. and L. Heimann, 1979.

4661. Heimann, Rolf, ed. *No Fission. A Collection of Anti-Nuclear Cartoons by Australian Artists*. Albert Park, Victoria: Access Magazine, 1983. 64 pp.

4662. Hutchinson, Garrie. *The Awful Australian: The Pick of Australian Cartoon Humour*. South Yarra, Victoria: Curry O'Neil Ross Pty. Ltd., 1984. 215 pp.

4663. Rideal, C.F. *People We Meet*. Field and Tuer, 1910. 24 pp.

4664. Robb, Brian. *My Middle East Campaigns*. Australian War Cartoons. London: Collins, 1944. 68 pp.

Awards and Competitions

4665. The Bulletin - Black and White Artists Annual Awards 1987. *Program*. Sydney: Bulletin, 1987.

4666. "Coffs Clock Up National Awards 4." *Inkspot*. Spring/Summer 1992, p. 13.

4667. David, Mark. "92 Stanleys Sees Leak Get His Fifth Gold." *Inkspot.* Spring/Summer 1992, p. 10.

4668. "1986 'Stanley' Awards." *Inkspot.* December 1986, p. 8.

4669. "The '93 Stanleys — A Night of Firsts." *Inkspot.* Summer 1993, p. 13.

4670. "Rotary National and International Cartoon Awards 1992." *Inkspot.* Spring/Summer 1992, pp. 29-33.

4671. "Rotary National and International Cartoon Awards 1993." *Inkspot.* Spring/Summer 1993, pp. 19-23.

4672. "'Stanley' Awards Portfolio." *Inkspot.* May 1987, p. 11.

4673. Szabo, Joe. "'For Gorsake, Stop Laughing, This Is Serious!'" *WittyWorld.* Winter/Spring 1994, p. 27.

4674. Worland, Lloyd. "Making It Big! The Birth of the Melbourne Comedy Festival Cartoon Competition!" *Inkspot.* Spring/Summer 1992, p. 12.

Black and White Artists' Club

4675. Buchanan, Cole. "You Just Can't Please Everybody." *Inkspot.* Summer 1993, p. 26.

4676. Lindesay, Vane. *Drawing From Life: A History of the Australian Black and White Artists' Club.* State Library of NSW Press, 1994.

4677. "The 1993 Report [Australian Black and White Artists]." *Inkspot.* Summer 1993, p. 10.

4678. Panozzo, Steve. "The 1992 Report." *Inkspot.* Spring/Summer 1992, p. 45.

Cartoonists and Their Works

4679. Baldwin, Wayne. "Artist in Profile: Brendan Akhurst. Country Boy Done Good." *Inkspot.* September 1988, pp. 8-9.

4680. Baldwin, Wayne. "Kaz Cooke: The Modern Cartoonist." *Inkspot.* Spring 1989, pp. 34-38.

4681. Baldwin, Wayne. "Kev Bailey, Black and White's Tassie Devil." *Inkspot.* Winter 1992, pp. 10-13.

4682. *Billabongs and Brolgas — An Australia Reader.* Sydney: Macmillan, 1992.

(Jimmy Bancks, Stan Cross, Eric Jolliffe, John Spooner, Michael Leunig, Ken Maynard, Doug Tainsh, S.T. Gill, David Low, Wep, Les Tanner, Leahy and Piper, Peter Nicholson, Bruce Petty).

4683. Bramwell, Murray and David Matthews. *Wanted for Questioning — Interviews with Australian Comic Artists*. Sydney: Allen and Unwin, 1992. (Patrick Cook, Jenny Coopes, Bruce Petty, Kaz Cooke, etc.).

4684. Cook, Patrick. *Ship of Fools. Cartoons by Cook*. Sydney: Allen and Unwin, 1991.

4685. Dove, Victor. "The Artist As Traveller." *Inkspot*. Autumn 1993, pp. 26-28.

4686. "Edd Aragon: A Touch of Oriental Class." *Inkspot*. Summer 1988, pp. 6-9.

4687. "Get To Know the Artist." *Inkspot*. Winter 1992, p. 27.

4688. "Get To Know the Artist." *Inkspot*. Spring/Summer 1992, p. 47. (Kerry Millard, Michael Dutkiewicz, Buddy Gross).

4689. "Get To Know the Artist." *Inkspot*. Summer 1993, p. 31. (Daniel Changer and Steve Zegarac).

4690. "Get To Know the Artist." *Inkspot*. Autumn 1993, p. 43.

4691. Hopkins, Livingston. *On the Hop!* Sydney, Australia: The Bulletin Newspaper Co., 1904.

4692. Horacek, Judy. *Life on the Edge*. Australia: Spinifex Press, 1992.

4693. "Inked in Mercier: Comic Master." *Inkspot*. Winter 1989, pp. 20-23.

4694. "John Jensen: An Ambidextrous Expatriate." *Inkspot*. September 1988, p. 5.

4695. "Jonsson Bletty 1890-1963." *Inkspot*. Spring 1989, pp. 39-42.

4696. Juddery, Mark. "Writer: David De Vries." *Comics Interview*. No. 108, 1992, pp. 14-19.

4697. "Leason 1889-1959: Rustic Skill." *Inkspot*. Autumn 1990, pp. 23-26.

4698. Lindesay, Vane. "Inked in Images: Miller, 1901-1983, Comic King." *Inkspot*. Winter 1992, pp. 20-22.

4699. Lindesay, Vane. "WEG: PROfile." *Inkspot*. Spring/Summer 1992, pp. 16-19.

4700. Lindsay, Jane. *Portrait of Pa*. Sydney: Angus and Robertson, 1993. (Norman Lindsay).

4701. "Lindsay, a Man Not To Cross Words With." *Inkspot*. Summer 1993, p. 9. (Lindsay Foyle).

4702. Lumsden, Glenn. "Strip Ease Artist." *Inkspot*. Autumn 1993, pp. 35-38.

4703. "Meet Your Fellow Members." *Inkspot*. March 1986, p. 7.

4704. "Meet Your Fellow Members." *Inkspot*. June 1986, p. 4.

4705. "Meet Your Fellow Members." *Inkspot*. September 1986, p. 6.

4706. "Meet Your Fellow Members." *Inkspot*. May 1987, pp. 12-13.

4707. "Meet Your Fellow Members." *Inkspot*. September 1988, p. 12.

4708. Muir, Marcie. *Australian Children's Book Illustrators*. Melbourne: Sun Books, 1977.

4709. "Norm Hetherington: Pulling the Right Strings." *Inkspot*. Spring 1989, pp. 14-17.

4710. *Pickering Recaptured*. Cartoons by Larry Pickering published in annual collection. This one was for 1980. Cartoons from *The Australian*.

4711. "Profile: Tony Rafty." *Inkspot*. Winter 1989, pp. 7-11.

4712. Rae, Richard. *Cartoonists of Australia*. Marrickville, NSW, Australia: View Productions, 1983. 95 pp.

4713. "Ralph Peverill, The Centre of Oz Cartooning." *Inkspot*. Winter 1989, pp. 24-27.

4714. Ryan, John. "Gibbs, Cecilia May (1876-1969)." In *Enciclopedia Mondiale del Fumetto*, edited by Maurice Horn and Luciano Secchi, p. 423. Milan: Editoriale Corno, 1978.

4715. Ryan, John. "Miller, Sydney Leon (1901-)." In *Enciclopedia Mondiale del Fumetto*, edited by Maurice Horn and Luciano Secchi, p. 566. Milan: Editoriale Corno, 1978.

4716. Ryan, John. "Nicholls, Sydney Wentworth (1896-)." In *Enciclopedia Mondiale del Fumetto*, edited by Maurice Horn and Luciano Secchi, p. 590. Milan: Editoriale Corno, 1978.

4717. Ryan, John. "Pitt, Stanley John (1925-)." In *Enciclopedia Mondiale del Fumetto*, edited by Maurice Horn and Luciano Secchi, p. 631. Milan: Editoriale Corno, 1978.

4718. Ryan, John. "Russell, James Newton (1909-)." In *Enciclopedia Mondiale del Fumetto*, edited by Maurice Horn and Luciano Secchi, pp. 665-666. Milan: Editoriale Corno, 1978.

4719. Spooner, John. *Bodies and Souls*. Melbourne: Sun/Macmillan Co. of Australia, 1989. 128 pp.

4720. "Vale: Keith Chatto, 1924-1992." *Inkspot*. Spring/Summer 1992, p. 13.

4721. West, Richard S. "Oliphant Down Under." *Target*. Summer 1984, pp. 16-19.

4722. Whitington, R.S. *Sir Frank*. Sydney: Cassell Australia, 1971.

4723. "WWII Nostalgia Department." *Cartoonews*. No. 11, 1975, p. 31-34. (Harold Barry Armstrong, political cartoonist).

4724. "WWII Nostalgia Department: Ted Scorfield." *Cartoonews*. June 1975, pp. 11-15.

Dixon, John

4725. "John Dangar Dixon." In *A History of Komiks of the Philippines and Other Countries*, by Cynthia Roxas and Joaquin Arevalo, Jr., p. 255. Manila: Islas Filipinas Publishing, 1985.

4726. "John Dixon — Artist, Author, Extraordinaire." *Comic Hotline*. 1:1 (1986), pp. 6-7.

Jolliffe, Eric

4727. *Jolliffe's Outback*. Collection of cartoons by E. Jolliffe, published by him regularly at Dee Why, N.S.W., Australia.

4728. "Profile: Eric Jolliffe, Gift Divine." *Inkspot*. Autumn 1990, pp. 12-15.

Petty, Bruce

4729. Herd, Nick, Susan Lambert, Barbara Alysen. "Bruce Petty." *Filmnews* (Sydney). May 1977.

4730. Starkiewicz, Antoinette. "Petty." *Cinema Papers*. July-August 1979.

Rigby, Paul

4731. Collins, Clive. ["Paul Rigby"]. *The Jester*. June 1992, p. 10.

4732. Rigby, Paul. *Rigby's New York and Beyond*. Carlstadt, New Jersey: Ardor Publishing Co., 1984.

4733. "Spotlight: Rigby." *Artsy.* 1:1 (1981), pp. 5-8.

Tainsh, Doug

4734. "Doug Tainsh: A True Blue Black and White." *Inkspot.* Summer 1988, pp. 17-20.

4735. "Profile: Doug Tainsh." *Inkspot.* Summer 1988, pp. 17-20.

Walsh, Richard

4736. Walsh, Richard. *Gortn the Act.* Melbourne: Sun Books, 1968.

4737. Walsh, Richard, ed. *Gough Syrup.* Melbourne: Sun Books, 1967.

4738. Walsh, Richard, ed. *No Holts Barred.* Melbourne: Sun Books, 1966.

Characters and Titles

4739. "Air Hawk and the Flying Doctors." In *A History of Komiks of the Philippines and Other Countries,* by Cynthia Roxas and Joaquin Arevalo, Jr., p. 229. Manila: Islas Filipinas Publishing, 1985.

4740. "Australian Comic Now in the U.S." *Editor and Publisher.* January 12, 1991, p. 34. ("Down Under").

4741. Brancatelli, Joe. "Out of the Silence (Australia)." In *Enciclopedia Mondiale del Fumetto,* edited by Maurice Horn and Luciano Secchi, p. 607. Milan: Editoriale Corno, 1978.

4742. Humphries, Barry and Nicholas Garland. *Bazza Pulls It Off.* London: A. Deutsch, 1971. 90 pp.

4743. Ryan, John. "Bib and Bub (Australia)." In *Enciclopedia Mondiale del Fumetto,* edited by Maurice Horn and Luciano Secchi, p. 185. Milan: Editoriale Corno, 1978.

4744. Ryan, John. "Bluey and Curley (Australia)." In *Enciclopedia Mondiale del Fumetto,* edited by Maurice Horn and Luciano Secchi, pp. 195-196. Milan: Editoriale Corno, 1978.

4745. Ryan, John. "Potts, The (Australia)." In *Enciclopedia Mondiale del Fumetto,* edited by Maurice Horn and Luciano Secchi, p. 635. Milan: Editoriale Corno, 1978.

4746. Ryan, John. "Rod Craig (Australia)." In *Enciclopedia Mondiale del Fumetto,* edited by Maurice Horn and Luciano Secchi, pp. 659-660. Milan: Editoriale Corno, 1978.

4747. Ryan, John. "Wally and the Major (Australia)." In *Enciclopedia Mondiale del Fumetto*, edited by Maurice Horn and Luciano Secchi, p. 755. Milan: Editoriale Corno, 1978.

"Fatty Finn"

4748. "Fatty Finn." In *A History of Komiks of the Philippines and Other Countries*, by Cynthia Roxas and Joaquin Arevalo, Jr., pp. 228-229. Manila: Islas Filipinas Publishing, 1985.

4749. Ryan, John. "Fatty Finn (Australia)." In *Enciclopedia Mondiale del Fumetto*, edited by Maurice Horn and Luciano Secchi, p. 323. Milan: Editoriale Corno, 1978.

"Ginger Meggs"

4750. "Ginger Meggs, Australia's Most Famous Comic Strip." *The World of Comic Art*. Fall 1966, pp. 32-35.

4751. "Ginger Meggs Is 65!" *Inkspot*. May 1987, p. 5.

4752. Gordon, Ian. "The Symbol of a Nation: Ginger Meggs and Australian National Identity." *Journal of Australian Studies*. September 1992.

4753. Ryan, John. "Ginger Meggs (Australia)." In *Enciclopedia Mondiale del Fumetto*, edited by Maurice Horn and Luciano Secchi, p. 425. Milan: Editoriale Corno, 1978.

"Snake"

4754. ["Snake Tales"]. *Editor & Publisher*. May 29, 1982, p. 52.

4755. Sols. *The Best of Snake*. No. 1. Kyabram, Victoria, Australia: Budget Books, 1984. 80 pp.

4756. Sols. *Call Me Snake*. New York: Berkley Books, 1984. 126 pp.

Animation

4757. "Aussies Offering Cartoon Feature." *Variety*. May 2, 1990, p. 282.

4758. "Australian Animation." *Cartoonist PROfiles*. December 1972, pp. 28-31.

4759. "Feds Enter Effort To Pitch Locations." *Variety*. April 26, 1993, p. 50.

4760. Fitzroy, Cosmo. "Animation from Australia." *Cartoonist PROfiles*. No. 16, 1972, pp. 28-31.

4761. Groves, Don. "Kids Power Oz Video Biz." *Variety*. January 31-February 6, 1994, p. 63.

4762. Groves, Don. "Oz Inks a Green Brick Road." *Variety*. June 20-26, 1994, pp. 32, 34.

4763. Hanlon, Bob. "Animation Down Under." *Animator's Newsletter* (St. Albans, U.K.). Winter 1983-1984.

4764. Knowles, Ann D. and Mary C. Nixon. "Children's Comprehension of a Television Cartoon's Emotional Theme." *Australian Journal of Psychology*. August 1990, pp. 115-121.

4765. Knowles, Ann D. and Mary C. Nixon. "Children's Comprehension of Expressive States Depicted in a Television Cartoon." *Australian Journal of Psychology*. April 1989, pp. 17-24.

4766. "The Koala May Take the Outfit to Nashville." *Variety*. February 18, 1991, p. 56.

4767. Mendham, Tim and Keith Hepper. "Animation in Australia." In *Industrial and Commercial Photography Yearbook 1978*. Sydney: 1978.

4768. Murdoch, Blake. "Financing Animation: Investors and Distribs." *Variety*. February 18, 1991, pp. 54, 56.

4769. Murdoch, Blake. "High Demand from U.S. Boosts Oz Animation Biz." *Variety*. February 18, 1991, p. 58.

4770. Murdoch, Blake. "Oz Thriving, Especially As a Supplier to Yanks." *Variety*. November 5, 1990, p. 66.

4771. Murdoch, Blake. "'Riddle' Poses Sales Questions." *Variety*. February 18, 1991, p. 57.

4772. Murdoch, Blake. "'Riddle' Prod Prompts Move to New Studio." *Variety*. February 18, 1991, p. 61.

4773. Murdoch, Blake. "Targeting TV and Debuting Two Blockbuster Features." *Variety*. February 18, 1991, pp. 53, 61.

4774. Murdoch, Blake. "Yoram Gross: The Mickey of Oz — Is He Blinky Bill?" *Variety*. February 18, 1991, pp. 53, 59.

4775. "Ninja Turtles Banned from Classrooms." *Asian Mass Communication Bulletin*. November-December 1990, p. 11.

4776. Starkiewicz, Antoinette. "Yoram Gross." *Cinema Papers* (Melbourne). October 1994.

4777. "What! Me Make Another Animated Feature? No Way!" *Industrial and Commercial Photography Yearbook*. Sydney: 1978.

Comic Books

4778. "Australian TV Show Features Comics Review Segment." *Comics Journal*. May 1989, p. 18.

4779. "Australia's Fox Comics Announces Distribution Deal with Fantagraphics." *Comics Buyer's Guide*. May 26, 1989, p. 61.

4780. Benjamin, Lesley. "Ian Jack." *Comics Interview*. August 1984, pp. 71-75.

4781. Boswell, Lawrence. "Aussie Comics' Dynamic Duo." *Inkspot*. Winter 1992, p. 6.

4782. Brannigan, A. "Crimes from Comics: Social and Political Determinants of Reform of the Victorian Obscenity Law 1938-1954." *Australian and New Zealand Journal of Criminology*. March 1986, pp. 23-42.

4783. Carr, Gerald. "AB & WAC at OZCON II." *Inkspot*. Autumn 1993, p. 11.

4784. Chaloner, Cary. "Comic Book Industry Celebrates at OZCON II." *Inkspot*. Autumn 1993, p. 10.

4785. Cosulich, Oscar. "Sesso e Dollari, per Sognare a Fumetti." *Comic Art*. October 1989, pp. 63-64.

4786. "Down Under But Not Out! Australian Cartoonist." *Cartoonist PROfiles*. June 1983, pp. 33-39.

4787. Foster, John. "From 'Ulla Dulla Mogo' to 'Serene Azure Vault of Heaven': Literary Style in Australian Children's Comic Books." *Journal of Popular Culture*. Winter 1991, pp. 63-77.

4788. "Last Rites for *Phantastique*?" *Comic Hotline*. 1:1 (1986), pp. 8-9.

4789. Norman, Albert E. "This World...Comic Books Put on Spot Down Under." *Christian Science Monitor*. September 8, 1952.

4790. Ridout, Cefn. "X Marks the Spot." *Speakeasy*. September 1989, pp. 68-70, 73.

4791. "Sydney's Comic Retailers." *Comic Hotline*. 1:1 (1986), pp. 11, 14-16, 18.

Comic Strips

4792. Baldwin, Wayne. "Australian Pub: from Cartoon Page to Thirst Quencher." *WittyWorld*. Autumn 1988, pp. 10-11.

4793. Blaikie, George. *Remember Smith's Weekly*. Adelaide: Rigby, 1966.

4794. Emmerson, Rod. "The Pub with No Peer...." *Inkspot*. Autumn 1993, pp. 16-19.

4795. Foster, Peter. *The Comic Strip Book*. Sydney: Ashton Scholastic, 1993.

Political Cartoons

4796. "Black and White Art in Australia." *Current Affairs Bulletin*. December 23, 1963.

4797. Heimann, Rolf. "Black and White Art in a Black and White Theme." *WittyWorld*. Winter/Spring 1990, pp. 30-31.

4798. "Report from Australia." *Target*. Winter 1984, pp. 30-31; Autumn 1984, p. 31.

NEW ZEALAND

Cartoonists

4799. Baskett, Pat. "How They Make Us Laugh." *New Zealand Herald*. March 4, 1992, Section 2, p. 6.

4800. Grant, Ian F. "Blo: Our Most Darling Cartoonist." *Insight*. December 1983-January 1984, pp. 26-27.

4801. Grant, Ian. "The Mirth Makers: Cartoonists and Their Clout." *Insight*. December 1983-January 1984, pp. 16-20, 22-25.

4802. McRae, Toni. "Television Cricket Cartoonist Is Out L.B.W. (Little Baby Wins)." *Sunday Star*. March 22, 1992.

4803. "Min's Brush with History." *New Zealand Herald*. February 20, 1992, Section 2, p. 1.

4804. "Sir Gordon Edward George Minhinnick." *Comics Journal*. May 1992, pp. 23-24.

4805. Ward, Tessa. "Kiwi Cartoonists Have Made Their Mark in UK." *The Jester*. April 1992, pp. 8-9.

4806. Wong, Gilbert. "Cartooning Is Not All Laughs." *New Zealand Herald*. February 27, 1992, p. 3.

Lye, Len

4807. Brownson, Ron, ed. *Len Lye—A Personal Mythology*. Auckland: Auckland City Art Gallery, 1980. 91 pp.

4808. Curnow, Wystan and Roger Horrocks, eds. *Figures of Motion—Len Lye, Selected Writings*. Auckland: Auckland University Press/Oxford University Press, 1984. 152 pp.

4809. "The Films of Len Lye." *Film Library Quarterly*. 14:3-5 (1981).

Characters and Titles

4810. Ball, Murray. *Bruce the Barbarian*. London: Quartet Books, 1973.

"Footrot Flats"

4811. Ball, Murray. *Footrot Flats*. Taita: INL Print, 1976.

4812. Ball, Murray. *Footrot Flats Two*. Victoria: Orin, 1979. 72 pp.

4813. Cawley, John. "A New Zeal (land) in Animation: Footrot Flats." *Cartoon Quarterly*. Winter 1988, pp. 11-14.

4814. "Kiwi 'Footrot' Has $A2-Mil in Oz B.O." *Variety*. May 13, 1987, pp. 55-56.

4815. Williamson, Lenora. "New Zealand Comic Strip Branching Out." *Editor and Publisher*. March 27, 1982, p. 46.

Animation

4816. McGilvary, Linda and Pat Penrose. "Living Happily with Television." Paper presented at Early Childhood Convention, Dunedin, New Zealand, September 8-11, 1991. 9 pp.

Comic Books

4817. "Dylan Horrocks Explores New Zealand and Comics in Pickle." *Comics Journal*. January 1994, pp. 15-17.

4818. "New Zealand Bans Some Comics, Restricts Others." *Comics Journal*. July 1991, pp. 13-14.

4819. "Sexual Comics Increase; So Do Challenges." *Comics Journal*. September 1990, pp. 12-13.

4820. Stone, Cornelius. "Art d'Ecco, Toys, New Zealand Comic Gazette Yearbook." *Ark*. No. 31, p. 63.

4821. Stone, Cornelius. "New Zealand: The Good, the Bad and the Ugly." *Ark*. No. 26, p. 41.

4822. Thompson, Mark. "New Zealand Customs Seize Comics." *Comics Journal*. May 1994, pp. 43-44.

4823. Townsend, Michael A., *et al.* "Student Perceptions of Verbal and Cartoon Humor in the Test Situation." *Educational Research Quarterly*. Winter 1983, pp. 17-23.

Comic Strips

4824. Corballis, Richard and Verson Small. "New Zealand Cartoon Strips." *Journal of Popular Culture*. Fall 1985, pp. 175-189.

4825. Lindesay, Vane. "White 1900-1986. Kiwi Wiz." *Inkspot*. Autumn 1993, pp. 32-34.

PAPUA NEW GUINEA

Comics

4826. "Fantom, Yu Pren Tru Bilong Mi." *Time*. September 26, 1977, p. 38.

4827. Smithies, Michael. "Reading Habits at a Third World Technological University." *Reading in a Foreign Language*. October 1983, pp. 111-118.

SOLOMON ISLANDS

Comic Books

4828. Roughan, John. "The Nongovernmental Organization Factor in Development: A View from the Solomon Islands." *Pacific Studies*. November 1990, pp. 95-108.

6

CENTRAL AND SOUTH AMERICA

REGIONAL AND INTER-COUNTRY PERSPECTIVES

Resources

4829. Méndez, José L. "Manipulación y Fabricación de Mitos en la Subliteratura." *Casa de las Américas*. 89 (1975), pp. 122-129.

4830. Miller, Gary, comp. "Graphics." In "Latin American Popular Culture: An Introductory Bibliography," edited by Roger Cunniff. *Proceedings of the Pacific Coast Council on Latin American Studies*. 5 (1976), pp. 188-191.

Periodical Directory

4831. *Boletim de HQ*. Newsletter of the Universidade de São Paulo, Escola de Comunicações e Artes, meant as outlet for program in comics. Articles on comics of Brazil and elsewhere. First issue, November-December 1991. Núcleo de Histórias em Quadrinhos/ECM, Av. Prof. Lúcio Martins Rodrigues, 443 05508, São Paulo, Brazil.

4832. *Comikaze para Matarse de Risa*. Tabloid humor magazine dealing with cartooning started in 1993. *Diario El Litoral*, 25 de Mayo 3536, 3000 Santa Fe, Argentina. Spanish.

4833. *La Semana Cómica* (The Comics Week). Managua, Nicaragua. Articles, comic strips, cartoons, erotic gag cartoons.

4834. *Motus Liber: Organo.* Fanzine published by Cómic Grupo de Estudio—México, after January 1973.

4835. *Puertitas. Historietas y Humor.* Periodical full of strips, with news and short articles. Esmeralda 779-6°F, Capital, Código Postal 1007, Argentina. No. 7, September 1990.

4836. *Trix Hemocomics.* Bimester magazine devoted to Argentine comics. Includes news, comic strips, reviews. Eight numbers appeared by November 1989. Félix Bravo, editor. Mendoza 415-1 er. Piso. Dpto. A, San Miguel de Tucumán C.P. 4000, Argentina.

General Sources

4837. Barahona, Salomón L. *Literatura de la Imagen.* Barcelona: Salvat, 1973.

4838. Baur, Elisabeth K. *La Historieta Como Experiencia Didáctica.* México: Nueva Imagen, 1978.

4839. Brickell, H. "Satire Transplanted: Francisco Rivero Gil." *Inter America.* April 1943, pp. 28-29.

4840. "The Dangerous Life of Latin American Cartoonists." *Group Media Journal.* 7:3/4 (1988), p. 27.

4841. Foster, David William. *From Mafalda to Los Supermachos. Latin American Graphic Humor As Popular Culture.* Boulder: Lynne Rienner, 1989. 129 pp. (Mexico, Peru, Argentina, and Brazil).

4842. Foster, David W. "On the Study of Popular Culture in America: Papers Presented at Workshop, Arizona State University, 23 March, 1984." In *Contemporary Latin American Culture: Unity and Diversity,* edited by L. Gail Guntermann, pp. 27-43. Tempe: Center for Latin American Studies, Arizona State University, 1984.

4843. Foster, David William. "Recent Works on Latin American Cartoon Art [Review Essay]." *Studies in Latin American Popular Culture.* 3 (1984), pp. 179-182.

4844. Haight, Anne Lyon, ed. *Portrait of Latin America As Seen by Her Print Makers.* New York, 1946, pp. 24-25.

4845. Helguera, J. León. "Nineteenth Century Cartoons: Colombian and Venezuelan Examples." *Studies in Latin American Popular Culture.* 2 (1983), pp. 220-222.

4846. Hinds, Harold E., ed. "Latin American Popular Culture." Special issues. *Journal of Popular Culture.* Winter 1980, pp. 405-534; Summer 1984, pp. 58-183.

4847. Massart, Pierre. "Literatura y Paraliteratura: El Estudio de la Literatura Infantil y Juvenil." *Revista Internacional de Ciencias Sociales.* 1 (1976), pp. 193-213.

4848. Moliterni, Claude. "Escola Panamericana de Arte." *Phénix* (Paris). No. 14, 1970.

4849. "Pan-American Accord As Seen by Cartoonists of Latin America." *Rotarian.* April 1942, p. 6.

4850. Reyes Hens, F. "How They Looked to Me." *Américas.* February 1959, pp. 34-35.

4851. Santiago. *Refandango e Outras Aventuras do Macanudo Taurino.* Porto Alegre: L&PM Editores, 1977.

4852. Williford, Miriam. *It's the Image That Counts: Cartoon Masters for Latin America Study.* Winthrop College Station, 1976.

4853. Zecchetto, Victorino. "Sketches, Comic Strips and Cartoons in 'Popular' Communications." *Group Media Journal.* 7:3/4 (1988), pp. 6-10. (South America).

Animation

4854. "Animación: Cinema y Video." Thematic issue. *Corto Circuito* (Lima). April 1992.

4855. "Latin America." In *Cartoons: One Hundred Years of Cinema Animation,* by Giannalberto Bendazzi. Bloomington: Indiana University Press, 1994. (Mexico, pp. 384-385; Cuba, pp. 385-388; Colombia, pp. 388-389; Venezuela, p. 389).

4856. Lenti, Paul. "Turner To Extend Reach of Its Cartoon Network." *Variety.* March 29, 1993, p. 54.

4857. Palmer, H. Marion. *Donald Duck Sees South America.* Boston, Massachusetts: D.C. Heath, 1945. 137 pp.

Caricature

4858. "Caricatures in Miniature; Exhibition of Sculptured Miniatures by F. Mendoza Limón." *Hobbies.* May 1944, p. 121.

4859. Johnson, James J. "Latin America in Caricature." *Latin American Digest.* Spring 1980, pp. 1-3.

4860. Kemchs, Arturo. *La Caricatura por la Paz*. Mexico: Editorial Oriental del Uruguay, 1988.

4861. Sánchez Quell, Hipólito. *El Caricaturista Miguel Acevedo*. Asunción: Casa América, 1974.

4862. "Sculptured Miniatures of Famous Personalities by F. Mendoza Limón." *Bulletin of Pan American Union*. March 1944, p. 154.

Comic Books

4863. Acevedo, Juan. *Para Hacer Historietas* (How To Make Comics). Madrid: Editorial Popular, 1981.

4864. Dineen, Louis. "Catechetics in Comics." *Columban Mission*. February 1977, pp. 6-7.

4865. Flora, Cornelia Butler. "Creative Choices for Latin American Photonovels and Comics." *Development Communication Report*. Autumn 1986, pp. 12-13.

4866. Flora, Cornelia Butler. "Roasting Donald Duck: Alternative Comics and Photonovels in Latin America." *Journal of Popular Culture*. Summer 1984, pp. 163-184.

4867. Fresnault Dreruelle, Pierre. "Diseños y Globos, La Historieta Como Medio de Expresión: El Montage." *C Línea; Revista Latinoamericana de Estudio de la Historieta*. 12 (1974), pp. 38-45.

4868. Hinds, Harold E., Jr. "Comics." In *Studies in Latin American Popular Culture*. 4 (1985), pp. 24-62.

4869. Llobera, José. *Dibujo del 'Cómic': Manuales Prácticas AFHA* (Comic Illustration...). Barcelona: Ediciones AFHA Internacional, 1973.

4870. "Medios Masivos de Comunicación." Special issue of *Referencias* (Havana). III (1972). (Catherine Wolfe and Marjorie Fiske, "Por Que Se Leen las Tiras Comicas," pp. 109-110; Humberto Eco, "El Mito de Superman," pp. 479 ff).

4871. Morales, Fidel. "La Historieta Pide Definirse." *C Línea; Revista Latinoamericana de Estudio de la Historieta*. 6 (1974), pp. 6-11.

4872. Nomez, Naim. "La Historieta en al Proceso de Cambio Social." *Comunicación y Cultura*. 2 (1974), pp. 109-123.

4873. North American Congress on Latin America, ed. "The United States Information Agency: Pushing the 'Big Lie.'" Issue of *Latin America and Empire Report*. September 1972, 31 pp.

4874. Ossa, Felipe. *El Mundo de la Historieta* (The World of Comics). Bogotá: Editores Colombia, 1978.

4875. Parlato, Ronald, Margaret Burns Parlato, and Bonnie J. Cain. *Fotonovelas and Comic Books: The Use of Popular Graphic Media in Development*. Washington, D.C.: Office of Education and Human Resources, Development Support Bureau, Agency for International Development, 1980.

4876. Perez-Yglesias, Maria and Mario Zeledon-Cambronero. *La B.D. Critique Latino-Américaine*. Louvain-La-Neuve: Cabay, 1982.

4877. Salwen, Michael B. and Bruce Garrison. *Latin American Journalism*. Hillsdale, New Jersey: Lawrence Erlbaum, 1991. ("Fotonovelas and Comic Books," pp. 138-139).

4878. Vega, Pastor. "Pequeña Crítica Ideológica de los Llamados Cómics en América Latina." *Cine Cubano*. Nos. 81-83, 1974, pp. 1-11.

4879. Vergueiro, Waldomiro. "Os Quadrinhos na América Latina." *Boletim de HQ*. May-June 1992, p. 3.

Fotonovelas

4880. Flora, Cornelia Butler. "The Fotonovela in America." *Studies in Latin American Popular Culture*. 1 (1982), pp. 15-26.

4881. Flora, Cornelia Butler. "Photonovels." In *Handbook of Latin American Popular Culture*, pp. 151-171. Westport, Connecticut: Greenwood, 1985.

4882. Flora, Cornelia Butler and Jan L. Flora. "The Fotonovela As a Tool for Class and Cultural Domination." New York: Women's International Resource Exchange Service, 1978-1983. 9 pp.

4883. Willis, Meredith S. "Spin-offs: The Fotonovela and the Marriage of Narrative and Art." *Teachers and Writers Collaborative*. 8:1 (1978), pp. 43-51.

ARGENTINA

Resources

4884. "Fanzines." *Trix*. No. 6 (n.d.), p. 46.

4885. "'Humor,' l'Argentina Che Ride." *Program*. Napoli 6. Mostra Internazionale del Fumetto e del Cinema d'Animazione. 1984, p. 34. (Humor periodical).

4886. "Nuevas Revistas de Historietas!" *Trix*. No. 5 (n.d), pp. 59-60.

4887. "Un Gran Organización al Servicio de la Historieta." *Dibujantes*. No. 4, 1953/1954, pp. 4-7.

General Sources

4888. Bróccoli, Alberto and Carlos Trillo. *El Humor Gráfico*. Buenos Aires: Centro Editor de América Latina, 1971, 1972.

4889. Cáceres, German. "The Argentine Graphic Humour: Today." Paper presented at First International Cartoon Festival, Budapest, Hungary, August 22, 1990.

4890. "Confraternidad." *Trix*. No. 6 (n.d), p. 46.

4891. Cuervo, Javier. "La Actividad de Buenos Aires: Las Putas y el Loco." *El Wendigo*. December 1985, pp. 4-5.

4892. Ferrer, Arturo Horacio. *El Libro del Tango; Historias e Imágenes*. Buenos Aires: Editorial Ossorio-Vargas, 1970.

4893. Fossati, Franco. *Il Fumetto Argentino* (The Argentine Comics). Genova: Pirella Editore, 1980. 73 pp.

4894. Jitrik, Noé. *La Revolución del 90*. Buenos Aires: Centro Editor de América Latina, 1971.

4895. Lindstrom, Naomi. "Latin American Cartooning: Between Lovers and Critics." *Studies in Latin American Popular Culture*. 1 (1982), pp. 246-251.

4896. Lindstrom, Naomi. "Social Commentary in Argentine Cartooning: From Description to Questioning." *Journal of Popular Culture*. Winter 1981, pp. 509-523.

4897. Lipszyc, David. "El Humor Argentino." *Inkspot*. Autumn 1993, p. 7.

4898. Masotta, Oscar. *Arte Pop y Semantica*. 2nd. Ed. Buenos Aires: Centro des Artes Visuales del Instituto Torcuato Di Tella, 1966. 64 pp.

4899. Masotta, Oscar. *El Pop-Art*. Buenos Aires: Editorial Columba, 1967. 120 pp.

4900. Ondarrabia, Martin. "Confluencias. Dibujos de Literatos." *La Nación* (Buenos Aires). August 1944.

4901. "Perros Ingleses." *Trix*. No. 6 (n.d.), p. 47.

4902. Rivera, Jorge. "Sonaste, Maneco! Historia del Humor Gráfico Argentino I." *Crisis* (Buenos Aires). 34 (1976), pp. 16-24; continued as "Una Compadrada Contra el Terror, Historia del Humor Gráfico Argentino II." 35 (1976), pp. 57-73.

4903. "Supervivencia Infantil." *Trix*. No. 6 (n.d.), p. 46.

4904. Trillo, Carlos and Guillermo Saccomanno. *Y Digo Yo....* Buenos Aires: Ediciones de la Flor, 1971.

4905. Various Authors. "De la Historieta a la Fotonovela." In *Capitulo Universal*. No. 143. Buenos Aires: Centro Editor de América Latina, S. A., 1971.

4906. Vázquez Lucio, Oscar E (Siulnas). *Historia del Humor Gráfico y Escrito en la Argentina*. Buenos Aires: Editorial Universitaria de Buenos Aires, 1985.

Cartoonists

4907. "Altuna i Bambini Post-Atomici." *Program*. Napoli 6. Mostra Internazionale del Fumetto e del Cinema d'Animazione. 1984, p. 31. (Horacio Altuna).

4908. "Así Naciéron: Aviato." *Dibujantes*. No. 18, 1956, p. 3.

4909. "Así Naciéron: Bólido." *Dibujantes*. No. 17, 1955, p. 13.

4910. Bendazzi, Giannalberto. *Due Volte l'Oceano—Vita di Quirino Cristiani, Pioniere del Cinema d'Animazione*. Florence: La Casa Usher, 1983. 138 pp.

4911. Brunoro, Gianni. "Dietro le Quinte delle Historietas." *Programma Lucca 14*. 1980, pp. 14-16. (Zerboni).

4912. Caceres, Germán. "Búsqueda Insaciable (Entrevista a Miguel Rep)." In *Así Se Lee la Historieta*. pp. 103-108. Buenos Aires: Beas Ediciones, 1994.

4913. Caceres, Germán. "Cita con la Aventura (Entrevista a Robin Wood)." In *Así Se Lee la Historieta*, pp. 69-76. Buenis Aires: Beas Ediciones, 1994.

4914. Caceres, Germán. "Defensa del Clasicismo (Entrevista a Lucho Olivera)." In *Así Se Lee la Historieta*, pp. 95-101. Buenos Aires: Beas Ediciones, 1994.

4915. Caceres, Germán. "La Historieta Como Sentimiento (Entrevista a Martha Barnes)." In *Así Se Lee la Historieta*, pp. 83-86. Buenos Aires: Beas Ediciones, 1994.

4916. Caceres, Germán. *Oesterheld*. Buenos Aires: Ediciones del Dock, 1992. 66 pp.

4917. Caloi. *Humor Libre de Caloi*. Buenos Aires: Editorial Nueva Senda, 1972.

4918. Cantón, Dario. *Gardel, ¿a Quién la Cantás?*. Buenos Aires: Ediciones de la Flor, 1972. (Carlos Gardel).

4919. "Carlos Enrique Vogt." *Dibujantes*. No. 13, 1955, pp. 32-33.

4920. "Conozca a Nuestros Argumentistas: Julio Almada." *Dibujantes*. No. 30, 1959, p. 33.

4921. "Entrepreneurs. Felix Bravo, 26 Años, 'Trix': Bravo por el Comic." *Noticias*. July 22, 1990, p. 75.

4922. "Es un Autentico Piantadino el Creador de Azonzato...." *Dibujantes*. No. 1, 1953, pp. 24-25, 34.

4923. Gasca, Luis. "Ianiro, Abel (1919-1960)." In *Enciclopedia Mondiale del Fumetto*, edited by Maurice Horn and Luciano Secchi. Milan: Editoriale Corno, 1978.

4924. Gasca, Luis. "Palacio, Lino (1910?-)." In *Enciclopedia Mondiale del Fumetto*, edited by Maurice Horn and Luciano Secchi, p. 609. Milan: Editoriale Corno, 1978.

4925. Gori, Leonardo. "Il Mistero de Marte." *Comic Art*. May 1994, p. 60. (Federico Pedrocchi).

4926. "La Figura, Que Surge: Pedro Flores." *Dibujantes*. No. 16, 1955, pp. 8-9.

4927. Legaristi, Francisco. "Entrevista: Horacio Lalia. El Sentido de Una Vida." *Trix*. May 1989, pp. 61-65.

4928. Legaristi, Francisco. "Entrevista a Osvaldo Viola." *Trix*. November 1989, pp. 24-29.

4929. Legaristi, Francisco. "Hemo Club." *Trix*. May 1989, pp. 19-20. (René Quirós).

4930. Legaristi, Francisco. "Juan Zanotto." *Trix*. No. 6 (n.d.), pp. 23-26.

4931. Legaristi, Francisco. "Monocomics." *Trix*. No. 6 (n.d.), pp. 25-28.

4932. Lezama, H.E. "They Make Argentina Laugh!" *Américas*. February 1960, pp. 22-27.

4933. Lipszyc, Enrique. *El Dibujo a Través del Temperamento de 150 Famosos Artistas*. Buenos Aires: Editor Enrique Lipszyc, 1953.

4934. "Monstruo Invitado—Peiro." *Trix*. No. 3 (n.d.), pp. 18-21.

4935. "Muñoz, 'Sudaca' Comics." *Program*. Napoli 6. Mostra Internazionale del Fumetto e del Cinema d'Animazione. 1984, p. 30. (José Muñoz).

4936. "Pratico, lo Humor in Galleria." *Program*. Napoli 6. Mostra Internazionale del Fumetto e del Cinema d'Animazione. 1984, p. 33. (Miguel Angel Pratico).

4937. Salzano, Daniel. "Monstruo Invitado: Crist." *Trix*. No. 4 (n.d.), p. 47.

4938. Siulnas. *Aquellos Personajes de Historieta (1912-1959)*. Buenos Aires: Puntosur Editores, 1987.

4939. "Walter Ciocca." In *A History of the Komiks of the Philippines and Other Countries*, by Cynthia Roxas and Joaquin Arevalo, Jr., p. 253. Manila: Islas Filipinas Publishing, 1985.

Breccia, Alberto

4940. "Alberto Breccia." In *A History of the Komiks of the Philippines and Other Countries*, by Cynthia Roxas and Joaquin Arevalo, Jr., pp. 253-254. Manila: Islas Filipinas Publishing, 1985.

4941. "Alberto Breccia Dead at 74." *Comics Journal*. December 1993, pp. 32-34.

4942. "Alberto Breccia, La Vie Est un Roman, Graphique." *La Quotidien de Paris*. January 22, 1992, p. xiv

4943. Cuccolini, Giulio C. "Breccia Portfolio Horror for Collectors." *Comic Art*. October 1986, p. 75.

4944. De La Croix, Arnaud. "Lovecraft - Breccia: L'Invisible Révélé." *Les Cahiers de la Bandes Dessinées*. 62, 1985, pp. 88-90.

4945. Gasca, Luis. "Breccia, Alberto (1919-)." In *Enciclopedia Mondiale del Fumetto*, edited by Maurice Horn and Luciano Secchi, p. 204. Milan: Editoriale Corno, 1978.

4946. Groensteen, Thierry. "Alberto Breccia. Repères Biographiques." *Les Cahiers de la Bande Dessinée*. 62, 1985, pp. 76-80.

4947. Groensteen, Thierry. "Conversation au Petit-Déjeuner." *Les Cahiers de la Bande Dessinée*. 62, 1985, p. 81.

4948. Jans, Michel. "Alberto Breccia im Gespräch." *Comic Info*. 1/1993, pp. 39-43.

4949. Kaps, Joachim. "Alberto Breccia." *Comic Info*. 1/1993, pp. 37-38.

4950. Lecigne, Bruno. "Breccia, Mode d'Emploi." *Les Cahiers de la Bande Dessinée*. 62, 1985, pp. 94-97.

4951. Rebière, Michel. "Alberto Breccia ou le Noir Éblouissant." *Charente Libre*. January 24, 1992, p. 11.

4952. Rivière, François. "Breccia, Noir Tango." *Liberation*. Supplement Special Angoulême 1992, pp. x-xi.

4953. "Vlamos Trabajar a Breccia." *Dibujantes*. No. 2, 1953, pp. 26-29.

Columba, Ramón

4954. Columba, Ramón. *Beba la Irresistible*. Buenos Aires: Edición del Autor, 1948.

4955. Columba, Ramón. *El Congreso Que yo He Visto*. Buenos Aires: Inter-American Congress for the Maintenance of Peace, 1948.

4956. Columba, Ramón. *El Congreso Que yo He Visto (1906-1943)*. Buenos Aires: Editorial Ramón Columba, 1951-1953. 3 Vols.

4957. Columba, Ramón. *Perfiles Pacifistas*. Buenos Aires: Inter-American Congress for the Maintenance of Peace, 1936.

4958. "Ramón Columba: Paséo Triunfante su Lapíz por el Mundo." *Dibujantes*. No. 4, 1953/1954, pp. 18-21.

Conti, Oscar

4959. Gasca, Luis. "Conti, Oscar (1914-)." In *Enciclopedia Mondiale del Fumetto*, edited by Maurice Horn and Luciano Secchi, p. 258. Milan: Editoriale Corno, 1978.

4960. Scout, A. "Oski, Maestro Internazionale del Cartoon." *Comics*. June 1975, pp. 28-30.

Copi (Raùl Damonte Taborde)

4961. Carabba, Claudio. "Copi." *Comma*. December 1968-January 1969.

4962. "Copi." *Enciclopedia dei Fumetti*. May 28, 1970, p. 201.

4963. Gasca, Luis. "Damonte Taborda, Raul (1939-)." In *Enciclopedia Mondiale del Fumetto*, edited by Maurice Horn and Luciano Secchi, p. 272. Milan: Editoriale Corno, 1978.

4964. "Raul Taborda." In *A History of Komiks of the Philippines and Other Countries*, by Cynthia Roxas and Joaquin Arevalo, Jr., p. 254. Manila: Islas Filipinas Publishing, 1985.

del Castillo, Arturo

4965. Fossati, Franco. "Arturo del Castillo, His Profile." *Comics Land*. June 1975, pp. 32-49.

4966. Fuchs, Wolfgang J. "Arturo del Castillo. Der Westernzeichner aus Südamerika." *Comic Forum. Das Österreichische Fachmagazin für Comicliteratur* (Vienna). 3:12 (1981), pp. 46-47.

4967. Gasca, Luis. "Del Castillo, Arturo (1925-)." In *Enciclopedia Mondiale del Fumetto*, edited by Maurice Horn and Luciano Secchi, p. 279. Milan: Editoriale Corno, 1978.

4968. Tschernegg, Markus. "Arturo del Castillo. Veröffentlichungen im Deutschsprachigen Raum." *Comic Forum. Das Österreichische Fachmagazin für Comicliteratur* (Vienna). 3:12 (1981), pp. 50-51.

Divito, Guillermo

4969. De Montaldo, M.E. "Divito: Hombre de Siglo XX y Dibujante del XXII." *Dibujantes*. No. 1, 1953, pp. 18-21.

4970. Divito, Guillermo. "Como Naciéron y Como Se Hacen las Chicas de Divito." *Dibujantes*. No. 15, 1955, pp. 26-27.

4971. Gasca, Luis. "Divito, Guillermo (1914-1969)." In *Enciclopedia Mondiale del Fumetto*, edited by Maurice Horn and Luciano Secchi, pp. 291-292. Milan: Editoriale Corno, 1978.

4972. "Guillermo Divito." In *A History of the Komiks of the Philippines and Other Countries*, by Cynthia Roxas and Joaquin Arevalo, Jr., p. 153. Manila: Islas Filipinas Publishing, 1985.

Fontanarrosa, Roberto

4973. Fontanarrosa, Roberto. *Boogie, el Aceitoso* (Boogie, the Greaser). Buenos Aires: Ediciones de la Flor, 1974-1990.

4974. Fontanarrosa, [Roberto]. *¿Quién Es Fontanarrosa?* Buenos Aires: Ediciones de la Flor, 1974.

4975. "Monstruo Invitado: Fontanarrosa." *Trix*. No. 2 (n.d.), pp. 36-37.

4976. Scout, A. "Fontanarrosa: L'Avventura in Chiave Umoristica." *Comics*. October 1975, pp. 12-13.

Gimenez, Juan

4977. Legaristi, Francisco. "Monocomics: Juan Antonio Gimenez." *Trix*. No. 2 (n.d.), p. 31.

4978. Stewart, Bhob. "An Interview with Juan Gimenez: Argentine Craftsman." *Comics Journal*. October 1984, pp. 86-89.

Grassi, Alfredo

4979. Grassi, Alfredo J. *¿Qué Es la Historieta?* Buenos Aires: Editorial Columba, Collección Esquemas, Vol. 88, 1968. 80 pp.

4980. "Monstruo Invitado: Alfredo Grassi." *Trix*. No. 1 (n.d.), pp. 34-35.

Landrú (Juan Carlos Columbres)

4981. "Así Opina: Landrú." *Dibujantes*. No. 29, 1956, p. 6.

4982. Columbres, Juan Carlos. *Gente Paqueta: Manual para Ser Finísimo*. Buenos Aires: Merlín, 1977.

4983. Columbres, Juan Carlos (Landrú). *Las Clases Magistrates de Landrú*. Buenos Aires: Merlín, 1972.

Mordillo, Guillermo

4984. A.K. "Mordillo." *Comixene*. July 1976, p. 39.

4985. Capet, B. and Th. Defert. "Mordillo." *Phénix*. No. 18, 1971.

4986. Gasca, Luis. "Mordillo, Guillermo (1933-)." In *Enciclopedia Mondiale del Fumetto*, edited by Maurice Horn and Luciano Secchi, p. 576. Milan: Editoriale Corno, 1978.

4987. Mordillo. "The International Pavilion of Humor of Montreal Presents Mordillo, 1977 Cartoonist of the Year." Montreal: 1977. 68 pp.

4988. Mordillo. *Toutes les Girafes*. Grenoble: Glénat, 1983.

4989. "Mordillo il Padre delle Giraffe." *Program*. Napoli 6. Mostra Internazionale del Fumetto e del Cinema d' Animazione. 1984, p. 32.

4990. Popov, Yordan. "Throbbing Eyes: Mordillo Presented by Yordan Popov." *Apropos*. No. 6, pp. 94-97.

4991. Salinas, José Luis and Eduardo Ferro. *Mordillo Football*. Paris: Éditions Glénat, 1981.

4992. "To Be Constantly in Despair Is a Waste of Time (A Talk with Mordillo)." *Apropos*. No. 6, pp. 84-93.

Quino (Joaquín S. Lavado)

4993. Cañizal, Eduardo Peñuela. "Quino: uma Proposta de Leitura." *Vozes 69*. No. 3, 1975, pp. 37-48.

4994. D'Adderio, Hugo. "Realización de un Dibujo al Lavado." *Dibujantes*. No. 2, 1953, pp. 10-13, 33.

4995. Gasca, Luis. "Lavado, Joaquin (1932-)." In *Enciclopedia Mondiale del Fumetto*, edited by Maurice Horn and Luciano Secchi, p. 521. Milan: Editoriale Corno, 1978.

4996. "La Figura Que Surge: Joaquin S. Lavado (Quino)." *Dibujantes*. No. 15, 1955, pp. 16-17.

4997. Lavado, Joaquin S. (Quino). *Bien, Gracias, ¿y Usted?* México: Imagen/Lumen, 1980.

4998. Lavado, Joaquin S. *Diez Años con Mafalda*. Barcelona: Lumen, 1973.

4999. Lavado, Joaquin S. *Gente en Su Sitio*. México: Nueva Imagen, 1978.

5000. Lavado, Joaquin S. *Hombres de Bolsillo*. Barcelona: Lumen, 1977.

5001. Lavado, Joaquin S. *Yo Que Usted*. Buenos Aires: Siglo Veintiuno, 1974.

5002. Martí, Agenor. "Quino Multiplied by 116." *Granma Weekly Review*. September 7, 1986, p. 7.

5003. Quino. *Ça Va Les Affaires?* Grenoble: Glénat, 1987. 64 pp.

5004. Quino. "The International Pavilion of Humor of Montreal Presents Quino. The Cartoonist of the Year 1982." Montreal: 1982. 71 pp.

5005. Quino. *Les Gaffes de Cupidon*. Grenoble: Glénat, 1988. 78 pp.

5006. Quino. *Provision d'Humeur*. Grenoble: Glénat, 1984. 48 pp.

5007. Quino. *Quino-Thérapie*. Grenoble: Glénat, 1985. 64 pp.

5008. "Quino." *Humour and Caricature*. August-September 1993.

5009. "Quino." *Informaciones Argentinas*. 49 (1972), p. 47.

5010. Resnick, Claudia Cairo and Paula K. Speck. "'Quino' after *Mafalda*: A Bittersweet Look at Argentine Reality." *Studies in Latin American Popular Culture*. 2 (1983), pp. 79-87.

Sábat, Hermenegildo

5011. Foster, David W. "Hermenegildo Sábat: Caricature As Cultural Dekitschification." *Latin American Digest*. 15:3/4 (1981), pp. 1-3, 27.

5012. Sábat, Hermenegildo. *Hermenegildo Sábat*. Quilmes, Argentina: Museo Municipal de Artes Visuales, 1980. (Exposition program).

Salinas, José Luis

5013. "José Luis Salinas: Señor de la Historieta y de la Ilustración." *Dibujantes*. No. 3, 1953, pp. 18-21.

5014. Tadeo Juan, Francisco. "El Císco Kid o la Caballerosídad Perdída." *Sunday*. January 1981, pp. 48-51.

Solano López, Francisco

5015. Solano López, F. and C. Sampayo. *Evarista: Deep City*. New York: Catalan Communications, 1986. 111 pp.

5016. Solano López, Gabriel and Francisco. "Ana, Capítulo Tercero." *Trix*. No. 6 (n.d.), pp. 5-15.

5017. "Solano López." *Trix*. 1:6 (1988), pp. 45-49.

Tati (Hector Omar Martin)

5018. Caceres, Germán. "La Maldición de los Gusanos (Entrevista a Tati)." In *Así Se Lee la Historieta*, pp. 77-81. Buenos Aires: Beas Ediciones, 1994.

5019. Cáceres, Germán. "Tati." In *Cartoonometer: Taking the Pulse of the World's Cartoonists*, edited by Joe Szabo and John A. Lent, p. 86. North Wales, Pennsylvania: WittyWorld Books, 1994.

5020. Cáceres, Germán. "The Curse of Worms: An Interview with Argentina's Tati." *WittyWorld*. Winter/Spring 1989, pp. 60-64.

Characters amd Titles

5021. Gasca, Luis. "Don Pancho Talero." In *Enciclopedia Mondiale del Fumetto*, edited by Maurice Horn and Luciano Secchi, p. 300. Milan: Editoriale Corno, 1978.

5022. Gasca, Luis. "Eternauta, El (Argentina)." In *Enciclopedia Mondiale del Fumetto*, edited by Maurice Horn and Luciano Secchi, p. 317. Milan: Editoriale Corno, 1978.

5023. Gasca, Luis. "Fallutelli (Argentina)." In *Enciclopedia Mondiale del Fumetto*, edited by Maurice Horn and Luciano Secchi, p. 321. Milan: Editoriale Corno, 1978.

5024. Gasca, Luis. "Hernan el Corsario (Argentina)." In *Enciclopedia Mondiale del Fumetto*, edited by Maurice Horn and Luciano Secchi, pp. 456-457. Milan: Editoriale Corno, 1978.

5025. Gasca, Luis. "Lindor Covas (Argentina)." In *Enciclopedia Mondiale del Fumetto*, edited by Maurice Horn and Luciano Secchi, p. 527. Milan: Editoriale Corno, 1978.

5026. Gasca, Luis. "Mangucho y Meneca (Argentina)." In *Enciclopedia Mondiale del Fumetto*, edited by Maurice Horn and Luciano Secchi, p. 549. Milan: Editoriale Corno, 1978.

5027. Gasca, Luis. "Mort Cinder (Argentina)." In *Enciclopedia Mondiale del Fumetto*, edited by Maurice Horn and Luciano Secchi, p. 577. Milan: Editoriale Corno, 1978.

5028. Gasca, Luis. "Negro Raul, El (Argentina)." In *Enciclopedia Mondiale del Fumetto*, edited by Maurice Horn and Luciano Secchi, p. 586. Milan: Editoriale Corno, 1978.

5029. Gasca, Luis. "Patoruzú (Argentina)." In *Enciclopedia Mondiale del Fumetto*, edited by Maurice Horn and Luciano Secchi, p. 612. Milan: Editoriale Corno, 1978.

5030. Perini, Barbara. "Randall (Argentina)." In *Enciclopedia Mondiale del Fumetto*, edited by Maurice Horn and Luciano Secchi, pp. 645-646. Milan: Editoriale Corno, 1978.

5031. Secchi, Luciano. "Sargento Kirk, El (Argentina)." In *Enciclopedia Mondiale del Fumetto*, edited by Maurice Horn and Luciano Secchi, p. 671. Milan: Editoriale Corno, 1978.

5032. Secchi, Luciano. "Wheeling (Argentina)." In *Enciclopedia Mondiale del Fumetto*, edited by Maurice Horn and Luciano Secchi, p. 762. Milan: Editoriale Corno, 1978.

"Don Fulgencio"

5033. "Don Fulgencio." In *A History of Komiks of the Philippines and Other Countries*, by Cynthia Roxas and Joaquin Arevalo, Jr., p. 228. Manila: Islas Filipinas Publishing, 1985.

5034. Gasca, Luis. "Don Fulgencio (Argentina)." In *Enciclopedia Mondiale del Fumetto*, edited by Maurice Horn and Luciano Secchi, pp. 299-300. Milan: Editoriale Corno, 1978.

"El Doctor Merengue"

5035. "El Doctor Merengue." In *A History of Komiks of the Philippines and Other Countries*, by Cynthia Roxas and Joaquin Arevalo, Jr., p. 228. Manila: Islas Filipinas Publishing, 1985.

5036. Gasca, Luis. "Doctor Merengue, El ." In *Enciclopedia Mondiale del Fumetto*, edited by Maurice Horn and Luciano Secchi, pp. 294-295. Milan: Editoriale Corno, 1978.

"Ernie Pike"

5037. "Ernie Pike." In *A History of Komiks of the Philippines and Other Countries*, by Cynthia Roxas and Joaquin Arevalo, Jr., p. 227. Manila: Islas Filipinas Publishing, 1985.

5038. Gasca, Luis. "Ernie Pike (Argentina)." In *Enciclopedia Mondiale del Fumetto*, edited by Maurice Horn and Luciano Secchi, p. 315. Milan: Editoriale Corno, 1978.

"Inodoro Pereyra"

5039. Acosta, Raúl. "Inodoro Pereyra: Una Historieta Argentina." *Crisis*. 13, 1974, pp. 70-72.

5040. Fontanarrosa, Roberto. *Las Aventuras de Inodoro Pereyra ¡El Renegau! Poema Telúrico de Fontanarrosa*. Buenos Aires: Ediciones de la Flor, 1974.

"Mafalda"

5041. Carlos, Antonio. "Toda Mafalda." *Boletim de HQ*. October 1991, p. 4.

5042. Cirne, Moacy. "Mafalda: Prática Semiológica e Prática Ideológica." *Revista de Cultura Vozes* (Petrópolis). September 1973, pp. 47-53.

5043. Eco, Umberto. "Mafalda la Disconforme." In *Joaquín Salvador Lavado, Mafalda: y Digo Yo.....* Barcelona: Noveno Arte, 1974.

5044. Escobar, Marina, Rebeca Orozco, and Marta Watts. "La Proxémica en Mafalda y Peanuts." In *El Cómic Es Algo Serio* (Comics Should Be Taken Seriously), pp. 145-163. México: Ediciones Eufesa, 1982.

5045. Foster, David W. "Mafalda: An Argentine Comic Strip." *Journal of Popular Culture.* Winter 1980, pp. 497-508.

5046. Foster, David W. "Mafalda...the Ironic Bemusement." *Latin American Digest.* June 1974, pp. 16-18.

5047. Gasca, Luis. "Mafalda (Argentina)." In *Enciclopedia Mondiale del Fumetto,* edited by Maurice Horn and Luciano Secchi, p. 545. Milan: Editoriale Corno, 1978.

5048. Hernández, Pablo José. *Para Leer a Mafalda* (How To Read Mafalda). Buenos Aires: Editorial Precursora, 1976.

5049. Koch, Dolores. "Mafalda: Recursos Narrativos de la Tira Cómica." In *Literature and Popular Culture in the Hispanic World: A Symposium,* edited by Rose S. Minc. Gaithersberg, Maryland: Hispamérica; Upper Montclair, New Jersey: Montclair State College, 1981.

5050. "Mafalda Hopes the World Solves Its Problems." *Maryknoll Magazine.* December 1976, pp. 34-36.

5051. "Mafalda: La Niña Cumple 17 Años y Está Muy Fuerte." *Superhumor.* 9 (1981), pp. 47-52.

5052. "Mafalda—the Intellectual Cartoon Character." *Group Media Jounal.* 7:3/4 (1988), p. 25.

5053. Meson, Danusia L. "Mafalda y la Crítica Pura (?) de la Razon y el Orden." In *Literature and Popular Culture in the Hispanic World: A Symposium,* edited by Rose S. Minc. Gaithersburg, Maryland: Hispamérica; Upper Montclair, New Jersey: Montclair State College, 1981.

5054. Quino (Lavado, Joaquín Salvador). *Encore Mafalda.* Paris: J'ai Lu., ca. 1988. 123 pp.

5055. Quino (Lavado, Joaquín Salvador). *Mafalda.* Buenos Aires: Ediciones de la Flor, 1967-1974.

5056. Quino (Lavado, Joaquín, Salvador). *Mafalda.* Mexico City: Neuva Imagen, 1977.

5057. Ravoni, Marcelo. "I Vent 'Anni di Mafalda." *Programma Lucca 16.* 1984, pp. 24-27.

5058. Steimberg, Oscar. "El Lugar de Mafalda." *Los Libros.* 17 (1971), pp. 6-7.

"Martín Fierro"

5059. Borges, Jorge Luis. *El "Martín Fierro."* Buenos Aires: Columba, 1953, 1965.

5060. Hernández, José. *El Gaucho Martín Fierro.* Buenos Aires: Imprenta de la Pampa, 1872. (Many subsequent editions).

5061. Hernández, José. *La Vuelta de Martín Fierro.* Buenos Aires: Librería del Plata, 1879. (Many subsequent editions).

5062. Jitrik, Noé. "El Tema del Canto en el Martín Fierro, de José Hernández." In *El Fuego de la Especie; Ensayos Sobre Seis Escritores Argentinos,* by Noé Jitrik. Buenos Aires: Siglo XXI Argentina, 1971.

Animation

5063. "Argentina: The World's First Animated Feature Film." In *Cartoons: One Hundred Years of Cinema Animation,* by Giannalberto Bendazzi, pp. 49-52. Bloomington: Indiana University Press, 1994.

5064. De Palos, Dante. "El Cine Necesita del Dibujo." *Dibujantes.* No. 1, 1953, pp. 4-5, 33.

5065. Lescaboura, Santos-Angel. *Cine y Dibujos Animados.* Caracas: Editorial Universitaria, 1949.

5066. Mujica, Martín. "La Animación y los Peines en Argentina." *Corto Circuito.* April 1992, pp. 16-17.

Caricature

5067. "Caricature in Argentina." Translated by Shahram Zarnadar." *Kayhan Caricature.* January 1993.

5068. Columba, Ramón. *¿Qué Es la Caricature?* Buenos Aires: Editorial Columba, Colleción Esquemas, No. 40, 1959. 80 pp.

5069. Dell'Acqua, Amado. *La Caricatura Politica Argentina.* Buenos Aires: Editorial Universitaria de Buenos Aires, 1960. 150 pp.

5070. Flax (Lino Palacio). *Historia de la Argentina Guerra.* Buenos Aires: Ediciones Lino Palacio, 1942, 1943, 1944, 1946. 4 Vols.

5071. Pahlen, Kurt. "La Música Atraves de la Caricatura." *La Nación* (Buenos Aires). December 17, 1944.

5072. Raul. "O Lápis Argentino." *Revista da Semana,* (Rio de Janeiro). Argentine edition. July 1940.

Comic Books

5073. Altuna, Horacio. *Grand Reporter.* Grenoble: Glénat, 1987. 79 pp.

5074. Altuna, Horacio. *Imaginaire.* Paris: Darguad, 1988. 56 pp.

5075. Battaglia, Roberto C. "Sentido Gráfico y Humanidad Son la Base del Dibujo Humoristico." *Dibujantes.* No. 2, 1953, pp. 4-5.

5076. "Bienal de la Historieta." *Crónica.* January 21, 1968.

5077. Birmajer, Marcelo. *Historieta: La Imaginación al Cuadrado.* Buenos Aires: Ediciones Dialéctica, 1988.

5078. Bróccoli, Alberto and Carlos Trillo. *Las Historietas.* Buenos Aires: Centro Editor de América Latina, 1971.

5079. Bullande, José. *El Nuevo Mundo de La Imagen, La Escuela en el Tiempo.* Buenos Aires: Eudeba, 1965.

5080. Caceres, Germán. "Trends of Argentine Comics." *WittyWorld.* Summer 1988, pp. 20-22.

5081. Caceres, Germán. "¡Huija por los 66!" In *Así Se Lee la Historieta,* pp. 51-54. Buenos Aires: Beas Ediciones, 1994.

5082. Castelli, Alfredo. "La Historieta Argentina." *Comics.* April 1966, pp. 3-5.

5083. "Círculo de la Historieta." *Trix.* No. 6 (n.d.), p. 47.

5084. "Como Naciéron los Grandes Personajes." *Dibujantes.* No. 29, 1959, p. 30.

5085. "Comoqueando." *Trix.* No. 6 (n.d.), p. 45.

5086. "Conozcamos a Nuestros Argumentistas." *Dibujantes.* No. 29, 1959, p. 35.

5087. Couste, Alberto. "El Triunfo de la Literatura Dibujada." *Primera Plana* (Buenos Aires). No. 303, 1968, pp. 44-49.

5088. Cuccolini, Giulio C. "Il Caso Argentino." *Comic Art .* September 1993, p. 59.

5089. "De Cuadros y Globitos." *Análisis*. September 18, 1968, pp. 73-75.

5090. De Santis, Pablo. *Historieta y Política en los '80s*. Buenos Aires: Ediciones Letra Buena, 1992.

5091. "Desde el Sur." *Trix*. No. 6 (n.d.), p. 49.

5092. "Editorial." *Trix*. No. 4 (n.d.), p. 4.

5093. "El Retocador de Historietas." *Dibujantes*. No. 6, 1954, pp. 8-10.

5094. Fernández, Norman. "Buenos Aires, Los Comics y el Loco." *El Wendigo*. No. 63, 1994, pp. 38-39.

5095. Fossati, Franco. *Il Fumetto Argentino*. Rome: Pirella, 1980.

5096. "Historietas: Amenaza de la Mitología Moderna." *Panorama* (Buenos Aires). No. 77, 1968.

5097. "Historietas Argentinas en Publicaciones del Exterior." *Dibujantes*. No. 5, 1954, pp. 29-31.

5098. "La Aventura de Vivir de Sueños." *La Gaceta*. May 31, 1992, p. 4.

5099. "La Caida del Dólar." *Adan* (Buenos Aires). No. 21, 1968, pp. 40-41.

5100. *La Historieta Mundial: Catálogo de I Bienal Mundial de la Historieta*. Buenos Aires, 1968.

5101. "Lectores Engañados." *Trix*. No. 6. (n.d.), pp. 48-49.

5102. Legaristi, Francisco. "Hemoclub." *Trix*. No. 4 (n.d.), pp. 57-60.

5103. Legaristi, Francisco. "Hemoclub." *Trix*. No. 5 (n.d.), pp. 56-58.

5104. Legaristi, Francisco. "Monocomics." *Trix*. No. 4 (n.d.), pp. 15-16.

5105. *Linea Latina! Fumetti Tra Italia e Argentina*. Rome: Ed. Carte Segrete, 1993. 112 pp.

5106. Lipszyc, Enrique. *La Historieta Mundial*. Buenos Aires: Editorial Lipszyc, 1958.

5107. "Los Secretos de la Historieta." *Dibujantes*. No. 2, 1953, pp. 8-10; No. 3, 1953, pp. 8-10; No. 4, 1953/4, pp. 30-31.

5108. Mas, Fernando. "La Historieta en la Argentina." *LINEA* (Buenos Aires). 2 (1969).

5109. Masotta, Oscar. *La Historieta en el Mundo Moderno* (Comics in the Modern World). Buenos Aires: Editorial Paidos, 1970.

5110. Masotta, Oscar. "La Historieta Mundial." Catalogo de Biennal Mundial de la Historieta, Buenos Aires, 1968.

5111. Masotta, Oscar. *Reflexiones Présemiologicas Sobre la Historieta: El Esquematismo.* Buenos Aires: Centro de Investigaciones Sociales, Instituto Torcuato Di Tella, October 1967. 29 pp.

5112. Masotta, Oscar. "Reflexiones Presemiológicas Sobre la Historieta: El 'Esquematismo.'" In *Conciencia y Estructura*, by Oscar Masotta. Buenos Aires: Jorge Alvarez, 1968.

5113. Masotta, Oscar. "Reflexiones Sobre la Historieta." In *Tecnica de la Historieta*, pp. 7-9. Buenos Aires: Escuela Panamericana de Arte, 1966.

5114. "Mazzone: Verdadero Ejemplo de Constania y Dedicación." *Dibujantes*. No. 5, 1954, pp. 18-21, 28.

5115. Morrow, Hugh. "El Éxito de un Fracaso Total." *Dibujantes*. No. 29, 1959, pp. 7-9.

5116. Panzera, Franco. "Güida: Un Dibujante con Propulsion a Chorro." *Dibujantes*. No. 9, 1954, pp. 18-21.

5117. "Plasmacomics. Editorial." *Trix*. No. 6 (n.d.), p. 53.

5118. Ravoni, Marcelo. "Il 'Gesto' Argentino." *Linus*. 5:47 (1969), pp. 1-17.

5119. "Reportaje Relampago a un Consagrado." *Dibujantes*. No. 29, 1959, p. 31.

5120. Rivera, Jorge B. *Panorama de la Historieta en la Argentina*. Buenos Aires: Libros del Quirquincho, 1992.

5121. Roque, Carlos. "Resurgimiento de la Historieta Argentina" (Resurgence of the Argentine Comic). *Análisis Latinoamericano* (New York). 1:2 (1979), pp. 47-49.

5122. Roux, Raul. "El Porqué una Afición y de una Especialidad." *Dibujantes*. No. 3, 1953, pp. 4-5, 30-31.

5123. Salomón, Antonio. *El Humor y la Historieta Que Leyó el Argentino* (Humor and Comics Read by Argentines). Córdoba, Argentina: Congreso Bianual de la Historieta de Córdoba, 1972, 1974, 1976, 1979 editions of conference proceedings.

5124. Sasturain, Juan. "Argentine. La Décennie du Renouveau." *Les Cahiers de la Bande Dessinée*. 70 (1986), pp. 48-51.

5125. Spadafino, Miguel. "Los Monitos Vendedores." *Dibujantes*. No. 4, 1953/1954, pp. 14-15.

5126. Steimberg, Oscar. "La Historieta Argentina." *Todo Es Historia* (Buenos Aires). April 1982, pp. 83-94.

5127. Steimberg, Oscar. *Leyendo Historietas*. Estilos y Sentidos en un "Arte Menor." Buenos Aires: Ediciones Nueva Visión, 1977.

5128. "Tebeo, Historieta o Comics." *Trix*. No. 6 (n.d.), p. 47.

5129. "Tiempo Moderno, Bang Splash." *Confirmado*. September 21, 1967, pp. 26-28.

5130. "Trayectoria y Destino de la Historieta Cómica." *Dibujantes*. No. 30, 1959, pp. 35-37.

5131. "Tres Pasiones de George Wunder." *Dibujantes*. No. 16, 1955, pp. 17-19.

5132. "Viva Córdoba." *Trix*. No. 6 (n.d.), p. 49.

5133. Watt-Evans, Lawrence. "Don't Cry for Me, Argentina!" *Comics Buyer's Guide*. May 25, 1984, pp. 26, 28, 30, 32.

Genres

5134. "Ahí Vienen los Gauchos." *Primera Plana*. No. 254, 1967.

5135. "Batman, Mandrake, Superman y Cia, Invaden la Argentina." *Gente* (Buenos Aires). No. 154, 1968, pp. 22-23.

5136. Brun, Noelle and Lionel Scanteié. *Héroes de Libros Maravillosos*. Buenos Aires: Editorial El Ateneo, 1964.

5137. Caceres, Germán. "La Historieta Policial Argentina." In *Así Se Lee la Historieta*, pp. 23-27. Buenos Aires: Beas Ediciones, 1994.

5138. Caceres, Germán. "La Historieta de Ciencia Ficción Argentina." In *Así Se Lee la Historieta*, pp. 17-22. Buenos Aires: Beas Ediciones, 1994.

5139. "Ciencia-Ficción en la Historieta." *2001*. No. 1, 1968, pp. 48-49.

5140. "Círculo Argentino de Ciencia Ficción y Fantasia." *Trix*. No. 6 (n.d.), p. 47.

5141. "Conversiones del Ilustre Tarzán." *Análisis*. October 16, 1968, p. 66.

5142. "Fantasio: Notable Ejemplo de Dedicación." *Dibujantes*. No. 17, 1955, pp. 17-19.

5143. Mactas, Mario. "Retornan los Héroes de Papel." *Atlantida*. No. 1217, 1968, pp. 30-32.

5144. "Un Cowboy Dibujante." *Dibujantes*. No. 4, 1953/1954, pp. 12-13.

Historical Aspects

5145. Costa, C. Diana. "Molas: Un Dibujante Argentino para la Historia Periodistica del Brasil." *Dibujantes*. No. 1, 1953, pp. 6-7.

5146. Lipszyc, Enrique. "Argentine." In *Histoire Mondiale de la Bande Dessinée*, edited by Pierre Horay, pp. 253-263. Paris: Pierre Horay Éditeur, 1989.

5147. Trillo, Carlos and Guillermo Saccomanno. *Historia de la Historieta Argentine*. Buenos Aires: Ediciones Record, 1980. 190 pp.

Technical Aspects

5148. Dowbley, Guillermo R. "La Pintura y la Historieta." *Dibujantes*. No. 6, 1954, pp. 28-29.

5149. Federico, G. "Técnica de la Historieta." *Dibujantes*. No. 1, 1953, pp. 10-16.

5150. Ferroni, Alfredo. "Creación y Realización de un Titulos de Historieta." *Dibujantes*. No. 3, 1953, pp. 26-28.

5151. Lipszyc, David and Enrique J. Vieytes, eds. *Técnica de la Historieta* (Technique of the Comics). Buenos Aires: La Escuala Panamericana de Arte, 1966. 182 pp.

5152. Lipszyc, Enrique, ed. *Técnica de la Historieta; Tratado de Dibujo Profesional Especializado*. Buenos Aires: Escuela Panamericana de Arte, 1967.

5153. Martínez, Marcos. "Vieytes: Un Espiritu Moderno al Servicio del Arte." *Dibujantes*. No. 13, 1955, pp. 18-21.

5154. Tencer, S.W. *Arte y Ciencia de la Historieta*. Buenos Aires: Editorial Hobby, 1948.

Comic Strips

5155. Carande, Bernardo V. "Explicación a un Cómic Sobre *El Sur* de Jorge Luis Borges." *Cuadernos Hispanoamericanos*. December 1988, pp. 45-54.

5156. Lipszyc, David and Oscar Masotta. "Argentina." In *La Historieta Mundial*, edited by World Congress of Comics. Buenos Aires: Escuela Panamericana de Arte, 1968.

5157. Medina, Enrique. *Strip-tease*. Buenos Aires: Editorial Corredigor, 1976.

5158. Vázquez Lucio, Oscar. "Comics in Argentina." *Apropos*. No. 7, 1991, pp. 120-121.

BOLIVIA

Animation

5159. Baraybar, Cecilia. "Bolivia: Entrevista a Liliana de la Quintana." *Corto Circuito*. April 1992, p. 48.

BRAZIL

General Sources

5160. Miranda, Orlando. *Tio Patinhas e os Mitos da Comunicação*. São Paulo:Summus, 1976.

5161. Peixoto, Afrânio. *Humour*. Rio de Janeiro: W.M. Jackson Inc., Editores, 1947. Vol. 18.

5162. Reinaldo, ed. *O Novo Humor Pasquim*. Rio de Janeiro: Codecri, 1977.

5163. Serra, Antônio. "O Fantasma, ou Atribulções dum Édipo no 3° Mundo." *Revista de Cultura Vozes* (Petrópolis). September 1973, pp. 55-65.

Cartoonists

5164. Abreu, Modesto. "Luís (Peixoto) Presidente." *Boletim da S.B.A.T.* (Rio de Janeiro). February 1950.

5165. Alvarus (Álvaro Cotrim). "O Natal e os Caricaturistas." *Vamos Ler!* (Rio de Janeiro). December 24, 1942.

5166. Alvarus (Álvaro Cotrim). "Santos Dumont e a Caricatura." *A Noite* (Rio de Janeiro). October 24, 1951.

5167. "A Mais Famosa Parceria de Caricaturistas." *Vamos Ler!* (Rio de Janeiro). January 21, 1943.

5168. *A Noite Ilustrada* (Rio de Janeiro). January 16, 1940. (Rafael Mendes de Carvalho).

5169. Armand, Abel. "Constantin Guys." *Vamos Ler!* (Rio de Janeiro). April 15, 1942.

5170. "Augusto Santos." *Planalto* (São Paulo). February 1, 1949.

5171. Barroso, Gustavo. "Gil Amora." In *Consulado de China*, 3.° Vol. de Memórias. Rio de Janeiro: Getúlio M. Costa, n.d.

5172. Belmiro (de Almeida). *Carta ao Dr. Pandiá Calógeras*. Paris: Les Éditions de l'Aquarelle, 1914.

5173. Belmonte (Benedito Bastos Barreto). "Como se Faz Um Caricaturista." *A Cigarra* (São Paulo). March 15, 1924. (Gelásio Pimenta).

5174. Bira. "Henfil." *Porrada*. August 1990, p. 25.

5175. Braga, Teodoro. *Artistas Pintores no Brasil*. São Paulo: Editôra Ltda., 1942.

5176. [Carlos Alberto da Costa Amoreim]. *Kayhan Caricature*. May 1993.

5177. de Carvalho, Leão. "Os Caricaturistas e o Teatro no Rio de Janeiro." *Vamos Ler!* (Rio de Janeiro). June 25, 1942.

5178. Chaves, Mauro. *Contraverbios: Illustrações de Gustavo Rosa*. Rio de Janeiro: Civilização Brasileira, 1977.

5179. Cirne, Moacy. *A Linguagem Dos Quadrinhos: O Universo Estrutural de Ziraldo e Maurício de Sousa* (The Comics' Language). Petrópolis: Editôra Vozes, 1971.

5180. de Almeida, Felinto. "Belmiro de Almeida." *A Semana* (Rio de Janeiro). May 7, 1887.

5181. de Castro Santos Vergueiro, Waldomiro. "Brazilian Comic Artists in the United States." *Brazilian Communication Research Yearbook 2*. 1993, pp. 99-106.

5182. "Desaparecerá o Caricaturista Brasileiro?" *Diretrizes* (Rio de Janeiro). October 24, 1947.

5183. de Sousa, J. A. Soares. *Um Caricaturista Brasileiro no Rio da Prata*. Rio de Janeiro: *Rev. I. H. G. Brasileiro*, Vol. 227, April 1955.

5184. Duque, Gonzaga. "Artur Lucas." In *Contemporâneos*. Rio de Janeiro: Tip. Benedito de Sousa, 1929.

5185. Duque, Gonzaga. "Aurélio de Figueiredo." In *Contemporâneos*. Rio de Janeiro: Tip. Benedito de Sousa, 1929.

5186. Faure, P. "Édmond Rostand, Retratista, Escultor, Arquiteto e Figurinista." *Vamos Ler!* (Rio de Janeiro). September 30, 1943.

5187. Firmo, Nélson. "Leônidas Freire e Sua Vida Singular." *A Noite Ilustrada* (Rio de Janeiro). December 22, 1942.

5188. Fragoso, Augusto. "Monteiro Lobato, Desenhista." *Ilustração Brasileira* (Rio de Janeiro). May 1954. (Monteiro Lobato).

5189. Gill, Ruben. "Caricaturistas do Rio de Janeiro." *Revista da Semana* (Rio de Janeiro). June 10, 1939.

5190. Gill, Ruben. "Era Uma Vez un Menino da Serra da Ibiapaba" (Leônidas). *A Noite Ilustrada* (Rio de Janeiro). November 11, 1937.

5191. Gill, Ruben. "Os Caricaturistas e o Teatro no Rio de Janeiro." *Vamos Ler!* (Rio de Janeiro). June 25, 1942.

5192. Gill, Ruben. "Os Caricaturistas Respeitam Os Poetas." *Dom Casmurro* (Rio de Janeiro). Number of Natal, 1943.

5193. Gill, Ruben. "O Século Boêmio." Series about writers and cartoonists. *Dom Casmurro* (Rio de Janeiro). *1-2*, "Memórias de Uma Época sem Ideologias Complexas e Outras Complicações Oportunistas," October 24 to 31, 1942; *3*, "Um Jornal Que Revelou Hermes Fontes, Lançou Bastos Tigre e Onde Costa Rêgo e Elói Pontes Foram Charadistas, etc.," November 7, 1942; *4*, "Gonzaga Duque," November 14, 1942; *5*, "Mário Pedemeiras," November 21, 1942; *6*, "J. Carlos," November 29, 1942; *7*, "Correia Dias," December 5, 1942, *8*, "V. da Cunha," December 12, 1942; *9*, "Leônidas," December 19, 1942 ; *10*, "Seth," December 26, 1942; *11*, "Raul," January 2, 1943; *12*, "K. Lixto," January 9, 1943; *13*, "Casanova," January 16, 1943; *14*, "Yantok," January 23, 1943; *15*, "Hélios," January 30, 1943; *16*, "Storni," February 5, 1943; *17*, "Fritz," February 13, 1943; *18*, "Belmonte," February 20, 1943; *19*, "Bambino," February 27, 1943; *20*, "Plácido Isasi," March 13, 1943; *21*, "Celso Hermínio," March 20, 1943; *22*, "Voltolino,"March 27, 1943; *23*, "Luís," April 3, 1943; *24*, "Rian," April 10, 1943; *25*, "Julião Machado," April 17, 1943; *26*, "Romano," April 24, 1943; *27*, "Gil," May 1, 1943; *28*, "Alvarus," May 15, 1943; *29*, "Vasco," May 22, 1943; *30*, "Angelo Agostini," May 29, 1943; *31*, "Emílio Cardosa Aires," June 5, 1943; *32*, "Nássara," June 12, 1943; *33*, "Trinas Fox," June 19, 1943; *34*, "A. Rocha," June 26, 1943; *35*, "Figueroa," July 3, 1943; *36*, "Isaltino Barbosa," July 10, 1943; *37*, "Néri," July 17, 1943; *38*, "Loureiro," July 24, 1943; *39*, "Teixeira da Rocha," July 31, 1943; *40*, "A. Delpino," August 7, 1943; *41*, "Malagutti," August 14, 1943; *42*, "Alberto Lima," August 21, 1943; *43*, "Teodoro Braga," August 28, 1943; *44*, "Francisco Acquarone," September 4, 1943; *45*, "João do Rio," September 11, 1943; *46*, "Basílio Viana," September 18, 1943; *47*, "João Brito," September 25, 1943; *48*, "Lobão," October 2, 1943; *49*, "Thoreau," October 9, 1943; *50*, "Mendez," October 16, 1943; *51*, "Ariosto," October 23, 1943; *52*, "Guevara," October 30, 1943; *53*,

"Elkins," November 6, 1943; *54*, "Ioiô, Caricaturisras do S. Paulo," November 13, 1943; *55*, "Jefferson," November 20, 1943; *56*, "Francisconi," November 27, 1943; *57*, "Rafael Bordalo Pinheiro," December 4, 1943; *58*, "Osvaldo," December 11, 1943; *59*, "Terra de Sena," January 15, 1944; *60*, "Antonius," January 22, 1944; *61*, "Cardoso de Meneses," January 29, 1944; *62*, "Carlos Bitencourt," February 5, 1944; *63*, "João do Norte," February 26, 1944; *64*, "Alfredo Cândido," March 4, 1944; *65*, "Henrique Fleiuss," March 11, 1944; *66*, "Martiniano," March 18, 1944; *67*, "Edmir," March 25, 1944; *67a*, "Os Fluminenses na Caricatura," April 1, 1944; *68*, "Sílvio," April 15, 1944; *69*, "J. Guerreiro," April 22, 1944; *70*, "Golpe de Vista à Caricatura em Pernambuco," April 29, 1944; *71*, "Raul Gomes," June 3, 1944; *72*, "J. Artur," June 17, 1944; *73*, "Gil," November 25, 1944; *74*, "Nemésio, Castro, Rebêlo, Rigoleto, Gastão Penalva," December 23, 1944; *75*, "Dudu," December 30, 1944; *76*, "Pereira Neto," January 20, 1945; *77*, "Breve Resumo de História da Caricatura Argentina," February 17, 1945; *77a*, "Caricaturistas Mineiros," February 24, 1945; *Extra*, Armando Miguéis, "Ruben Gill," July 3, 1945.

5194. Gill, Ruben, "O Século Boêmio." *Dom Casmurro* (Rio de Janeiro). September 4, 1943. (Francisco Acquarone).

5195. Gill, Ruben, "O Século Boêmio." *Dom Casmurro* (Rio de Janeiro). October 2, 1943. (J. Ramos Lobão).

5196. Gill, Ruben. "O Século Boêmio." *Dom Casmurro* (Rio de Janeiro). October 23, 1943. (Ariosto Duncan).

5197. Gill, Ruben. "O Século Boêmio." *Dom Casmurro* (Rio de Janeiro). November 20, 1943.

5198. Gill, Ruben. "O Século Boêmio." *Dom Casmurro* (Rio de Janeiro). February 26, 1944. (Gustavo Barroso).

5199. Gill, Ruben. "O Século Boêmio." *Dom Casmurro* (Rio de Janeiro). March 4, 1944. (Alfredo Cândido).

5200. Gill, Ruben. "O Século Boêmio." *Dom Casmurro* (Rio de Janeiro). April 15, 1944. (Sílvio de Figueiredo).

5201. Gill, Ruben. "O Século Boêmio." *Dom Casmurro* (Rio de Janeiro). December 30, 1944. (Cícero Valadares [Dudu]).

5202. Guerra, Paulo de Sales. Series of interviews with J. Carlos, K. Lixto, Raul, Augusto Rodrigues, Yantok, Loureiro, and Storni. *Revista da Semana* (Rio de Janeiro). August-September 1944.

5203. Jorge, Fernando. *Vidas de Grandes Pintores do Brasil*. São Paulo: Livraria Martins Editôra, 1954.

5204. J.M. (Joseph Mill?). "Caricaturistas. Esboceto." *O Figaro* (Rio de Janeiro). November 1, 1876.

5205. Kantor. *Auto-Caricatura del Caricaturista Adolescente.* Buenos Aires: Ediciones Botella, 1956.

5206. Leão, Múcio. "Notas para um Perfil." *Autores & Livros* (Rio de Janeiro). June 13, 1943.

5207. Lima, Herman. "Escritores Caricaturistas." In *Revista do Livro*. Rio de Janeiro: Ministério da Educação e Cultura, Instituto Nacional do Livro, September 1957.

5208. Lima, Herman. "Lápis x Pena. Os Caricaturistas Brasileiros Sempre Andaram de Braco dado com os Escritores." *Jornal de Letras* (Rio de Janeiro). June 1950.

5209. Lima, Herman. "Sotero Cosme, Caricaturista Romântico." *Rio Magazine.* December 1950

5210. Olveira, Carlos. "Os Bonecos de Borjalo Correm Mundo." *A Cigarra-Magazine* (Rio de Janeiro). May 1957. (Borjalo).

5211. Pacheco, Armando, "Existe Caricatura Moderna no Brasil?" Series of interviews with Belmonte, J. Carlos, Augusto Rodrigues, Nássara, Mendez, Alvarus, K. Lixto, Raul. *Dom Casmurro* (Rio de Janeiro). August 9, 16, 23, 30 and September 12, 27, 1941.

5212. Paraguaçu (Manuel). *O Caricaturista.* Bahia: n.p., n.d.

5213. Penalva, Gastão. "Caricatura e Caricaturistas." Series of articles. *D Quixote.* (Rio de Janeiro). February 24 to March 17, 1926.

5214. Pinto, Estêvão. "D. Pedro II e a Caricatura." *Diário de Pernambuco* (Recife). December 2, 1925.

5215. Pontes, Elói. *A Vida Inquieta de Raul Pompéia.* Rio de Janeiro: Livraria José Olympio Editôra, 1935.

5216. Rangel, Alberto. *Dom Pedro e a Marquesa de Santos.* n.p.: n.p., 1928. 2nd Ed.

5217. Romero, Ricardo. "O Natal e os Caricaturistas." *Vamos Ler!* (Rio de Janeiro). December 24, 1942.

5218. "Sociais." *O País.* December 18, 1911. (Crispin do Amaral).

5219. Sousa, J.A. "*A Lanterna Mágica.* Suas Personagens e Seu Caricaturista." *Jornal do Brasil* (Rio de Janeiro). August 11, 1957.

5220. Sousa, J.A. "Um Caricaturista Brasileiro no Rio da Prata." *Revista do Instituto*

Histórico e Geográfico Brasileiro. June 1955.

5221. Terra de Sena. "A Figura de Jeca Tatu na Irreverência dos Nossos Caricaturistas." *Vamos Ler!* (Rio de Janeiro). November 18, 1943.

5222. "Três Caricaturistas da Velha Guarda: Storni, Yantok e Loureiro." *Revista da Semana* (Rio de Janeiro). March 31, 1945.

5223. Vieira, Gilda. "Cartoonists Urge Reform in Brazil." *Group Media Journal.* 7: 3/4 (1988), pp. 18-21.

Agostini, Angelo

5224. "Angelo Agostini." *O País* (Rio de Janeiro). January 24, 1910.

5225. Barata, Mario. "Desenhos de Carnaval de A. Agostini." *Diário de Notícias* (Rio de Janeiro). February 28, 1958.

5226. Brício Filho. "O Lápis da Abolição." *Autores & Livros* (Rio de Janeiro). June 18, 1943.

5227. Bruma, Hélio. "Ângelo Agostini e a Caricatura Entre Nós." *A Tribuna* (Santos). February 21, 1910.

5228. Cremona, Ercole. "Angelo Agostini." *Para Todos* (Rio de Janeiro). March 15, 1923.

5229. da Silva Arújo, Carlos. "Angelo Agostini e o Salão de 1884." *Boletim de Belas-Artes* (Rio de Janeiro). September-December 1945.

5230. de Andrade, Teófilo. "Angelo Agostini, Campeão da Abolição." *A Noite Ilustrada* (Rio de Janeiro). May 17, 1938.

5231. Fernando, Jorge. *Vidas de Grandes Pintores do Brasil (incluindo os Grandes Caricaturistas).* São Paulo; Livraria Martins Editôra, 1954.

5232. Gill, Ruben. "O Século Boêmio." *Dom Casmurro* (Rio de Janeiro). May 29, 1943.

5233. "Grande Figura Que os Historiadores Esqueceram, Uma." *A Noite* (Rio de Janeiro). September 28, 1925.

5234. Kelly, Celso. "Um Esplêndido Material, Ainda Inexplorado para o Estudo da Nossa História. O Sentido Político e Social das *Charges* de Angelo Agostini, Caricaturista do Império." *Vamos Ler!* (Rio de Janeiro). September 28, 1939.

5235. Leão, Múcio. "Notas para um Perfil de Angelo Agostini." *Autores e Livros* (Rio de Janeiro). June 13, 1943.

5236. Leão, Múcio. "Notícia Sôbre Angelo Agostini." *Autores e Livros* (Rio de Janeiro). June 13, 1943.

5237. Lima, Herman. "Angelo Agostini." *Revista da Semana* (Rio de Janeiro). April 3, 1943.

5238. Lima, Herman. "Angelo Agostini, Criador da Caricatura Política no Brasil." *Revista Sul América* (Rio de Janeiro). June 1954.

5239. Lima, Herman. "Angelo Agostini. Os Mestres da Caricatura Brasileira." *Pensamento da América* (Rio de Janeiro). August 16, 1947.

5240. Lima, Herman. "Angelo Agostini. Os Mestres do Lápis Brasileiro." *O Jornal* (Rio de Janeiro). November 18, 1951.

5241. Lima, Herman. "Angelo Agostini, Precursor da Caricatura Brasileira." *Vitrina* (Rio de Janeiro). April 1943.

5242. Matos, Adalberto. "Um Artista Que Deve Ser Lembrado." *O Malho* (Rio de Janeiro). March 24, 1928.

5243. Monteiro, Lobato. "A Caricatura no Brasil. Angelo Agostini." In *Idéias de Jeca Tatu*. São Paulo: Edição de Monteiro Lobato e Cia., 1922.

5244. Patrocínio, José. "Angelo Agostini." *Euclides* (Rio de Janeiro). January 15, 1941.

5245. Rubens, Carlos. "Angelo Agostini." In *Pequena História das Artes Plásticas no Brasil*. São Paulo: Cia. Editôra Nacional, 1941.

5246. Rubens, Carlos. "Angelo Agostini." *Boletim de Belas-Artes* (Rio de Janeiro). September 1946.

5247. Silva, Araújo. "Angelo Agostini." *Boletim de Belas-Artes* (Rio de Janeiro). September 1946.

5248. Verim, Júlio (Luís de Andrade). "A. Agostini." *Revista Ilustrada* (Rio de Janeiro). October 13, 1888.

5249. Xisto Grafite. "A. Agostini." *Revista Ilustrada* (Rio de Janeiro). April 12, 1890.

Alvarus (Álvaro Cotrim)

5250. de Bettencourt, Gastão. "Alvarus, um Grande Caricaturista Brasileiro." *Notícias Ilustradas* (Lisbon). July 24, 1932.

5251. Eneida. "Alvarus e os Seus Bonecos." *Diário de Notícias* (Rio de Janeiro). July 2, 1954.

5252. Eneida. "Alvarus no Peru." *Diário de Notícias* (Rio de Janeiro). January 6, 1958.

5253. Gill, Ruben. "O Século Boêmio." *Dom Casmurro* (Rio de Janeiro). May 15, 1943.

5254. Guerra, Paulo de Sales. "Penicilina para a Caricatura." *Revista da Semana* (Rio de Janeiro). October 14, 1944.

5255. Lima, Herman. "Alvarus e os Bonecos do Seu Circo." *Rio-Magazine*. February 1949.

5256. Lima, Herman. *Alvarus e os Seus Bonecos*. Rio de Janeiro: Ministério da Educação e Cultura, Serviço de Documentacão, 1954.

5257. Magalháes, Júnior, R. "Alvarus e os Seus Bonecos." *Diário de Notícias* (Rio de Janeiro). March 20, 1954.

5258. Milano, Atílio. "O Álbum de Alvarus." *O Jornal* (Rio de Janeiro). May 23, 1954.

5259. Moreyra, Álvaro. "Alvarus." *Hoje Tem Espetáculo*. Rio de Janeiro: Zélio Valverde, 1945.

5260. Pacheco, Armando. "Alvarus Afirma: 'Os Parlamentares Feios do Brasil Devem Acabar com a Charge!" *O Globo* (Rio de Janeiro). August 2, 1948.

5261. Pacheco, Armando. "Existe Caricatura Moderna no Brasil?" *Dom Casmurro* (Rio de Janeiro). September 6, 1941.

5262. Velarde, Hernan. "Cotrim, Genio de la Caricatura." *La Crónica Dominical* (Lima, Peru). October 6, 1957.

5263. Wilson, Carlos. "A Caricatura como Antídoto do Veneno Literário." *Mundo Ilustrado* (Rio de Janeiro). February 5, 1931.

Américo, Pedro

5264. Amaral Júnior, Amadeu. "Pedro Américo Caricaturista." *Vamos Ler!* (Rio de Janeiro). August 13, 1942.

5265. de Oliveira, J.M. Cardoso. *Pedro Américo. Sua Vida e Suas Obras*. Rio de Janeiro: Ministério da Educação e Saúde, 1943.

5266. Duque, Gonzaga A. *Arte Brasileira*. Rio de Janeiro: Impr. H. Rombaerts, 1988.

5267. Guimarães, Luís. *Biografia do Pintor Pedro Américo*. Rio de Janeiro: Henrique Brown e João de Almeida, 1871.

5268. Lima, Herman. "O Caricaturista Pedro Américo." *Revista da Samana* (Rio de Janeiro). April 24, 1943.

5269. Lima, Herman. "Pedro Américo Caricaturista." *Cultura Política* (Rio de Janeiro). October 1944.

5270. Lima, Herman. "Pedro Américo e um Enigma Artístico." *Rio-Magazine*. April 1949.

Azevedo, Aluísio

5271. Alvarus (Álvaro Cotrim). "Artur Azevedo e a Caricatura." *Boletim da S.B.A.T.* (Rio de Janeiro). May-June 1955.

5272. Barbosa, Domingos. "Os Irmãos Azevedo." In *Conferências*. Rio de Janeiro: Federação das Academias de Letras do Brasil, F. Briguiet and Cia., 1939.

5273. Coelho Neto. "Reminiscências." In *Frutos do Tempo*. Bahia: Livraria Catilina, 1920.

5274. Lima, Herman. "O Caricaturista Aluísio Azevedo." *Jornal de Letras* (Rio de Janeiro). April 1957.

5275. Lima, Herman. "Escritores Caricaturistas." In *Revista do Livro*. Rio de Janeiro: Instituto Nacional do Livro, September 1957.

5276. Montelo, Josué. "Aluísio Azevedo e a Caricatura do Tempo do Império." *Histórias da Vida Literária*. Rio de Janeiro: Nosso Livro Editôra, 1944.

5277. Peixoto, Afrânio, "Lembranças de Aluísio Azevedo." In *Poeira da Estrada*. Rio de Janeiro: W.M. Jackson Inc. Editôres, 1947. Vol. 10.

Barbosa, Bento

5278. Coimbra, Figueiredo. "Bento Barbosa." *A Semana* (Rio de Janeiro). July 23, 1887.

5279. "Notícia da Redação." *Revista Ilustrada* (Rio de Janeiro). December 1894.

Barbosa, Rui

5280. Barbosa, Francisco de Assis. "Uma Biografia de Rui Barbosa Pela Caricatura." *Fôlha da Noite* (São Paulo). October 29, 1949.

5281. Bento, Antônio. "Rui e a Caricatura." *Diário Carioca* (Rio de Janeiro). June 18, 1950.

5282. de Aquino, Flávio. "Rui e a Caricatura." *Diário de Notícias* (Rio de Janeiro). June 16, 1950.

5283. de Queiroz, Rachel. "Caricatura." *O Cruzeiro* (Rio de Janeiro). June 24, 1950.

5284. do Rêgo, José Lins. "A Vida de Rui Barbosa Pela Caricatura." *O Jornal* (Rio de Janeiro). July 17, 1950.

5285. Freyre, Gilberto. "Rui e a Caricatura." *Jornal de Letras* (Rio de Janeiro). June 1950.

5286. Leão, Múcio. "As Caricaturas de Mestre Rui." *Jornal do Brasil* (Rio de Janeiro). June 17, 1950.

5287. Lima, Herman. "Cândido de Faria, um Mestre Esquecido." *Diário de Notícias* (Rio de Janeiro). August 16, 1954.

5288. Lima, Herman. "O Ciclo das Caricaturas contra Bernardo Pereira de Vasconcelos." *Diário de Notícias* (Rio de Janeiro). November 29, 1953.

5289. Lima, Herman. "Rui e a Caricatura." *Revista do Servico Público* (Rio de Janeiro). November 1949.

5290. Lima, Herman. "Rui e a Caricatura." *Rio Magazine.* November 1949.

5291. Lima, Herman. *Rui e a Caricatura.* Biografia política de Rui Barbosa, pela caricatura (1879-1949). Rio de Janeiro: Ministério da Educação e Saúde, Casa de Rui Barbosa, 1949; Gráfica Olímpica Editôra, 1950. 2nd Ed.

5292. Montenegro, Braga. "As Caricaturas de Rui Barbosa." *O Povo* (Fortaleza). October 11, 1950.

5293. Rêgo, Costa. "As Caricaturas de Rui Barbosa." *Correio da Manhã* (Rio de Janeiro). June 6, 1950.

5294. Soares, Ubaldo. "Rui e a Caricatura." *Carioca* (Rio de Janeiro). July 27, 1950.

5295. Tys, Hélio. "Rui e a Caricatura." *Idéias e Livros* (Rio de Janeiro). October 15, 1950.

Belmonte (Benedito Bastos Barreto)

5296. Alvarus. "Morreu Belmonte." *Boletim de Belas-Artes* (Rio de Janeiro). May 1947.

5297. Belmonte (Benedito Bastos Barreto). *Assim Falou Juca Pato.* Crônicas ilustradas pelo Autor. São Paulo: Cia. Editôra Nacional, 1933.

5298. Belmonte (Benedito Bastos Barreto). *Caricatura dos Tempos*. São Paulo: Edições Melhoramentos, 1948.

5299. Belmonte (Benedito Bastos Barreto). *Idéias de João-Ninguém*. Crônicas ilustradas pelo Autor. Rio de Janeiro: Livraria José Olympio Editôra, 1935.

5300. Belmonte (Benedito Bastos Barreto). *Música, Maestro!* São Paulo: Emprêsa Fôlha da Manhã, Ltda., 1940.

5301. Belmonte (Benedito Bastos Barreto). *No Tempo dos Bandeirantes*. São Paulo: Edições Melhoramentos, n.d. 3rd Ed.

5302. Belmonte (Benedito Bastos Barreto). *O Amor Através os Séculos*. Rio de Janeiro: Editôra Frou-Frou, 1928.

5303. Cavalheiro, Edgar. "Tentativa Testamentária." In *Testamento de Uma Geração*. Pôrto Alegre: Livraria do Globo, 1944.

5304. Gill, Ruben. "O Século Boêmio." *Dom Casmurro* (Rio de Janeiro). February 20, 1943.

5305. Lima, Herman. "Belmonte, Juca Pato e o Homem da Rua." *Rio-Magazine* (Rio de Janeiro). December 1953.

5306. Morel, Edmar. "Belmonte Verde-Amarelo." *Revista do Globo* (Pôrto Alegre). January 25, 1947.

5307. Pacheco, Armando. "Depoimento de Uma Geração." *Dom Casmurro* (Rio de Janeiro). February 7, 1942.

5308. Pacheco, Armando. "Tem a Palavra o Autor de Juca Pato." *Vamos Ler!* (Rio de Janeiro). January 29, 1943.

5309. Peixoto, Silveira. "Belmonte." In *Falam os Escritores*. São Paulo: Edições Cultura Brasileira S.A., 1940.

5310. Peixoto, Silveira. "Quem Ouviu Falar em Benedito Bastos Barreto?" *Fôlha Carioca* (Rio de Janeiro). April 25, 1947.

5311. Silveira, Celestino. "A Caricatura é Uma Arma Que Deve Ser Usada na Luta." *Revista da Semana* (Rio de Janeiro). March 3, 1945.

5312. Vainer, Nelson. "Belmonte. Vida e Obra do Criador de Juca Pato." *Fôlha da Noite* (São Paulo). May 16, 1957 to July 12, 1957.

5313. Vainer, Nelson. "Belmonte. No 10º Aniversário do Desaparecimento do Grande Caricaturista Bandeirante." *Correio da Manhã* (Rio de Janeiro). May 25, 1957.

5314. Vainer, Nelson. "Depois de Dez Anos do Desaparecimento de Belmonte Surgirá Sua Biografia." *O Globo* (Rio de Janeiro). September 10, 1956.

5315. Vainer, Nelson. "Um Prefácio Inédito de Monteiro Lobato." *Revista da Semana* (Rio de Janeiro). April 5, 1947.

Borgomainerio, Luigi

5316. "Notícia de Sua Morte." *O Mosquito* (Rio de Janeiro). March 4, 1876.

5317. "Notícia de Sua Morte." *Revista Ilustrada* (Rio de Janeiro). March 4, 1876.

Cardosa Aires, Emílio

5318. Aires, Emílio Cardoso. [Album] Paris: Distribuidora Livraria Briguiet, 1912.

5319. "Aires, Caricaturista da Elegância." *Revista da Semana* (Rio de Janeiro). December 23, 1916.

5320. Alvarus (Álvaro Cotrim). "O Caricaturista Emílio Cardoso Aires." *Vamos Ler!* (Rio de Janeiro). January 7, 1943.

5321. Alvarus. "Um Caricaturista da Aristocracia." *Vitrina* (Rio de Janeiro). September 1942.

5322. Cavalcanti, Valdemar. "O Chá da Cavé." *O Jornal* (Rio de Janeiro). February 29, 1948.

5323. de Albuquerque, Mateus. "O Domínio da Caricatura." *Sensações e Reflexões*. Lisbon: Editôra Portugal-Brasil Ltda., n.d.

5324. Gill, Ruben. "O Século Boêmio." *Dom Casmurro* (Rio de Janeiro). June 5, 1943.

5325. Lima, Herman. "Emílio Cardoso Aires." *Rio*. November 1946.

Cortez, Jayme

5326. Cortez, Jayme. *A Arte de Jayme Cortez*. São Paulo: Press Editorial, 1986. (Includes Wagner Augusto. "A Cronologia Biográfica do Mestre").

5327. de Moya, Alvaro. "Jayme Cortez Brasiliano di Adozione." *1986 Lucca 20 Anni*. 1986, p. 23.

Cunha Dias, Ronaldo

5328. Cunha Dias, Ronaldo. *O Homem Que Ri*. Porto Alegre, Brazil: Tche! Editora Ltda., 1987.

5329. "Ronaldo Cunha Dias, 'Brazil,' Presents His Cartoonbook." *FECO News*. No. 6, 1988, p. 2.

de Almeida, Belmiro

5330. de Almeida, Felinto. "Belmiro de Almeida." *A Semana* (Rio de Janeiro). May 7, 1887.

5331. Duque, Gonzaga. "Belmiro de Almeida." In *A Arte Brasileira*. Rio de Janeiro: Imprensa H. Rombaerts, 1888.

5332. Gill, Ruben. "Homens Que Riem." *Dom Casmurro* (Rio de Janeiro). April 6, 1946.

5333. Luso, João. "Belmiro de Almeida." In *Assim Falou Polidoro*. Rio de Janeiro: Cia. Editôra Americana S. A., 1941.

5334. Ribeiro, Flexa. "A Pintura-Sátira de Belmiro de Almeida." *Illustração Brasileira* (Rio de Janeiro). August 1935.

de Sousa, Mauricio

5335. Hurd, Jud. "Brazilian Cartoonist Mauricio." *Cartoonist PROfiles*. No. 30, 1976, pp. 8-13.

5336. "Mauricio De Sousa, Brazilian Cartoonist, Creator of Monica." *Cartoonist PROfiles*. No. 30, 1976, pp. 8-13.

5337. Silva, Mayra Cristina. "Mauricio de Sousa: Disney do Brasil." *Fumetti d'Italia*. Winter 1993, pp. 8-9.

Dias, Correia

5338. de Barros, João. "Correia Dias, Caricaturista e Decorador." *Gazeta de Notícias* (Rio de Janeiro). May 17, 1914.

5339. de Carvalho, Ronald. "O Irreal na Arte." *Seleta* (Rio de Janeiro). September 29, 1914.

5340. Gill, Ruben. "O Século Boêmio." *Dom Casmurro* (Rio de Janeiro). December 5, 1942.

5341. Pinto, Álvaro. "Um Poeta da Beleza." *Diário de Lisboa*. Literary Supplement. November 29, 1935.

5342. X. "A Exposição de Correia Dias." *Gazeta de Notícias* (Rio de Janeiro). May 10, 1914.

Di Cavalcanti, Emiliano

5343. di Cavalcanti, Emiliano. *A Realidade Brasileira.* São Paulo: Published by author, n.d.

5344. di Cavalcanti, Emiliano. *Viagem da Minha Vida.* Rio de Janeiro: Civilização Brasileira, 1955.

Figueroa, Enrique

5345. Gill, Ruben. "Figueroa." *Dom Casmurro* (Rio de Janeiro). March 3, 1945.

5346. Gill, Ruben. "O Século Boêmio." *Dom Casmurro* (Rio de Janeiro). July 3, 1943.

5347. Martins, Carlos. "Enrique Figueroa." *A Pacotilha* (S. Luís). February 21, 1925.

Fleiuss, Henrique

5348. Fleiuss, Max. "Centenário de Henrique Fleiuss." *Páginas de História.* Rio de Janeiro: Dep. Imprensa Nacional, 1930.

5349. Fleiuss, Max. "Meu Pai." In *Recordando. Cenas e Perfis,* Rio de Janeiro: da *Rev. do I.H.G. Brasileiro,* 1941.

5350. Gill, Ruben. "O Século Boêmio." *Dom Casmurro* (Rio de Janeiro). March 11, 1944.

5351. Pinto, Odorico Pires. "Henrique Fleiuss." *Correio da Manhã* (Rio de Janeiro). January 16, 1949.

5352. Pinto, Odorico Pires. "O Número Inaugural da *Semana Ilustrada.*" *Jornal do Comércio* (Rio de Janeiro). December 9, 1956.

Fritz (Anísio Oscar da Mota)

5353. Amarante, Newton. "A Repercussão Social da Obra de um Caricaturista." *Correio da Manhã* (Rio de Janeiro). January 13, 1957.

5354. "Há Quarenta Anos o Lápis de Fritz Alegra o Carioca." *O Semanário* (Rio de Janeiro). August 16-23, 1956.

5355. Moreyra, Álvaro. "Fritz." In *Havia Uma Oliveira no Jardim.* Rio de Janeiro: Jotapê Livreiro Editor, 1958.

Gil (Carlos Lenoir)

5356. "Caricaturas de Gil." *D. Quixote* (Rio de Janeiro). December 25, 1918.

5357. Gill, Ruben. "O Século Boêmio." *Dom Casmurro* (Rio de Janeiro). May 1, 1943.

5358. Lima, Herman. "Gil e o Seu Famoso Bal-de-Têtes." *Rio Magazine*. October 1950.

5359. Raul. "O Gil." *Jornal do Brasil* (Rio de Janeiro). January 14, 1906.

Hélios (Hélios Seelinger)

5360. Duque, Gonzaga. "Hélios Seelinger." In *Contemporâneos*. Rio de Janeiro: Tip. Benedito de Sousa, 1929.

5361. Edmundo, Luís. "Hélios Seelinger." In *De um Livro de Memórias*. Rio de Janeiro: Imp. Nacional, 1958. 3 Vols.

5362. "50 Anos de Vida Artística e Boêmia." *Revista da Semana* (Rio de Janeiro). April 17, 1943.

5363. Lima, Herman. "Cinqüenta Años de Vida Artística e Boêmia." *Revista da Semana* (Rio de Janeiro). April 17, 1943.

Hermínio, Celso

5364. "Celso Hermínio." *Jornal do Brasil* (Rio de Janeiro). November 1, 1897.

5365. "O Caricaturista Celso Hermínio." *Ilustração Portuguêsa* (Lisbon). March 14, 1904.

5366. Gill, Ruben. "O Século Boêmio." *Dom Casmurro* (Rio de Janeiro). March 20, 1943.

Hofmann

5367. Ferraz, Geraldo. "Hofmann e a Caricatura." Literary Supplement. *Estado de São Paulo*. May 16, 1959.

5368. Godwin, John. "Incrível Conto de Hofmann." *O Globo* (Rio de Janeiro). March 28, 1958.

J. Artur

5369. Gill, Ruben. "O Século Boêmio." *Dom Casmurro* (Rio de Janeiro). June 17, 1944.

5370. "J. Artur." *Fôlha do Norte*. November 16, 1911.

J. Carlos (José Carlos de Brito e Cunha)

5371. "A Caricatura Está Agonizando—Declara J. Carlos." *Revista da Semana* (Rio de Janeiro). August 26, 1944.

5372. Alvarus. "J. Carlos." *Rio-Magazine*. November 1950.

5373. Amado, Genolino. "Jota Carlos e o Seu Tempo." *O Cruzeiro* (Rio de Janeiro). June 16, 1951.

5374. Amado, Genolino. "Luzes da Cidade. Jota Carlos e o Seu Tempo." *O Cruzeiro* (Rio de Janeiro). June 16, 1951.

5375. Aquino, Flávio. "J. Carlos." *Diário de Notícias* (Rio de Janeiro). December 31, 1950.

5376. Ariel (Miranda Neto). "Uma Época e o Seu Pintor." *A Noite* (Rio de Janeiro). March 7, 1951.

5377. Bento, Antônio. "J. Carlos." *Diário Carioca* (Rio de Janeiro). December 31, 1950.

5378. Broca, Brito. "A Caricatura Política." *A Manhã* (Rio de Janeiro). December 31, 1950.

5379. Campofiorito, Quirino. "J. Carlos." *O Jornal* (Rio de Janeiro). October 4, 1950.

5380. Campofiorito, Quirino. "O Livro J. Carlos." *O Jornal* (Rio de Janeiro). January 4, 1951.

5381. Carmo, Mauro. "J. Carlos." *A Noite* (Rio de Janeiro). January 31, 1951.

5382. Cascudo, Luís da Câmara. "J. Carlos." *Diário de Natal* (Natal). May 23, 1951.

5383. Celso, Maria Eugênia. "J. Carlos." *Jornal do Brasil* (Rio de Janeiro). June 18, 1951.

5384. Fernandes, Sebastião. "J. Carlos." *Sul-América* (Rio de Janeiro). December 1951.

5385. Gill, Ruben. "O Século Boêmio." *Dom Casmurro* (Rio de Janeiro). November 29, 1942.

5386. *J. Carlos*. Álbum de Desenhos. Introduction by Herman Lima. Rio de Janeiro: Min. Educação e Saúde, Serv. de Documentação, 1950.

5387. J. Carlos (José Carlos de Brito e Cunha). "Meus Segredos." *Dom Quixote* (Rio de Janeiro). December 25, 1918.

5388. J. Carlos. *Minha Babá*. Rio de Janeiro: Biblioteca d'*O Tico-Tico*, 1933.

5389. Kelly, Celso. "A Rua J. Carlos." *A Noite* (Rio de Janeiro). June 19, 1951.

5390. Leão, Múcio. "A Evocação de Um Artista." *Jornal do Brasil* (Rio de Janeiro). February 17, 1951.

5391. Lima, Herman. "A Carioca na Arte de J. Carlos." *Rio Magazine*. December 1947.

5392. Lima, Herman. "Em Louvor de um Mestre." *Rio Magazine*. October 1951.

5393. Lima, Herman. "Êste Homem Embalou a Nossa Infância." *O Malho* (Rio de Janeiro). January 1950.

5394. Lima, Herman. "J. Carlos." *Coletânea* (Rio de Janeiro). August 1952.

5395. Lima, Herman. "J. Carlos." *Rio*. December 1949.

5396. Lima, Herman. "J. Carlos, Caricaturista da Vida Moderna." *Diário de Notícias* (Rio de Janeiro). May 7, 1950.

5397. Lima, Herman. "J. Carlos, Caricaturista da Vida Moderna." *Vitrina* (Rio de Janeiro). November 1942.

5398. Lima, Herman. "J. Carlos, Cronista do Rio Dêste Século." *Jornal de Letras* (Rio de Janeiro). October 1950.

5399. Lima, Herman. "J. Carlos. Os Mestres do Lápis Brasileiro." *O Jornal* (Rio de Janeiro). November 4, 1951.

5400. Lima, Herman. "Meio Século de Caricatura." *Revista do Globo* (Pôrto Alegre). August 19, 1950.

5401. Lima, Herman. "O Natal na Arte de J. Carlos." *Rio Magazine*. December 1948.

5402. Lima, Herman. "Pinheiro Machado e o Lápis de J. Carlos." *Rio Magazine*. June 1951.

5403. Magalhães Júnior, R. "Um Mestre da Caricatura." *Diário de Notícias* (Rio de Janeiro). October 3, 1950.

5404. Marques, Sara. "J. Carlos." *Diário Popular* (Rio de Janeiro). November 30, 1950.

5405. Milano, Atílio. "O Gênio da Caricatura." *O Jornal* (Rio de Janeiro). December 3, 1950.

5406. Milliet, Sérgio. "J. Carlos." In *Diário Crítico*. Vol. 7. São Paulo: Livraria Martins Editôra, 1953.

5407. Moreyra, Manuel. "Um Mestre do Lápis." *Careta* (Rio de Janeiro). June 20, 1953.

5408. Olinto, Antônio. "J. Carlos." *O Globo* (Rio de Janeiro). January 31, 1951.

5409. "O Primeiro Desenho de J. Carlos." *A Noite* (Rio de Janeiro). August 23, 1952.

5410. Ouro-Prêto, Maluh. "Exposição de J. Carlos." *Tribuna da Imprensa* (Rio de Janeiro). December 5, 1950.

5411. Pacheco, Armando. "A Palavra de J. Carlos, Mestre da Sua Arte no Brasil." *O Globo* (Rio de Janeiro). June 26, 1948.

5412. Pacheco, Armando. "Dois Dedos de Prosa com J. Carlos." *Vamos Ler!* January 6, 1944.

5413. Pacheco, Armando. "Existe Caricatura Moderna no Brasil?" *Dom Casmurro* (Rio de Janeiro). August 16, 1941.

5414. Pongetti, Henrique. "O Silêncio." *O Globo* (Rio de Janeiro). January 19, 1951.

5415. Rêgo, José Lins do. "O Álbum de J. Carlos." *O Jornal* (Rio de Janeiro). December 24, 1950.

5416. Rêgo, José Lins do. "Sôbre a Caricatura." *O Jornal.* August 10, 1951.

5417. Rio Branco, Miguel Paranhos do. "J. Carlos." *Ilustração Brasileira* (Rio de Janeiro). November 1950.

5418. Rosa, Santa. "A Exposição de J. Carlos." *Letras e Artes* (Rio de Janeiro). December 10, 1950.

5419. Silveira, Joel. "Não Quero Ser Parafuso da Máquina Nazista." *Diretrizes* (Rio de Janeiro). June 6, 1942.

5420. Silveira, Joel. "Um Álbum." *Diário de Notícias* (Rio de Janeiro). December 24, 1950.

5421. Theo. "O Grande Artista Que o Brasil Perdeu." *O Globo* (Rio de Janeiro). November 20, 1950.

5422. Vítor, Leo. "J. Carlos, Historiador." *A Cigarra* (São Paulo). 1928.

K. Lixto (Calixto Cordeiro)

5423. Baciu, Stefan. "Depoimento de Mestre Kalixto." *Tribuna da Imprensa* (Rio de Janeiro). October 16, 1954.

5424. Bandeira, Manuel. "Calixto." *Jornal do Brasil* (Rio de Janeiro). September 12, 1956.

5425. Cajás, Paulo. "Desapareceu o Último Fraque do Brasil." *Mundo Ilustrado* (Rio de Janeiro). February 20, 1957.

5426. Cajás, Paulo. "O Samba de Kalixto." *Leitura* (Rio de Janeiro). November 1957.

5427. Campofiorito, Quirino. "K. Lixto." *O Jornal* (Rio de Janeiro). September 9, 1956.

5428. Ciarla, Lêda. "Calixto Cordeiro." *Revista ABD* (Rio de Janeiro). August 1950.

5429. "Com a Morte de Kalixto Também Desaparece o Rio de Outrora." *Jornal do Brasil* (Rio de Janeiro). February 12, 1957.

5430. Costallat, Benjamin. "O Chapelão e o France." *Jornal do Brasil* (Rio de Janeiro). February 17, 1957.

5431. da Rocha, Mário Pena. "K. Lixto o Lápis Que Marcou uma Época." *Brasil Rotário* (Rio de Janeiro). March 1956.

5432. "Desaparece aos 80 Anos Calixto Cordeiro—o Famoso K. Lixto." *A Gazeta* (S. Paulo). February 15, 1957.

5433. Duque, Gonzaga. "Calixto Cordeiro." *Contemporâneos*. Rio de Janeiro: Tip. Benedito Sousa, 1929.

5434. Gill, Ruben. "O Século Boêmio." *Dom Casmurro* (Rio de Janeiro). January 9, 1943.

5435. Gomes, Raul. "Mestre Kalixto." *Correio da Manhã* (Rio de Janeiro). October 7, 1956.

5436. "Kalixto Nunca se Acostumou com a Evoluçao do Vestuário." *O Globo* (Rio de Janeiro). September 3, 1956.

5437. K. Lixto (Calixto Cordeiro). "Autobiocalungografia." *D. Quixote* (Rio de Janeiro). December 25, 1918.

5438. Laus, Lasimar. "Kalixto." *Jornal do Brasil* (Rio de Janeiro). February 17, 1957.

5439. Lima, Herman. "Calixto Cordeiro, Cronista do Esnobismo Carioca." *Rio-Magazine*. November 1948.

5440. Lima, Herman. "Calixto Cordeiro e a Sua Grande Arte." *Vitrina* (Rio de Janeiro). March 1943.

5441. Lima, Herman. "Cinqüenta Anos de Caricatura." *Vamos Ler!* (Rio de Janeiro). June 21, 1947.

5442. Lima, Herman. "K. Lixto e a Sua Grande Arte." *Tribuna da Imprensa* (Rio de Janeiro). October 17, 1954.

5443. Lima, Herman. "Meio Século de Caricatura. Dois Mestres Brasileiros. K. Lixto e Raul." *O Malho* (Rio de Janeiro). July 1948.

5444. Lima, Herman. "Os Mestres do Lápis Brasileiro. Calixto Cordeiro." *O Jornal* (Rio de Janeiro). July 29, 1951.

5445. "Meu Dia Não Chegou, O." *Revista da Semana* (Rio de Janeiro). September 9, 1944.

5446. Pacheco, Armando. "Existe Caricatura Moderna no Brasil?" *Dom Casmurro* (Rio de Janeiro). September 13, 1941.

5447. Pacheco, Armando. "Há Meio Século Iniciavam-se na Consagração e na Popularidade Dois dos Maiores Artistas do Lápis no Brasil." *O Globo* (Rio de Janeiro). July 29, 1948.

5448. Silveira, Joel. "Vendedores de Humor." *Diretrizes* (Rio de Janeiro). June 26, 1941.

5449. "Última Pilhéria Que Eu ia Dizer Será Encaixotada Comigo, A." *A Noite* (Rio de Janeiro). February 12, 1957.

5450. Vanderlei, Eustórgio. "Tipos Populares." *Correio da Manhã* (Rio de Janeiro). June 6, 1941.

Lima, Herman

5451. "Caricatura a Grande Paixão Literária de Herman Lima." *O Povo* (Fortaleza). May 19, 1956.

5452. "Dez Minutos com Herman Lima. A Primeira História da Caricatura no Brasil." *A Gazeta* (São Paulo). January 8, 1955.

5453. "Do Ceará para a Europa Herman Lima Foi Presença na Caricatura do Brasil." *Gazeta de Notícias* (Fortaleza). June 3, 1962.

5454. "Herman Lima Abre os Seus Arquivos e Nos Mostra Mais de Cem Anos de Caricatura." *A Cigarra Magazine* (Rio de Janeiro). June 1956.

5455. "Herman Lima Apresenta a Caricatura Brasileira." *Tribuna da Imprensa* (Rio de Janeiro). July 17-18, 1954.

5456. Schneider, Otto. "Herman Lima e as Caricaturas." *O Jornal* (Rio de Janeiro). April 11, 1954.

Loureiro (Luís Gomes Loureiro)

5457. Gill, Ruben. "O Século Boêmio." *Dom Casmurro* (Rio de Janeiro). July 24, 1943.

5458. "O Pai de Chiquinho." *Tribuna da Imprensa* (Rio de Janeiro). September 6-7, 1952.

5459. "Três Caricaturistas da Velha Guarda: Loureiro, Yantok e Storni." *Revista da Semana* (Rio de Janeiro). March 31, 1945.

Luís (Luís Peixoto)

5460. Carioca, Lulu. "Boêmios do Meu Tempo." *Vamos Ler!* (Rio de Janeiro). April 26, 1947.

5461. de Abreu, Modesto. "Luís, Presidente." *Boletim da SBAT* (Rio de Janeiro). February 1950.

5462. Edmundo, Luís. "Luís Peixoto." In *De um Livro de Memórias*. Rio de Janeiro: Departamento de Imprensa Nacional, 1958. Vol. III.

5463. Gill, Ruben. "O Século Boêmio." *Dom Casmurro* (Rio de Janeiro). April 3, 1943.

5464. Labanca. "Luís Peixoto: Uma Época do Teatro Brasileiro de Revista." *Para Todos*. June 15, 1957.

Machado, Julião

5465. Boaventura, Armando. "Julião Machado e as Iluminuras Incompletas de *Os Lusíadas*." *Voz de Portugal* (Rio de Janeiro). October 31, 1946.

5466. Duque, Gonzaga. "Os Aquarelistas de 1907." In *Contemporâneos*. Rio de Janeiro: Tip. Benedito de Sousa, 1929.

5467. Edmundo, Luís. "Julião Machado." In *O Rio de Janeiro do Meu Tempo*. Rio de Janeiro: Imp. Nacional, 1938. Vol. 2.

5468. Gill, Ruben. "O Século Boêmio." *Dom Casmurro* (Rio de Janeiro). April 17, 1943.

5469. Lima, Herman. "Julião Machado. Os Mestres do Lápis Brasileiro." *O Jornal* (Rio de Janeiro). December 16, 1951.

5470. Lima, Herman. "Julião Machado, um Grande da Arte do Traço e da Ironia." *Rio Magazine*. January 1949.

5471. Luso, João. "Julião Machado." In *Louvores*. Rio de Janeiro: Edições Dois Mundos, Brasil-Portugal, n.d.

5472. Machado, Julião. "A Greve dos Micróbios." *Era Nova* (Rio de Janeiro). August 21, 1915.

5473. Machado, Julião. "A Morte do Bardo." *Álbum d'O País*. Rio de Janeiro: 1903.

5474. Machado, Julião. "Notas Autobiográficas." *D. Quixote* (Rio de Janeiro). December 25, 1918.

5475. Machado, Julião. "O Luto do Escrupuloso Mota." *Dom Quixote* (Rio de Janeiro). March 12, 1919.

5476. Machado, Julião. *O Modêlo*. Rio de Janeiro: Tip. do Jornal do Comércio, 1916.

5477. Machado, Julião. "Uber Alles." In *Almanaque d'A Noite*. Rio de Janeiro: 1917.

Mendez (Mário Mendes)

5478. Chiacchio, Carlos. "Mario Mendez." *A Tarde* (Salvador). January 3, 1934.

5479. Gill, Ruben. "O Século Boêmio." *Dom Casmurro* (Rio de Janeiro). October 16, 1943.

5480. Leite, Barbosa. "Arte das Américas." *Revista ABD* (Rio de Janeiro). December 1950.

5481. Lima, Herman. "Mendez e o Seu Mundo Hilariante." *Rio Magazine*. March 1951.

5482. Lima, Herman. "Mendez e o Seu Mundo Hilariante." *Vitrina* (Rio de Janeiro). September 1944.

5483. Lima, Herman. "O Pintor Mendez." *Vamos Ler!* (Rio de Janeiro). December 27, 1945.

5484. Mendez (Mário Mendes). *Aprenda a Desenhar Caricaturas*. Rio de Janeiro: Editôra Gertum Carneiro, 1950.

5485. Mendez (Mário Mendes). *Tipos e Costumes do Negro no Brasil*. Catálogo de Exposição na Bahia, 1938.

5486. "Mendez." *Vamos Ler!* (Rio de Janeiro). July 3, 1944.

5487. Pacheco, Armando. "Depoimento de uma Geração." *Vamos Ler!* (Rio de Janeiro). January 21, 1943.

5488. Pacheco, Armando. "Entrevista." *O Globo* (Rio de Janeiro). August 9, 1948.

5489. "Vestiram a Blusa de Marujos e Receberam os Louros da Vitória." *A Noite* (Rio de Janeiro). October 5, 1956.

Nássara

5490. "Eu Comecei Como Hitler, Sujando as Paredes." *Revista da Semana* (Rio de Janeiro). April 14, 1945.

5491. Gill, Ruben. "O Século Boêmio." *Dom Casmurro* (Rio de Janeiro). June 12, 1943.

5492. Moschovsky, Simão. "Nássara Recorda Mr. Evans e Fala da Estatística e da Filosofia." *O Globo* (Rio de Janeiro). November 11, 1953.

5493. "Nássara." *O Cruzeiro* (Rio de Janeiro). February 18, 1939.

5494. Pacheco, Armando. "Entrevista." *O Globo* (Rio de Janeiro). August 16, 1945.

5495. Pacheco, Armando. "Existe Caricatura Moderna no Brasil?" *Dom Casmurro* (Rio de Janeiro). August 23, 1941.

5496. Pedrosa, Milton. "Nássara, o Rei do Papo." *Manchete* (Rio de Janeiro). January 10, 1953.

5497. Squeff, Egídio. "Nássara, Sôbre Música Popular." *Para Todos*. October 1956.

Nemésio (Nemésio Dutra)

5498. de Miranda, Floresta. "Meu Amigo Embaixador." *Correio da Manhã* (Rio de Janeiro). January 6, 1956.

5499. Gill, Ruben. "O Século Boêmio." *Dom Casmurro* (Rio de Janeiro). November 25, 1944.

Neto, Pereira

5500. Azevedo, Artur. "Palestra." *O País* (Rio de Janeiro). January 10, 1907.

5501. Gill, Ruben. "O Século Boêmio." *Dom Casmurro* (Rio de Janeiro). January 20, 1945.

5502. "Pereira Neto." *Revista Ilustrada* (Rio de Janeiro). February 22, 1890.

Pôrto-Alegre, Manuel de Araújo

5503. Antunes, de Paranhos. "Araújo Pôrto-Alegre e a Caricatura." *Diário de Notícias* (Rio de Janeiro). January 1, 1954.

5504. Antunes, de Paranhos. *O Pintor do Romantismo*. Rio de Janeiro: Zélio Valverde Ed., 1943.

5505. *Autores e Livros*. Number dedicated to Pôrto-Alegre. August 15, 1943.

5506. de Sousa, J.A. Soares. "Vasconcelos e as Caricaturas." *Revista do I.H.G. Brasileiro* (Rio de Janeiro). January-March 1953.

5507. Lima, Herman. "Manuel de Araújo Pôrto-Alegre, o Primeiro Caricaturista Brasileiro?" *Diário de Notícias* (Rio de Janeiro). December 20, 1953.

5508. Lôbo, Hélio. *Manuel de Araújo Pôrto-Alegre*. Rio de Janeiro: Emprêsa ABC Ltda., 1938.

5509. Pôrto-Alegre, Manuel de Araújo. "Apontamentos Biográficos." *Revista da Academia Brasileira de Letras* (Rio de Janeiro). December 1931.

5510. Pôrto-Alegre, Manuel de Araújo. *Diário Intimo*. Manuscript. Biblioteca do D.P.H.A.N.

Raul (Raul Pederneiras)

5511. Abreu, Modesto. "Raul." *Boletim da SBAT* (Rio de Janeiro). May-June 1952.

5512. Calmon, Pedro. "Raul, Patriarca Dos Bonecos." *Revista da Semana* (Rio de Janeiro). June 3, 1953.

5513. Costa, Nelson. "O Bom Raul." *Correio da Manhã* (Rio de Janeiro). May 13, 1953.

5514. Costa, Nelson. "Raul." *Correio da Manhã* (Rio de Janeiro). May 11, 1955.

5515. Costa, Nelson. "Raul e a Geringonça Carioca." *Correio da Manhã* (Rio de Janeiro). December 11, 1958.

5516. "Figura Que Encarnava uma Época." *O Globo* (Rio de Janeiro). May 11, 1953.

5517. Gill, Ruben. "Jubileu do Historiador da Caricatura Nacional." *Dom Casmurro* (Rio de Janeiro). January 5, 1946.

5518. Gill, Ruben. "O Século Boêmio." *Dom Casmurro* (Rio de Janeiro). January 2, 1943.

5519. "Lápis Que Resta, O." *O Globo* (Rio de Janeiro). May 14, 1953.

5520. Lima, Herman. "Cinqüenta Anos de Caricatura." *Vamos Ler!* (Rio de Janeiro). June 21, 1947.

5521. Lima, Herman. "Meio Século de Caricatura. Dois Mestres Brasileiros: K. Lixto e Raul." *O Malho* (Rio de Janeiro). July 1948.

5522. Lima, Herman. "Predestinação da Popularidade, A." *O Globo* (Rio de Janeiro). July 22, 1946.

5523. Lima, Herman. "Raul." *Rio-Magazine*. December 1951.

5524. Lima, Herman. "Raul. Os Mestres do Lápis Brasileiro." *O Jornal* (Rio de Janeiro). July 8, 1951.

5525. Luso, João. "O Jubileu de um Humorista." *Revista da Semana*. May 1, 1926.

5526. Magalhães Júnior, R. "A Rua Raul." *Diário de Notícias* (Rio de Janeiro). August 15, 1951.

5527. Martins, Claudinier. "Raul." *Revista da Semana* (Rio de Janeiro). February 17, 1940.

5528. Matos, Adalberto. "A Obra de Raul." *Para Todos...* (Rio de Janeiro). September 6, 1924.

5529. "Obra Teatral de Raul, A." *Boletim da SBAT* (Rio de Janeiro). July 1947.

5530. Pacheco, Armando. "50 Anos de Glória." *A Noite Ilustrada* (Rio de Janeiro). April 15, 1952.

5531. Paulo Filho, M. "Memórias de Barros Franco: Raul Pederneiras." *Correio da Manhã* (Rio de Janeiro). June 16, 1956.

5532. Pongetti, Henrique. "Encontro." *O Globo* (Rio de Janeiro). May 14, 1953.

5533. Raul. "A Caricatura de 1822 a 1922." *Jornal do Brasil* (Rio de Janeiro). September 7, 1922.

5534. Raul. "A Gravura." *O Imparcial* (Rio de Janeiro). February 19, 1922.

5535. Raul. *A Máscara do Riso. Ensaios de Anátomo-Fisiologia Artística.* Rio de Janeiro, Ofs. Gráficas do *Jornal do Brasil.* Rio de Janeiro: 1917. 2nd Ed.

5536. Raul. "Amor e Mêdo." *Boletim da SBAT* (Rio de Janeiro). July 1947.

5537. Raul. *Cenas da Vida Carioca. Primeiro Álbum.* Rio de Janeiro: Published by author, 1924.

5538. Raul. *Cenas da Vida Carioca. Segundo Álbum.* Rio de Janeiro: Published by author, 1935.

5539. Raul. *Chá de Sabugueiro.* Rio de Janeiro: Coleção "Teatro Brasileiro," Edição da SBAT, n.d.

5540. Raul. "Dom Pedro II e os Lápis do Seu Tempo." *Revista da Semana* (Rio de Janeiro). January 1, 1921.

5541. Raul. *Figurações Onomásticas.* Rio de Janeiro: Published by author, 1927.

5542. Raul. *Geringonça Carioca. Verbêtes para um Dicionário da Giria.* Rio de Janeiro: F. Briguiet & Cia. Editôres, 2nd. Ed.

5543. Raul. *Lições de Caricatura. Método de Raul.* Rio de Janeiro: F. Briguiet & Cia. Editôres, 1946.

5544. Raul. *Musa Travêssa. Rumas de Rimas sem Rumo.* Rio de Janeiro: Published by author, 1936.

5545. Raul. "Na Cozinha dos Jornals." *Revista da Semana* (Rio de Janeiro). April 30, 1921.

5546. Raul. *Nos Pelas Costas. Notas Sôltas de um Caderno de Viagem.* Rio de Janeiro: Ofs. Gráfs. do *Jornal do Brasil,* 1930.

5547. Raul. "O Calemburgo." *Kosmos* (Rio de Janeiro). May 1906.

5548. Raul. "O Irredentismo em Arte." *Jornal do Brasil* (Rio de Janeiro). June 18, 1911.

5549. Raul. "O Lápis, de 1822 a 1922." *A Noite* (Rio de Janeiro). September 7, 1922.

5550. Raul. "Um Caricaturista Sôbre a Arte Dos Calungas." In *A Caricatura na Imprensa Brasileira,* by Frei Pedro Sinzig. Petrópolis: Edição das Vozes de Petrópolis, 1911.

5551. Rocha, Daniel. "Raul Pederneiras, um Espírito Alegre Que Sempre Levou a Vida a Sério." *Boletim da SBAT* (Rio de Janeiro). July 1947.

5552. "Reminiscências de um Bacharel de 1895." *O Globo* (Rio de Janeiro). December 21, 1945.

5553. Schmidt, Augusto Frederico. "A Morte de Raul." *Correio da Manhã* (Rio de Janeiro). May 13, 1953.

5554. Silveira, Celestino. "Raul Conta-nos como Apareceu a *Revista da Semana*." *Revista da Semana* (Rio de Janeiro). June 17, 1944.

5555. Terra de Sena. "Raul." *O Malho* (Rio de Janeiro). July 1953.

5556. Vieira, Celso. "Raul." *O Malho* (Rio de Janeiro). June 1953.

Rian (Nair de Teffé)

5557. Barbosa, Francisco de Assis. "Nair de Teffé, Aristocrata da Primeira República." *Diretrizes* (Rio de Janeiro). May 7, 1943.

5558. Gill, Ruben. "O Século Boêmio." *Dom Casmurro* (Rio de Janeiro). April 10, 1943.

5559. Lima, Herman. "Nair de Teffé. Caricaturista da Alta Roda." *Rio-Magazine*. December 1952.

5560. Lima, Herman. "Nair de Teffé. Os Mestres do Nosso Lápis." *O Jornal* (Rio de Janeiro). January 6, 1952.

5561. Lima, Herman. "Nossa Primeira Caricaturista: Nair de Teffé." *Revista do Livro*. Rio de Janeiro: Ministério da Educação e Cultura, Instituto Nacional do Livro, March-June 1961.

5562. Vidal, Barros. "Nair de Teffé." In *Precursoras Brasileiras*. Rio de Janeiro: Editôra A Noite, 1953.

Rocha, Teixeira da

5563. Correia, Magalhães. "Os Últimos Prêmios de Imperial Academia de Belas-Artes." *Jornal do Brasil* (Rio de Janeiro). April 9, 1941.

5564. Gill, Ruben. "O Século Boêmio." *Dom Casmurro* (Rio de Janeiro). July 31, 1943.

5565. Raul. "Teixeira da Rocha." *Jornal do Brasil* (Rio de Janeiro). May 1, 1941.

5566. "Teixeira da Rocha." *Revista da Semana* (Rio de Janeiro). March 15, April 26, 1941.

Rodrigues, Augusto

5567. Amado, Genolino. "Augusto Rodrigues, o Inesgotável." *O Cruzeiro* (Rio de Janeiro). June 24, 1950.

5568. Anísio, Pedro. "Pintura Não é o Sorriso da Sociedade." *Planalto* (São Paulo). September 15, 1941.

5569. Aulicus, Coelius. "Arte Não Leva Enderêço." *Revista da Semana* (Rio de Janeiro). December 30, 1944.

5570. de Aquino, Flávio. "Augusto Rodrigues Prêmio do Salão de 53." *Jornal de Letras* (Rio de Janeiro). September 1953.

5571. Lima, Herman. "Augusto Rodrigues, o Imprevisto." *Rio-Magazine.* September 1951.

5572. Pacheco, Armando. "Entrevista." *O Globo* (Rio de Janeiro). August 23, 1948.

5573. Pacheco, Armando. "Existe Caricatura Moderna no Brasil?" *Dom Casmurro* (Rio de Janeiro). August 23, 1941.

5574. Rodrigues, Augusto. "Caricaturas e Caricaturistas." *Revista da Semana* (Rio de Janeiro). July 10, 1937.

5575. Silveira, Joel. "Retrato de Augusto Rodrigues." *Revista do Globo* (Pôrto Alegre). October 27, 1945.

5576. Silveira, Joel. "Retrato em Prêto e Branco." *Vamos Ler!* (Rio de Janeiro). January 29, 1942.

Romano

5577. "Fêz a Caricatura do Professor e Ficou Prêso...." *A Noite* (Rio de Janeiro). September 28, 1953.

5578. Gill, Ruben. "O Século Boêmio." *Dom Casmurro* (Rio de Janeiro). April 24, 1943.

5579. "Os Príncipes do Nosso Lápis." *A Maçã* (Rio de Janeiro). March 14, 1925.

5580. Romano. "Boneco-Biografia." *D. Quixote* (Rio de Janeiro). December 25, 1918.

Seth (Álvaro Marins)

5581. "Faleceu o Caricaturista Seth." *A Noite* (Rio de Janeiro). January 29, 1949.

5582. Gill, Ruben. "O Século Boêmio." *Dom Casmurro* (Rio de Janeiro). December 26, 1942.

5583. Seth (Álvaro Marins). "Nas Asas da Memória. Viagem de um Artista em Torno de Si Mesmo." *Gazeta de Notícias* (Rio de Janeiro). August-October 1947.

5584. Seth (Álvaro Marins). *O Brasil Pela Imagem.* Rio de Janeiro: Indústria do Livro Ltda., 1943.

Silva, Nestor

5585. Andrade, Gilberto Osório. "Elogio da Sensibilidade." *Jornal do Comércio* (Recife). June 22, 1941.

5586. "Arte Pernambucana no Salão Nacional de 1941." *Diário de Manhã* (Recife). November 6, 1941.

5587. Campelo, José. "A Significação da Arte de Nestor Silva." *Jornal do Comércio* (Recife). June 15, 1941.

5588. Lopes, Silvino. "Um Artista." *Diário da Manhã* (Recife). February 11, 1942.

5589. "Nestor Silva." *A Noite* (Rio de Janeiro). June 3, 1941.

5590. "Nestor Silva." *Diário da Manhã* (Recife). June 1, 3, 1941.

5591. Teixeira, Luís. "Luz e Sombra." *Meio-Dia* (Rio de Janeiro). February 12, 1942.

5592. Varejão, Lucilo. "Nestor Silva." In *Figura e Paisagem.* Recife: n.p., 1956.

Storni

5593. Gill, Ruben. "O Século Boêmio." *Dom Casmurro* (Rio de Janeiro). February 5, 1943.

5594. Lima, Herman. "Storni, Artilheiro Político do Lápis." *Rio Magazine.* April 1952.

Theo

5595. Lima, Herman. "Theo e os Seus Bonecos de Carne e Osso." *Rio-Magazine.* July 1950.

5596. Theo (Djalma Pires Ferreira). *A Bola do Dia. Charges* publicadas no *Globo.* Rio de Janeiro: Published by author, 1945.

5597. Theo. *Na Berlinda.* Rio de Janeiro: Editôra Civilização Brasileira, S. A., 1947.

Vasco (Vasco Lima)

5598. Canalini, Sabino. "Cinqüenta Anos de Jornalismo." *Revista da Semana* (Rio de Janeiro). October 1944.

5599. Gill, Ruben. "O Século Boêmio." *Dom Casmurro* (Rio de Janeiro). May 22, 1943.

5600. Lima, Herman. "O Caricaturista Vasco Lima, Homem de Imprensa Integral." *Diário de Notícias* (Rio de Janeiro). December 5, 1954.

5601. Martins, Guimarães and Byron de Freitas. "Vasco Lima." *Dom Casmurro* (Rio de Janeiro). February 13, 1943.

5602. "Meio Século de Imprensa. Jubileu de Vasco Lima." *Diário da Noite* (Rio de Janeiro). October 17, 1944.

Voltolino (Lemmo Lemmi)

5603. de Almeida, Guilherme. "Eco ao Longo dos Meus Passos." *O Estado de São Paulo*. September 20, 1958.

5604. de Almeida, Guilherme. "Voltolino." *O Estado de São Paulo*. September 20, 1957.

5605. Gill, Ruben. "O Século Boêmio." *Dom Casmurro* (Rio de Janeiro). March 27, 1943.

5606. "Lemmo Lemmi, Voltolino, o Grande Esquecido." *A Gazeta* (São Paulo). January 10, 1958.

5607. Lima, Herman. "Um Grande do Lápis Bandeirante." *Rio-Magazine*. January 1950.

5608. Machado, Antônio de Alcântara. "Voltolino." *Cavaquinho e Saxofone*. Rio de Janeiro: Livraria José Olympio Editôra, 1940.

5609. N. "A Caricatura." (Exposition of Voltolino). *Revista do Brasil* (São Paulo). April 1916.

5610. Schmidt, Afonso. "Voltolino." *Paulistana* (São Paulo). March-April 1949.

5611. "Voltolino." *Gazeta Magazine* (São Paulo). January 4, 1942.

5612. "Voltolino." *Vamos Ler!* (Rio de Janeiro). January 29, 1948.

Weber, Hilde

5613. Gullar, Ferreira. "Hilde." *Jornal do Brasil* (Rio de Janeiro). November 18, 1956.

5614. Miranda, Macedo. "Hilde." In *Catálogo da Exposição da Artista*, Galeria do IBEU.

Yantok (Max Cesarino)

5615. Augusto, Sergio. "O Velho Toque de Max Yantok." *Jornal do Brasil* (Rio de Janeiro). February 9, 1968.

5616. Gill, Ruben. "O Século Boêmio." *Dom Casmurro* (Rio de Janeiro). January 23, 1943.

5617. Lima, Herman. "Yantok." *Rio Magazine*. July 1952.

5618. Lima, Herman. "Yantok. Os Mestres do Lápis Brasileiro." *O Jornal* (Rio de Janeiro). January 20, 1952.

5619. Silveira, Joel. "Vendedores de Humor." *Diretrizes* (Rio de Janeiro). June 21, 1941.

5620. "Três Caricaturistas da Velha Guarda: Yantok, Loureiro e Storni." *Revista da Semana* (Rio de Janeiro). March 31, 1945.

5621. Yantok (Max Cesarino). "Autobonecografia." *Dom Quixote* (Rio de Janeiro). December 25, 1918.

Ziraldo (Alves Pinto)

5622. Castañeda, Mireya. "Artist, Singular and Plural." *Granma International*. May 5, 1991, p. 9.

5623. Foster, David W. "Disjunctive Strategies in Ziraldo's Cartoons: *Jeremias, o Bom.*" Unpublished paper.

5624. Ziraldo, (Alves Pinto). *A Última do Brasileiro: Quatro Años de História Nos Charges do Jornal do Brasil*. Rio de Janeiro: Codecri, 1975.

5625. Ziraldo (Alves Pinto). *Jeremias, o Bom*. Rio de Janeiro/São Paulo: Expressão e Cultura, 1969.

Animation

5626. Alvarus (Álvaro Cotrim). "Grove." *A Noite* (Rio de Janeiro). May 22, 1957.

5627. Moreno, Antonio. *A Experiencia Brasileira no Cinema de Animação.* Rio de Janeiro: Artenova/Embrafilme, 1978. 127 pp.

Caricature, Cartooning

5628. Alvarus (Álvaro Cotrim). "A Caricatura e o Teatro." Conferência na A. B. I. *Boletim da S. B. A. T.* (Rio de Janeiro). January-February 1954.

5629. Alvarus (Álvaro Cotrim). *A Caricatura no Brasil.* Conference held in Instituto Peruano-Brasileiro, Lima, Peru, November 14, 1957.

5630. Amoroso Neto, João. "Diabo Coxo." *Boletim Municipal* (São Paulo). 11(1948).

5631. Auler, Guilherme. "A Revista *Horas Vagas.*" *Jornal do Brasil* (Rio de Janeiro). April 13, 1958.

5632. Azevedo, Fernando. "Caricatura e Desenho Humorístico." In *A Cultura Brasileira.* São Paulo: Edições Melhoramentos, 1959. 3rd Ed.

5633. Baciu, Stefan. "Bons Tempos de Outrora." *Diário Carioca* (Rio de Janeiro). August 1, 1954.

5634. Barroso, Gustavo. "A Caricatura Inglêsa no Museu Histórico." *Anais do Museu Histórico Nacional.* Rio de Janeiro: Ministério da Educação e Saúde, 1941.

5635. Borba, Osório. "O Grande Jota." *Diário de Notícias* (Rio de Janeiro). June 24, 1951.

5636. Borges, Roberto. "O Rio de Janeiro Que Não Foi do Meu Tempo." *Dom Casmurro* (Rio de Janeiro). December 23, 1941.

5637. Campanela Neto, F. "O Homem Que Insiste e Não Desiste de Usar Fraque." *A Noite Ilustrada* (Rio de Janeiro). August 24, 1954.

5638. "Caricaturas." *Anhembi* (São Paulo). April 1955.

5639. "Caricaturas de Outrora Profetizavam os Inventos Modernos, As." *Eu Sei Tudo* (Rio de Janeiro). February 1943.

5640. "Caricaturas e Medicina." *Revista Roche* (Rio de Janeiro). July to October 1953.

5641. Carreno, Francisco. "A Arte Social e a Caricatura." *Leitura* (Rio de Janeiro). June 1943.

5642. C. D. A. (Carlos Drummond de Andrade). "Tudo é Caricatura." *Correio da Manhã* (Rio de Janeiro). July 25, 1954.

5643. Ciarla, Lêda. "A Arte da Caricatura." *Revista ABD* (Rio de Janeiro). March-April 1950.

5644. Couto, Ribeiro. "Confissões de um Bárbaro Arrependido." *Revista da Semana* (Rio de Janeiro). December 19, 1942.

5645. Damasceno, Athos. "A Lente." *Correio do Povo* (Pôrto Alegre). March 27 and April 4, 1959.

5646. Damasceno, Athos. "Artes Plásticas no Rio Grande do Sul." *Correio do Povo* (Pôrto Alegre). November 1, 1958.

5647. Damasceno, Athos. "Artes Plásticas no Rio Grande do Sul." *Correio do Povo* (Pôrto Alegre). April 11 and May 1, 1959.

5648. Damasceno, Athos. "O Figaro." *Correio do Povo* (Pôrto Alegre). June 28, July 5, 12, 19, 1958.

5649. Damasceno, Athos. "Periódicos Críticos e Ilustrados do Rio Grande do Sul. O Chargista Tadeo Amorim." *Correio do Povo* (Pôrto Alegre). Series of 4 articles, May 3, 10, 17, 24, 1958.

5650. Dantas, Raimundo Sousa. "A Caricatura Não é um Nariz Apenas." *Vamos Ler!* (Rio de Janeiro). October 30, 1941.

5651. de Andrade, Gilberto Osório. *A Cólera-Morbo. Um Momento Crítico da Medicina em Pernambuco.* Recife: Secretaria da Educação, "Cadernos de Pernambuco," 1956.

5652. "Defesa e Elogio da Caricatura." *Vida Doméstica* (Rio de Janeiro). November 1938.

5653. de Oliveira, Cordeiro. "A Reportagem Que Eu Não Escrevi." *Correio da Manhã* (Rio de Janeiro). February 17, 1957.

5654. de Sousa, J. A. Soares. "Vasconcelos e as Caricaturas." *Revista do Instituto Histórico e Geográfico Brasileiro* (Rio de Janeiro). January-March 1951.

5655. de Sousa, Otávio Tarquínio. "Uma Tradição Brasileira." *Correio da Manhã* (Rio de Janeiro). April 15, 1945.

5656. Diniz, Oscar. *Flagrantes Lusos. Desenhos e Sátiras.* Rio de Janeiro: Author, 1928.

5657. dos Santos, Francisco Marques. "As Belas-Artes na Regência." *Estudos Brasileiros* (Rio de Janeiro). July-December 1942.

5658. Duque, Gonzaga. *A Arte Brasileira*. Pintores e Escultores. Rio de Janeiro: Impr. H. Lombaerts, 1888.

5659. Duque, Gonzaga. "Comentando uma Conferência." *Diário de Notícias* (Rio de Janeiro). July 24, 1955.

5660. Duque, Gonzaga. "Os Pintores do Grosseiro." *Kosmos* (Rio de Janeiro). January 1955.

5661. Eneida. "Comentando uma Conferência." *Diário de Notícias* (Rio de Janeiro). July 24, 1955.

5662. Figueiredo, Sílvio. *Quixote*. Rio de Janeiro: Published by author, 1934.

5663. Fleiuss, Max. "Meu Pai." *Recordando. Cenas e Perfis*. Supplement. *Rev. do I. H.G. Brasileiro*. (Rio de Janeiro). 1941.

5664. "Fôrça Expressiva da Caricatura, A." *Correio da Manhã* (Rio de Janeiro). December 31, 1945.

5665. Garibaldi, Sadi. "A Caricatura no Brasil de Ontem." *Vamos Ler!* (Rio de Janeiro). July 11, 1940.

5666. Gill, Ruben. "A Caricatura Contemporânea." *Dom Casmurro* (Rio de Janeiro). Natal number, 1942.

5667. Gill, Ruben. "A Caricatura Mundana." *Vamos Ler!* (Rio de Janeiro). December 25, 1941.

5668. Gill, Ruben. "O Rio de Janeiro Que Não Foi do Meu Tempo." *Dom Casmurro* (Rio de Janeiro). December 23, 1941.

5669. Gill, Ruben. "O Século Boêmio." *Dom Casmurro* (Rio de Janeiro). February 27, 1943.

5670. Gomes, Raul. "Caricatura." *Correio da Manhã* (Rio de Janeiro). September 17, 1953.

5671. "Guerra Não Muda...na Caricatura, A." *Vamos Ler!* (Rio de Janeiro). June 8, 1944.

5672. Lima, Herman. "A Beleza, o Tempo e a Moda." *Rio Magazine*. July 1948.

5673. Lima, Herman. "A Caricatura, Arte Anciã e Sempre Nova." *Revista ABD* (Rio de Janeiro). January-April 1952.

5674. Lima, Herman. "A Caricatura e os Antigos." *Vamos Ler!* (Rio de Janeiro). February 1, 1945.

5675. Lima, Herman. "A Caricatura na Antiguidade." *Vamos Ler!* (Rio de Janeiro). January 18, 1945.

5676. Lima, Herman. "A Caricatura na Imprensa Carioca." Relação dos Periódicos Ilustrados com Caricaturas, no Brasil. *Diário de Notícias* (Rio de Janeiro). January 1, 1955.

5677. Lima, Herman. "A Caricatura no Império." *Rio Magazine.* March 1949.

5678. Lima, Herman. "A Caricatura Nos Salões Cariocas." *Rio Magazine.* April, May 1944.

5679. Lima, Herman. "A Caricatura Vendo os Costumes Cariocas." *Coletânea* (Rio de Janeiro). June 1958.

5680. Lima, Herman. "A Mulher, a Moda e a Caricatura." *Rio Magazine.* March 1948.

5681. Lima, Herman. "Análise Espectral da Caricatura." *Revista Brasileira* (Rio de Janeiro). July-December 1958 and January-June 1959.

5682. Lima, Herman. "Caricatura. Conceito e Considerações Gerais." *A Tarde* (Salvador). April 22, 1954.

5683. Lima, Herman. "Curiosidades da Imprensa Brasileira." *A Noite Ilustrada* (Rio de Janeiro). October 26, 1954.

5684. Lima, Herman. "Humoristas do Lápis e da Pena." *Jornal do Brasil* (Rio de Janeiro). December 29, 1957 and January 5, 1958.

5685. Lima, Herman. "O Rio de Janeiro e a Caricatura." *Para Todos* (Rio de Janeiro). September 15, 1957.

5686. Lima, Herman. *O Rio de Janeiro na Caricatura.* Conferência no Salão Nobre da Câmara Municipal do Rio de Janeiro, September 12, 1953.

5687. Lima, Herman. "O Sentido do Trágico e do Grotesco na Antiguidade." *Vamos Ler!* (Rio de Janeiro). February 8, 1945.

5688. Lima, Herman. "O Sete de Abril e a Caricatura." *Diário de Notícias* (Rio de Janeiro). November 22, 1953.

5689. Lima, Herman. "Senhores Congressistas, Não Matem a Caricatura!" *O Globo* (Rio de Janeiro). June 17, 1948.

5690. Lubbers, Frits. "Fen Zwitsers Sprookje." *Sick.* No. 22/23, 1991, pp. 28-29.

5691. Magalháes Júnior, R. "A Caricatura nos Museus." *Diário de Notícias* (Rio de Janeiro). September 6, 1952. (Reprinted in *Europa 52*. Rio de Janeiro: Livraria José Olympio Editôra, 1953).

5692. Magalháes Júnior, R. "A Caricatura Também Faz Blitzkrieg." *Vamos Ler!* (Rio de Janeiro). January 28, 1943.

5693. Magalháes Júnior, R. "Um Homem Que Faz Graças." (Vão Gogo). *Diário de Notícias* (Rio de Janeiro). August 1, 1956.

5694. Meyer, Augusto. "O Caruncho." *Correio da Manhã* (Rio de Janeiro). July 14, 1956.

5695. "O Outro Lado do Riso." *Visão* (Rio de Janeiro). September 16, 1955.

5696. *O Rio na Caricatura*. Rio de Janeiro: Biblioteca Nacional/Jornal do Brasil, 1965.

5697. Paraguaçu, João. "O Fardão." *Correio da Manhã* (Rio de Janeiro). June 12, 1949.

5698. Péricles. *O Amigo da Onça*. Rio de Janeiro: Edições *O Cruzeiro*, 1946.

5699. Ribeiro, Emanuel. *Considerações Sôbre a Arte da Caricatura*. Pôrto: Author, n.d.

5700. Rocha, Luís. "A Divina Dama da Voz de Ouro. Sarah Bernhardt Vista Pelo Lápis dos Grandes Caricaturistas Mundiais." *Vamos Ler!* (Rio de Janeiro). October 26, 1944.

5701. Roitman, Maurício. "Um Século de Caricatura no Brasil." *Revista do Globo* (Pôrto Alegre). November 27, 1945.

5702. Rosa, Santa. "Sôbre a Arte da Ilustração." *Roteiro de Arte*, Cadernos de Cultura. Rio de Janeiro: Ministério da Educação e Saúde, Serviço de Documentação, 1952.

5703. Santone, Adolfo. "La Caricatura en la Prensa del Rio de Janeiro." *Tribuna* (Rosário, Argentina). September 19, 1954.

5704. Teixeira, Floriano Bicudo. "A Gravura no Brasil." *Política e Letras* (Rio de Janeiro). July 22, 1948.

5705. Terra de Sena. "Nos Tempos Áureos do *Tagarela*." *Vamos Ler!* (Rio de Janeiro). October 26, 1944.

5706. Terra de Sena. "Os Evadidos da Caricatura." *Vamos Ler!* (Rio de Janeiro). October 12, 1944.

5707. Wilson, Carlos. "A Caricatura como Antídoto do Veneno Literário." *Mundo Ilustrado* (Rio de Janeiro). February 5, 1931.

Anthologies

5708. Augusto, Sergio. "Uma Antologia Que Nao e Obra-Prima." *Jornal do Brasil*. July 7, 1967.

5709. Brentani, Gerda. *Atrás da Fachada*. Caricaturas. Preface by Sérgio Milliet. São Paulo: Habitat Editôra Ltda., 1955.

5710. Caruso, Chico. *Chico. Nova República. Novo Testamento*. São Paulo: Circo Editorial, 1987. 159 pp.

5711. Fossai, Donnyos. *Antología Brasileira de Humor*. Pôrto Alegre, Brazil: Editora Pôrto Alegre, 1976.

5712. Gê, Luis. *Os Anos 77-80 nas Charges*. São Paulo: T. A. Queiroz, 1981.

5713. Jaguar y Fortunas, Claudius. *¿Hoy Gobierno?* Rio de Janeiro: Civilização Brasileira, 1964.

Historical Aspects

5714. Albuquerque, Medeiros, E. "As Memórias d'*O Malho*." *O Malho* (Rio de Janeiro). August 17, 1933.

5715. Alvarus (Álvaro Cotrim). "A Caricatura Também é História." *A Noite* (Rio de Janeiro). July 30, 1951.

5716. Alves, Constâncio. "A Caricatura no Segundo Império." *Revista da Semana* (Rio de Janeiro). December 30, 1922 and January 6, 1923.

5717. Armand, Abel. "A Caricatura Alemã na Guerra de 1914-18." *Vamos Ler!* (Rio de Janeiro). February 11, 1945.

5718. "Caricatura, A." *L'Iride Italiana* (Rio de Janeiro). October 4, 1855.

5719. "Caricature au Brésil, La." *L'Argus* (Rio de Janeiro). March 3, 1838.

5720. Costa, Licurgo and Barros Vidal. *História e Evolução da Imprensa Brasileira*. Rio de Janeiro: 1940.

5721. da Fonseca, Gondim. *Biografia do Jornalismo Carioca. 1808-1908*. Rio de Janeiro: Quaresma Editôra, 1941.

5722. Damasceno, Athos. *Imprensa Caricata no Rio Grande do Sul no Século XIX*. Pôrto Alegre: Editôra Globo, 1962.

5723. Damasceno, Athos. *Jornais Críticos e Humorísticos de Pôrto Alegre no Século XIX.* Pôrto Alegre: Livraria do Globo, 1944.

5724. da Silva, H. Pereira. "Artistas de Ontem e de Hoje. Uma História da Caricatura." *Carioca* (Rio de Janeiro). Januray 13, 1951.

5725. da Silva, Osvaldo P. *Gravuras e Gravadores em Madeira. Origem, Evolução e Técnica da Xilografia.* Rio de Janeiro: Imprensa Nacional, 1941.

5726. de Morais, Evaristo. *A Campanha Abolicionista (1879-1888).* Rio de Janeiro: Leite Ribeiro, 1924.

5727. "Doença na Arte e na Caricatura, A." *O País* (Rio de Janeiro). May 21, 1906.

5728. Duque, Gonzaga. "A Caricatura no Brasil. Os Caricaturistas de Costumes." In *Contemporâneos.* Rio de Janeiro: Tip. Benedito Sousa, 1929.

5729. Eneida. "História da Caricatura no Brasil." *Diário de Notícias* (Rio de Janeiro). December 28, 1958.

5730. *Exposição Comemorativa do 1.º Centenário da Imprensa Periódica no Brasil, Promovida Pelo I. H. G. Brasileiro. Rev. do I. H. G. Bras.* Rio de Janeiro: 1908. 2 Vols.

5731. Ferraz, Áidano do Couto. "História da Caricatura no Brasil." *Diretrizes* (Rio de Janeiro). May 8, 1941.

5732. Fleiuss, Max. "A Caricatura no Brasil." *Rev. do I. H. G. Brasileiro* (Rio de Janeiro). Tomo 80, Vol. 134, 1917.

5733. Guimaraes, Argeu. "As Artes Plásticas no Brasil." In *Dicionário Histórico, Geográfico e Etnográfico do Brasil. (História Artística).* Rio de Janeiro: Impr. Nacional, 1922.

5734. Lima, Herman. *A Caricatura, Arma Secreta da Liberdade.* Rio de Janeiro: Ministério da Educação e Saúde, Serviço de Documentação, 1949.

5735. Lima, Herman. "A Caricatura, Arma Secreta da Liberdade." *Vamos Ler!* (Rio de Janeiro). December 28, 1944.

5736. Lima, Herman. *A Caricatura, Arte Subsidiária da História e da Sociologia.* Five conferences held at Universidade de Bahia, April 1954.

5737. Lima, Herman. "A Caricatura Brasileira tem Cem Anos." *Vamos Ler!* (Rio de Janeiro). December 21, 1944.

5738. Lima, Herman. *História da Caricatura no Brasil.* Rio de Janeiro: Livraria José Olympio Editôra, 1963. 4 Vols. 1,796 pp.

5739. Lima, Herman. "Nasce a Caricatura no Brasil." *Diário de Notícias* (Rio de Janeiro). November 8, 1953.

5740. Lima, Herman. "Nascimento da Caricatura no Brasil." *Diário de Notícias* (Rio de Janeiro). November 15, 1953.

5741. Lima, Herman. "Origens da Sátira Política no Brasil." *Revista do Livro* (Rio de Janeiro, Ministério da Educação e Cultura, Instituto Nacional do Livro), December 1958.

5742. Lima, Herman. "Rio, 1904-14." *Rio Magazine*. October 1948.

5743. Lima, Herman. "Zé Pereira Faz Cem Anos." *Rio Magazine*. March 1952.

5744. Lys, Edmundo. "O Centenário da Caricatura." *O Globo* (Rio de Janeiro). October 17, 1944.

5745. Magalháes Júnior, R. "A Caricatura como Documento Histórico." *Diário de Notícias* (Rio de Janeiro). May 30, 1950.

5746. Milliet, Sérgio. *Marginalidade de Pintura Moderna, in A Evolução Social da Pintura*. São Paulo: Departamento de Cultura, 1942. Vol. 28.

5747. Passos, Alexandre. *A Imprensa no Período Colonial*. Rio de Janeiro: Ministério da Educação e Saúde, Serviço de Documentação, Cadernos de Cultura, 1952.

5748. "Representação Caricatural do Brasil." *Fon-Fon!* (Rio de Janeiro). April 14, 1908.

5749. Rizzini, Carlos. *O Livro, o Jornal e a Tipografia no Brasil. 1500-1822. Com um Breve Estudo Geral Sôbre a Informação*. Rio de Janeiro: Livraria Kosmos Editôra, 1945.

5750. Rubens, Carlos. *Impressões de Arte*. Rio de Janeiro: Tip. do *Jornal do Comércio*, 1921.

5751. Rubens, Carlos. *Pequena História das Artes Plásticas no Brasil*. São Paulo: Cia. Editôra Nacional, 1941.

5752. Sgarbi, Otávio. "Introdução à História da Caricatura Brasileira." *Anuário da Imprensa Brasileira*. Rio de Janeiro: D. I. P., 1942.

5753. Silveira, Joel. "Vendedores de Humor. A História Pouco Alegre dos Humoristas Brasileiros. Entrevista com Raul, K. Lixto e Yantok." *Diretrizes* (Rio de Janeiro). June 26, 1941. Reprinted in *Os Homens Não Falam Demais....*Rio de Janeiro: Alba Editôra, 1942.

5754. Simões, Nuno. *Gente Risonha. Palavras Sôbre a Caricatura.* Pôrto Alegre: n.p., 1915.

5755. Sinzig, Frei Pedro. *A Caricatura na Imprensa Brasileira. Contribuição para um Estudo Histórico-Social.* Petrópolis: Tip. das Vozes de Petrópolis, 1911.

5756. Storni, Alfredo. "A Caricatura no Brasil." *Almanaque d'"O Malho.".* Rio de Janeiro: 1913.

5757. Teixeira, Floriano Bicudo. "Primeiras Manifestaçoes da Gravura no Brasil." In *A Biblioteca.* Publicação da Biblioteca do DASP. Rio de Janeiro: Vol 3, Nos. 1, 2, January-February 1946.

5758. Terra de Sena (Lauro Carmeliano Pereira Nunes). "O Espírito da Caricatura." *Correio da Manhã* (Rio de Janeiro). September 24, 1933.

5759. Viana, Ernesto da Cunha Araújo. "Das Artes Plásticas no Brasil em Geral e no Rio de Janeiro em Particular." *Revista do Instituto Histórico e Geográfico Brasileiro* (Rio de Janeiro). Tomo 78, Vol. 132, 1915.

5760. Viana, Hélio. *Contribuição à História da Imprensa Brasileira (1812-1869).* Rio de Janeiro: Ministério da Educação e Saúde, Instituto Nacional do Livro, 1946.

Historical Aspects: Careta

5761. "*Careta*: 50 Anos de História do Brasil." *PN* (Rio de Janeiro). October 13, 1958.

5762. Lima, Herman. "Meio Século de um Jornal do Riso e da Sátira." *Jornal do Brasil* (Rio de Janeiro). June 15, 1958.

5763. Magalháes Júnior, R. "O Drama de um Jornal Que Faz Rir." *A Noite* (Rio de Janeiro). November 28, 1945.

Historical Aspects: Charge

5764. Lima, Herman. "O Teatro e a *Charge*." *Rio Magazine.* July 1949.

5765. Lima, Herman. "O Verão e a *Charge*." *Rio Magazine.* January 1951.

5766. Lima, Herman. "Uma *Charge* Famosa." *Rio Magazine.* February 1951.

Historical Aspects: O Tico-Tico

5767. Cavalcanti, Valdemar. "Um Cinqüentenário (of *O Tico-Tico*)." *O Jornal* (Rio de Janeiro). October 16, 1955.

5768. C.D.A. (Carlos Drummond de Andradea). "Um Passarinho" (O Cinqüentenário de *O Tico-Tico*). *Correio da Manhã* (Rio de Janeiro). October 9, 1955.

5769. Duque, Gonzaga. "O Tico-Tico." *Diário de Notícias* (Rio de Janeiro). October 16, 1955.

5770. Freyre, Gilberto. "O Tico-Tico." *O Jornal* (Rio de Janeiro). October 25, 1955.

5771. Lôbo, Flávia da Silveira. "Virar Criança de Nôvo" (Propósito do Cinqüentenário de *O Tico-Tico*). *Correio da Manhã* (Rio de Janeiro). December 8, 1955.

Comic Books

5772. "A Bienal Val Exibir Historia em Quadrinhos." *O Estado de São Paulo*. September 29, 1965.

5773. André, A. "World Menace in Brazil." *Américas*. February 1955, p. 39.

5774. Augusto, Sergio. "A Moda de Muitos Anos." *Jornal do Brasil* (Rio de Janeiro). March 17, 1967.

5775. Augusto, Sergio. "As Bandas Francesas." *Jornal do Brasil* (Rio de Janeiro). March 3, 1967.

5776. Augusto, Sergio. "As Criancas de Verdade." *Jornal do Brasil* (Rio de Janeiro). April 14, 1967.

5777. Augusto, Sergio. "As Relacoes Perigosas Sob o Balaozinho." *Jornal do Brasil* (Rio de Janeiro). August 4, 1967.

5778. Augusto, Sergio. "LBJ Vai de Super." *Jornal do Brasil* (Rio de Janeiro). November 22, 1967.

5779. Augusto, Sergio. "O Americano Tranquilo de Cachimbo na Bôca." *Jornal do Brasil*. July 14, 1967.

5780. Augusto, Sergio. "O Bom Espirito do Espirito." *Jornal do Brasil* (Rio de Janeiro). May 12, 1967.

5781. Augusto, Sergio. "O Dia da Maria Cebola." *Jornal do Brasil* (Rio de Janeiro). November 17, 1967.

5782. Augusto, Sergio. "Os Demonios de Milao." *Jornal do Brasil* (Rio de Janeiro). March 8, 1968.

5783. Augusto, Sergio. "Quadrinho è Coisa Cada Vez Mais Séria." *Visao* (São Paulo). March 4, 1966.

5784. Augusto, Sergio. "Um Gibi Marginal na Base do Suspiro." *Jornal do Brasil* (Rio de Janeiro). March 1, 1968.

5785. Caceres, Germán. "Quadrinhos Versus Comics (La Historieta en Brasil)." In *Asi Se Lee la Historieta*, pp. 29-33. Buenos Aires: Beas Ediciones, 1994.

5786. Cagnin, Antônio Luiz. *Os Quadrinhos*. São Paulo: Editora Ática, 1975.

5787. Calazans, Flavio. "O Poder do Riso." *Leopoldianum*. April 1991, pp. 75-80.

5788. Cirne, Moacy. *A Linguagem dos Quadrinhos*. Petrópolos: Editôra Vozes, 1971.

5789. Cirne, Moacy. "Os Novos Quadrinhos Brasileiros (New Brazilian Comics)." *Revista de Cultura Vozes* (Petrópolis). September 1973, pp. 65-68.

5790. Cirne, Moacy. *Para Ler os Quadrinhos: Da Narrativa Cinematográfica à Narrativa Quadrinizada* (How To Read the Funnies). Petrópolis: Editôra Vozes, 1972.

5791. Cirne, Moacy. *Vanguarda: Um Projeto Semiológico*. Petrópolis: Editôra Vozes, 1975.

5792. Conça, Paulo. "Quadrinhos: A Arte de Ler." *Boletim de HQ*. May-June 1992, p. 4.

5793. Cortez, Jayme. *A Tecnica do Desenho*. São Paulo: Ind. Gráfica Bentivegna Editora Ltda., 1965. 200 pp.

5794. Cortez, Jayme. *Mestres da Ilustração*. São Paulo: Hemus-Livraria e Editôres, 1970.

5795. Del Picchia, Menotti. "Vitória dos Quadrinhos." *A Gazeta* (São Paulo). January 3, 1955.

5796. de Moya, Alvaro. "Comics in Brazil." *Studies in Latin American Popular Culture*. 7 (1988), pp. 227-239.

5797. "Domingo Pace Triunfa en Brasil." *Dibujantes* (Buenos Aires). No. 9, 1954, p. 22.

5798. Imaguire, Key, Jr. "I Fumetti in Brasile." *Il Fumetto*. November 1973, pp. 39-41.

5799. Junior, Zoe. *Vorwort zu "A Tecnica de Desenho."* São Paulo: Bentivegna Editora, 1965.

5800. Lopes, Irasson. "O Poder das HQs." *Boletim de HQ*. October 1991, p. 2.

5801. Pierce, John G. "Comics in Brasil." *Comics Buyer's Guide*. June 29, 1984, pp. 20, 24.

5802. "Quadrinhos e Ideologia." Entire issue. *Revista de Cultura Vozes* (Petrópolis). September 1973.

5803. Silva, Renato. *A Arte de Desenhar*. Rio de Janeiro: Editôra Conquista, 1957.

5804. Thomasz, Aylton. *Desenho Comico*. São Paulo: Editôra Bentivegna, 1971.

5805. Vieira, José G. "Fola de São Paulo." *O Estado de São Paulo*. April 30, 1965.

Business Aspects

5806. de Moya, Álvaro. "O Fascínio dos Quadrinhos na Bienal Internacional do Rio." *Abigraf*. November-December 1991, pp. 66-69.

5807. Zimbres, Fabio. "Brazilian Comics Creators Find Conditions Slowly Improving for Original Material." *Comics Journal*. December 1991, pp. 31-32.

5808. Zimbres, Fabio. "Economy Zaps Brazilian Comics." *Comics Journal*. February 1993, pp. 39-40.

5809. Zimbres, Fabio. "Rio de Janeiro Comics Biennial '93." *Comics Journal*. February 1994, pp. 47-48.

Culture and Education

5810. Augusto, Sergio. "A Cultura Horizontal." *Jornal do Brasil*. February 6, 1966.

5811. Augusto, Sergio. "A Tentacao dos Quadrinhos." *Jornal do Brasil* (Rio de Janeiro). January 13, 1967.

5812. Augusto, Sergio. "Uma Cultura Fechada." *Jornal do Brasil* (Rio de Janeiro). May 26, 1967.

5813. Conocer Nuestro Tiempo. No. 4. *Las Historietas: Una Nueva Forma de Comunicación*. São Paulo: Abril, S. A. Cultural e Industrial, 1973.

Genres

5814. Augusto, Sergio. "A Visao Russa do Superhomem." *Jornal do Brasil* (Rio de Janeiro). December 29, 1967.

5815. Augusto, Sergio. "O Aposentado Cowboy de Cabelos de Fogo." *Jornal do Brasil* (Rio de Janeiro). October 20, 1967.

5816. Augusto, Sergio. "Os Fantasticos Musculosos." *Jornal do Brasil* (Rio de Janeiro). Spring 1967.

5817. Augusto, Sergio. "Os Hérois Estao Cansados." *Jornal do Brasil* (Rio de Janeiro). April 20, 1967.

5818. Augusto, Sergio. "O Velho Fanatismo." *Jornal do Brasil* (Rio de Janeiro). January 20, 1967.

5819. Augusto, Sergio. "Um Héroi Sem Aquêle Algo Mais." *Jornal do Brasil* (Rio de Janeiro). July 28, 1967.

5820. "Bamba: as Mais Belas Historias de Heroismo." *A Imprensa* (São Paulo). No. 22, 1951, p. 2.

5821. "Brazilian Classics Update." *The Classics Collector.* February-March 1990, p. 12.

5822. Calisi, Romano. "L'Avventurosa Storia dei Fumetti Brasiliani." *Comics, Archivio Italiano della Stampa a Fumetti* (Rome). September 1966, pp. 15-21.

5823. Hylio. "Músicae Quadrinhos." *Boletim de HQ.* January-February 1992, pp. 5-6.

5824. Lins do Rego, José. "Romances em Quadrinhos." *O Globo* (Rio de Janeiro). 1967.

5825. Various Authors. "O Mundo dos Super Herois." *Vozes.* No. 4, 1971.

Histórias

5826. Anselmo, Zilda Augusta. *Histórias em Quadrinhos.* Petrópolis: Editôra Vozes, 1975.

5827. Augusto, Sergio. *A Evolução da Historia em Quadrinhos.* Rio de Janeiro: Museo de Arte Moderna, 1967.

5828. "Como Se Faz Historia em Quadrinhos." *O Tempo* (São Paulo). Supplement. March 23, 1952.

5829. de Castro Santos Vergueiro, Waldomiro. "A ECA e as Histórias em Quadrinhos." *Comunicacoes e Artes.* May 1992, p. 27.

5830. De Moya, Alvaro. "Brésil." In *Histoire Mondiale de la Bande Dessinée*, edited by Pierre Horay, pp. 264-267. Paris: Pierre Horay Éditeur, 1989.

5831. Freyre, Gilberto. "Ainda as Historias em Quadrinhos." *O Cruzeiro* (São Paulo). 1967.

5832. Freyre, Gilberto. "A Proposito de Historias em Quadrinhos." *O Cruzeiro* (São Paulo). 1967.

5833. Freyre, Gilberto. "Historias em Quadrinhos." *O Cruzeiro* (São Paulo). 1967.

5834. Katz, Chaim Samuel. "Ideologia e Centro Mas Histórias em Quadrinhos." *Revista de Cultura* (Petrópolis). September 1973, pp. 5-20.

5835. Lipszyc, Enrique. "Publicações Brasileiras de Histórias em Quadrinhos." In *Catálogo da Exposição Internacional de História em Quadrinhos*. São Paulo: 1970.

5836. Morato, Cláudio. "Ecologia e as Histórias em Quadrinhos." *Boletim de HQ*. May-June 1992, p. 9.

5837. Silveira de Queiroz, Dinah. "Aizen, o Pequeno Imperador." *Jornal do Comercio* (Rio de Janeiro). January 5, 1955.

Titles

5838. Augusto, Sergio. "Jodelle Veio, Viu e Vencen." *Jornal do Brasil*. September 29, 1967.

5839. Augusto, Sergio. "Tarza o Homem e o Mito. (I) A Atualidade do Faz de Conta; (II) O Pai do Homem-macaco; (III) No Principio Foi o Berro; (IV) As Chaves do Reino; (V) As Faces do Homem-macaco." *Jornal do Brasil*. January 4, 5, 6, 7, 9, 1966.

5840. Cirne, Moacy. *Bum! A Explosão Criativa dos Quadrinhos*. 4th Ed. Petrópolis: Editôra Vozes, 1974. 1st Ed., 1970.

5841. de Aquino, José Jefferson Barbosa. "The Saga of the Original Marvel Family in Brazil." *FCA S.O.B.* April 1980, p. 3.

5842. de Moya, Alvaro, ed. *Shazam!* São Paulo: Editôra Perspectiva, 1970, 1972.

5843. Horn, Maurice. "Raymondo o Cangaceiro (Brasile)." In *Enciclopedia Mondiale del Fumetto*, edited by Maurice Horn and Luciano Secchi, pp. 647-648. Milan: Editoriale Corno, 1978.

5844. Nanci. "Amazônia em Chamas." *Boletim de HQ*. May-June 1992, p. 9.

5845. Pierce, John. "Captain Marvel Meets the Human Torch?" *Amazing Heroes*. June 15, 1984, pp. 50, 52-54, 56.

Comic Strips

5846. Augusto, Sergio. "O Protesta de Al Capp." *Jornal do Brasil* (Rio de Janeiro). January 27, 1967.

5847. Ramos, Luciano. "Comics Made in Brasil." *Comics*. June 1975, pp. 34-35.

CHILE

General Sources

5848. Cardenio. *Todo el Mondo Sabe Que Esto Son Diez Dedos*. Santiago de Chile: Edición del Autor, 1936.

5849. de la Vega, D. "Graphic Journalism in Chile." *Pan American Magazine*. September 1917, pp. 255-256.

5850. Dorfman, Ariel. *Ensayos Quemados en Chile: Inocencia y Neocolonialismo*. Buenos Aires: Ediciones de la Flor, 1974.

5851. Lukas, [Arturo]. *Bestiario del Reyno de Chile*. Valparaíso: Ediciones Universitarias de Valparaíso, 1972.

5852. Romera. *Apuntes del Olimpo*. Santiago de Chile: Nascimento, 1949.

Caricature

5853. Delano, Jorge. "Quando Nasceu a Caricatura?" *Américas*. February 1953.

5854. Romera, Antônio. *Caricaturas*. Santiago de Chile: Editorial Orbe, 1942.

Cartooning, Cartoons

5855. Bascuñan, H. "Chilean Mickey Mouse." *Américas*. December 1954, pp. 35-36.

5856. Donoso, Ricardo. *La Sátira Política en Chile*. Santiago de Chile: Imprenta Universitaria, 1950.

5857. Schnell, Jim. "Governmental Use of Cartoons in Chile As a Means of Informing and Persuading Voters." EDRS. 1990. 17 pp.

Delano, Jorge

5858. "Cartoons in Chile; Topaze's Delano and Creatures." *Time*. September 20, 1943, p. 75.

5859. Delano, Jorge. *Yo Soy Tu*. Argumento de Jorge Delano. Dirección de "Coke." Santiago de Chile: Empresa Editora Zig-Zig S.A., 1954.

5860. De Pascal, V. "Professor Topaze Goes to Town; Chilean Politicos Are Target of Persistent and Merciless Lampooning by Cartoonist Coke." *Inter America*. December 1943, pp. 18-22.

Comic Books and Strips

5861. Dorfman, Ariel and Manuel Jofré. *Superman y Sus Amigos del Alma*. Buenos Aires: Ediciones Galerna, 1974.

5862. Gastón, Enrique. *La Propaganda Dirigida a los Niños* (Propaganda Directed at Children). Valparaíso, Chile: Ediciones Universitarias de Valparaíso, 1971.

5863. Hall, Wendell and Enrique Lafourcade. "Teaching Aspects of the Foreign Culture Through Comic Strips." In *Teaching Cultural Concepts in Spanish Classes*, edited by H. Ned Seelye, pp. 86-92. Springfield, Illinois: Office of the Superintendent of Public Instruction, 1972.

5864. *I Fumetti do Unidad Popular: Uno Strumento di Informazione Populare Nel Cile di Allende*. Milan: Celuc, 1974.

5865. Kunzle, David. "Art of the New Chile: Mural, Poster, and Comic Book in a 'Revolutionary Process.'" In *Art and Architecture in the Service of Politics*, edited by Henry A. Millon and Linda Nochlin, pp. 356-381. Cambridge, Massachusetts: The MIT Press, 1978.

5866. Kunzle, David. "The Chilean Worker as Mythic Hero: 'The Shanks of Juan.'" *Praxis*. Winter 1976, pp. 199-219.

5867. Kunzle, David. "Chile's *La Firme* Versus ITT." *Latin American Perspectives*. Winter 1978, pp. 119-133.

5868. Nómez, Naín. "La Historieta en al Proceso de Cambio Social. Un Ejemplo: De lo Exótico a lo Rural" (Comics During the Process of Social Change). *Comunicación y Cultura* (Mexico). 2nd. ed., 1978, pp. 109-124.

5869. Osses Asenjo, Luis. "Militarism and Economics Hinder Contents, Circulation of Chilean Comic Books." *WittyWorld*. Summer/Autumn 1989, p. 42.

5870. Serafini, Horacio and Roberto Bardin. "La Inocencia de la Historieta." *Cambio*. 1976, pp. 49-53.

5871. Woll, Allen L. "The Comic Book in a Socialist Society: Allende's Chile, 1970-1973." *Journal of Popular Culture*. Spring 1976, pp. 1039-1045.

COLOMBIA

References

5872. Ortega Ricaurte, Carmen. *Diccionario de Artistas en Colombia*. Bogotá: Ediciones Tercer Mundo, 1965.

5873. Santo Molano, Enrique and Jaime Zárate Valero, comps. *Enciclopedia Ilustrada de las Grandes Noticias Colombianas, 1483-1983*. Bogotá: Ediciones Avance Ltda., for Universidad Central, 1983.

Cartoonists

5874. Cafetero, Banco, comp. *Gloria Arte y Humor en José Maria Espinosa*. Bogotá: Italgraf Ltda., 1968. Unpaginated.

Morenclavijo (Clavijo Moreno)

5875. Moreno, Clavijo. *85 Colombianos en el Lápiz de Morenclavijo*. Bogotá: O.K., 1946.

5876. Moreno, Clavijo. *El Hombre Que Hacía Monitos y Otras Estampas Bogotanas*. Bogotá: Ediciones Tercer Mundo, 1969.

5877. Moreno, Clavijo (Morenclavijo). *Mi Generación en Líneas*. Bogotá: Kelly, 1951.

Rendón, Ricardo

5878. Celis, Carlos Uribe. *Los Años Veinte en Colombia: Ideologia y Cultura*. Bogotá: Ediciones Aurora, 1984. (Pages 139-149 on Rendón's place within 1920's Colombia).

5879. Colmenares, Germán. *Ricardo Rendón. Una Fuente para la Historia de la Opinión Pública*. Bogotá: Fondo Cultural Cafetero, 1984.

5880. Rendón, Ricardo. *Caricaturas*. Bogotá: Cromos, 1931.

5881. *Rendón*. Medellin: Editorial Colina, 1976.

5882. *Rendón. Caricaturas.* 2 Vols. Bogotá: Editorial El Grafico, [1930].

Yayo (Diego Herrera)

5883. Yayo (Diego Herrera). *Le Carton de Yayo.* Montreal: Editions du Phylactère, 1990.

5884. Yayo (Diego Herrera). *Zooillogique.* Montreal: Éditions du Phylactère, 1991.

5885. "Yayo, Diego Herrera." *FECO News.* No. 7, 1989, pp. 6-7.

Animation

5886. Bernal Jiménez, Augusto. "Anima Sociedad Anónima." *Corto Circuito.* April 1992, p. 52.

Comic Books

5887. *Evaluation of the Effectiveness of Illustrated Print Media (Nonverbal) in Family Planning Attitudes Among Colombians.* Program of Policy Studies in Science and Technology. Washington, D.C.: George Washington University, 1974.

5888. Montalvo P., Carlos, ed. *Ensayos Marxistas Sobre los Cómics.* Bogotá: Los Comuneros, 1978.

5889. Pareja, Reynaldo. *El Nuevo Lenguaje del Cómic* (The Comics' New Language). Bogotá: Ediciones Tercer Mundo, 1982.

Political Cartoons

5890. Arciniegas, Germán. *El Zancudo: La Caricatura Política en Colombia (Siglo XIX)* (The Mosquito: Political Caricature in Colombia [XIXth Century]). Bogotá: Editora Arco, 1975. 215 pp.

5891. Giraldo Jaramillo, Gabriel. *La Pintura en Colombia, Colección Tierra Firme, 36.* Mexico: Fondo de Cultura Económica, 1946.

5892. Helguera, J. León. "Notes on a Century of Colombian Political Cartooning: 1830-1930." *Studies in Latin American Popular Culture.* No. 6, 1987, pp. 259-280.

5893. Helguera, J. León. "Some Observations on the Cartoon As a Source for

Colombian Social History." Presented at Latin American Studies Association, 1986.

5894. Santos Molano, Enrique. "Introduccion." In *1880-1980. Un Siglo do Publicidad Gráfica en Colombia*, edited by José María Reventos R., *et al.* Bogotá: Puma Editores, 1984.

ECUADOR

Comics and Children

5895. Guevaba, D. *Sicopatologia del Cuento Infantil*. Quito: Casa de la Cultura Ecuatoriana, 1955.

EL SALVADOR

Comic Books

5896. Waldron, Vince. "El Salvador Enlists Comic Books." *Comics Buyer's Guide*. October 7, 1983, p. 24.

GUATEMALA

General Sources

5897. Jacob, Jeffrey C. "The Children of Santa María: A Study of Culture and Poverty in Urban Latin America." Ph.D. dissertation, Syracuse Universtiy, 1974.

5898. Jacob, Jeffrey C. "Urban Poverty, Children, and the Consumption of Popular Culture: A Perspective on Marginality Theses from a Latin American Squatter Settlement." *Human Organization*. Fall 1980, pp. 233-241.

5899. López, Róger. *¿Cómo Es Quién en Gautemala? Figuras Conocidas*. Guatemala: Arte Gráficas, 1945.

5900. López, Róger. *Róger López Presenta Su Exposición de Caricaturas: Folleto de Guía*. Guatemala: Artes Gráficas, 1945.

5901. Vigano, Oscar. "Estudio Sobre Aceptación y Efectividad de las Fotonovelas e Historietas en la Comunicación de Conocimientos en Áreas Rurales de Guatemala" (Study of the Acceptance and Effectiveness of Photonovels and Comics in Communicating Knowledge in Rural Guatemala). Rural Education and

Extra Scholastic Programs of Guatemala. Guatemala: Academy of Educational Development, 1976.

HONDURAS

Comic Books

5902. Viganó, Oscar. "Comic Books Carry Health Messages to Rural Children in Honduras." *Development Communication Report*. March 1983, pp. 3-4.

MEXICO

Resources

5903. *Artes de México* (México). 158 (n.d.). Titled *"La Historieta Mexicana,"* devoted to the Mexican comic book.

5904. *Artes Visuales* (México). June-August 1979. Special issue on comics.

5905. Hinds, Harold E., Jr. "Mexican Popular Culture: A Basic Bibliography." *Studies in Latin American Popular Culture*. 4 (1985), pp. 247-249.

5906. "Mexican Comics." Clipping file. 1 portfolio. Russel B. Nye Popular Culture Collection's Popular Culture Vertical File, Michigan State University, East Lansing, Michigan.

General Studies

5907. *Cultura, Comunicación de Masas y Lucha de Clases*. Translated by Aurora Chiaramonte. México: Editorial Nueva Imagen, 1978.

5908. Fernández Márquez, P. "Panorama de las Artes Plásticas." *El Nacional*. June 17, 1951, p. 9.

5909. Gandique J., Labrador. "Sentido del Humorismo, I and II." *Abside*. April-May 1940, pp. 55-63.

5910. Glennie B., E. "Revistas para Niños." *Apreciaciones*. September 4, 1943, p. 2.

5911. Hinds, Harold E., Jr. "Tradiciones y Leyendas de la Colonia: Folklore and Colonial History for Popular Consumption." *Folklore Americano*. June 1978, pp. 101-119.

5912. J. F. T. "Mora por Teléfono." *SNIF: El Mitín del Nuevo Comic.* August 1980, p. 23.

5913. Jodorowsky, Alexandro. "El Pato Donald y el Budismo ZEN." *El Heraldo Cultural*, 1967.

5914. Monsiváis, Carlos. "Impresiones Sobre la Cultura Popular Urbana en México: Segunda Parte" (Impressions on Mexican Urban Life). *Cuadernos Comunicación* (México). April 1977, pp. 6-15.

5915. Parent, Georges A. "Focalization: A Narratological Approach to Mexican Illustrated Stories." *Studies in Latin American Popular Culture.* 1 (1982), pp. 201-215.

5916. Ponce de León, Salvador. "La Pornografía al Día." *El Universal.* May 4, 1972, pp. 4, 7.

5917. Rota, Josep. "Mexican Children's Use of the Mass Media As a Source of Need Gratification." *Studies in Latin American Popular Culture.* 2 (1983), pp. 44-58.

Fotonovelas

5918. Aurrecoechea, Juan Manuel. "Los Verdaderos Antecedentes de la Fotonovela Actual." *Artes de México.* 15 Anniversary Extraordinary No. 119, 1969, pp. 18-27.

5919. Foster, David W. "Verdad y Ficción en una Fotonovela Mexicana: la Duplicidad Genera el Texto." *Confluencia; Revista Hispánica de Cultura y Literatura.* 2:2 (1986), pp. 50-59.

5920. Hill, Jane H. and Carole Browner. "Gender Ambiguity and Class Stereotyping in the Mexican Fotonovela." *Studies in Latin American Popular Culture.* 1 (1982), pp. 43-64.

5921. Montoya, Alberto and Ma. Antonieta Rebeil. "El Carácter Clasista de las Fotonovelas." Work Document, UAM, México, 1982.

5922. Pavlo Tenorio, Jesús. "Fotonovelas y Comics Son la Lectura Habitual del Mexicano." *Señal.* November 29, 1980, pp. 24-25.

5923. Torres, Kay. "Colectivo El Ojo y la Fotonovela." *Obscur: Magazine of the Los Angeles Center for Photographic Studies.* 2:5 (1983), pp. 18-23.

5924. Wischmann, Christine. *Die Mexikanische Fotonovela: Eine Untersuchung über Struktur, Ideologie und Rezeption von Massenliteratur in Mexiko und Lateinamerika.* Wiesbaden: Heymann, 1976.

Government and Legal Aspects

5925. "Del Plagio Como una de las Bellas Artes" (Plagiarism as One of the Fine Arts). *SNIF: El Mitín del Nuevo Comic* (México). 3 (n.d.), p. 59.

5926. Lara Barragán, Antonio. "Prohiben la Circulación de 25 Publicaciones Pornográficas." *El Universal*. March 11, 1972, p. 1.

5927. Silva O., José L. "Un Asunto Censurable, la Censura" (A Censurable Subject: Censorship). *Motus Liber: Organo* (fanzine) (México). January 1973, pp. 3-10.

5928. Stevens, Evelyn P. *Protest and Response in Mexico*. Cambridge: MIT Press, 1974, pp. 53-58.

Historical Aspects

5929. Charlot, Jean. *The Mexican Mural Renaissance: 1920-1925*. New York: Hacker Art Books, 1979.

5930. Vega, Santiago R. de la. "Cristalería de los Hermanos Avalos Que Viven y Soplan y Pintan." *El Universal*. April 13, 1934, pp. 5, 8.

5931. Zuno, Hernández, José Guadalupe. *Historia de la Ironía Plástica en Jalisco*. Guadalajara: Biblioteca de Autores Jaliscienses Modernos, 1972.

Caricature

5932. Alcocer, José Antonio. "Estética. La Caricatura." *Abside*. October 1940, pp. 56-58.

5933. Arenas Guzmán, Diego. "En el Mundo de la Caricatura." *El Universal*. December 14, 1947, pp. 4-11.

5934. Aurrecoechea, Juan Manuel and Armando Barata. "La Caricatura Política del Signo XIX, Tarsa e Historia." *Libros de México*. April, May, June 1988, pp. 35-39.

5935. Beals, Carleton. "La Caricatura." In *Panorama Mexicano*. Santiago de Chile: Edición Zig-Zag S. A., 1942.

5936. Capistrán Garza, René. "El Merolico (Caricatura de la Curandero)." *El Universal*. December 26, 1946, pp. 1, 16.

5937. Caso, Antonio. *La Caricatura*. Mexico: Publicaciones de la Secretaría de Educación, 1925.

5938. Castro, Rosa. "Historia de la Caricatura en Nuestra Nación." *Excélsior*. October 9, 1949, p. 4.

5939. Colmenares, Octavio. "La Caricatura en México." *Jueves de Excélsior*. December 11, 1947, p. 25.

5940. Enciso, Enrique Félix. "Los Caricaturistas Ambulantes." *Revista de Revistas*. April 3, 1949, pp. 10-11.

5941. Fernández, Justino. "La Caricatura." In *El Arte Moderno en México*, pp. 379-384. Mexico: Antigua Librería Robredo, José Porrúa e Hijos, 1937.

5942. Fernández, Justino. "La Caricatura." *Forma*. October 1926.

5943. García, Mario T. "Chistes and Caricaturas in the Mexican-American Press. Los Angeles, 1926-1927." *Studies in Latin American Popular Culture*. 1 (1982), pp. 74-90.

5944. González Ramírez, Manuel. "La Caricatura." *Novedades*. November 13, 20, 1949, p. 8.

5945. Ibarra de Anda, Fortina. *El Periodismo en México. La Caricatura y los Caricaturistas*. Mexico: Imprenta Mundial, 1934.

5946. J. G. Z. (José Guadalupe Zuno). "Sobre la Caricatura." *Bandera de Provincias*. December 1-15, 1929.

5947. "La Caricatura." In *El Ateneo*, pp. 141-142. Mexico: Imprenta de Vicente G. Torres, 1844.

5948. "Las Caricaturas." *La Antorcha Católica*. August 9, 1873.

5949. Mejía Corona, Alfonso. "La Caricatura Hace Veinte Mil Años." *El Universal*. May 2, 1950, p. 4, 30.

5950. Ontiveros, Alfonso. "Three Caricature Studies." *Mexican Life*. July 1933, p. 15.

5951. Piñó Sandoval, Jorge. "Los Brujos Gemelos." *Todo*. October 8, 1935, pp. 18-19.

5952. Ramos, Samuel. "La Caricatura." *Forma*. October 1926, pp. 8-9.

5953. René, Idisago. "La Caricatura en México." *Todo*. December 4, 1947, p. 64.

5954. Rodríguez, Antonio. "La Caricatura en México. Exposición de la Hemeroteca Nacional." *El Nacional*. December 14, 1947, p. 6.

5955. Toro, Alfonso. "Caricatura Grabada en Acero." *Mexican Art and Life*. January 1939, p. 21.

404 **Comic Art in Africa, Asia, Australia, and Latin America**

5956. Torres, Teodoro. "La Caricatura en México." In *El Humorismo y la Sátira en México*, pp. 113-140. Mexico: Talleres Tipográficos Modelo, S.A., 1943.

5957. Toussaint, Manuel. "Political Caricature in Mexico." *Mexican Art and Life.* October 1938, pp. 26-29.

5958. Vega, Santiago R. de la. "La Caricatura en México." *El Universal.* March 4, 5, 1948, pp. 4, 14 and 4, 19.

5959. Zuno Hernández, José Guadalupe. *Historia de la Caricatura en México.* Guadalajara: Biblioteca de Autores Jaliscienses Modernos, 1967.

5960. Zuno Hernández, José Guadalupe. "Historia de la Caricatura." *Bandera de Provincias.* 1 and 2 Quincenas of November 1929, pp. 5-6.

5961. Zuno Hernández, José Guadalupe. *Historia General de la Caricatura y la Ironía Plástica.* Guadalajara: Biblioteca de Autores Jaliscienses Modernos, 1972.

5962. Zuno Hernández, José Guadalupe. "Introducción a la Historia General de la Caricatura y de la Ironía Plástica." *El Nacional.* October 1952, pp. 4-12.

Comics

5963. Acosta, Miguel M., *et al. Primer Almanaque Humorístico Zacatecano.* Zacatecas: Imprenta Sucursal, 1881. Bibliografía Zacatecas.

5964. Aguilar Zinser, Carmen. "La Historieta Surge del Códice Prehispánico y Originó Obras de Arte." *Excélsior.* October 10, 1971, pp. B1-B2.

5965. Aguilar Zinser, Carmen. " 79 Años de Historieta Mexicana." *Excélsior.* October 9, 1971, pp. 1-28.

5966. Aurrecoechea, Juan Manuel and Armando Barata. "Heraldos de la Historieta Moderna." *Libros de México.* October-November-December 1987, pp. 33-37.

5967. Aurrecoechea, Juan Manuel and Armando Barata. *Puros Cuentos. 1: La Historia de la Historieta en Mexico 1874-1934.* Mexico, D. F.: Consejo Nacional para La Cultura y las Artes, Museo Nacional de Culturas Populares, 1988. 291 pp.

5968. Bastien, Remy. "History of Mexican Comics Got Off to Smoky Start." *Mexico City News.* January 24, 1986. pp. 23, 26.

5969. Delhumeau, Antonio. "Historia Cómica de la Tragedia" (Apuntes Acerca de las Virtudes del Subdesarrollo en las Historietas Cómicas Mexicanas). *Revista Mexicana de Ciencia Política.* 19: 74 (1973), pp. 19-23.

5970. de Pérez Valdés, Rosalva. "Crónica General de la Historieta" (General Chronicle of the Comics). *Artes de México* (México). 19:158 (1972), pp. 9-13, 84-86, 89-90.

5971. de Pérez Valdés, Rosalva. "Mexique." In *Histoire Mondiale de la Bande Dessinée*, edited by Pierre Horay, pp. 268-272. Paris: Pierre Horay Éditeur, 1989.

5972. González, José Carlos. "Entrevista con Carlos Monsiváis [on Mexican comics]." *Artes Visuales* (México). June-August 1979, pp. 25-29, 44-46.

5973. Jiménez Codinach, Estela Guadalupe. "Historia e Historieta: *Episodios Mexicanos* (Estudio de Caso)." Paper presented at the VI Conference of Mexican and United States Historians, Chicago, Illinois, September 10, 1981.

5974. Siller, David. "Historia de la Historieta" (History of the Comics). *Revista Comunidad (CONACYT)* (México). August 1977, pp. 23-26.

5975. Trejo, Patricia. "La Historieta Mexicana." *Hoy* (México). October 23, 1971, pp. 32-37.

Political Cartoons

5976. Alba, Victor and W. A. Coupe. "The Mexican Revolution and the Cartoon." *Comparative Studies in Society and History*. January 1967, pp. 121-136.

5977. del Río, Eduardo [Ríus]. *Un Siglo de Caricatura en Mexico* (A Century of Mexican Cartooning). Mexico City: Editorial Grijalbo, 1984. 167 pp.

5978. González Ramírez, Manuel. *La Caricatura Política, Fuentes para la Historia de la Revolución Mexicana*. México: Fondo de Cultura Económica, 1955.

5979. "These Cartoons by Bernal Dynamited Nazis in Mexico." *Life*. February 9, 1942, pp. 8-9.

5980. Zorrilla S., Ramón. "Humor Político de México en la Historia de Sus Caricaturas. 122 Años." *Jueves de Excélsior*. December 11, 1947, p. 25.

Cartooning, Cartoons

5981. Kreiner, Rich. "Textbooks from Cartoon U." *Comics Journal*. September 1990, pp. 53-58.

5982. Tollison, Hal. *Cartooning*. Tustin, California: Walter Foster Publishing, 1989. 64 pp.

5983. Velarde, Víctor, ed. *Siete Dibujantes con Una Idea*, México: Editorial Libros y Revistas, 1954.

Cartoonists

5984. Bailey, Joyce Waddell. "José Clemente Orozco (1883-1949): Formative Years in the Narrative Graphic Tradition." *Latin American Research Review.* 15:3 (1980), pp. 74-93.

5985. Cardoso, Antonio and Orlando Ortiz. "Autoentrevista: [Antonio] Cardoso y Orlando Ortiz Se Confiesan." (Self-Interview...). *SNIF: El Mitín del Nuevo Comic* (México). September 1980, pp. 45-46.

5986. "Carlos Alcalde y Su Nacionalismo." *Revista de Revistas.* October 7, 1917, p. 12.

5987. Castro, Rosa. "Verdaderos Maestros de la Caricaturas en Vidrio." *Ultimas Noticias de Excélsior.* August 26, 1949. p. 3.

5988. Dial, Eleanore Maxwell and John E. Dial. "Cartoons and Covers: The World of Luis de la Torre in Hoy [*Today*] in the 1970s." *Studies in Latin American Popular Culture.* 2 (1983), pp. 131-140.

5989. Gualti Rojo, Alfredo. "El Destino Heroico de Santiago Hernández." *Novedades.* June 29, 1952, pp. 2-3.

5990. Helm, MacKinley. *Modern Mexican Painters.* New York: Harper Brothers, 1941.

5991. Kraft, David A. "Rémy Bastìen." *Comics Interview.* No. 92, 1991, pp. 10-11, 13-18.

5992. Mendoza, Miguel Angel. "Un Grande del Arte Mexicano: Ernesto García Cabral." *Hoy.* March 3, 1951, pp. 61-62.

5993. *México Arte Moderno II: Diego Rivera, José Luis Cuevas, Rafael Coronel, Francisco Toledo, Leonora Carrington, Pedro Friedeberg, Miguel Covarrubias, Leonardo Nierman, Tomás Parra, and Ernesto Paulsen.* Mexico City: Cámara Nacional de Comercio, 1977.

5994. Reboredo, Aída. "Sin las Historietas Millones de Mexicanos Serían Analfabetos Funcionales: Javier Barros, de la SEP." *Uno Más Uno.* July 11, 1981, p. 19.

5995. Rodríguez, Antonio. "La Litografía Mexicana en el Siglo Pasado. Con Motivo de la Exposición de Tres Litógrafos Mexicanos en la Biblioteca 'Cervantes' de Esta Ciudad. *Los Grandes Caricaturistas.*" *El Nacional.* August 20, 1950, p. 7.

5996. Serrano, Carlos. "Desde Tierras de Francia. Anécdotas de Algunos Caricaturistas Mexicanos del Pasado: José María Villasana, Carlos Alcalde, etc." *Excélsior.* May 23, 1951, pp. 6, 13.

5997. Stewart, Virginia. *Forty-Five Contemporary Mexican Artists.* Stanford, California: 1951.

5998. Taibo, Paco Ignacio, II. "De La Historia Marginal a el Desempleado." *SNIF: El Mitín del Nuevo Cómic* (México). September 1980, p. 29. (Víctor Uhthoff).

5999. Wolfe, Bertram D. *The Fabulous Life of Diego Rivera.* New York: Stein and Day, 1963.

Covarrubias, Miguel

(For fuller treatment of Covarrubia's career, especially in the United States, see pages 280-281 of *Animation, Caricature, and Gag and Political Cartoons in the United States and Canada: An International Bibliography,* compiled by John A. Lent. Westport, Connecticut: Greenwood Press, 1994.)

6000. Aguilar Zinser, Carmen. "Miguel Covarrubias: La Maravilla de Lápiz." *Excélsior.* January 16, 1971.

6001. Ali, Ben. "La Obra del Chamaco en Nueva York." *El Universal Ilustrado.* June 6, 1925.

6002. Barreda, Octavio. "Elena Poniatowska Reconstruye la Vida de Miguel Covarrubias." *Novedades.* April 22, 1957.

6003. Covarrubias, Miguel. "El Arte 'Olmeca' o de La Vente." *Cuadernos Americanos.* July-August 1950, p. 153+.

6004. Covarrubias, Miguel. *Indian Art of Mexico and Central America.* New York: Alfred A. Knopf, 1957.

6005. Covarrubias, Miguel. *Island of Bali.* New York: Alfred A. Knopf, 1937.

6006. Covarrubias, Miguel. *Mexico South: The Isthmus of Tehuantepec.* New York: Alfred A. Knopf, 1962.

6007. Covarrubias, Miguel. "Notas Sobre Máscaras Mexicanas." *Mexican Folkways.* 5:3 (1929-1930), pp. 116+.

6008. Covarrubias, Miguel. *Obras Selectas del Arte Popular.* No. 5. Mexico City: Museo Nacional de Artes e Industrias Populares, 1953.

6009. Covarrubias, Miguel. "Slapstick and Venom." *Theatre Arts Monthly.* August 1938, pp. 593+.

6010. Covarrubias, Miguel. "Tlatilco, Archaic Mexican Art and Culture." *DYN: The Review of Modern Art*. No. 4-5, 1943, pp. 40+.

6011. Covarrubias, Miguel. "Tlatilco: El Arte y la Cultura Preclásica del Valle de México." *Cuadernos Americanos*. May-June 1950, pp. 153+.

6012. Covarrubias, Miguel. "The World and the Theatre." *Theatre Arts Monthly*. August 1936, pp. 578+.

6013. Covarrubias, Miguel and Daniel F. Rubín de la Borbolla, eds. *El Arte Indígena de Norteamérica*. Mexico City: Fondo de Cultura Económica México, 1945.

6014. "Covarrubias, Mexican Artist of Negro, Says Paris Lacks of 'Popular Art.'" *Paris Herald*. November 1927.

6015. "Covarrubias on Paper." *Smithsonian*. November 1984, pp. 174-178.

6016. Crespo de la Serna, J.J. "Miguel Covarrubias." *Novedades*. March 24, 1957.

6017. Fernández Bustamante, Adolfo. "Miguel Covarrubias, el Gran Caricaturista Mexicano." *Revista Nuestro México*. August 1932.

6018. Freund, Giselle. "Miguel y Rosa Covarrubias en Su Hogar." *Novedades*. October 14, 1951.

6019. Gamboa, Fernando. "Fernando Gamboa y Daniel Rubín de la Borbolla Hablan de Miguel Covarrubias." *Novedades*. May 5, 1957.

6020. Gilmore, Cecile. "Gaiety of Bali Woos Jaded Gothamites: Covarrubias Is the Designer of New Prints." *Evening Post*. December 30, 1937.

6021. Grana, Teresa. "Miguel Covarrubias, Drawings and Caricatures of Harlem." Master's thesis, George Washington University, 1985.

6022. Grau, Corazón. "Covarrubias Doesn't Believe in Teachers." *The Tribune Magazine* (Manila). July 1930.

6023. Grieder, Terence. "The Divided World of Miguel Covarrubias." *Americas*. May 5, 1971, pp. 24+.

6024. Gutiérrez Nájera, Manuel. "Miguel Covarrubias y Sus Caricaturas Neoyorquinas." *El Universal Ilustrado*. February 21, 1924.

6025. Haldeman-Julius, Margaret. "Miguel Covarrubias." *Haldeman-Julius Quarterly*. January 1927, pp. 60-62+.

6026. McBride, Henry. "Gifted Young Caricaturist Has All Harlem in His Debt." *New York Sun*. December 24, 1927.

6027. McLean, Lou. "Mexico's Great Caricaturist Is a Union Man and a Progressive." *People's World* (San Francisco). January 12, 1939.

6028. Medina, Andrés. "Miguel Covarrubias y el Romanticismo en la Antropología." In *Nueva Antropología*. Mexico City: NNAM, 1976.

6029. "Men of Mexico." *Vanity Fair*. June 1929, p. 62.

6030. "Mexican Artist, Twenty-One, Famous." *New York Times*. November 24, 1925.

6031. "Miguel Covarrubias: 'El Chamaco.'" *Revista de Revistas*. February 24, 1957.

6032. *Miguel Covarrubias: Homenaje*. Exhibition catalogue. Mexico City: CCAC, 1987.

6033. Mountsier, Roberto. "Mexican Artist 'Paints' Mexico." *New York Sun*. January 22, 1938.

6034. Pach, Walter. "An Artist Looks on Harlem." *New York Herald Tribune*. November 6, 1927, p. 89.

6035. Poniatowska, Elena. "Alfonso Caso, Harry Block y Diego Rivera Hablan de Miguel Covarrubias." *Novedades*. May 12, 1957.

6036. Poniatowska, Elena. "En Memoria de Miguel Covarrubias." *Novedades*. April 28, 1957.

6037. Poniatowska, Elena. "Un Acontecimiento Editorial. México Rescata a Miguel Covarrubias Traduciéndolo por Primera Vez al Español." *Novedades*. October 15, 1961.

6038. "Raoul Fournier, Carlos Solórzano y Justino Fernández Hablan de Miguel Covarrubias." *Novedades*. May 9, 1957.

6039. Rodrígues, Antonio. "Muerte de Miguel Covarrubias." *El Nacional* (Mexico City). February 1957.

6040. Rubín de la Borbolla, Daniel. "Miguel Covarrubias 1905-1957." *American Antiquity*. July 1957, p. 64.

6041. Terry, Walter. "Mexico Produces a New Triumvirate: Limón, Chávez, Covarrubias." *Dance Magazine*. June 1951, pp. 17-18, 40.

6042. Williams, Adriana. *Covarrubias*. Austin: University of Texas Press, 1994. 318 pp.

6043. Ybarra-Frausto, Tomás. "Miguel Covarrubias: Cartógrafo." *Miguel Covarrubias: Homenaje*. Mexico City: CCAC, 1987.

del Río, Eduardo (Ríus)

6044. Barata, Armando. "De Monitos: El Fenómeno Ríus." *SNIF: El Mitín del Nuevo Cómic* (México). 4 (n.d.), pp. 11-14.

6045. Cornejo, Leobardo. "Elementos de Retórica en Ríus." *Cuadernos de Semiótica* (Mexico). August 1982, pp. 1-16.

6046. del Río, Eduardo (Ríus). *A B Che*. Mexico City: Editorial Grijalbo, 1978.

6047. del Río, Eduardo (Ríus). *Como Suicidarse sin Método en 30 Lecciones*. Mexico City: Editorial Posada, 1972.

6048. del Río, Eduardo (Ríus). *Cristo de Carne y Hueso*. n.p., 1972.

6049. del Río, Eduardo (Ríus). *Cuba Libre*. Mexico City: Editorial Posada, 1977.

6050. del Río, Eduardo (Ríus). *Cuba para Principiantes*. Mexico City: Ediciones de Cultura Popular, 1966.

6051. del Río, Eduardo (Ríus). *Del Detritus Federal a Laguna Verde* (From the Federal Detritus to Laguna Verde). Mexico City: Editorial Posada, 1989. 153 pp.

6052. del Río, Eduardo (Ríus). *El Museo de Ríus*. Mexico City: Editorial Posada, 1977.

6053. del Río, Eduardo (Ríus). *El Yerberito Ilustrado*. Mexico City: Editorial Posada, 1975.

6054. del Río, Eduardo (Ríus). *¿Hay Lidertad de Prensa en Mexico?* (Is There Freedom of the Press in Mexico?) Mexico City: Editorial Posada, 1989. 127 pp.

6055. del Río, Eduardo (Ríus). *Huele a Gas*. Mexico City: Editorial Posada, 1978.

6056. del Río, Eduardo (Ríus). *La Deuda (y Como No Pagarla...)*. (The Debt [And How Not To Pay It]). Mexico City: Editorial Grijalbo, 1985. 93 pp.

6057. del Río, Eduardo (Ríus). *La Interminable Conquista de Mexico* (The Unending Conquest of Mexico). Mexico City: Editorial Grijalbo, 1984. 151 pp.

6058. del Río, Eduardo (Ríus). *La Joven Alemania*. Mexico City: Ediciones de Cultura Popular, 1967.

6059. del Río, Eduardo (Ríus). *La Panza Es Primero*. Mexico City: Editorial Posada, 1972.

6060. del Río, Eduardo (Ríus). *La Revolución Feminina de las Mujures*. Mexico City: Editorial Grijalbo, 1979.

6061. del Río, Eduardo (Ríus). *La Revolución Mexicana.* Mexico City: Editorial Posada, 1978.

6062. del Río, Eduardo (Ríus). *La Trukulenta Historia del Kapitalismo.* Mexico City: Editorial Posada, 1976.

6063. del Río, Eduardo (Ríus). *Lenín para Principiantes.* Mexico City: Ediciones de Cultura Popular, 1975.

6064. del Río, Eduardo (Ríus). *Manifiesto Comunista. Marx, Engels, Ríus.* Mexico City: Editorial Nueva Sociedad, 1975.

6065. del Río, Eduardo (Ríus). *Manual del Perfecto Ateo.* Mexico City: Editorial Grijalbo, 1980.

6066. del Río, Eduardo (Ríus). *Mao.* Mexico City: Editorial Grijalbo, 1979.

6067. del Río, Eduardo (Ríus). *Marx para Principiantes.* Mexico City: Ediciones de Cultura Popular, 1972.

6068. del Río, Eduardo (Ríus). *No Consulte a Su Médico.* Mexico City: Editorial Posada, 1975.

6069. del Río, Eduardo (Ríus). "Pequeño Ríus Ilustrado." In *Diccionario de Humor, Violencia, Sexo y Agruras.* Mexico City: Ediciones de Cultura Popular, 1971.

6070. del Río, Eduardo (Ríus). *¿Qué Tal URSS?* Mexico City: Editorial Posada, 1973.

6071. del Río, Eduardo (Ríus). *Ríus a la China.* Mexico City: Editorial Posada, 1978.

6072. del Río, Eduardo (Ríus). *Ríus: Caricaturas Rechazadas.* Mexico City: Ediciones de Cultura Popular, 1967.

6073. del Río, Eduardo (Ríus). *Ríus en Política.* Mexico City: Ediciones de Cultura Popular, 1974.

6074. del Río, Eduardo (Ríus). *Ríus (1955-1958), Primeras Porquerías.* Mexico City: Editorial Heterodixia, 1973.

6075. del Río, Eduardo (Ríus). *Ríus (1959-1961). El Segundo Aire.* Mexico City: Editorial Heterodixia, 1973.

6076. Fernández Aguilar, Javier. "Ríus." *Presagio; Pensamiento y Acción de la Juventud.* 11 (1969), pp. 32-33.

6077. Frenzel, Martin. "Ríus. Ein Anwalt der Verdammten Dieser Erde." *Comic Forum. Das Magazin für Comicliteratur.* 7:30 (1985), pp. 52-55.

6078. Herner, Irene. "La Odisea Ríus." In *Mitos y Monitos: Historietas y Fotonovelas en México*, by Irene Herner, pp. 147-153. Mexico: Editorial Nueva Imagen, 1979.

6079. Pint, John J. "Of Virgins and Demons." *Comics Journal*. June 1991, p. 51.

6080. Pint, John J. "Who's This Ríus?" *Comics Journal*. September 1990, pp. 27-32.

6081. Poniatowska, Elena. "Ríus, Ese Seminarista." *Siempre* 800 (1968), pp. 40-41.

6082. Riding, Alan. "Humorist Tickles Mexico While Tweaking Official Noses." *New York Times*. August 27, 1979, p. A-2.

6083. Riding, Alan. "Maverick Cartoonist Struggles Against Censors." *New York Times* release in *Las Cruces* (New Mexico) *Sun-News*. September 3, 1979, p. B-13.

6084. Speck, Paula K. "Ríus for Beginners: A Study in Comicbook Satire." *Studies in Latin American Popular Culture*. 1 (1982), pp. 113-124.

6085. Tatum, Charles M. "Eduardo del Río: Comic Book Writer As Social Gadfly." Paper presented at VI Conference of Mexican and United States historians, Chicago, September 8-12, 1981.

6086. Tatum, Charles M. "Rius: Comic Book Writer As Social Critic and Political Gadfly." Unpublished paper.

6087. Tatum, Charles M. "Ruis [sic]: der Comics-Autor als Sozialkritiker und Politischer Unruhestifter." *Iberoamericana*. 13/14 (1982), pp. 78-91.

6088. Tatum, Chuck [Charles], and Harold Hinds. "Eduardo del Río (Rius): An Interview and Introductory Essay." *Chasqui*. November 1979, pp. 3-23.

Mora, Angel J.

6089. Malvido, Adriana. "Ganó Angel Mora el Primer Concurso de Historietas de México." *Uno Más Uno*. August 26, 1981, p. 4.

6090. Malvido, Adriana. "Las Historietistas Mexicanos Enajenan Sus Derechos de Autor; Ningún Regalía ha Recibido Angel Mora." *Uno Más Uno*. August 23, 1981, p. 19.

Picheta (Gabriel V. Gahona)

6091. Nelken, Margarita. "Significación de Picheta." *Excélsior*. October 28, 1951, p. 9.

6092. Orosa Díaz, Jaime. *Picheta (Gabriel Vicente Gahona, 1828-1899)*. Mérida: Gobierno del Estado de Yucatán, 1948.

Posada, José Guadalupe

6093. Ades, Dawn. "Posada and the Popular Graphic Tradition." In *Art in Latin America. The Modern Era, 1820-1980,* edited by Dawn Ades, *et al.*, pp. 111-123. London: The South Bank Centre, 1989.

6094. Berdicio, Roberto and Stanley Applebaum, eds. *Posada's Popular Prints.* New York: Dover, 1972.

6095. Carrillo A [zpéitia], Rafael. *Posada y el Grabado Mexicano desde el Famoso Grabador de Temas Populares Hasta los Artistas Contemporáneos* (Posada and the Mexican Engraving from the Famed Engraver of Popular Themes up to Contemporary Artists). 3rd Ed. Mexico: Panorama Editorial, 1983. 80 [+71] pp.

6096. Goeldi, Osvaldo. "O Grande Gravador Mexicano Posadas." *Pensamento da América.* (Rio de Janeiro). June 15, 1947.

6097. Guido, Angel. "José Guadalupe Posadas y las *Calaveras.*" In *Redescubrimiento de América.* Buenos Aires: Libreria y Editorial "El Ateneo," 1944.

6098. Haces, Carlos and Pulido, Marco Antonio, comps. *José Guadalupe Posada y el Amor. Para Iluminar* (José Guadalupe Posada and Love. For Coloring). Mexico: SEP, Ediciones del Ermitano, 1984. 41 pp.

6099. Hasegawa, Nina Yui de. "Posada o Fūshi No Wakugumi de Kangaeru." (To Think about Posada Within the Framework of Satire). *Fūshiga Kenkyū.* July 20, 1992, pp. 4-5.

6100. Hiriart, Hugo. *El Universo de Posada. Estética de la Obsolescencia* (Posada's Universe. The Aesthetic of Obsolescence). Memoria y Olvido, VIII (Memory and Oblivion, VIII). Mexico: SEP Martín Casillas Editores, 1982. 71 [+4] pp.

6101. "Homenaje en el Primer Centenario del Nacimiento de José Guadalupe Posada. 1852-1952." *El Nacional.* February 24, 1952. 16 pp. (16 articles on Posada).

6102. Macazaga, Carlos, *et al. Las Calaveras Vivientes de Posada.* Mexico City: Editorial Cosmos, 1977; Editorial Innovación, 1979.

6103. Middleton, Michael. "Posada y Presente de la Caricatura en Gran Bretaña." *El Diario* (La Paz). July 22, 1951.

6104. Palencia, Ceferino. "José Guadalupe Posada y el Posadismo." *Novedades.* February 13, 1949, p. 4.

6105. Rothenstein, Julian, ed. *José Guadalupe Posada: Mexican Popular Prints.* Boston: Shambhala Redstone Editions, 1993.

6106. Tyler, Ron. *Posada's Mexico.* Washington, D.C.: Library of Congress, 1979.

Quezada, Abel

6107. "Abel Quezada." *Comics Journal*. April 1991, p. 24.

6108. Camp, Roderic A. "The Cartoons of Abel Quezada." *Studies in Latin American Popular Culture*. 4 (1985), pp. 125-138.

Vargas Dulché, Yolanda

6109. Miller, Beth and Alfonso González. *26 Autores del México Actual*. Mexico City: B. Costa-Amic Editor, 1978. (Yolanda Vargas Dulché, pp. 375-384).

6110. Vargas Dulché, Yolanda. "¿Qué Es la Historieta para Mí?" *Artes de México* (México). 158 (n.d.), pp. 14, 87, 90-91.

Vargas, Gabriel

6111. B[arata] A[rmando]. "De Monitos: Gabriel Vargas e Hijos Sin Succesores." *SNIF: El Mitín del Nuevo Cómic* (México). 3 (n.d.), p. 40.

6112. Poniatowska, Elena. "Gabriel Vargas y *Familia Burrón*." *El Gallo Ilustrado*. Supplement of *El Día*. February 10, 1963, p. 2.

Vigil, Carlos and Guillermo Zubieta

6113. *Cromofantasías de Guillermo Zubieta Vigil*. Mexico City: Creaciones Luhec, n.d.

6114. Silva, José Luis. "Interview: Carlos Vigil on Mexican Comic Books and Photonovels." *Studies in Latin American Popular Culture*. 5 (1986), pp. 196-210.

6115. Vigil, Guillermo Z. " Ensayo Sobre la Personalidad de los Principales Personajes del Cómic 'Los Supersabios,' del Dibujante y Argumentista Mexicano Germán Butze." *Motus Liber: Organo* (México). January 1973, pp. 12-15.

Characters and Titles

6116. Curiel, Fernando. *Mal de Ojo Iniciación a la Literatura Icónica*. Mexico City: Universidad Nacional Autónoma de México, 1989.

6117. Gasca, Luis. "Annibal 5 (Messico)." In *Enciclopedia Mondiale del Fumetto*, edited by Maurice Horn and Luciano Secchi, p. 156. Milan: Editoriale Corno, 1978.

6118. Gasca, Luis. "Fantomas (Messico)." In *Enciclopedia Mondiale del Fumetto*, edited by Maurice Horn and Luciano Secchi. p. 323. Milan: Editoriale Corno, 1978.

6119. Guillermoprieto, Alma. "*El Caballo del Diablo*: un Estudio de Caso." Presented at Primer Simposio Mexicano Centroamericano de Investigación sobre La Mujer, Mexico, November 7-9, 1977.

6120. Hinds, Harold E., Jr. "Arandu: Mexican Adventure Comics." *WittyWorld*. Spring 1988, pp. 22-23.

6121. Malvido, Adriana. " Reunidos en Cocoyoc, Trece de los Más Importantes Historietistas del Momento." *Uno Más Uno*. August 18, 1981, p. 20.

6122. Reséndiz, Rafael C. "El Mito de Rarotonga" (The Myth of Rarotonga). In *El Comic Es Algo Serio*, pp. 129-243. México: Ediciones Eufesa, 1982.

6123. Reséndiz, Rafael C. "Ultraman: La Impotencia de Una Potencia." In *Comunicación e Ideologia: Dependencia y Liberacion de los Medios*, pp. 11-20. Mexico: December 1974-January 1975.

6124. Steele, Cynthia. "Ideology and Mexican Mass Culture: The Case of *Sangre India: Chamula.*" *Studies in Latin American Popular Culture*. 2 (1983), pp. 14-23.

6125. "South-of-the-Border Fun with *La Mama del Abulon*. " *Comics Journal*. July 1991, p. 31.

"Alma Grande"

6126. "Alma Grande." In *A History of Komiks of the Philippines and Other Countries*, by Cynthia Roxas and Joaquin Arevalo, Jr., p. 227. Manila: Islas Filipinas Publishing, 1985.

6127. Gasca, Luis. "Alma Grande (Messico)." In *Enciclopedia Mondiale del Fumetto*, edited by Maurice Horn and Luciano Secchi, pp. 148-149. Milan: Editoriale Corno, 1978.

"Chanoc"

6128. "Chanoc." In *A History of Komiks of the Philippines and Other Countries*, by Cynthia Roxas and Joaquin Arevalo, Jr., p. 227. Manila: Islas Filipinas Publishing, 1985.

6129. Gasca, Luis. "Chanoc (Messico)." In *Enciclopedia Mondiale del Fumetto*, edited by Maurice Horn and Luciano Secchi, p. 244. Milan: Editoriale Corno, 1978.

6130. Hinds, Harold E., Jr. "*Chanoc*: Adventure and Slapstick on Mexico's Southeast Coast." *Journal of Popular Culture*. Winter 1980, pp. 424-436.

"Chupamirto"

6131. "Chupamirto" In *A History of Komiks of the Philippines and Other Countries*, by

Cynthia Roxas and Joaquin Arevalo, Jr., pp. 227-228. Manila: Islas Filipinas Publishing, 1985.

6132. Horn, Maurice. "Chupamirto (Messico)." In *Enciclopedia Mondiale del Fumetto*, edited by Maurice Horn and Luciano Secchi, p. 250. Milan: Editoriale Corno, 1978.

"El Cuarto Reich"

6133. Hunt, Nancy L. and David G. LaFrance. "'El Cuarto Reich': Economic Disaster, Torture and Other Laughs." *Studies in Latin American Popular Culture*. 2 (1983), pp. 36-43.

6134. Polomo, José. *El Cuarto Reich*. Mexico City: Editorial Nueva Imagen, 1979-82. (Anthology of four volumes).

6135. Palomo, José. *El Cuarto Reich: Es Una Creación de la ITT, Anaconda, Kennecott, Chase Manhattan Bank...*2d Ed. México: Nueva Imagen, 1980.

"El Payo"

6136. Barata, Armando. "De Monitos: Réquiem por *El Payo*." *SNIF: El Mitín del Nuevo Cómic* (México). October 1980, p. 25.

6137. Erreguerena, María Josefa. "El Payo ¡Un Hombre Contra el Mundo!" *Revista de la Universidad de México* (México). October-November 1978, pp. 85-86.

6138. Gasca, Luis. "Payo, El (Messico)." In *Enciclopedia Mondiale del Fumetto*, edited by Maurice Horn and Luciano Secchi, p. 614. Milan: Editoriale Corno, 1978.

6139. Hinds, Harold E., Jr. "El Payo: A Man Against His World!—A Mexican 'Western' Comic Book." *North Dakota Quarterly*. Spring 1980, pp. 31-55.

6140. Hinds, Harold E., Jr. "*El Payo*: Una Solución a la Lucha Mexicana Entre los Robatierras y los Descamisados." *Hispamérica* (Buenos Aires). April 1982, pp. 33-49.

6141. Vigil, Guillermo Z. *El Payo: O Cómo Escribo Mi Historieta*. Mexico: Edamex, 1981.

"Fabulas Panicas"

6142. "Fabulas Panicas." In *A History of Komiks of the Philippines and Other Countries*, by Cynthia Roxas and Joaquin Arevalo, Jr., p. 227. Manila: Islas Filipinas Publishing, 1985.

6143. Gasca, Luis. "Fabulas Panicas (Messico)." In *Enciclopedia Mondiale del Fumetto*, edited by Maurice Horn and Luciano Secchi, p. 319. Milan: Editoriale Corno, 1978.

"Kaliman"

6144. Dienhart, Mort. "Superman Go Home, We've Got Kaliman." *University of Minnesota Update*. October 1984, p. 12.

6145. Hinds, Harold E., Jr. "Kaliman: A Mexican Superhero." *Journal of Popular Culture*. Fall 1979, pp. 229-238.

6146. Hinds, Harold E., Jr. "*Kaliman:* Mexico's Most Popular Superhero." *Studies in Latin American Popular Culture*. 4 (1985), pp. 27-42.

6147. Hinds, Harold E., Jr. "Literatura Popular: 'No Hay Fuerza Más Poderosa Que la Mente Humana'—Kaliman." *Hispamérica* (Buenos Aires). December 1977, pp. 31-46.

6148. Robledo, Elisa. "El Éxito Loco de Kaliman." *Contenido 227*. April 1982, p. 59.

6149. Romero, Norma. "Análisis de un Episodio Completo de la Historieta Seriada Kaliman." Thesis, UIA, México 1980.

"La Familia Burrón"

6150. Gasca, Luis. "Familia Burrón, La (Messico)." In *Enciclopedia Mondiale del Fumetto*, edited by Maurice Horn and Luciano Secchi, p. 321. Milan: Editoriale Corno, 1978.

6151. Pérez Cruz, Emiliano. "La Familia Burrón." *Nexos*. March 1980, pp. 57-58.

6152. Tatum, Charles. "*La Familia Burrón*: Inside a Lower Middle Class Family." *Studies in Latin American Popular Culture*. 4 (1985), pp. 43-62.

6153. Wicke, Charles R. "The Burron Family: Class Warfare and the Culture of Poverty." *Studies in Latin American Popular Culture*. 2 (1983), pp. 59-70.

"Lágrimas, Risas y Amor"

6154. Tatum, Charles M. "*Lágrimas, Risas y Amor*: La Historieta Más Popular de México." *Hispamérica* (Buenos Aires). Fall 1983, pp. 101-108.

6155. Tatum, Charles M. "*Lágrimas, Risas y Amor*: Mexico's Most Popular Romance Comic Book." *Journal of Popular Culture*. Winter 1980, pp. 413-424.

6156. Tatum, Charles M. "*Lágrimas, Risas y Amor:* Mexico's Most Popular Romance Comic Book." *Journal of Popular Culture*. Spring 1983, pp. 117-126.

"Los Agachados"

6157. del Río, Eduardo (Rius). *Números Agotados de 'Los Agachados.'* Vol. 2. Mexico: Editorial Posada, 1974, pp. 12-44.

6158. Gasca, Luis. "Agachados, Los (Messico)." In *Enciclopedia Mondiale del Fumetto*, edited by Maurice Horn and Luciano Secchi, pp. 138-139. Milan: Editoriale Corno, 1978.

6159. "Los Agachados." In *A History of Komiks of the Philippines and Other Countries*, by Cynthia Roxas and Joaquin Aievalo, Jr., pp. 226-227. Manila: Islas Filipinas Publishing, 1985.

"Los Supermachos"

6160. Cornejo, Leobardo. "Semiótica de Los Supermachos y Los Agachados de Rius." In *El Cómic Es Algo Serio*, pp. 121-128. México: Ediciones Eufesa, 1982.

6161. del Río, Eduardo [Rius]. "Rius Denuncia a los Lectores y Amigos de *Los Supermachos*." *La Voz de México*. November 26, 1967, p. 4.

6162. Eisler, Ken. "Mexico's New Race: 'Los Supermachos.'" *Texas Quarterly*. 10:4 (1967), pp. 182-197.

6163. Gasca, Luis. "Supermachos, Los (Messico)." In *Enciclopedia Mondiale del Fumetto*, edited by Maurice Horn and Luciano Secchi, pp. 711-712. Milan: Editoriale Corno, 1978.

6164. *Golpe de Estado en San Garabato*. Los Supermachos 575. Mexico City: Editorial Meridiano, 1977.

6165. "Los Supermachos." *Mexico/This Month*. October 1967, pp. 26-28.

6166. Palacios Franco and Julia Emilia. "Los Supermachos (98 Números): Rius." *Motus Liber: Organo* (México). January 1973, p. 10.

6167. Patten, Fred. "Superman South." *Alter Ego*. August 1965 and Winter 1965, pp. 24-28 and 4-12. Parts III and IV available only in manuscript form as *Alter Ego* ceased publication.

6168. Proctor, Phyllis A. "Mexico's *Supermachos*: Satire and Social Revolution in Comics by Rius." Ph.D. dissertation, University of Texas, 1972.

6169. Tatum, Charles M. "Eduardo del Rio's *Los Agachados* and *Los Supermachos*." *Praxis*. Forthcoming.

"Torbellino"

6170. Palacios Franco, Julia Emilia. "Proposiciones para el Análisis de un Cómic Mexicano: El Caso de *Torbellino*." M.A. thesis, Iberoamerican University, 1978.

6171. Palacios Franco, Julia Emilia. "*Torbellino*: Toward an Alternative Comic Book." *Studies in Latin American Popular Culture*. 5 (1986), pp. 186-195.

Animation

6172. Alcántara Pastor, Angel. "La Caricatura en la Pantalla Cinematográfica." *El Universal*. January 23, 1948, p. 8.

6173. Escalona, Enrique. *Tlacuilo*. Mexico City: Universidad Nacional Autónoma de México, 1989.

6174. Santacruz Moctezuma, Lino. "El Cine de Animación en México." *Corto Circuito*. April 1992, pp. 36-37.

Caricature

6175. *Anuario de la Caricaturas 1992*. Mexico City: Sociedad Mexicana de Caricaturistas S. de A. de I. P., 1993. 146 pp.

6176. Aragón, Etcheagaray, Enríque. "La Caricatura de la Ciudad." *Excélsior*. June 21, 1953, pp. 7C, 11C.

6177. Avilés, René. "La Señora de Pallares y una Caricatura Inolvidable." *El Nacional*. June 11, 1950, pp. 3, 7.

6178. Bermejo, Manuel M. "La Caricatura Musical." *El Universal Gráfico*. July 21, 1953, pp. 6, 17.

6179. Carrasco Puente, Rafael. *La Caricatura en México*. México: Imprenta Universitaria, 1953. 322 pp.

6180. Carrasco Puente, Rafael. *La Caricatura en Mexico*. México: Talleres de Gráfica Cervantina, 1962.

6181. del Río, Eduardo (Rius). *Caricaturas Rechazadas*. México: Fondo de Cultura Popular, 1968.

6182. del Río, Eduardo (Rius). "La Caricatura Mexicana." Special Issue. *Los Agachados*. 104, 1972.

6183. Fernández, Justino. *Arte Moderno y Contemporaneo de Mexico*. Mexico: 1952, pp. 446-448, 458, 478.

6184. "La Caricatura Mexicana." In *Cartoons 1988*. Catalogue of Cartoonfestival Knokke-Heist, Belgium. June-September 1988. Knokke-Heist: 1988.

6185. Lan, Federica. "27 Caricaturas." *Excélsior*. August 3, 1952, pp. 9, 11.

6186. Lara Pardo, Luis. "La Caricatura Mexicana." *Excélsior*. August 17, 1952, p. 16.

6187. Medina Ruiz, Fernando. "Exposición de Caricatura Periodística." *Jueves de Excélsior*. August 7, 1952, p. 30.

6188. Pruneda, Salvador. *La Caricatura Como Arma Política*. México: Instituto Nacional de Estudios Históricos de la Revolución Méxicana, 1958.

Comic Books

6189. Acosta, Mariclaire. "La Historieta Cómica en México." *Revista de la Universidad de México*. June 1973, pp. 14-19.

6190. Aguilar Zinser, Carmen. "La Historieta como Instrumento para Politizar a los Lectores." *Excélsior*. October 16, 1971, p. 5-B

6191. Alfie, David. "Semiologia del Cómic." In *El Cómic Es Algo Serio*, pp. 47-57. México: Ediciones Eufesa, 1982.

6192. Allegri, Luigi. "Historieta y Estructuras Narrativas." In *Cultura, Comunicación de Masas y Lucha de Clases*, translated by Aurora Chiaramonte, pp. 57-80. México: Editorial Nueva Imagen, 1978.

6193. Aurrecoechea, Juan Manuel. "La Historieta Mexicana: Fascículo Desprendible y Coleccionable." *SNIF: El Mitín del Nuevo Cómic* (México). August 1980, September 1980, October 1980, 4 (n.d.). All appeared as unpaginated inserts.

6194. B[arta], A[rmando]. "De Monitos: Del Cartón a la Historieta." *SNIF: El Mitín del Nuevo Cómic* (México). 3 (n.d.), p. 82.

6195. Baur, Elisabeth K. *La Historieta Como Experiencia Didáctica*. México: Editorial Nueva Imagen, 1978.

6196. BHU. "Historietas Preferidas." *El Gallo Ilustrado: Suplemento Dominical de El Día*. February 10, 1963, p. 3.

6197. "Cinco Empresas Monopolizan la Historieta, Explotan al Trabajador e Impiden Sus Reivindicaciones." *Uno Más Uno*. August 21, 1981, p. 17.

6198. "Comics y Televisión." *Revista Mexicana de Ciencia Política.* 19:74 (1973), pp. 5-60.

6199. "Comic: Una Historieta Popular, la Paraliteratura en México." *Revista Semana* (Sunday supplement, *El Universal*). July 10, 1977, p. 3.

6200. Couch, Chris. "In Mexico, Nearly Everybody Reads Comics." *Comics Buyer's Guide.* July 8, 1983, pp. 20, 22, 24, 26, 28, 30.

6201. Delhumeau, Antonio. "Historia Cómica de la Tragedia: Apuntes Acerca de las Virtudes del Subdesarrollo en las Historietas Cómicas Mexicanas." *Revista Mexicana de Ciencia Política.* October-December 1973, pp. 19-23.

6202. de Lourdes Solórzano, Luz. "Psicología en la Historieta." *Artes de México.* 19:158 (1972), pp. 4-5, 83-84, 88.

6203. del Río, Eduardo (Rius). "Las Historietas." (The Comics). *Los Agachados* (México). April 4, 1971.

6204. *El Cómic Es Algo Serio.* Mexico: Ediciones Eufesa, 1982.

6205. Erreguerena, Josefa. "Análisis Semiológico del Comic Como Medio de Comunicación Aplicado." Thesis, México, 1977.

6206. Gaddis, Walter. "Zowie!! Comics Are Hot in Mexico." *Mexico City News.* January 24, 1986, p. 17.

6207. Gallo, Miguel Angel. *Los Comics: Un Enfoque Sociológico.* Mexico City: Ediciones Quinto Sol, n.d.

6208. Gutiérrez Oropeza, Manuel. "Las Revistas en México." *Libros de México.* 1 (1985), pp. 34-35.

6209. Gutiérrez Vega, Hugo. *Informacion y Sociedad.* Mexico: Fondo de Cultura Economica, 1974. (Rius and Quino books).

6210. Gutiérrez Vega, Hugo. "Observaciones Sobre el Cine, la Radio, la Televisión y las Historietas Cómicas." *Revista Mexicana de Ciencia Política.* October-December 1973, pp. 5-11.

6211. "Heraclio Bernal. El Payo de Sinaloa." *SNIF: El Mitín del Nuevo Comic.* 5:2.

6212. Herner, Irene. "El Museo y la Historieta." *Revista Mexicana de Ciencia Política* (México). April-June 1974, pp. 51-61.

6213. Herner, Irene. *Mitos y Monitos: Historietas y Fotonovelas en México* (Myths and the Funnies). México: Universidad Nacional Autónoma de México, Editorial Nueva Imagen, 1979.

6214. Hinds, Harold E., Jr. "Algunas Reflexiones Sobre la Historieta Mexicana." *Artes Visuales* (México). Vol. 22, June-August, pp. 30-31, 46-47.

6215. Hinds, Harold E., Jr. "Comics." In *Handbook of Latin American Popular Culture*, edited by Harold E. Hinds, Jr. and Charles M. Tatum, pp. 81-110. Westport, Connecticut: Greenwood Press, 1985.

6216. Hinds, Harold E., Jr. "Comics: An Introduction to Mexico's Most Popular Literature." In *Popular Culture in Mexico and in the American Southwest* (tentative title), edited by Linda B. Hall. San Antonio, Texas: Trinity University Press, forthcoming.

6217. Hinds, Harold E., Jr. "If You've Been to Mexico Lately, Did You Notice What Most Mexicans Are Reading? Would You Believe It's Comics and Photonovels [Review Essay]." *Canadian and International Education.* 11:1 (1982), pp. 73-79.

6218. Hinds, Harold E., Jr. "*La Novela Policiaca*: Crime, Detectives, and Escapism." Paper presented at the VI Conference of Mexican and United States Historians, Chicago, Illinois, September 8-12, 1981.

6219. Hinds, Harold and Charles Tatum. "Images of Women in Mexican Comic Books." *Journal of Popular Culture.* Summer 1984, pp. 146-162.

6220. Hinds, Harold E., Jr. and Charles Tatum. "Mexican and American Comic Books in a Comparative Perspective." In *Mexico and the United States: Intercultural Relations in the Humanities*, edited by Juanita Luna Lawhr, *et al.*, pp. 67-84. San Antonio, Texas: San Antonio College, 1984.

6221. Hinds, Harold E., Jr. and Charles M. Tatum. *Not Just For Children: The Mexican Comic Book in the Late 1960s and 1970s.* Westport, Connecticut: Greenwood Press, 1992. 264 pp.

6222. Horn, Maurice. "Recent Mexican Scholarship on Comics [A Review Essay]." *Studies in Latin American Popular Culture.* 2 (1983), pp. 208-212.

6223. Jarque Andrés, Francisco. "La Paraliteratura: Producción y Consumo." *Hispamérica* (Buenos Aires). December 1978, pp. 37-52.

6224. "La Historieta Mexicana." *Artes de México.* 19:158 (1972), pp. 2-91.

6225. "Le Scaglie del Serpente Piumato." *Comics.* May 1974, p. 34.

6226. Malvido, Adriana and Teresa Martínez Arana. "La Historieta en México: Un Mundo Ancho y Ajeno." *Casa del Tiempo.* July 1984, p. 21.

6227. Manjarrez, Froylan C. "Comics: l'Ecole de la Violence." *Revolution* (Paris). December 1964-January 1965, pp. 42-56.

6228. Meisler, Stanley. "Best Sellers in Mexico: Comic Books." *Los Angeles Times.* March 29, 1974, pp. 1A-3A.

6229. Mejía G., Francisco. "Edipín Pingüín." *Motus Liber: Organo* (México). January 1973, p. 11.

6230. Monsiváis, Carlos. "Picaresca y Moraleja de la Historieta Mexicana." *El Gallo Ilustrado* (Sunday supplement of *El Día*). February 10, 1963, p. 2.

6231. Mott, Gordon D. "In Mexico, an Insatiable Appetite for the Comic Book and Its Heroes." *Philadelphia Inquirer.* April 18, 1982, p. 5-C.

6232. Mott, Gordon D. "Where Comic Books Are King." *San Francisco Examiner and Chronicle.* April 18, 1982, p. A-3.

6233. Pérez Cruz, Emiliano and José Suárez Lozano. "La Historieta Mexicana." *Artes de México.* 158 (1979).

6234. Pérez Valdés, Jorge. "Dal Nostro Corrispondente in Messico." *Comic Art.* December 1984, p. 4.

6235. Piho, Virve. "La Obrera Textil: Encuesta Sobre su Trabajo, Ingreso y Vida Familiar." *Acta Sociológica.* 4 (1974), pp. 35-135.

6236. "Popolari per il Messico." *If.* November 1982, p. 36.

6237. "Proyecto para una Exposición Sobre la Historieta Mexicana." *Libros de México.* 8 (1987), p. 59.

6238. Reynoso, Ricardo. "Una Mancha en Un Cómic" (A Blot on a Comic). *Motus Liber: Organo* (México). January 1973, p. 16.

6239. Riding, Alan. "Mexico's Passionate Affair with the Comics." *New York Times.* September 5, 1977, p. 19.

6240. Rubinstein, Anne. "Seduction of the Mexican Innocent." *Comics Journal.* March 1993, pp. 45-48.

6241. Sewell, Dorita. "The Comics in Mexico." Paper presented at seventh convention, Popular Culture Association, Baltimore, Maryland, April 28, 1977.

6242. Silva, Ludovico. *Teoria y Practica de la Ideologia.* Mexico City: Editorial Nuestro Tiempo, 1971.

6243. Simard, Jean Claude and Francisco Jarque Andrés. "La Paraliteratura Mexicana." Report, Conseil des Arts du Canada, Groupe de Recherche en Paraliterature Mexicane [sic], Département des Littératures, Université Laval, August 1976.

6244. *SNIF: El Mitín del Nuevo Comic.* 4 Vols. México: SEP/Editorial Penélope, August 1980.

6245. Suárez Lozano, José, ed. "La Historieta Mexicana." *Artes de México.* 19 (1972), pp. 1-91.

6246. Taibo, Paco Ignacio, II. "Muñoz, Sampayo y Alack." *SNIF: El Mitín del Nuevo Cómic* (México). 4 (n.d.), p. 50.

6247. Tatum, Charles. "Images of the United States in Selected Mexican Comic Books." In *The Americanization of the Global Village,* edited by Roger Rollin, pp. 33-60. Bowling Green, Ohio: Popular Press, 1989.

6248. Tron, Carlos. "Growing Up with Comics in Mexico." In *San Diego Comic Comvention 1989* program book, pp. 82-84. San Diego: San Diego Comic-Con Committee, 1989.

6249. Vásquez González, Modesto. *La Historiética: Todo lo Relativo al Lenguaje Lexipictográfico* (The Comic Book Compendium). México: Promotora K, S.A., 1981.

6250. "Venta de Historietas Supera a Libros en México." *Chasqui.* January-March 1985, p. 68.

Culture

6251. Alcover, Marta and Alicia Molina. "Mexican Comics As Culture Industry." In *Comics and Visual Culture: Research Studies from Ten Countries,* edited by Alphons Silbermann and H.-D. Dyroff, pp. 196-212. Munich: K. G. Saur, 1986.

6252. Alvarez Constantino, Higilio. *La Magia de los 'Cómics' Coloniza Nuestra Cultura.* México: By the Author, Angel Urraza 272-2, 1978.

6253. Alvarez Constantino, Higilio. "La Magia de los Cómics Coloniza Nuestra Cultura." *Audiovisión* (México). September-October 1975, November-December 1975, January-February 1976, pp. 459-464, 573-583, 67-77.

6254. Alvarez Constantino, Higilio. "La Magia de los Cómics Coloniza Nuestra Cultura." *Respuesta: La Opinión Educativa en México* (México). March-April 1979, pp. 23-26.

6255. Herner Reiss, Irene. "Las Historietas y la Cultural Nacional." *Sábado: Suplemento de Uno Más Uno.* August 18, 1979, p. 8.

6256. Sotres Mora, Bertha Eugenia. "La Cultura de los Cómics." *Revista Mexicana de Ciencia Política.* October-December 1973, pp. 13-17.

Education

6257. Carrillo, Bert B. "The Use of Mexican Comics As Teaching Material in Bilingual Classes." *Hispania*. March 1976, pp. 126-128.

6258. Fernández Paz, Agustín. "Práctica: Los Cómics en la Escuela." *Cuadernos de Pedagogías* (México). February 1981, pp. 47-53.

6259. Guerra, Georgina. *El Cómic o la Historieta en la Enseñanza* (The Comic Strip and Comic Book in Education). México: Editorial Grijalbo, 1982.

6260. Malvido, Adriana. "La Historieta, Un Elemento de Educación Visual, Sostiene el Español Luis García." *Uno Más Uno*. August 20, 1981, p. 19.

Comic Strips

6261. del Río, Eduardo (Rius). *La Vida de Cuadritos: Guia Incompleta de la Historieta* (Life Within the Drawings: An Incomplete Guide to the Comic Strip). Mexico City: Editorial Grijalbo, 1984. 207 pp.

6262. Jis y Trino. *El Santos Contra le Tetona Mendoza*. Mexico City: Ediciones La Jornada, 1993. (Sunday strips in *La Jornada*).

6263. Matluck, Joseph H. "The Comic-Strip: A Source of Anglicism in Mexican Spanish." *Hispania*. 43 (1960), pp. 227-233.

6264. "Mexican Artist Adopts Novel to Comic Strip Form." *Cartoonist PROfiles*. No. 15, 1972, pp. 65-67.

Political Cartoons

6265. Henestrosa, Andrés. "La Caricatura Política." *Excélsior*. August 13, 1950, pp. 9, 15.

6266. Pruneda, Salvador. "El Cartón del Dia." S. p. i. (Mexico, 1930).

6267. Ramirez, Manuel González, *La Caricatura Política*. Mexico, D. F.: Fondo de Cultura Económica, 1955.

6268. Ross, Oakland. "The Mighty Pens of Mexico." Toronto *Globe and Mail*. June 28, 1983.

6269. Taller de Gráfica Popular. *Calaveras Resurrectas: 16 Años de Calaveras Políticas del Taller da Gráfica Popular*. México: Beltrán, 1954.

NICARAGUA

General Sources

6270. Barahona, Salomón L. (Chilo). *Historia de la Caricatura y Personajes Nicaragüenses, por Chilo*. Managua: Editorial San José, 1955.

6271. "El Tayacán—A Newspaper for the People." *Group Media Journal*. 7:3/4 (1988), p. 26.

6272. Sewell, Edward H., Jr. and Arnoldo J. Martinez Salvo. "No Light at the End of the Tunnel. U.S.—Nicaraguan Images in Editorial Cartoons." Presented at Fifth Intercultural Conference on Communication in Latin America and the Caribbean, Miami, February 5, 1988.

Rogér

6273. *Cartoons from Nicaragua: The Revolutionary Humor of Rogér*. Translated by Philip Beisswenger. Managua, Nicaragua: Committee of U.S. Citizens Living in Nicaragua. 1984. 49 pp.

6274. Clark, Christian. "Cartoonist Rogér Drew Humor and Truth." *Guardian*. December 19, 1990, p. 19.

6275. Rosen, David. "Cartoonist for the Sandinistas." *Target*. Winter 1986, pp. 4-6.

PANAMA

General Sources

6276. Buckman, Robert. "Panamanian President Sues Political Cartoonist." *Editor and Publisher*. September 21, 1991, pp. 16-17.

6277. Escovar, Luis and Peggy L. de Escovar. "Motivación al Logro y Motivación al Poder en el Contenido de Historietas Populares" (Achievement Motivation and Power Motivation in the Content of Popular Comics). *Revista Interamericana de Psicología*. 7:3-4 (1973), pp. 233-238.

6278. "Some People Just Can't Take a Joke." *CAPS*. November 1991, p. 8.

PARAGUAY

Animation

6279. de Tone, José Luis. "Testimonio de Marcial Ruíz Díaz: La Animación en Paraguay." *Corto Circuito*. April 1992, pp. 24-25.

Guevara, Andres

6280. "Guevara: o Jornal de Ontem e de Amanhã." *Diretrizes* (Rio de Janeiro). January 20, 1944.

6281. "Guevara, o Único Paraguaio Que Conseguiu Vencer o Brasil." *Revista da Semana* (Rio de Janeiro). June 17, 1944.

6282. Lima, Herman. "Guevara, o Único Paraguaio Que Nos Venceu." *Rio Magazine* (Rio de Janeiro). May 1949.

6283. Sam. "A Reabilitação da Caricatura, Através Duma Entrevista com Andres Guevara." *Diário Carioca* (Rio de Janeiro). December 17, 1944.

PERU

Animation

6284. García Miranda, Nelson. "El Cine Animado en el Perú." *Corto Circuito*. April 1992, pp. 30-33.

Caricature

6285. Eneida. "Alvarus no Peru." *Diário de Notícias* (Rio de Janeiro). January 6, 1958.

6286. Grenet, Julio Malaga. "La Caricatura en el Peru." *La Crónica* (Lima). April 7, 1953.

6287. Velarde, Hernan. "Cotrim, Geio de la Caricatura." *La Crónica Dominical* (Lima). October 6, 1957.

Comics

6288. Delgado, Hector. "Quadrinhos Depoimento de um Peruano." *Boletim de HQ.* October 1991, p. 3.

6289. Kagelmann, H. Jürgen and Rosi Zimmermann. "Comics in Peru." *Comixene. Das Comicfachmagazin.* 7:29 (1980), pp. 9-11.

6290. SUCESO. Suplemento Dominical del Diario. *Correo.* Edición especial sobre el 9°. Arte: La Historieta. (Various authors). Lima, February 22, 1976.

6291. Wolfe, Catherine M. and Marjorie Fiske. "Por Que Se Leen las Tiras Comicas." In *Imperialismo y Medios Masivos de Comunicación,* Vol. 2, pp. 97 ff. Lima: Editorial Causchun, 1973.

URUGUAY

General Sources

6292. Bello, Luis. *Un Lápiz Contra un Régimen: Dibujos y Textos.* Montevideo: Private Edition, 1946.

6293. *Raquel Orzuj: 25 Años de Pintora.* Montevideo: Comision Interamericana de Mujeres de la OEA, 1983. 340 pp.

6294. Tomeo, Humberto. "La Historieta: Una Forma de Arte Visual." *Boletin Pedagogico de Artes Visuales* (Montevideo). Serie 2, No. 9, 1965.

Animation

6295. Mendizábal, Iván Rodrigo. "La Animación Como Proceso Alternativo de Creación: Las Experiencias de Bolivia y Uruguay." *Corto Circuito.* April 1992, pp. 18-21. (Also Bolivia).

6296. Sanjurjo Toucón, Alvaro. "Breve Panorama del Cine de Animación en Uruguay." *Corto Circuito.* April 1992, p. 35.

6297. Sanjurjo Toucón, Alvaro. "Entrevista a Walter Tournier." *Corto Circuito.* April 1992, pp. 45-46.

VENEZUELA

Cartooning

6298. "Comic Strip Portrays Colonisation." *Action*. November/December 1992, p. 7.

6299. Pérez Vila, Manuel. *La Caricatura Política en el Siglo XIX* (Political Caricature in the XIXth Century). Caracas: Cromotip, 1979. 71 pp.

6300. Valencia, Mayte. "Venezuela: Nuevos Equipos para el Centro de Imágenes Animadas y Efectos Especiales de la USB." *Corto Circuito*. April 1992, p. 47. (Animation).

Caricature

6301. Kit. *Caricaturas*. Caracas: Editorial Elite, 1944.

6302. Kit. *Esa Bella Humanidad*. Caracas: 1952.

6303. Nazoa, Aquiles, ed. *Leoncio Martínez, Genial e Ingenioso: La Obra Literaria y Gráfica del Gran Artista Caraqueño*. Caracas: Consejo Municipal, 1976.

7

CARIBBEAN

REGIONAL AND INTER-COUNTRY PERSPECTIVES

General Sources

6304. Auld, A. Michael. "Anansesem." *Jamaica Journal.* 16:2 (1983), pp. 35-36.

6305. "Cartoon—As an Instrument for Development." *Caribbean Contact.* February 1975, p. 16.

6306. "Cartoonists at Work." *Caribbean Contact.* April 1975, p. 4.

6307. "Cartoons Are No Laughing Matter." *The Nation* (Barbados). November 30, 1975, p. 40.

6308. Lent, John A. *Bibliographic Guide to Caribbean Mass Communication.* Westport, Connecticut: Greenwood Press, 1992. (Comics, Cartoons, No. 1315—In Barbados, 1143: in Caribbean, 358, 363, 820-821; in Guyana, 1269).

6309. Lent, John A. "Caribbean Cartoonists Strive To Overcome Isolation, Anonymity and Low Wages." *Comics Journal.* October 1991, pp. 33-35.

6310. Lent, John A. "Cartooning and Development in the Caribbean." Paper presented at CALACS Conference, Ottawa, Canada, October 23, 1993.

6311. Lent, John A. "Comic Arts in the Caribbean." Paper presented at Caribbean Studies Association, Havana, Cuba, May 1991.

6312. "Off, BBC News, Cartoons." *Caribbean Contact*. July 1975, p. 18.

CUBA

General Sources

6313. Armada, Chago. "Gnosis, Information and True Vanguard Graphic Humor." *CEMEDIM*. May-June 1985, pp. 6-7.

6314. Cánovas Fabelo, Alexis Mario. "(III) Esa Categoría Ilamada Lo Cómico." *UPEC*. May-June 1983, pp. 34-43.

6315. Castañeda, Mireya. "Humor for Peace." *Granma Weekly Review*. April 2, 1989, p. 6.

6316. "A Common Human Denominator." *Granma Weekly Review*. June 19, 1983, p. 7.

6317. Franco-Lao, Méri. *Cuba Rie*. Gabriele Mazzotta Editore, 1972. 240 pp.

6318. Kunzle, David. "Public Graphics in Cuba: A Very Cuban Form of Internationalist Art." *Latin American Perspectives*. Issue 7. Supplement 1975, 2:4 (1975), pp. 89-110.

6319. López García, Sergio. "Cuban Graphic Arts in Brazil." *Granma Weekly Review*. October 27, 1985, p. 6.

6320. Martí, Agenor. "Humour in Today's Cuba." *Democratic Journalist*. March 1979, pp. 11-16.

6321. Piñera, Tony. "The Cuban Humor Boom." *Granma Weekly Review*. May 19, 1985, p. 7.

6322. Santiano, Armando [Chago]. *El Humor Otro*. Havana: Ediciones Revolucionarias, 1973.

6323. Ysla, Nelson Herrera. "Humor Found." *Granma Weekly Review*. June 15, 1986, p. 7.

Historical Aspects

6324. Arango, Rodolfo. "Periodismo Humorístico." In *El Periodismo en Cuba, 1935*, pp. 59-61. Havana, 1935.

6325. Armada, Santiago. "El Humorismo en la Sierra Maestra." *CEMEDIM*. May- June 1984, p. 6.

6326. Castellanos, Israel. "El Comic y Su Historia." *Despegue* (Havana). May 15, 1974, p. 5.

6327. de Juan, Adelaida. "Caricatura y Política, 1868-1959." In *El Dibujo Político en Cuba, 1868-1959*. Havana: Consejo Nacional de Cultura, 1975.

6328. Gálvez, Wenceslao. "La Caricatura." *El Figaro* (Havana). 5:20 (1889), p. 6.

6329. Goldman, Shifra M. "Painters into Poster Makers: Two Views Concerning the History, Aesthetics and Ideology of the Cuban Poster Movement." *Studies in Latin American Popular Culture*. 3 (1984), pp. 162-173.

6330. Verdés Plana, Raoul. "La Caricatura Satírica Como Elemento de Combate." In *El Periodismo en Cuba, 1935* (Havana). 1, 1935, pp. 169-170.

Revolution

6331. de la Nuez, René. "Editorial Cartoons in the Struggle for Peace." *CEMEDIM*. May-June 1986, pp. 5-6.

6332. Latona, Robert. "Comics: Castro Style." *Vanguard*. No. 1, 1966, pp. 31-43.

6333. Mariana Arteaga, Luísa." "'El Humorismo Es Un Arma de Combate.'" *UPEC*. January-February 1983, pp. 3-6.

6334. Miani, Rozinaldo. "Che: Um Revolucionário Que Virou Mito." *Boletim de HQ*. May-June 1992, p. 7.

6335. Piñera, Toni. "Humorists in Action." *Granma Weekly Review*. September 28, 1986, p. 7.

Cartooning, Cartoons

6336. Castañeda, Mireya. "Look and Laugh." *Granma Weekly Review*. May 28, 1989, p. 12.

6337. Castañeda, Mireya. "Taking Humor and Cartoons Seriously." *Granma International*. April 28, 1991, p. 5.

6338. Lent, John A. *Bibliography of Cuban Mass Communications*. Westport, Connecticut: Greenwood Press, 1992. (Nos. 554-629, 4151, 4153-4154, 4157, 4163).

6339. Lent, John A. "Cuba's Comic Art Tradition." *Studies in Latin American Popular Culture.* 14 (1995), pp. 1-20.

6340. Lent, John A. "Lively Cartooning in the Land of Castro." *Comics Journal.* September 1991.

6341. Lent, John A. "The Situation of Comic Art in Cuba: Not a Laughing Matter." Paper presented at Caribbean Studies Asscociation, St. George's, Grenada, May 27, 1992.

6342. "Smiles and Denunciation in Cartoons." *Democratic Journalist.* July-August 1987, pp. 16-18.

6343. Tamayo, Évora. "Humor para Atrapar el Lector." *UPEC.* March-April 1985, pp. 46-49.

Bienal Internacional de Humorismo

6344. "V Bienal del Humor Internacional de San Antonio de los Baños." *Boletin Comision Nacional Cubana de la Unesco.* January- June 1987, p. 10.

6345. *Cuarta Bienal Internacional de Humorismo 1985.* San Antonio de los Baños, Cuba. Havana: 1987.

6346. "Discurso de Ernesto Vera en la Inauguracion de la I Bienal de Humorismo." *UPEC.* May-June 1979, pp. 8-9.

6347. "5th International Biennial Festival of Humor Cuba '87." *IOJ Newsletter.* October 1986, p. 2.

6348. "The Fifth International Biennial of Humor in San Antonio de los Baños." *Democratic Journalist.* July-August 1987, pp. 16-18.

6349. "Fourth Biennale of Humor in Cuba." *IOJ Newsletter.* May 1985, p. 6.

6350. "The 4th International Biennial of Humour and Political Satire 1985." *Democratic Journalist.* October 1985, pp. 14, 19.

6351. "Fourth International Biennial of Humour Convoked in Cuba." *IOJ Newsletter.* August 15, 1984, p. 2.

6352. "Humor Biennial." *Granma Weekly Review.* May 19, 1985, p. 6.

6353. "La I Bienal Internacional de Humorismo y de Gráfica Militante." *UPEC.* January-February 1979, pp. 41-43.

6354. "7th International Biennial Festival of Humour." *IOJ Newsletter.* April 1990, p. 3.

6355. "VI Salón Nacional de Humoristas Horacio Rodríguez." *UPEC* (Havana). November-December 1975, pp. 14-21.

6356. "Third International Biennial of Humour CUBA 1983." *IOJ Newsletter*. March 1982, p. 4.

Dedeté

6357. "*Dedeté* Incluímos 183 Premios Internacionales del Humor Gráfico Cubano." Special edition. *Lapiztola* (Mexico). No. 3, 1993, pp. 1-22. (Cartoons, listing of award winning cartoonists of Cuba).

6358. "XV Aniversario de DDT." *UPEC*. May-June 1983, pp. 24-25.

6359. Medina, Jorge Oliver. *Dedeté*. Havana: Editora Abril de la UJC, Colección Caimán, 1985. 191 pp.

6360. Piñera, Toni. "'Dedeté': A Champion of Cuban Humor." *Granma Weekly Review*. October 27, 1985, p. 6.

Palante

6361. *25 Años de Humor en Palante*. Havana: Editora Abril, 1986. 256 pp. (Profiles of many cartoonists of Cuba).

6362. Tamayo, Evora. "Palante: 25 Años de Humor." *UPEC*. November-December 1986, pp. 40-48.

Cartoonists

6363. Aiguesvives, Eduardo. "Nicholás Guillén, a Cartoonist." *Grnama Weekly Review*. September 9, 1990, p. 7.

6364. Avilés, Cecilio. "Aucas y Aleluyas: Uno de los Antecedantes Más Cercanos a la Historieta." *UPEC*. November-December 1986, pp. 20-22.

6365. Castañeda, Mireya. "Adigio Benítez: An Artist Who Lives Silently in His World." *Granma Weekly Review*. January 31, 1988, p. 6.

6366. Castañeda, Mireya. "Ajubel: The Laughing Man." *Granma Weekly Review*. September 13, 1987, p. 8.

6367. Fariñas Rodríguez, Gilda. "Street Chronicler." *Granma Weekly Review*. September 24, 1989, p. 12.

6368. "Historietas: Orestes Suarez Lemus." *UPEC*. March-April 1984, pp. 44-46.

6369. "Historietas: Roberto Alfonso." *UPEC*. July- August 1983, pp. 28-33.

6370. "Historietistas: Emilio Fernandez." *UPEC*. May- June 1984, pp. 46-48.

6371. Jiménez Sánchez, Martha. " Con Roberto Figueredo: Cada Modalidad del Diseño Grafico Tiene su Encanto." *UPEC*. May-June 1986, pp. 38-41.

6372. Rodríguez Garcia, Mercedes. "Pedro Mendez Piensa y Habla en Serio del Humor." *UPEC*. January-February 1983, pp. 7-9.

6373. Rodríguez Ruiz, Francisco. *Humor Posada Por Panchito*. Havana: Editorial Pablo de la Torriente, 1989. 96 pp.

6374. Tamayo, Évora. "Tomy: A Humorist for the Year 2000." *Granma Weekly Review*. November 2, 1986, p. 7.

Ares *(Aristides Esteban Hernández Guerrero)*

6375. Ares. *Entrar Por el Aro (Ares)*. Havana: Editorial Pablo de la Torriente, 1989.

6376. Lent, John A. "Ares." In *Cartoonometer: Taking the Pulse of the World's Cartoonists*, edited by Joe Szabo and John A. Lent, p. 42. North Wales, Pennsylvania: WittyWorld Books, 1994.

6377. Lent, John A. and José E. Polo Madeira. "The Shrink with the Pen and Ink." *Kayhan Caricature*. June 1993.

6378. Lent, John A. and José E. Polo Madeira. "The Shrink with Pen and Ink: Cuban Cartoonist/Psychiatrist Ares." *WittyWorld*. Winter/Spring 1992, pp. 33-36.

Blanco, Rafael

6379. Blanco, Francisco. "Rafael Blanco en Su Centenario." *UPEC*. January-February 1986, pp. 16-18.

6380. Suárez Solís, Rafael. "En la Muerte de un Humorista." *Carteles* (Havana). August 21, 1955.

Carlucho

6381. Castañeda, Mireya. "Carlucho: A Man of Few Words." *Granma Weekly Review*. November 11, 1990, p. 12.

6382. Piñera, Toni. "Carlucho: A Distinctive Personal Style." *Granma Weekly Review*. June 9, 1985, p. 6.

de la Nuez, René

6383. Armada, Chago. "Nuez: His Mastery and His Latest Book." *Granma Weekly Review*. July 14, 1985, p. 7.

6384. Castañeda, Mireya. "Nuez Talks About the 5th International Humor Biennal." *Granma Weekly Review*. February 22, 1987, p. 7.

6385. Colina, Cino. "Nuez in Concert." *Granma Weekly Review*. September 21, 1986, p. 6.

6386. Martí, Agenor. "Nuez' New Symbol and Mystery." *Granma Weekly Review*. June 7, 1987, p. 6.

6387. Nuez, René de la. *El Humor Nuestro de Cada Día*. Havana: Orbe, 1976.

6388. "René de la Nuez." *Apropos*. No. 7, 1988, pp. 32-34.

6389. Sarusky, Jaime. "René de la Nuez: A Cartoonist Who Heralds Victory." *Granma Weekly Review*. June 19, 1983, p. 6.

Massaguer, Conrado W.

6390. Capote, Maria H. "The Penetrating Glance of Conrado W. Massaguer." *Granma Weekly Review*. June 11, 1989, p. 6.

6391. de Fornaro, C. "Impaling Celebrities on a Pen-point; a Sketch of Conrado Massaguer, the Cuban Caricaturist." *Arts and Decoration*. April 1923, pp. 22-23.

6392. Lima, Herman. "Um Grande Caricaturista Cubano." *Vamos Ler!* (Rio de Janeiro). February 7, 1948.

6393. "Nostalgia! Massaguer's Foneygraphs of Funny Fellows." *Cartoonist PROfiles*. No. 17, p. 47.

Padrón, Juan

6394. "The Cartoonist and His 'Baby'—Juan Padrón and Elpidio Valdés." *Granma Weekly Review*. February 27, 1983, p. 5.

6395. "Cuban Cartoons: Vampires in Havana." *Granma Weekly Review*. September 22, 1985, p. 4.

6396. Evora, José Antonio. "Cuba: Las Aventuras de Juan Padrón." *Corto Circuito*. April 1992, pp. 10-13.

6397. Evora, José Antonio. "Las Aventuras de Juan Padrón." *Cine Cubano*. No. 131 (1991), pp. 7-12.

6398. Herrera Ysla, Nelson. "Juan Padrón: Humor Found." *Granma Weekly Review*. June 15, 1986, p. 7.

Characters and Titles

"El Bobo"

6399. Gay Galbó, Enrique. *El Bobo; Ensayo Sobre el Humorismo de Abela*. Havana: 1949. 127 pp.

6400. Vasconcelos, Ramón. "Envocación y Resurrección Imposible del 'Bobo.'" *Bohemia*. January 26, 1947, pp. 46-47, 56.

"Elpidio Valdes"

6401. Chijona, Gerardo. "Elpidio Valdes en el Pais del Largometraje." *Cine Cubano*. No. 98, 1980, pp. 110-114.

6402. Colina, Enrique. "Elpidio Valdes Contra Dolar y Cañon." *Cine Cubano*. No. 107, 1983, pp. 90-92.

6403. Gonzalez Acosta, Alejandro. "Las Dos Caras de Elpidio Padron." *Cine Cubano*. No. 107, 1983, pp. 1-4.

6404. Johoy, Silvia. "Elpidio Valdés." *Trabajadores* (Havana). April 19, 1977, p. 5.

6405. Linares, Cecilia and Vivian Gamoneda. "SOS Vampiros en Habana." *Cine Cubano*. No. 114, 1985, pp. 89-91.

6406. Muriente Pérez, Julio Antonio. "Elpidio Valdés y la Hermandad de Cuba y Puerto Rico." *Cine Cubano*. No. 107, 1983, pp. 92-93.

6407. Palaez, Rosa Elvira. "A Circumstantial Chat with Elpidio Valdés." *Granma Weekly Review*. August 28, 1988, p. 6.

Animation

6408. "Apuntes Sobre el Departamento de Dibujos Animados del ICAIC." *Cine Cubano*. March 1964, pp. 38-44.

6409. Branley, Roberto. "Un Largo Metraje, Seis Cortos y Un Dibujo Animado Cubanos." *Gaceta de Cuba* (Havana). April 1977, pp. 22-24.

6410. Chijona, Gerardo. "Vida, Suerte y Milagros del Dibujo Animado Cubano." *Cine*

Cubano. Nos. 91/92, 1978, p. 147.

6411. Cobas, Roberto. "Notas para una Cronología del Dibujo Animado Cubano." *Cine Cubano*. No. 110, 1984.

6412. Dueñas Díaz, Ovidio, *et al*. "El Dibujo Animado en Cuba." *Bohemia* (Havana). April 1974.

6413. "El Dibujo Animado en Cuba." *Cine Cubano*. September-December 1964, pp. 36-38.

6414. González Acosta, Alejandro. "Veinte Años Hacienda Reir...y Pensar: Entrevistas con Eduardo Muñoz Bach, Hernán Henríquez, Manuel Pérez y Juan Padrón, Creadores de Dibujos Animados." *Cine Cubano*. No. 95, 1979, pp. 123-134.

6415. Lent, John A. *Bibliography of Cuban Mass Communications*. Westport, Connecticut: Greenwood Press, 1992. (Nos. 266, 805-823).

6416. Linares, Cecilia and Pablo Ramos. "Cine y Juventud." *Cine Cubano*. No. 117, 1987, pp. 9-13.

6417. Manet, Eduardo. "Dibujos Animados de Aquí y de Allá." *Cine Cubano*. Decenber 1963, pp. 37-44.

6418. Pérez, Manolo. "El Personaje Histórico en el Dibujo Animado." *C. Linea*. April-June 1977, p. 12-14.

6419. Puñal, Francisco. "La Musica, Un Actor Anonimo." *Cine Cubano*. No. 117 (1987), pp. 42-45.

6420. "Reportaje Sobre Dibujo Animado." *Cine Cubano*. September 1960, pp. 44-49.

6421. Rivero, Angel. "El Joven de Animación." *Revolucíon y Cultura* (Havana). November 11, 1977, p. 4.

6422. Rodríguez, Raul. "Una Historia Recuperada." *Cine Cubano*. No. 124, 1988, pp. 16-19.

6423. Sanchez, Juan Carlos. "Con Animos de Animar." *Cine Cubano*. No. 124, 1988, pp. 20-24.

6424. Santovenia, Rodolfo. "Tony de Peltrie y la Animacion Computarizada." *Cine Cubano*. No. 123, 1988, pp. 64-66.

Caricature

6425. Barroz, Bernardo G. *La Caricatura Contemporánea*. Madrid: Editorial América, 1931. 2 vols. (Cuba in Vol. 2).

6426. Cotta Benítez, Ramón. "La Caricatura en el Periodismo Cubano." In *Album del Cincuentenario de la Asociación de Reporters de la Habana*, pp. 332-334. Havana: Editorial Lex, 1952.

6427. David, Juan. "Cuando la Caricatura Fue por Primera Vez Cubana." *Bohemia* (Havana). September 19, 1975, pp. 10-13.

6428. de Juan, Adelaida. *Caricatura de la República* (Caricature of the Republic). Havana: Editorial Letras Cubanas, 1982.

6429. Herrera, Alicia. "La Fiesta de los Caricaturistas Cubanos." *UPEC*. March-April 1985, pp. 1-3.

6430. Tamayo, Évora. "La Caricatura Critica." *UPEC*. March-April 1984, pp. 11-12.

Comic Books and Strips

6431. Arango, Rodolfo. "Periodismo Humorístico." In *El Periodismo en Cuba, 1935*, pp. 59-61. Havana: 1935.

6432. Avilés, Cecilio. "Comics: A Language of the 20th Century." *CEMEDIM*. January-February 1987, p. 5.

6433. Avilés, Cecilio. *La Historieta Cubana. Sesenta Narradores Graficos Contemporaneos*. Havana: Editorial Pablo de la Torriente, 1990. 166 pp.

6434. Avilés, Cecilio. "La Historieta Poderoso Instrumento Ideológico." *UPEC*. September-October 1985, pp. 12-13.

6435. Avilés, Cecilio. "No a la Historieta?" *UPEC*. No. 5, 1981, pp. 48-49.

6436. Blanco Avila, Francisco. "Comics and Ideological Manipulation." *Granma Weekly Review*. August 5, 1984, p. 8.

6437. Durán, Alexis. *A Punto y Seguido*. Santiago de Cuba: Editorial Oriente, 1988. 169 pp.

6438. Faur, Jean-Claude. "La Bande Dessinée Latino-Américaine à Cuba et les Objectifs de la Tricontinale." Marseilles: Adibédé, 1979. 3 pp.

6439. Guerra, Felix. "Humor without Borders." *Granma Weekly Review*. July 5, 1987, p. 7.

6440. "La Batalla de los Comics." *Bohemia*. No. 49, 1958, p. 23.

6441. *LINEA. Revista Latinoamericana de Estudio de la Historieta*. (N. ° 1-12). Habana: Prensa Latina, 1973-1975.

6442. Santana, Joaquín. "Uncle Scrooge Died in Cuba." *Granma Weekly Review*. November 27, 1983, p. 6.

6443. Vergara, Jorge. "*Comics* y Relaciones Mercantiles." *Casa de las Américas*. March-April 1973, pp. 126 ff.

Political Cartoons

6444. Castañeda, Mireya. "Humor's Universal Language." *Granma Weekly Review*. April 19, 1987, p. 9.

6445. Duchesne, Concepción. "La Política Cómica de la Frustración Nacional." *Bohemia* (Havana). June 4, 1976, pp. 86-91.

6446. "La Política Cómica." In *Castañas. Frías y Calientes*, by Juan J Mirabet, pp. 74-75. Havana: Imprenta La Prueba, 1907.

6447. Piñero, Tony. "International Political Satire Contest/Exhibit on Foreign Debt." *Granma Weekly Review*. June 22, 1986, p. 7.

6448. Tamayo, Évora and Juan Blas Rodríguez. *Cuba. Cien Años de Humor Político*. Havana: Instituto del Libro, 1971. 349 pp.

6449. Tamayo, Évora, Juan Blas Rodríguez, and Oscar Hurtado. *Más de Cien Años de Humor Politico*. Tomo I. Santiago de Cuba: Editorial Oriente, 1984. 123 pp.

6450. Tamayo, Évora, Juan Blas Rodríguez, and Oscar Hurtado. *Más de Cien Años de Humor Politico*. Tomo 2. Santiago de Cuba: Editorial Oriente, 1984. 121 pp.

GUYANA

Political Cartoons

6451. *Cartoons from the Mirror*. Georgetown, Guyana: New Guyana Co. Ltd., October 1974.

HAITI

General Sources

6452. "Cartoonists Focus on Haiti's Poor." *Windsor Star*. October 10, 1987.

6453. Tarter, William V. "'Many Hands—Load Not Heavy'; A Study of Participatory Communication in Rural Haiti." MA thesis, University of Washington, 1985.

JAMAICA

Political Cartoons

6454. Boothe, Diahann V. "A Comparative Content Analysis of Political Cartoons in the Daily and Sunday Gleaner and The Jamiaca Daily News During the 1976 General Elections." BA graduation paper, University of West Indies, Mona, 1993. 74 pp.

6455. Buchanan, Charles. "A Content Analysis of Editorial Cartoons Appearing in the Gleaner and Jamaica Record on Four Selected Topics." Graduation paper, University of West Indies, Mona, 1992.

6456. Callender, Andrea. "Urban Leandro on the 1976 and 1980 Elections. The Cartoon As Social Commentary." BA graduation paper, Universtiy of West Indies, Mona, 1987.

6457. Gradussov, Alex. "Carl Abrahams: Painter and Cartoonist." *Jamaica Journal*. 3:1 (1969), pp. 43-46.

6458. McIntosh, Sandy. *One Mac's Worth a Million Words*. In *Livingston McLaren—Selected Editorial Cartoons*. Kingston: Jamaica *Daily News*, 1979.

PUERTO RICO

General Sources

6459. Arbona, Ramón. "El Humor Es Una Cosa Muy Seria." *Layout*. December 1985, pp. 36-37.

TRINIDAD

Political Cartoons

6460. Hitchins, William E. *J.M. and Other Cartoonists from the Trinidad Guardian.* Port of Spain: Trinidad Publishing Co., 1954.

8

ADDENDUM

ASIA

General Sources

6461. Lent, John A. "Clandestine Cartoonists." *Notebook* of the Association of American Editorial Cartoonists. Winter 1995, pp. 16-18

6462. Sandler, Adam and Brian Lowry. "DreamWorks Harbors Plan for Movies, Toons." *Variety*. January 30-February 5, 1995, pp. 13, 16.

Periodical Directory

6463. *Animania*. German-language fanzine on Japanese anime. Weird Visions Media, Postfach 73, 56239 Selters/Ww, Germany.

6464. *Animenia*. Dutch-language fanzine on Japanese anime. Postcode 2048, 3000 CA Rotterdam, The Netherlands.

6465. *J.A.M.M.* English-language fanzine on Japanese anime. Emmanuel Van Melkebeke, Parkplein 5, B-9000 Ghent, Belgium.

6466. *M.A.G.+.* French-language anime fanzine from Philippe Verhelst, 80 rue de la Pastorale, 1080 Bruxelles, Belgium.

6467. *Mangazine Scandinavia.* Japanese comics fanzine in English. Mega Scandinavia A/S, Linnesgade 14A, DK-1361 Copenhagen K, Denmark.

6468. *Video J.A.F..* Spanish anime fanzine. Apdo. 180, D.P. 18690, Almunecar, Granada, Spain.

6469. *Yamage Fanzine.* English-language anime fanzine. Weth. Wierdelsstr. 18, 1107 DK Amsterdam, The Netherlands.

China

6470. Clark, Paul. "Uproar in Heaven." In *The Hawai'i International Film Festival*, p. 56. Honolulu: East-West Center, 1985. (Animation).

6471. Kaye, Lincoln. "Trading Rights." *Far Eastern Economic Review.* March 9, 1995, p. 16. (Property rights).

Hong Kong

6472. do Rosario, Louise. "Drawing the Line: Zunzi, Hong Kong. Political Cartoonist Takes Aim at China's Communist Elite." *Far Eastern Economic Review.* March 9, 1995, p. 70.

6473. Moore, Jack. "Cartooning Characters." *Sunday Post-Herald Magazine.* May 25, 1969, p. 5. (Daniel Zabo and Chris Wren).

India

6474. Ambroise, Yvon. *Animation for Social Change.* New Delhi: Caritas, 1992.

Japan

6475. "Aozora Shojotai, Blue Sky Girl Squadron." *Anime UK.* March 1995, pp. 30-32. (Anime title: "Aozora Shojotai").

6476. "CBG Video News." *Comics Buyer's Guide.* March 31, 1995, p. 50. (Anime).

6477. Clements, Jonathan. "Japan Rocks." *Anime UK.* March 1995, pp. 42-43. (Anime music: "Luna Sea").

6478. Davies, Robert L. *et al.* "Videoscan." *Anime UK*. March 1995, pp. 48-51.

6479. Dean, P. "Japanese Animation 'Akira,' Video Rentals and Sales." *Sight and Sound*. November 1994, p. 63.

6480. Katsura, H. "Yunomae Cartoon Museum and Community Center Kuma." *Architectural Design*. No. 107, 1994, pp. 46-47.

6481. Kyte, Steve. "A to Z of Anime. Part One, A-L." *Anime UK*. March 1995, 8 pp. insert.

6482. Kyte, Steve. "SFXpress." *Anime UK*. March 1995, pp. 20. (Anime).

6483. Lipari, Phil and Martin King. "Enter the Dragonball." *Anime UK*. March 1995, pp. 36-41. (Anime title: "Dragonball").

6484. McCarthy, Helen. "Con Report: AnimEast 94." *Anime UK*. March 1995, p. 11.

6485. McCarthy, Helen. "Go, Go Power Rangers... Here Comes Dinosaur Task Force Zyuranger." *Anime UK*. March 1995, pp. 20-23. (Anime title: "Power Rangers").

6486. McCarthy, Helen. "Green Legend Ran." *Anime UK*. March 1995, pp. 34-35. (Anime title: "Green Legend Ran").

6487. McCarthy, Helen. "Koichi Ohata." *Anime UK*. March 1995, p. 12. (Cartoonist).

6488. McCarthy, Helen. "Lupin the 3rd: The Secret Files." *Anime UK*. March 1995, pp. 28-29, 44-45. (Anime title: "Lupin").

6489. McCarthy, Helen. "Monkey Punch." *Anime UK*. March 1995, p. 13. (Cartoonist).

6490. Munson-Siter, Patricia A. "Bio Booster Armor Guyver." *Anime UK*. March 1995, pp. 14-17. (Anime title: "Guyver").

6491. "Newsline." *Anime UK*. March 1995, pp. 6-7.

6492. "Oscar Nomination for Studio Ghibli at Last?" *Anime UK*. March 1995, p. 6.

6493. Overton, Wil. "Final Fantasy, the Animation." *Anime UK*. March 1995, p. 19. (Anime title: "Final Fantasy").

6494. Schodt, Frederik L. "The Osamu Tezuka Manga Museum." *Anime UK*. March 1995, p. 10.

6495. Sertori, Julia. "Friends Forever: Ushio and Tora." *Anime UK*. March 1995, pp. 24-27. (Anime title: "Ushio and Tora").

6496. Sertori, Julia. "Lore Breakers: Sex, Religion and Devil-Hunting." *Anime UK*. March 1995, pp. 46-47. (Anime title: "Devil Hunter Yohko").

6497. "U.S. Division, Otomo Film Are Launched." *Comics Buyer's Guide*. March 10, 1995, p. 76.

6498. "Viz Collects Urusei Yatsura." *Comics Buyer's Guide*. March 10, 1995, p. 76.

6499. Watson, Paul. "Games Capsule: Final Fantasy VI." *Anime UK*. March 1995, pp. 18-19. (Anime games).

Korea

6500. Chung, Saehyang P. "Kim Hongdo's 'Ssirum' (Wrestling) Painting." *Korean Culture*. Spring 1995, pp. 4-7.

6501. Lent, John A. "Korean Cartooning: Historical and Contemporary Perspectives." *Korean Culture*. Spring 1995, pp. 8-19.

AUSTRALIA

6502. Sanson, A. and C. DiMuccio. "The Influence of Aggressive and Neutral Cartoons and Toys on the Behavior of Preschool Children." *Australian Psychologist*. July 1993, pp. 93-99.

CENTRAL AND SOUTH AMERICA

Argentina

6503. Fontanarrosa, R. "It Was Up to Us To Make People Laugh: A Selection of the Cartoon Humor of Fontanarrosa Reflecting 20 Years of Argentine Life and Politics." *Cuadernos Hispanoamericanos*. July-September 1993, pp. 352-359.

6504. Loiseau, C. "Through the Window: A Short Autobiography of the Argentine Cartoonist and Feature Writer Loiseau, Carlos (Caloi), with Samples of His Cartoon Humor." *Cuadernos Hispanoamericanos*. July-September 1993, pp. 360-368.

CARIBBEAN

Periodical Directory

6505. *Chronique "Laisse-Moi te Dire."* Cartoon periodical poking fun at France and its relationships with French Antilles. No. 1 published in May 1990; No. 2 in November 1990. Editions Exbrayat, Morne l' Eventée No. 5, Route de Balata, 97200 Fort-de-France, Martinique.

MIDDLE EAST

General Sources

6506. Shaheen, Jack G. "Arab Images in American Comic Books." *Journal of Popular Culture*. Summer 1994, pp. 123-133.

AUTHOR INDEX

Avilés, René, 6177
Azevedo, Artur, 5500
Azevedo, Fernando, 5632
Azitah Azmi, 4120
Aziza, Mohamed, 177
Aznam, Suhaini, 4040

Bachmayer, Eva, 3543
Baciu, Stefan, 5423, 5633
Bader, A.L., 614
Badr, Anwar, 319
Badrudin, Ramli, 1616-1617, 1623-1624
Baek Eun-Hyun, 3854
Bailey, James, 3286-3287
Bailey, Joyce Waddell, 5984
Baina, Mohammed, 176
Baker, Ed, 2338, 2674, 2777
Bakhti, B., 45
Bakshi, Rajni, 1528
Ba'labakkî, Fâtima, 316
Balachandran, Chhaya, 1479
Baldwin, Wayne, 4679-4681, 4792
Balein, Jose, 4156, 4163
Bales, Elizabeth, 1782, 2073
Balfour, Brad, 3490
Ball, Murray, 4810-4812
Baltake, Joe, 2302
Bandeira, Manuel, 5424
Bang Hak-Ki, 3754
Bantzogi, 4016
Bao Siwen, 1040
Barahona, Salomón L. (Chilo), 4873, 6270
Barata, Armando, 5934, 5966-5967, 6044, 6136
Barata, Mario, 5225, 6111, 6194
Baraybar, Cecilia, 5159
Barber, Karin, 18
Barber, Lee, 2779
Barbosa, Domingos, 5272
Barbosa, Francisco de Assis, 5280, 5557
Bardin, Roberto, 5870
Bardy, John, 2433
Baria, Farah, 1503
Barnett, Will, 1243
Barreda, Octavio, 6002
Barrett, Hope, 1224, 1318

Barroso, Gustavo, 5171, 5634
Barroz, Bernardo G., 6425
Barson, Michael S., 3491
Bascuñan, H., 5855
Baskett, Pat, 4799
Baskin, Marg, 2145
Basler, Barbara, 1225
Bastien, Remy, 5968
Batio, Christopher, 3393
Battaglia, Roberto C., 5075
Bauer, Wolfgang, 1160
Baur, Elisabeth K., 4838, 6195
Bauregard, Olivier, 73
Bayram, Muhammad, 319
Beals, Carleton, 5935
Beatty, Terry, 2532, 3492
Beauchamp, Marc, 2146
Beeson, Diana, 4568
Behl, Karuna, 1350
Bejo, Noel B., 4237
Bello, Luis, 6292
Belmiro (de Almeida), 5172
Belmonte (Benedito Bastos Barreto), 5173, 5297-5302
Bendazzi, Giannalberto, 4910
ben Hafsi, H., 181
Benjamin, Lesley, 4780
Bento, Antônio, 5281, 5377
Benziman, Uzi, 286
Berceño, Marila A., 4283
Berckman, Edward M., 1161
Berdicio, Roberto, 6094
Bermejo, Manuel M., 6178
Bernal Jiménez, Augusto, 5886
Bernardi, Luigi, 2303
Bernardo, Carmen, 2781, 3289
Bernhardi, Jill, 3290
Bertieri, Claudio, 3671, 4361
Bessaih, B., 45
Bessman, Jim, 3033
Bhade, Abhijit, 1449
Bhaskaran, Gautaman, 1368
Bi Keguan, 563-567, 615, 648-656, 744-749, 808-811, 823, 839, 886-897, 1018-1019, 1033, 1059, 1069, 1071-1072, 1077, 1237-1238, 1307
Biagini, Alessandra, 1134
Bierbaum, Mary, 2363

SUBJECT INDEX

CHARACTERS AND TITLES

COMPANIES, FANZINES, and PERIODICALS

GENERAL SUBJECTS

About the Compiler

JOHN A. LENT is managing editor of *WittyWorld International Cartoon Magazine*. The other three volumes of this international study of comic art literature are *Animation, Caricature, and Gag and Political Cartoons in the United States and Canada: An International Bibliography* (Greenwood, 1994), *Comic Art of Europe: An International Comprehensive Bibliography* (Greenwood, 1994), and *Comic Books and Comic Strips in the United States: An International Bibliography* (Greenwood, 1994).

ISBN 0-313-29343-0

EAN

9 780313 293436

90000>

HARDCOVER BAR CODE